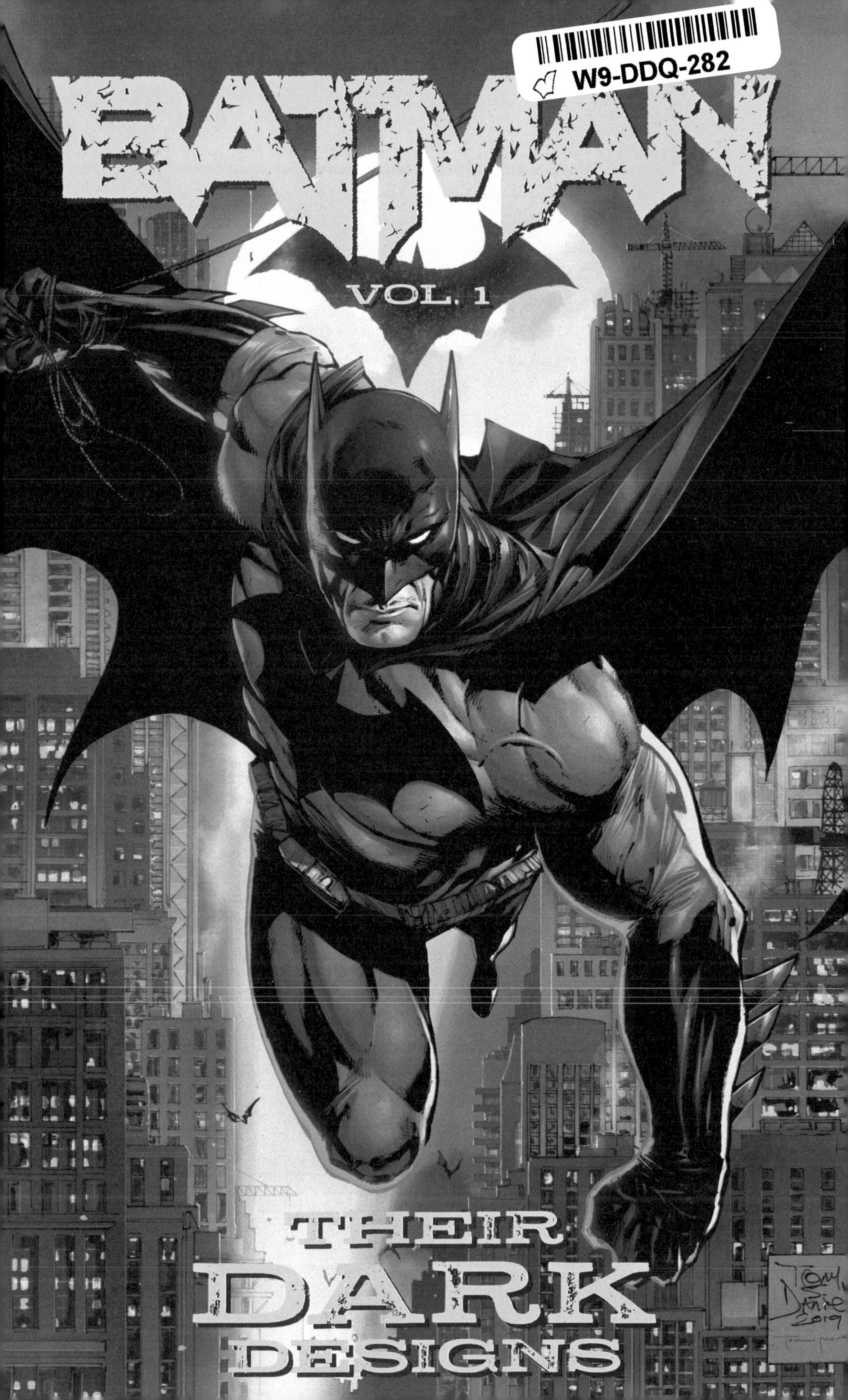
BATMAN
VOL. 1
THEIR
DARK
DESIGNS

BATMAN

VOL. 1

BEN ABERNATHY
JAMIE S. RICH
Editors – Original Series
DAVE WIELGOSZ
Associate Editor – Original Series
ROBIN WILDMAN
Editor – Collected Edition
STEVE COOK
Design Director – Books
DAMIAN RYLAND
Publication Design
SUZANNAH ROWNTREE
Publication Production

MARIE JAVINS
Editor-in-Chief, DC Comics

DANIEL CHERRY III
Senior VP – General Manager
JIM LEE
Publisher & Chief Creative Officer
JOEN CHOE
VP – Global Brand & Creative Services
DON FALLETTI
VP – Manufacturing Operations & Workflow
Management
LAWRENCE GANEM
VP – Talent Services
ALISON GILL
Senior VP – Manufacturing & Operations
NICK J. NAPOLITANO
VP – Manufacturing Administration & Design
NANCY SPEARS
VP – Revenue

BATMAN VOL. 1: THEIR DARK DESIGNS

Published by DC Comics. Compilation and all new
material Copyright © 2020 DC Comics. All Rights
Reserved. Originally published in single magazine
form in *Batman* 85-94, *Batman Secret Files* 3.
Copyright © 2020 DC Comics. All Rights Reserved.
All characters, their distinctive likenesses, and
related elements featured in this publication are
trademarks of DC Comics. The stories, characters,
and incidents featured in this publication are
entirely fictional. DC Comics does not read or accept
unsolicited submissions of ideas, stories, or artwork.
DC – a WarnerMedia Company.

DC Comics,
2900 West Alameda Ave.,
Burbank, CA 91505.
Printed by LSC Communications,
Owensville, MO, USA. 8/23/21.
First Printing. ISBN: 978-1-77950-801-0

Library of Congress Cataloging-in-Publication
Data is available.

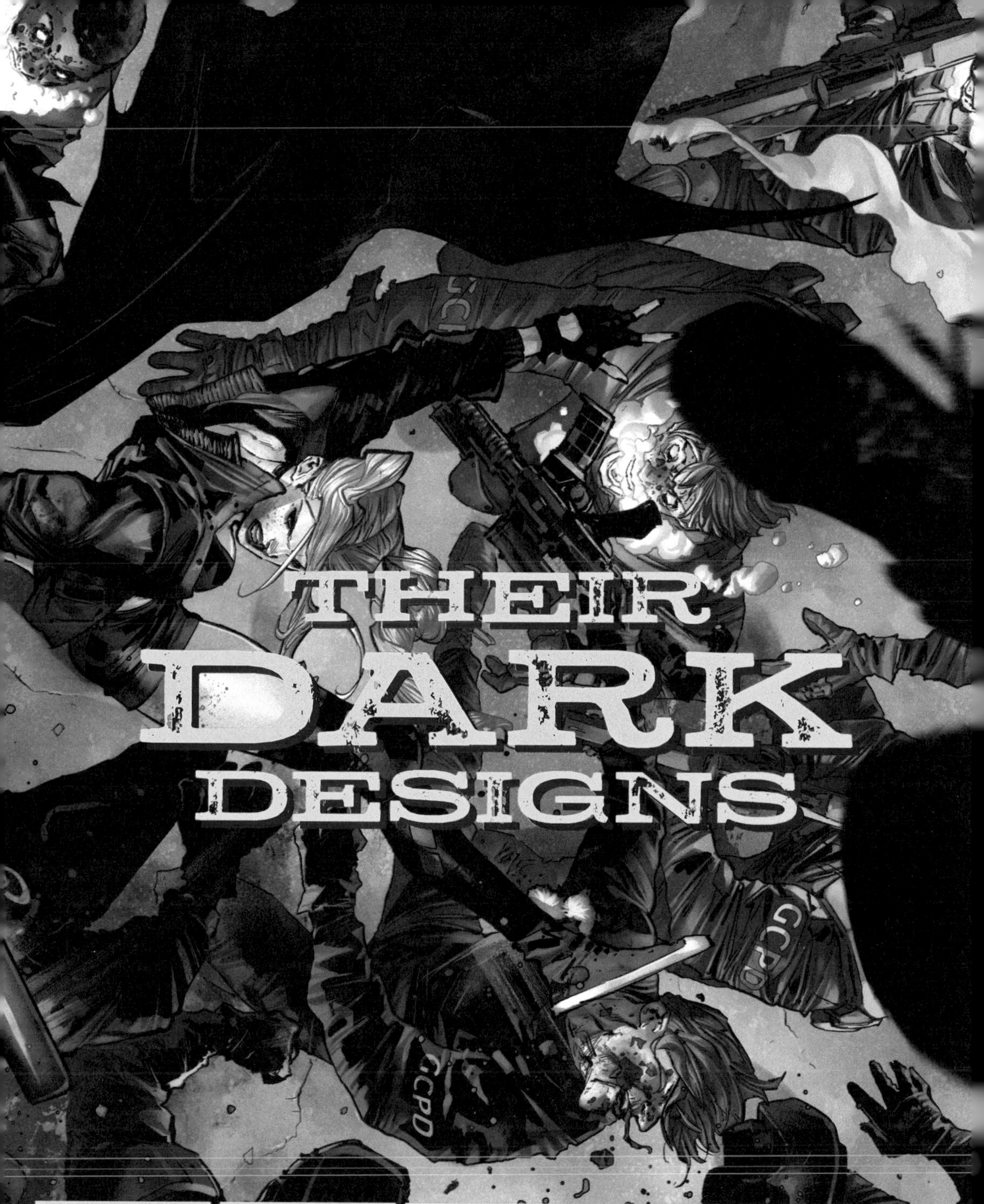
GCPD

THEIR DARK DESIGNS

WRITERS

JAMES TYNION IV
VITA AYALA
PHILLIP KENNEDY JOHNSON
MARIKO TAMAKI
DAN WATTERS

ARTISTS

GUILLEM MARCH
TONY S. DANIEL
CARLO PAGULAYAN
JORGE JIMENEZ
RAFAEL ALBUQUERQUE
JAVIER FERNANDEZ
DANNY MIKI
ANDIE TONG
VICTOR IBÁÑEZ
RILEY ROSSMO
JOHN PAUL LEON
SUMIT KUMAR

COLORISTS

TOMEU MOREY
DAVID BARON
ALEJANDRO SÁNCHEZ
JORDIE BELLAIRE
IVAN PLASCENCIA
JOHN PAUL LEON
FCO PLASCENCIA

LETTERERS

CLAYTON COWLES
ROB LEIGH
TROY PETERI
TOM NAPOLITANO
DERON BENNETT
CARLOS M. MANGUAL

COLLECTION COVER ARTISTS

JORGE JIMENEZ & TOMEU MOREY

BATMAN CREATED BY

BOB KANE WITH **BILL FINGER**

EPILOGUE

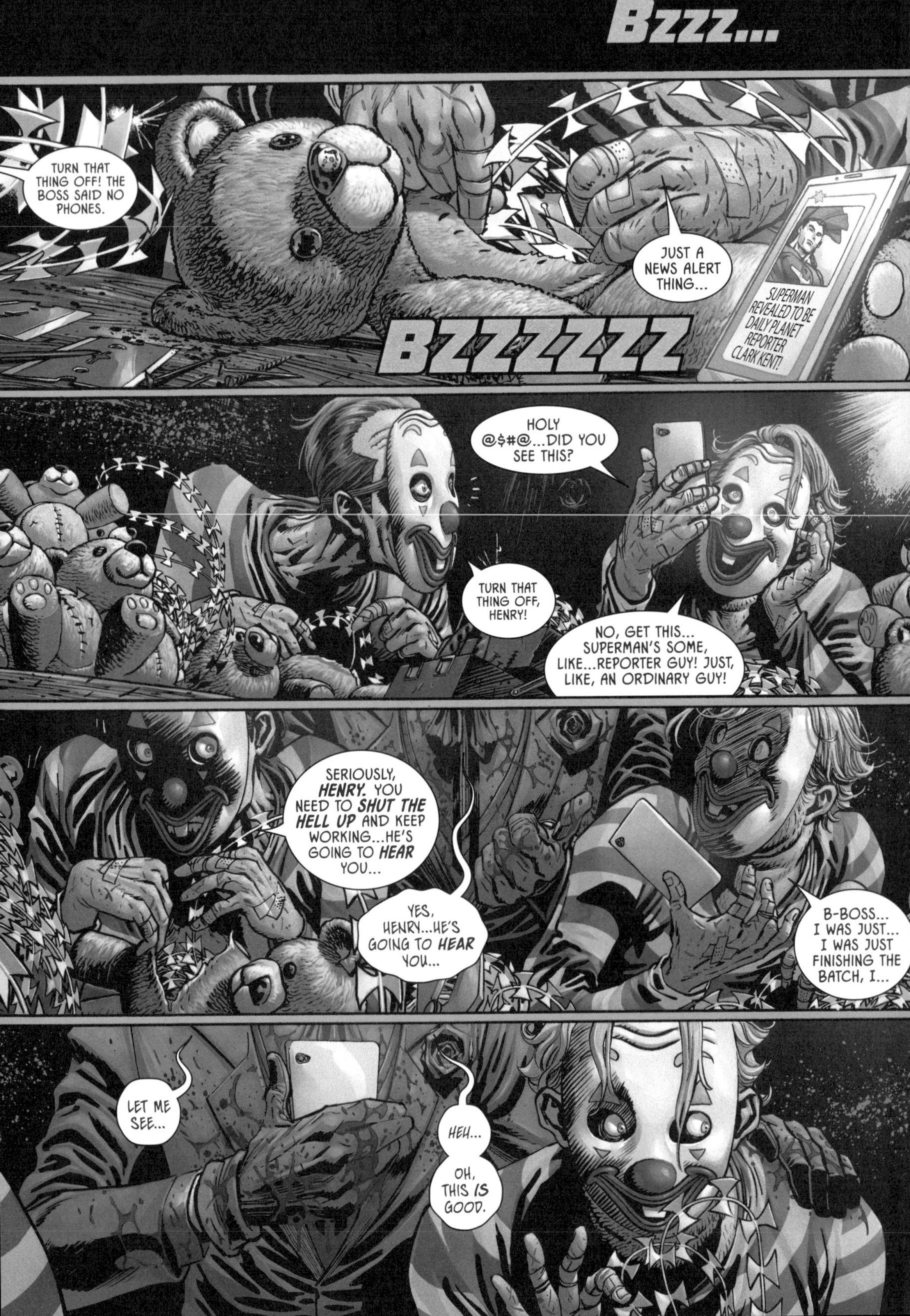

Bzzz...
TURN THAT THING OFF! THE BOSS SAID NO PHONES.
JUST A NEWS ALERT THING...
SUPERMAN REVEALED TO BE DAILY PLANET REPORTER CLARK KENT!
BZZZZZZ
HOLY @$#@...DID YOU SEE THIS?
TURN THAT THING OFF, HENRY!
NO, GET THIS... SUPERMAN'S SOME, LIKE...REPORTER GUY! JUST, LIKE, AN ORDINARY GUY!
SERIOUSLY, HENRY. YOU NEED TO SHUT THE HELL UP AND KEEP WORKING...HE'S GOING TO HEAR YOU...
YES, HENRY...HE'S GOING TO HEAR YOU...
B-BOSS... I WAS JUST... I WAS JUST FINISHING THE BATCH, I...
LET ME SEE...
HEH...
OH, THIS IS GOOD.

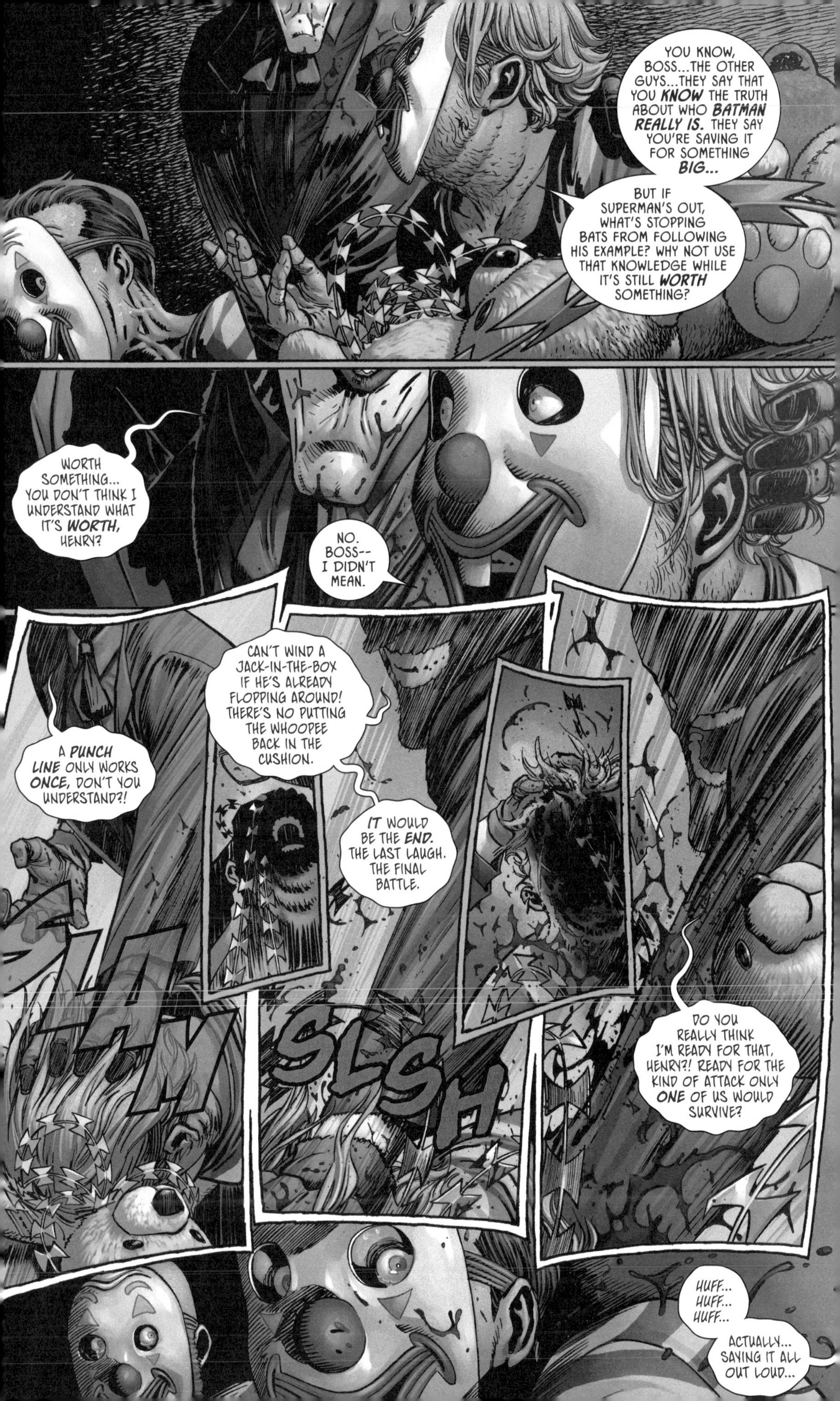

YOU KNOW, BOSS...THE OTHER GUYS...THEY SAY THAT YOU KNOW THE TRUTH ABOUT WHO BATMAN REALLY IS. THEY SAY YOU'RE SAVING IT FOR SOMETHING BIG...
BUT IF SUPERMAN'S OUT, WHAT'S STOPPING BATS FROM FOLLOWING HIS EXAMPLE? WHY NOT USE THAT KNOWLEDGE WHILE IT'S STILL WORTH SOMETHING?
WORTH SOMETHING... YOU DON'T THINK I UNDERSTAND WHAT IT'S WORTH, HENRY?
NO. BOSS-- I DIDN'T MEAN.
A PUNCH LINE ONLY WORKS ONCE, DON'T YOU UNDERSTAND?!
CAN'T WIND A JACK-IN-THE-BOX IF HE'S ALREADY FLOPPING AROUND! THERE'S NO PUTTING THE WHOOPEE BACK IN THE CUSHION.
IT WOULD BE THE END. THE LAST LAUGH. THE FINAL BATTLE.
SLSH
DO YOU REALLY THINK I'M READY FOR THAT, HENRY?! READY FOR THE KIND OF ATTACK ONLY ONE OF US WOULD SURVIVE?
HUFF... HUFF... HUFF...
ACTUALLY... SAYING IT ALL OUT LOUD...

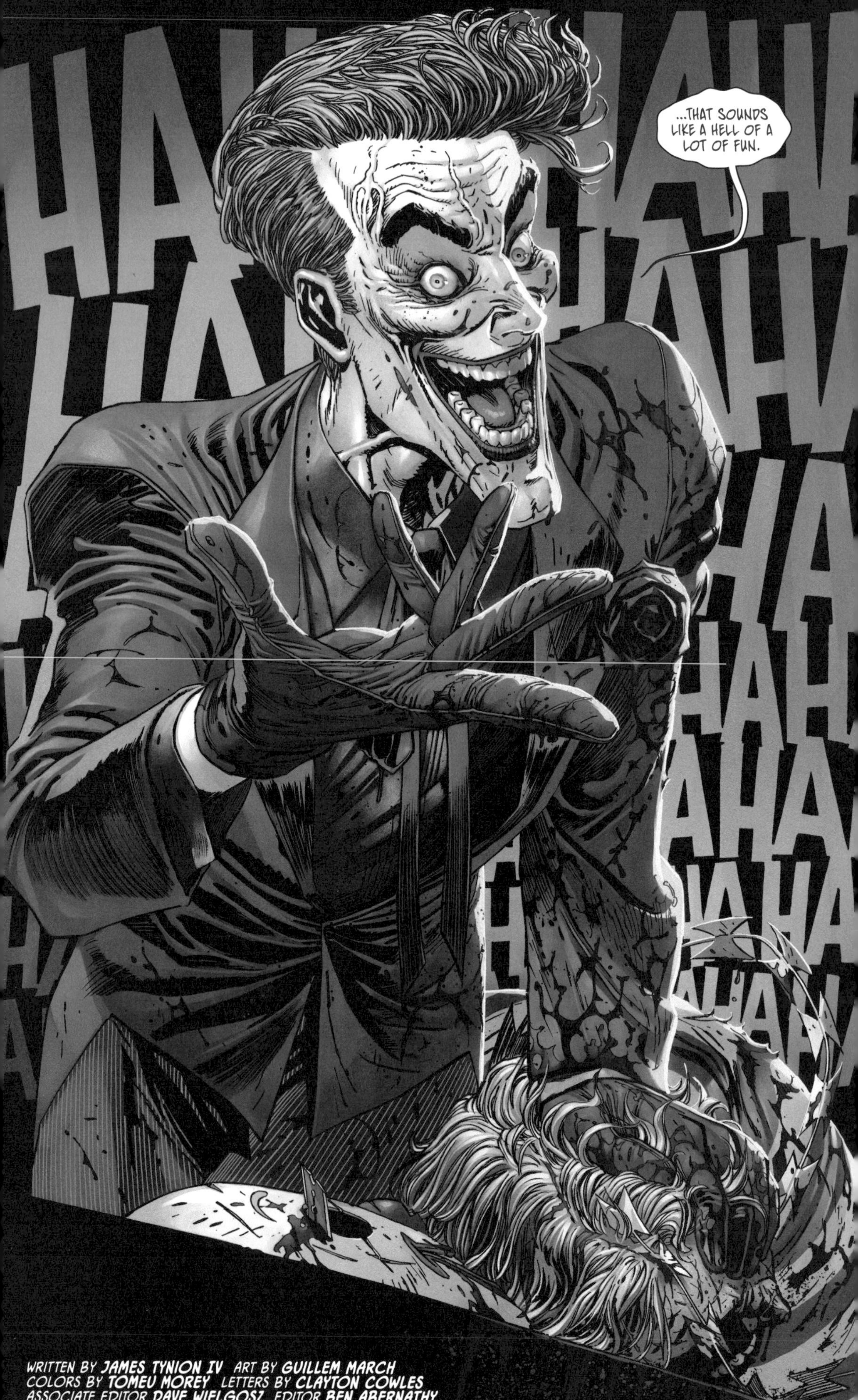

...THAT SOUNDS LIKE A HELL OF A LOT OF FUN.

WRITTEN BY **JAMES TYNION IV** ART BY **GUILLEM MARCH**
COLORS BY **TOMEU MOREY** LETTERS BY **CLAYTON COWLES**
ASSOCIATE EDITOR **DAVE WIELGOSZ** EDITOR **BEN ABERNATHY**

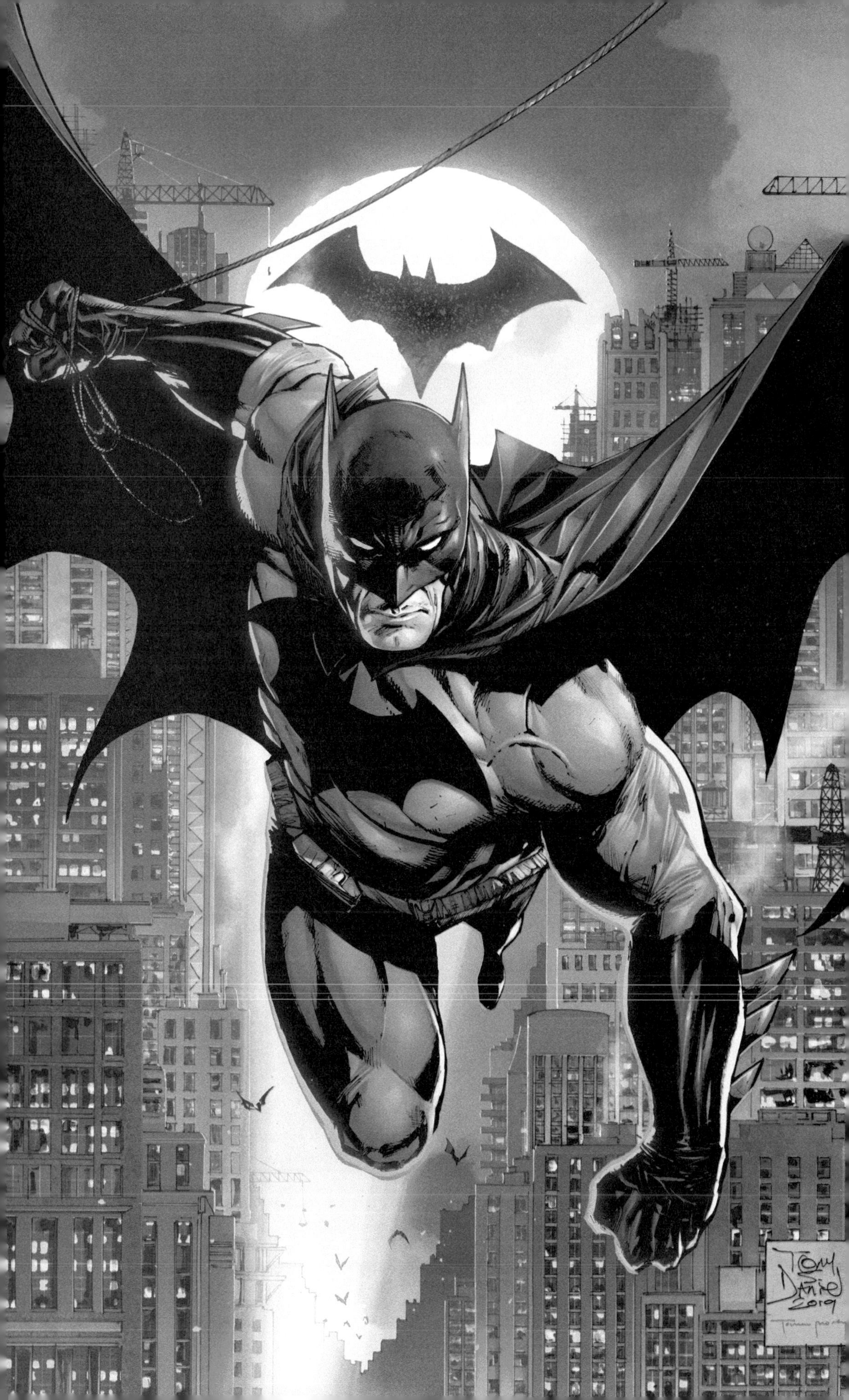

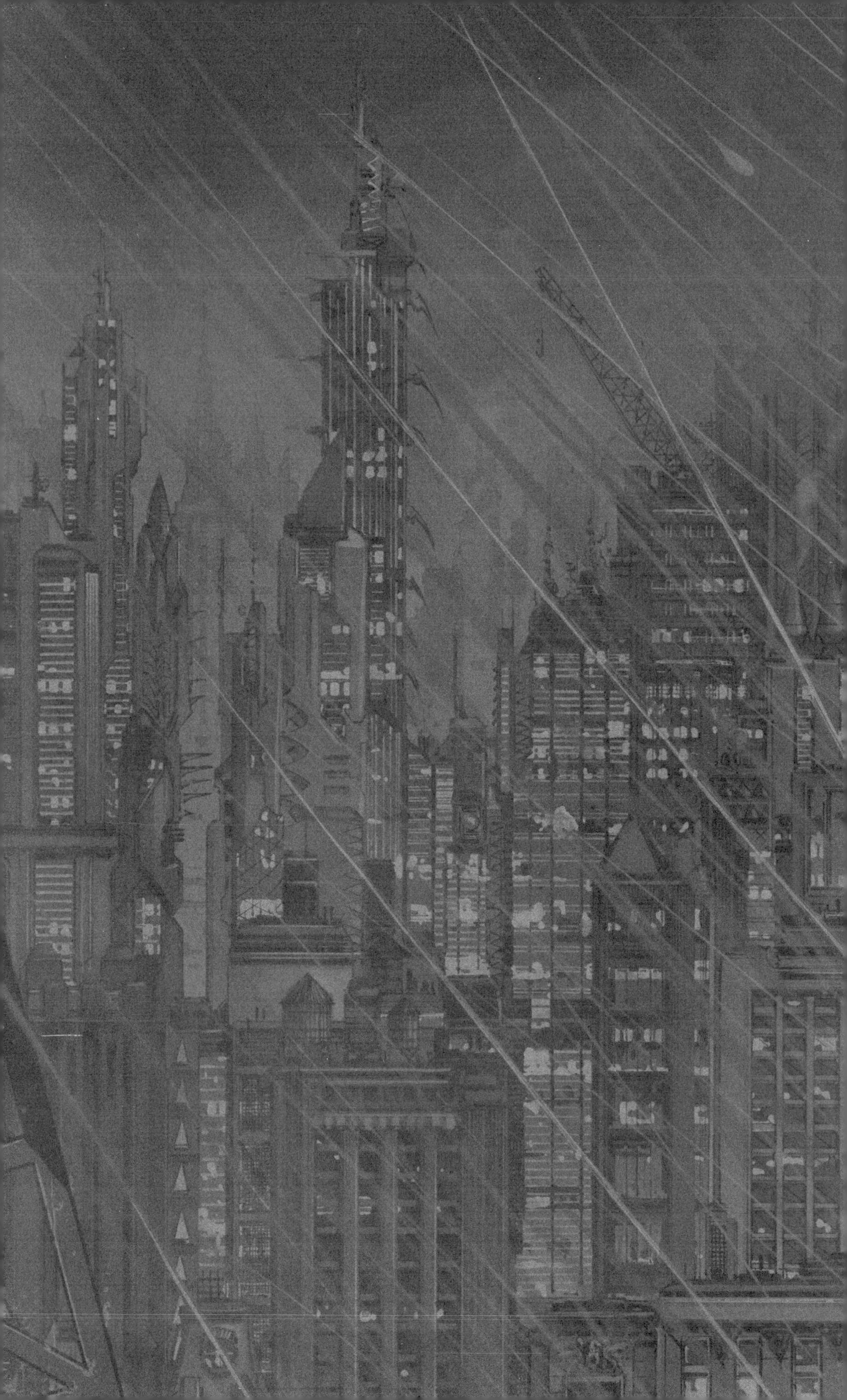

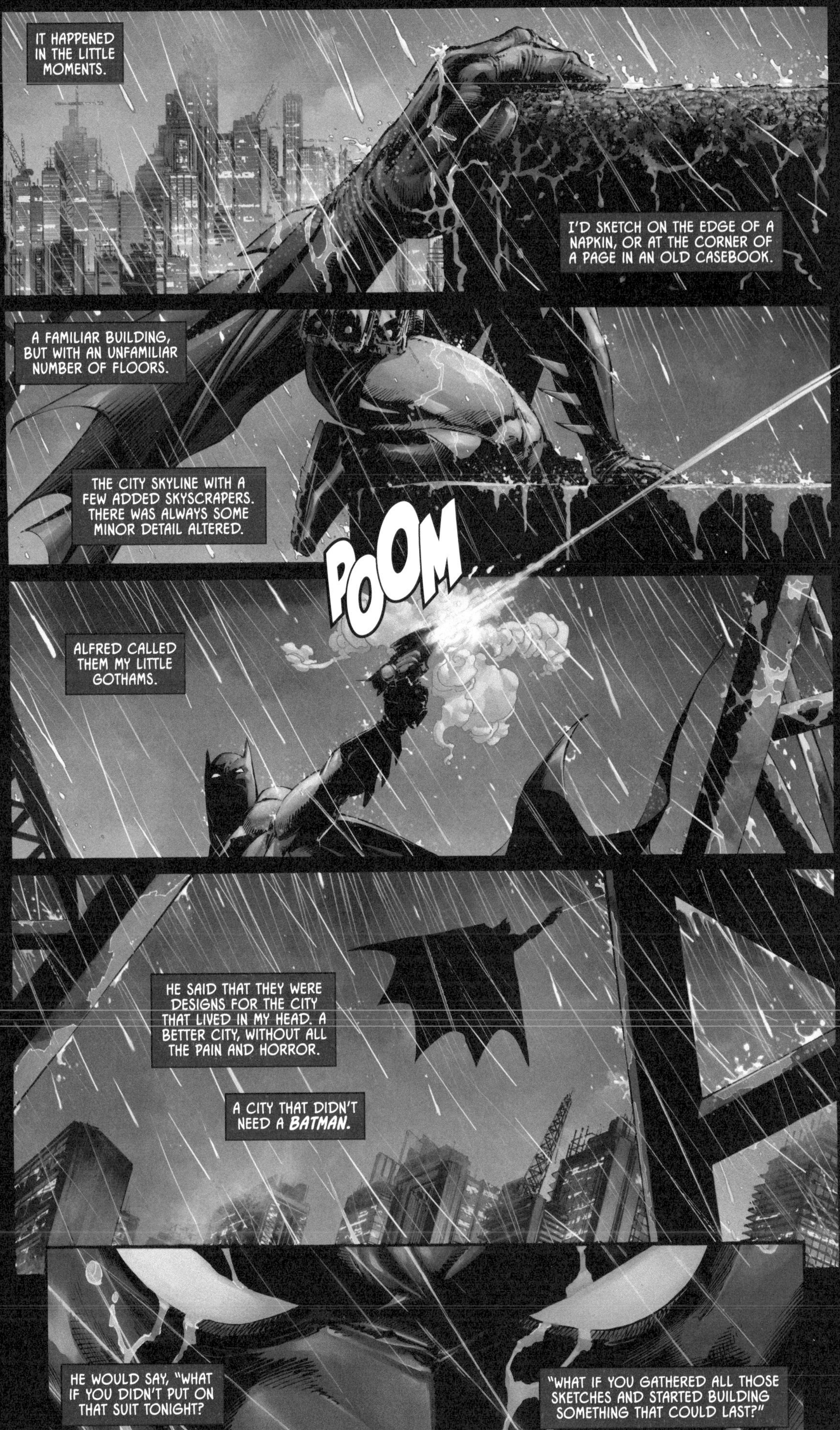
IT HAPPENED IN THE LITTLE MOMENTS.
I'D SKETCH ON THE EDGE OF A NAPKIN, OR AT THE CORNER OF A PAGE IN AN OLD CASEBOOK.
A FAMILIAR BUILDING, BUT WITH AN UNFAMILIAR NUMBER OF FLOORS.
THE CITY SKYLINE WITH A FEW ADDED SKYSCRAPERS. THERE WAS ALWAYS SOME MINOR DETAIL ALTERED.
POOM
ALFRED CALLED THEM MY LITTLE GOTHAMS.
HE SAID THAT THEY WERE DESIGNS FOR THE CITY THAT LIVED IN MY HEAD. A BETTER CITY, WITHOUT ALL THE PAIN AND HORROR.
A CITY THAT DIDN'T NEED A *BATMAN.*
HE WOULD SAY, "WHAT IF YOU DIDN'T PUT ON THAT SUIT TONIGHT?
"WHAT IF YOU GATHERED ALL THOSE SKETCHES AND STARTED BUILDING SOMETHING THAT COULD LAST?"

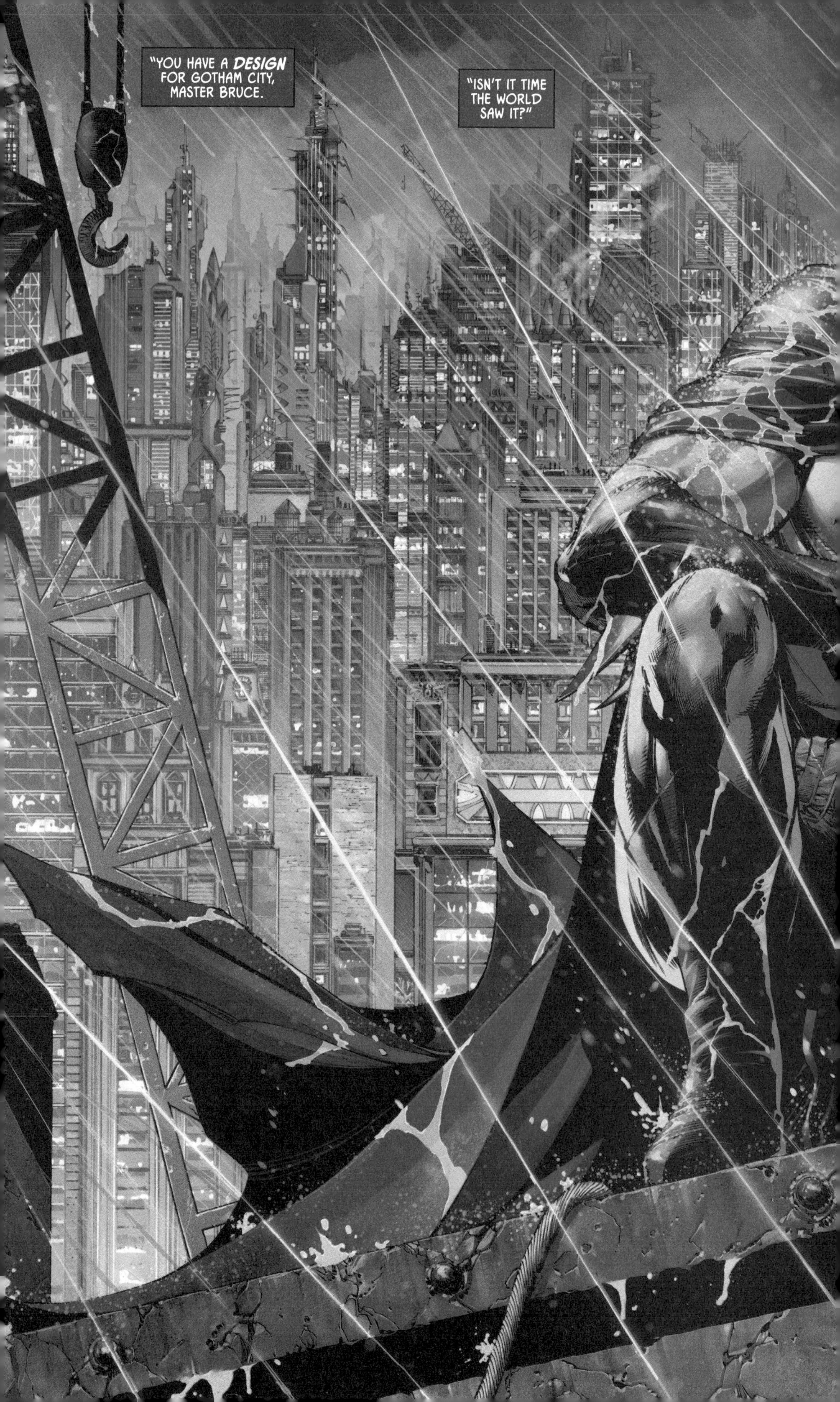
"YOU HAVE A DESIGN FOR GOTHAM CITY, MASTER BRUCE.
"ISN'T IT TIME THE WORLD SAW IT?"

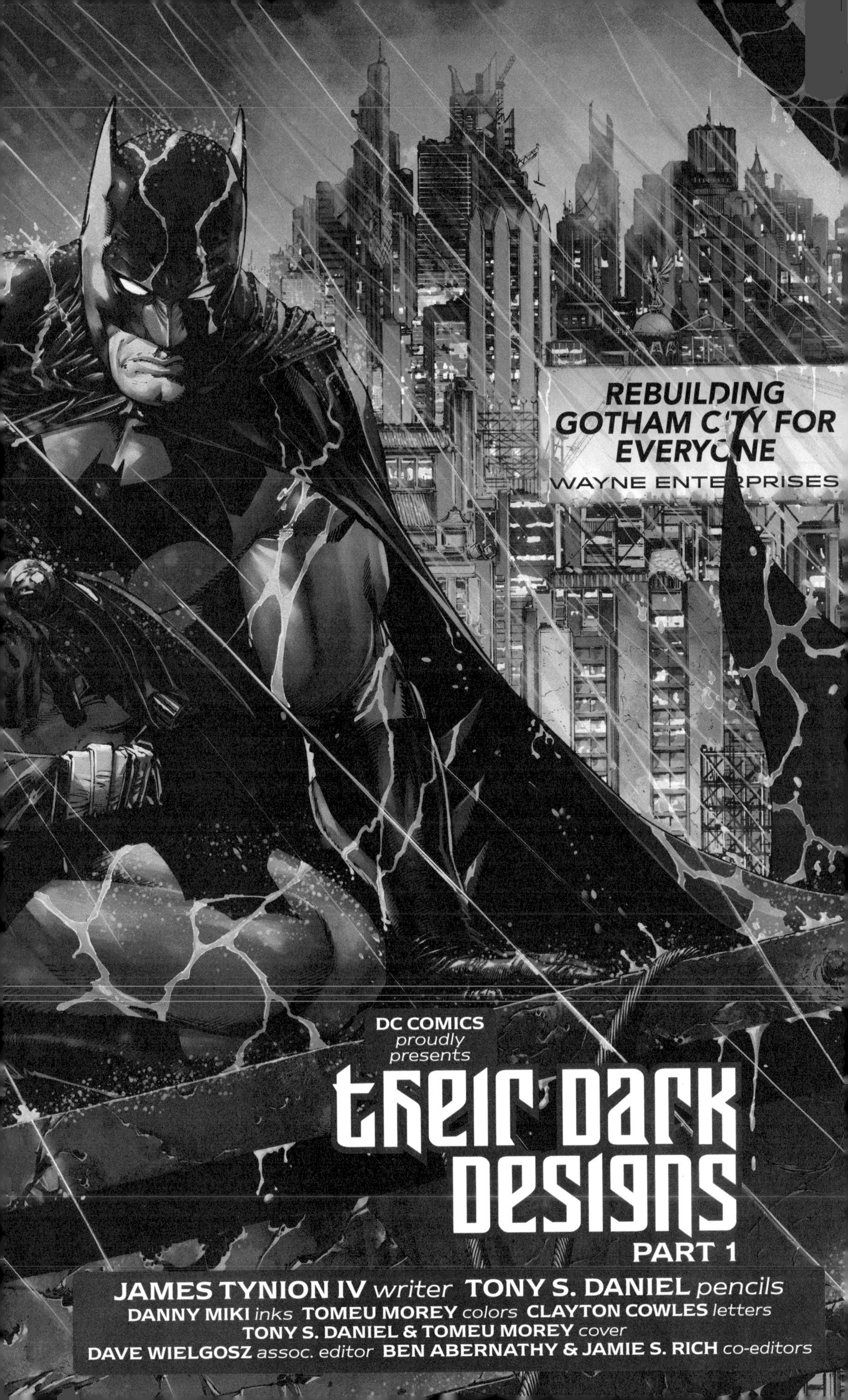
REBUILDING GOTHAM CITY FOR EVERYONE
WAYNE ENTERPRISES
DC COMICS proudly presents
THEIR DARK DESIGNS
PART 1
JAMES TYNION IV writer TONY S. DANIEL pencils
DANNY MIKI inks TOMEU MOREY colors CLAYTON COWLES letters
TONY S. DANIEL & TOMEU MOREY cover
DAVE WIELGOSZ assoc. editor BEN ABERNATHY & JAMIE S. RICH co-editors

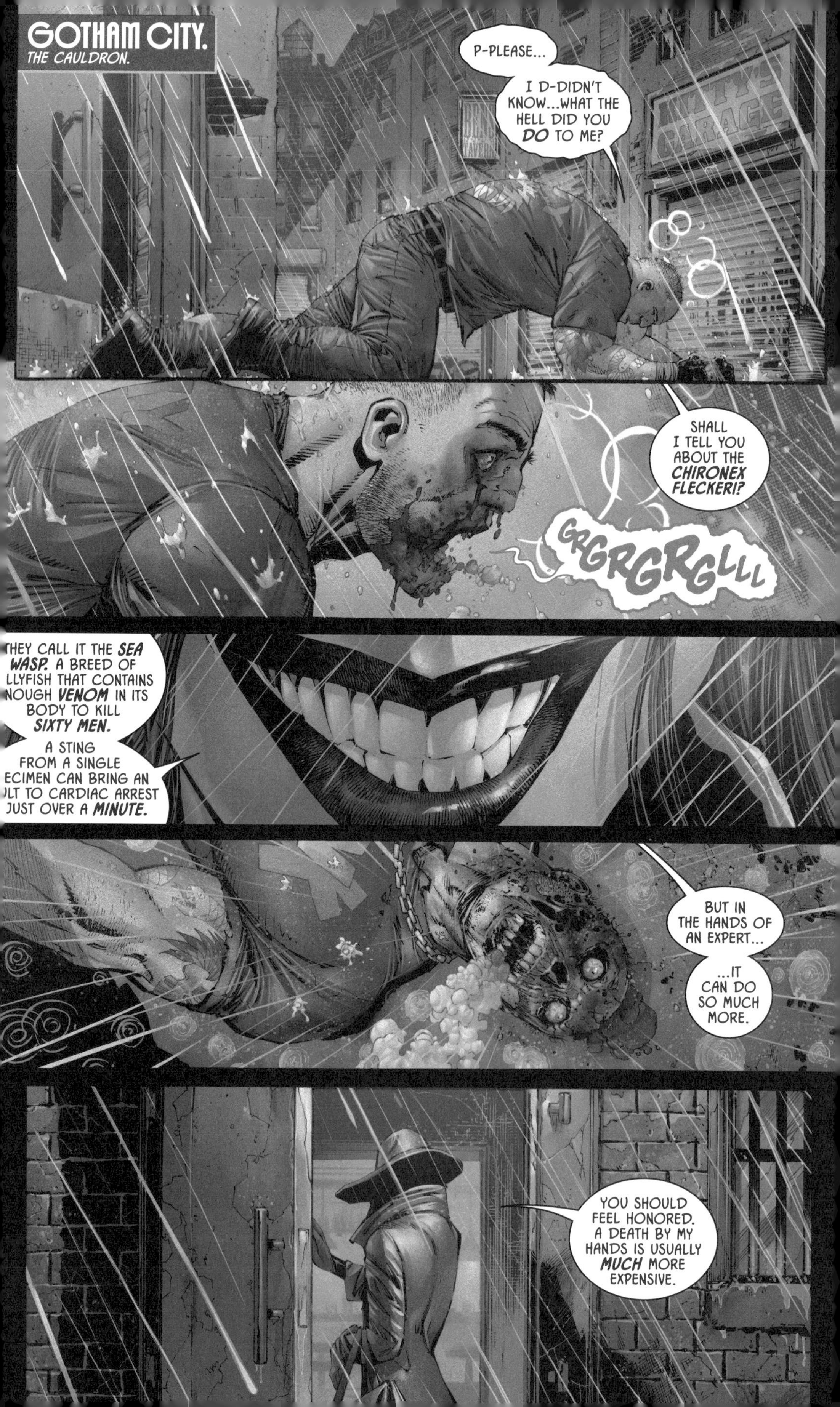
GOTHAM CITY.
THE CAULDRON.
P-PLEASE...
I D-DIDN'T KNOW...WHAT THE HELL DID YOU DO TO ME?
SHALL I TELL YOU ABOUT THE CHIRONEX FLECKERI?
GRGRGRGRGLLLL
HEY CALL IT THE SEA WASP. A BREED OF LLYFISH THAT CONTAINS NOUGH VENOM IN ITS BODY TO KILL SIXTY MEN.
A STING FROM A SINGLE ECIMEN CAN BRING AN ULT TO CARDIAC ARREST JUST OVER A MINUTE.
BUT IN THE HANDS OF AN EXPERT...
...IT CAN DO SO MUCH MORE.
YOU SHOULD FEEL HONORED. A DEATH BY MY HANDS IS USUALLY MUCH MORE EXPENSIVE.

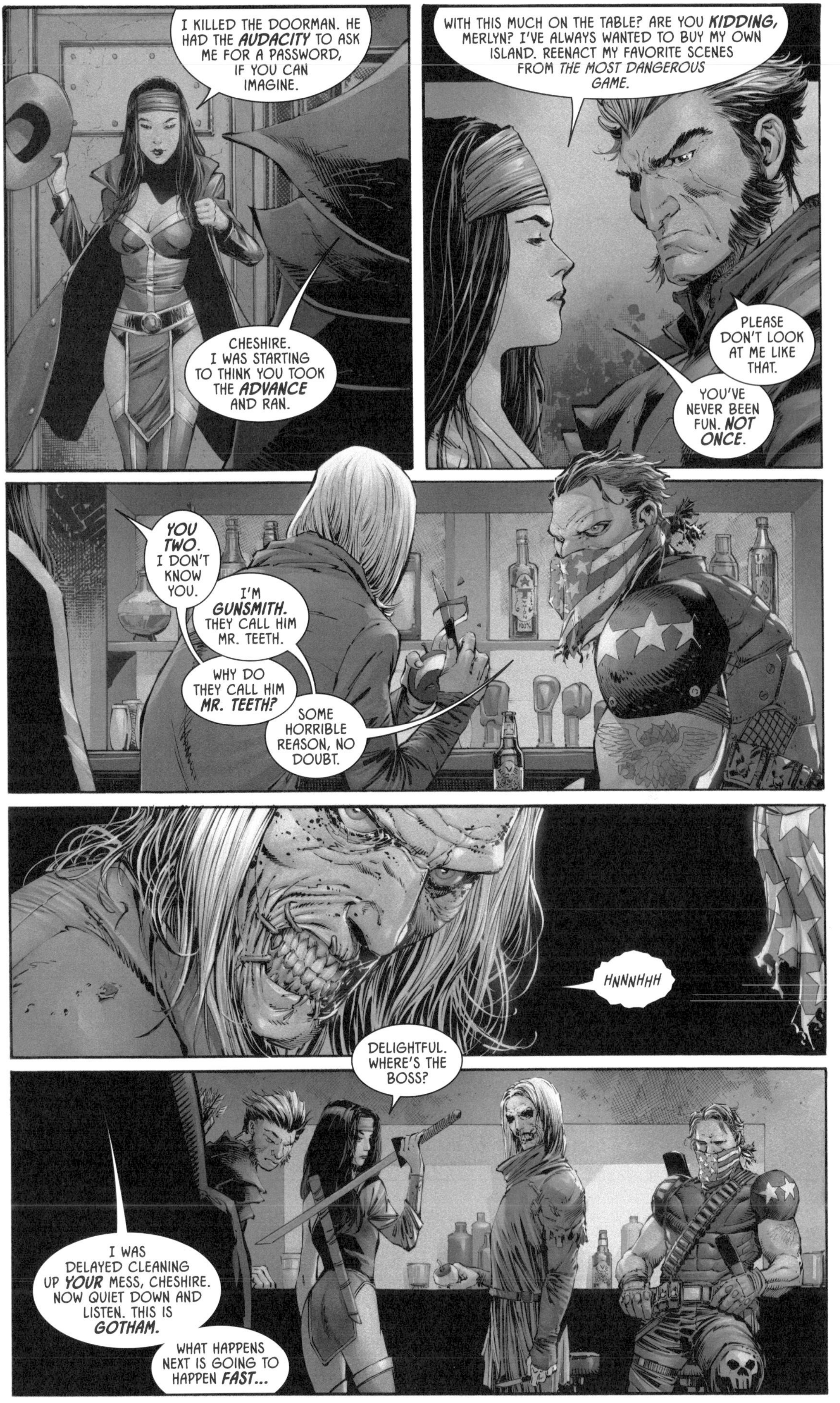
I KILLED THE DOORMAN. HE HAD THE *AUDACITY* TO ASK ME FOR A PASSWORD, IF YOU CAN IMAGINE.
CHESHIRE. I WAS STARTING TO THINK YOU TOOK THE *ADVANCE* AND RAN.
WITH THIS MUCH ON THE TABLE? ARE YOU *KIDDING,* MERLYN? I'VE ALWAYS WANTED TO BUY MY OWN ISLAND. REENACT MY FAVORITE SCENES FROM *THE MOST DANGEROUS GAME.*
PLEASE DON'T LOOK AT ME LIKE THAT.
YOU'VE NEVER BEEN FUN. ***NOT ONCE.***
YOU TWO. I DON'T KNOW YOU.
I'M ***GUNSMITH.*** THEY CALL HIM MR. TEETH.
WHY DO THEY CALL HIM ***MR. TEETH?***
SOME HORRIBLE REASON, NO DOUBT.
HNNNHHH
DELIGHTFUL. WHERE'S THE BOSS?
I WAS DELAYED CLEANING UP ***YOUR*** MESS, CHESHIRE. NOW QUIET DOWN AND LISTEN. THIS IS ***GOTHAM.***
WHAT HAPPENS NEXT IS GOING TO HAPPEN ***FAST...***

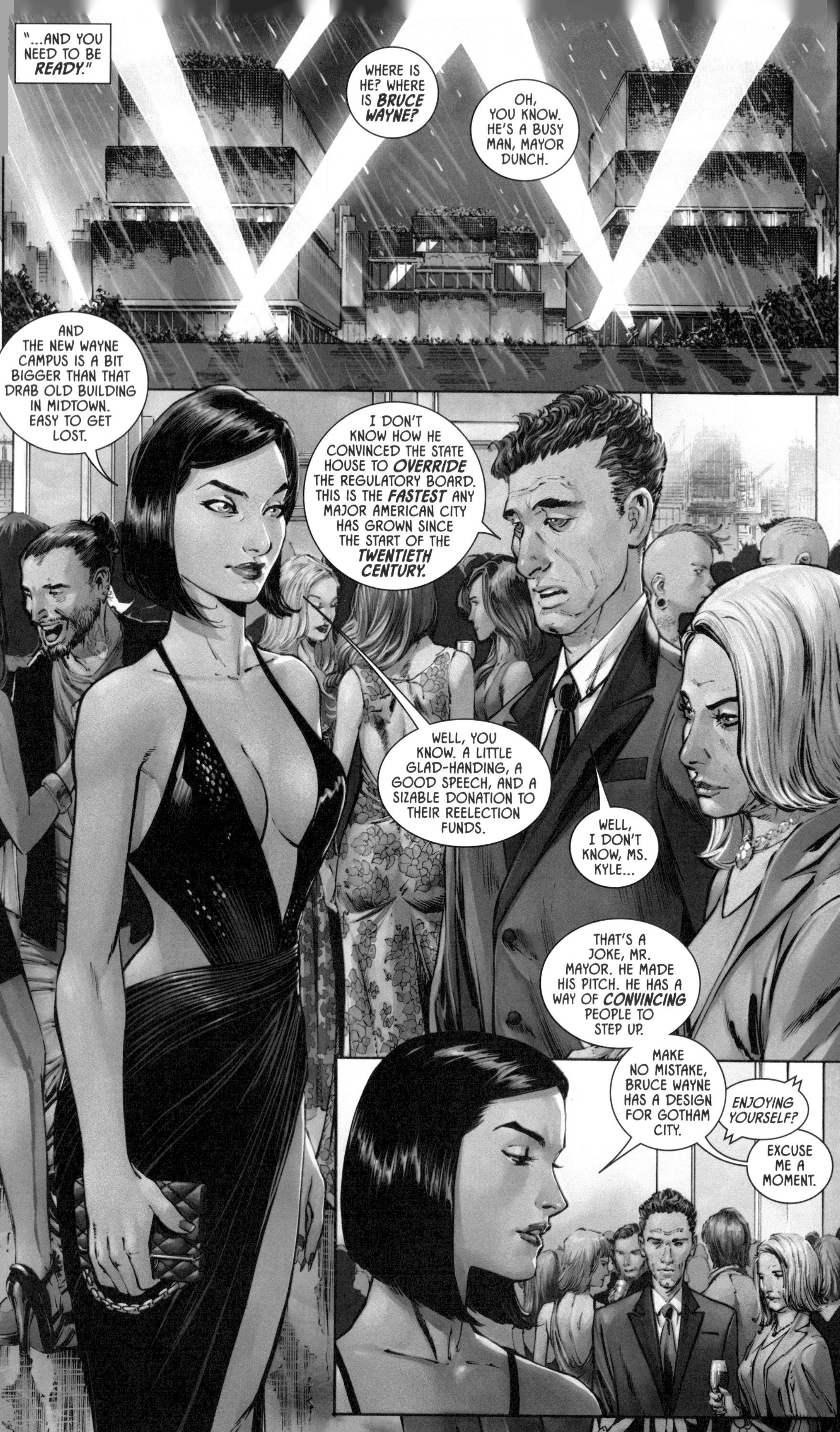

"...AND YOU NEED TO BE READY."
WHERE IS HE? WHERE IS BRUCE WAYNE?
OH, YOU KNOW. HE'S A BUSY MAN, MAYOR DUNCH.
AND THE NEW WAYNE CAMPUS IS A BIT BIGGER THAN THAT DRAB OLD BUILDING IN MIDTOWN. EASY TO GET LOST.
I DON'T KNOW HOW HE CONVINCED THE STATE HOUSE TO OVERRIDE THE REGULATORY BOARD. THIS IS THE FASTEST ANY MAJOR AMERICAN CITY HAS GROWN SINCE THE START OF THE TWENTIETH CENTURY.
WELL, YOU KNOW. A LITTLE GLAD-HANDING, A GOOD SPEECH, AND A SIZABLE DONATION TO THEIR REELECTION FUNDS.
WELL, I DON'T KNOW, MS. KYLE...
THAT'S A JOKE, MR. MAYOR. HE MADE HIS PITCH. HE HAS A WAY OF CONVINCING PEOPLE TO STEP UP.
MAKE NO MISTAKE, BRUCE WAYNE HAS A DESIGN FOR GOTHAM CITY.
ENJOYING YOURSELF?
EXCUSE ME A MOMENT.

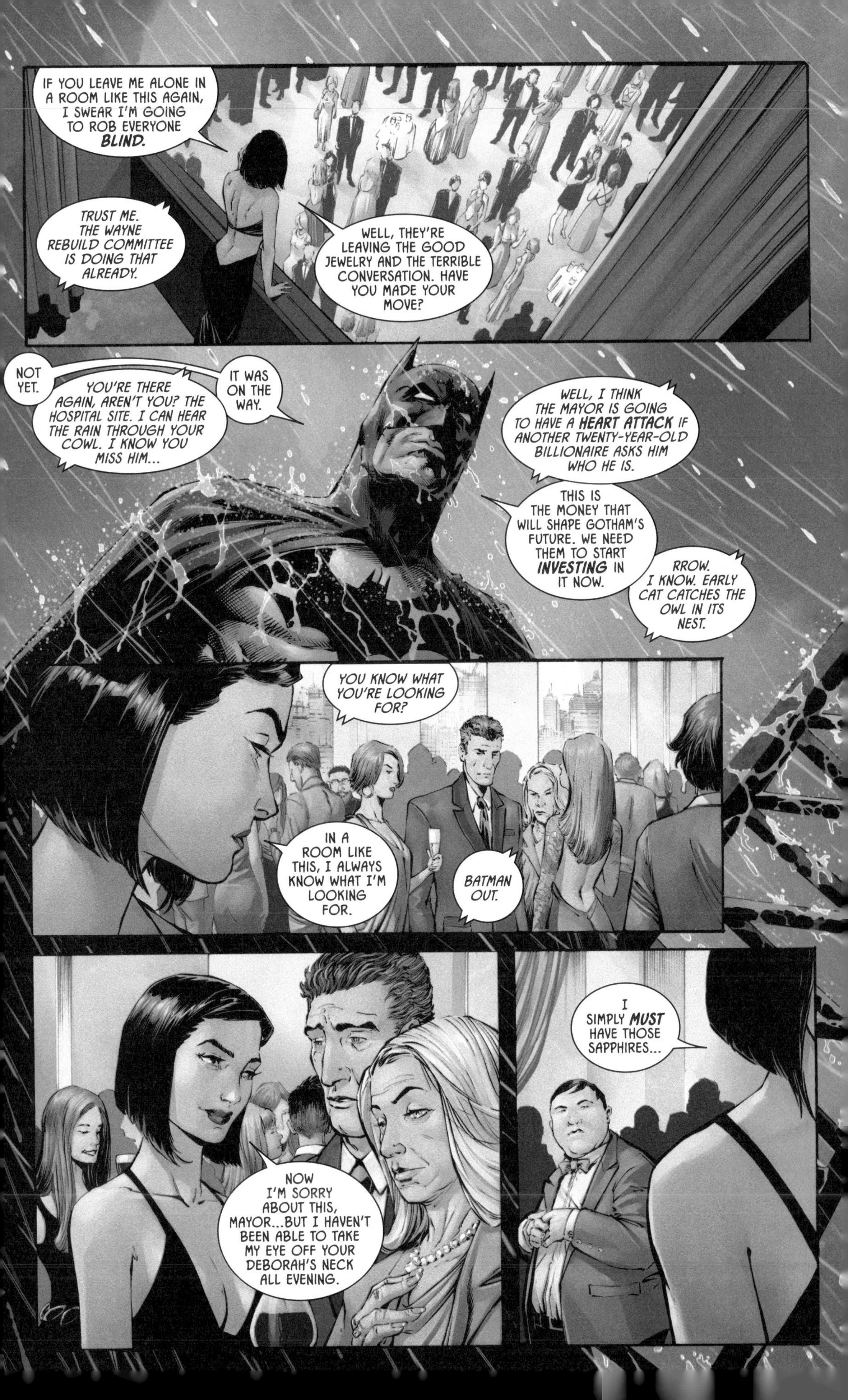
IF YOU LEAVE ME ALONE IN A ROOM LIKE THIS AGAIN, I SWEAR I'M GOING TO ROB EVERYONE **BLIND.**
TRUST ME. THE WAYNE REBUILD COMMITTEE IS DOING THAT ALREADY.
WELL, THEY'RE LEAVING THE GOOD JEWELRY AND THE TERRIBLE CONVERSATION. HAVE YOU MADE YOUR MOVE?
NOT YET.
IT WAS ON THE WAY.
YOU'RE THERE AGAIN, AREN'T YOU? THE HOSPITAL SITE. I CAN HEAR THE RAIN THROUGH YOUR COWL. I KNOW YOU MISS HIM...
WELL, I THINK THE MAYOR IS GOING TO HAVE A **HEART ATTACK** IF ANOTHER TWENTY-YEAR-OLD BILLIONAIRE ASKS HIM WHO HE IS.
THIS IS THE MONEY THAT WILL SHAPE GOTHAM'S FUTURE. WE NEED THEM TO START **INVESTING** IN IT NOW.
RROW. I KNOW. EARLY CAT CATCHES THE OWL IN ITS NEST.
YOU KNOW WHAT YOU'RE LOOKING FOR?
IN A ROOM LIKE THIS, I ALWAYS KNOW WHAT I'M LOOKING FOR.
BATMAN OUT.
NOW I'M SORRY ABOUT THIS, MAYOR...BUT I HAVEN'T BEEN ABLE TO TAKE MY EYE OFF YOUR DEBORAH'S NECK ALL EVENING.
I SIMPLY **MUST** HAVE THOSE SAPPHIRES...

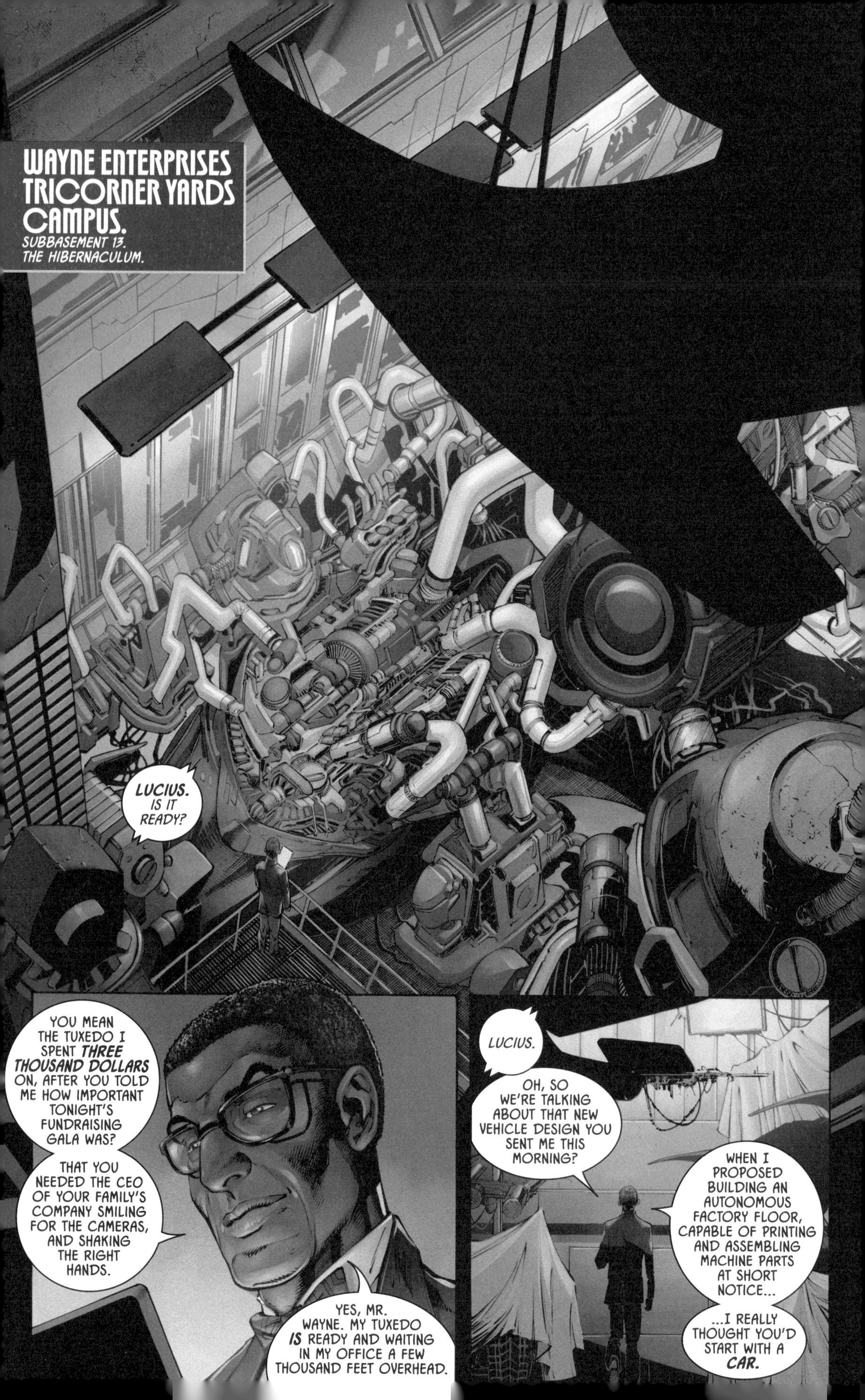
WAYNE ENTERPRISES TRICORNER YARDS CAMPUS.
SUBBASEMENT 13. THE HIBERNACULUM.
LUCIUS. IS IT READY?
YOU MEAN THE TUXEDO I SPENT THREE THOUSAND DOLLARS ON, AFTER YOU TOLD ME HOW IMPORTANT TONIGHT'S FUNDRAISING GALA WAS?
THAT YOU NEEDED THE CEO OF YOUR FAMILY'S COMPANY SMILING FOR THE CAMERAS, AND SHAKING THE RIGHT HANDS.
YES, MR. WAYNE. MY TUXEDO IS READY AND WAITING IN MY OFFICE A FEW THOUSAND FEET OVERHEAD.
LUCIUS.
OH, SO WE'RE TALKING ABOUT THAT NEW VEHICLE DESIGN YOU SENT ME THIS MORNING?
WHEN I PROPOSED BUILDING AN AUTONOMOUS FACTORY FLOOR, CAPABLE OF PRINTING AND ASSEMBLING MACHINE PARTS AT SHORT NOTICE...
...I REALLY THOUGHT YOU'D START WITH A CAR.

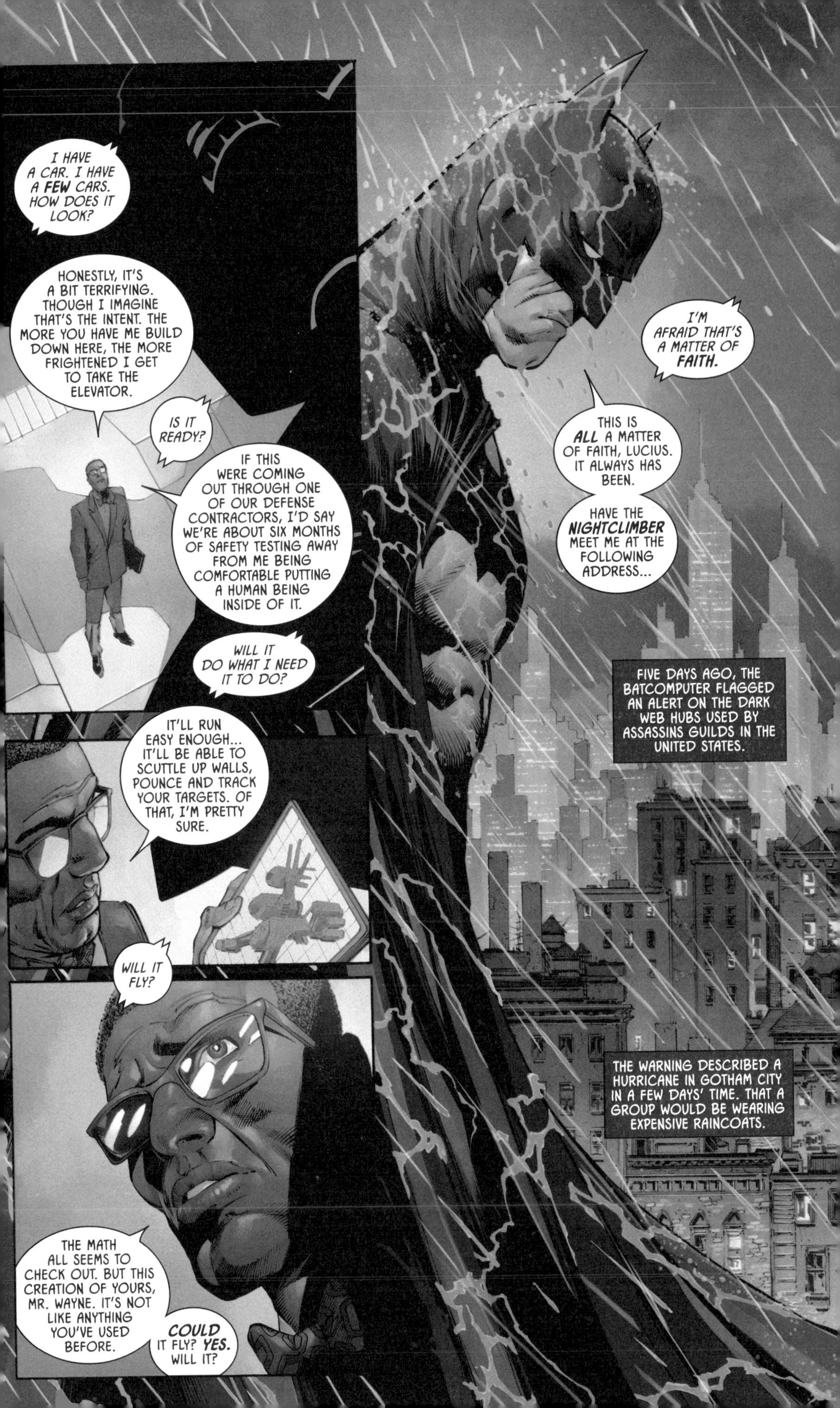
I HAVE A CAR. I HAVE A **FEW** CARS. HOW DOES IT LOOK?
HONESTLY, IT'S A BIT TERRIFYING. THOUGH I IMAGINE THAT'S THE INTENT. THE MORE YOU HAVE ME BUILD DOWN HERE, THE MORE FRIGHTENED I GET TO TAKE THE ELEVATOR.
IS IT READY?
IF THIS WERE COMING OUT THROUGH ONE OF OUR DEFENSE CONTRACTORS, I'D SAY WE'RE ABOUT SIX MONTHS OF SAFETY TESTING AWAY FROM ME BEING COMFORTABLE PUTTING A HUMAN BEING INSIDE OF IT.
WILL IT DO WHAT I NEED IT TO DO?
IT'LL RUN EASY ENOUGH... IT'LL BE ABLE TO SCUTTLE UP WALLS, POUNCE AND TRACK YOUR TARGETS. OF THAT, I'M PRETTY SURE.
WILL IT FLY?
THE MATH ALL SEEMS TO CHECK OUT. BUT THIS CREATION OF YOURS, MR. WAYNE. IT'S NOT LIKE ANYTHING YOU'VE USED BEFORE.
COULD IT FLY? **YES.** WILL IT?
I'M AFRAID THAT'S A MATTER OF **FAITH.**
THIS IS **ALL** A MATTER OF FAITH, LUCIUS. IT ALWAYS HAS BEEN.
HAVE THE **NIGHTCLIMBER** MEET ME AT THE FOLLOWING ADDRESS...
FIVE DAYS AGO, THE BATCOMPUTER FLAGGED AN ALERT ON THE DARK WEB HUBS USED BY ASSASSINS GUILDS IN THE UNITED STATES.
THE WARNING DESCRIBED A HURRICANE IN GOTHAM CITY IN A FEW DAYS' TIME. THAT A GROUP WOULD BE WEARING EXPENSIVE RAINCOATS.

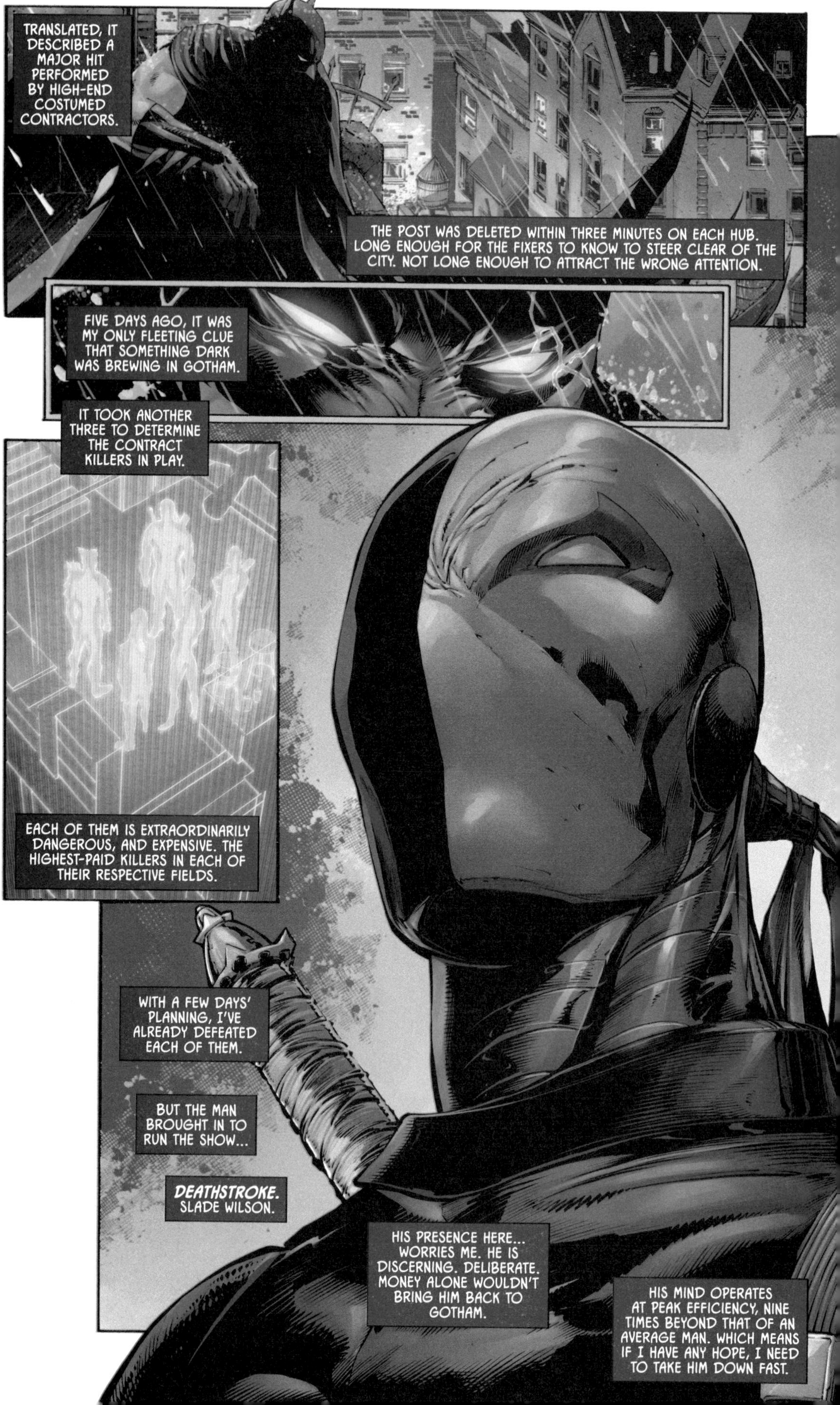
TRANSLATED, IT DESCRIBED A MAJOR HIT PERFORMED BY HIGH-END COSTUMED CONTRACTORS.
THE POST WAS DELETED WITHIN THREE MINUTES ON EACH HUB. LONG ENOUGH FOR THE FIXERS TO KNOW TO STEER CLEAR OF THE CITY. NOT LONG ENOUGH TO ATTRACT THE WRONG ATTENTION.
FIVE DAYS AGO, IT WAS MY ONLY FLEETING CLUE THAT SOMETHING DARK WAS BREWING IN GOTHAM.
IT TOOK ANOTHER THREE TO DETERMINE THE CONTRACT KILLERS IN PLAY.
EACH OF THEM IS EXTRAORDINARILY DANGEROUS, AND EXPENSIVE. THE HIGHEST-PAID KILLERS IN EACH OF THEIR RESPECTIVE FIELDS.
WITH A FEW DAYS' PLANNING, I'VE ALREADY DEFEATED EACH OF THEM.
BUT THE MAN BROUGHT IN TO RUN THE SHOW...
DEATHSTROKE. SLADE WILSON.
HIS PRESENCE HERE... WORRIES ME. HE IS DISCERNING. DELIBERATE. MONEY ALONE WOULDN'T BRING HIM BACK TO GOTHAM.
HIS MIND OPERATES AT PEAK EFFICIENCY, NINE TIMES BEYOND THAT OF AN AVERAGE MAN. WHICH MEANS IF I HAVE ANY HOPE, I NEED TO TAKE HIM DOWN FAST.

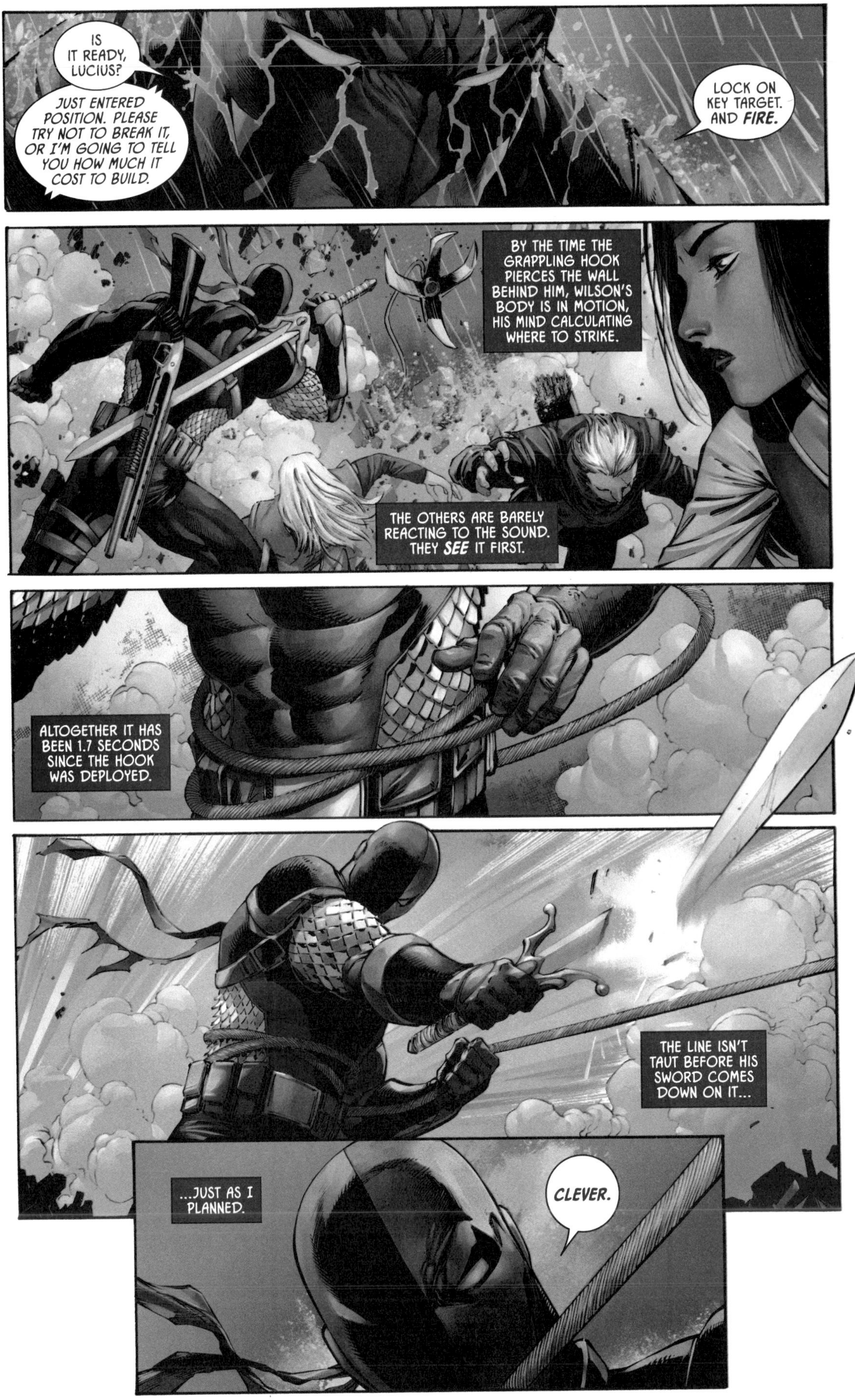
IS IT READY, LUCIUS?
JUST ENTERED POSITION. PLEASE TRY NOT TO BREAK IT, OR I'M GOING TO TELL YOU HOW MUCH IT COST TO BUILD.
LOCK ON KEY TARGET. AND FIRE.
BY THE TIME THE GRAPPLING HOOK PIERCES THE WALL BEHIND HIM, WILSON'S BODY IS IN MOTION, HIS MIND CALCULATING WHERE TO STRIKE.
THE OTHERS ARE BARELY REACTING TO THE SOUND. THEY SEE IT FIRST.
ALTOGETHER IT HAS BEEN 1.7 SECONDS SINCE THE HOOK WAS DEPLOYED.
THE LINE ISN'T TAUT BEFORE HIS SWORD COMES DOWN ON IT...
...JUST AS I PLANNED.
CLEVER.

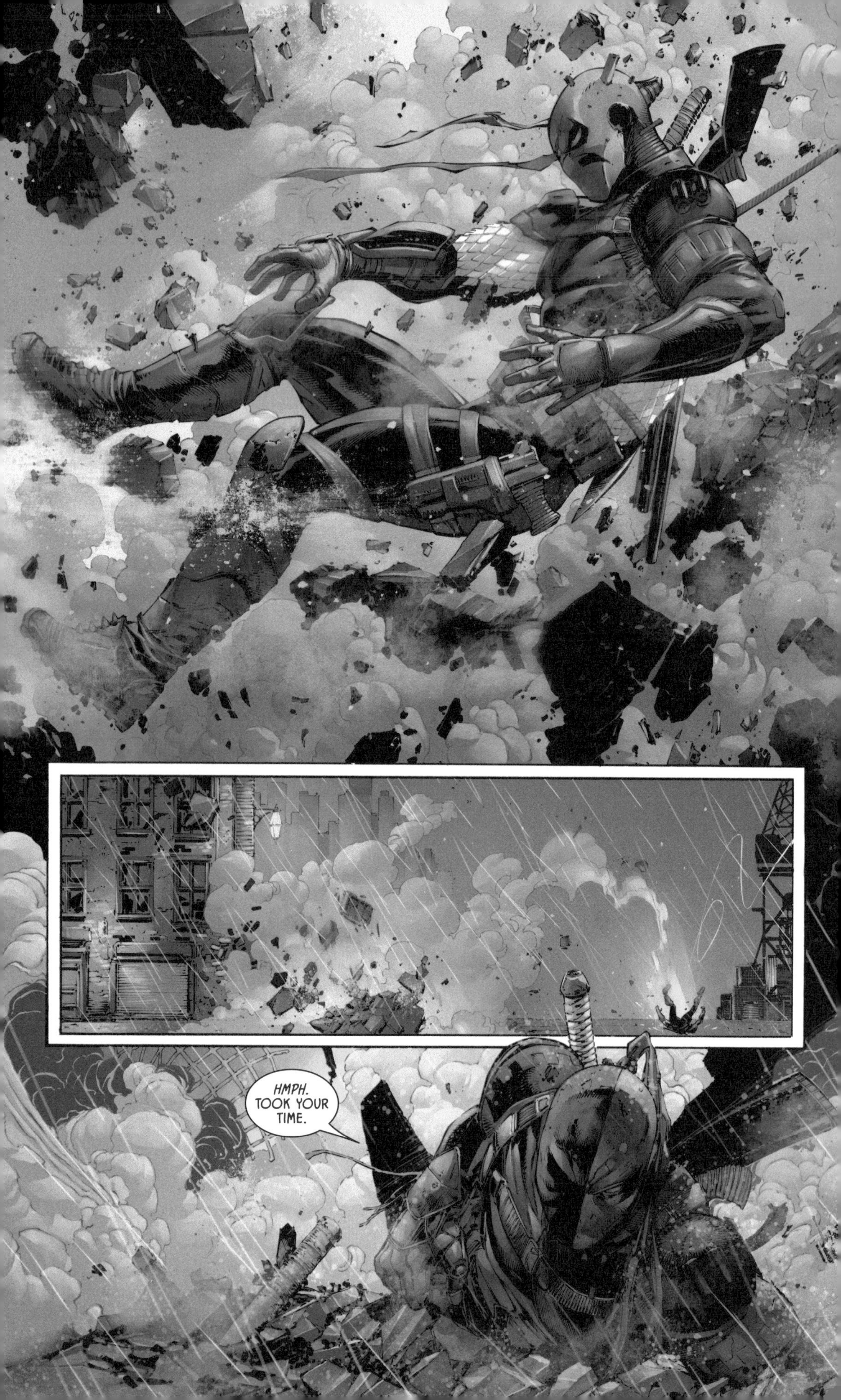
HMPH. TOOK YOUR TIME.

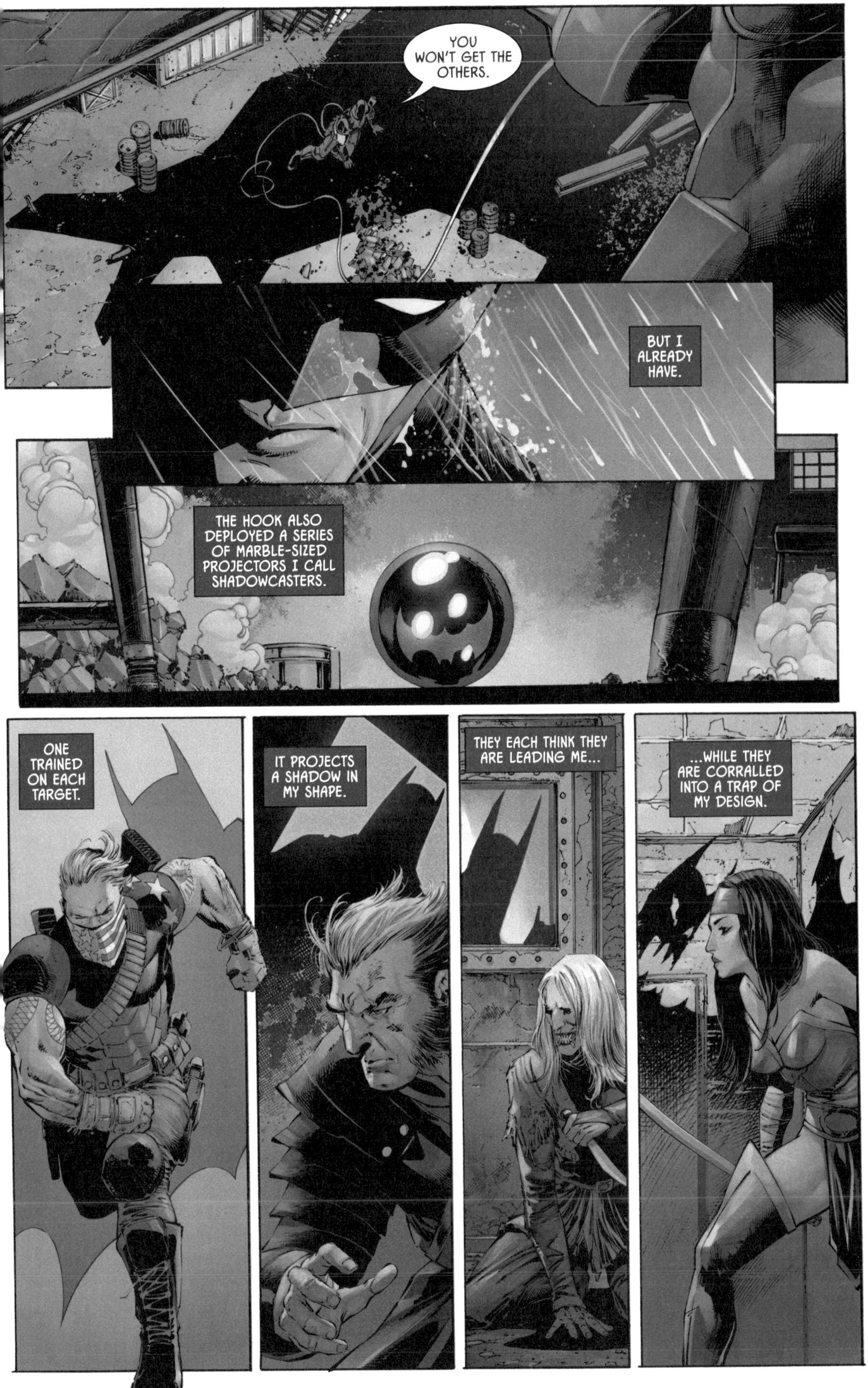
YOU WON'T GET THE OTHERS.
BUT I ALREADY HAVE.
THE HOOK ALSO DEPLOYED A SERIES OF MARBLE-SIZED PROJECTORS I CALL SHADOWCASTERS.
ONE TRAINED ON EACH TARGET.
IT PROJECTS A SHADOW IN MY SHAPE.
THEY EACH THINK THEY ARE LEADING ME...
...WHILE THEY ARE CORRALLED INTO A TRAP OF MY DESIGN.

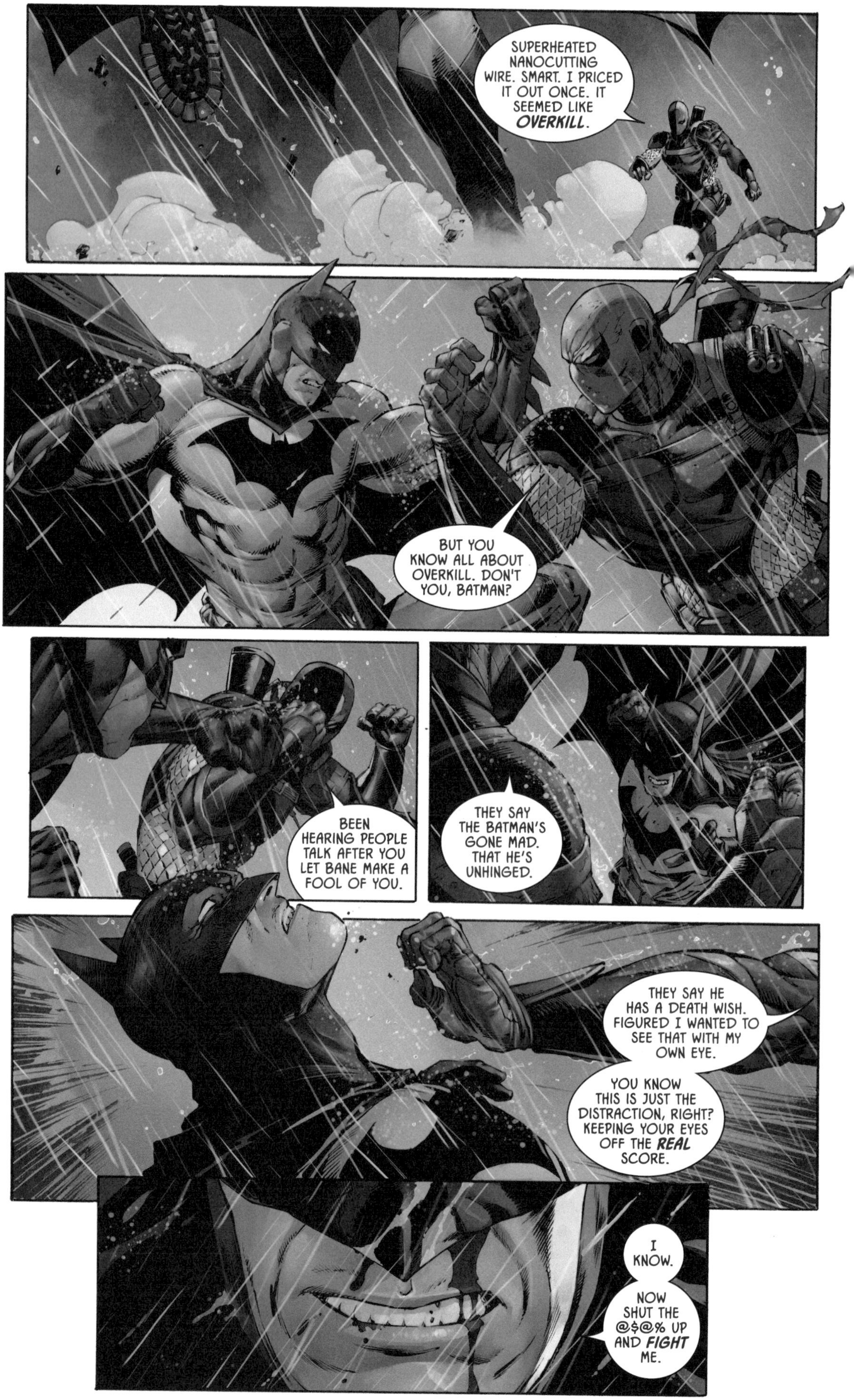
SUPERHEATED NANOCUTTING WIRE. SMART. I PRICED IT OUT ONCE. IT SEEMED LIKE OVERKILL.
BUT YOU KNOW ALL ABOUT OVERKILL. DON'T YOU, BATMAN?
BEEN HEARING PEOPLE TALK AFTER YOU LET BANE MAKE A FOOL OF YOU.
THEY SAY THE BATMAN'S GONE MAD. THAT HE'S UNHINGED.
THEY SAY HE HAS A DEATH WISH. FIGURED I WANTED TO SEE THAT WITH MY OWN EYE.
YOU KNOW THIS IS JUST THE DISTRACTION, RIGHT? KEEPING YOUR EYES OFF THE REAL SCORE.
I KNOW.
NOW SHUT THE @$@% UP AND FIGHT ME.

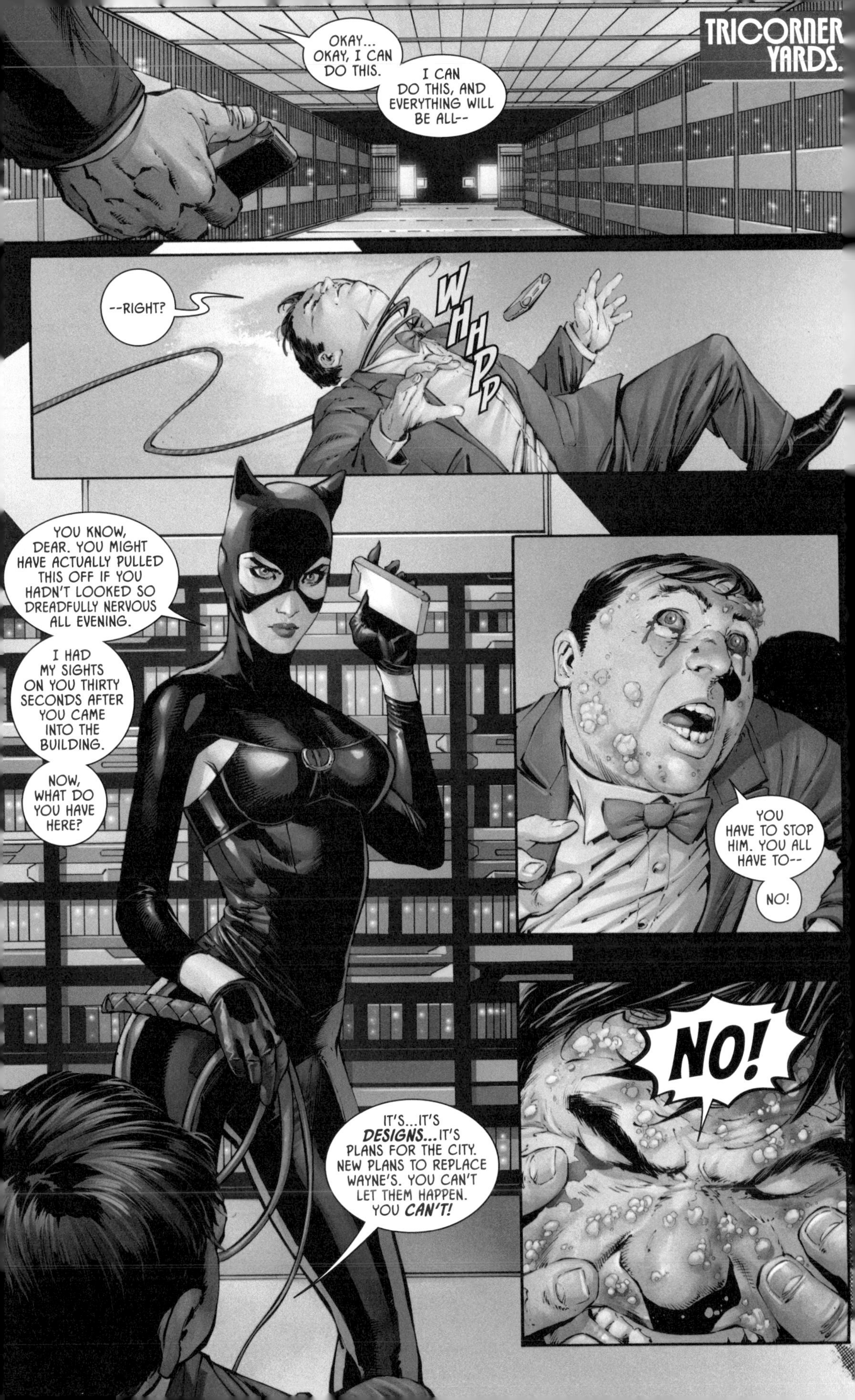
TRICORNER YARDS.
OKAY... OKAY, I CAN DO THIS.
I CAN DO THIS, AND EVERYTHING WILL BE ALL--
--RIGHT?
WHHPP
YOU KNOW, DEAR. YOU MIGHT HAVE ACTUALLY PULLED THIS OFF IF YOU HADN'T LOOKED SO DREADFULLY NERVOUS ALL EVENING.
I HAD MY SIGHTS ON YOU THIRTY SECONDS AFTER YOU CAME INTO THE BUILDING.
NOW, WHAT DO YOU HAVE HERE?
YOU HAVE TO STOP HIM. YOU ALL HAVE TO--
NO!
IT'S...IT'S DESIGNS...IT'S PLANS FOR THE CITY. NEW PLANS TO REPLACE WAYNE'S. YOU CAN'T LET THEM HAPPEN. YOU CAN'T!
NO!

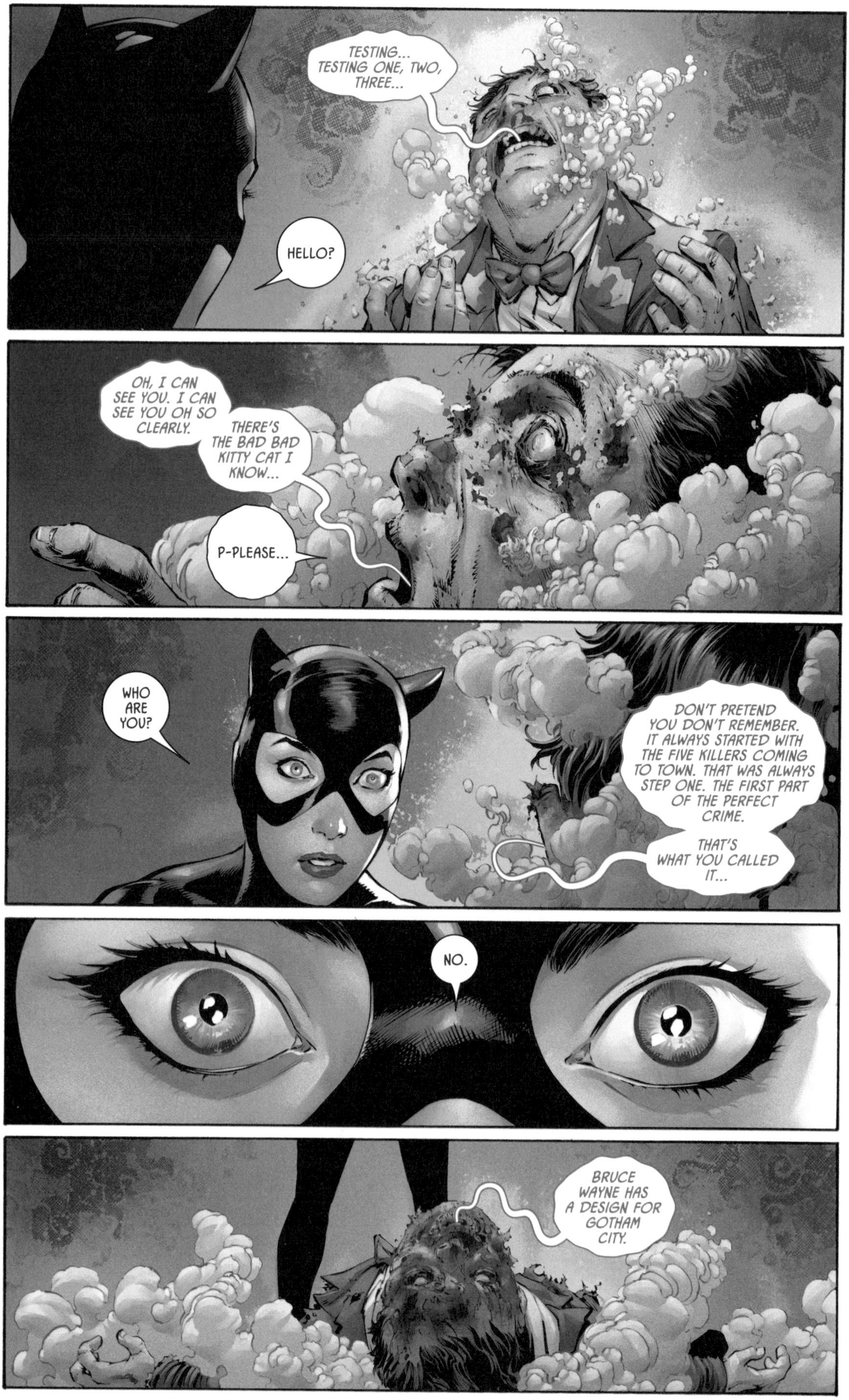
TESTING... TESTING ONE, TWO, THREE...
HELLO?
OH, I CAN SEE YOU. I CAN SEE YOU OH SO CLEARLY.
THERE'S THE BAD BAD KITTY CAT I KNOW...
P-PLEASE...
WHO ARE YOU?
DON'T PRETEND YOU DON'T REMEMBER. IT ALWAYS STARTED WITH THE FIVE KILLERS COMING TO TOWN. THAT WAS ALWAYS STEP ONE. THE FIRST PART OF THE PERFECT CRIME.
THAT'S WHAT YOU CALLED IT...
NO.
BRUCE WAYNE HAS A DESIGN FOR GOTHAM CITY.

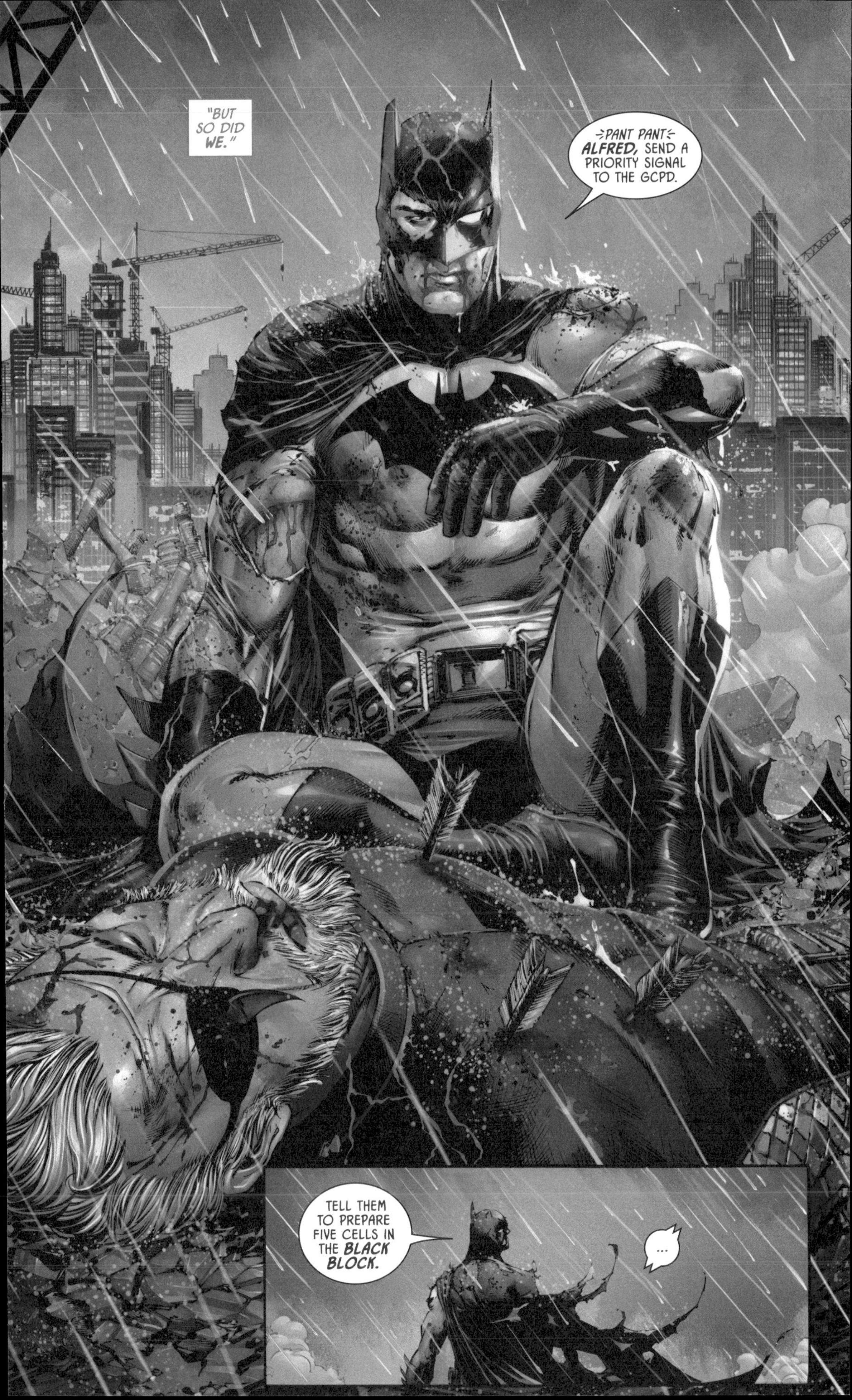
"BUT
SO DID
WE."
PANT PANT
ALFRED, SEND A
PRIORITY SIGNAL
TO THE GCPD.
TELL THEM
TO PREPARE
FIVE CELLS IN
THE BLACK
BLOCK.
...

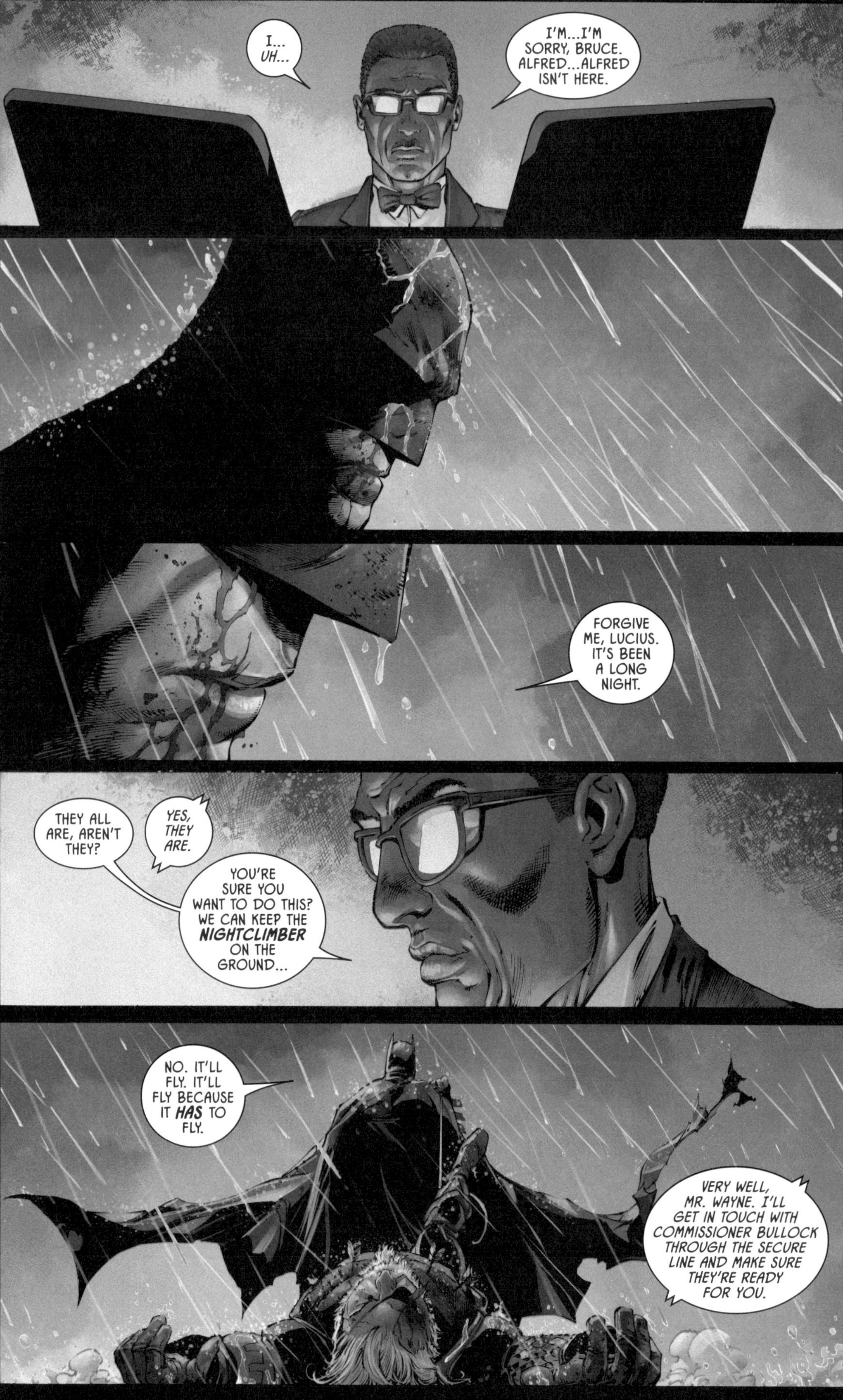
I... UH...
I'M...I'M SORRY, BRUCE. ALFRED...ALFRED ISN'T HERE.
FORGIVE ME, LUCIUS. IT'S BEEN A LONG NIGHT.
THEY ALL ARE, AREN'T THEY?
YES, THEY ARE.
YOU'RE SURE YOU WANT TO DO THIS? WE CAN KEEP THE NIGHTCLIMBER ON THE GROUND...
NO. IT'LL FLY. IT'LL FLY BECAUSE IT HAS TO FLY.
VERY WELL, MR. WAYNE. I'LL GET IN TOUCH WITH COMMISSIONER BULLOCK THROUGH THE SECURE LINE AND MAKE SURE THEY'RE READY FOR YOU.

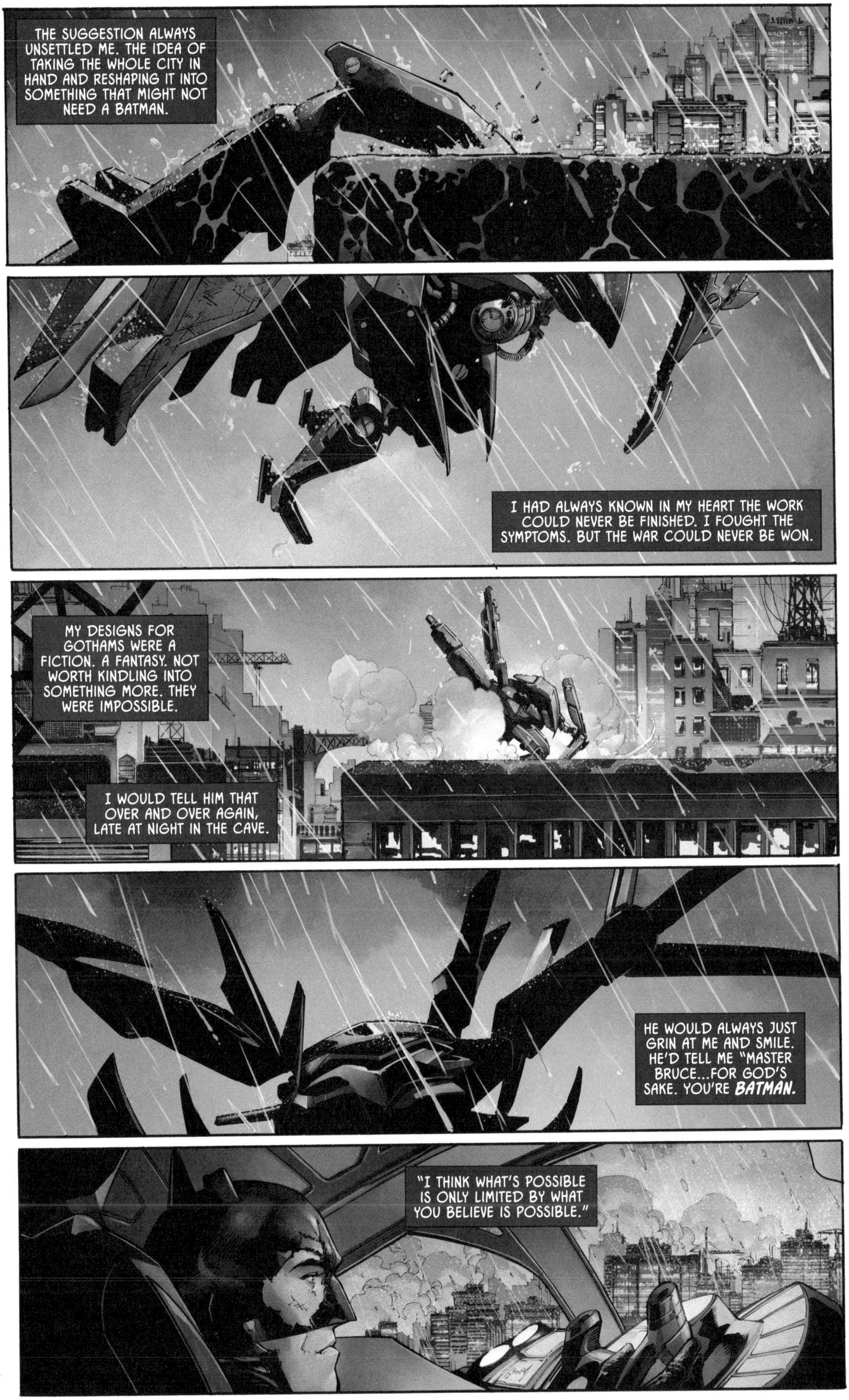
THE SUGGESTION ALWAYS UNSETTLED ME. THE IDEA OF TAKING THE WHOLE CITY IN HAND AND RESHAPING IT INTO SOMETHING THAT MIGHT NOT NEED A BATMAN.
I HAD ALWAYS KNOWN IN MY HEART THE WORK COULD NEVER BE FINISHED. I FOUGHT THE SYMPTOMS. BUT THE WAR COULD NEVER BE WON.
MY DESIGNS FOR GOTHAMS WERE A FICTION. A FANTASY. NOT WORTH KINDLING INTO SOMETHING MORE. THEY WERE IMPOSSIBLE.
I WOULD TELL HIM THAT OVER AND OVER AGAIN, LATE AT NIGHT IN THE CAVE.
HE WOULD ALWAYS JUST GRIN AT ME AND SMILE. HE'D TELL ME "MASTER BRUCE...FOR GOD'S SAKE. YOU'RE ***BATMAN.***
"I THINK WHAT'S POSSIBLE IS ONLY LIMITED BY WHAT YOU BELIEVE IS POSSIBLE."

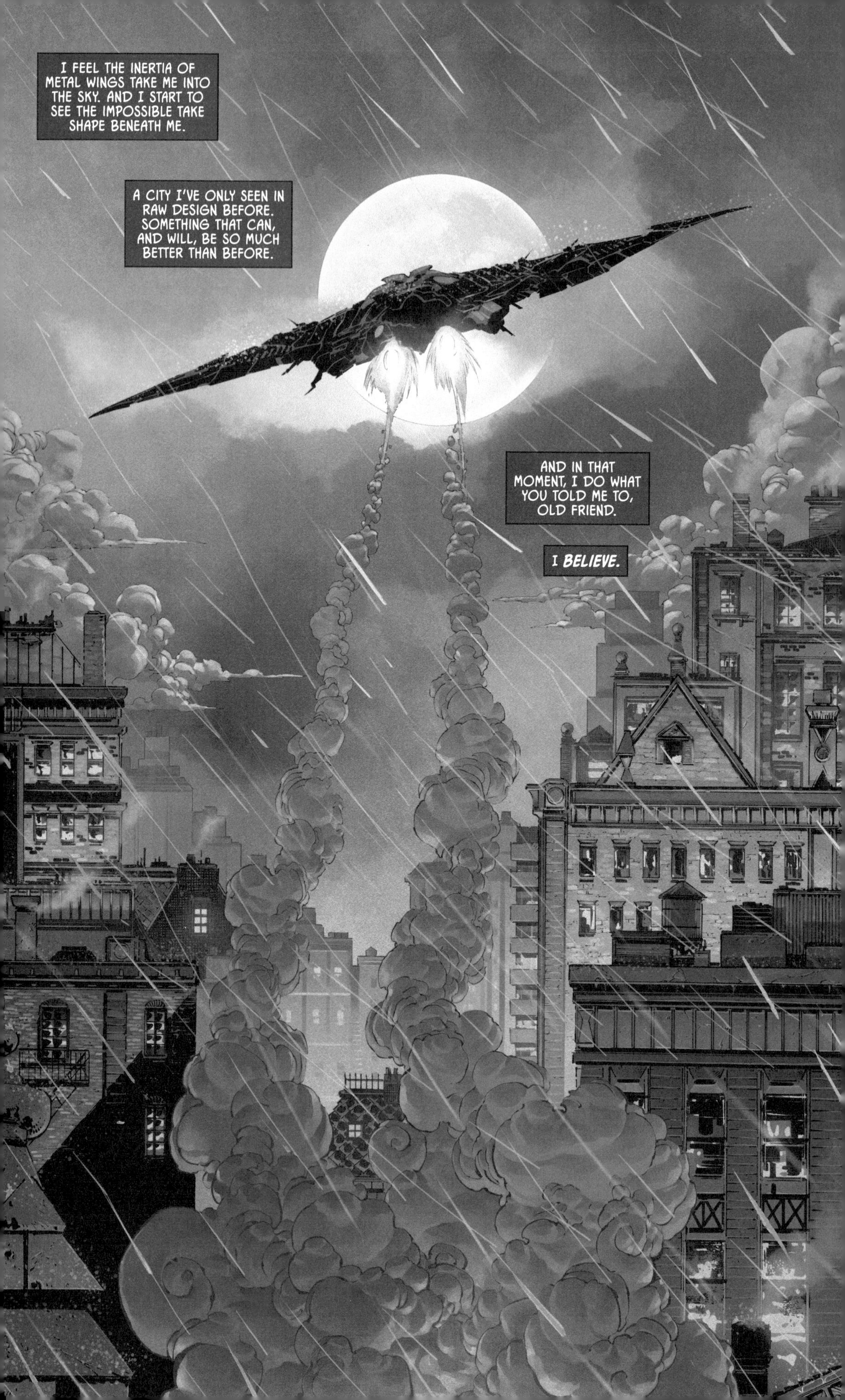
I FEEL THE INERTIA OF METAL WINGS TAKE ME INTO THE SKY. AND I START TO SEE THE IMPOSSIBLE TAKE SHAPE BENEATH ME.
A CITY I'VE ONLY SEEN IN RAW DESIGN BEFORE. SOMETHING THAT CAN, AND WILL, BE SO MUCH BETTER THAN BEFORE.
AND IN THAT MOMENT, I DO WHAT YOU TOLD ME TO, OLD FRIEND.
I *BELIEVE.*

EPILOGUE

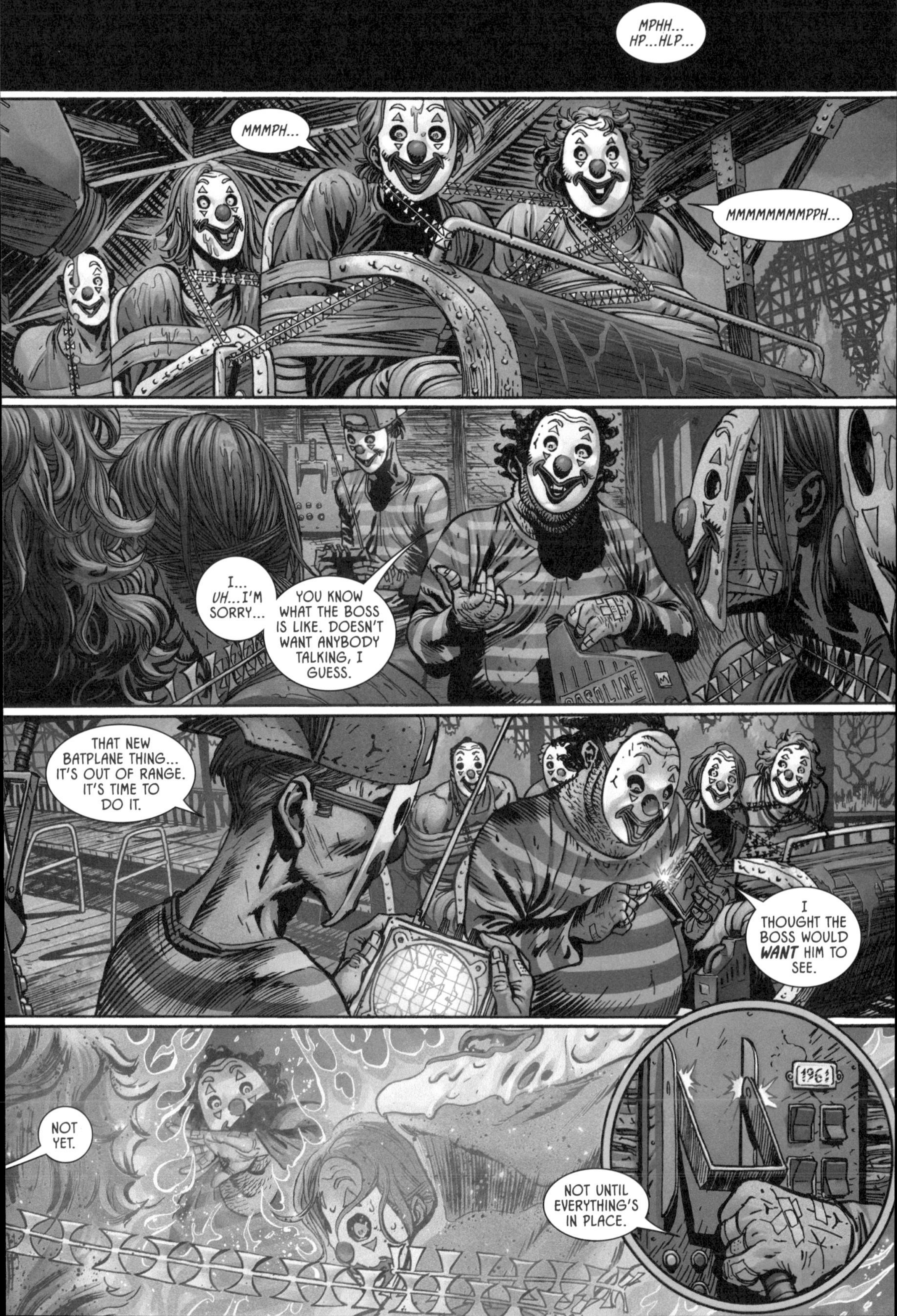
MPHH...
HP...HLP...
MMMPH...
MMMMMMMMPPH...
I...
UH...I'M
SORRY...
YOU KNOW WHAT THE BOSS IS LIKE. DOESN'T WANT ANYBODY TALKING, I GUESS.
GASOLINE
THAT NEW BATPLANE THING... IT'S OUT OF RANGE. IT'S TIME TO DO IT.
I THOUGHT THE BOSS WOULD ***WANT*** HIM TO SEE.
NOT YET.
1961
NOT UNTIL EVERYTHING'S IN PLACE.

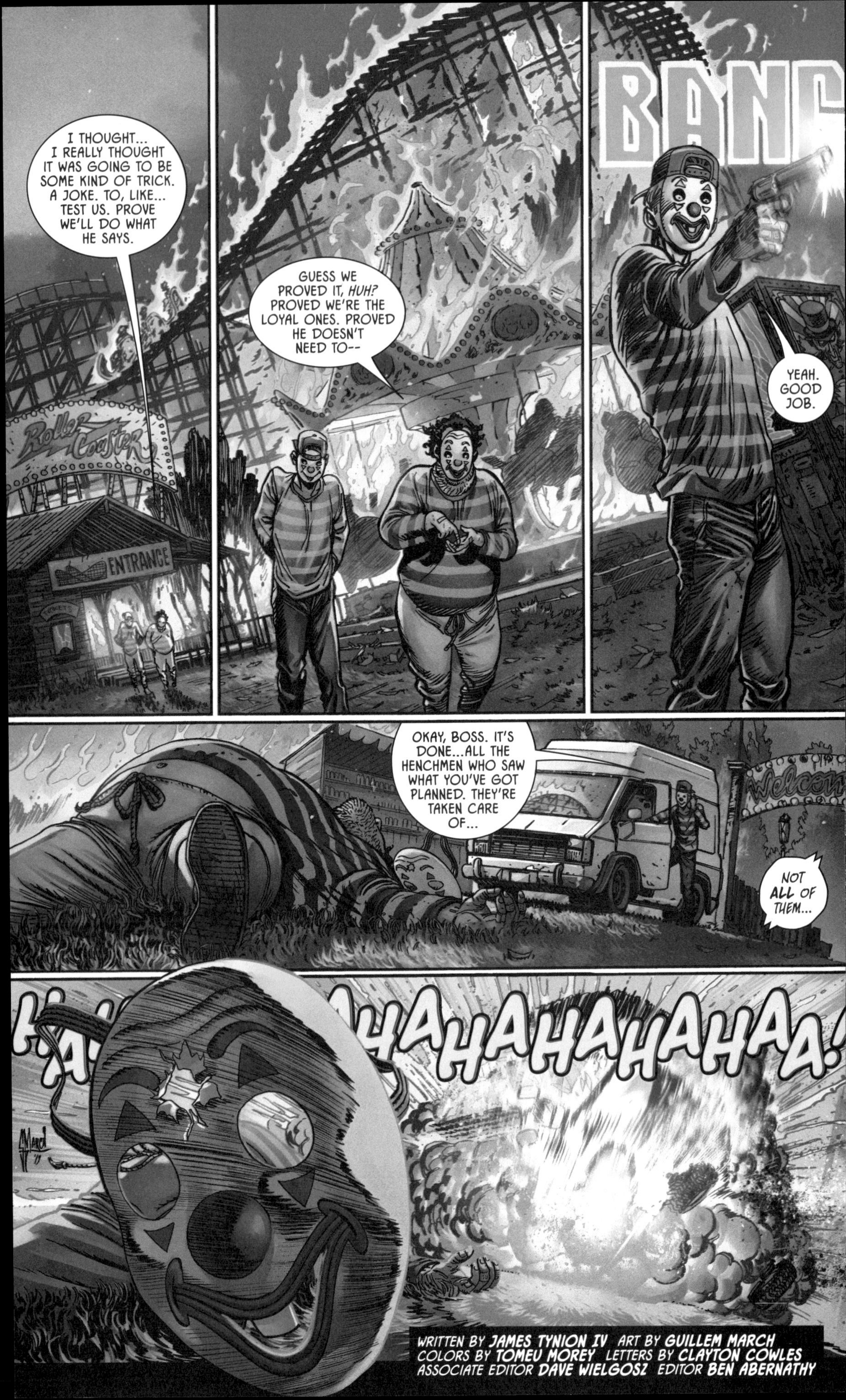

I THOUGHT... I REALLY THOUGHT IT WAS GOING TO BE SOME KIND OF TRICK. A JOKE. TO, LIKE... TEST US. PROVE WE'LL DO WHAT HE SAYS.
Roller Coaster
ENTRANCE
GUESS WE PROVED IT, *HUH?* PROVED WE'RE THE LOYAL ONES. PROVED HE DOESN'T NEED TO--
BANG
YEAH. GOOD JOB.
OKAY, BOSS. IT'S DONE...ALL THE HENCHMEN WHO SAW WHAT YOU'VE GOT PLANNED. THEY'RE TAKEN CARE OF...
NOT **ALL** OF THEM...
HAHAHAHAHAHAA!
WRITTEN BY **JAMES TYNION IV** ART BY **GUILLEM MARCH**
COLORS BY **TOMEU MOREY** LETTERS BY **CLAYTON COWLES**
ASSOCIATE EDITOR **DAVE WIELGOSZ** EDITOR **BEN ABERNATHY**

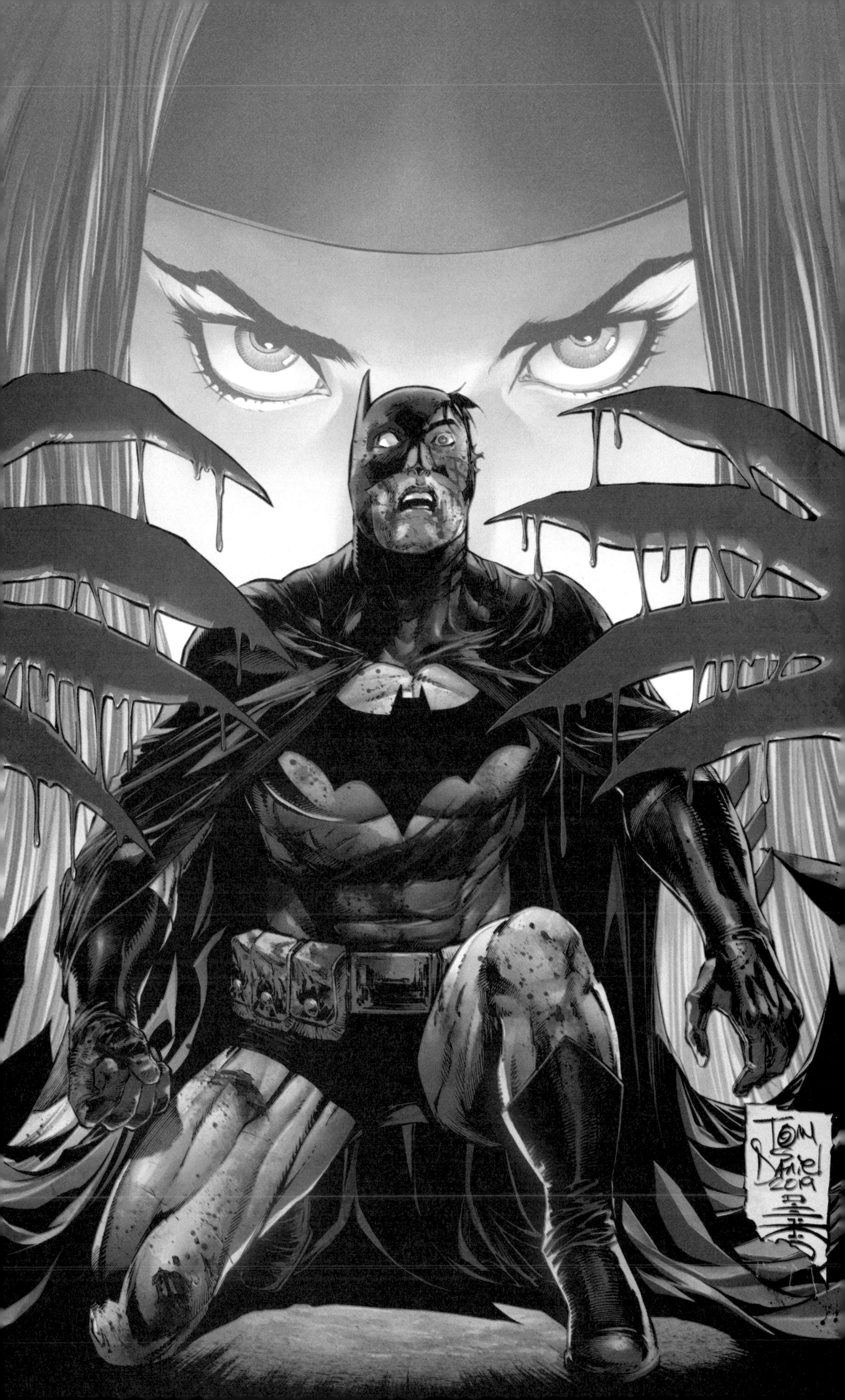

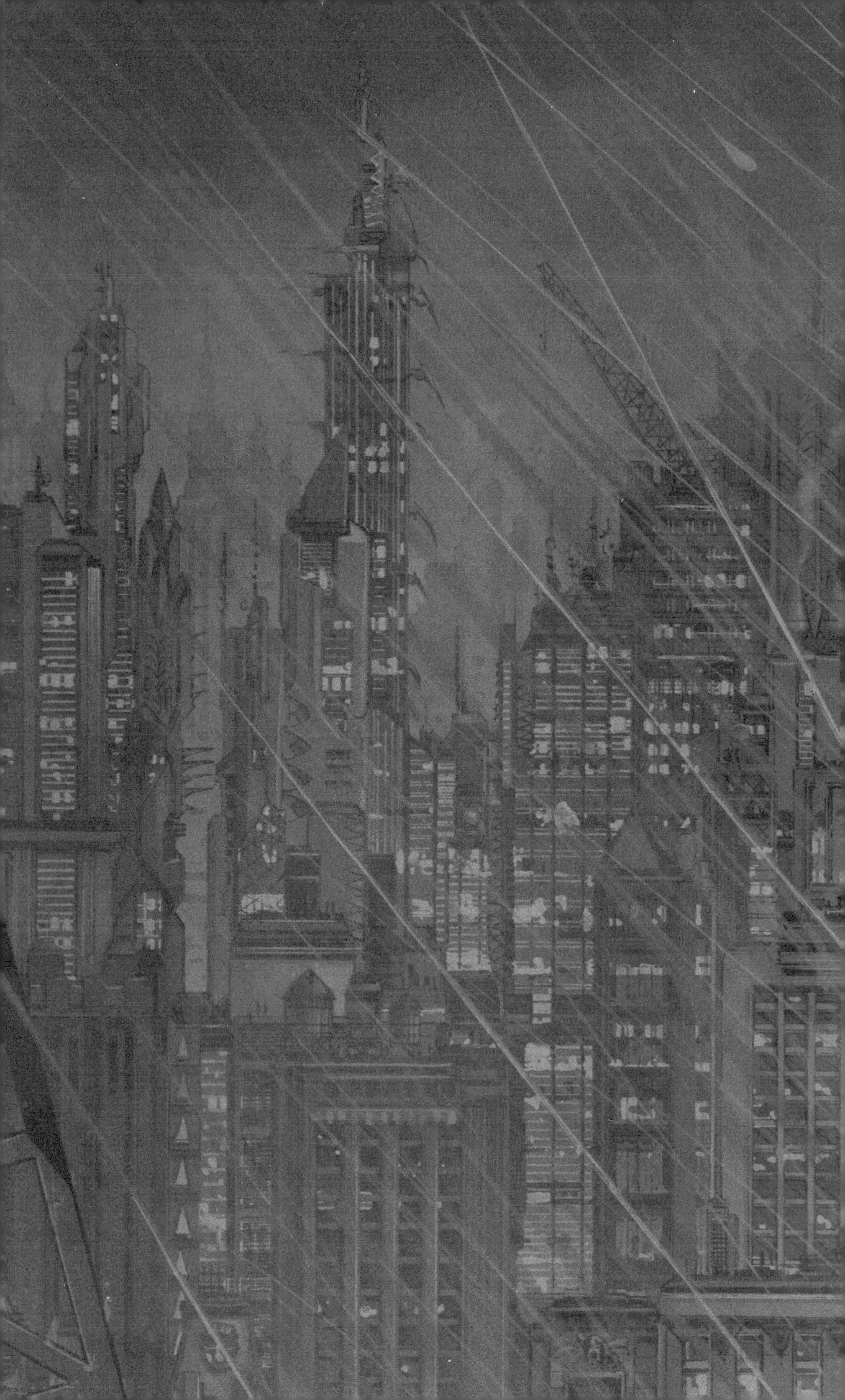

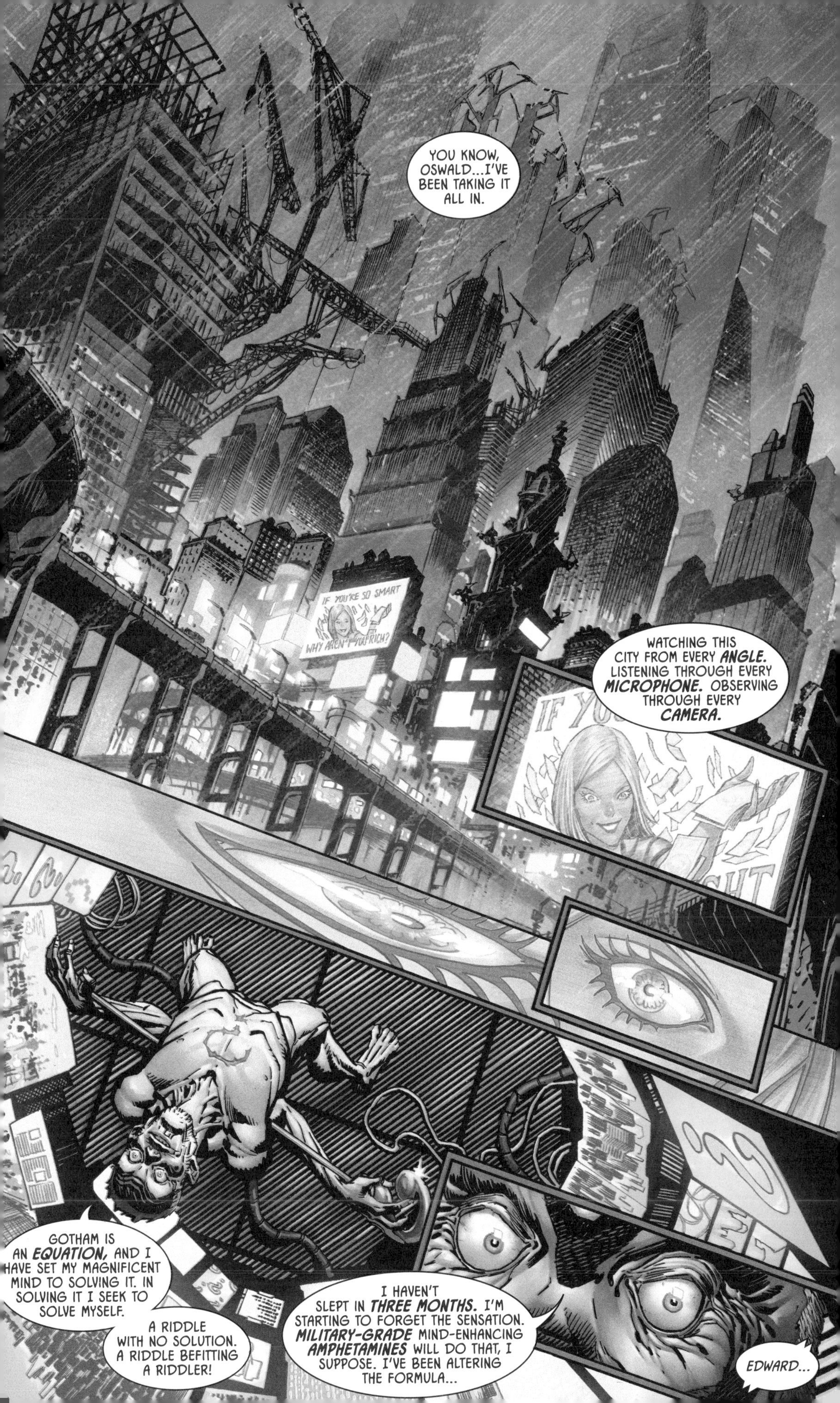

YOU KNOW, OSWALD...I'VE BEEN TAKING IT ALL IN.
IF YOU'RE SO SMART WHY AREN'T YOU RICH?
WATCHING THIS CITY FROM EVERY ANGLE. LISTENING THROUGH EVERY MICROPHONE. OBSERVING THROUGH EVERY CAMERA.
GOTHAM IS AN EQUATION, AND I HAVE SET MY MAGNIFICENT MIND TO SOLVING IT. IN SOLVING IT I SEEK TO SOLVE MYSELF.
A RIDDLE WITH NO SOLUTION. A RIDDLE BEFITTING A RIDDLER!
I HAVEN'T SLEPT IN THREE MONTHS. I'M STARTING TO FORGET THE SENSATION. MILITARY-GRADE MIND-ENHANCING AMPHETAMINES WILL DO THAT, I SUPPOSE. I'VE BEEN ALTERING THE FORMULA...
EDWARD...

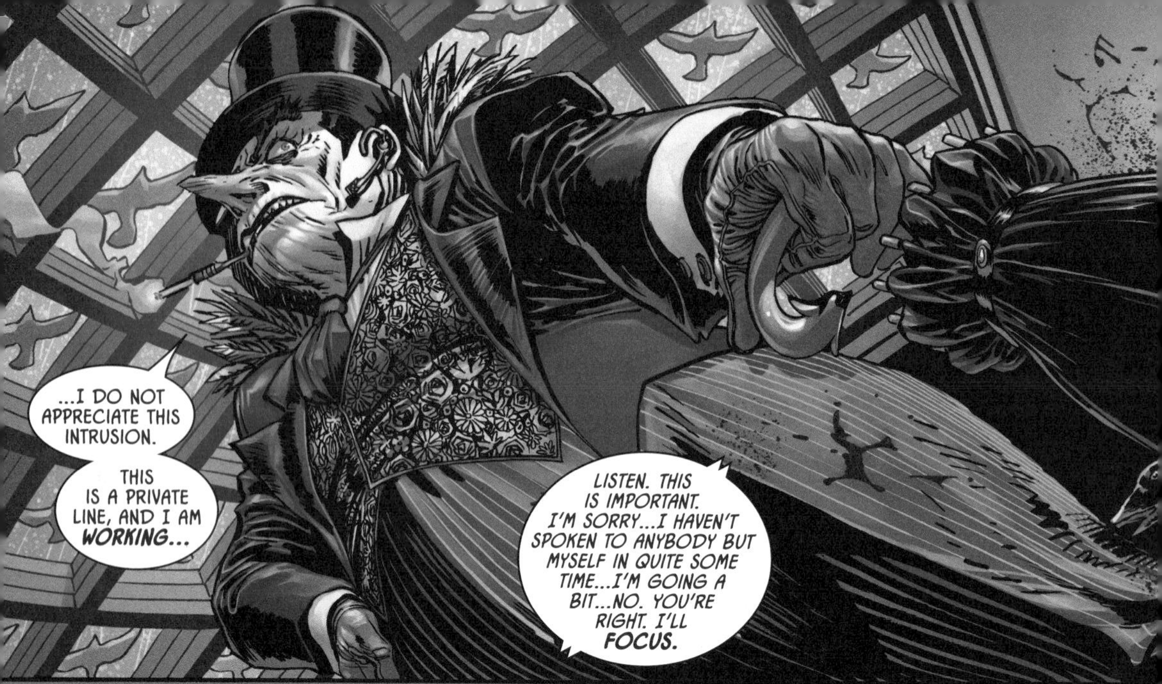
...I DO NOT APPRECIATE THIS INTRUSION.
THIS IS A PRIVATE LINE, AND I AM **WORKING...**
LISTEN. THIS IS IMPORTANT. I'M SORRY...I HAVEN'T SPOKEN TO ANYBODY BUT MYSELF IN QUITE SOME TIME...I'M GOING A BIT...NO. YOU'RE RIGHT. I'LL **FOCUS.**

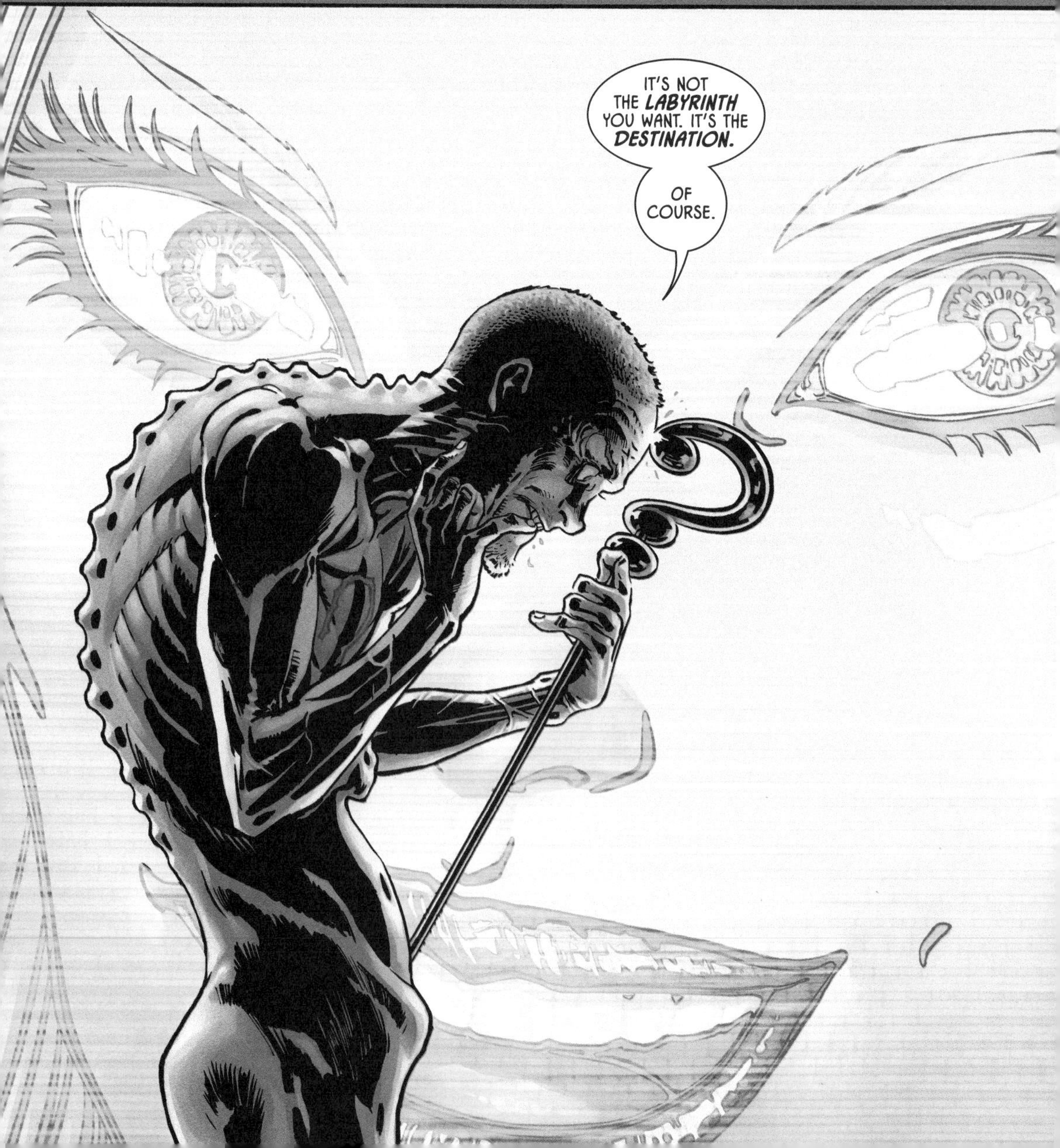
IT'S NOT THE **LABYRINTH** YOU WANT. IT'S THE **DESTINATION.**
OF COURSE.

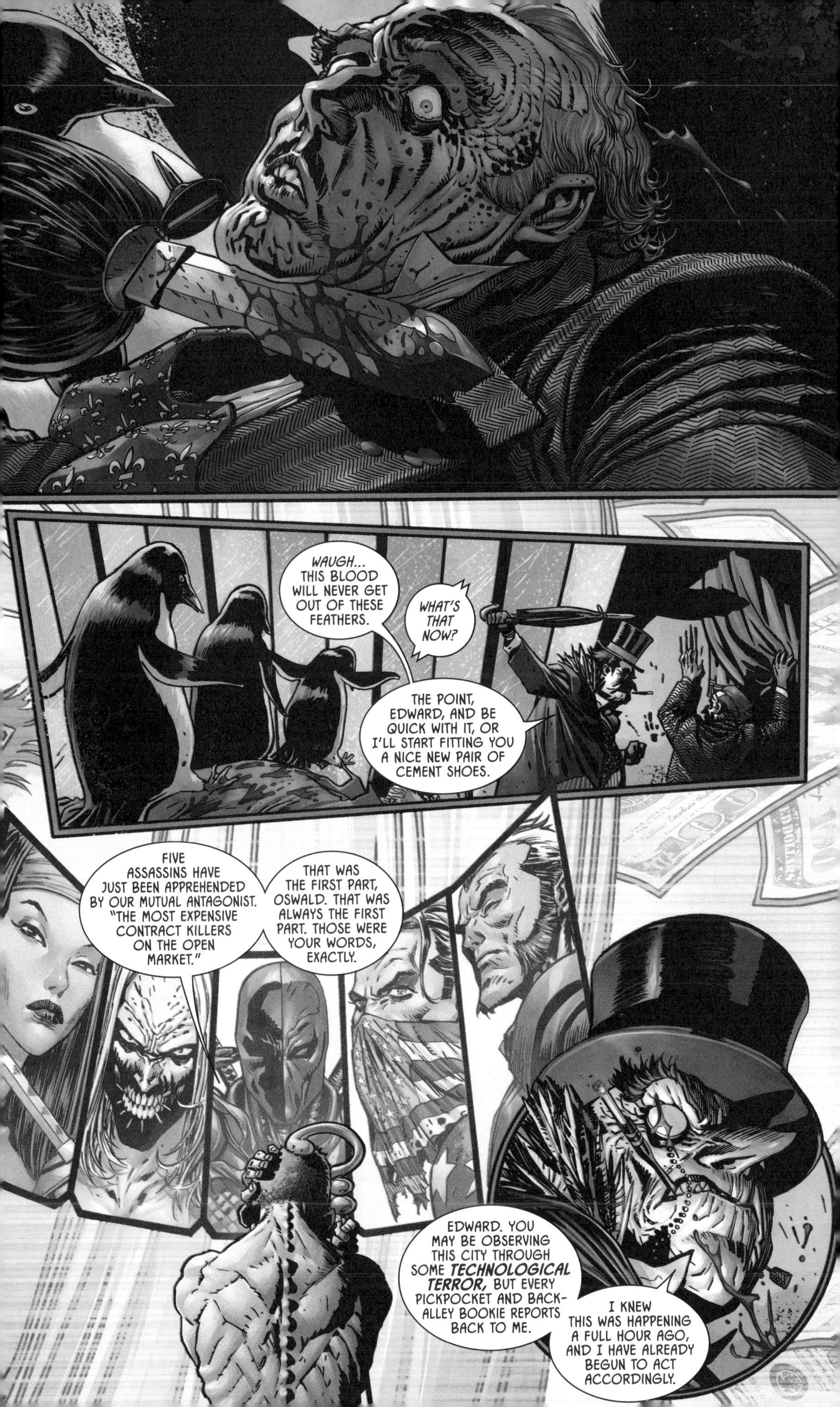
WAUGH... THIS BLOOD WILL NEVER GET OUT OF THESE FEATHERS.
WHAT'S THAT NOW?
THE POINT, EDWARD, AND BE QUICK WITH IT, OR I'LL START FITTING YOU A NICE NEW PAIR OF CEMENT SHOES.
FIVE ASSASSINS HAVE JUST BEEN APPREHENDED BY OUR MUTUAL ANTAGONIST. "THE MOST EXPENSIVE CONTRACT KILLERS ON THE OPEN MARKET."
THAT WAS THE FIRST PART, OSWALD. THAT WAS ALWAYS THE FIRST PART. THOSE WERE YOUR WORDS, EXACTLY.
EDWARD. YOU MAY BE OBSERVING THIS CITY THROUGH SOME **TECHNOLOGICAL TERROR,** BUT EVERY PICKPOCKET AND BACK-ALLEY BOOKIE REPORTS BACK TO ME.
I KNEW THIS WAS HAPPENING A FULL HOUR AGO, AND I HAVE ALREADY BEGUN TO ACT ACCORDINGLY.

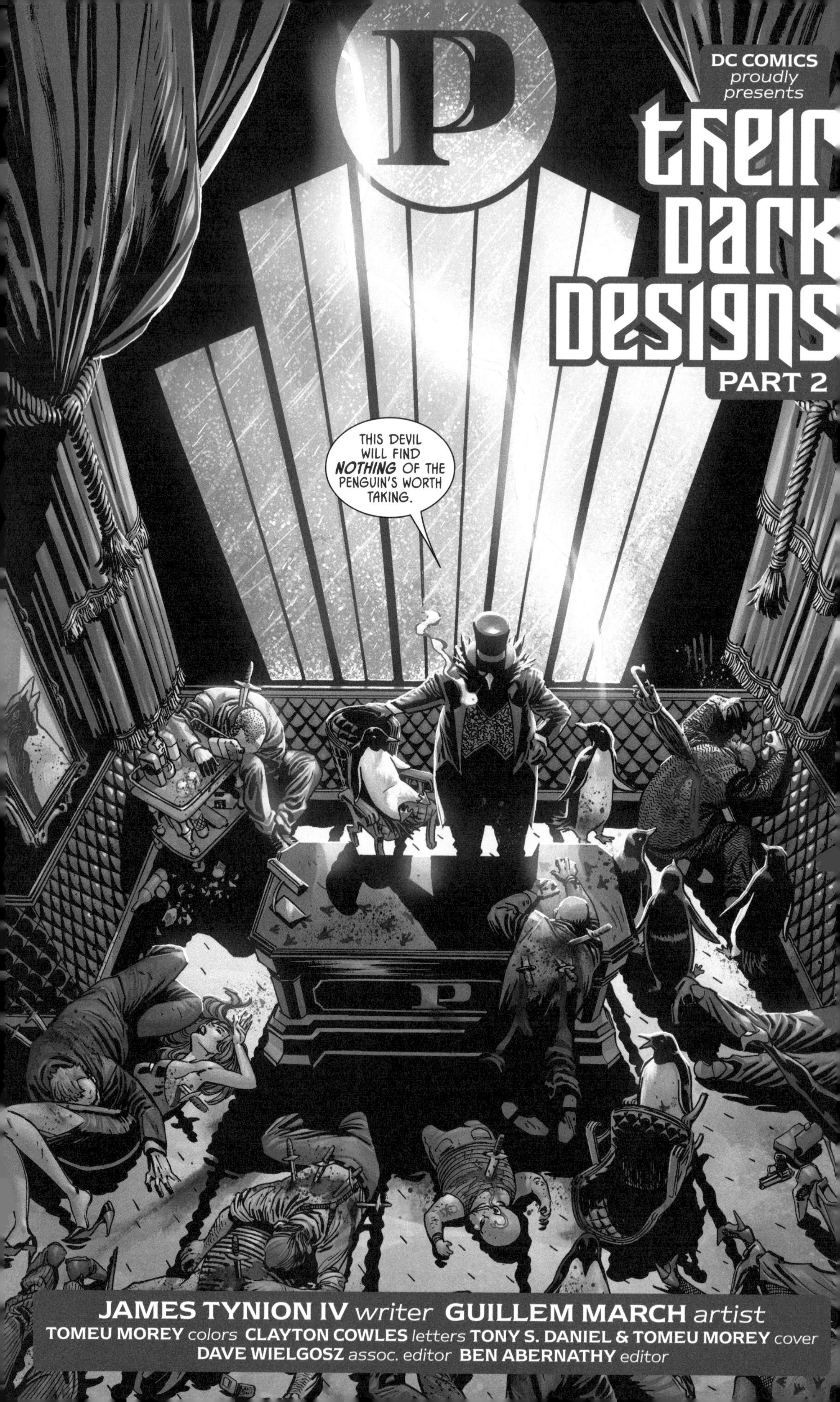

DC COMICS proudly presents
THEIR DARK DESIGNS
PART 2
THIS DEVIL WILL FIND NOTHING OF THE PENGUIN'S WORTH TAKING.
JAMES TYNION IV writer GUILLEM MARCH artist
TOMEU MOREY colors CLAYTON COWLES letters TONY S. DANIEL & TOMEU MOREY cover
DAVE WIELGOSZ assoc. editor BEN ABERNATHY editor

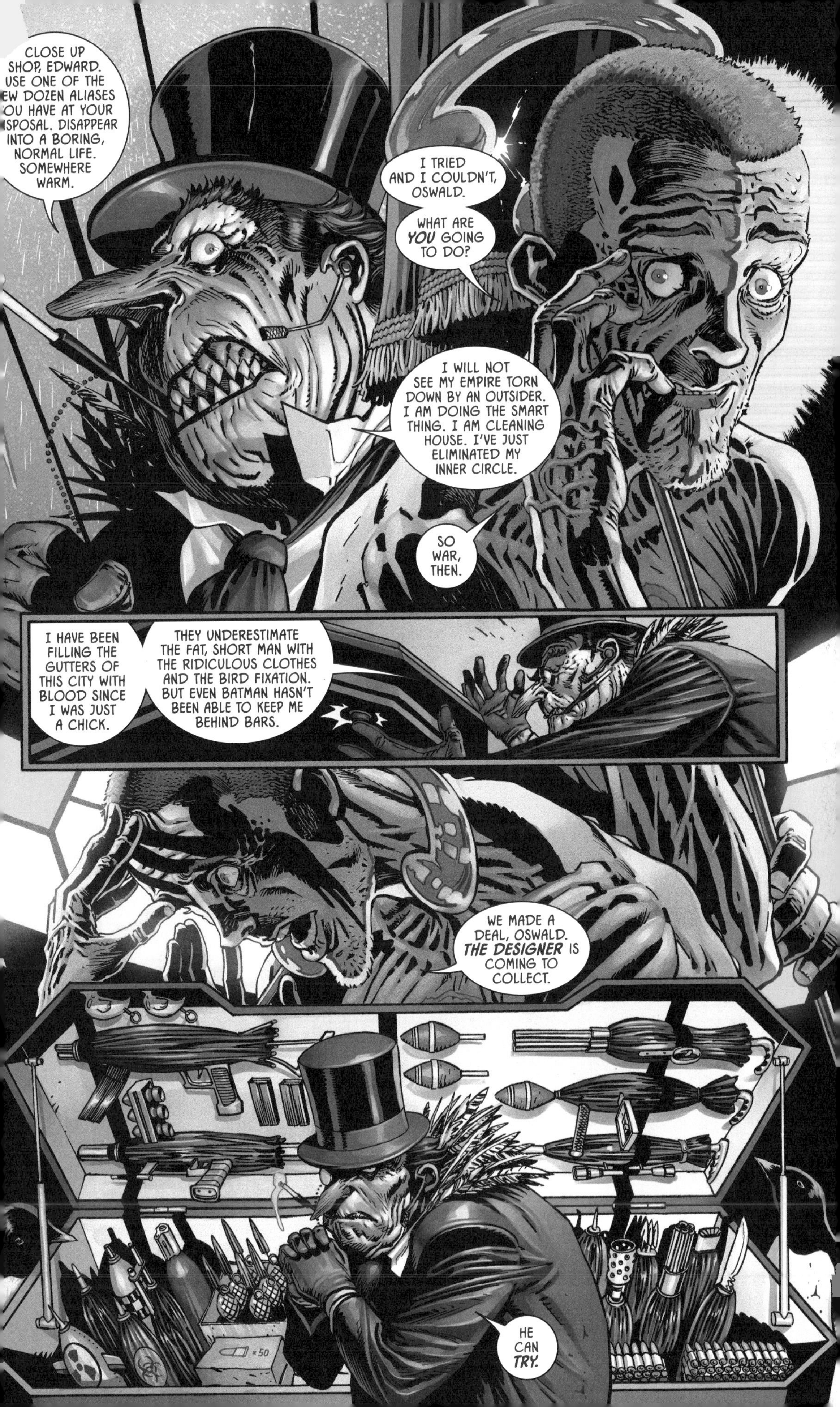
CLOSE UP SHOP, EDWARD. USE ONE OF THE EW DOZEN ALIASES OU HAVE AT YOUR SPOSAL. DISAPPEAR INTO A BORING, NORMAL LIFE. SOMEWHERE WARM.
I TRIED AND I COULDN'T, OSWALD.
WHAT ARE YOU GOING TO DO?
I WILL NOT SEE MY EMPIRE TORN DOWN BY AN OUTSIDER. I AM DOING THE SMART THING. I AM CLEANING HOUSE. I'VE JUST ELIMINATED MY INNER CIRCLE.
SO WAR, THEN.
I HAVE BEEN FILLING THE GUTTERS OF THIS CITY WITH BLOOD SINCE I WAS JUST A CHICK.
THEY UNDERESTIMATE THE FAT, SHORT MAN WITH THE RIDICULOUS CLOTHES AND THE BIRD FIXATION. BUT EVEN BATMAN HASN'T BEEN ABLE TO KEEP ME BEHIND BARS.
WE MADE A DEAL, OSWALD. THE DESIGNER IS COMING TO COLLECT.
HE CAN TRY.

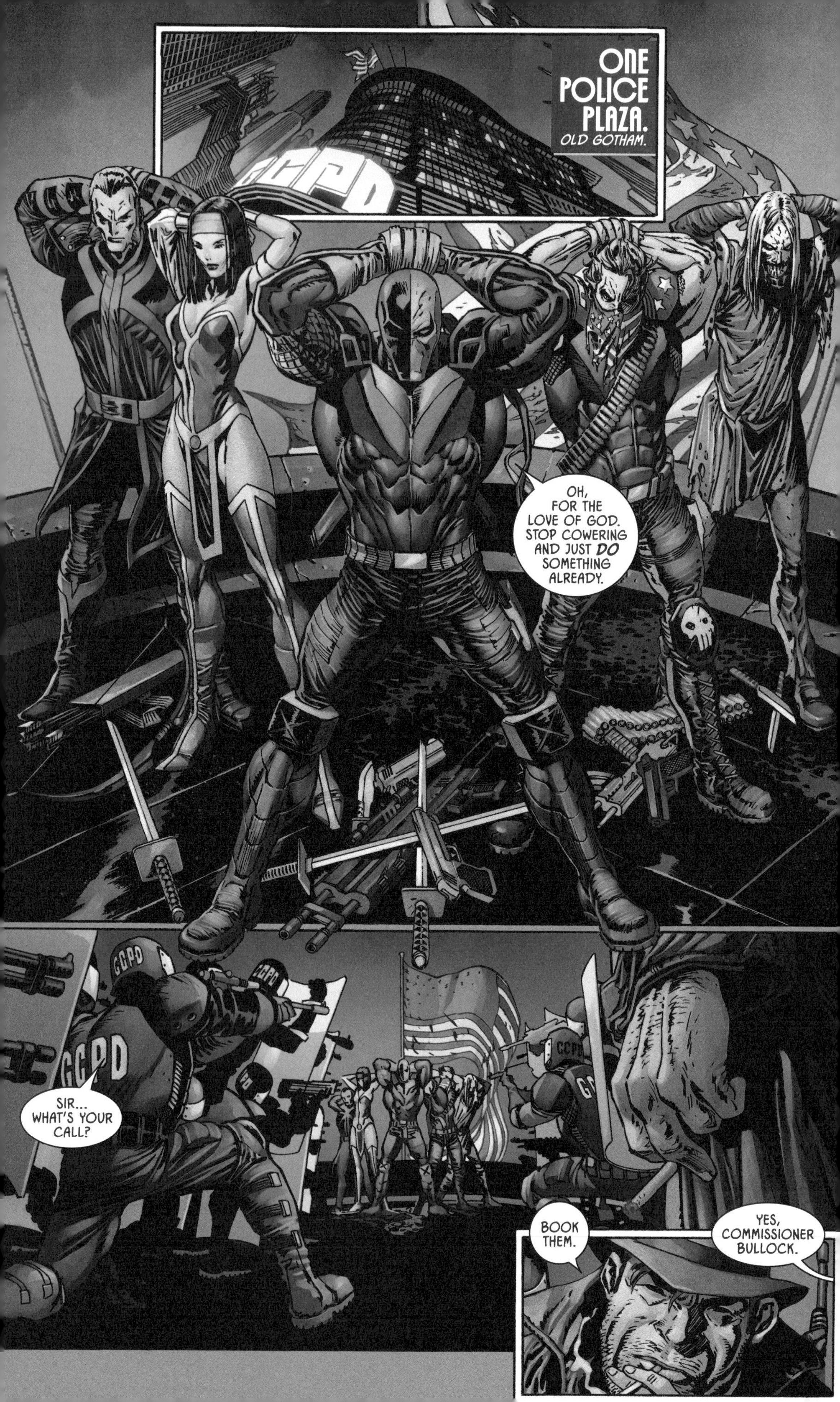

ONE POLICE PLAZA.
OLD GOTHAM.
OH, FOR THE LOVE OF GOD. STOP COWERING AND JUST DO SOMETHING ALREADY.
GCPD
SIR... WHAT'S YOUR CALL?
BOOK THEM.
YES, COMMISSIONER BULLOCK.

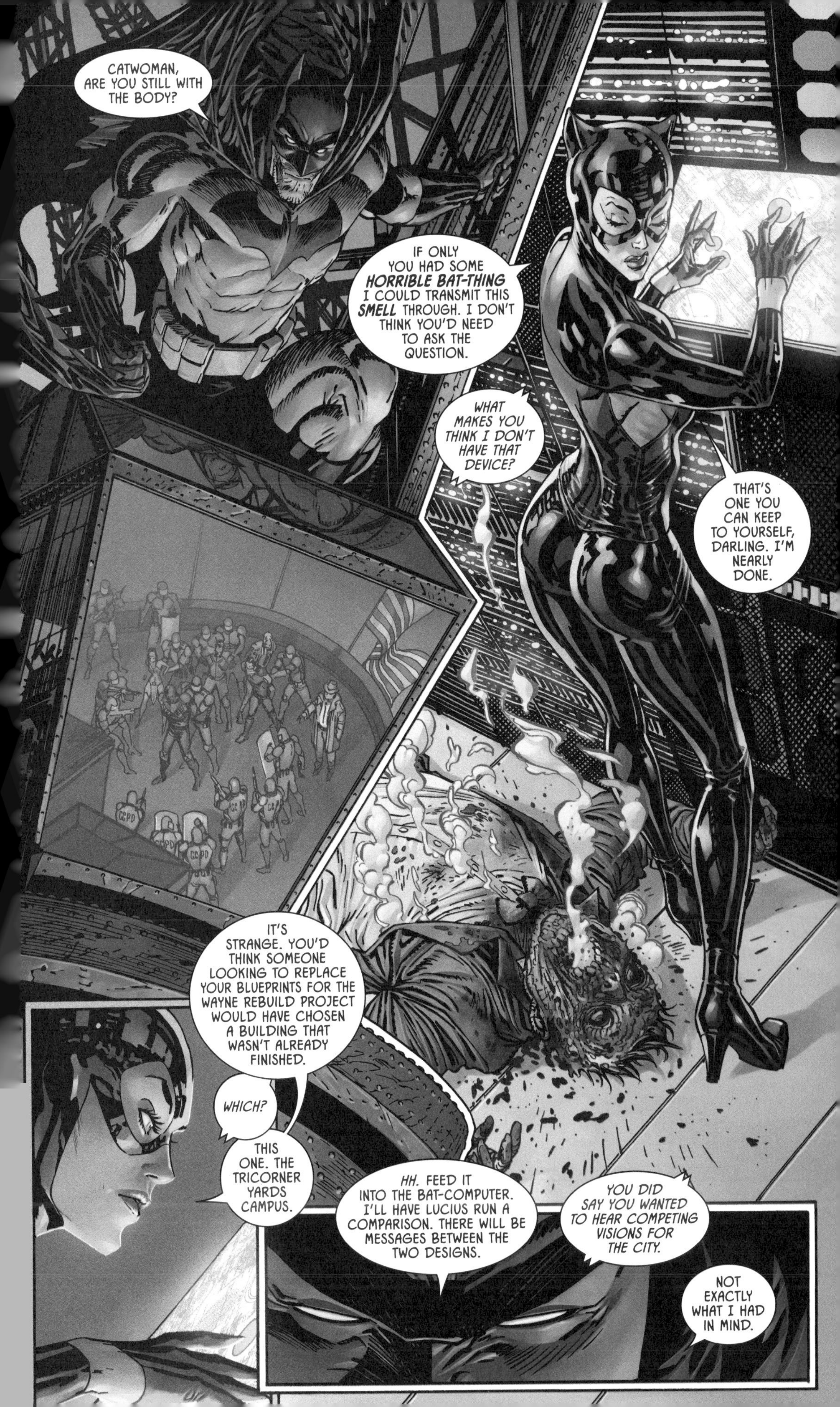
CATWOMAN, ARE YOU STILL WITH THE BODY?
IF ONLY YOU HAD SOME HORRIBLE BAT-THING I COULD TRANSMIT THIS SMELL THROUGH. I DON'T THINK YOU'D NEED TO ASK THE QUESTION.
WHAT MAKES YOU THINK I DON'T HAVE THAT DEVICE?
THAT'S ONE YOU CAN KEEP TO YOURSELF, DARLING. I'M NEARLY DONE.
IT'S STRANGE. YOU'D THINK SOMEONE LOOKING TO REPLACE YOUR BLUEPRINTS FOR THE WAYNE REBUILD PROJECT WOULD HAVE CHOSEN A BUILDING THAT WASN'T ALREADY FINISHED.
WHICH?
THIS ONE. THE TRICORNER YARDS CAMPUS.
HH. FEED IT INTO THE BAT-COMPUTER. I'LL HAVE LUCIUS RUN A COMPARISON. THERE WILL BE MESSAGES BETWEEN THE TWO DESIGNS.
YOU DID SAY YOU WANTED TO HEAR COMPETING VISIONS FOR THE CITY.
NOT EXACTLY WHAT I HAD IN MIND.

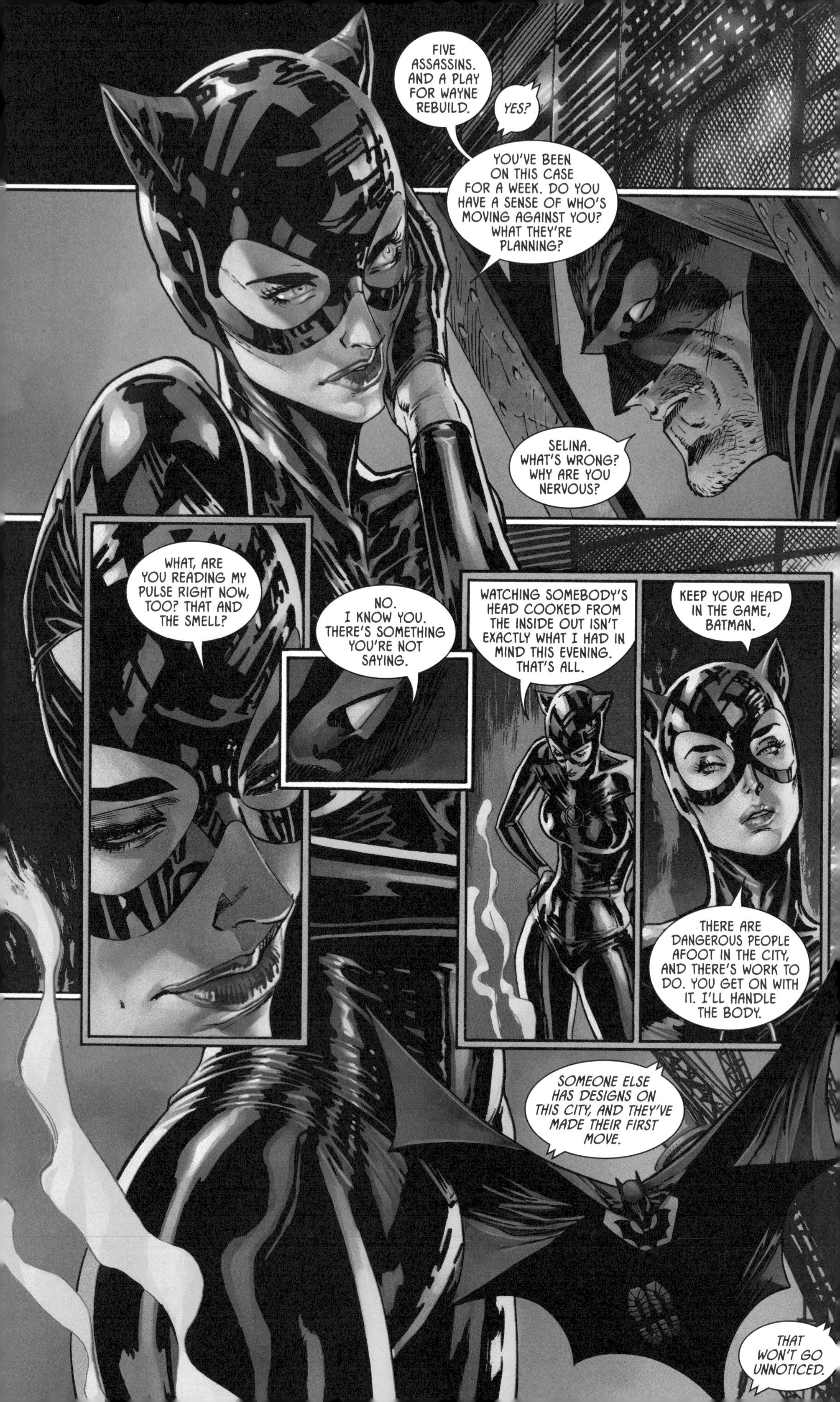
FIVE ASSASSINS. AND A PLAY FOR WAYNE REBUILD.
YES?
YOU'VE BEEN ON THIS CASE FOR A WEEK. DO YOU HAVE A SENSE OF WHO'S MOVING AGAINST YOU? WHAT THEY'RE PLANNING?
SELINA. WHAT'S WRONG? WHY ARE YOU NERVOUS?
WHAT, ARE YOU READING MY PULSE RIGHT NOW, TOO? THAT AND THE SMELL?
NO. I KNOW YOU. THERE'S SOMETHING YOU'RE NOT SAYING.
WATCHING SOMEBODY'S HEAD COOKED FROM THE INSIDE OUT ISN'T EXACTLY WHAT I HAD IN MIND THIS EVENING. THAT'S ALL.
KEEP YOUR HEAD IN THE GAME, BATMAN.
THERE ARE DANGEROUS PEOPLE AFOOT IN THE CITY, AND THERE'S WORK TO DO. YOU GET ON WITH IT. I'LL HANDLE THE BODY.
SOMEONE ELSE HAS DESIGNS ON THIS CITY, AND THEY'VE MADE THEIR FIRST MOVE.
THAT WON'T GO UNNOTICED.

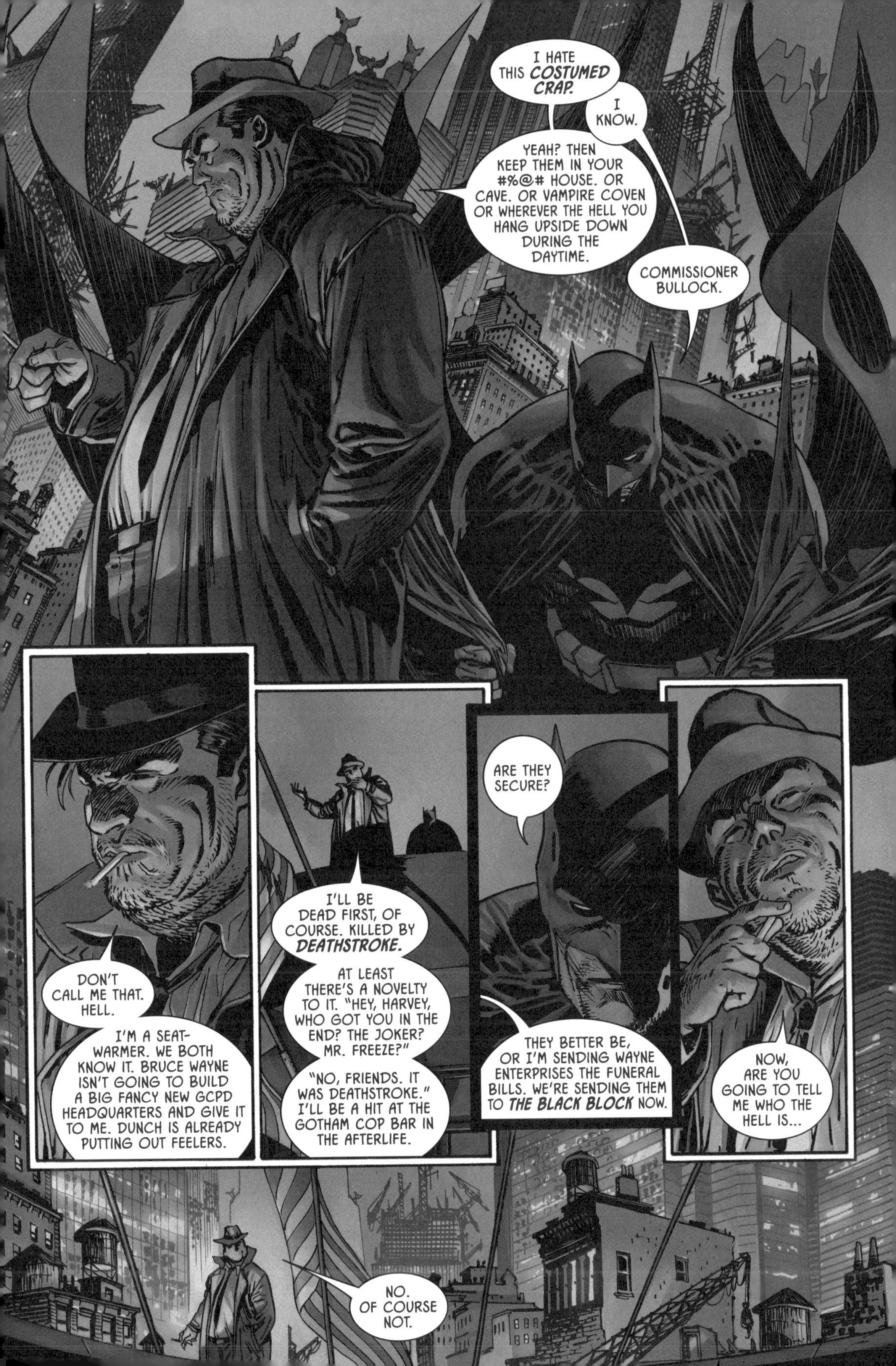

I HATE THIS COSTUMED CRAP.
I KNOW.
YEAH? THEN KEEP THEM IN YOUR #%@# HOUSE. OR CAVE. OR VAMPIRE COVEN OR WHEREVER THE HELL YOU HANG UPSIDE DOWN DURING THE DAYTIME.
COMMISSIONER BULLOCK.
DON'T CALL ME THAT. HELL.
I'M A SEAT-WARMER. WE BOTH KNOW IT. BRUCE WAYNE ISN'T GOING TO BUILD A BIG FANCY NEW GCPD HEADQUARTERS AND GIVE IT TO ME. DUNCH IS ALREADY PUTTING OUT FEELERS.
I'LL BE DEAD FIRST, OF COURSE. KILLED BY DEATHSTROKE.
AT LEAST THERE'S A NOVELTY TO IT. "HEY, HARVEY, WHO GOT YOU IN THE END? THE JOKER? MR. FREEZE?"
"NO, FRIENDS. IT WAS DEATHSTROKE." I'LL BE A HIT AT THE GOTHAM COP BAR IN THE AFTERLIFE.
ARE THEY SECURE?
THEY BETTER BE, OR I'M SENDING WAYNE ENTERPRISES THE FUNERAL BILLS. WE'RE SENDING THEM TO THE BLACK BLOCK NOW.
NOW, ARE YOU GOING TO TELL ME WHO THE HELL IS...
NO. OF COURSE NOT.

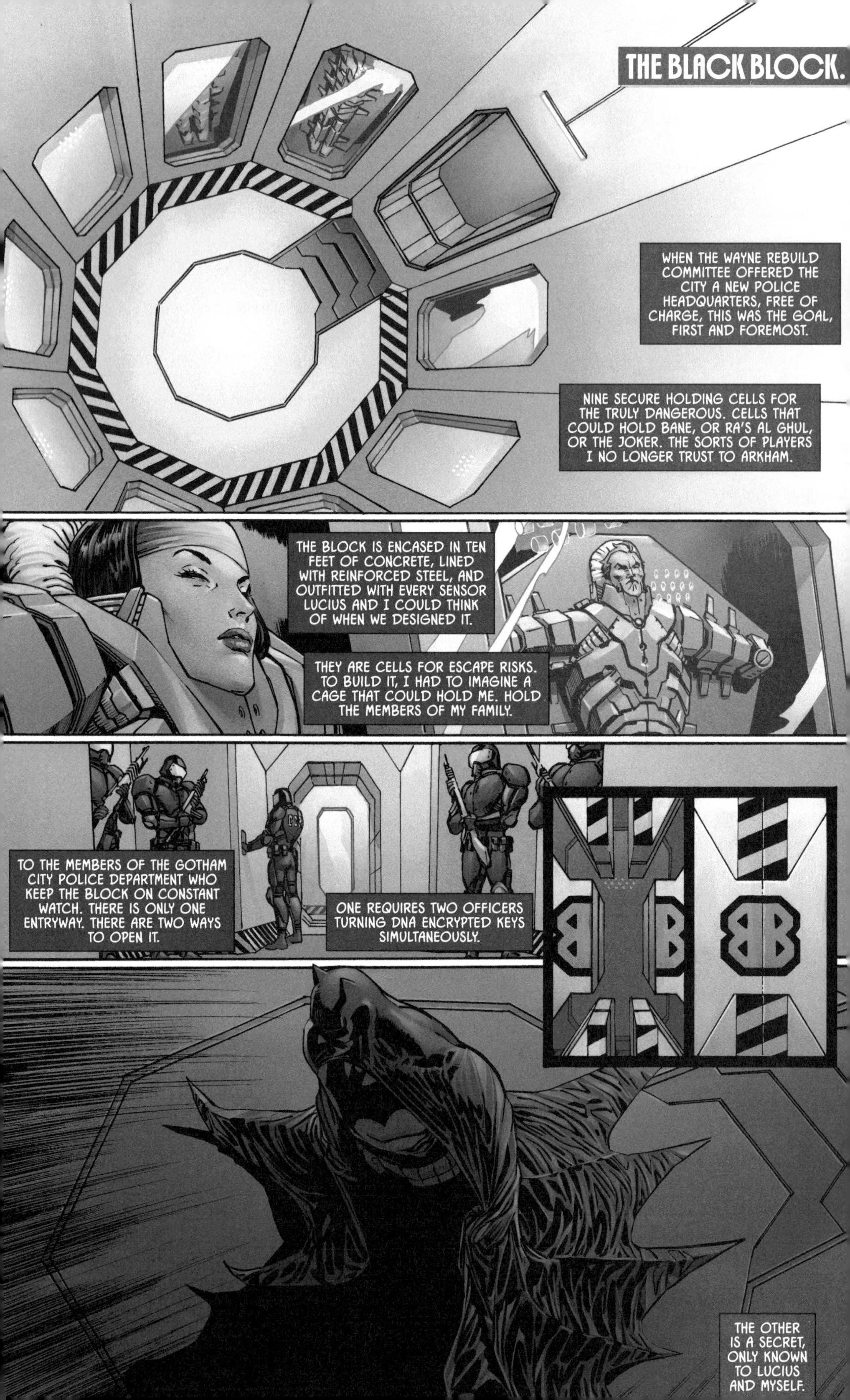
THE BLACK BLOCK.
WHEN THE WAYNE REBUILD COMMITTEE OFFERED THE CITY A NEW POLICE HEADQUARTERS, FREE OF CHARGE, THIS WAS THE GOAL, FIRST AND FOREMOST.
NINE SECURE HOLDING CELLS FOR THE TRULY DANGEROUS. CELLS THAT COULD HOLD BANE, OR RA'S AL GHUL, OR THE JOKER. THE SORTS OF PLAYERS I NO LONGER TRUST TO ARKHAM.
THE BLOCK IS ENCASED IN TEN FEET OF CONCRETE, LINED WITH REINFORCED STEEL, AND OUTFITTED WITH EVERY SENSOR LUCIUS AND I COULD THINK OF WHEN WE DESIGNED IT.
THEY ARE CELLS FOR ESCAPE RISKS. TO BUILD IT, I HAD TO IMAGINE A CAGE THAT COULD HOLD ME. HOLD THE MEMBERS OF MY FAMILY.
TO THE MEMBERS OF THE GOTHAM CITY POLICE DEPARTMENT WHO KEEP THE BLOCK ON CONSTANT WATCH. THERE IS ONLY ONE ENTRYWAY. THERE ARE TWO WAYS TO OPEN IT.
ONE REQUIRES TWO OFFICERS TURNING DNA ENCRYPTED KEYS SIMULTANEOUSLY.
THE OTHER IS A SECRET, ONLY KNOWN TO LUCIUS AND MYSELF.

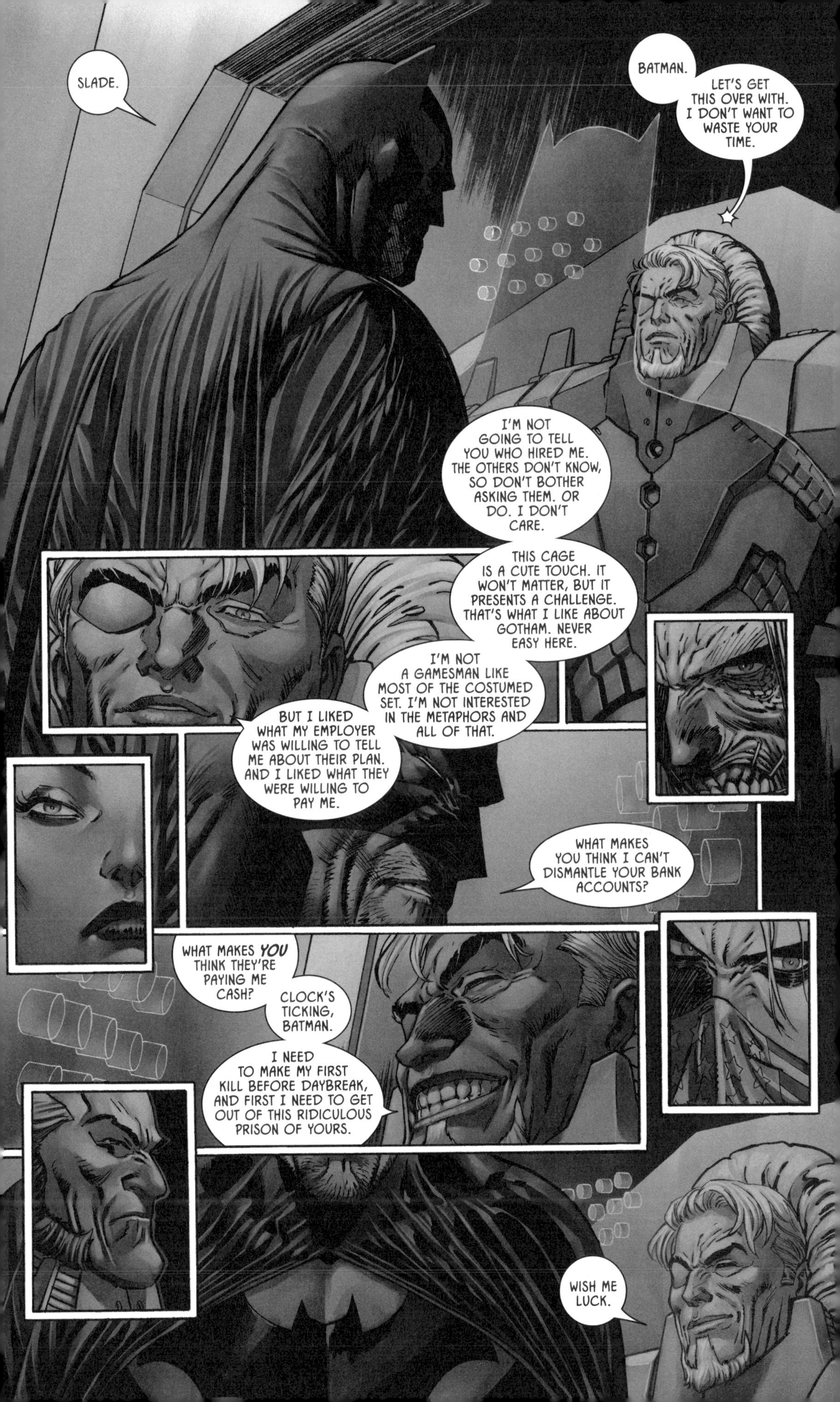
SLADE.
BATMAN.
LET'S GET THIS OVER WITH. I DON'T WANT TO WASTE YOUR TIME.
I'M NOT GOING TO TELL YOU WHO HIRED ME. THE OTHERS DON'T KNOW, SO DON'T BOTHER ASKING THEM. OR DO. I DON'T CARE.
THIS CAGE IS A CUTE TOUCH. IT WON'T MATTER, BUT IT PRESENTS A CHALLENGE. THAT'S WHAT I LIKE ABOUT GOTHAM. NEVER EASY HERE.
I'M NOT A GAMESMAN LIKE MOST OF THE COSTUMED SET. I'M NOT INTERESTED IN THE METAPHORS AND ALL OF THAT.
BUT I LIKED WHAT MY EMPLOYER WAS WILLING TO TELL ME ABOUT THEIR PLAN. AND I LIKED WHAT THEY WERE WILLING TO PAY ME.
WHAT MAKES YOU THINK I CAN'T DISMANTLE YOUR BANK ACCOUNTS?
WHAT MAKES ***YOU*** THINK THEY'RE PAYING ME CASH?
CLOCK'S TICKING, BATMAN.
I NEED TO MAKE MY FIRST KILL BEFORE DAYBREAK, AND FIRST I NEED TO GET OUT OF THIS RIDICULOUS PRISON OF YOURS.
WISH ME LUCK.

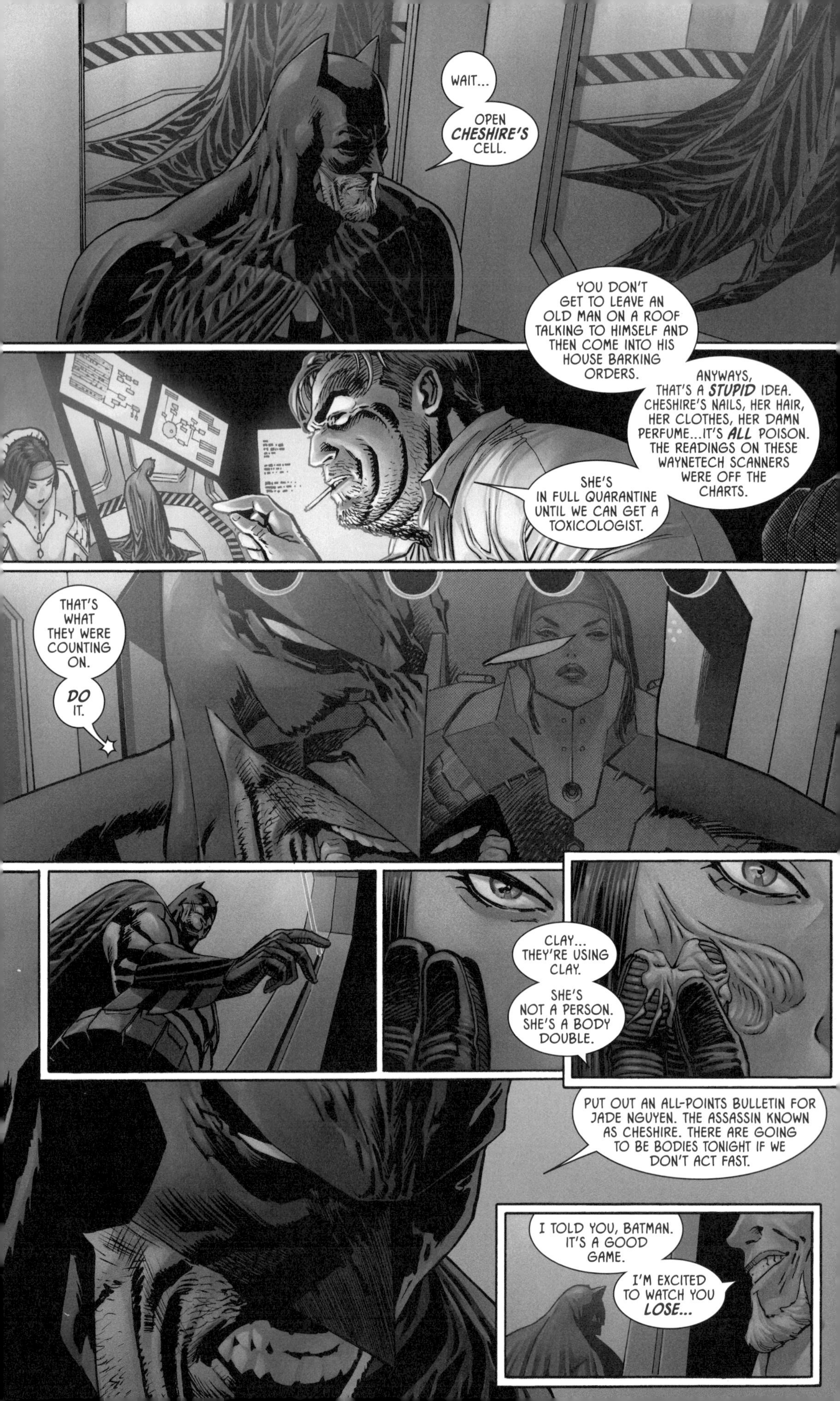

WAIT...
OPEN CHESHIRE'S CELL.
YOU DON'T GET TO LEAVE AN OLD MAN ON A ROOF TALKING TO HIMSELF AND THEN COME INTO HIS HOUSE BARKING ORDERS.
ANYWAYS, THAT'S A STUPID IDEA. CHESHIRE'S NAILS, HER HAIR, HER CLOTHES, HER DAMN PERFUME...IT'S ALL POISON. THE READINGS ON THESE WAYNETECH SCANNERS WERE OFF THE CHARTS.
SHE'S IN FULL QUARANTINE UNTIL WE CAN GET A TOXICOLOGIST.
THAT'S WHAT THEY WERE COUNTING ON.
DO IT.
CLAY... THEY'RE USING CLAY.
SHE'S NOT A PERSON. SHE'S A BODY DOUBLE.
PUT OUT AN ALL-POINTS BULLETIN FOR JADE NGUYEN. THE ASSASSIN KNOWN AS CHESHIRE. THERE ARE GOING TO BE BODIES TONIGHT IF WE DON'T ACT FAST.
I TOLD YOU, BATMAN. IT'S A GOOD GAME.
I'M EXCITED TO WATCH YOU LOSE...

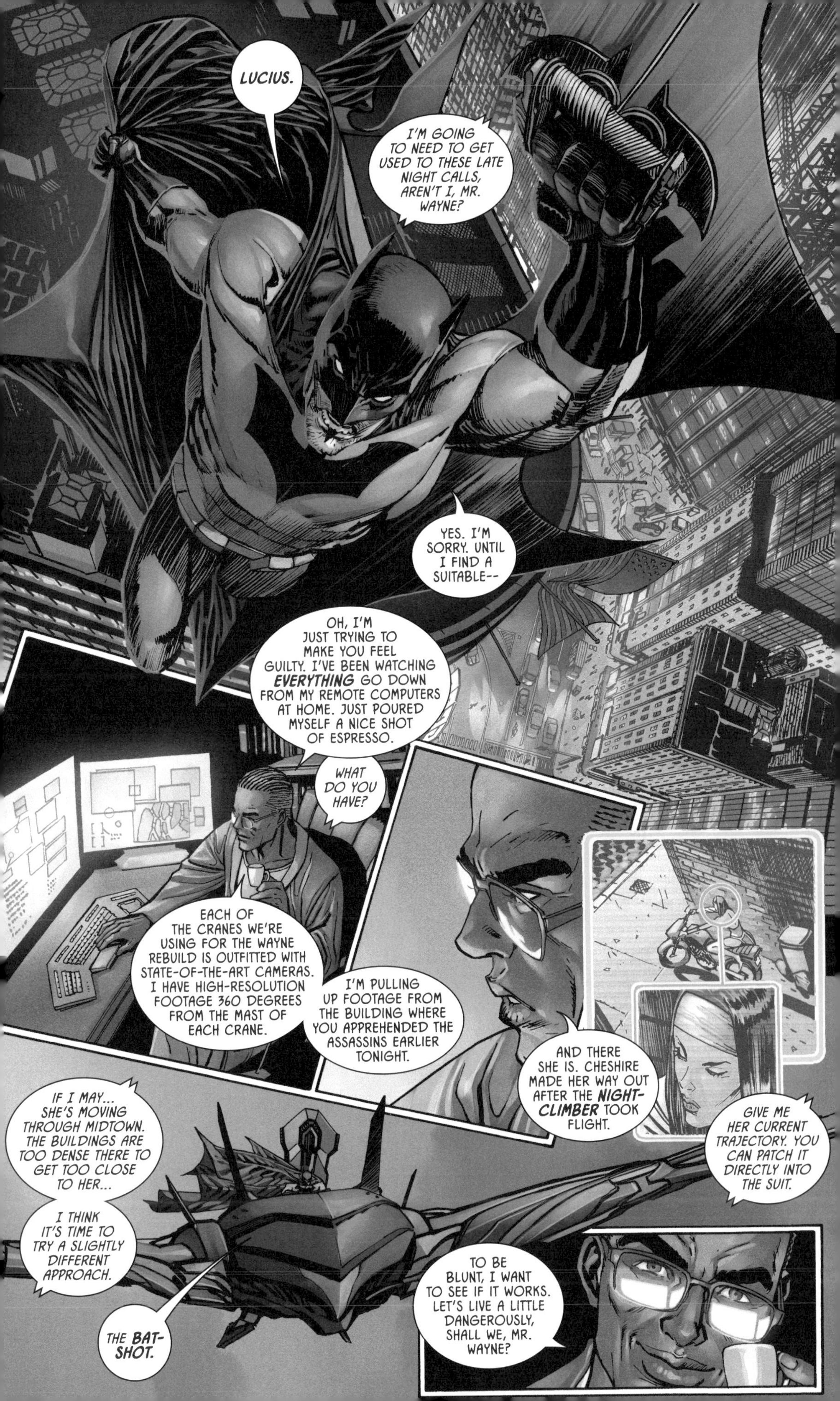
LUCIUS.
I'M GOING TO NEED TO GET USED TO THESE LATE NIGHT CALLS, AREN'T I, MR. WAYNE?
YES. I'M SORRY. UNTIL I FIND A SUITABLE--
OH, I'M JUST TRYING TO MAKE YOU FEEL GUILTY. I'VE BEEN WATCHING EVERYTHING GO DOWN FROM MY REMOTE COMPUTERS AT HOME. JUST POURED MYSELF A NICE SHOT OF ESPRESSO.
WHAT DO YOU HAVE?
EACH OF THE CRANES WE'RE USING FOR THE WAYNE REBUILD IS OUTFITTED WITH STATE-OF-THE-ART CAMERAS. I HAVE HIGH-RESOLUTION FOOTAGE 360 DEGREES FROM THE MAST OF EACH CRANE.
I'M PULLING UP FOOTAGE FROM THE BUILDING WHERE YOU APPREHENDED THE ASSASSINS EARLIER TONIGHT.
AND THERE SHE IS. CHESHIRE MADE HER WAY OUT AFTER THE NIGHT-CLIMBER TOOK FLIGHT.
GIVE ME HER CURRENT TRAJECTORY. YOU CAN PATCH IT DIRECTLY INTO THE SUIT.
IF I MAY... SHE'S MOVING THROUGH MIDTOWN. THE BUILDINGS ARE TOO DENSE THERE TO GET TOO CLOSE TO HER...
I THINK IT'S TIME TO TRY A SLIGHTLY DIFFERENT APPROACH.
THE BAT-SHOT.
TO BE BLUNT, I WANT TO SEE IF IT WORKS. LET'S LIVE A LITTLE DANGEROUSLY, SHALL WE, MR. WAYNE?

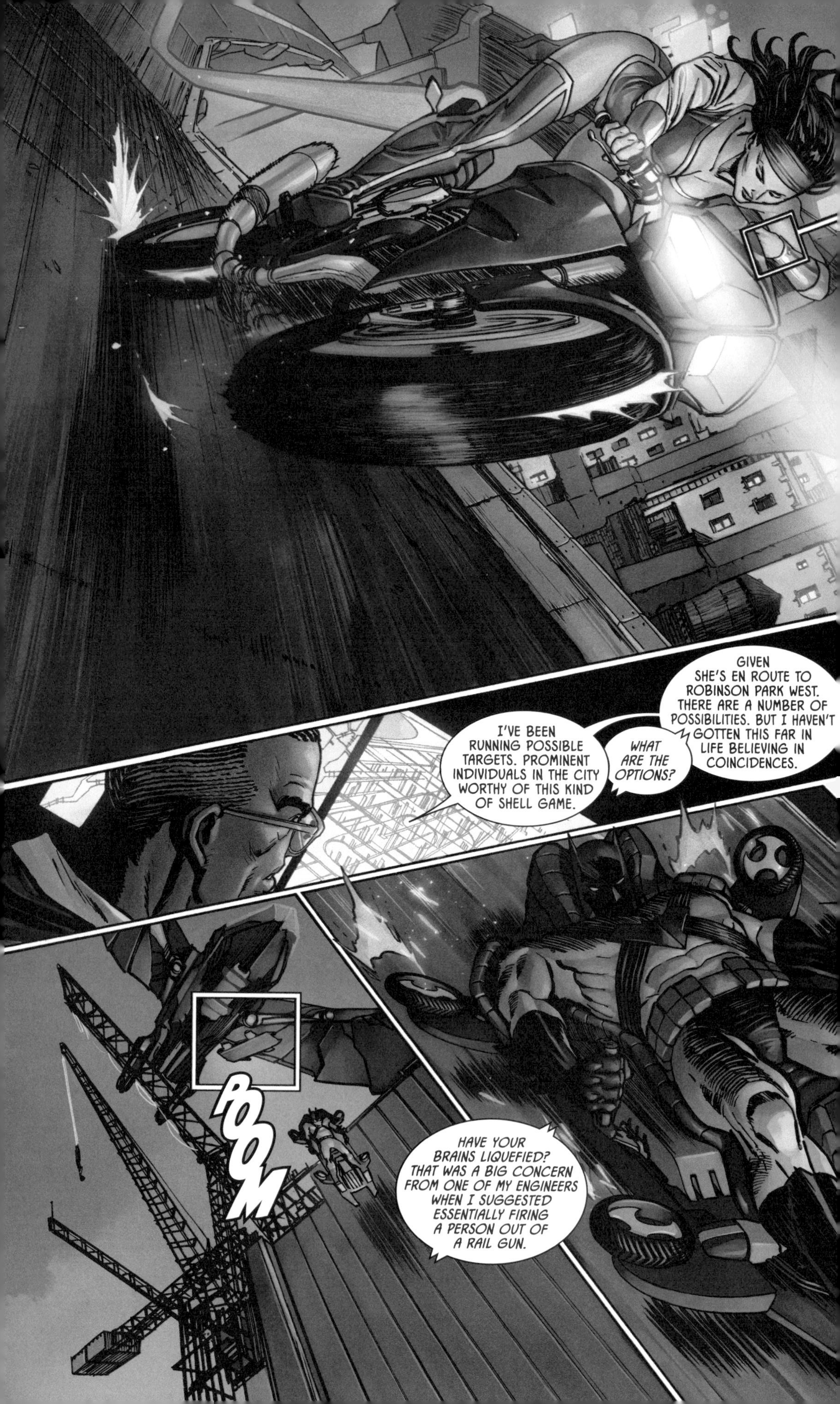
I'VE BEEN RUNNING POSSIBLE TARGETS. PROMINENT INDIVIDUALS IN THE CITY WORTHY OF THIS KIND OF SHELL GAME.
WHAT ARE THE OPTIONS?
GIVEN SHE'S EN ROUTE TO ROBINSON PARK WEST. THERE ARE A NUMBER OF POSSIBILITIES. BUT I HAVEN'T GOTTEN THIS FAR IN LIFE BELIEVING IN COINCIDENCES.
VROOM
HAVE YOUR BRAINS LIQUEFIED? THAT WAS A BIG CONCERN FROM ONE OF MY ENGINEERS WHEN I SUGGESTED ESSENTIALLY FIRING A PERSON OUT OF A RAIL GUN.

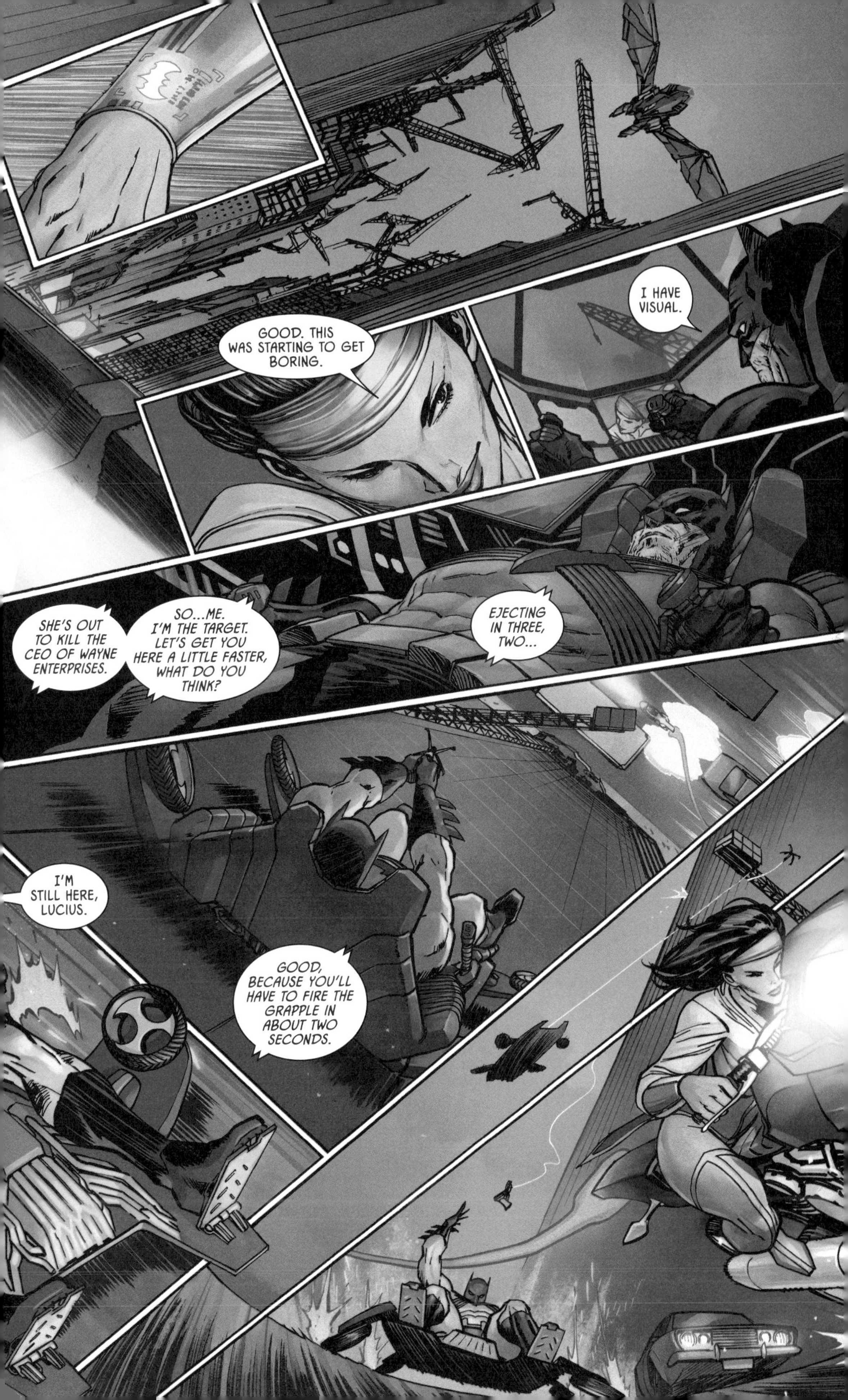
I HAVE VISUAL.
GOOD. THIS WAS STARTING TO GET BORING.
SHE'S OUT TO KILL THE CEO OF WAYNE ENTERPRISES.
SO...ME. I'M THE TARGET. LET'S GET YOU HERE A LITTLE FASTER, WHAT DO YOU THINK?
EJECTING IN THREE, TWO...
I'M STILL HERE, LUCIUS.
GOOD, BECAUSE YOU'LL HAVE TO FIRE THE GRAPPLE IN ABOUT TWO SECONDS.

SSSZZZHHH

MOVING INTO POSITION NOW...

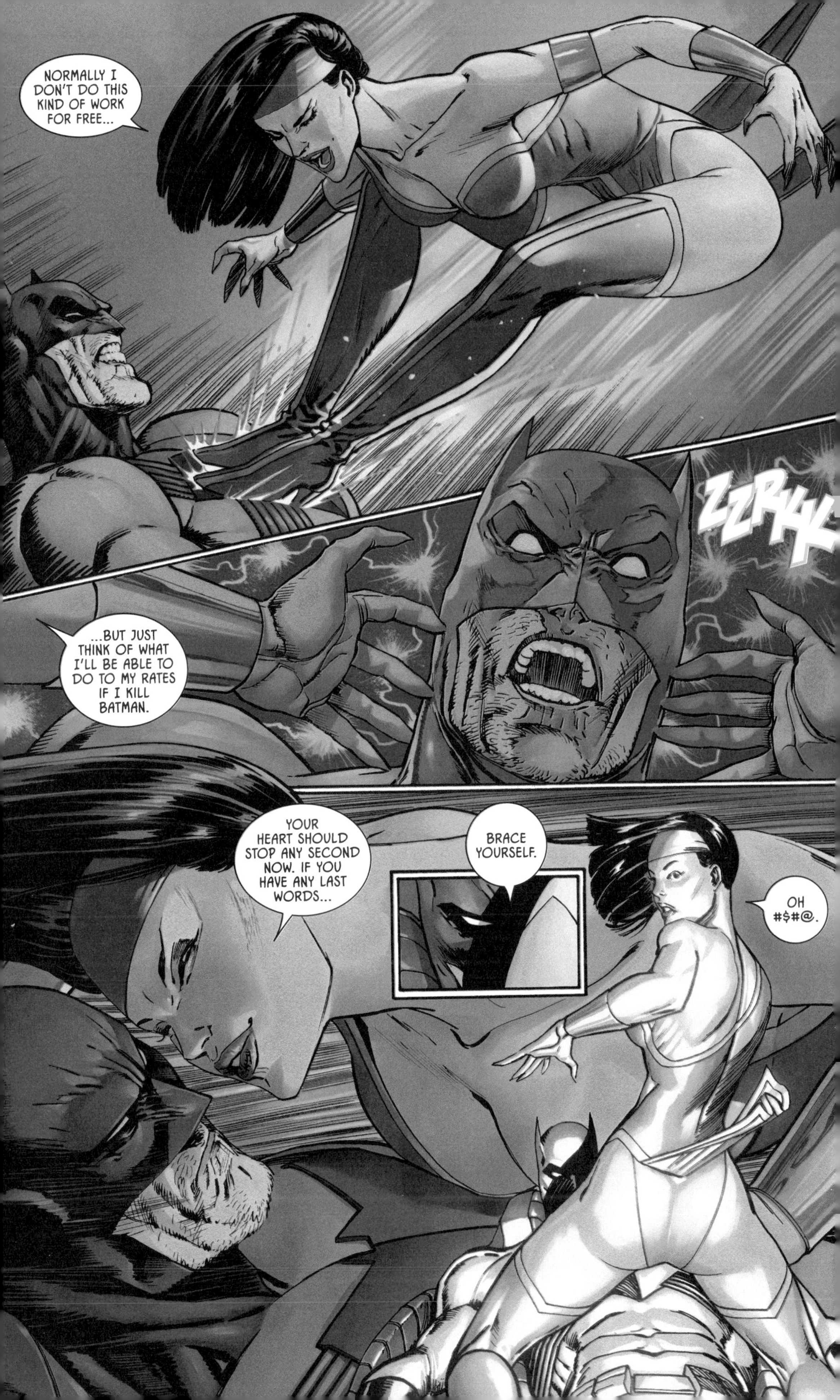

NORMALLY I DON'T DO THIS KIND OF WORK FOR FREE...
ZZRKKK
...BUT JUST THINK OF WHAT I'LL BE ABLE TO DO TO MY RATES IF I KILL BATMAN.
YOUR HEART SHOULD STOP ANY SECOND NOW. IF YOU HAVE ANY LAST WORDS...
BRACE YOURSELF.
OH #$#@.

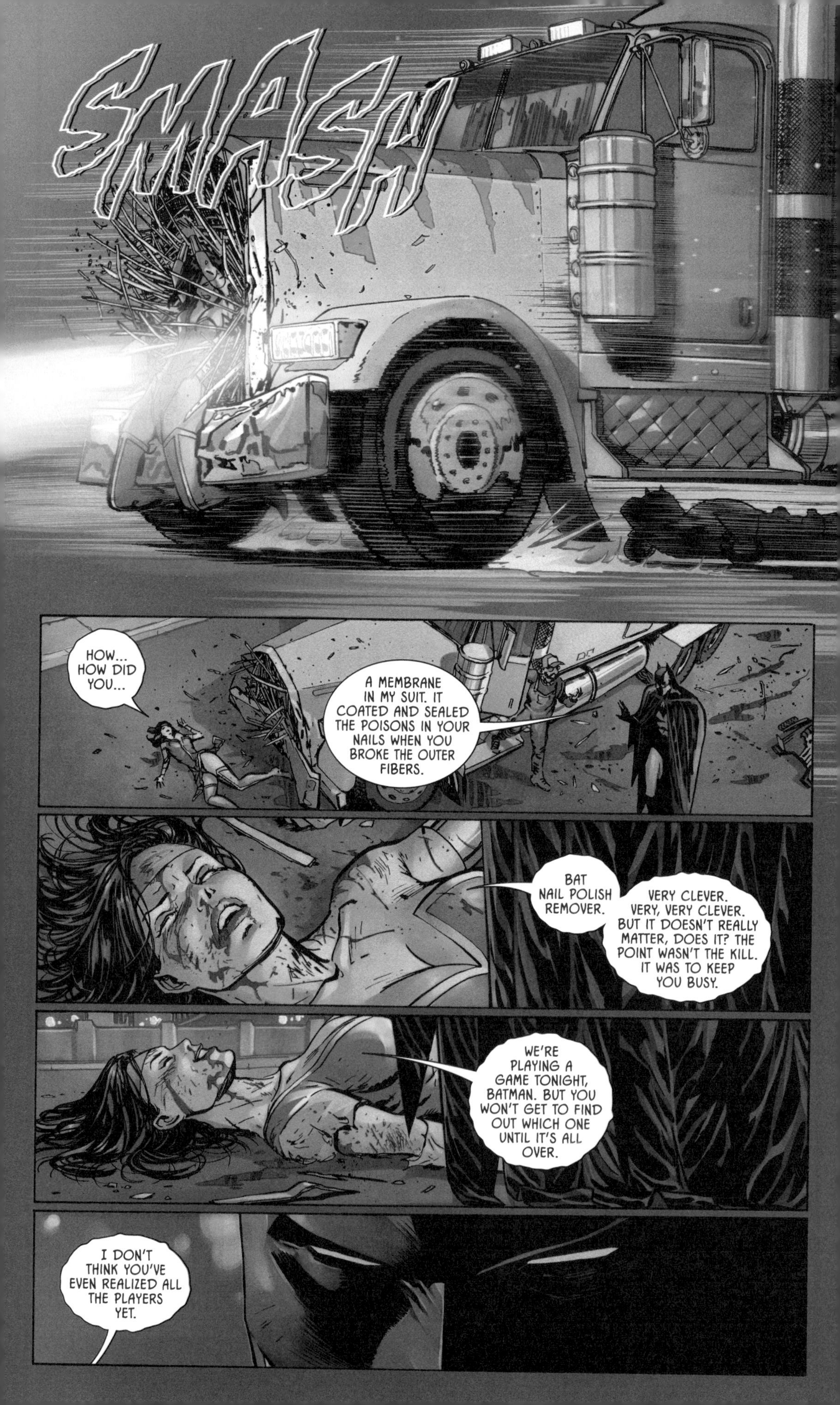
SMASH
HOW... HOW DID YOU...
A MEMBRANE IN MY SUIT. IT COATED AND SEALED THE POISONS IN YOUR NAILS WHEN YOU BROKE THE OUTER FIBERS.
BAT NAIL POLISH REMOVER.
VERY CLEVER. VERY, VERY CLEVER. BUT IT DOESN'T REALLY MATTER, DOES IT? THE POINT WASN'T THE KILL. IT WAS TO KEEP YOU BUSY.
WE'RE PLAYING A GAME TONIGHT, BATMAN. BUT YOU WON'T GET TO FIND OUT WHICH ONE UNTIL IT'S ALL OVER.
I DON'T THINK YOU'VE EVEN REALIZED ALL THE PLAYERS YET.

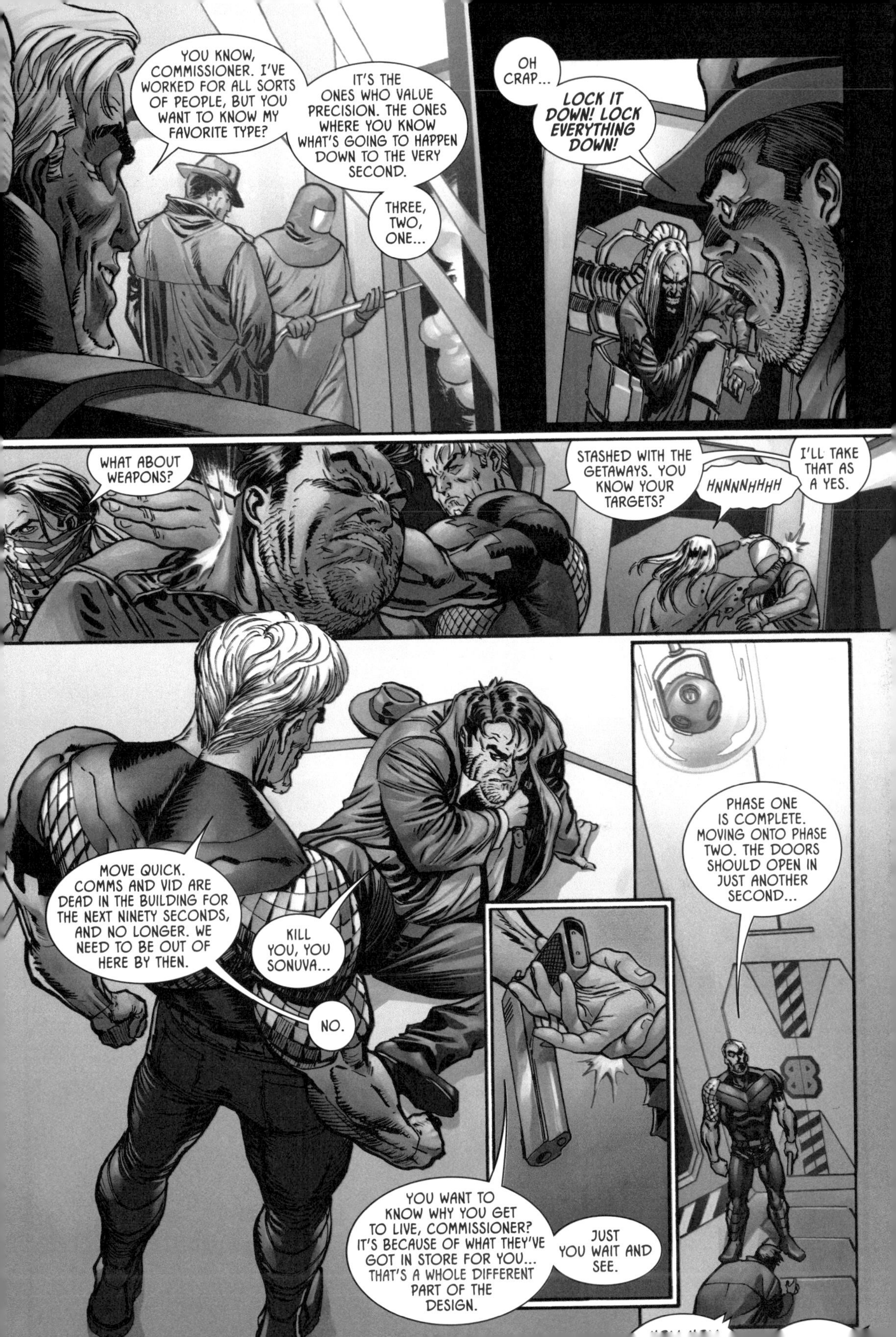

YOU KNOW, COMMISSIONER. I'VE WORKED FOR ALL SORTS OF PEOPLE, BUT YOU WANT TO KNOW MY FAVORITE TYPE?
IT'S THE ONES WHO VALUE PRECISION. THE ONES WHERE YOU KNOW WHAT'S GOING TO HAPPEN DOWN TO THE VERY SECOND.
THREE, TWO, ONE...
OH CRAP...
LOCK IT DOWN! LOCK EVERYTHING DOWN!
WHAT ABOUT WEAPONS?
STASHED WITH THE GETAWAYS. YOU KNOW YOUR TARGETS?
HNNNNHHHH
I'LL TAKE THAT AS A YES.
MOVE QUICK. COMMS AND VID ARE DEAD IN THE BUILDING FOR THE NEXT NINETY SECONDS, AND NO LONGER. WE NEED TO BE OUT OF HERE BY THEN.
KILL YOU, YOU SONUVA...
NO.
PHASE ONE IS COMPLETE. MOVING ONTO PHASE TWO. THE DOORS SHOULD OPEN IN JUST ANOTHER SECOND...
YOU WANT TO KNOW WHY YOU GET TO LIVE, COMMISSIONER? IT'S BECAUSE OF WHAT THEY'VE GOT IN STORE FOR YOU... THAT'S A WHOLE DIFFERENT PART OF THE DESIGN.
JUST YOU WAIT AND SEE.

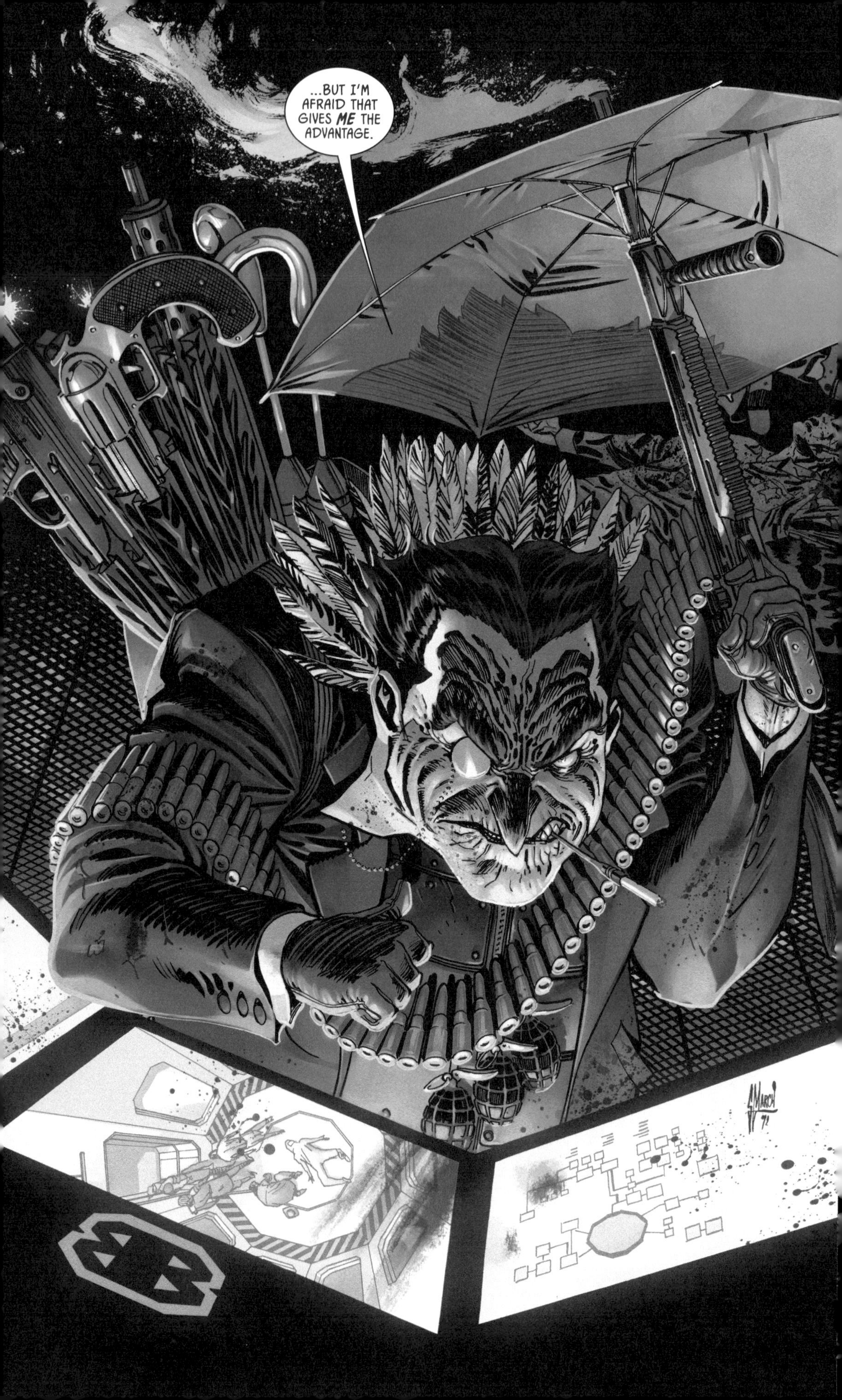
...BUT I'M AFRAID THAT GIVES ME THE ADVANTAGE.

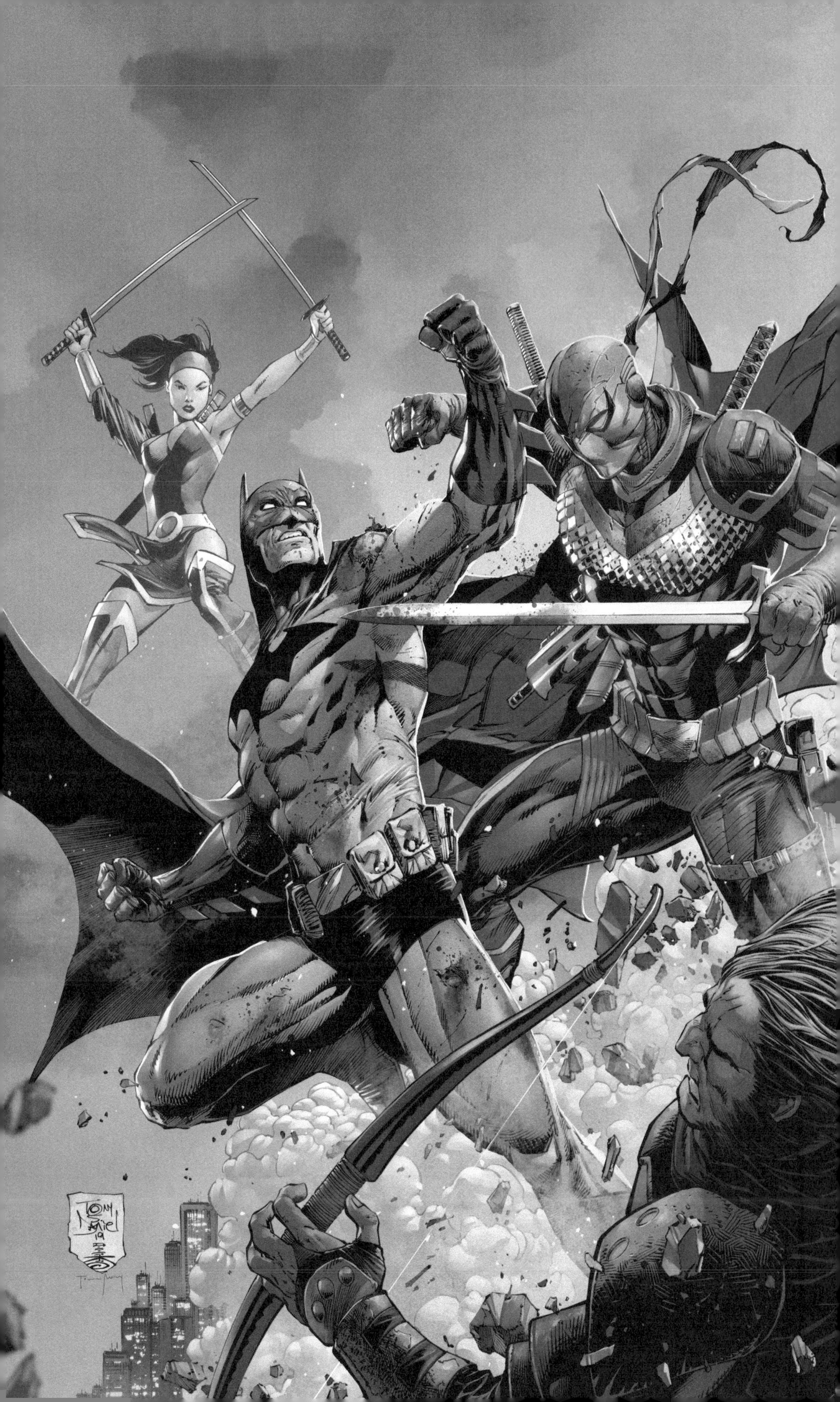

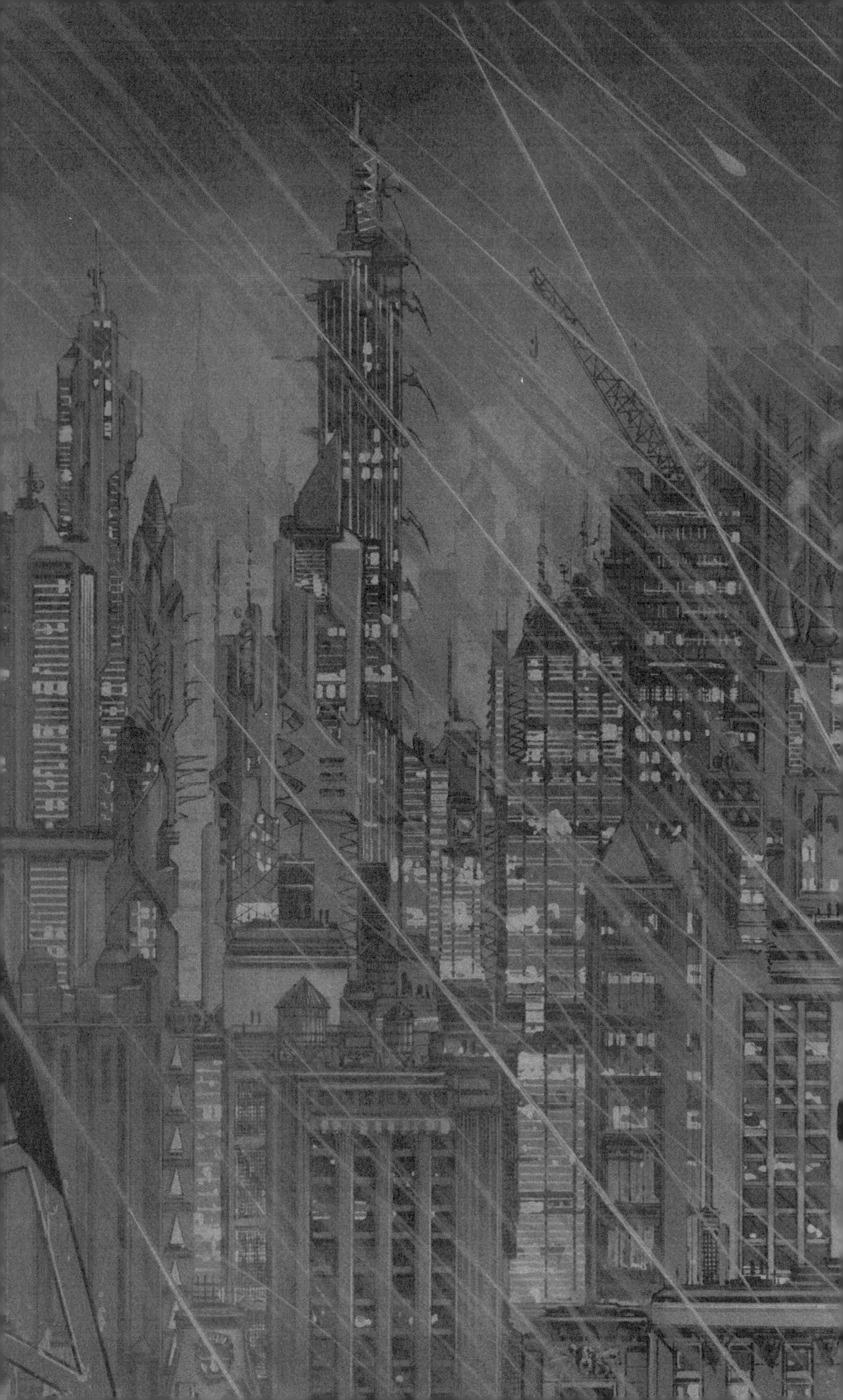

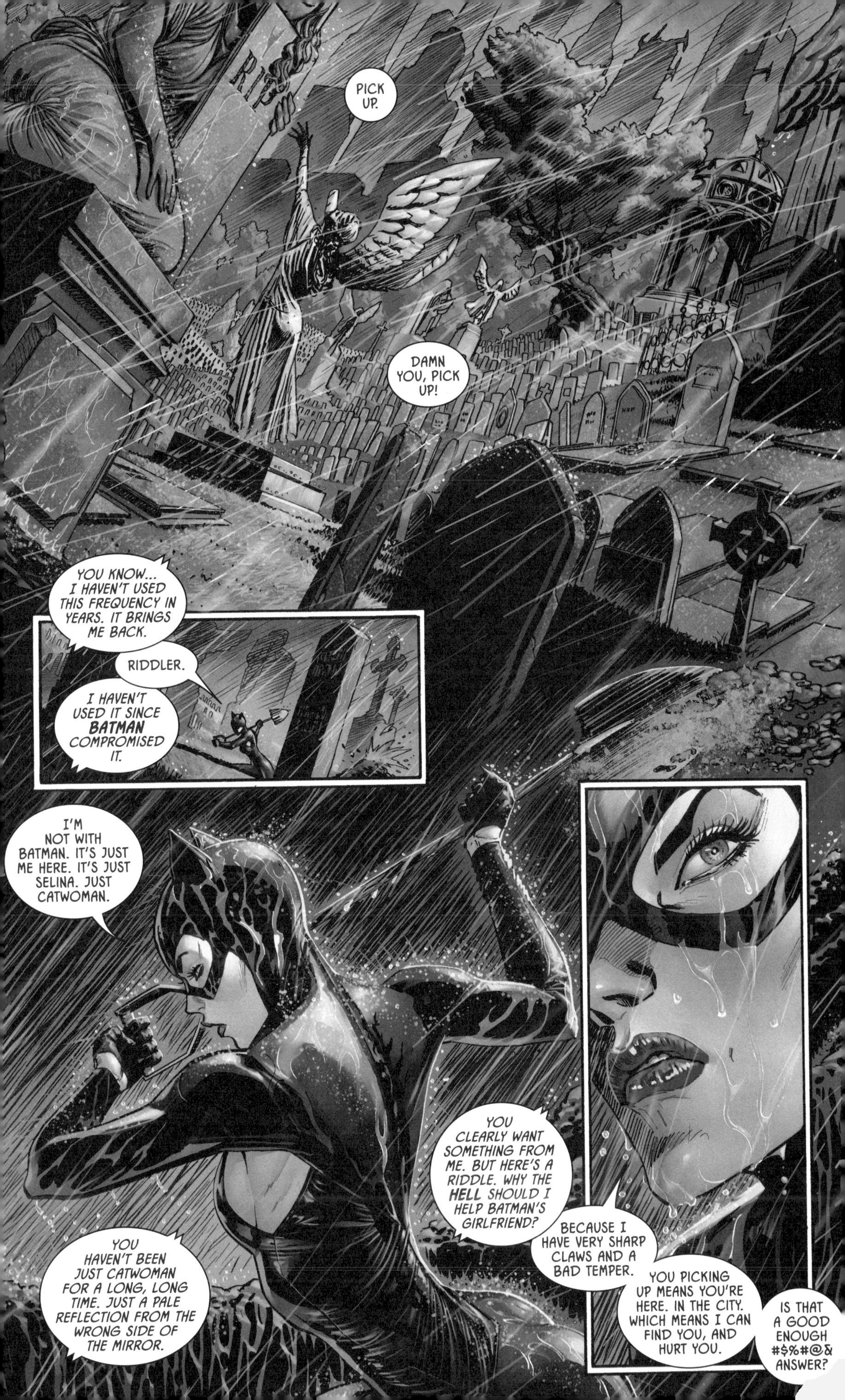
RIP
PICK UP.
DAMN YOU, PICK UP!
YOU KNOW... I HAVEN'T USED THIS FREQUENCY IN YEARS. IT BRINGS ME BACK.
RIDDLER.
I HAVEN'T USED IT SINCE BATMAN COMPROMISED IT.
I'M NOT WITH BATMAN. IT'S JUST ME HERE. IT'S JUST SELINA. JUST CATWOMAN.
YOU HAVEN'T BEEN JUST CATWOMAN FOR A LONG, LONG TIME. JUST A PALE REFLECTION FROM THE WRONG SIDE OF THE MIRROR.
YOU CLEARLY WANT SOMETHING FROM ME. BUT HERE'S A RIDDLE. WHY THE HELL SHOULD I HELP BATMAN'S GIRLFRIEND?
BECAUSE I HAVE VERY SHARP CLAWS AND A BAD TEMPER.
YOU PICKING UP MEANS YOU'RE HERE. IN THE CITY. WHICH MEANS I CAN FIND YOU, AND HURT YOU.
IS THAT A GOOD ENOUGH #$%#@& ANSWER?

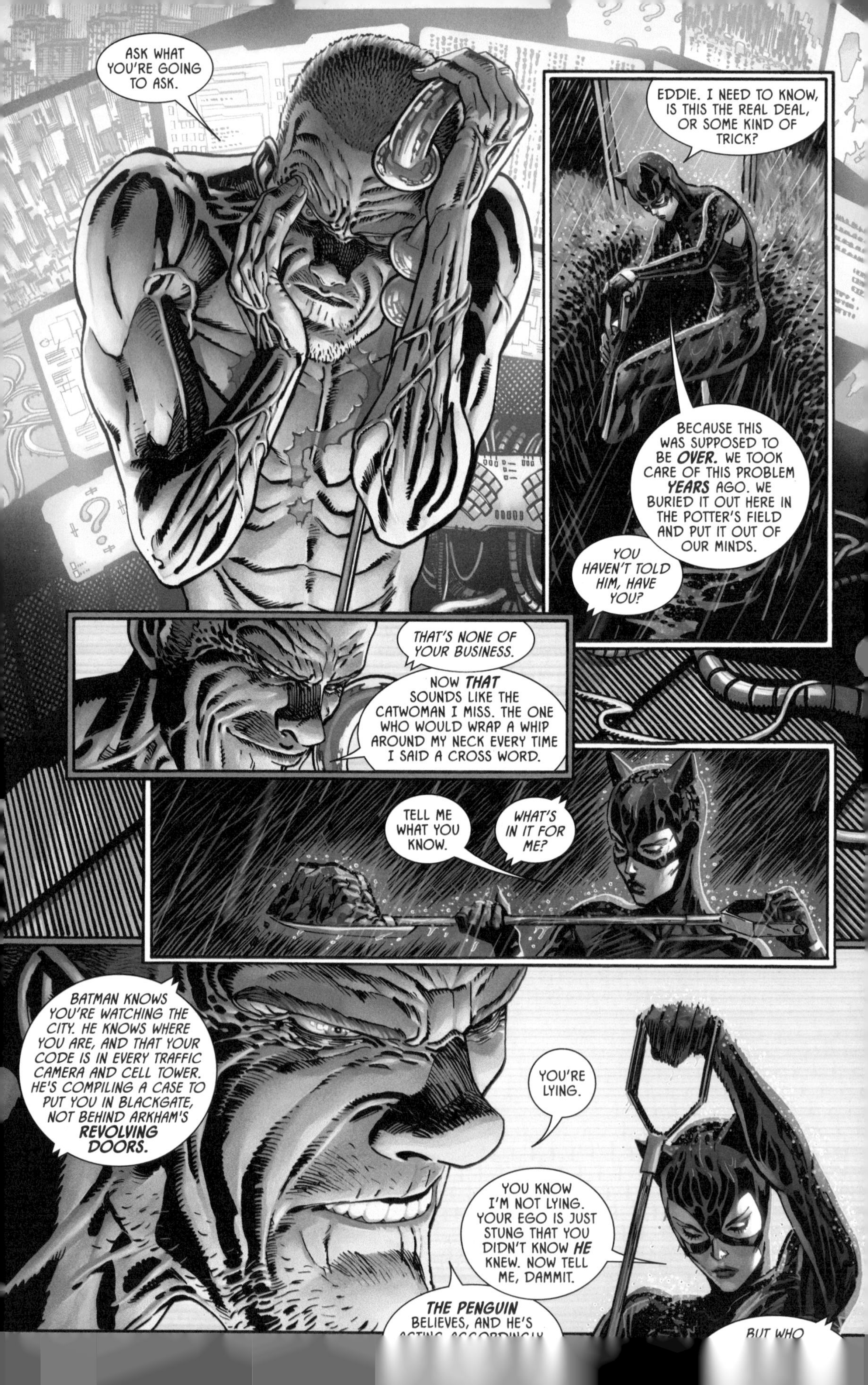
ASK WHAT YOU'RE GOING TO ASK.
EDDIE. I NEED TO KNOW, IS THIS THE REAL DEAL, OR SOME KIND OF TRICK?
BECAUSE THIS WAS SUPPOSED TO BE OVER. WE TOOK CARE OF THIS PROBLEM YEARS AGO. WE BURIED IT OUT HERE IN THE POTTER'S FIELD AND PUT IT OUT OF OUR MINDS.
YOU HAVEN'T TOLD HIM, HAVE YOU?
THAT'S NONE OF YOUR BUSINESS.
NOW THAT SOUNDS LIKE THE CATWOMAN I MISS. THE ONE WHO WOULD WRAP A WHIP AROUND MY NECK EVERY TIME I SAID A CROSS WORD.
TELL ME WHAT YOU KNOW.
WHAT'S IN IT FOR ME?
BATMAN KNOWS YOU'RE WATCHING THE CITY. HE KNOWS WHERE YOU ARE, AND THAT YOUR CODE IS IN EVERY TRAFFIC CAMERA AND CELL TOWER. HE'S COMPILING A CASE TO PUT YOU IN BLACKGATE, NOT BEHIND ARKHAM'S REVOLVING DOORS.
YOU'RE LYING.
YOU KNOW I'M NOT LYING. YOUR EGO IS JUST STUNG THAT YOU DIDN'T KNOW HE KNEW. NOW TELL ME, DAMMIT.
THE PENGUIN BELIEVES, AND HE'S
BUT WHO

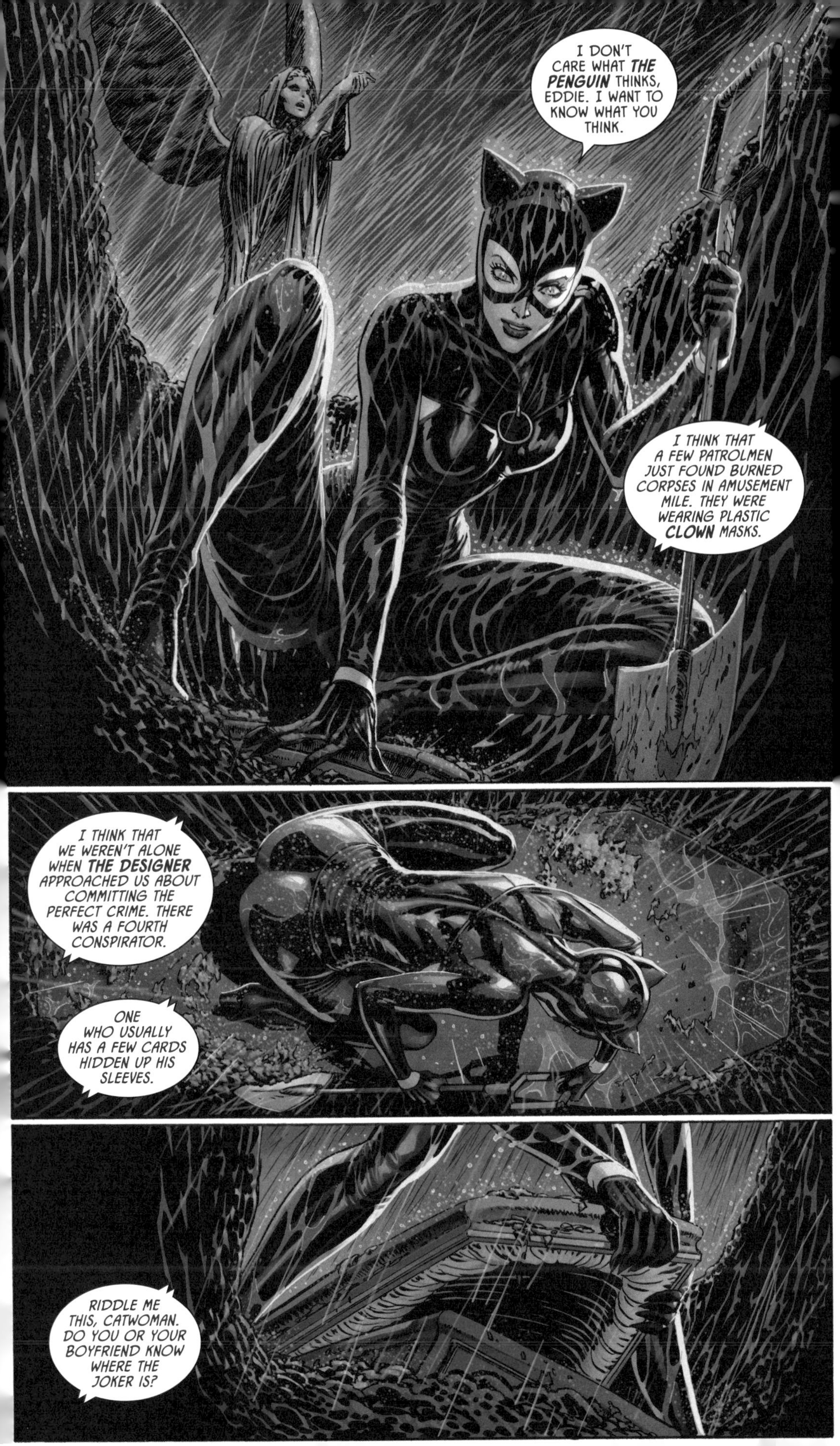
I DON'T CARE WHAT THE PENGUIN THINKS, EDDIE. I WANT TO KNOW WHAT YOU THINK.
I THINK THAT A FEW PATROLMEN JUST FOUND BURNED CORPSES IN AMUSEMENT MILE. THEY WERE WEARING PLASTIC CLOWN MASKS.
I THINK THAT WE WEREN'T ALONE WHEN THE DESIGNER APPROACHED US ABOUT COMMITTING THE PERFECT CRIME. THERE WAS A FOURTH CONSPIRATOR.
ONE WHO USUALLY HAS A FEW CARDS HIDDEN UP HIS SLEEVES.
RIDDLE ME THIS, CATWOMAN. DO YOU OR YOUR BOYFRIEND KNOW WHERE THE JOKER IS?

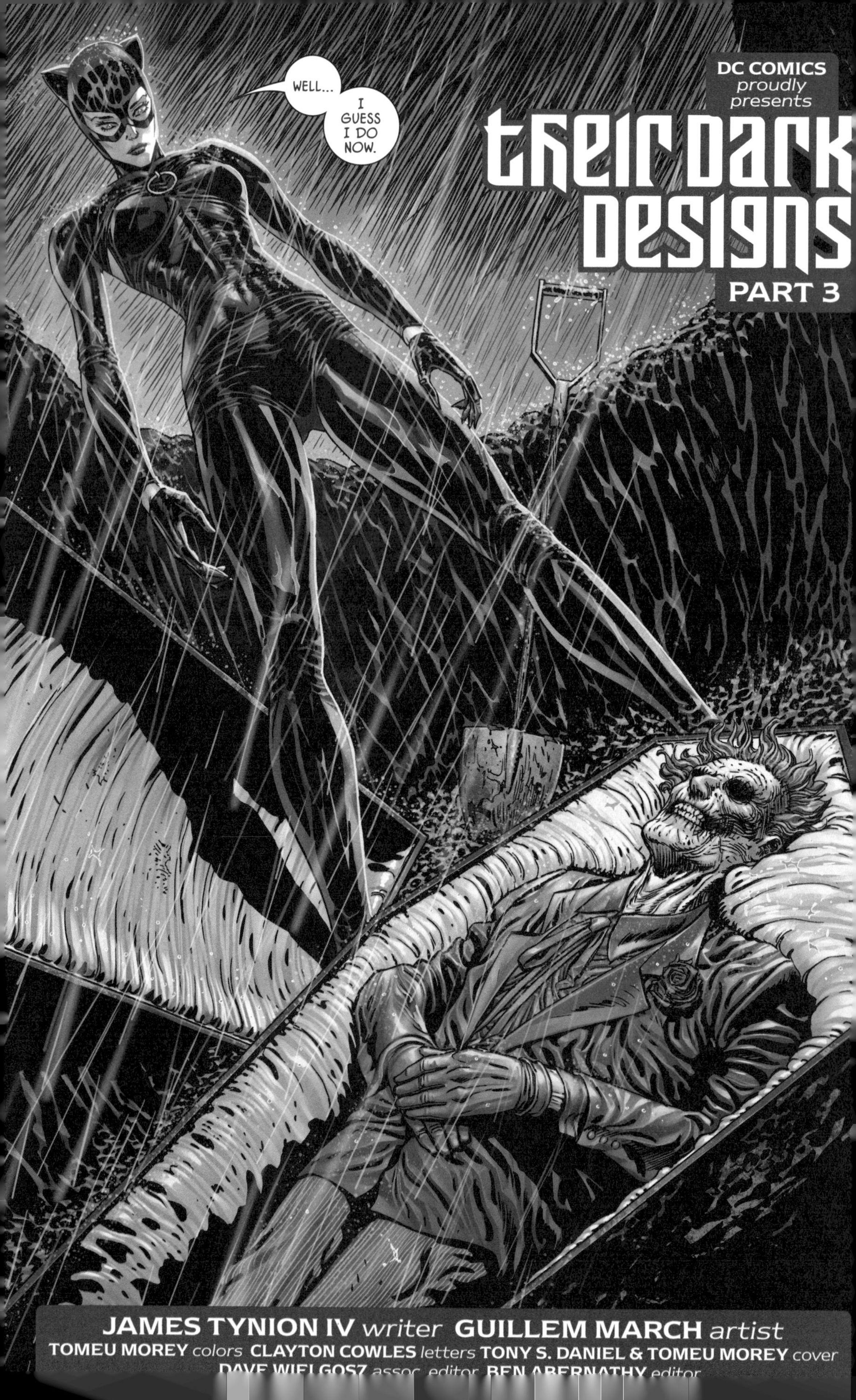

WELL...
I GUESS I DO NOW.
DC COMICS proudly presents
THEIR DARK DESIGNS
PART 3
JAMES TYNION IV writer GUILLEM MARCH artist
TOMEU MOREY colors CLAYTON COWLES letters TONY S. DANIEL & TOMEU MOREY cover
DAVE WIELGOSZ assoc. editor BEN ABERNATHY editor

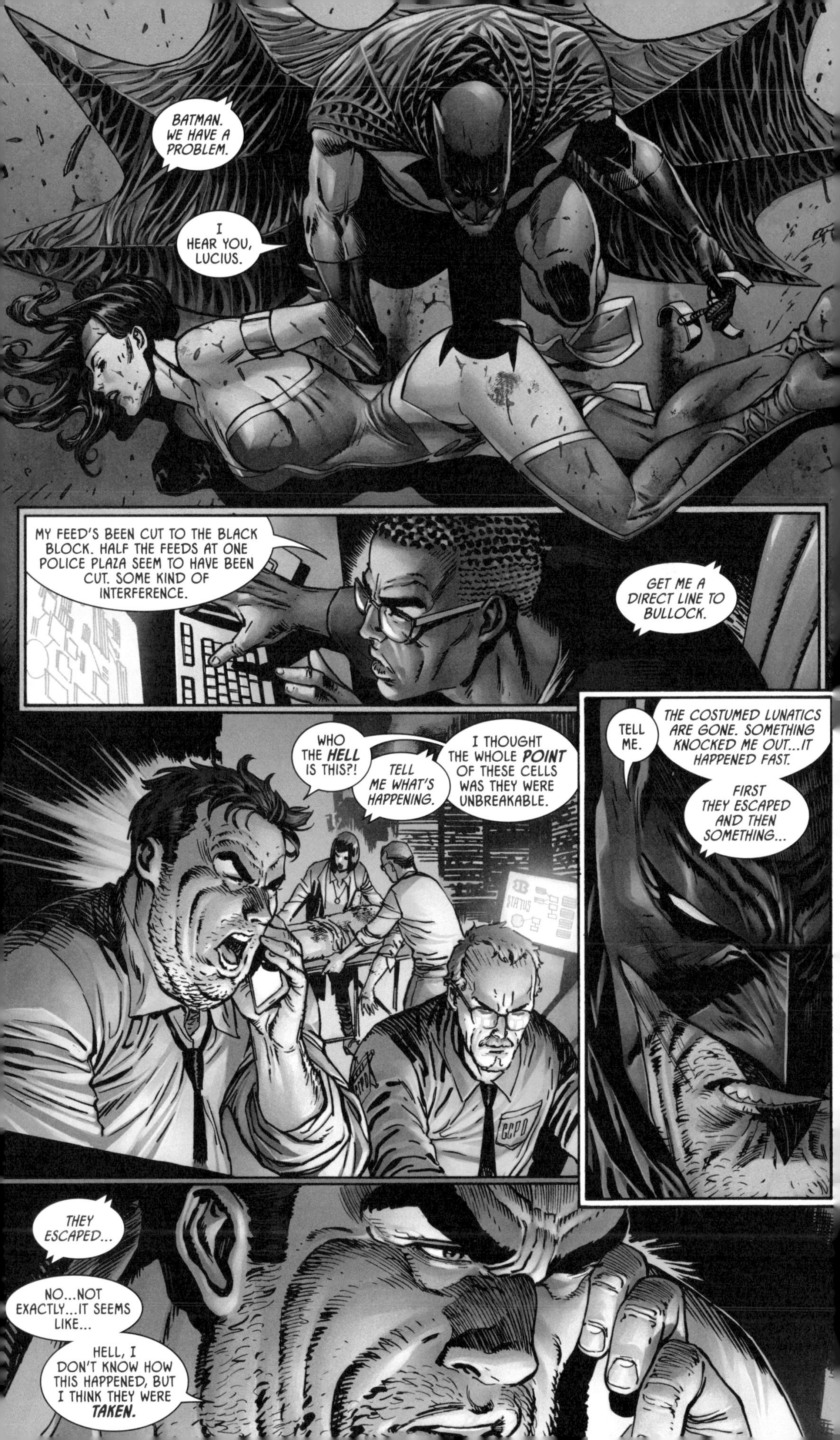
BATMAN. WE HAVE A PROBLEM.
I HEAR YOU, LUCIUS.
MY FEED'S BEEN CUT TO THE BLACK BLOCK. HALF THE FEEDS AT ONE POLICE PLAZA SEEM TO HAVE BEEN CUT. SOME KIND OF INTERFERENCE.
GET ME A DIRECT LINE TO BULLOCK.
WHO THE HELL IS THIS?!
TELL ME WHAT'S HAPPENING.
I THOUGHT THE WHOLE POINT OF THESE CELLS WAS THEY WERE UNBREAKABLE.
TELL ME.
THE COSTUMED LUNATICS ARE GONE. SOMETHING KNOCKED ME OUT...IT HAPPENED FAST.
FIRST THEY ESCAPED AND THEN SOMETHING...
STATUS
GCPD
THEY ESCAPED...
NO...NOT EXACTLY...IT SEEMS LIKE...
HELL, I DON'T KNOW HOW THIS HAPPENED, BUT I THINK THEY WERE TAKEN.

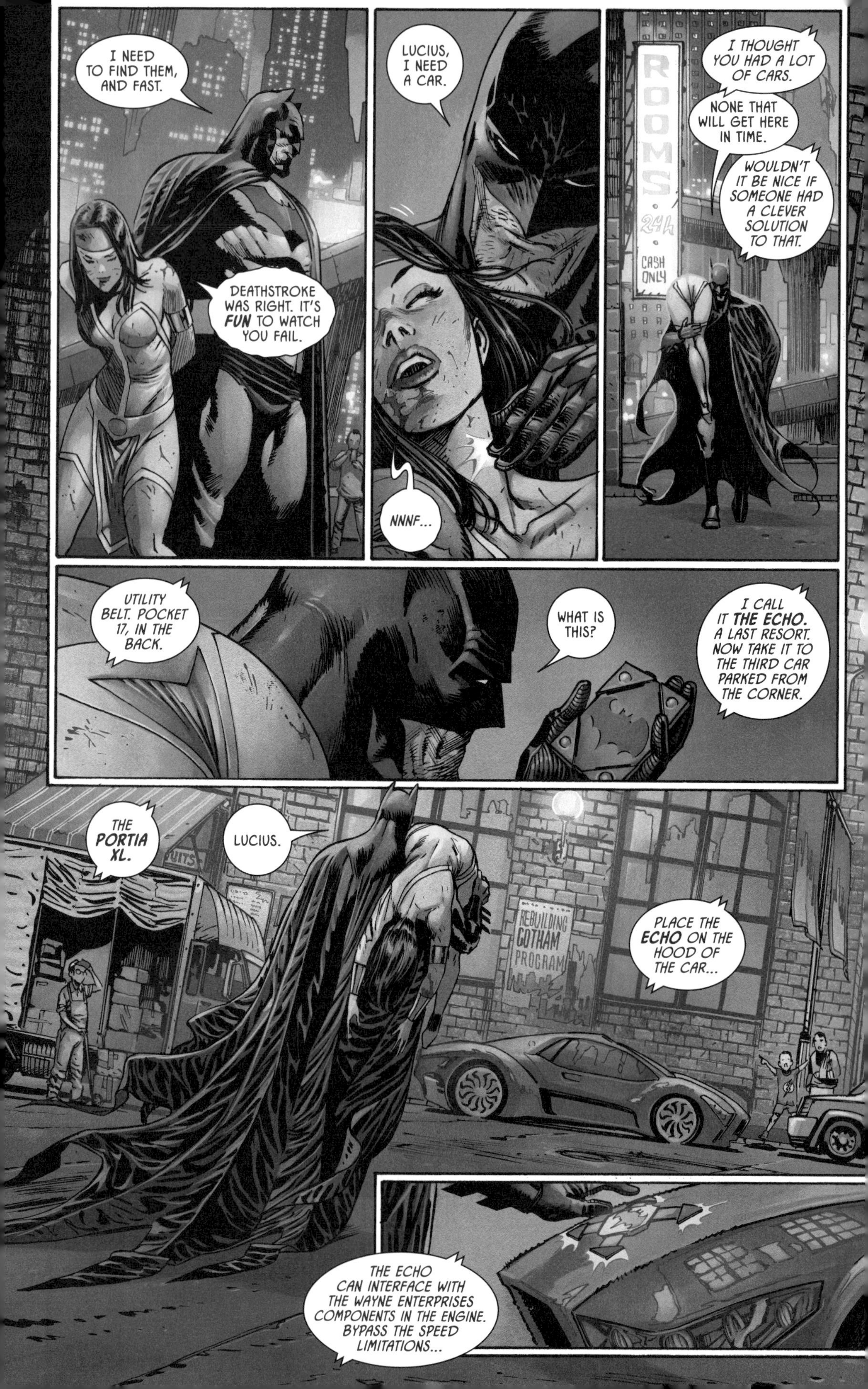
I NEED TO FIND THEM, AND FAST.
DEATHSTROKE WAS RIGHT. IT'S FUN TO WATCH YOU FAIL.
LUCIUS, I NEED A CAR.
NNNF...
ROOMS 24h CASH ONLY
I THOUGHT YOU HAD A LOT OF CARS.
NONE THAT WILL GET HERE IN TIME.
WOULDN'T IT BE NICE IF SOMEONE HAD A CLEVER SOLUTION TO THAT.
UTILITY BELT. POCKET 17, IN THE BACK.
WHAT IS THIS?
I CALL IT THE ECHO. A LAST RESORT. NOW TAKE IT TO THE THIRD CAR PARKED FROM THE CORNER.
THE PORTIA XL.
LUCIUS.
REBUILDING GOTHAM PROGRAM
PLACE THE ECHO ON THE HOOD OF THE CAR...
THE ECHO CAN INTERFACE WITH THE WAYNE ENTERPRISES COMPONENTS IN THE ENGINE. BYPASS THE SPEED LIMITATIONS...

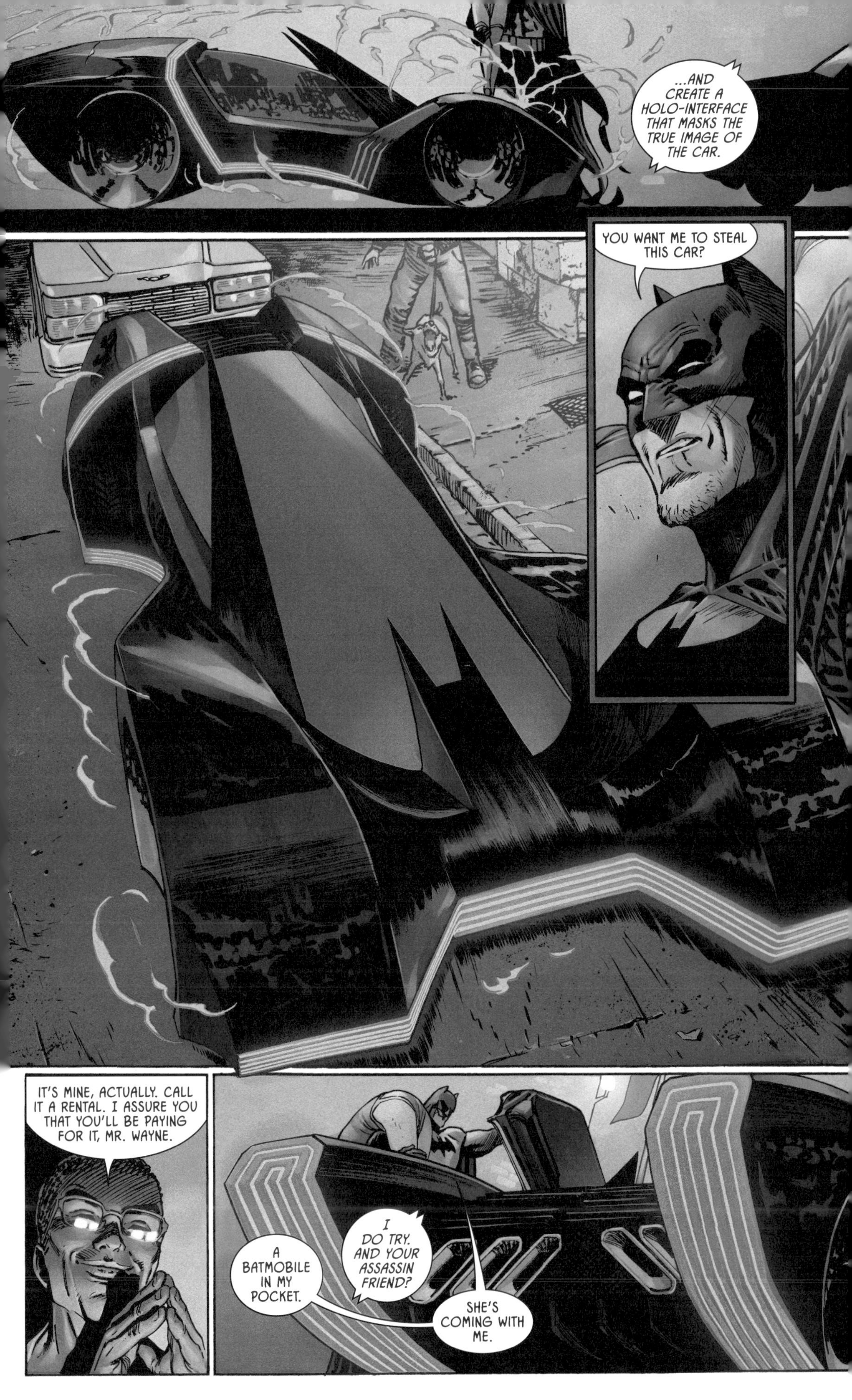
...AND CREATE A HOLO-INTERFACE THAT MASKS THE TRUE IMAGE OF THE CAR.
YOU WANT ME TO STEAL THIS CAR?
IT'S MINE, ACTUALLY. CALL IT A RENTAL. I ASSURE YOU THAT YOU'LL BE PAYING FOR IT, MR. WAYNE.
A BATMOBILE IN MY POCKET.
I DO TRY. AND YOUR ASSASSIN FRIEND?
SHE'S COMING WITH ME.

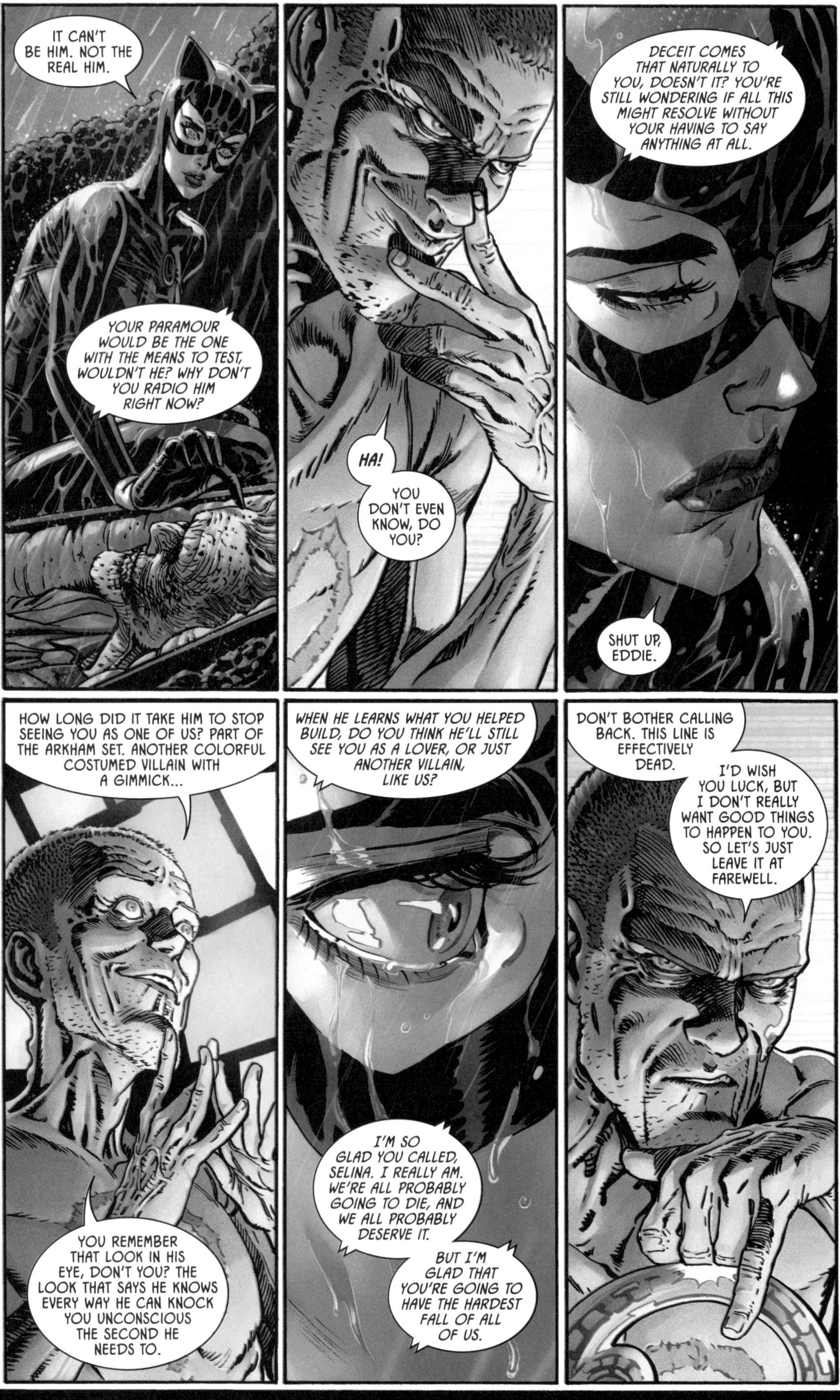
IT CAN'T BE HIM. NOT THE REAL HIM.
YOUR PARAMOUR WOULD BE THE ONE WITH THE MEANS TO TEST, WOULDN'T HE? WHY DON'T YOU RADIO HIM RIGHT NOW?
HA!
YOU DON'T EVEN KNOW, DO YOU?
DECEIT COMES THAT NATURALLY TO YOU, DOESN'T IT? YOU'RE STILL WONDERING IF ALL THIS MIGHT RESOLVE WITHOUT YOUR HAVING TO SAY ANYTHING AT ALL.
SHUT UP, EDDIE.
HOW LONG DID IT TAKE HIM TO STOP SEEING YOU AS ONE OF US? PART OF THE ARKHAM SET. ANOTHER COLORFUL COSTUMED VILLAIN WITH A GIMMICK...
YOU REMEMBER THAT LOOK IN HIS EYE, DON'T YOU? THE LOOK THAT SAYS HE KNOWS EVERY WAY HE CAN KNOCK YOU UNCONSCIOUS THE SECOND HE NEEDS TO.
WHEN HE LEARNS WHAT YOU HELPED BUILD, DO YOU THINK HE'LL STILL SEE YOU AS A LOVER, OR JUST ANOTHER VILLAIN, LIKE US?
I'M SO GLAD YOU CALLED, SELINA. I REALLY AM. WE'RE ALL PROBABLY GOING TO DIE, AND WE ALL PROBABLY DESERVE IT.
BUT I'M GLAD THAT YOU'RE GOING TO HAVE THE HARDEST FALL OF ALL OF US.
DON'T BOTHER CALLING BACK. THIS LINE IS EFFECTIVELY DEAD.
I'D WISH YOU LUCK, BUT I DON'T REALLY WANT GOOD THINGS TO HAPPEN TO YOU. SO LET'S JUST LEAVE IT AT FAREWELL.

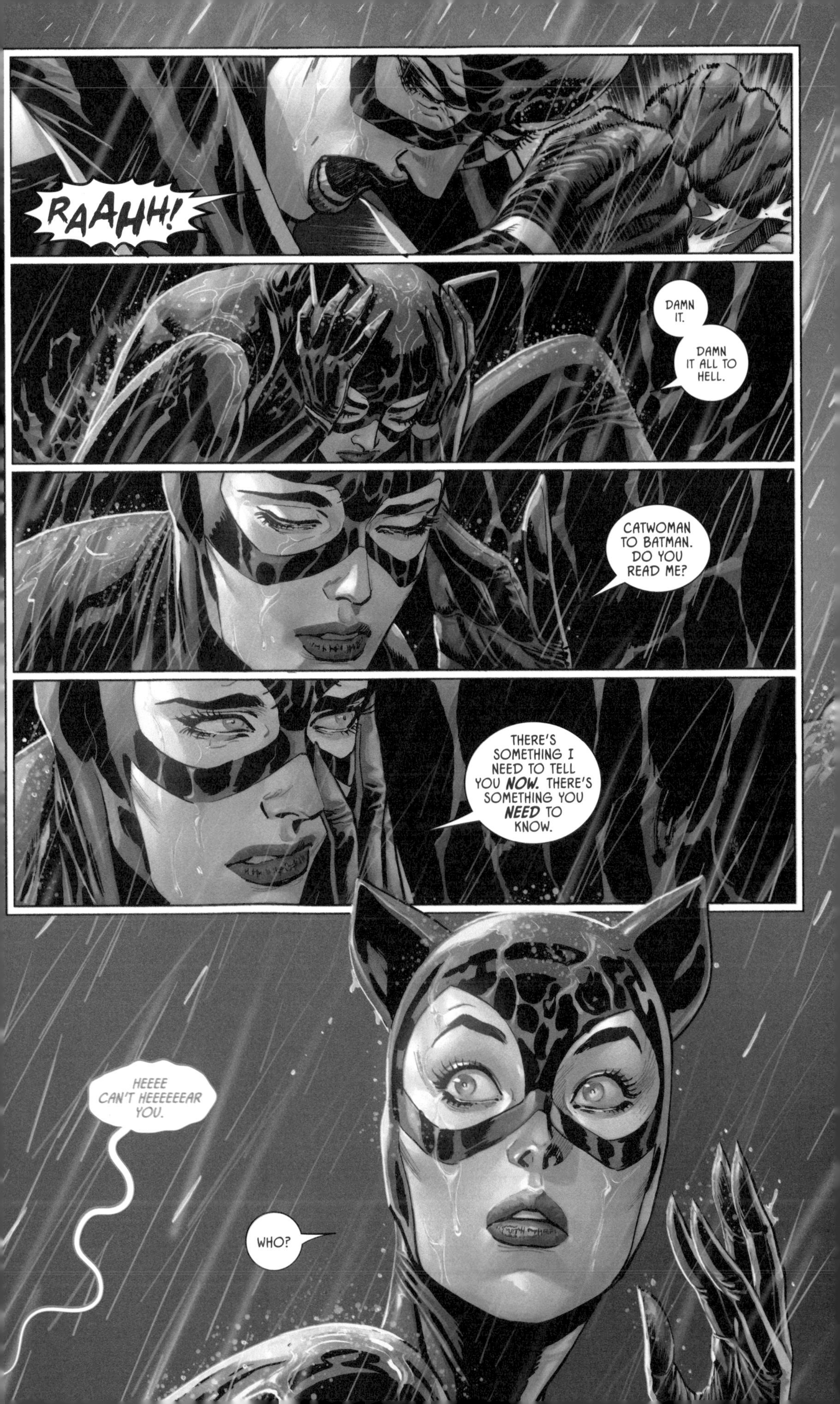
RAAHH!
DAMN IT.
DAMN IT ALL TO HELL.
CATWOMAN TO BATMAN. DO YOU READ ME?
THERE'S SOMETHING I NEED TO TELL YOU NOW. THERE'S SOMETHING YOU NEED TO KNOW.
HEEEE CAN'T HEEEEEEAR YOU.
WHO?

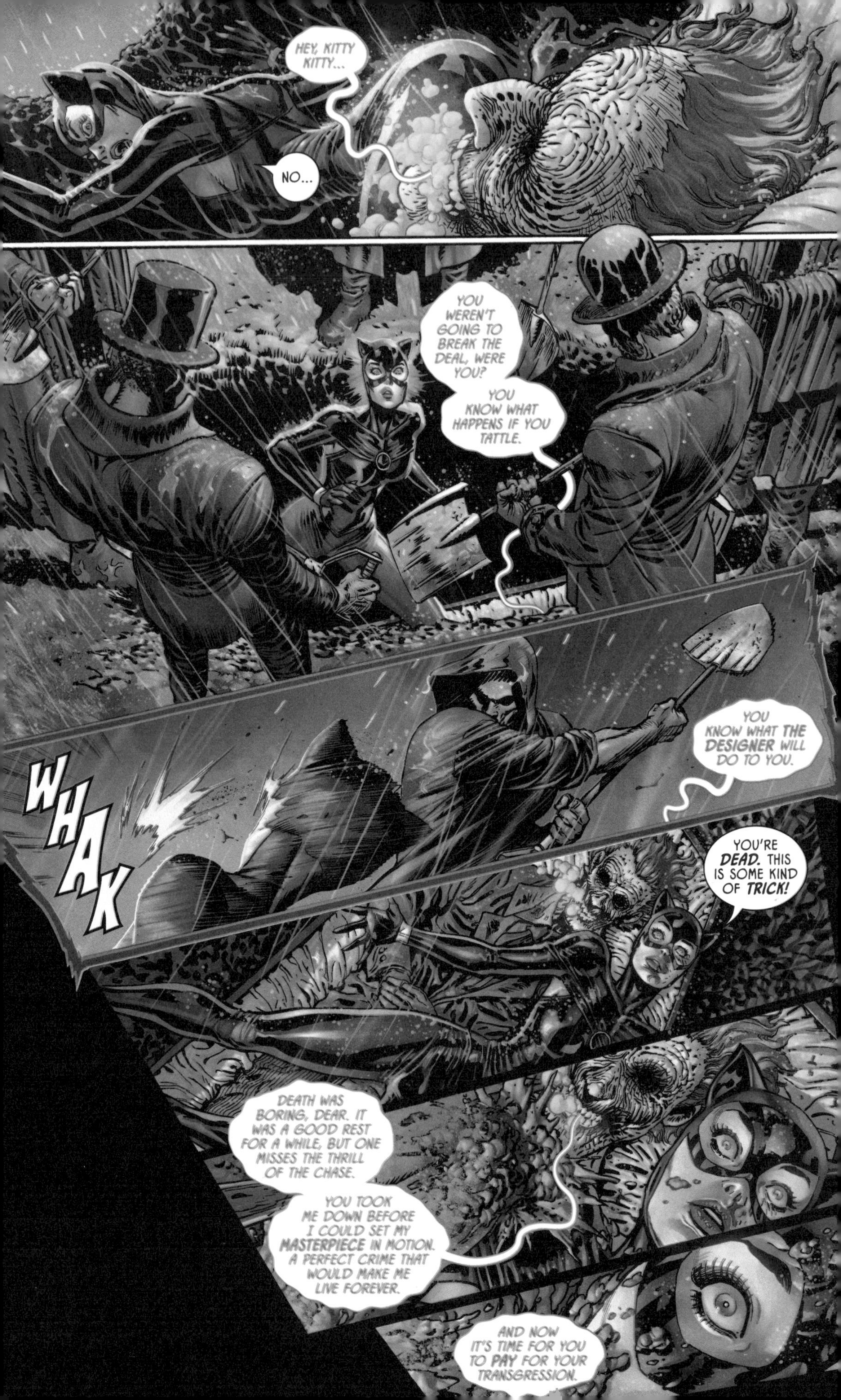

HEY, KITTY KITTY...
NO...
YOU WEREN'T GOING TO BREAK THE DEAL, WERE YOU?
YOU KNOW WHAT HAPPENS IF YOU TATTLE.
YOU KNOW WHAT THE DESIGNER WILL DO TO YOU.
WHAK
YOU'RE DEAD. THIS IS SOME KIND OF TRICK!
DEATH WAS BORING, DEAR. IT WAS A GOOD REST FOR A WHILE, BUT ONE MISSES THE THRILL OF THE CHASE.
YOU TOOK ME DOWN BEFORE I COULD SET MY MASTERPIECE IN MOTION. A PERFECT CRIME THAT WOULD MAKE ME LIVE FOREVER.
AND NOW IT'S TIME FOR YOU TO PAY FOR YOUR TRANSGRESSION.

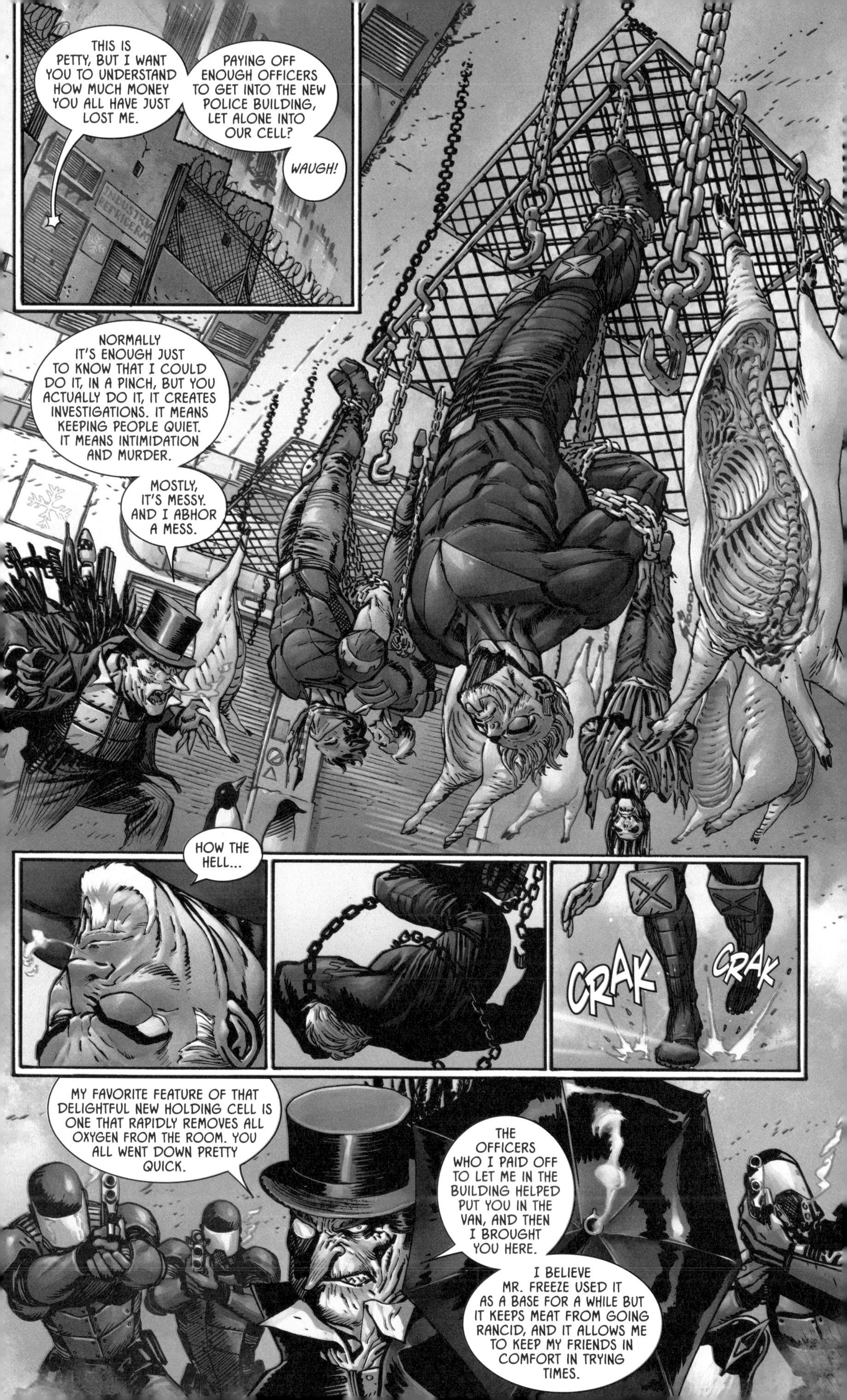
THIS IS PETTY, BUT I WANT YOU TO UNDERSTAND HOW MUCH MONEY YOU ALL HAVE JUST LOST ME.
PAYING OFF ENOUGH OFFICERS TO GET INTO THE NEW POLICE BUILDING, LET ALONE INTO OUR CELL?
WAUGH!
NORMALLY IT'S ENOUGH JUST TO KNOW THAT I COULD DO IT, IN A PINCH, BUT YOU ACTUALLY DO IT, IT CREATES INVESTIGATIONS. IT MEANS KEEPING PEOPLE QUIET. IT MEANS INTIMIDATION AND MURDER.
MOSTLY, IT'S MESSY. AND I ABHOR A MESS.
HOW THE HELL...
CRAK
CRAK
MY FAVORITE FEATURE OF THAT DELIGHTFUL NEW HOLDING CELL IS ONE THAT RAPIDLY REMOVES ALL OXYGEN FROM THE ROOM. YOU ALL WENT DOWN PRETTY QUICK.
THE OFFICERS WHO I PAID OFF TO LET ME IN THE BUILDING HELPED PUT YOU IN THE VAN, AND THEN I BROUGHT YOU HERE.
I BELIEVE MR. FREEZE USED IT AS A BASE FOR A WHILE BUT IT KEEPS MEAT FROM GOING RANCID, AND IT ALLOWS ME TO KEEP MY FRIENDS IN COMFORT IN TRYING TIMES.

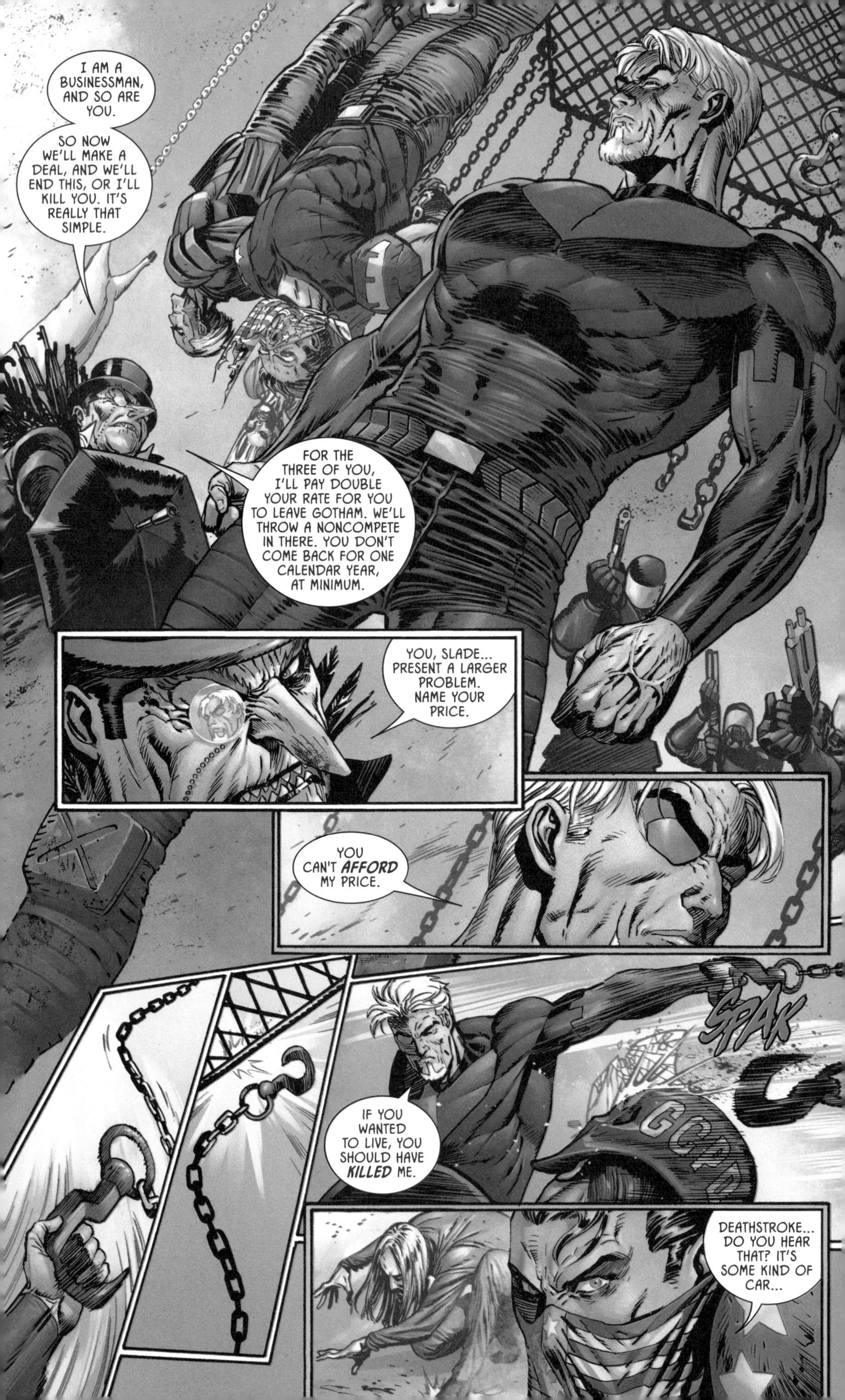
I AM A BUSINESSMAN, AND SO ARE YOU.
SO NOW WE'LL MAKE A DEAL, AND WE'LL END THIS, OR I'LL KILL YOU. IT'S REALLY THAT SIMPLE.
FOR THE THREE OF YOU, I'LL PAY DOUBLE YOUR RATE FOR YOU TO LEAVE GOTHAM. WE'LL THROW A NONCOMPETE IN THERE. YOU DON'T COME BACK FOR ONE CALENDAR YEAR, AT MINIMUM.
YOU, SLADE... PRESENT A LARGER PROBLEM. NAME YOUR PRICE.
YOU CAN'T ***AFFORD*** MY PRICE.
SPAK
IF YOU WANTED TO LIVE, YOU SHOULD HAVE ***KILLED*** ME.
GCPD
DEATHSTROKE... DO YOU HEAR THAT? IT'S SOME KIND OF CAR...

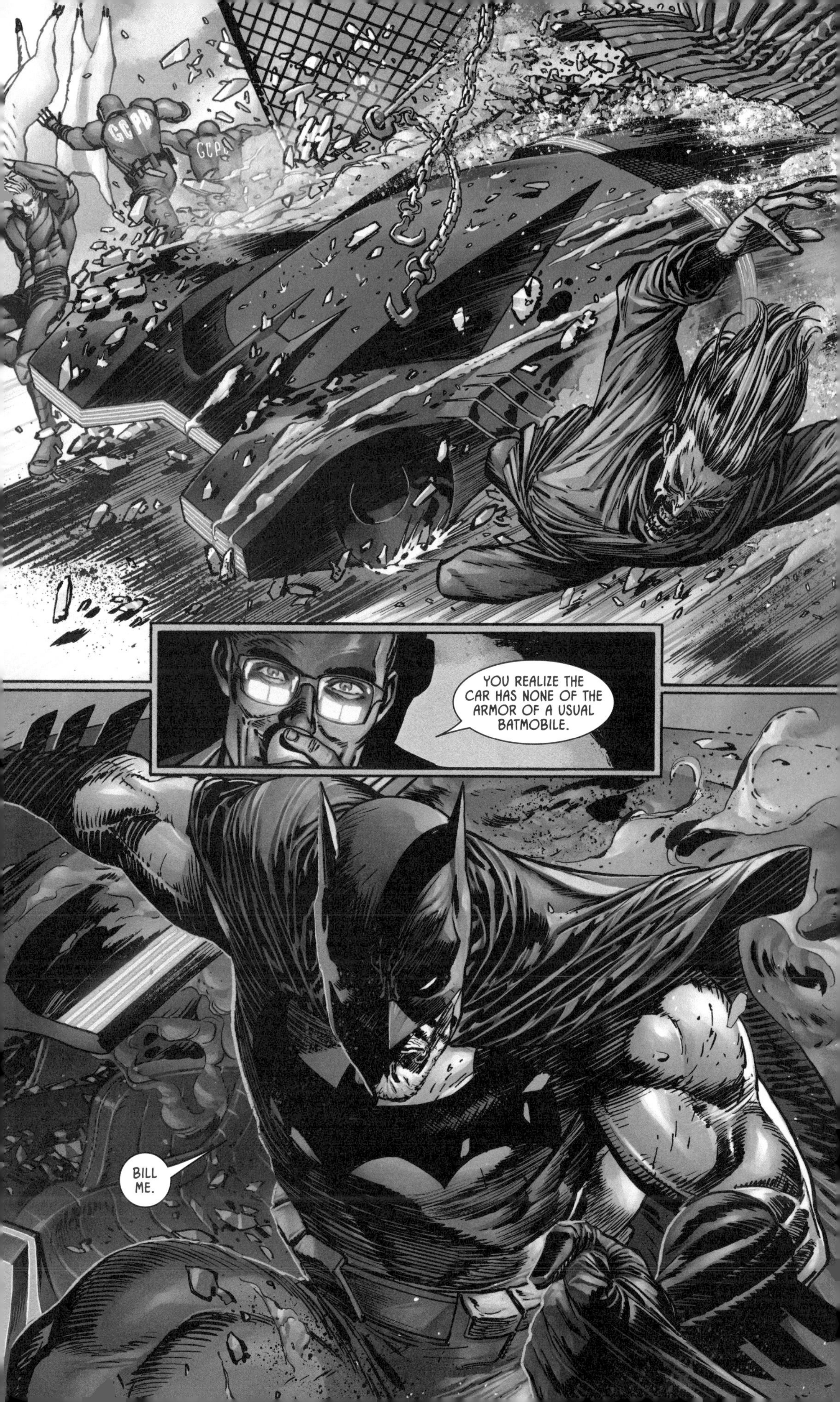
GCPD
GCPD
YOU REALIZE THE CAR HAS NONE OF THE ARMOR OF A USUAL BATMOBILE.
BILL ME.

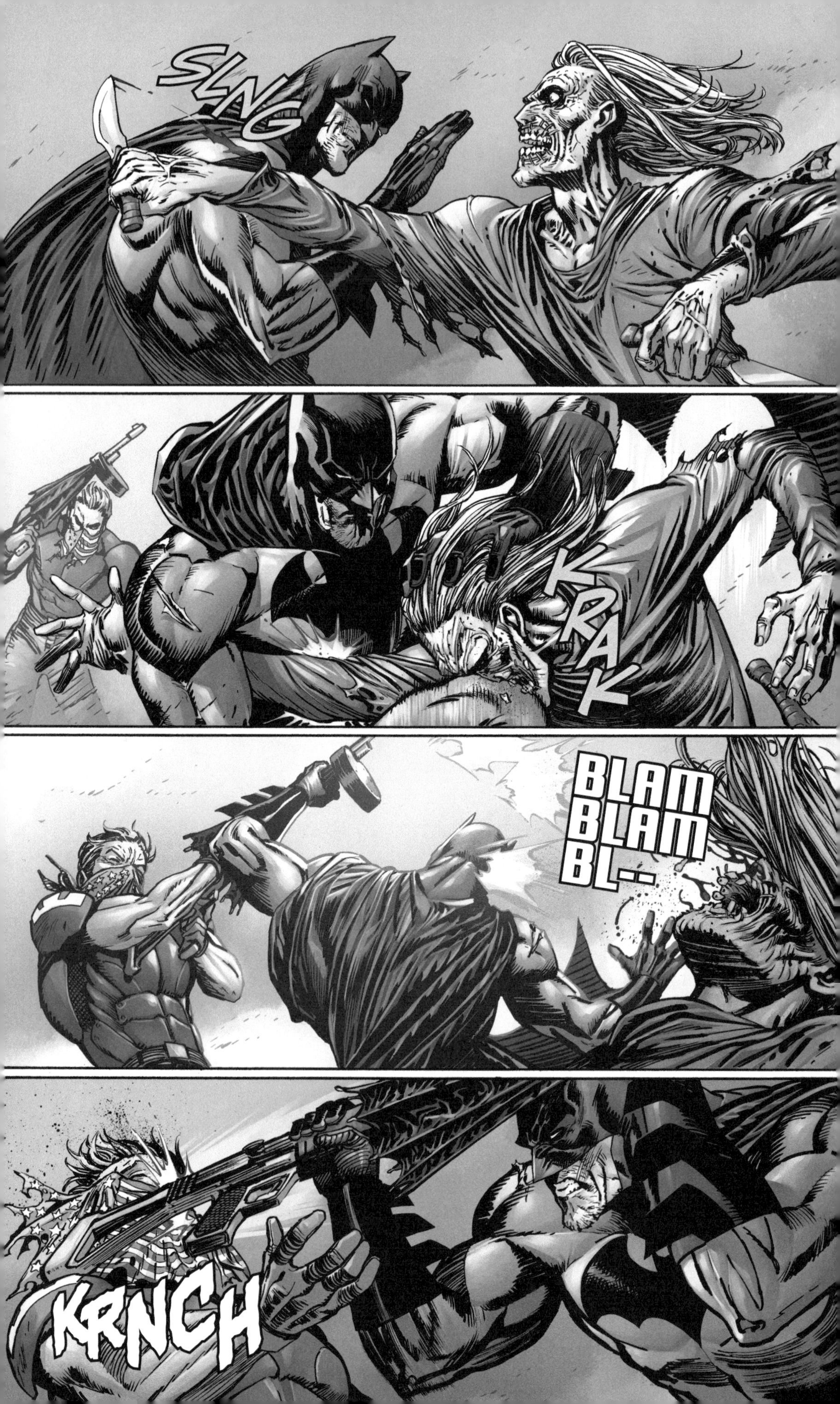
SLNG
KRAK
BLAM
BLAM
BL--
KRNCH

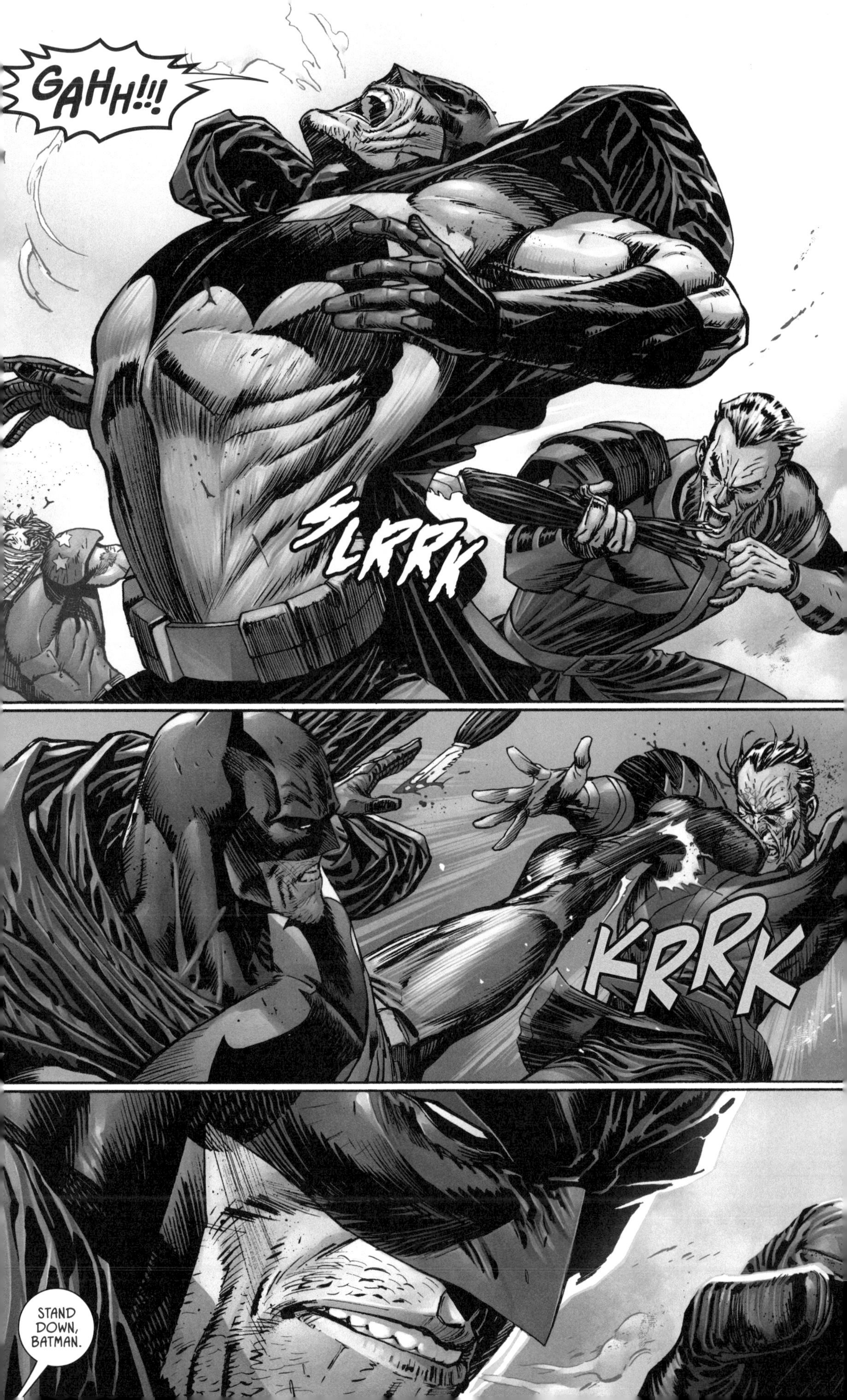
GAHH!!!
SLRRK
KRRK
STAND DOWN, BATMAN.

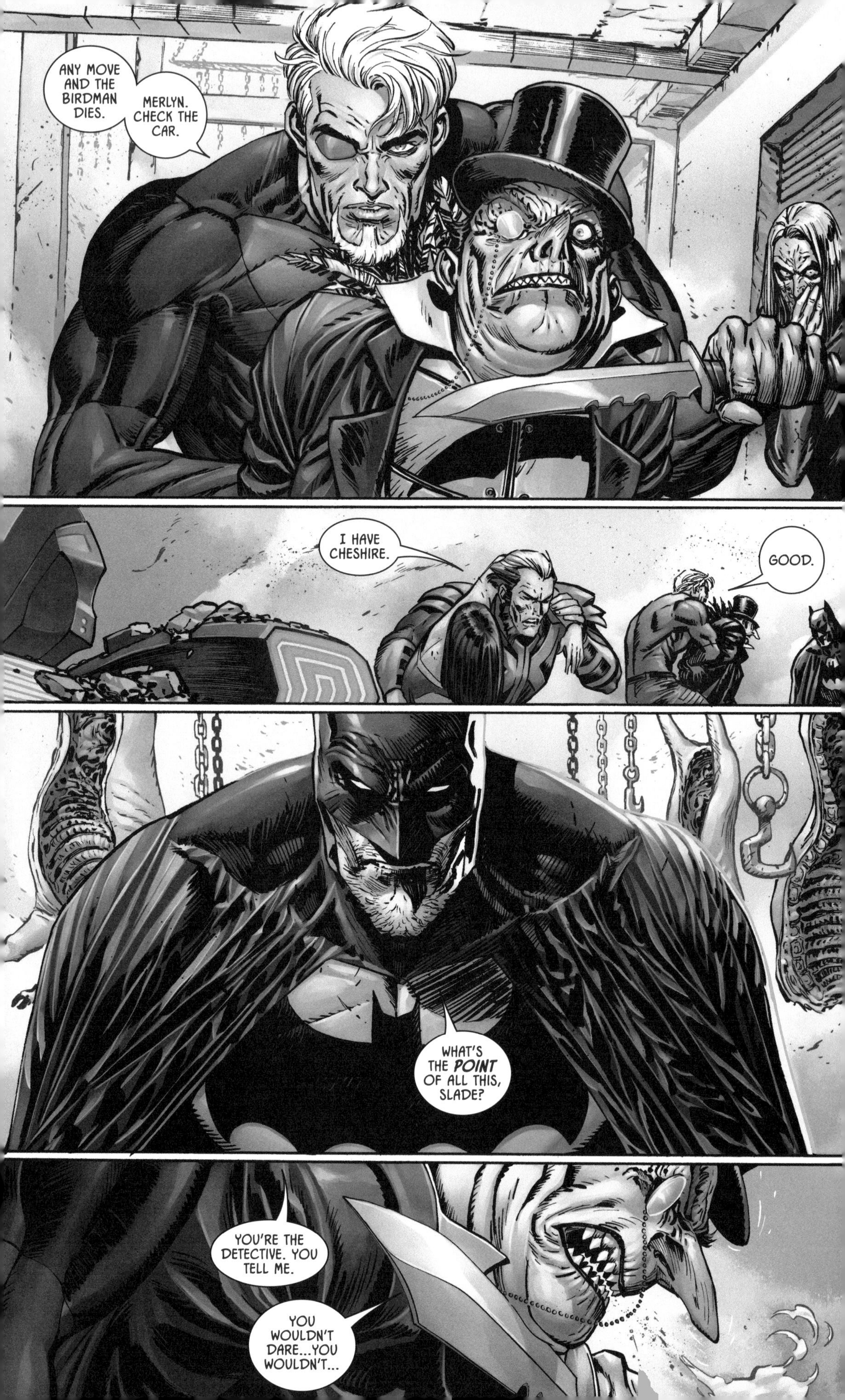
ANY MOVE AND THE BIRDMAN DIES.
MERLYN. CHECK THE CAR.
I HAVE CHESHIRE.
GOOD.
WHAT'S THE *POINT* OF ALL THIS, SLADE?
YOU'RE THE DETECTIVE. YOU TELL ME.
YOU WOULDN'T DARE...YOU WOULDN'T...

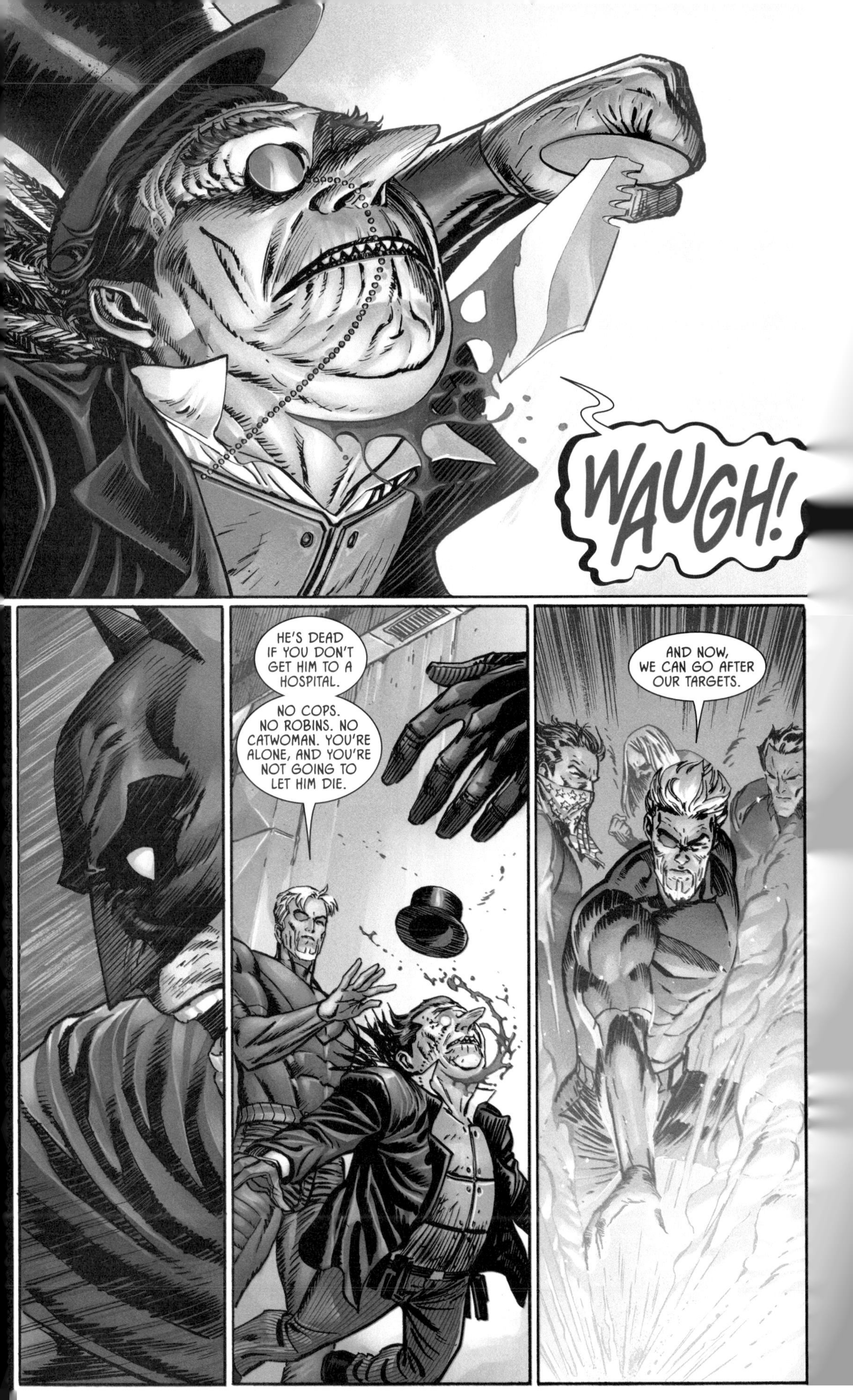
WAUGH!
HE'S DEAD IF YOU DON'T GET HIM TO A HOSPITAL.
NO COPS. NO ROBINS. NO CATWOMAN. YOU'RE ALONE, AND YOU'RE NOT GOING TO LET HIM DIE.
AND NOW, WE CAN GO AFTER OUR TARGETS.

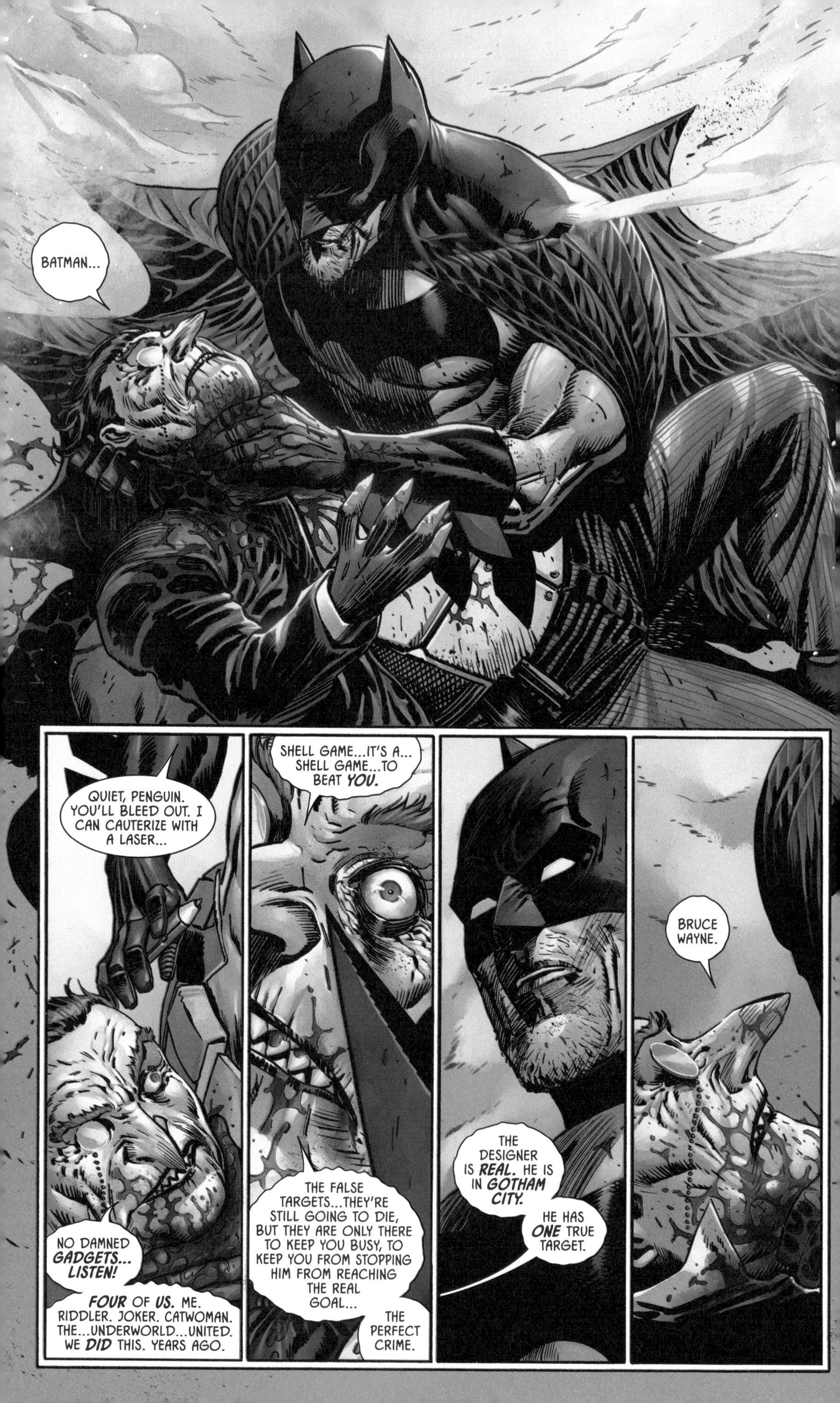
BATMAN...
QUIET, PENGUIN. YOU'LL BLEED OUT. I CAN CAUTERIZE WITH A LASER...
NO DAMNED **GADGETS... LISTEN!**
FOUR OF **US.** ME. RIDDLER. JOKER. CATWOMAN. THE...UNDERWORLD...UNITED. WE **DID** THIS. YEARS AGO.
SHELL GAME...IT'S A... SHELL GAME...TO BEAT **YOU.**
THE FALSE TARGETS...THEY'RE STILL GOING TO DIE, BUT THEY ARE ONLY THERE TO KEEP YOU BUSY, TO KEEP YOU FROM STOPPING HIM FROM REACHING THE REAL GOAL...
THE PERFECT CRIME.
THE DESIGNER IS **REAL.** HE IS IN **GOTHAM CITY.**
HE HAS **ONE** TRUE TARGET.
BRUCE WAYNE.

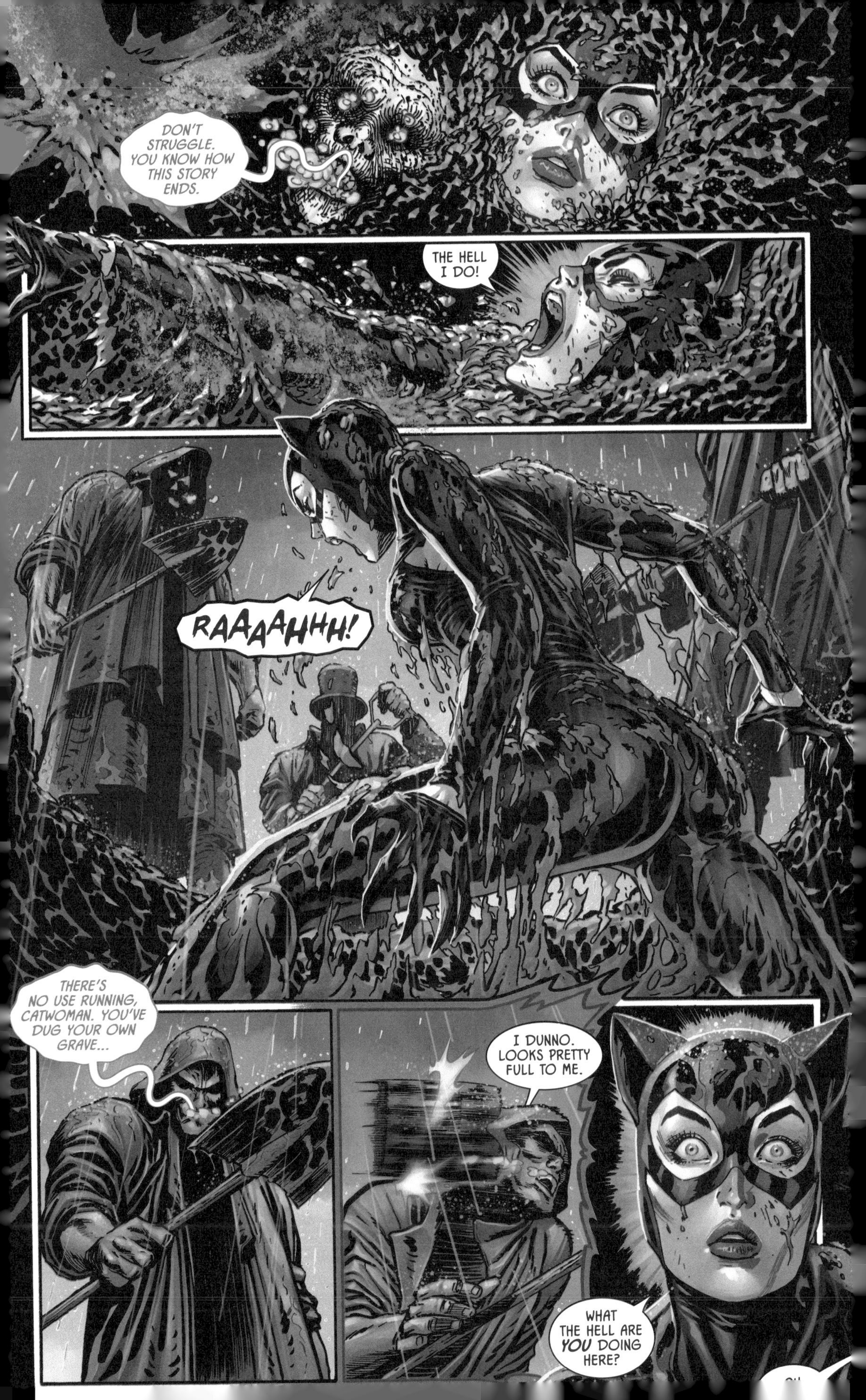
DON'T STRUGGLE. YOU KNOW HOW THIS STORY ENDS.
THE HELL I DO!
RAAAAHHH!
THERE'S NO USE RUNNING, CATWOMAN. YOU'VE DUG YOUR OWN GRAVE...
I DUNNO. LOOKS PRETTY FULL TO ME.
WHAT THE HELL ARE YOU DOING HERE?

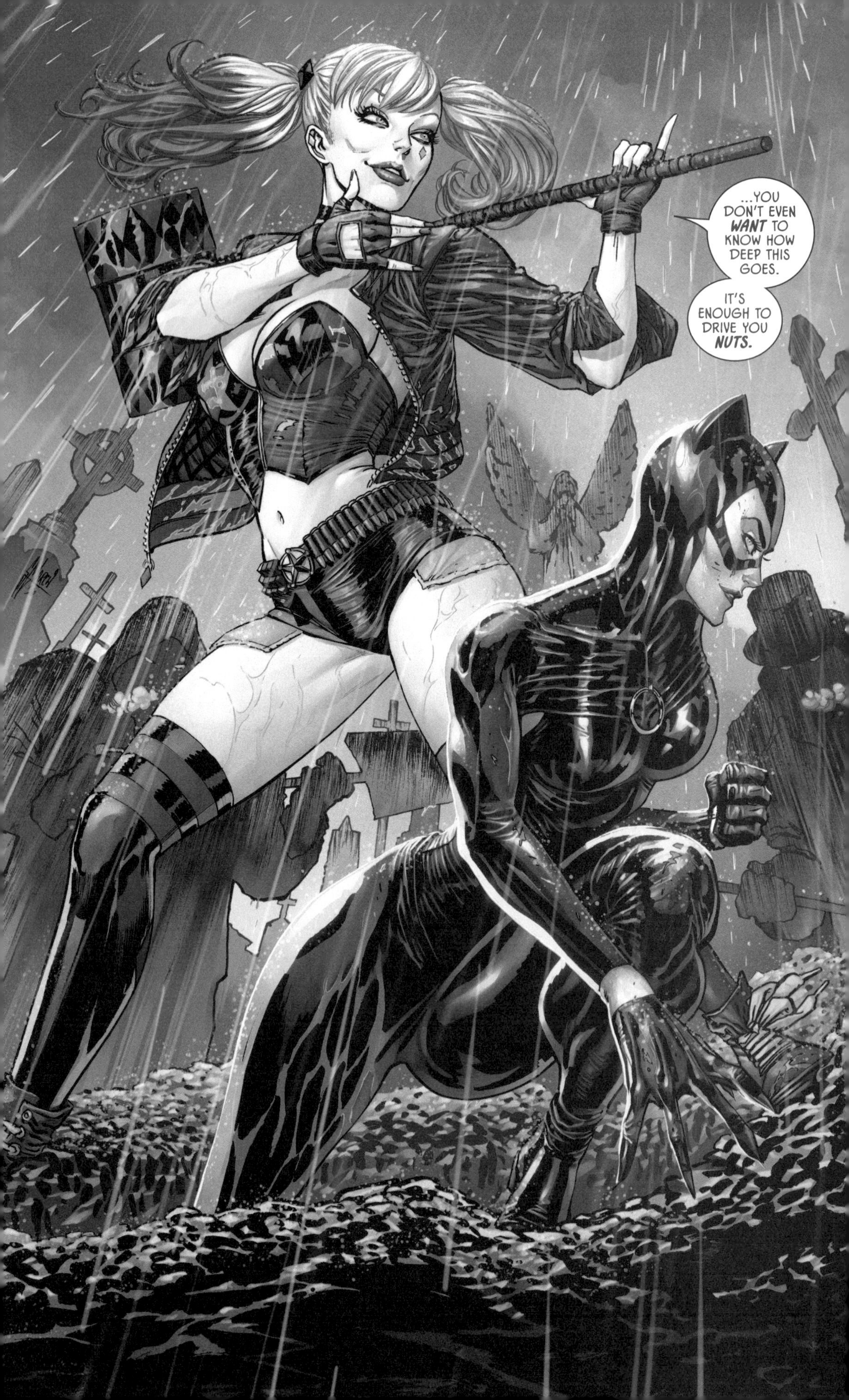
...YOU DON'T EVEN WANT TO KNOW HOW DEEP THIS GOES.
IT'S ENOUGH TO DRIVE YOU NUTS.

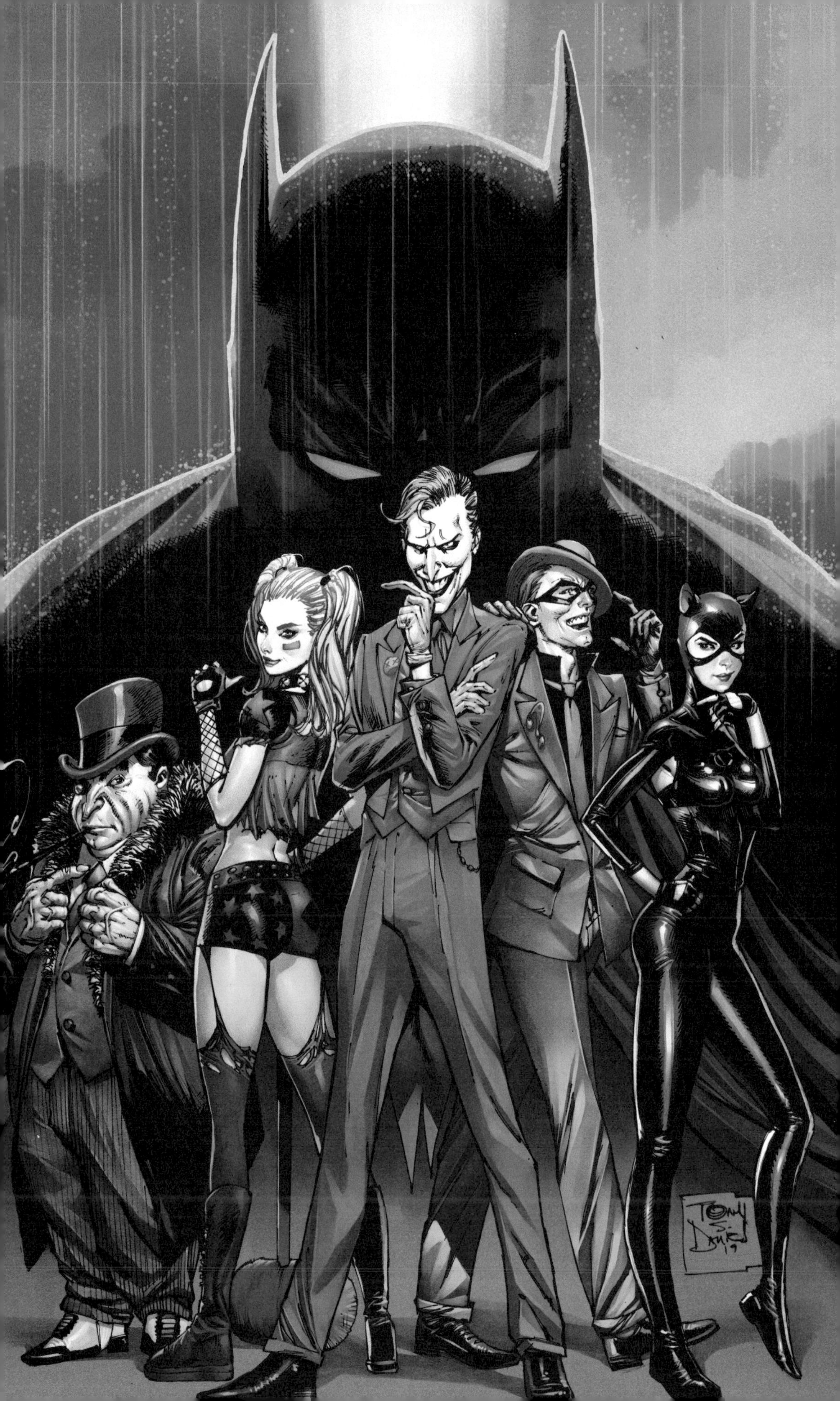

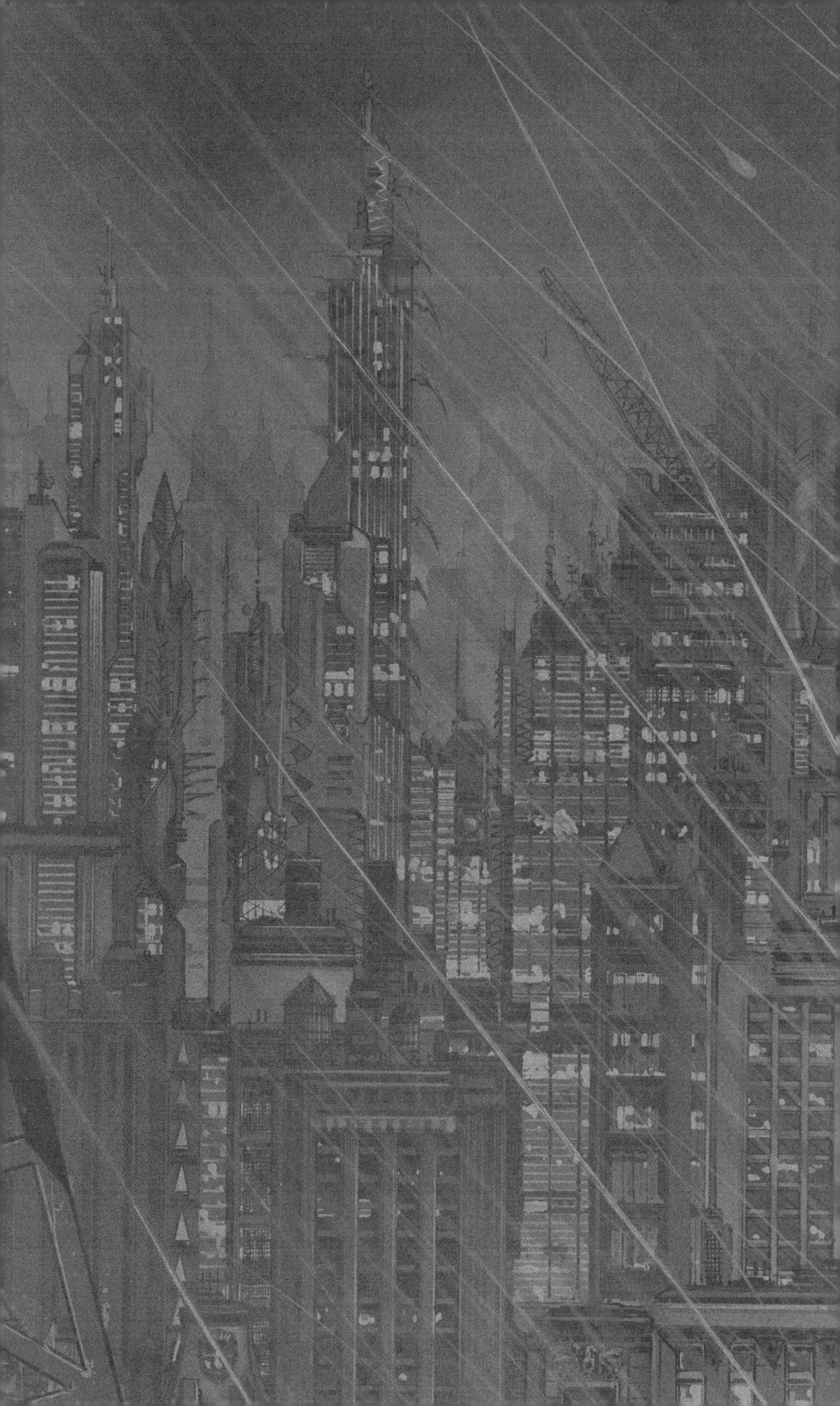

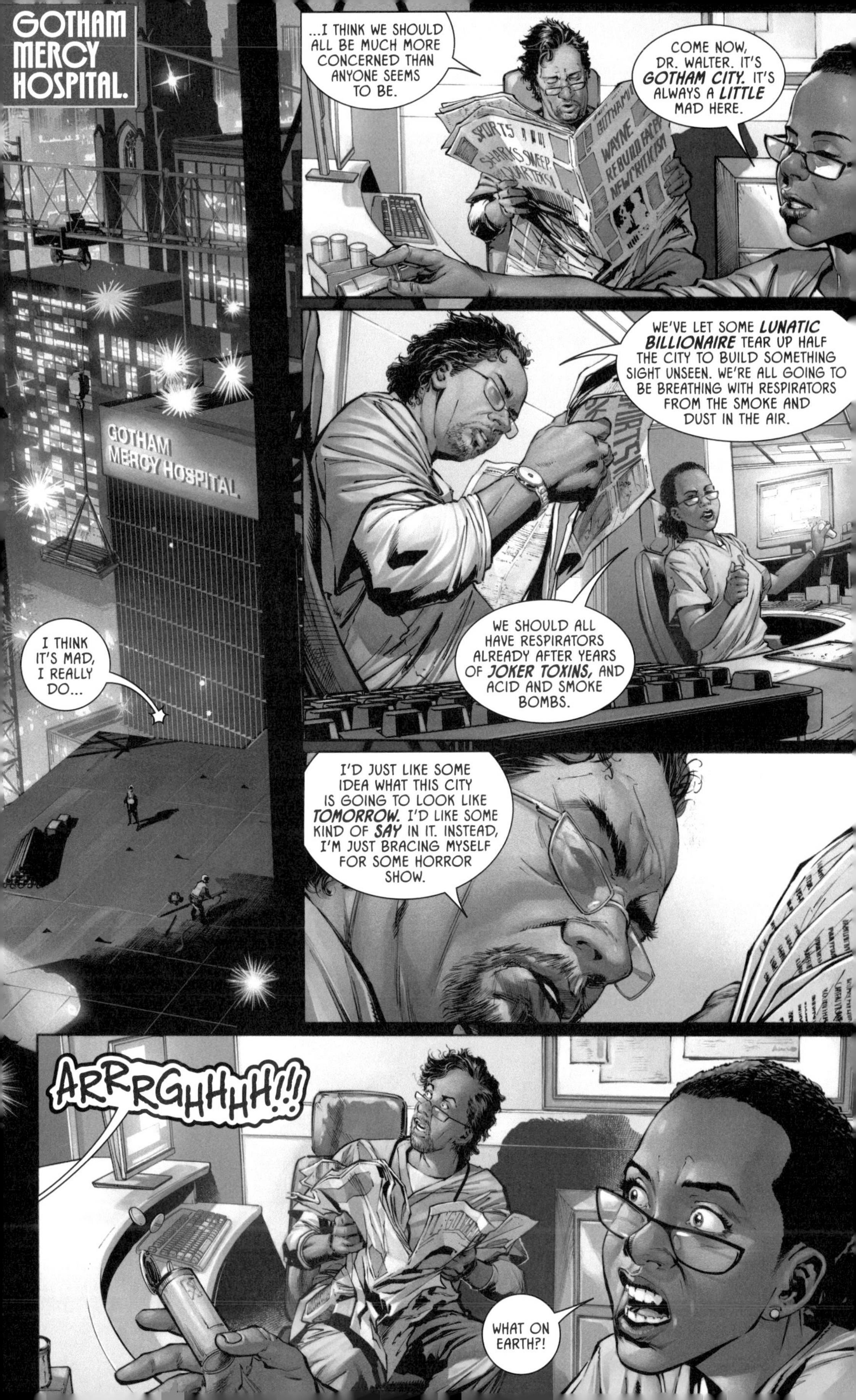
GOTHAM MERCY HOSPITAL.
GOTHAM MERCY HOSPITAL
I THINK IT'S MAD, I REALLY DO...
...I THINK WE SHOULD ALL BE MUCH MORE CONCERNED THAN ANYONE SEEMS TO BE.
COME NOW, DR. WALTER. IT'S GOTHAM CITY. IT'S ALWAYS A LITTLE MAD HERE.
WE'VE LET SOME LUNATIC BILLIONAIRE TEAR UP HALF THE CITY TO BUILD SOMETHING SIGHT UNSEEN. WE'RE ALL GOING TO BE BREATHING WITH RESPIRATORS FROM THE SMOKE AND DUST IN THE AIR.
WE SHOULD ALL HAVE RESPIRATORS ALREADY AFTER YEARS OF JOKER TOXINS, AND ACID AND SMOKE BOMBS.
I'D JUST LIKE SOME IDEA WHAT THIS CITY IS GOING TO LOOK LIKE TOMORROW. I'D LIKE SOME KIND OF SAY IN IT. INSTEAD, I'M JUST BRACING MYSELF FOR SOME HORROR SHOW.
ARRRGHHHH!!!
WHAT ON EARTH?!

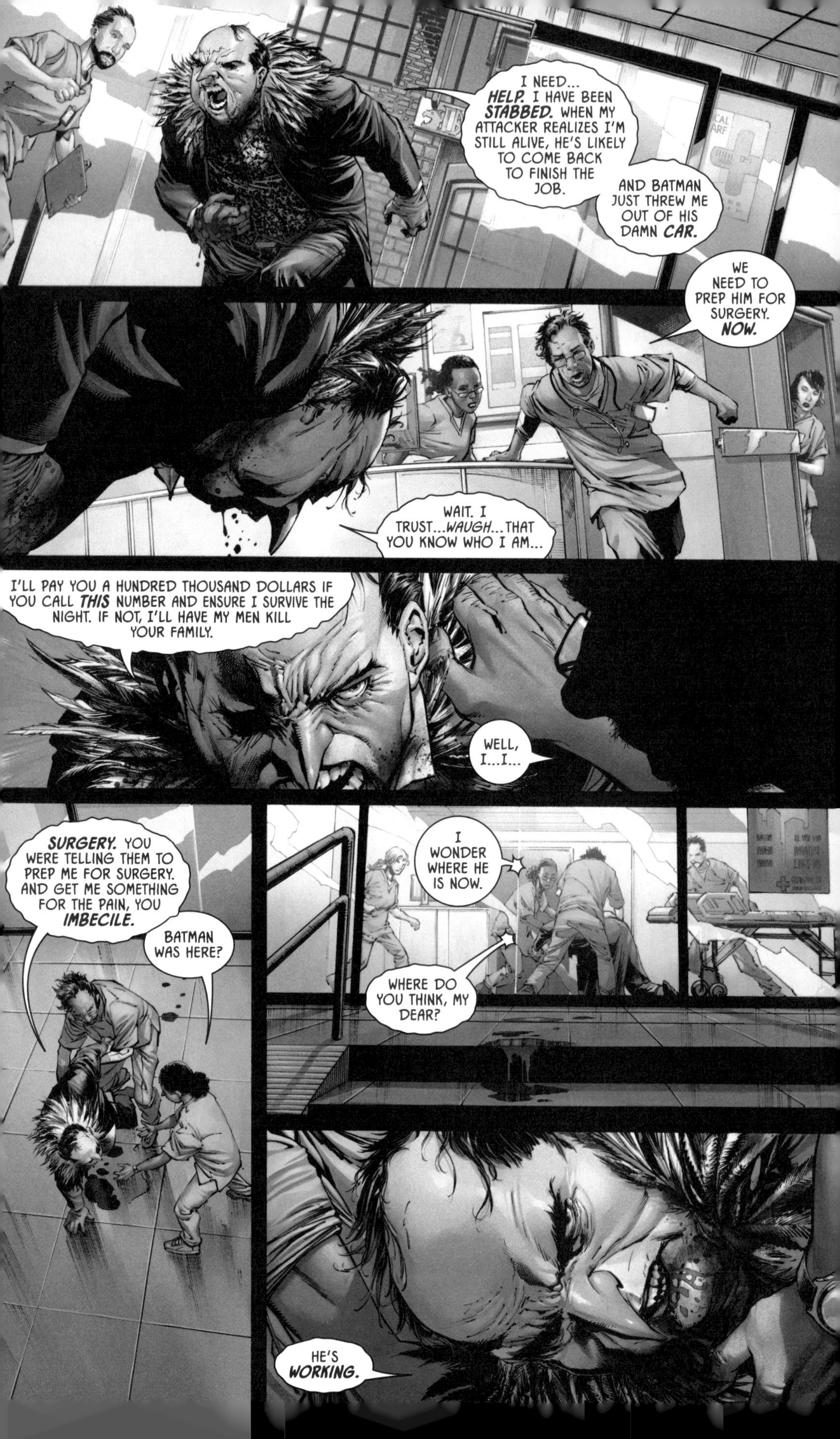
I NEED... HELP. I HAVE BEEN STABBED. WHEN MY ATTACKER REALIZES I'M STILL ALIVE, HE'S LIKELY TO COME BACK TO FINISH THE JOB.
AND BATMAN JUST THREW ME OUT OF HIS DAMN CAR.
WE NEED TO PREP HIM FOR SURGERY. NOW.
WAIT. I TRUST...WAUGH...THAT YOU KNOW WHO I AM...
I'LL PAY YOU A HUNDRED THOUSAND DOLLARS IF YOU CALL THIS NUMBER AND ENSURE I SURVIVE THE NIGHT. IF NOT, I'LL HAVE MY MEN KILL YOUR FAMILY.
WELL, I...I...
SURGERY. YOU WERE TELLING THEM TO PREP ME FOR SURGERY. AND GET ME SOMETHING FOR THE PAIN, YOU IMBECILE.
BATMAN WAS HERE?
I WONDER WHERE HE IS NOW.
WHERE DO YOU THINK, MY DEAR?
HE'S WORKING.

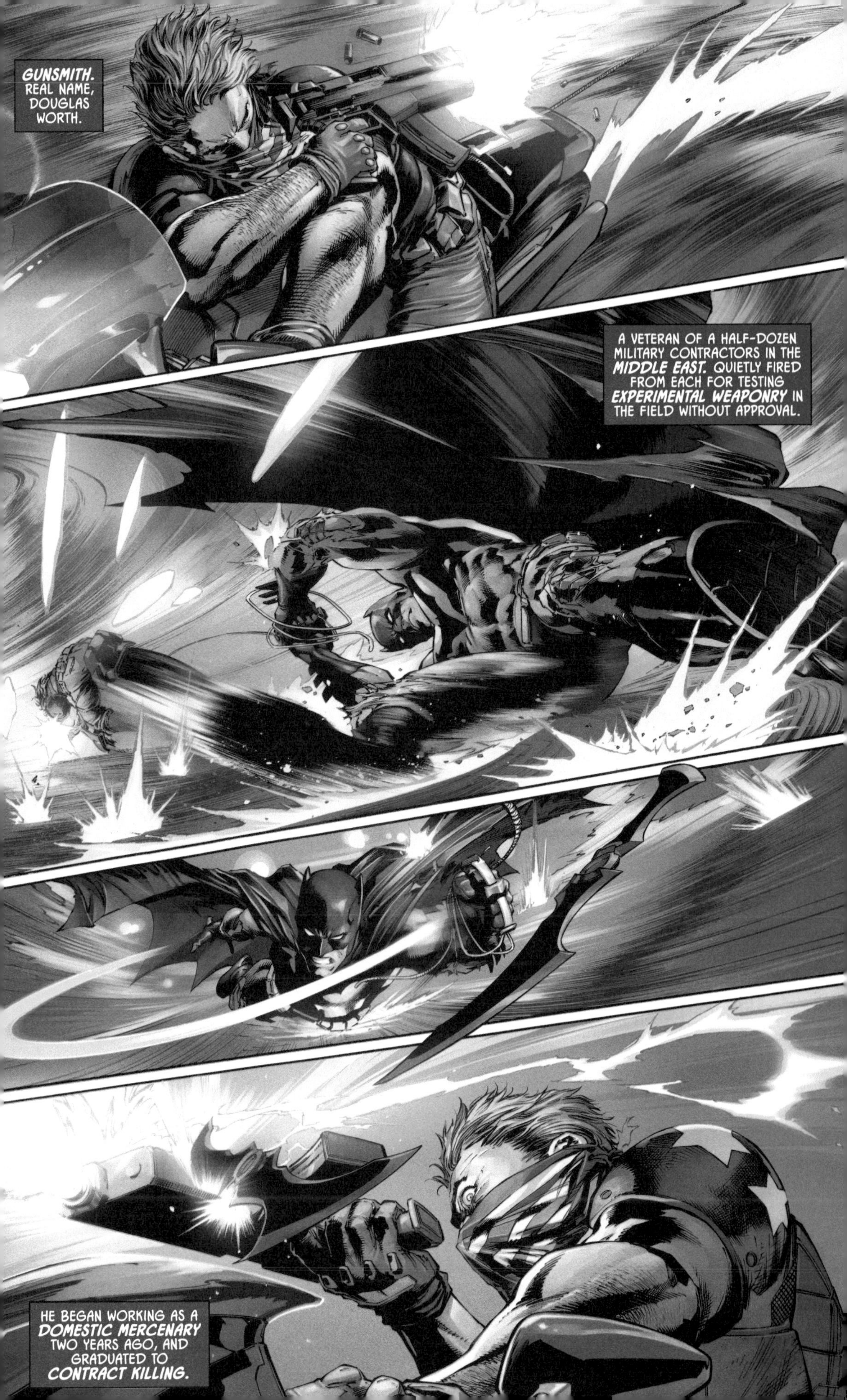
GUNSMITH. REAL NAME, DOUGLAS WORTH.
A VETERAN OF A HALF-DOZEN MILITARY CONTRACTORS IN THE MIDDLE EAST. QUIETLY FIRED FROM EACH FOR TESTING EXPERIMENTAL WEAPONRY IN THE FIELD WITHOUT APPROVAL.
HE BEGAN WORKING AS A DOMESTIC MERCENARY TWO YEARS AGO, AND GRADUATED TO CONTRACT KILLING.

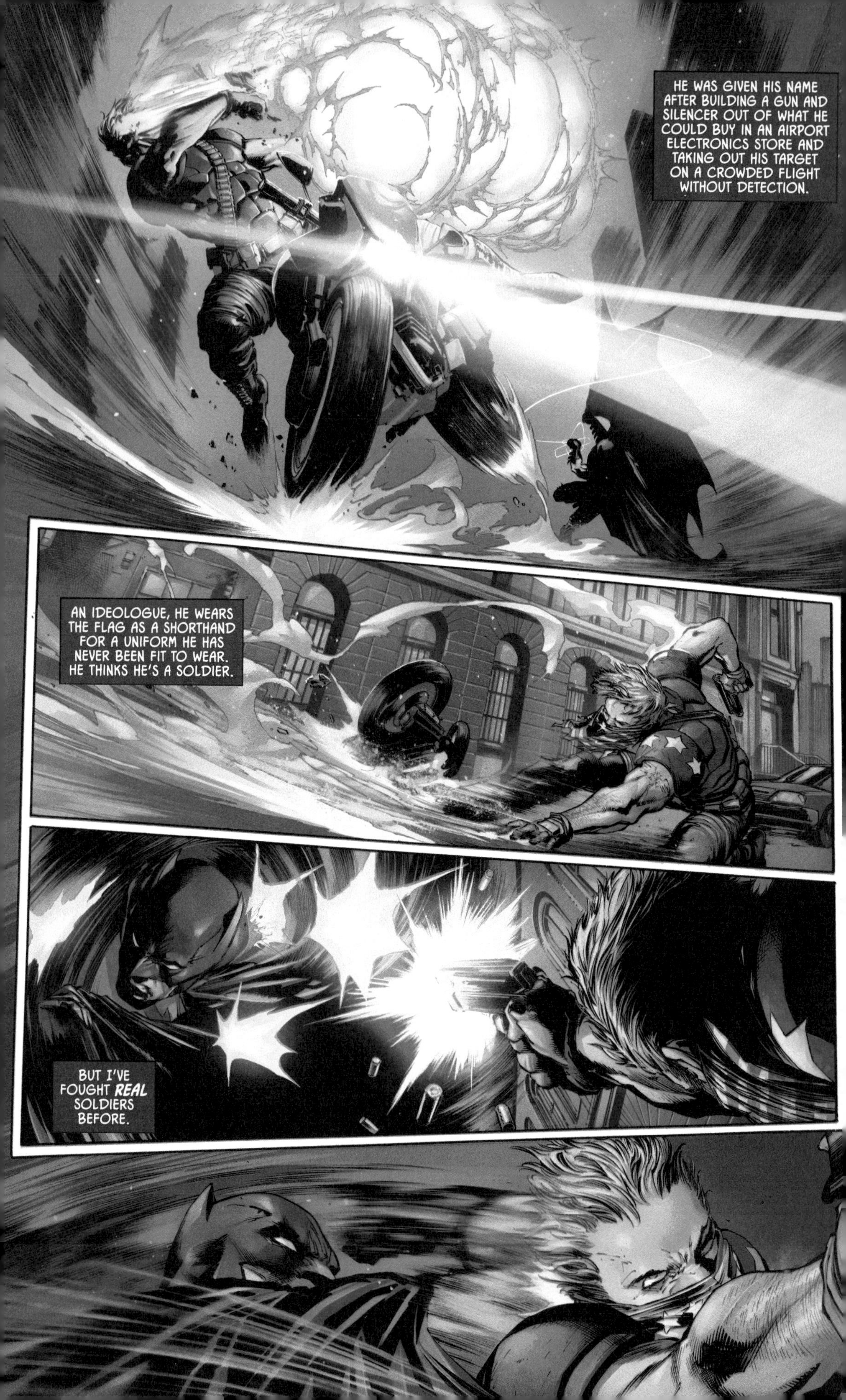
HE WAS GIVEN HIS NAME AFTER BUILDING A GUN AND SILENCER OUT OF WHAT HE COULD BUY IN AN AIRPORT ELECTRONICS STORE AND TAKING OUT HIS TARGET ON A CROWDED FLIGHT WITHOUT DETECTION.
AN IDEOLOGUE, HE WEARS THE FLAG AS A SHORTHAND FOR A UNIFORM HE HAS NEVER BEEN FIT TO WEAR. HE THINKS HE'S A SOLDIER.
BUT I'VE FOUGHT REAL SOLDIERS BEFORE.

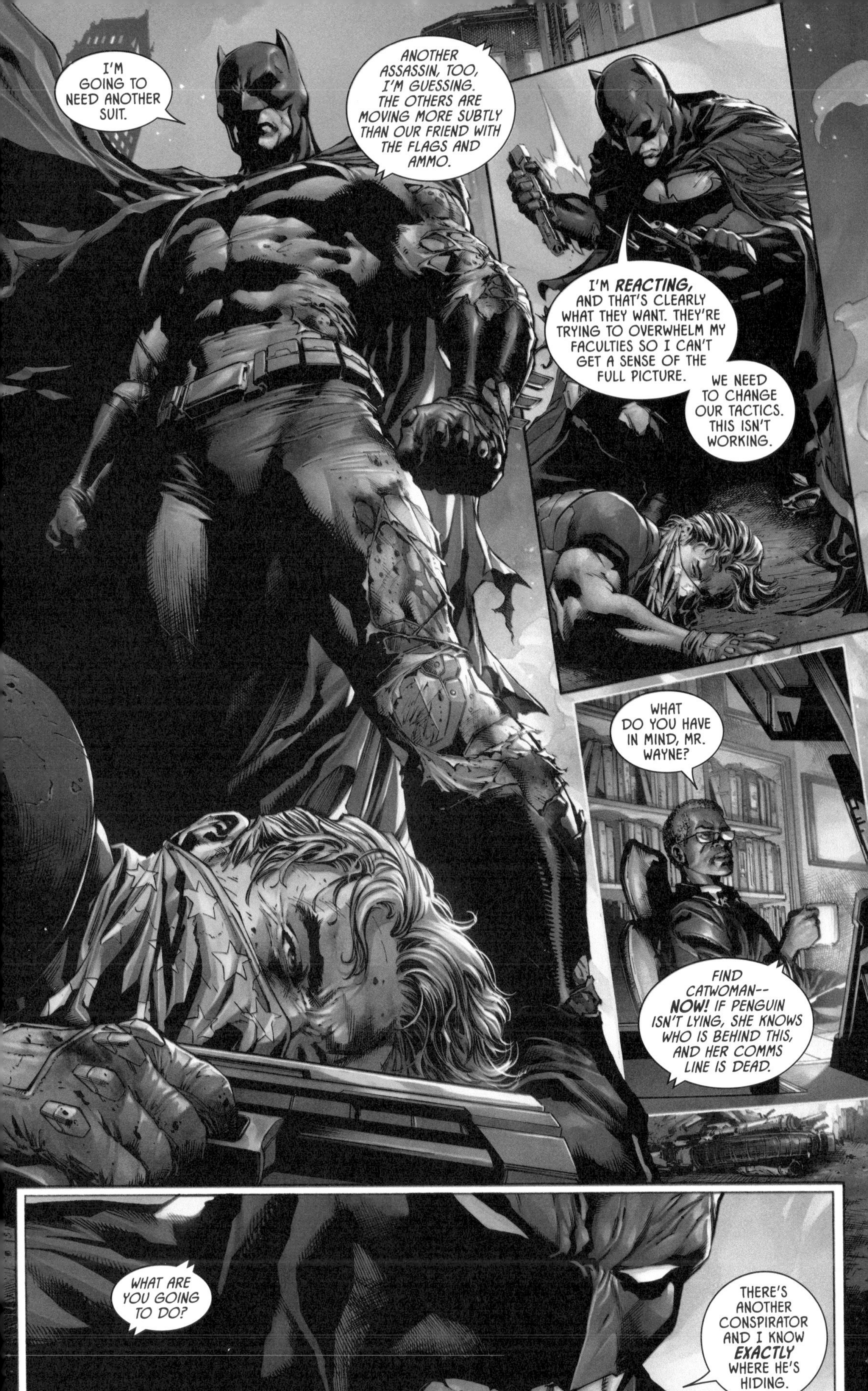

I'M GOING TO NEED ANOTHER SUIT.
ANOTHER ASSASSIN, TOO, I'M GUESSING. THE OTHERS ARE MOVING MORE SUBTLY THAN OUR FRIEND WITH THE FLAGS AND AMMO.
I'M **REACTING,** AND THAT'S CLEARLY WHAT THEY WANT. THEY'RE TRYING TO OVERWHELM MY FACULTIES SO I CAN'T GET A SENSE OF THE FULL PICTURE.
WE NEED TO CHANGE OUR TACTICS. THIS ISN'T WORKING.
WHAT DO YOU HAVE IN MIND, MR. WAYNE?
FIND CATWOMAN-- **NOW!** IF PENGUIN ISN'T LYING, SHE KNOWS WHO IS BEHIND THIS, AND HER COMMS LINE IS DEAD.
WHAT ARE YOU GOING TO DO?
THERE'S ANOTHER CONSPIRATOR AND I KNOW **EXACTLY** WHERE HE'S HIDING.

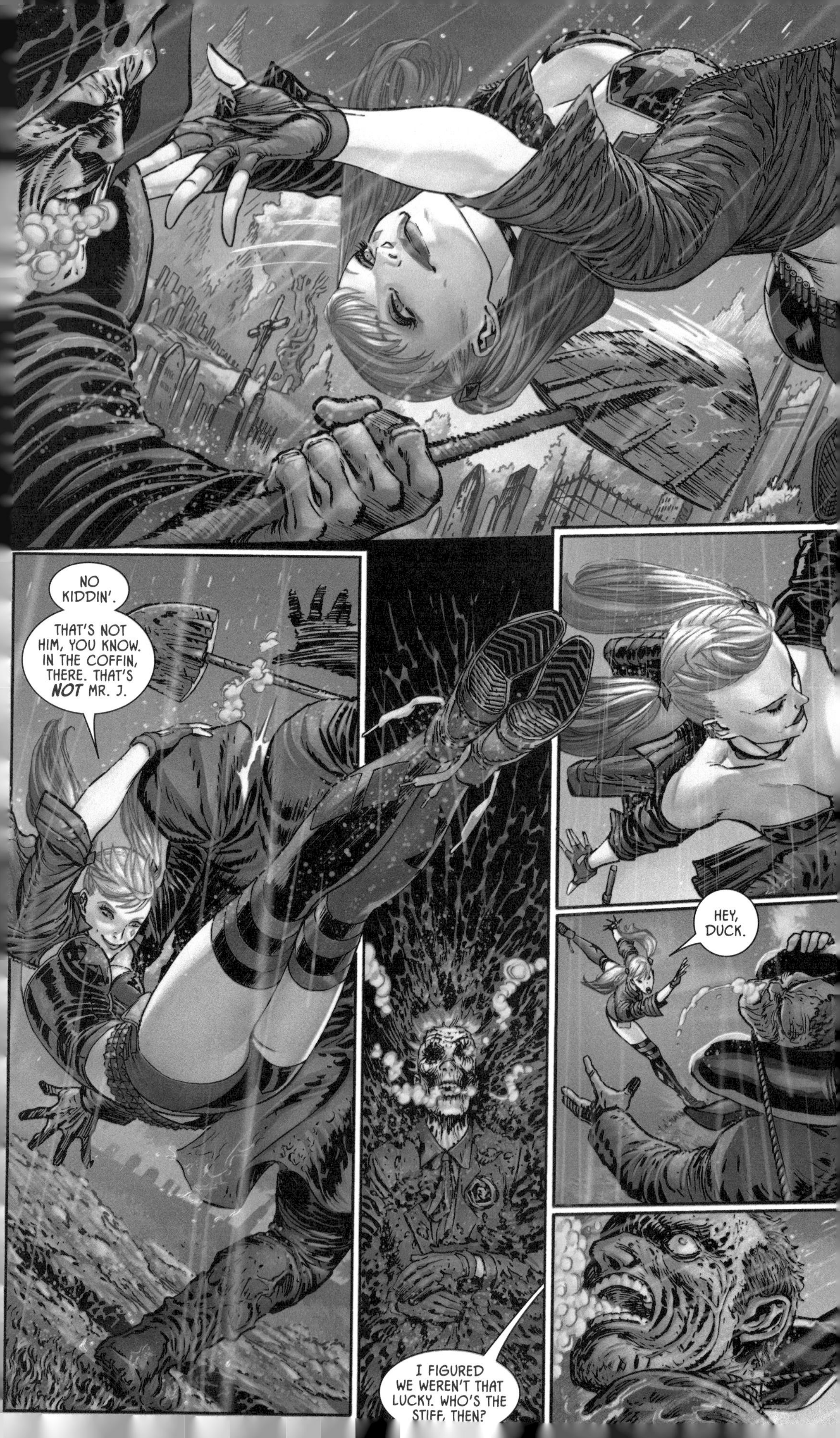
NO KIDDIN'.
THAT'S NOT HIM, YOU KNOW. IN THE COFFIN, THERE. THAT'S NOT MR. J.
I FIGURED WE WEREN'T THAT LUCKY. WHO'S THE STIFF, THEN?
HEY, DUCK.

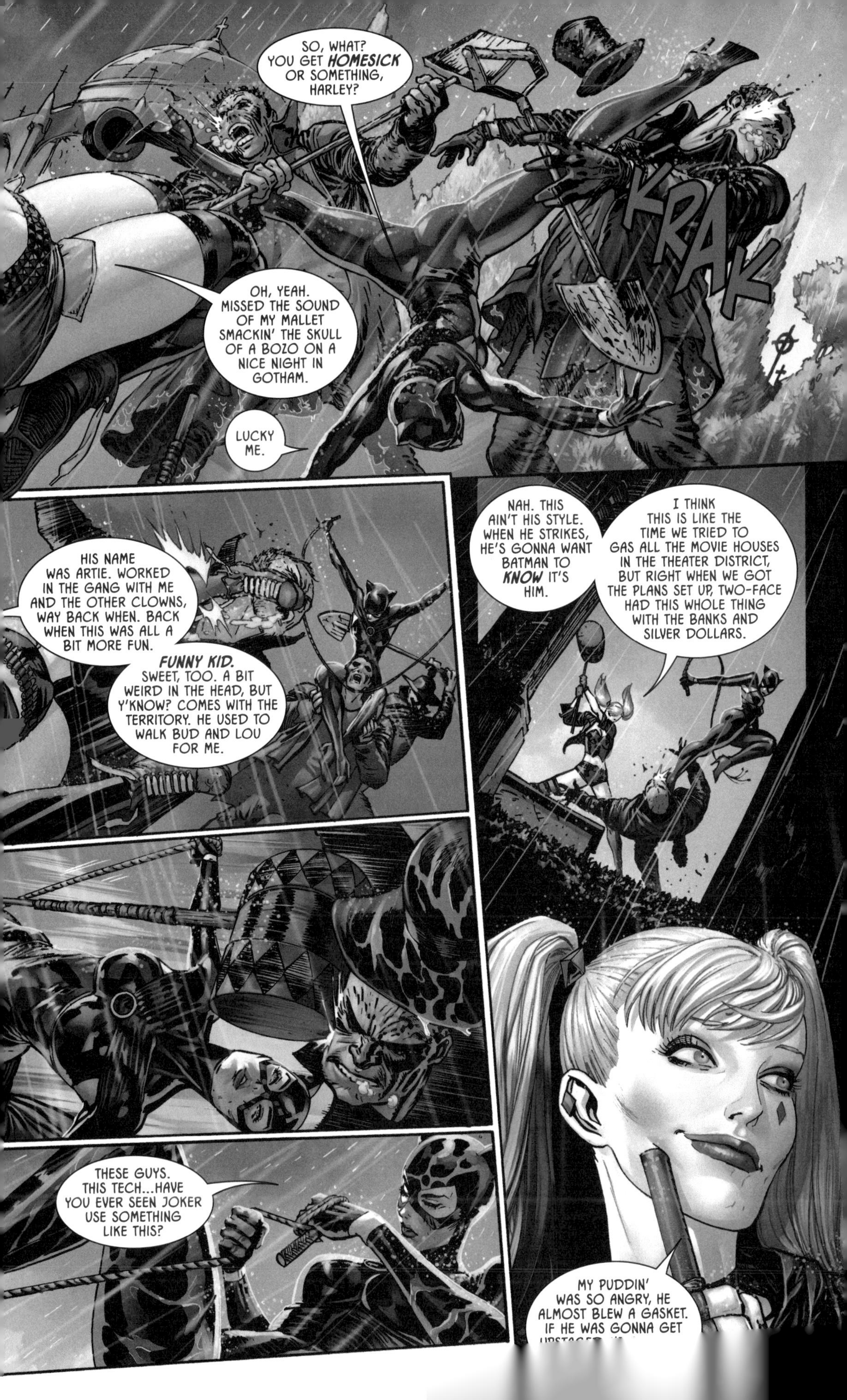
SO, WHAT? YOU GET *HOMESICK* OR SOMETHING, HARLEY?
KRAK
OH, YEAH. MISSED THE SOUND OF MY MALLET SMACKIN' THE SKULL OF A BOZO ON A NICE NIGHT IN GOTHAM.
LUCKY ME.
HIS NAME WAS ARTIE. WORKED IN THE GANG WITH ME AND THE OTHER CLOWNS, WAY BACK WHEN. BACK WHEN THIS WAS ALL A BIT MORE FUN.
FUNNY KID. SWEET, TOO. A BIT WEIRD IN THE HEAD, BUT Y'KNOW? COMES WITH THE TERRITORY. HE USED TO WALK BUD AND LOU FOR ME.
NAH. THIS AIN'T HIS STYLE. WHEN HE STRIKES, HE'S GONNA WANT BATMAN TO *KNOW* IT'S HIM.
I THINK THIS IS LIKE THE TIME WE TRIED TO GAS ALL THE MOVIE HOUSES IN THE THEATER DISTRICT, BUT RIGHT WHEN WE GOT THE PLANS SET UP, TWO-FACE HAD THIS WHOLE THING WITH THE BANKS AND SILVER DOLLARS.
THESE GUYS. THIS TECH...HAVE YOU EVER SEEN JOKER USE SOMETHING LIKE THIS?
MY PUDDIN' WAS SO ANGRY, HE ALMOST BLEW A GASKET. IF HE WAS GONNA GET

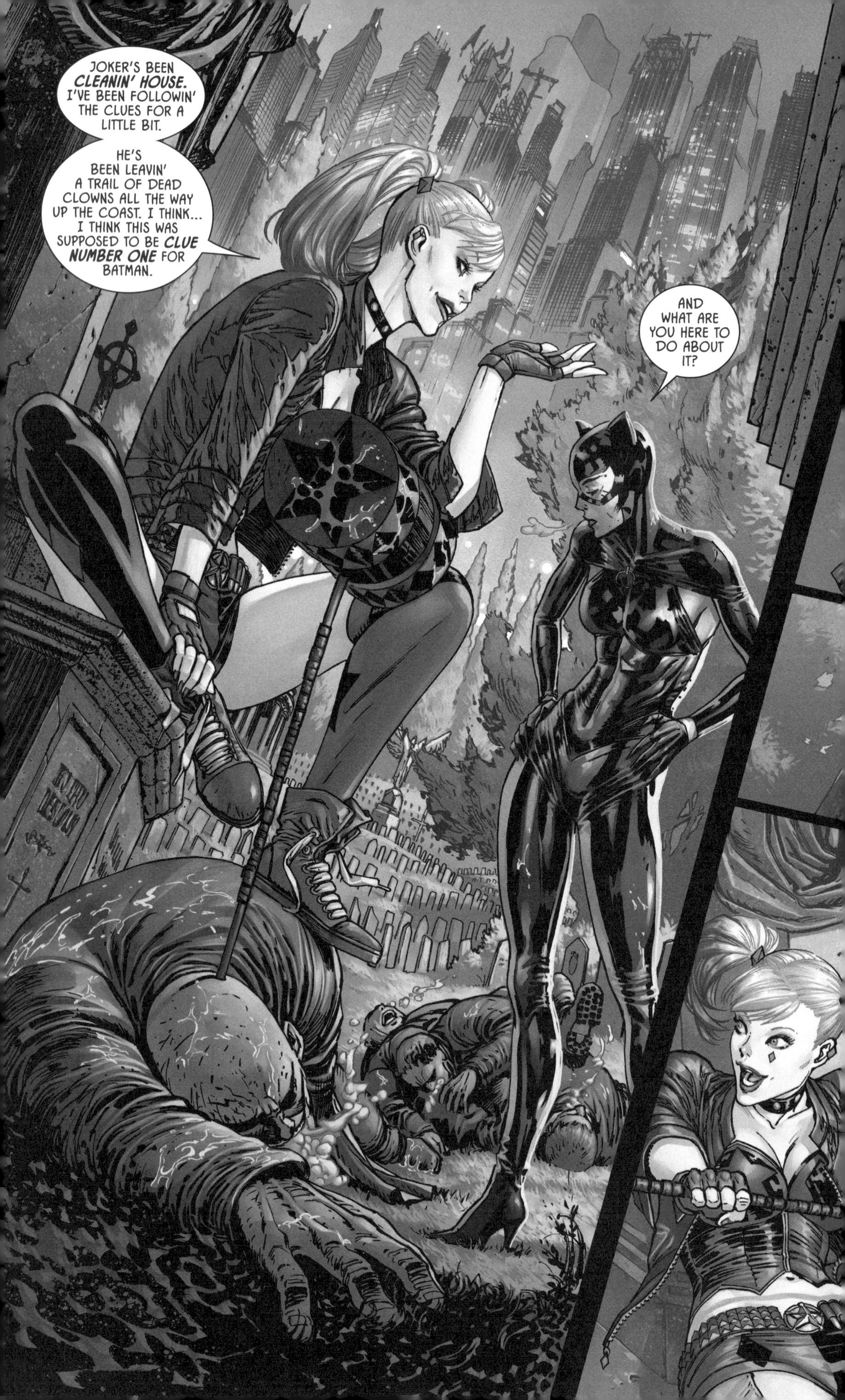

JOKER'S BEEN CLEANIN' HOUSE. I'VE BEEN FOLLOWIN' THE CLUES FOR A LITTLE BIT.
HE'S BEEN LEAVIN' A TRAIL OF DEAD CLOWNS ALL THE WAY UP THE COAST. I THINK... I THINK THIS WAS SUPPOSED TO BE CLUE NUMBER ONE FOR BATMAN.
AND WHAT ARE YOU HERE TO DO ABOUT IT?

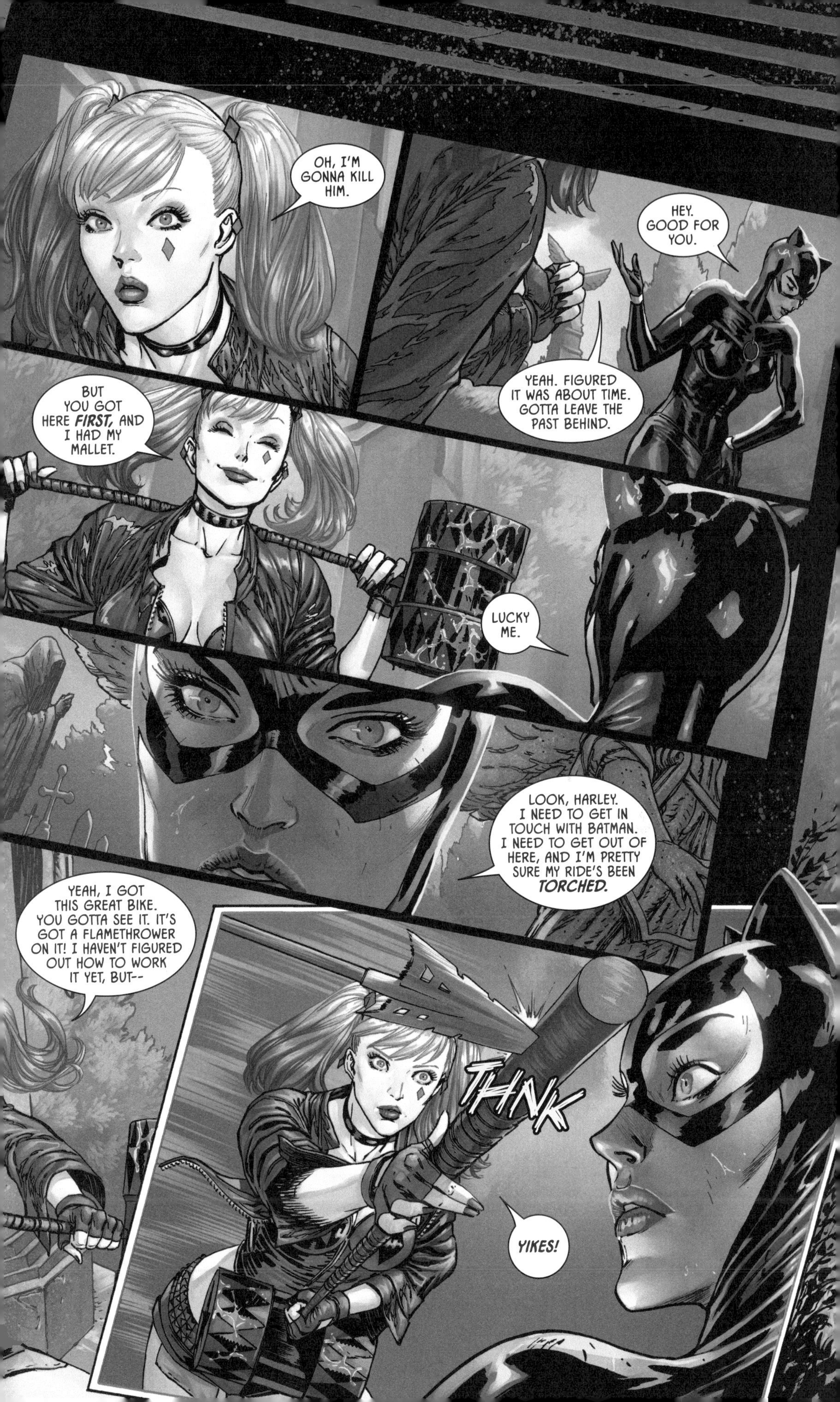
OH, I'M GONNA KILL HIM.
HEY. GOOD FOR YOU.
YEAH. FIGURED IT WAS ABOUT TIME. GOTTA LEAVE THE PAST BEHIND.
BUT YOU GOT HERE FIRST, AND I HAD MY MALLET.
LUCKY ME.
LOOK, HARLEY. I NEED TO GET IN TOUCH WITH BATMAN. I NEED TO GET OUT OF HERE, AND I'M PRETTY SURE MY RIDE'S BEEN TORCHED.
YEAH, I GOT THIS GREAT BIKE. YOU GOTTA SEE IT. IT'S GOT A FLAMETHROWER ON IT! I HAVEN'T FIGURED OUT HOW TO WORK IT YET, BUT--
THNK
YIKES!

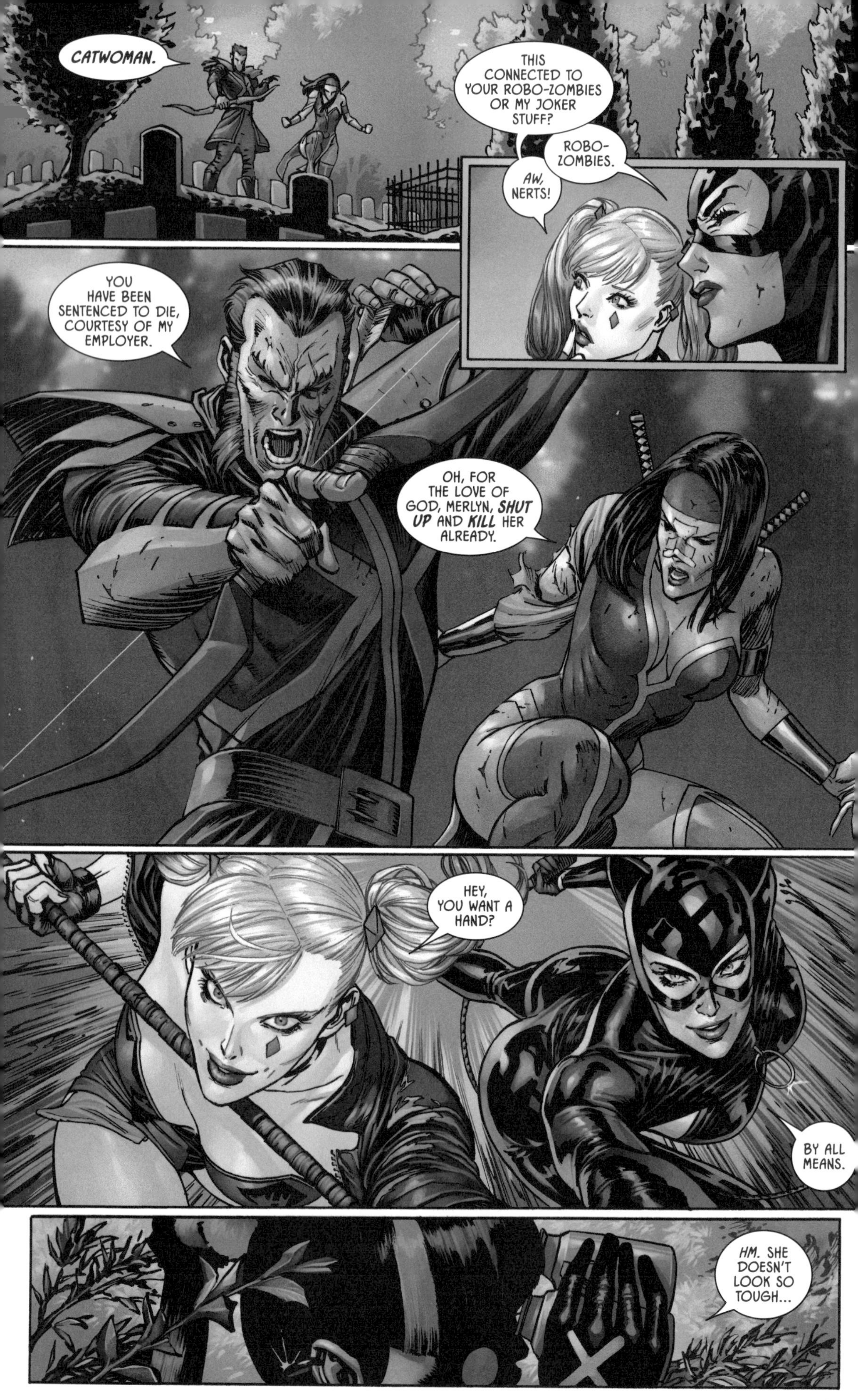

CATWOMAN.
THIS CONNECTED TO YOUR ROBO-ZOMBIES OR MY JOKER STUFF?
ROBO-ZOMBIES.
AW, NERTS!
YOU HAVE BEEN SENTENCED TO DIE, COURTESY OF MY EMPLOYER.
OH, FOR THE LOVE OF GOD, MERLYN, SHUT UP AND KILL HER ALREADY.
HEY, YOU WANT A HAND?
BY ALL MEANS.
HM. SHE DOESN'T LOOK SO TOUGH...

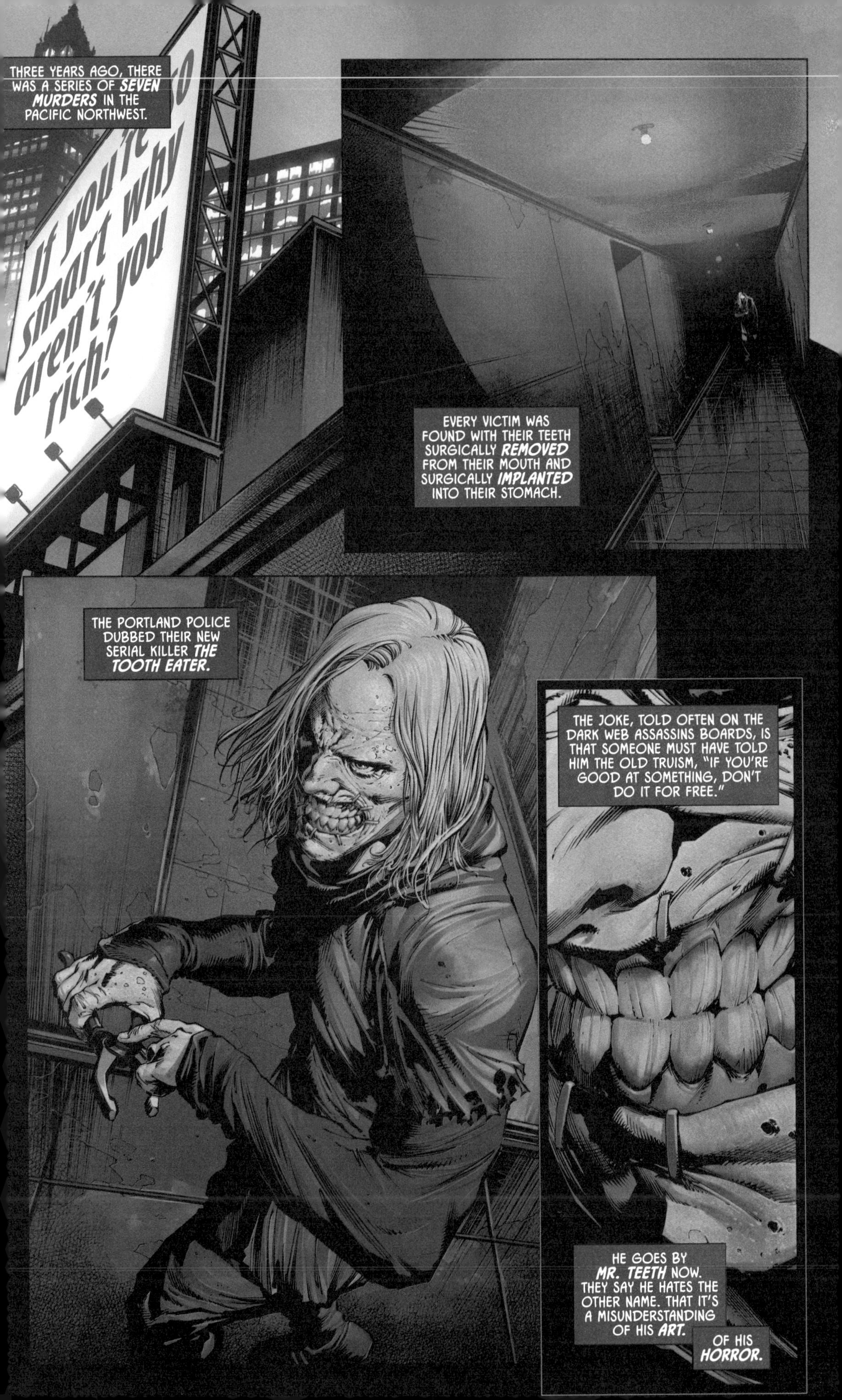
THREE YEARS AGO, THERE WAS A SERIES OF SEVEN MURDERS IN THE PACIFIC NORTHWEST.
If you're so smart why aren't you rich?
EVERY VICTIM WAS FOUND WITH THEIR TEETH SURGICALLY REMOVED FROM THEIR MOUTH AND SURGICALLY IMPLANTED INTO THEIR STOMACH.
THE PORTLAND POLICE DUBBED THEIR NEW SERIAL KILLER THE TOOTH EATER.
THE JOKE, TOLD OFTEN ON THE DARK WEB ASSASSINS BOARDS, IS THAT SOMEONE MUST HAVE TOLD HIM THE OLD TRUISM, "IF YOU'RE GOOD AT SOMETHING, DON'T DO IT FOR FREE."
HE GOES BY MR. TEETH NOW. THEY SAY HE HATES THE OTHER NAME. THAT IT'S A MISUNDERSTANDING OF HIS ART.
OF HIS HORROR.

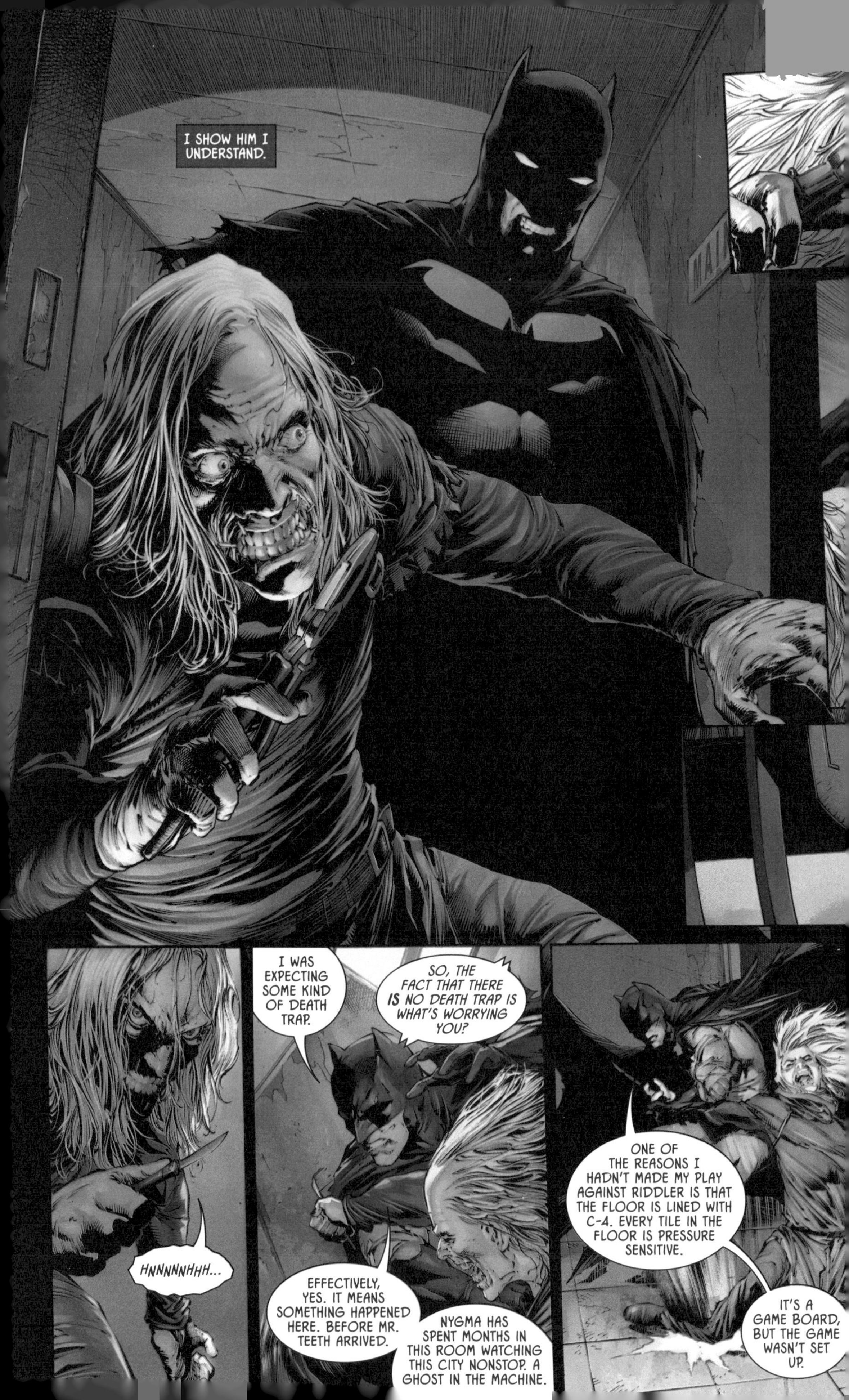
I SHOW HIM I UNDERSTAND.
HNNNNNHHH...
I WAS EXPECTING SOME KIND OF DEATH TRAP.
SO, THE FACT THAT THERE IS NO DEATH TRAP IS WHAT'S WORRYING YOU?
EFFECTIVELY, YES. IT MEANS SOMETHING HAPPENED HERE. BEFORE MR. TEETH ARRIVED.
NYGMA HAS SPENT MONTHS IN THIS ROOM WATCHING THIS CITY NONSTOP. A GHOST IN THE MACHINE.
ONE OF THE REASONS I HADN'T MADE MY PLAY AGAINST RIDDLER IS THAT THE FLOOR IS LINED WITH C-4. EVERY TILE IN THE FLOOR IS PRESSURE SENSITIVE.
IT'S A GAME BOARD, BUT THE GAME WASN'T SET UP.

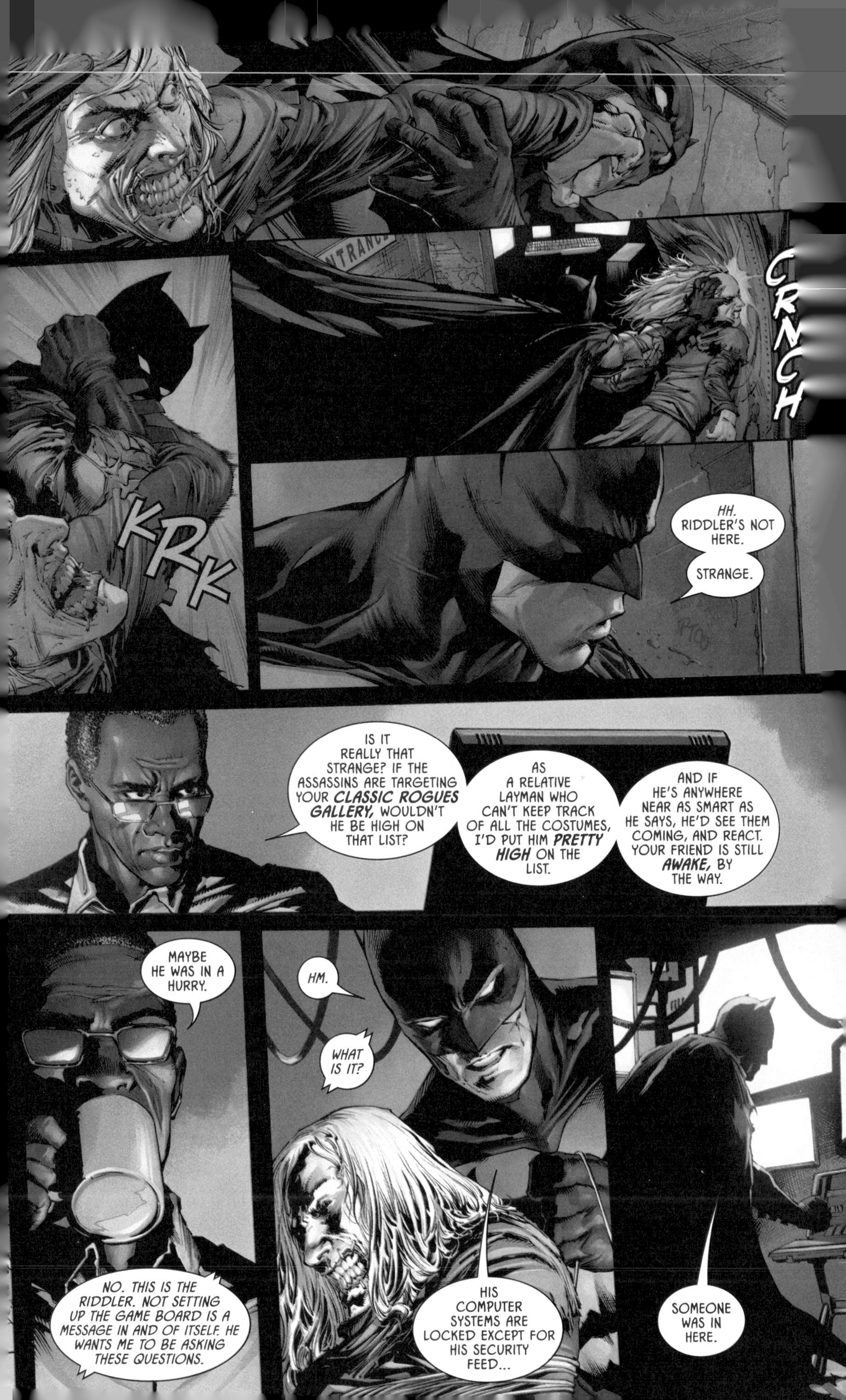
CRNCH
KRK
HH. RIDDLER'S NOT HERE.
STRANGE.
IS IT REALLY THAT STRANGE? IF THE ASSASSINS ARE TARGETING YOUR CLASSIC ROGUES GALLERY, WOULDN'T HE BE HIGH ON THAT LIST?
AS A RELATIVE LAYMAN WHO CAN'T KEEP TRACK OF ALL THE COSTUMES, I'D PUT HIM PRETTY HIGH ON THE LIST.
AND IF HE'S ANYWHERE NEAR AS SMART AS HE SAYS, HE'D SEE THEM COMING, AND REACT. YOUR FRIEND IS STILL AWAKE, BY THE WAY.
MAYBE HE WAS IN A HURRY.
NO. THIS IS THE RIDDLER. NOT SETTING UP THE GAME BOARD IS A MESSAGE IN AND OF ITSELF. HE WANTS ME TO BE ASKING THESE QUESTIONS.
HM.
WHAT IS IT?
HIS COMPUTER SYSTEMS ARE LOCKED EXCEPT FOR HIS SECURITY FEED...
SOMEONE WAS IN HERE.

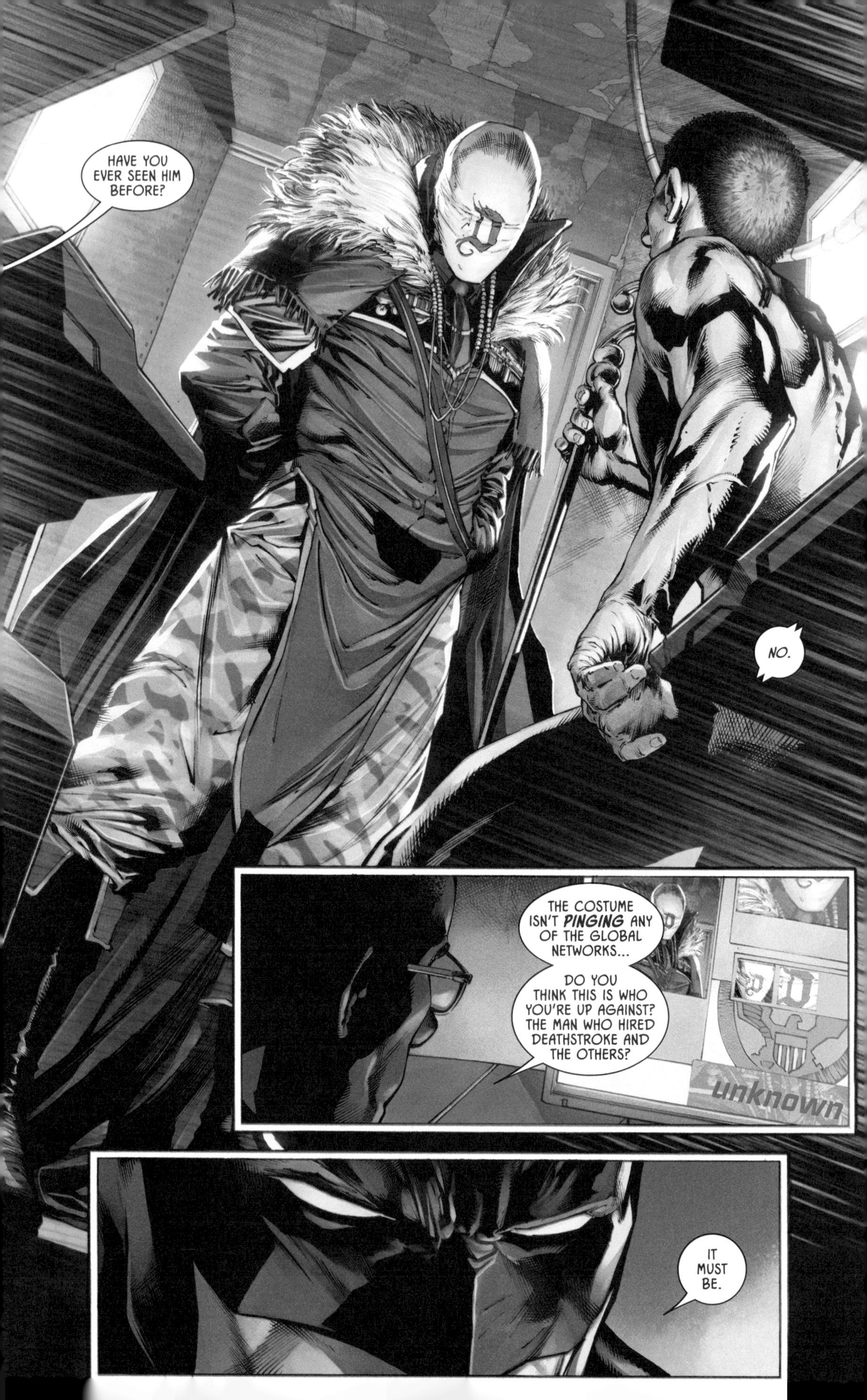
HAVE YOU EVER SEEN HIM BEFORE?
NO.
THE COSTUME ISN'T *PINGING* ANY OF THE GLOBAL NETWORKS...
DO YOU THINK THIS IS WHO YOU'RE UP AGAINST? THE MAN WHO HIRED DEATHSTROKE AND THE OTHERS?
unknown
IT MUST BE.

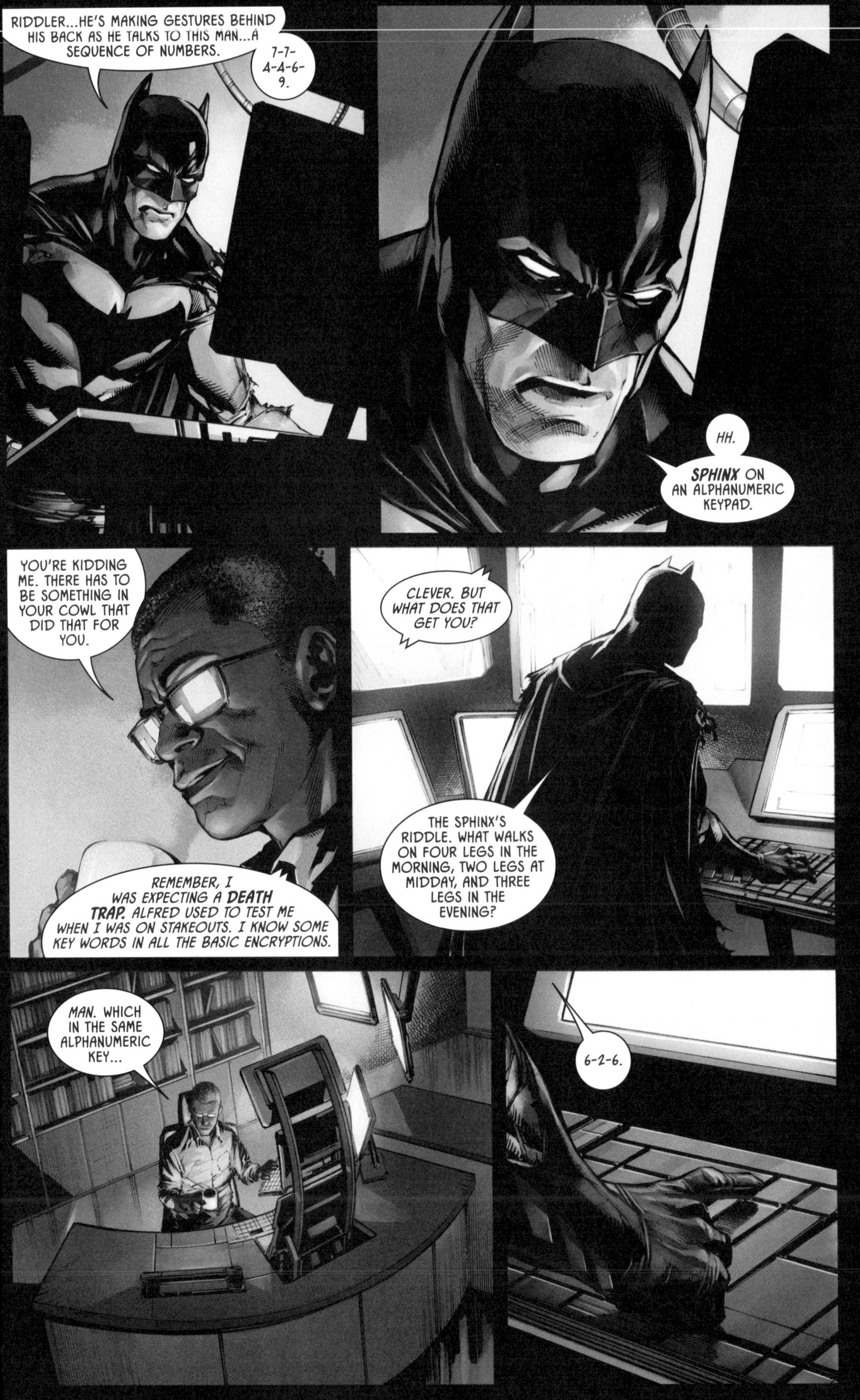
RIDDLER...HE'S MAKING GESTURES BEHIND HIS BACK AS HE TALKS TO THIS MAN...A SEQUENCE OF NUMBERS.
7-7-4-4-6-9.
HH.
SPHINX ON AN ALPHANUMERIC KEYPAD.
YOU'RE KIDDING ME. THERE HAS TO BE SOMETHING IN YOUR COWL THAT DID THAT FOR YOU.
REMEMBER, I WAS EXPECTING A DEATH TRAP. ALFRED USED TO TEST ME WHEN I WAS ON STAKEOUTS. I KNOW SOME KEY WORDS IN ALL THE BASIC ENCRYPTIONS.
CLEVER. BUT WHAT DOES THAT GET YOU?
THE SPHINX'S RIDDLE. WHAT WALKS ON FOUR LEGS IN THE MORNING, TWO LEGS AT MIDDAY, AND THREE LEGS IN THE EVENING?
MAN. WHICH IN THE SAME ALPHANUMERIC KEY...
6-2-6.

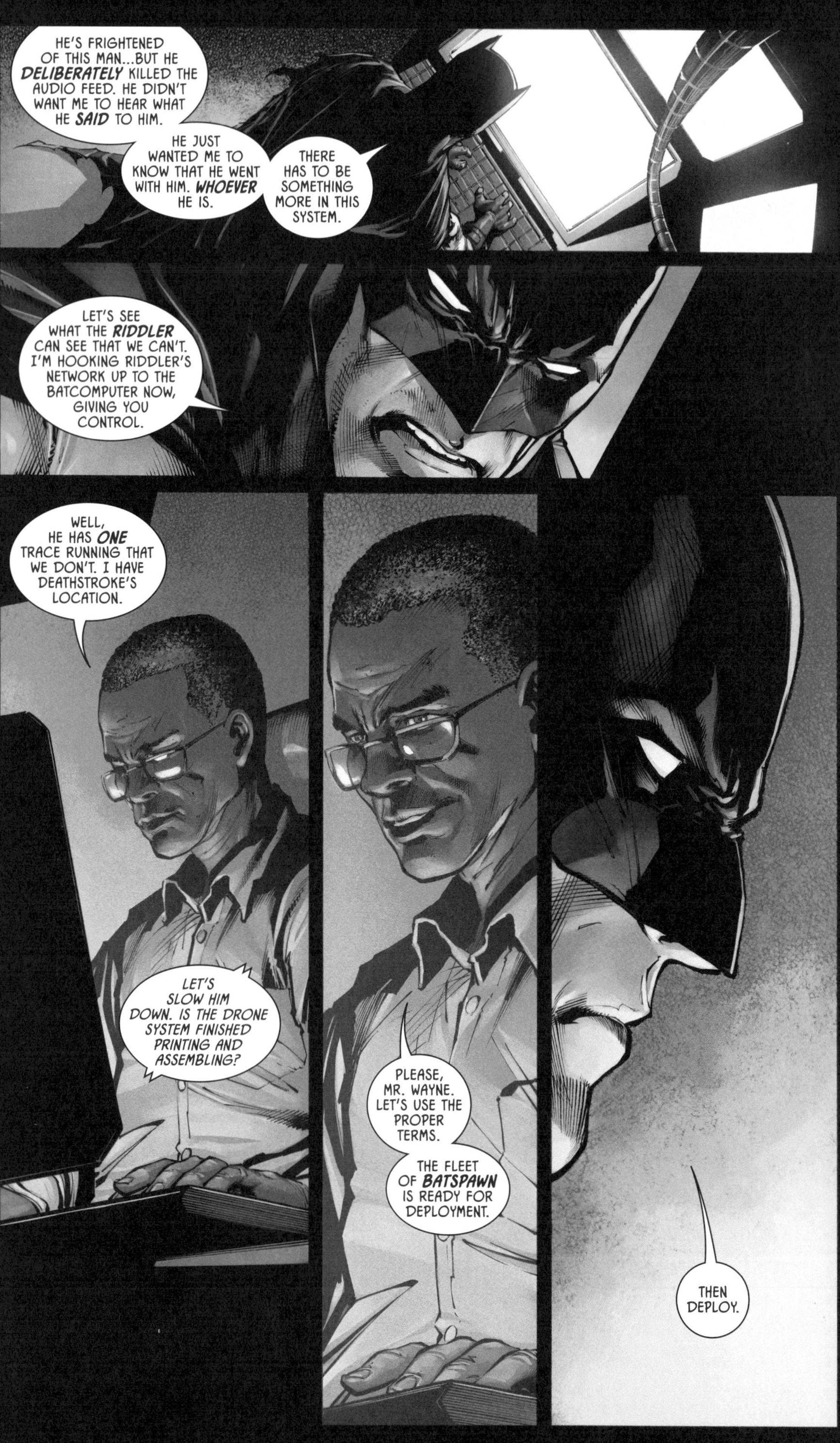
HE'S FRIGHTENED OF THIS MAN...BUT HE DELIBERATELY KILLED THE AUDIO FEED. HE DIDN'T WANT ME TO HEAR WHAT HE SAID TO HIM.
HE JUST WANTED ME TO KNOW THAT HE WENT WITH HIM. WHOEVER HE IS.
THERE HAS TO BE SOMETHING MORE IN THIS SYSTEM.
LET'S SEE WHAT THE RIDDLER CAN SEE THAT WE CAN'T. I'M HOOKING RIDDLER'S NETWORK UP TO THE BATCOMPUTER NOW, GIVING YOU CONTROL.
WELL, HE HAS ONE TRACE RUNNING THAT WE DON'T. I HAVE DEATHSTROKE'S LOCATION.
LET'S SLOW HIM DOWN. IS THE DRONE SYSTEM FINISHED PRINTING AND ASSEMBLING?
PLEASE, MR. WAYNE. LET'S USE THE PROPER TERMS.
THE FLEET OF BATSPAWN IS READY FOR DEPLOYMENT.
THEN DEPLOY.

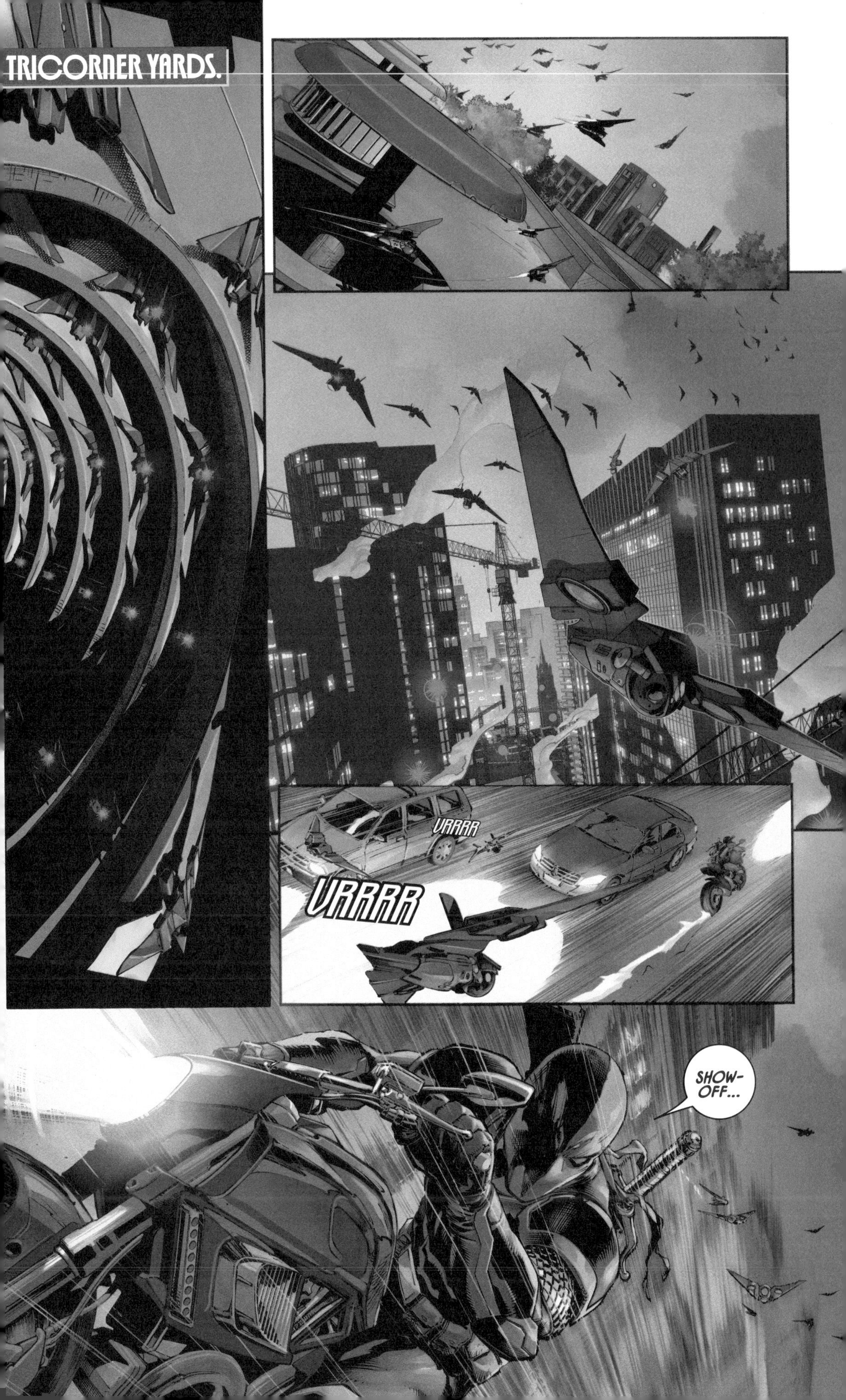
TRICORNER YARDS.
VRRRR
VRRRR
SHOW-OFF...

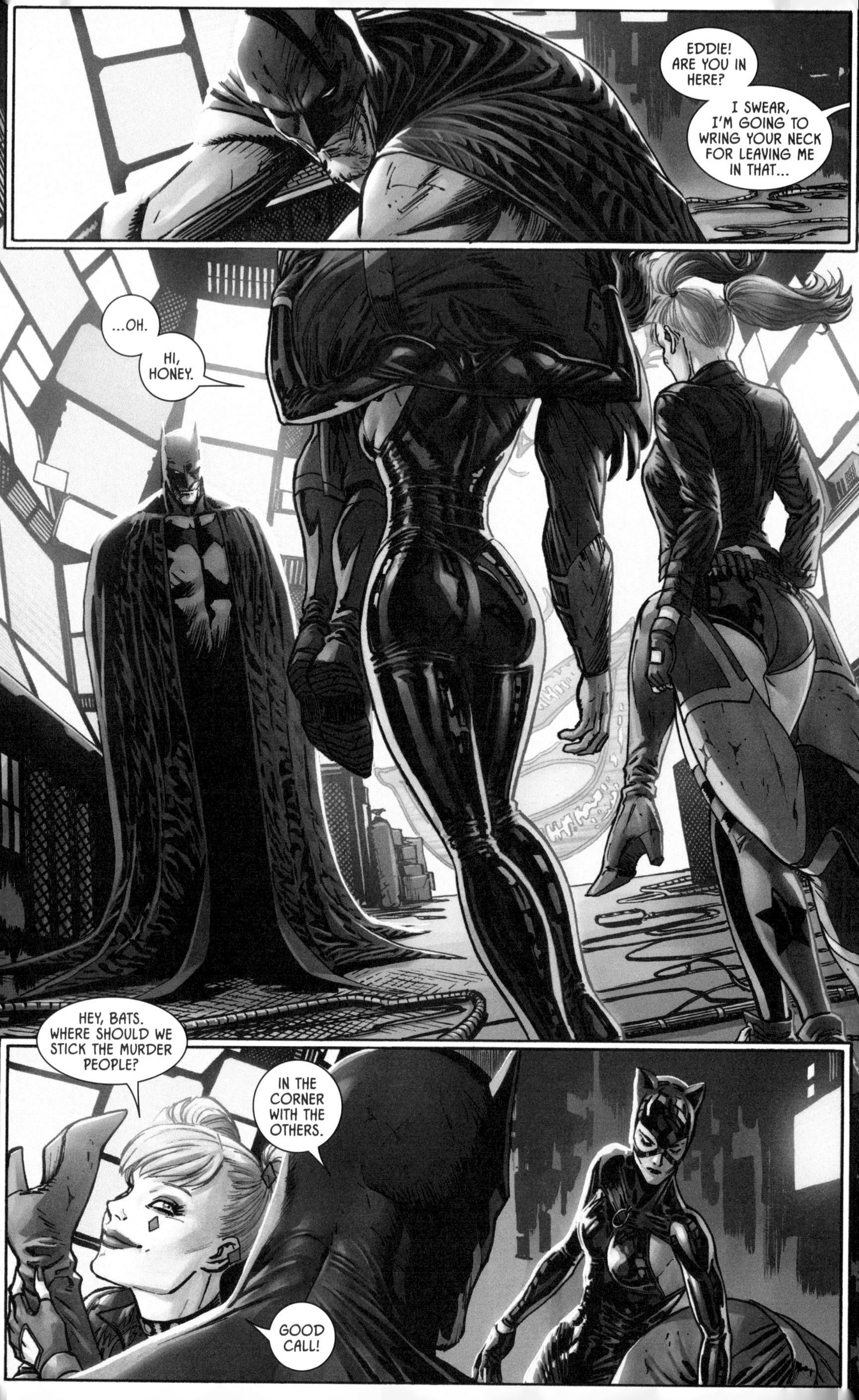
EDDIE! ARE YOU IN HERE?
I SWEAR, I'M GOING TO WRING YOUR NECK FOR LEAVING ME IN THAT...
...OH.
HI, HONEY.
HEY, BATS. WHERE SHOULD WE STICK THE MURDER PEOPLE?
IN THE CORNER WITH THE OTHERS.
GOOD CALL!

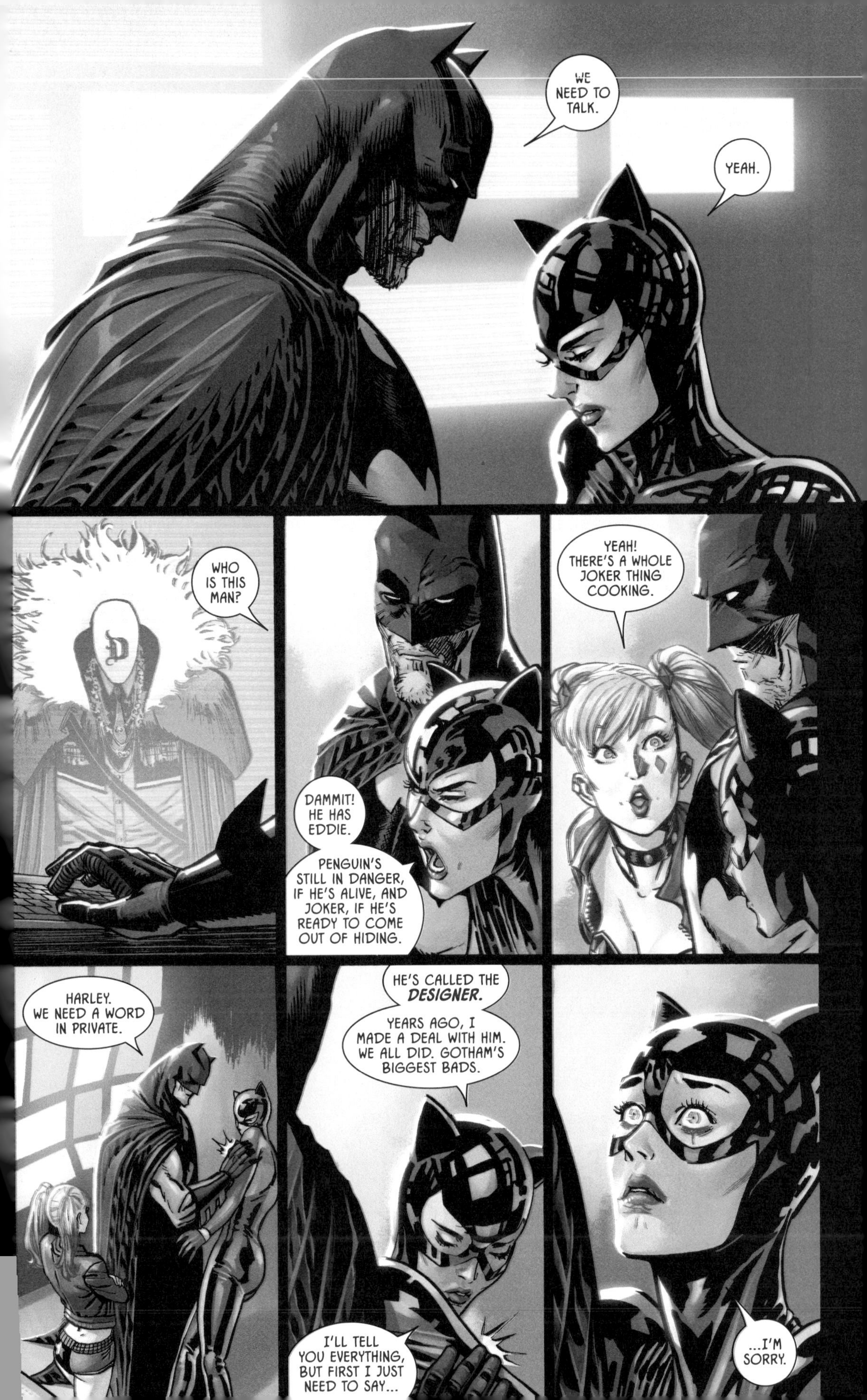
WE NEED TO TALK.
YEAH.
WHO IS THIS MAN?
DAMMIT! HE HAS EDDIE.
PENGUIN'S STILL IN DANGER, IF HE'S ALIVE, AND JOKER, IF HE'S READY TO COME OUT OF HIDING.
YEAH! THERE'S A WHOLE JOKER THING COOKING.
HARLEY. WE NEED A WORD IN PRIVATE.
HE'S CALLED THE ***DESIGNER.***
YEARS AGO, I MADE A DEAL WITH HIM. WE ALL DID. GOTHAM'S BIGGEST BADS.
I'LL TELL YOU EVERYTHING, BUT FIRST I JUST NEED TO SAY...
...I'M SORRY.

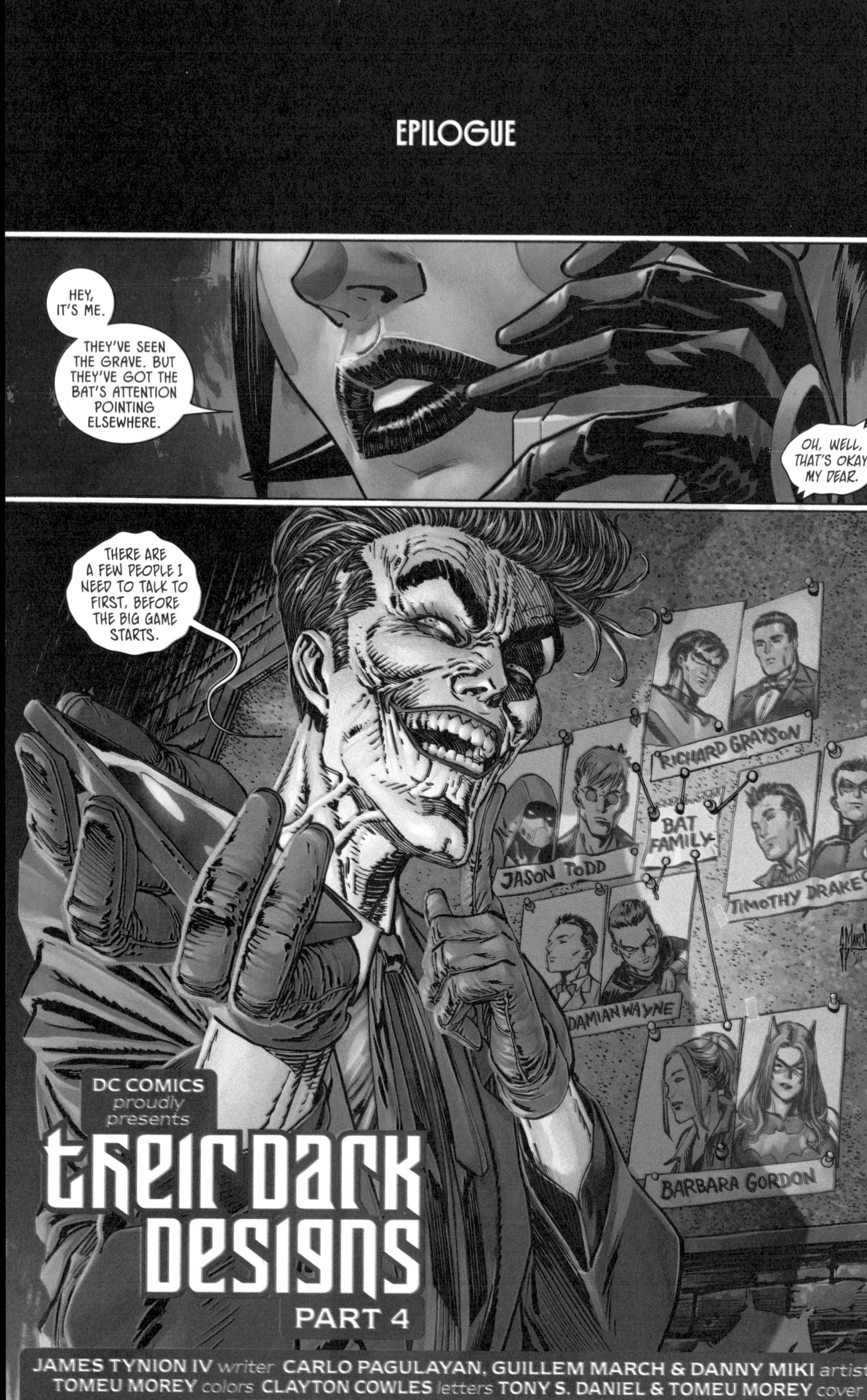
EPILOGUE
HEY, IT'S ME.
THEY'VE SEEN THE GRAVE. BUT THEY'VE GOT THE BAT'S ATTENTION POINTING ELSEWHERE.
OH, WELL, THAT'S OKAY MY DEAR.
THERE ARE A FEW PEOPLE I NEED TO TALK TO FIRST, BEFORE THE BIG GAME STARTS.
RICHARD GRAYSON
BAT FAMILY
JASON TODD
TIMOTHY DRAKE
DAMIAN WAYNE
BARBARA GORDON
DC COMICS proudly presents
THEIR DARK DESIGNS
PART 4
JAMES TYNION IV writer CARLO PAGULAYAN, GUILLEM MARCH & DANNY MIKI artis
TOMEU MOREY colors CLAYTON COWLES letters TONY S. DANIEL & TOMEU MOREY cover

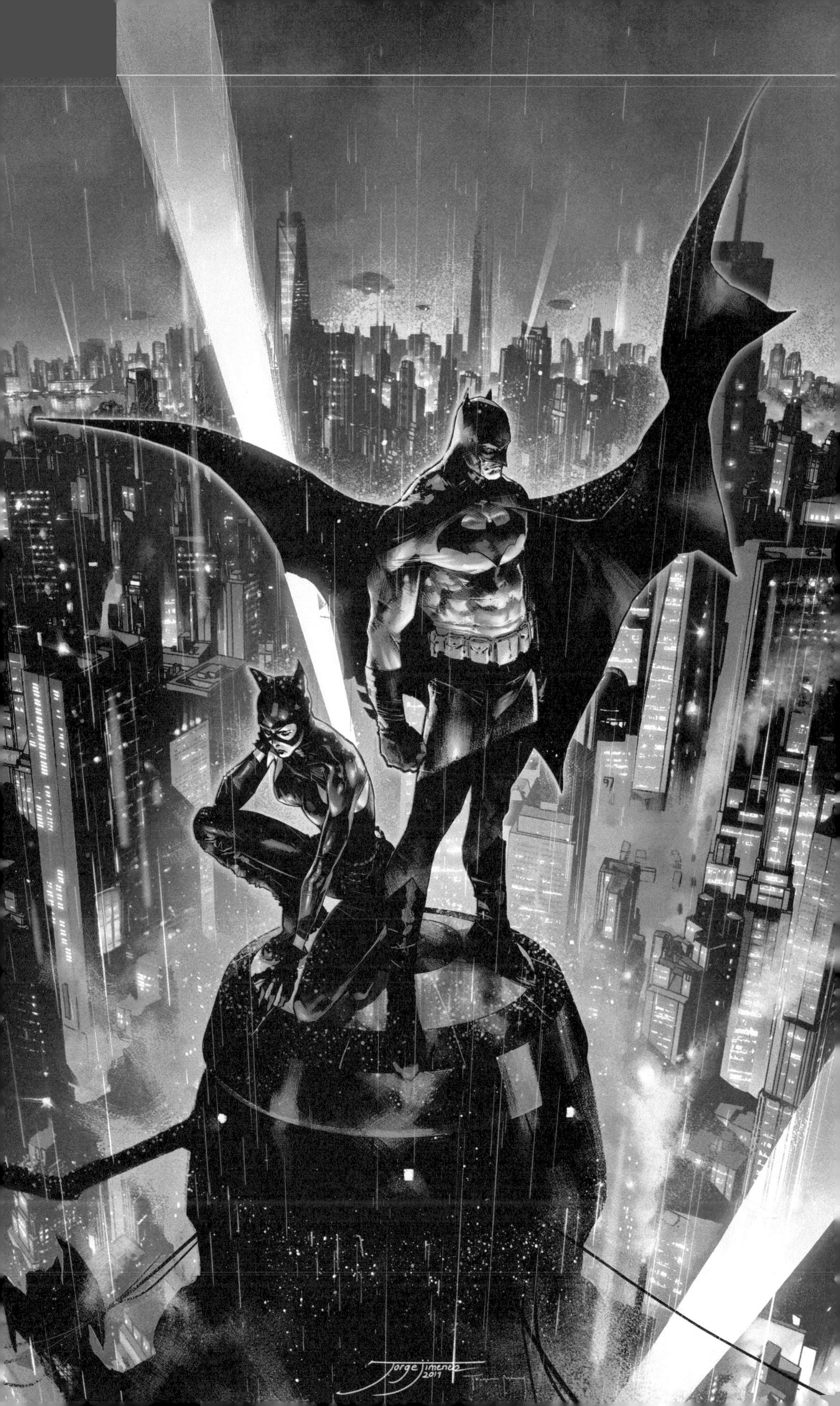

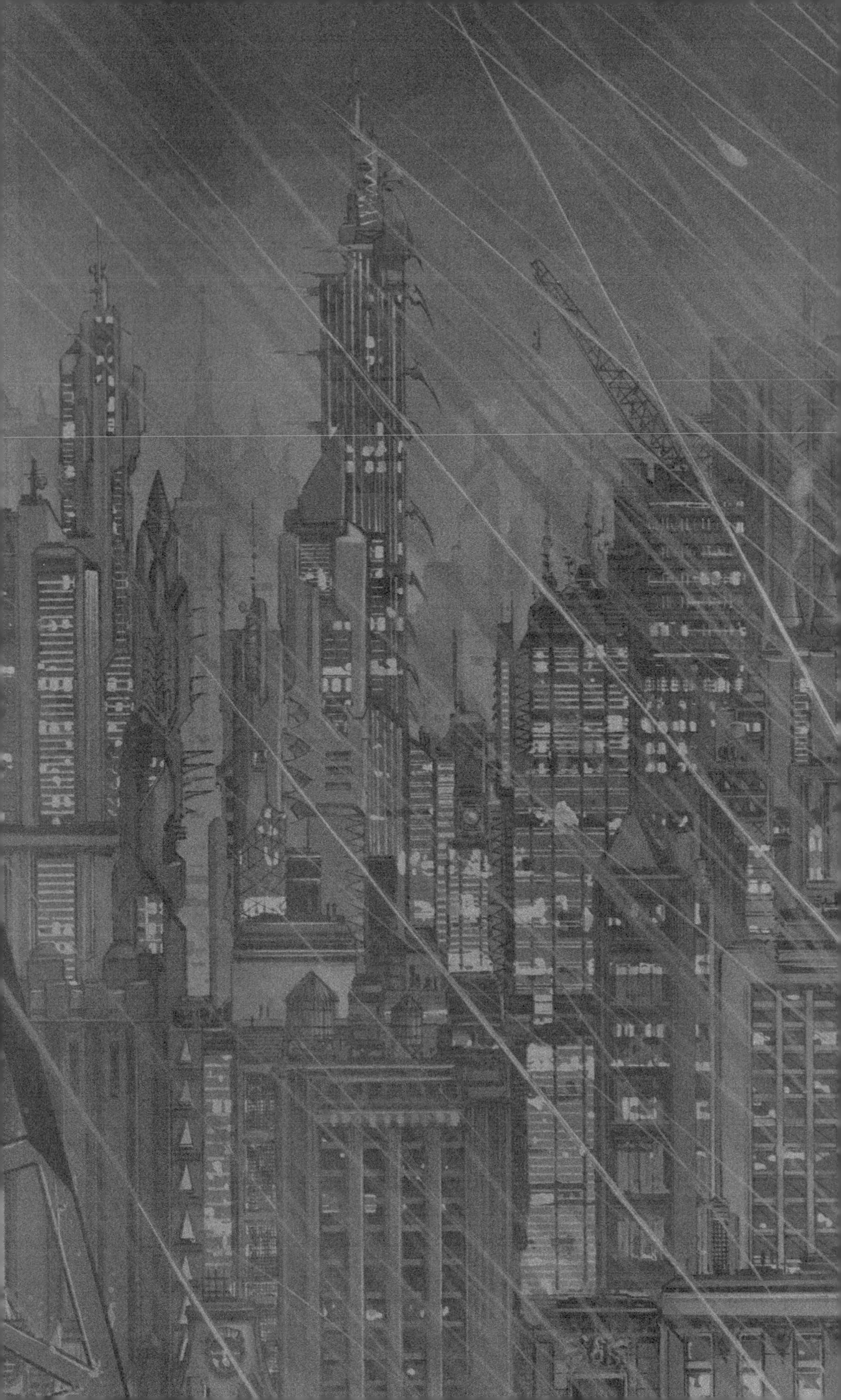

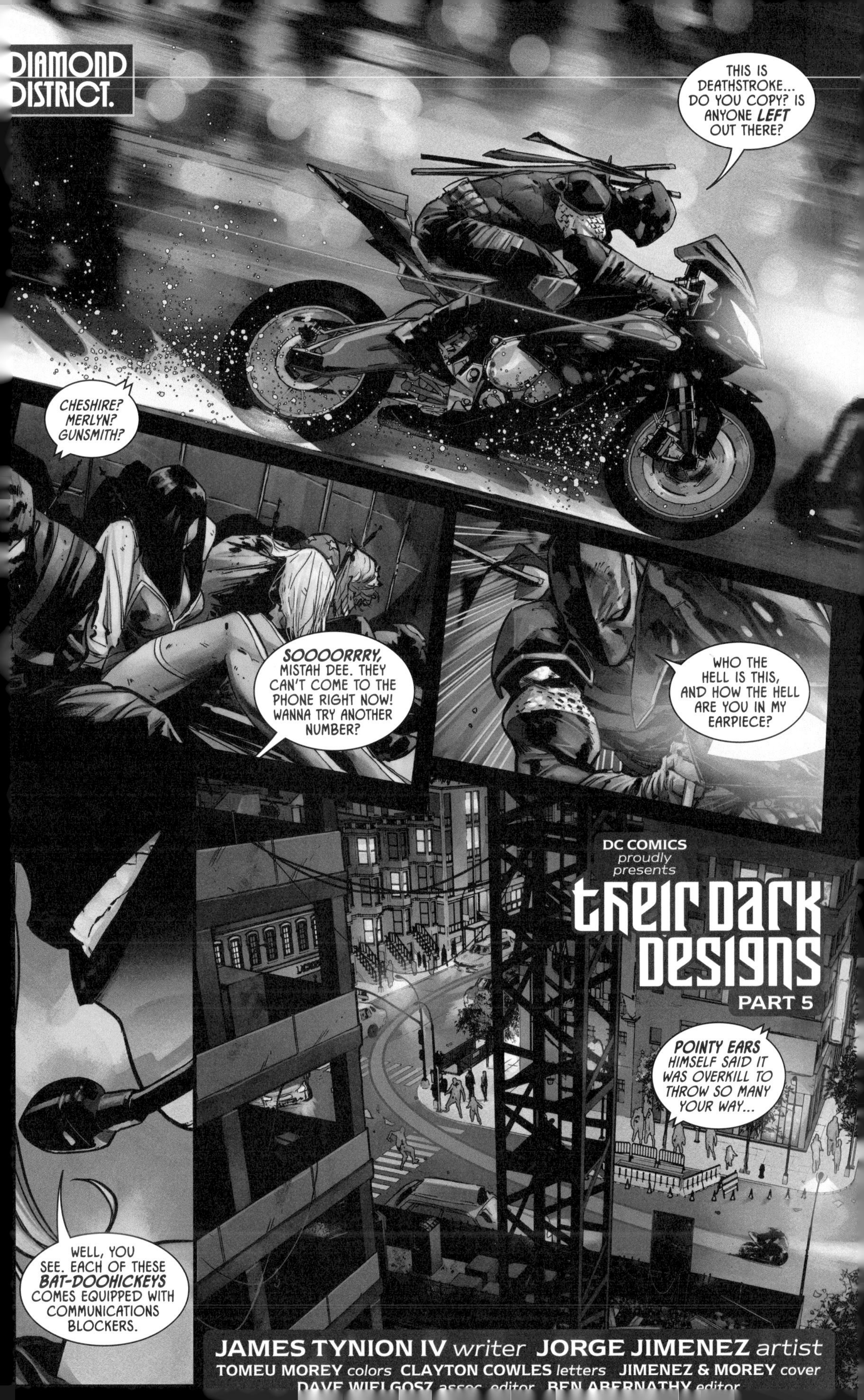

DIAMOND DISTRICT.
THIS IS DEATHSTROKE... DO YOU COPY? IS ANYONE *LEFT* OUT THERE?
CHESHIRE? MERLYN? GUNSMITH?
SOOOORRRY, MISTAH DEE. THEY CAN'T COME TO THE PHONE RIGHT NOW! WANNA TRY ANOTHER NUMBER?
WHO THE HELL IS THIS, AND HOW THE HELL ARE YOU IN MY EARPIECE?
DC COMICS proudly presents
THEIR DARK DESIGNS
PART 5
POINTY EARS HIMSELF SAID IT WAS OVERKILL TO THROW SO MANY YOUR WAY...
WELL, YOU SEE. EACH OF THESE *BAT-DOOHICKEYS* COMES EQUIPPED WITH COMMUNICATIONS BLOCKERS.
JAMES TYNION IV writer JORGE JIMENEZ artist
TOMEU MOREY colors CLAYTON COWLES letters JIMENEZ & MOREY cover
DAVE WIELGOSZ assoc. editor BEN ABERNATHY editor

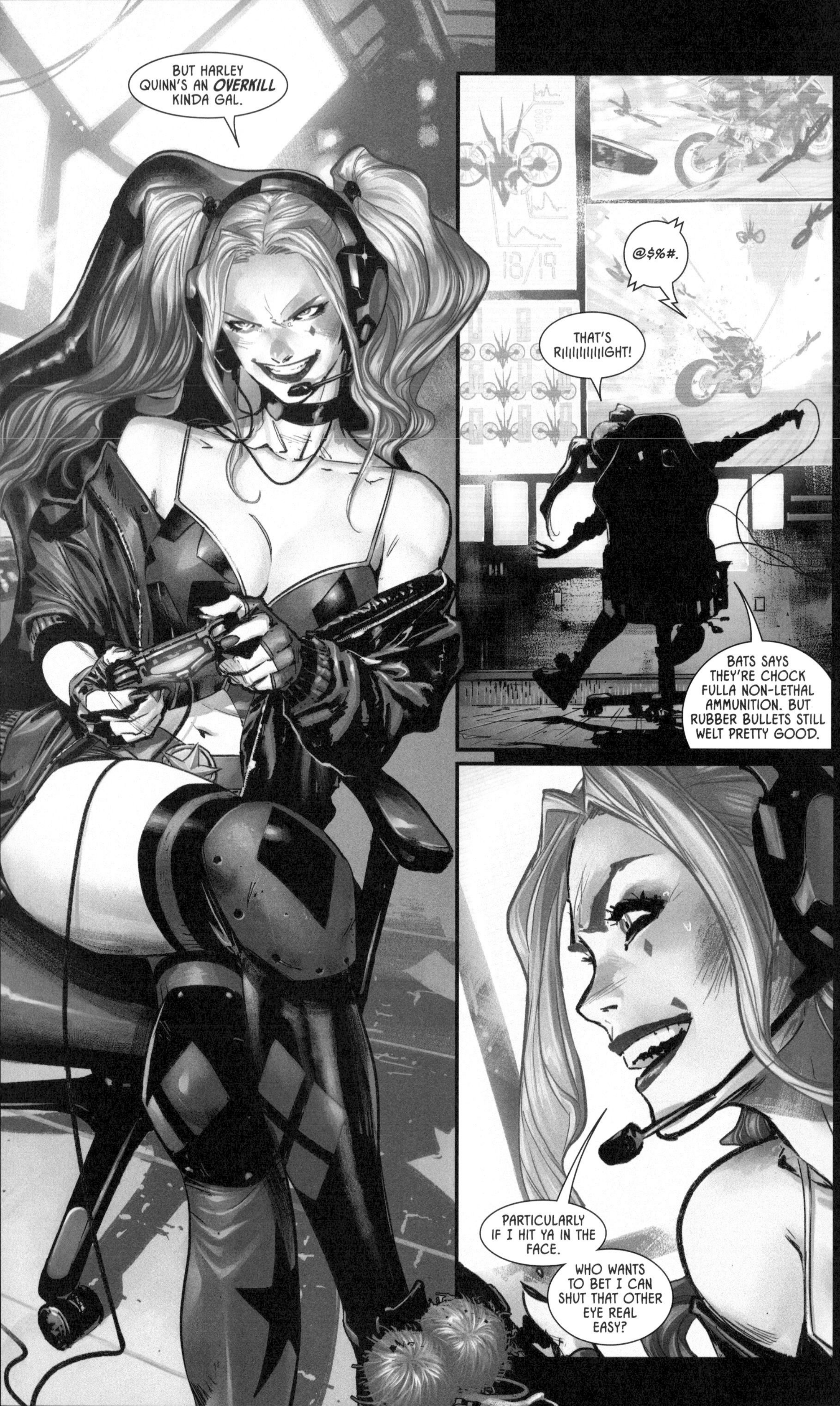
BUT HARLEY QUINN'S AN OVERKILL KINDA GAL.
@$%#.
THAT'S RIIIIIIIIIGHT!
BATS SAYS THEY'RE CHOCK FULLA NON-LETHAL AMMUNITION. BUT RUBBER BULLETS STILL WELT PRETTY GOOD.
PARTICULARLY IF I HIT YA IN THE FACE.
WHO WANTS TO BET I CAN SHUT THAT OTHER EYE REAL EASY?

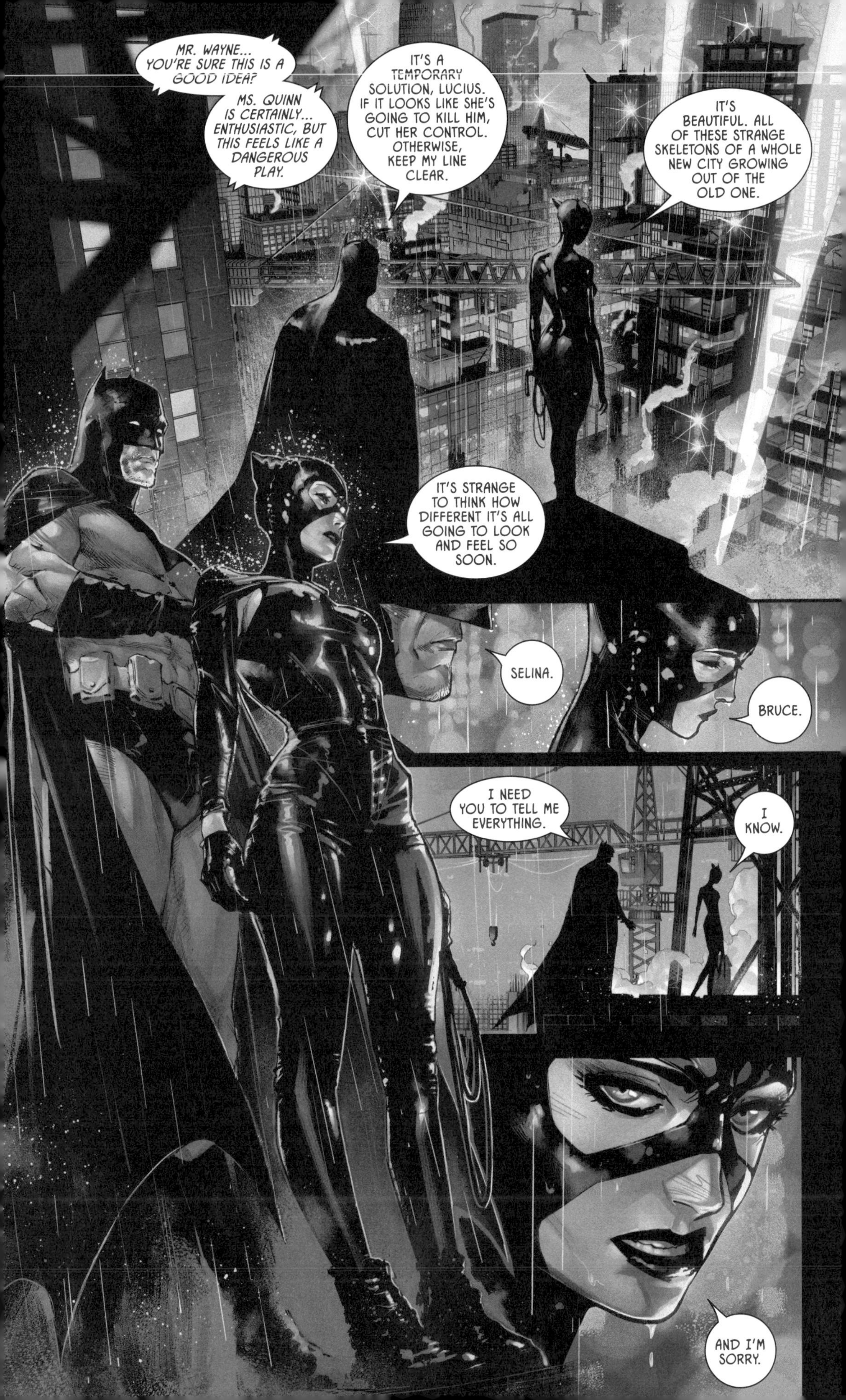
MR. WAYNE... YOU'RE SURE THIS IS A GOOD IDEA?
MS. QUINN IS CERTAINLY... ENTHUSIASTIC, BUT THIS FEELS LIKE A DANGEROUS PLAY.
IT'S A TEMPORARY SOLUTION, LUCIUS. IF IT LOOKS LIKE SHE'S GOING TO KILL HIM, CUT HER CONTROL. OTHERWISE, KEEP MY LINE CLEAR.
IT'S BEAUTIFUL. ALL OF THESE STRANGE SKELETONS OF A WHOLE NEW CITY GROWING OUT OF THE OLD ONE.
IT'S STRANGE TO THINK HOW DIFFERENT IT'S ALL GOING TO LOOK AND FEEL SO SOON.
SELINA.
BRUCE.
I NEED YOU TO TELL ME EVERYTHING.
I KNOW.
AND I'M SORRY.

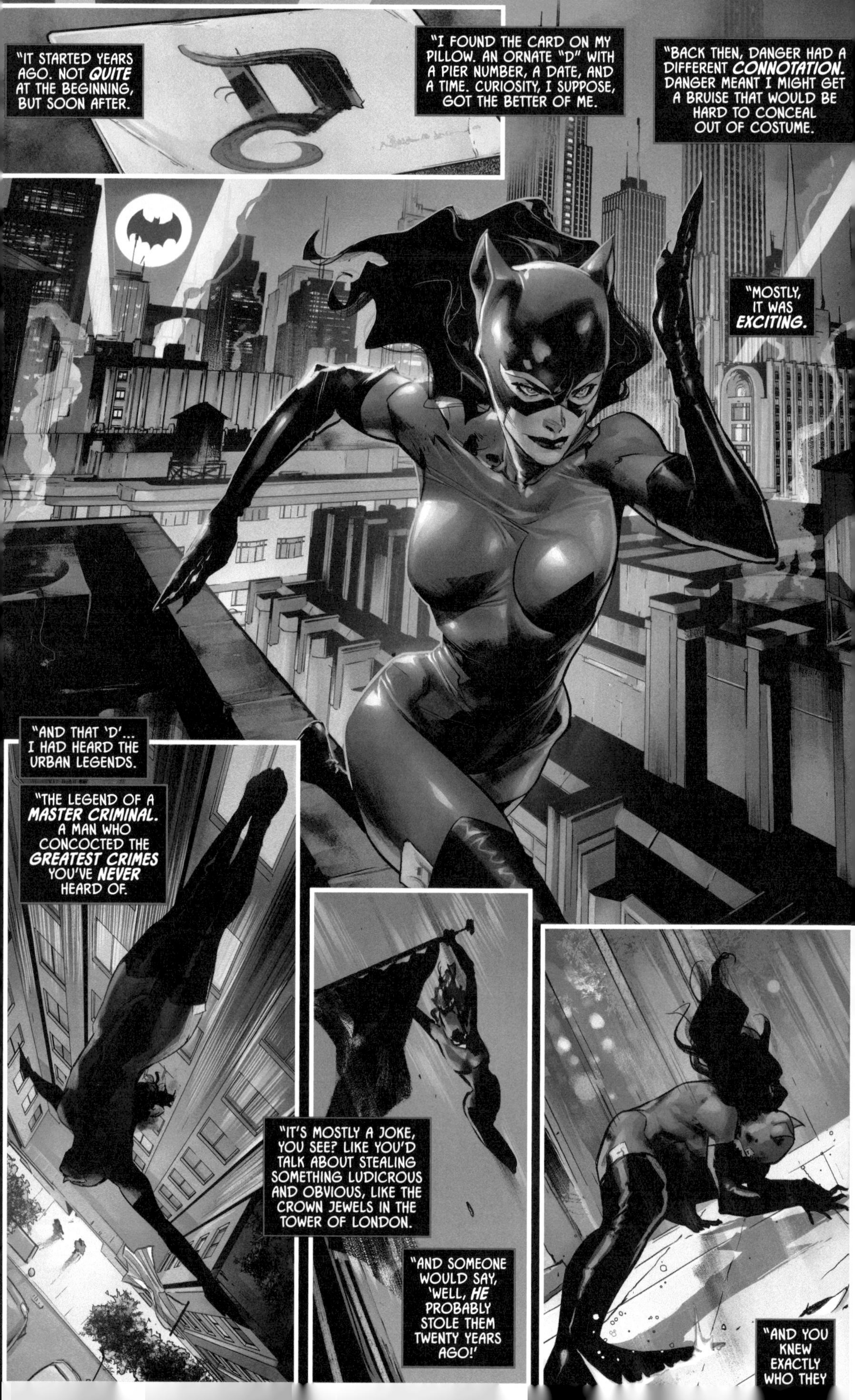
"IT STARTED YEARS AGO. NOT QUITE AT THE BEGINNING, BUT SOON AFTER.
"I FOUND THE CARD ON MY PILLOW. AN ORNATE "D" WITH A PIER NUMBER, A DATE, AND A TIME. CURIOSITY, I SUPPOSE, GOT THE BETTER OF ME.
"BACK THEN, DANGER HAD A DIFFERENT CONNOTATION. DANGER MEANT I MIGHT GET A BRUISE THAT WOULD BE HARD TO CONCEAL OUT OF COSTUME.
"MOSTLY, IT WAS EXCITING.
"AND THAT 'D'... I HAD HEARD THE URBAN LEGENDS.
"THE LEGEND OF A MASTER CRIMINAL. A MAN WHO CONCOCTED THE GREATEST CRIMES YOU'VE NEVER HEARD OF.
"IT'S MOSTLY A JOKE, YOU SEE? LIKE YOU'D TALK ABOUT STEALING SOMETHING LUDICROUS AND OBVIOUS, LIKE THE CROWN JEWELS IN THE TOWER OF LONDON.
"AND SOMEONE WOULD SAY, 'WELL, HE PROBABLY STOLE THEM TWENTY YEARS AGO!'
"AND YOU KNEW EXACTLY WHO THEY

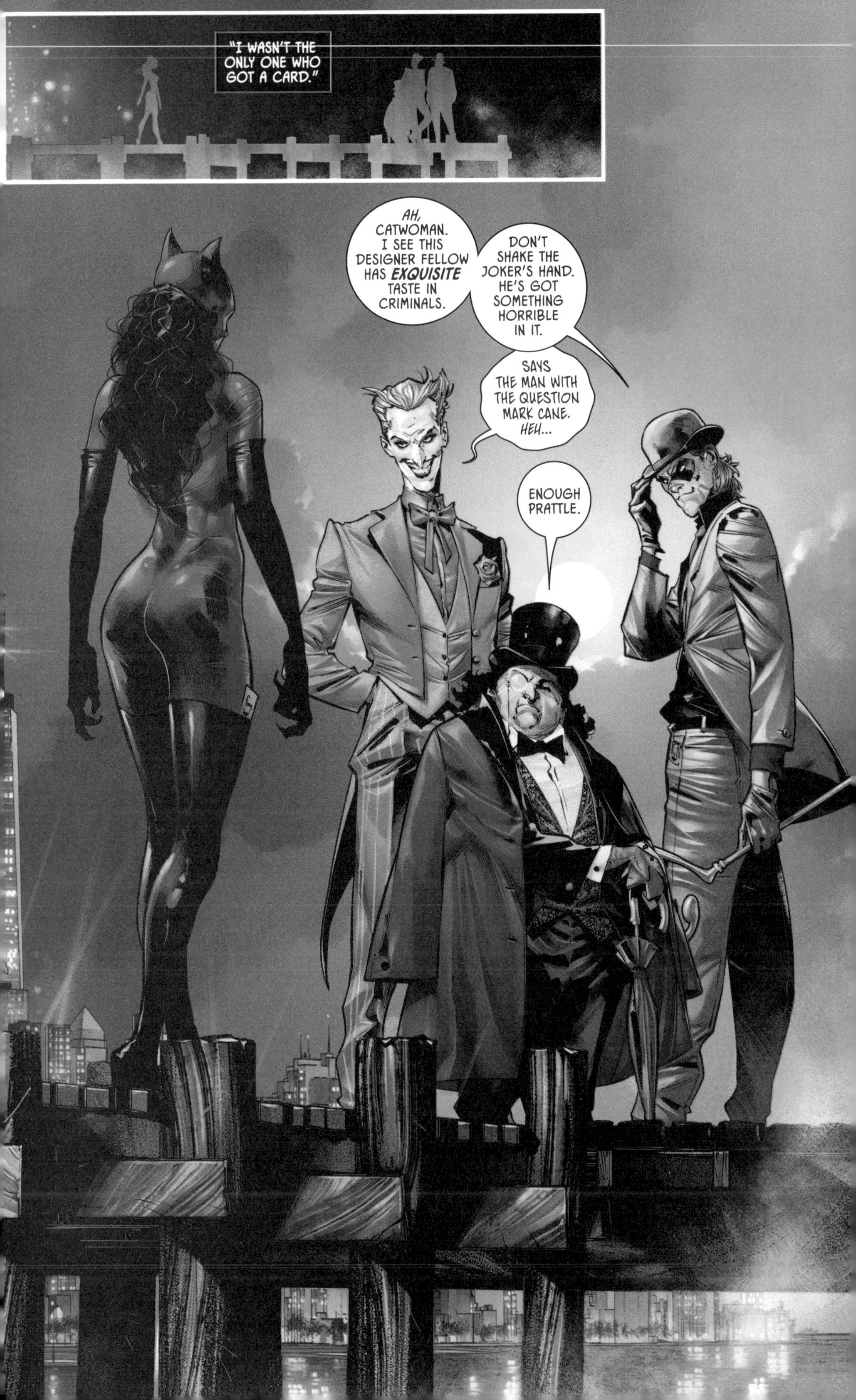

"I WASN'T THE ONLY ONE WHO GOT A CARD."
AH, CATWOMAN. I SEE THIS DESIGNER FELLOW HAS *EXQUISITE* TASTE IN CRIMINALS.
DON'T SHAKE THE JOKER'S HAND. HE'S GOT SOMETHING HORRIBLE IN IT.
SAYS THE MAN WITH THE QUESTION MARK CANE. *HEH...*
ENOUGH PRATTLE.

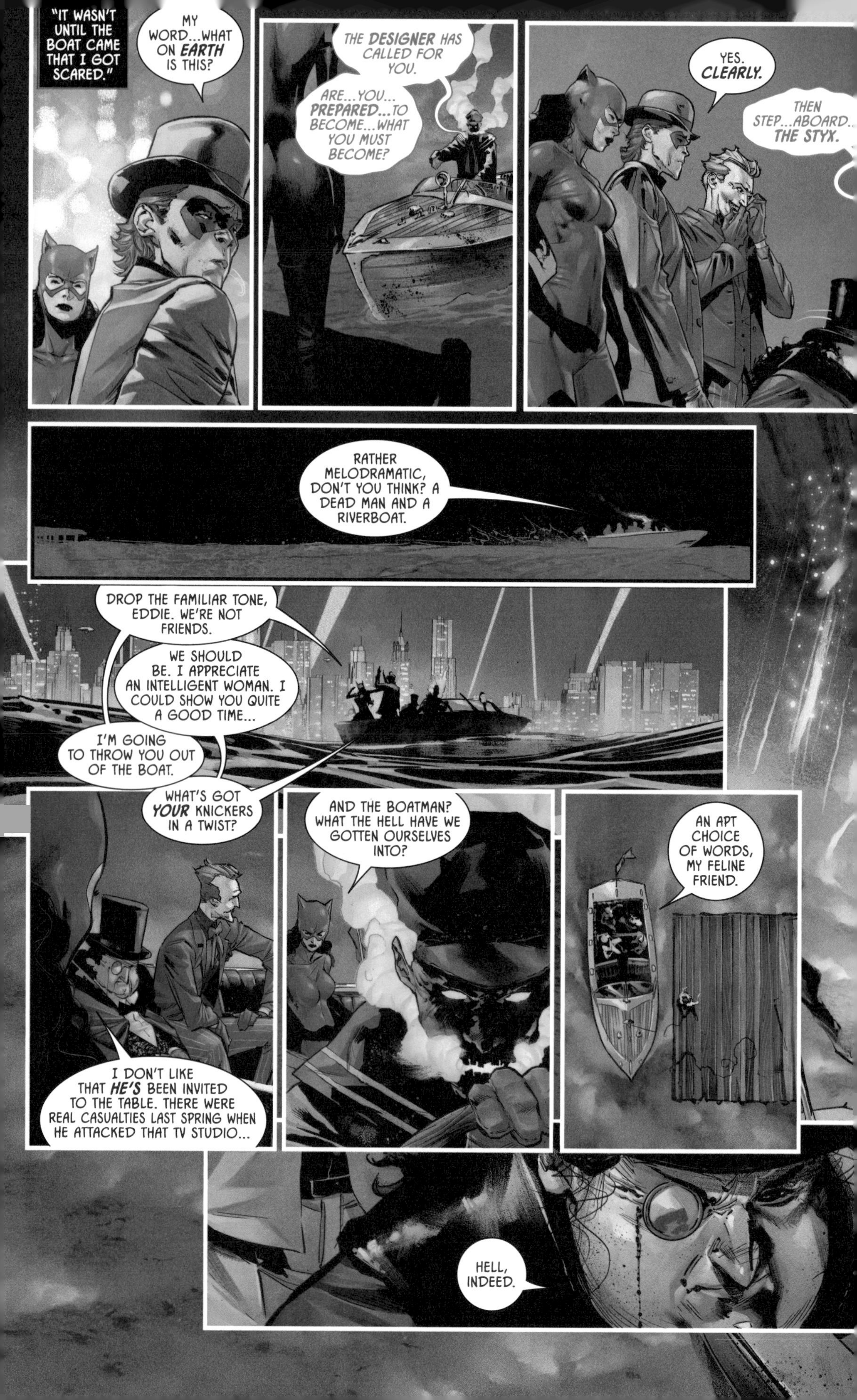

"IT WASN'T UNTIL THE BOAT CAME THAT I GOT SCARED."
MY WORD...WHAT ON EARTH IS THIS?
THE DESIGNER HAS CALLED FOR YOU.
ARE...YOU... PREPARED...TO BECOME...WHAT YOU MUST BECOME?
YES. CLEARLY.
THEN STEP...ABOARD... THE STYX.
RATHER MELODRAMATIC, DON'T YOU THINK? A DEAD MAN AND A RIVERBOAT.
DROP THE FAMILIAR TONE, EDDIE. WE'RE NOT FRIENDS.
WE SHOULD BE. I APPRECIATE AN INTELLIGENT WOMAN. I COULD SHOW YOU QUITE A GOOD TIME...
I'M GOING TO THROW YOU OUT OF THE BOAT.
WHAT'S GOT YOUR KNICKERS IN A TWIST?
I DON'T LIKE THAT HE'S BEEN INVITED TO THE TABLE. THERE WERE REAL CASUALTIES LAST SPRING WHEN HE ATTACKED THAT TV STUDIO...
AND THE BOATMAN? WHAT THE HELL HAVE WE GOTTEN OURSELVES INTO?
AN APT CHOICE OF WORDS, MY FELINE FRIEND.
HELL, INDEED.

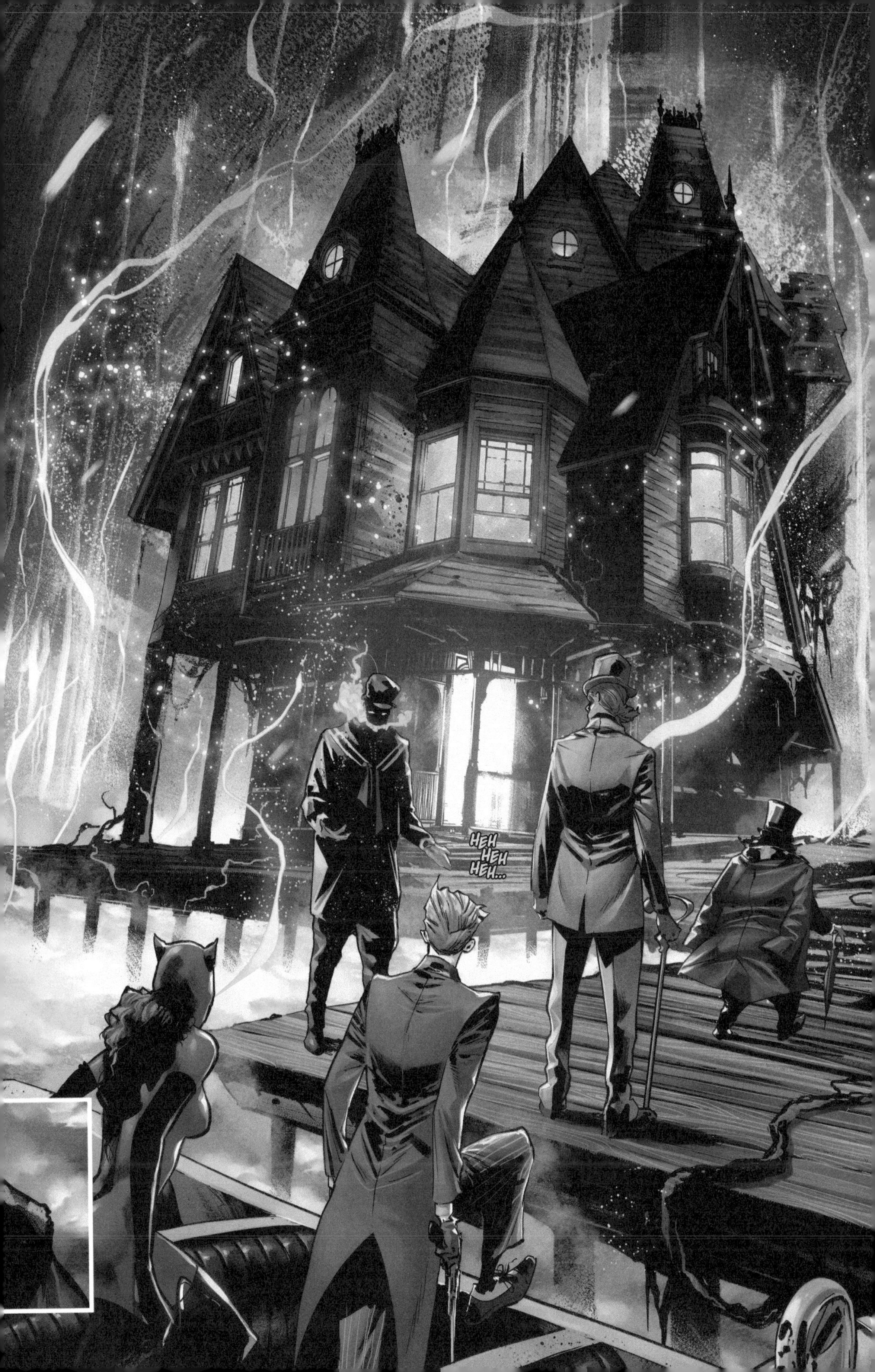
HEH HEH HEH...

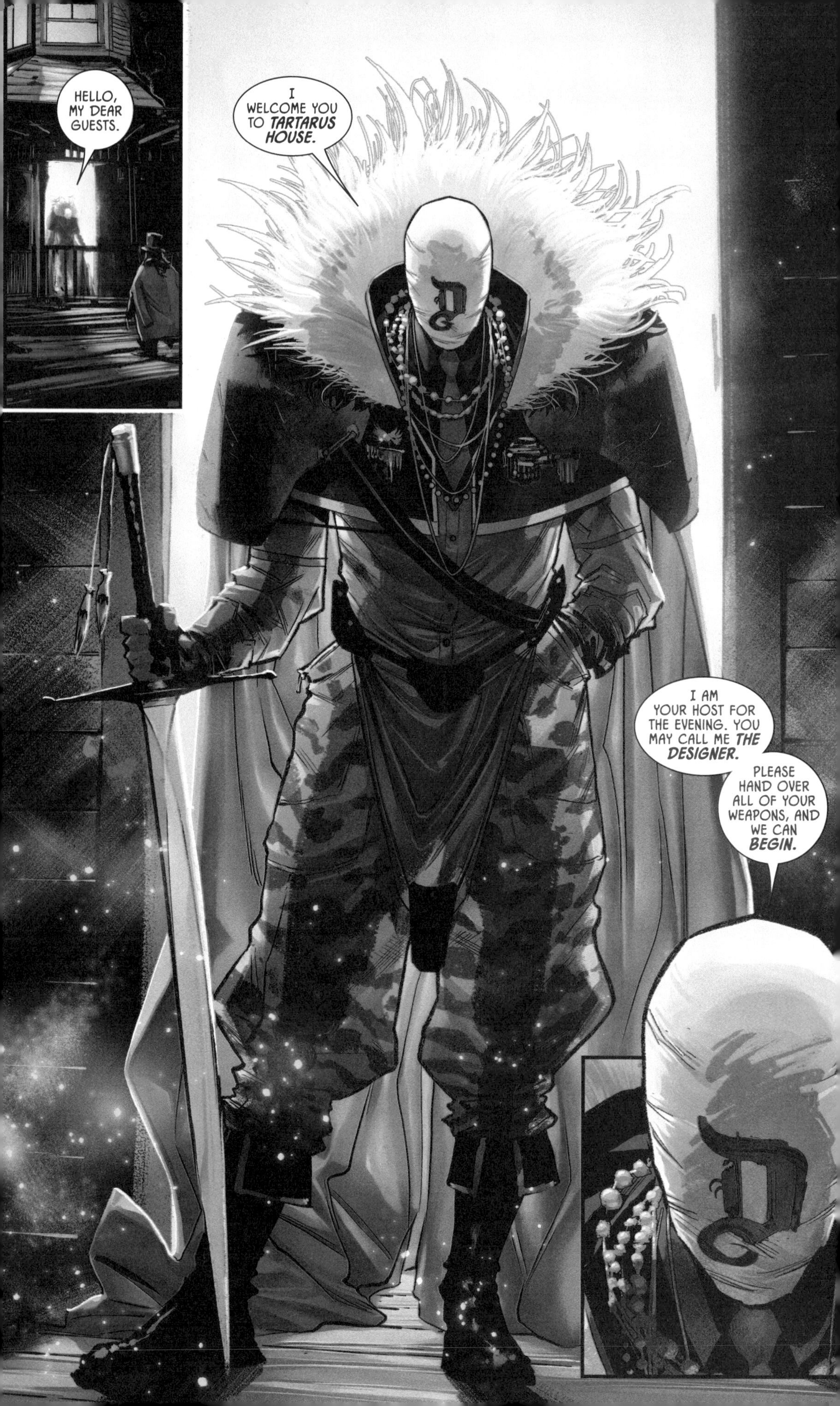
HELLO, MY DEAR GUESTS.
I WELCOME YOU TO TARTARUS HOUSE.
I AM YOUR HOST FOR THE EVENING. YOU MAY CALL ME THE DESIGNER.
PLEASE HAND OVER ALL OF YOUR WEAPONS, AND WE CAN BEGIN.

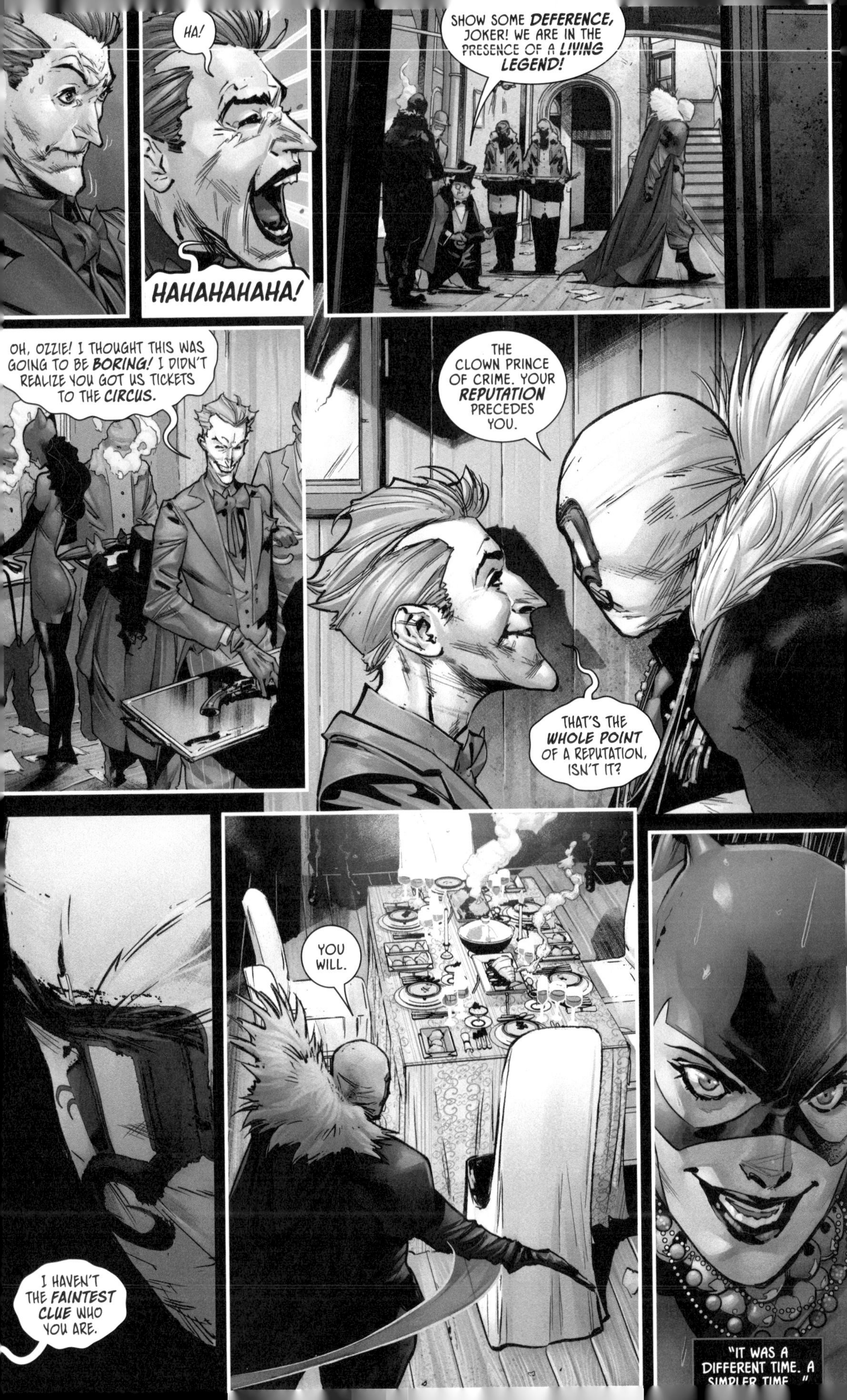
HA!
HAHAHAHAHA!
SHOW SOME DEFERENCE, JOKER! WE ARE IN THE PRESENCE OF A LIVING LEGEND!
OH, OZZIE! I THOUGHT THIS WAS GOING TO BE BORING! I DIDN'T REALIZE YOU GOT US TICKETS TO THE CIRCUS.
THE CLOWN PRINCE OF CRIME. YOUR REPUTATION PRECEDES YOU.
THAT'S THE WHOLE POINT OF A REPUTATION, ISN'T IT?
I HAVEN'T THE FAINTEST CLUE WHO YOU ARE.
YOU WILL.
"IT WAS A DIFFERENT TIME. A SIMPLER TIME..."

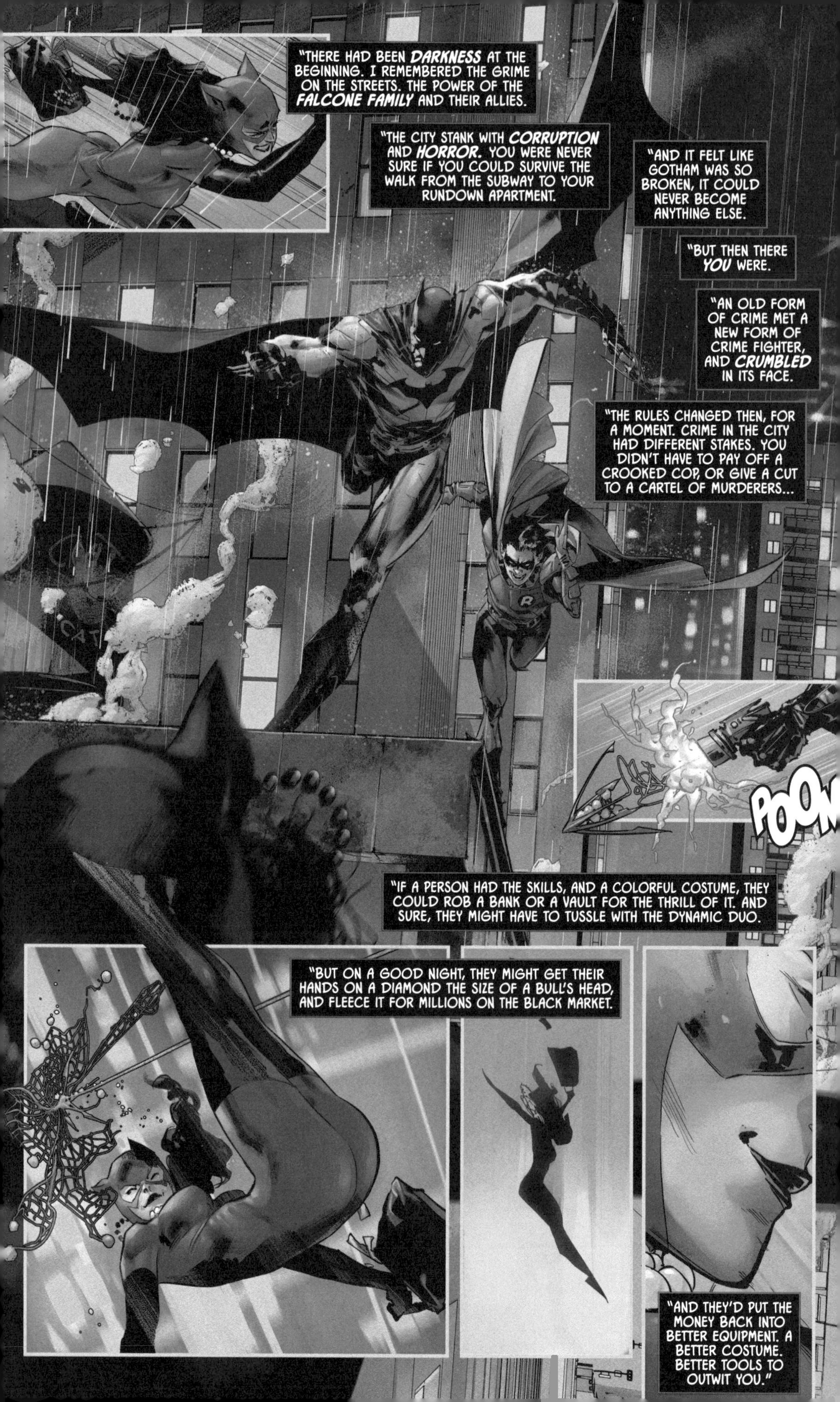
"THERE HAD BEEN DARKNESS AT THE BEGINNING. I REMEMBERED THE GRIME ON THE STREETS. THE POWER OF THE FALCONE FAMILY AND THEIR ALLIES.
"THE CITY STANK WITH CORRUPTION AND HORROR. YOU WERE NEVER SURE IF YOU COULD SURVIVE THE WALK FROM THE SUBWAY TO YOUR RUNDOWN APARTMENT.
"AND IT FELT LIKE GOTHAM WAS SO BROKEN, IT COULD NEVER BECOME ANYTHING ELSE.
"BUT THEN THERE YOU WERE.
"AN OLD FORM OF CRIME MET A NEW FORM OF CRIME FIGHTER, AND CRUMBLED IN ITS FACE.
"THE RULES CHANGED THEN, FOR A MOMENT. CRIME IN THE CITY HAD DIFFERENT STAKES. YOU DIDN'T HAVE TO PAY OFF A CROOKED COP, OR GIVE A CUT TO A CARTEL OF MURDERERS...
POOM
"IF A PERSON HAD THE SKILLS, AND A COLORFUL COSTUME, THEY COULD ROB A BANK OR A VAULT FOR THE THRILL OF IT. AND SURE, THEY MIGHT HAVE TO TUSSLE WITH THE DYNAMIC DUO.
"BUT ON A GOOD NIGHT, THEY MIGHT GET THEIR HANDS ON A DIAMOND THE SIZE OF A BULL'S HEAD, AND FLEECE IT FOR MILLIONS ON THE BLACK MARKET.
"AND THEY'D PUT THE MONEY BACK INTO BETTER EQUIPMENT. A BETTER COSTUME. BETTER TOOLS TO OUTWIT YOU."

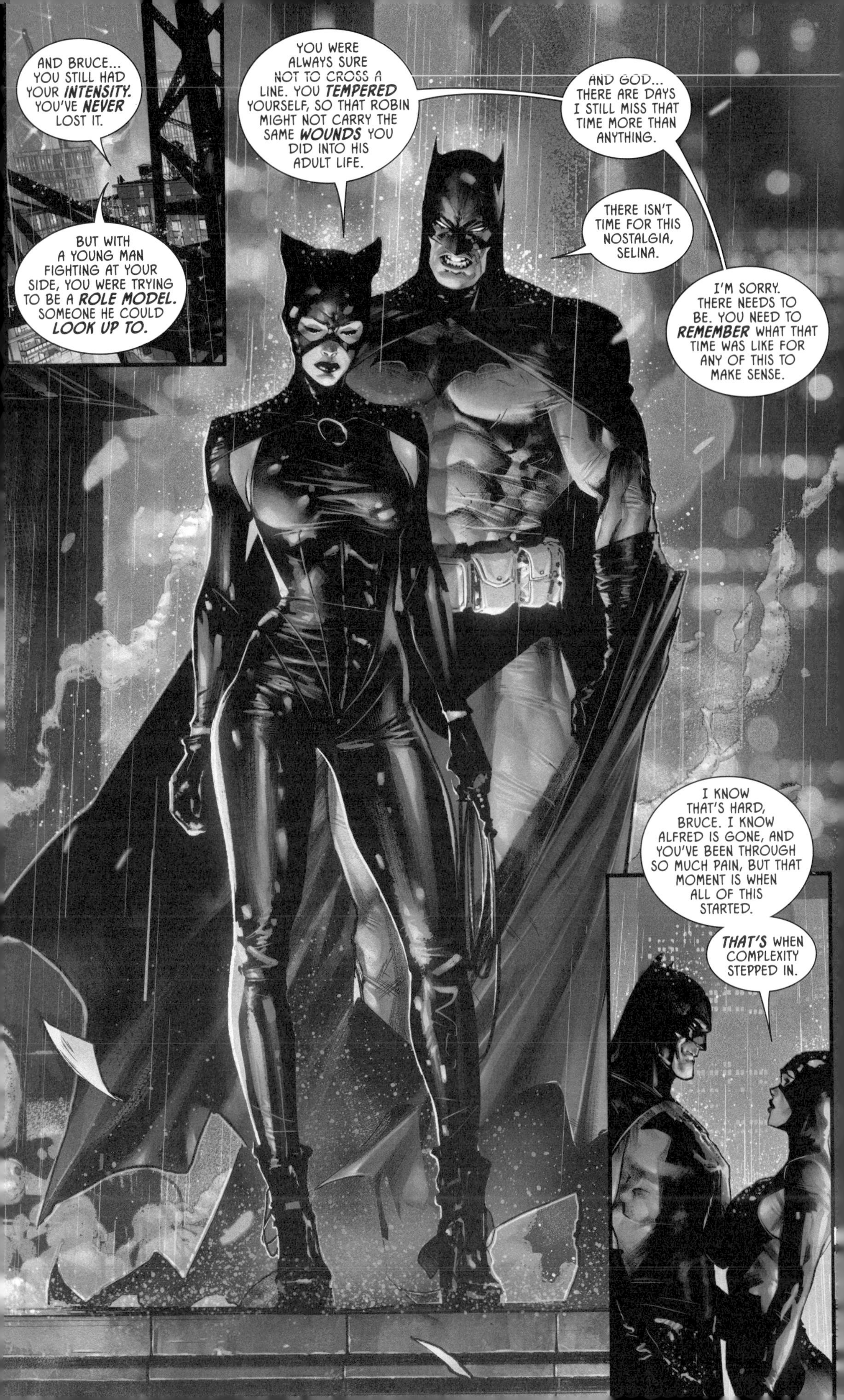
AND BRUCE... YOU STILL HAD YOUR INTENSITY. YOU'VE NEVER LOST IT.
BUT WITH A YOUNG MAN FIGHTING AT YOUR SIDE, YOU WERE TRYING TO BE A ROLE MODEL. SOMEONE HE COULD LOOK UP TO.
YOU WERE ALWAYS SURE NOT TO CROSS A LINE. YOU TEMPERED YOURSELF, SO THAT ROBIN MIGHT NOT CARRY THE SAME WOUNDS YOU DID INTO HIS ADULT LIFE.
AND GOD... THERE ARE DAYS I STILL MISS THAT TIME MORE THAN ANYTHING.
THERE ISN'T TIME FOR THIS NOSTALGIA, SELINA.
I'M SORRY. THERE NEEDS TO BE. YOU NEED TO REMEMBER WHAT THAT TIME WAS LIKE FOR ANY OF THIS TO MAKE SENSE.
I KNOW THAT'S HARD, BRUCE. I KNOW ALFRED IS GONE, AND YOU'VE BEEN THROUGH SO MUCH PAIN, BUT THAT MOMENT IS WHEN ALL OF THIS STARTED.
THAT'S WHEN COMPLEXITY STEPPED IN.

I THANK YOU ALL FOR JOINING ME AT TARTARUS HOUSE TONIGHT. I HAVE BEEN LOOKING FORWARD TO THIS DINNER FOR QUITE SOME TIME.

I HAVE BEEN WATCHING EACH OF YOUR CAREERS WITH GREAT FONDNESS, AND YOU HAVE IMPRESSED ME WITH YOUR SPIRIT AND YOUR STYLE.

BUT IN WATCHING, I HAVE SEEN YO[U] LOSE, TIME AN[D] TIME AGAIN...A[ND] THAT IS WHY [I] HAVE COME HERE.

TO OFFER MY.. EXPERTISE.

"IN MY YOUTH, I FACED A YOUNG ADVERSARY MUCH LIKE YOUR OWN. THE FINEST DETECTIVE THIS WORLD HAS EVER SEEN.

"IN THE BEGINNING, I THOUGHT OF HIM AS A NUISANCE. I WAS AFTER REAL, TANGIBLE ASSETS, AND HE WAS MERELY THE FLY IN MY OINTMENT. HE WOULD THWART ME AT EVERY TURN.

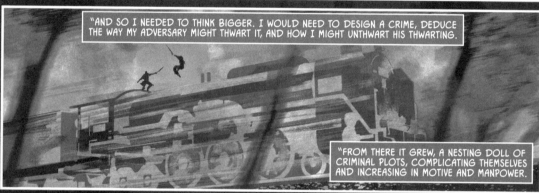

"AND SO I NEEDED TO THINK BIGGER. I WOULD NEED TO DESIGN A CRIME, DEDUCE THE WAY MY ADVERSARY MIGHT THWART IT, AND HOW I MIGHT UNTHWART HIS THWARTING.

"FROM THERE IT GREW, A NESTING DOLL OF CRIMINAL PLOTS, COMPLICATING THEMSELVES AND INCREASING IN MOTIVE AND MANPOWER.

"IN TIME, I WASN'T PLOTTING CRIMES FOR PERSONAL GAIN. I WAS SIMPLY TRYING TO BEAT THE DAMNED DETECTIVE AT HIS OWN GAME.

"VICTORY ELUDED ME AT EVERY TURN, AND I WAS DRIVEN TO THE BRINK OF MADNESS AND BEYOND...

"WHICH IS WHERE A SIMPLE TRUTH PRESENTED ITSELF TO ME, AND CHANGED MY LIFE."

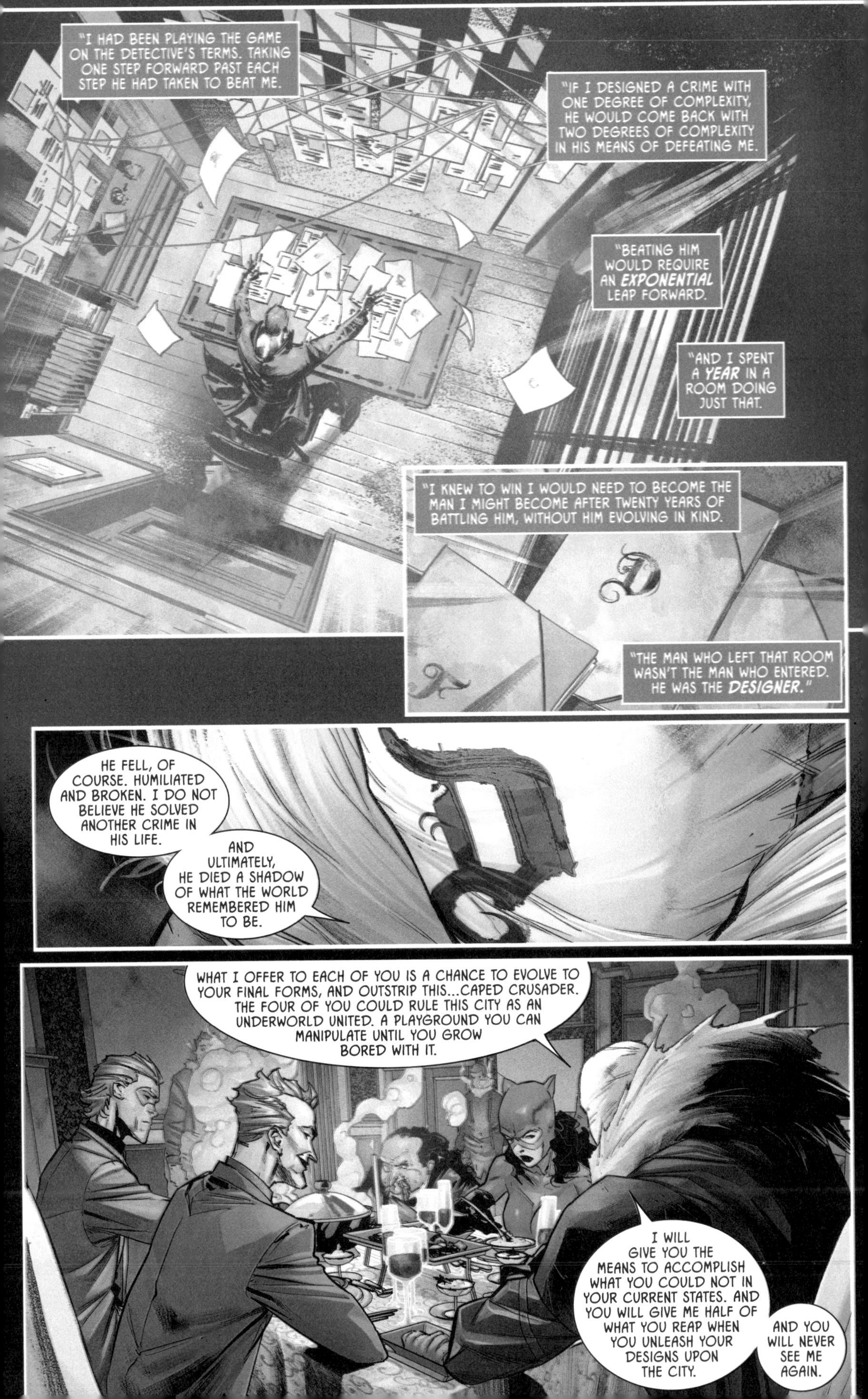
"I HAD BEEN PLAYING THE GAME ON THE DETECTIVE'S TERMS. TAKING ONE STEP FORWARD PAST EACH STEP HE HAD TAKEN TO BEAT ME.
"IF I DESIGNED A CRIME WITH ONE DEGREE OF COMPLEXITY, HE WOULD COME BACK WITH TWO DEGREES OF COMPLEXITY IN HIS MEANS OF DEFEATING ME.
"BEATING HIM WOULD REQUIRE AN *EXPONENTIAL* LEAP FORWARD.
"AND I SPENT A *YEAR* IN A ROOM DOING JUST THAT.
"I KNEW TO WIN I WOULD NEED TO BECOME THE MAN I MIGHT BECOME AFTER TWENTY YEARS OF BATTLING HIM, WITHOUT HIM EVOLVING IN KIND.
"THE MAN WHO LEFT THAT ROOM WASN'T THE MAN WHO ENTERED. HE WAS THE *DESIGNER*."
HE FELL, OF COURSE. HUMILIATED AND BROKEN. I DO NOT BELIEVE HE SOLVED ANOTHER CRIME IN HIS LIFE.
AND ULTIMATELY, HE DIED A SHADOW OF WHAT THE WORLD REMEMBERED HIM TO BE.
WHAT I OFFER TO EACH OF YOU IS A CHANCE TO EVOLVE TO YOUR FINAL FORMS, AND OUTSTRIP THIS...CAPED CRUSADER. THE FOUR OF YOU COULD RULE THIS CITY AS AN UNDERWORLD UNITED. A PLAYGROUND YOU CAN MANIPULATE UNTIL YOU GROW BORED WITH IT.
I WILL GIVE YOU THE MEANS TO ACCOMPLISH WHAT YOU COULD NOT IN YOUR CURRENT STATES. AND YOU WILL GIVE ME HALF OF WHAT YOU REAP WHEN YOU UNLEASH YOUR DESIGNS UPON THE CITY.
AND YOU WILL NEVER SEE ME AGAIN.

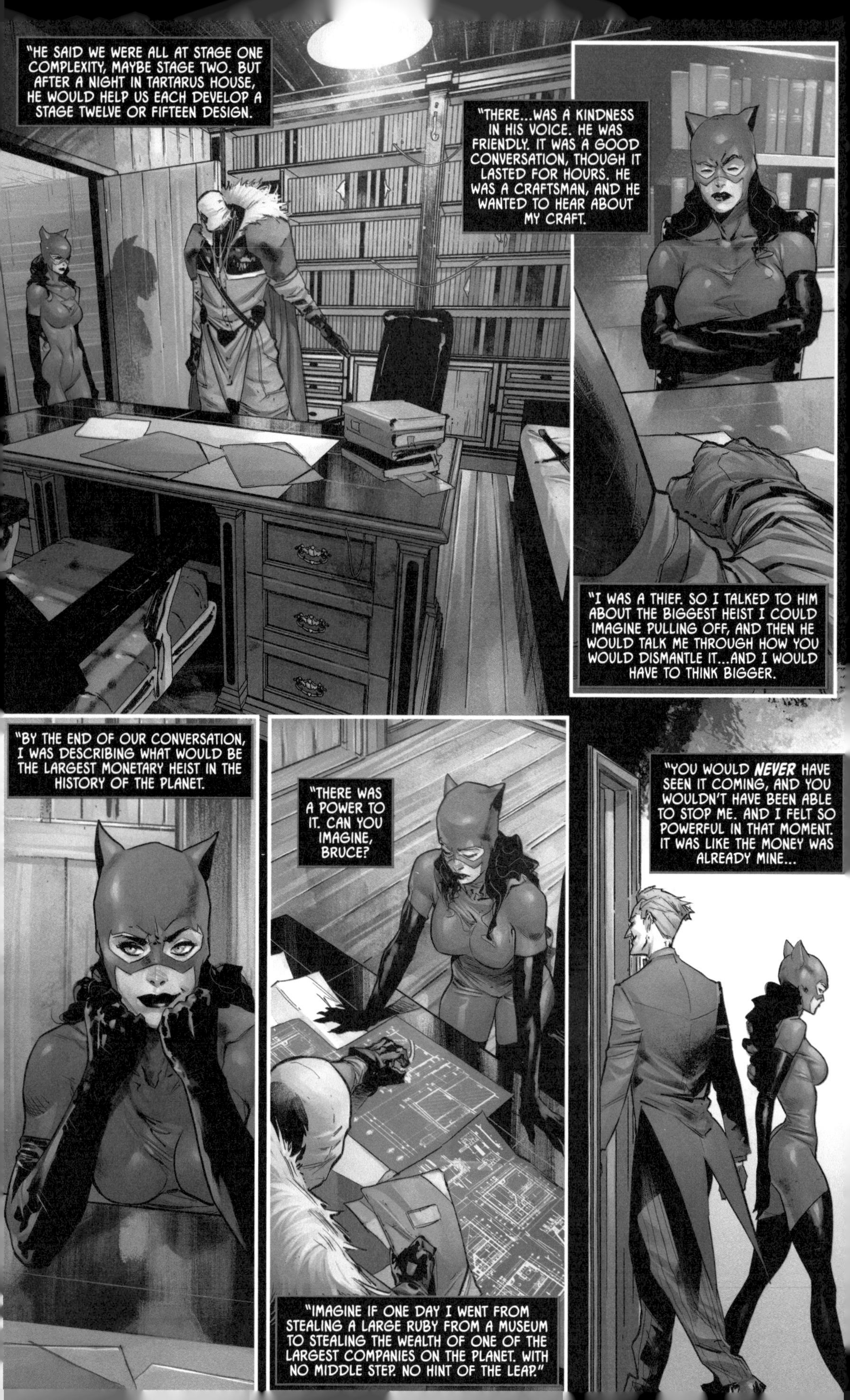

"HE SAID WE WERE ALL AT STAGE ONE COMPLEXITY, MAYBE STAGE TWO. BUT AFTER A NIGHT IN TARTARUS HOUSE, HE WOULD HELP US EACH DEVELOP A STAGE TWELVE OR FIFTEEN DESIGN.
"THERE...WAS A KINDNESS IN HIS VOICE. HE WAS FRIENDLY. IT WAS A GOOD CONVERSATION, THOUGH IT LASTED FOR HOURS. HE WAS A CRAFTSMAN, AND HE WANTED TO HEAR ABOUT MY CRAFT.
"I WAS A THIEF. SO I TALKED TO HIM ABOUT THE BIGGEST HEIST I COULD IMAGINE PULLING OFF, AND THEN HE WOULD TALK ME THROUGH HOW YOU WOULD DISMANTLE IT...AND I WOULD HAVE TO THINK BIGGER.
"BY THE END OF OUR CONVERSATION, I WAS DESCRIBING WHAT WOULD BE THE LARGEST MONETARY HEIST IN THE HISTORY OF THE PLANET.
"THERE WAS A POWER TO IT. CAN YOU IMAGINE, BRUCE?
"IMAGINE IF ONE DAY I WENT FROM STEALING A LARGE RUBY FROM A MUSEUM TO STEALING THE WEALTH OF ONE OF THE LARGEST COMPANIES ON THE PLANET. WITH NO MIDDLE STEP. NO HINT OF THE LEAP."
"YOU WOULD ***NEVER*** HAVE SEEN IT COMING, AND YOU WOULDN'T HAVE BEEN ABLE TO STOP ME. AND I FELT SO POWERFUL IN THAT MOMENT. IT WAS LIKE THE MONEY WAS ALREADY MINE...

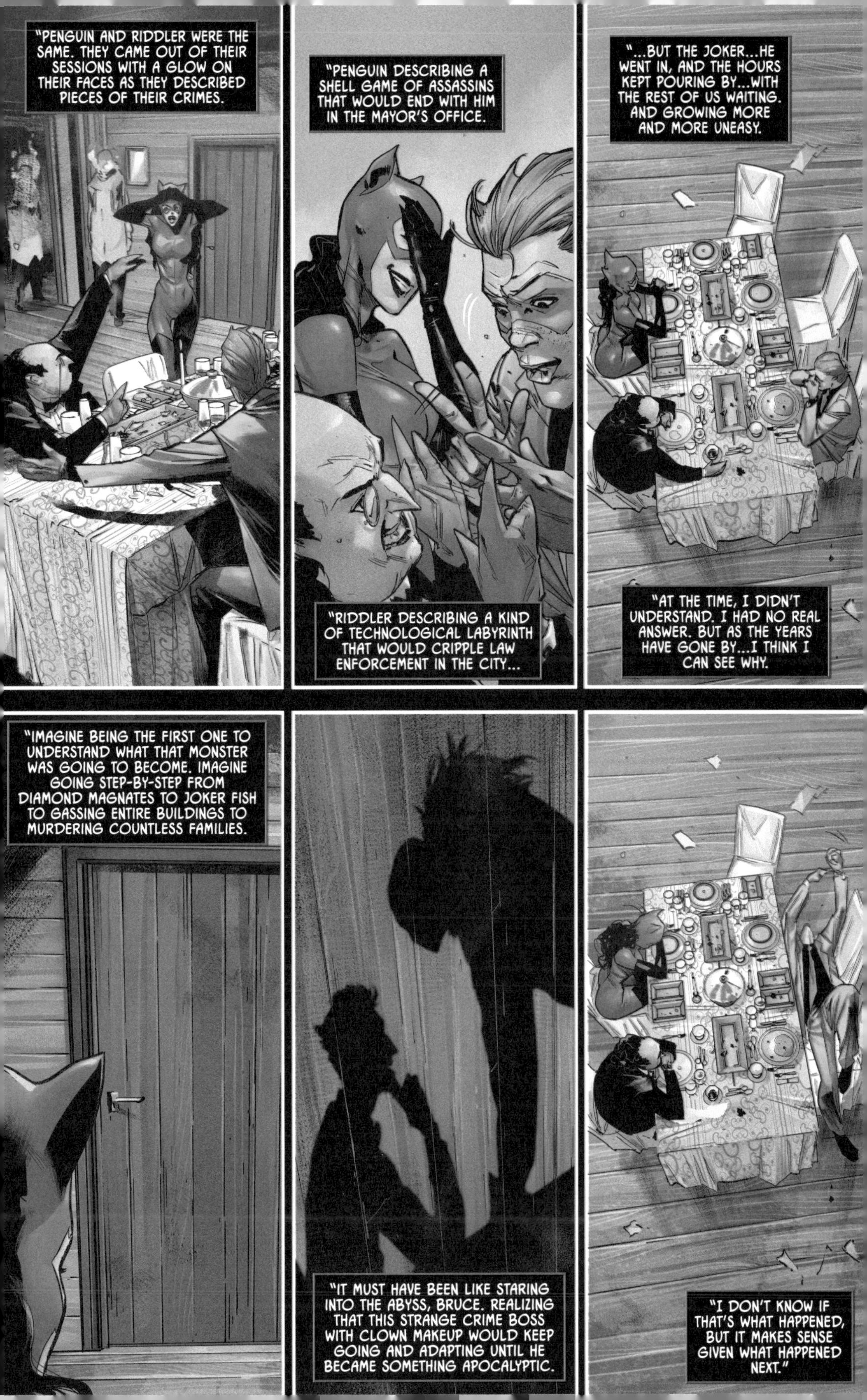
"PENGUIN AND RIDDLER WERE THE SAME. THEY CAME OUT OF THEIR SESSIONS WITH A GLOW ON THEIR FACES AS THEY DESCRIBED PIECES OF THEIR CRIMES.
"PENGUIN DESCRIBING A SHELL GAME OF ASSASSINS THAT WOULD END WITH HIM IN THE MAYOR'S OFFICE.
"RIDDLER DESCRIBING A KIND OF TECHNOLOGICAL LABYRINTH THAT WOULD CRIPPLE LAW ENFORCEMENT IN THE CITY...
"...BUT THE JOKER...HE WENT IN, AND THE HOURS KEPT POURING BY...WITH THE REST OF US WAITING. AND GROWING MORE AND MORE UNEASY.
"AT THE TIME, I DIDN'T UNDERSTAND. I HAD NO REAL ANSWER. BUT AS THE YEARS HAVE GONE BY...I THINK I CAN SEE WHY.
"IMAGINE BEING THE FIRST ONE TO UNDERSTAND WHAT THAT MONSTER WAS GOING TO BECOME. IMAGINE GOING STEP-BY-STEP FROM DIAMOND MAGNATES TO JOKER FISH TO GASSING ENTIRE BUILDINGS TO MURDERING COUNTLESS FAMILIES.
"IT MUST HAVE BEEN LIKE STARING INTO THE ABYSS, BRUCE. REALIZING THAT THIS STRANGE CRIME BOSS WITH CLOWN MAKEUP WOULD KEEP GOING AND ADAPTING UNTIL HE BECAME SOMETHING APOCALYPTIC.
"I DON'T KNOW IF THAT'S WHAT HAPPENED, BUT IT MAKES SENSE GIVEN WHAT HAPPENED NEXT."

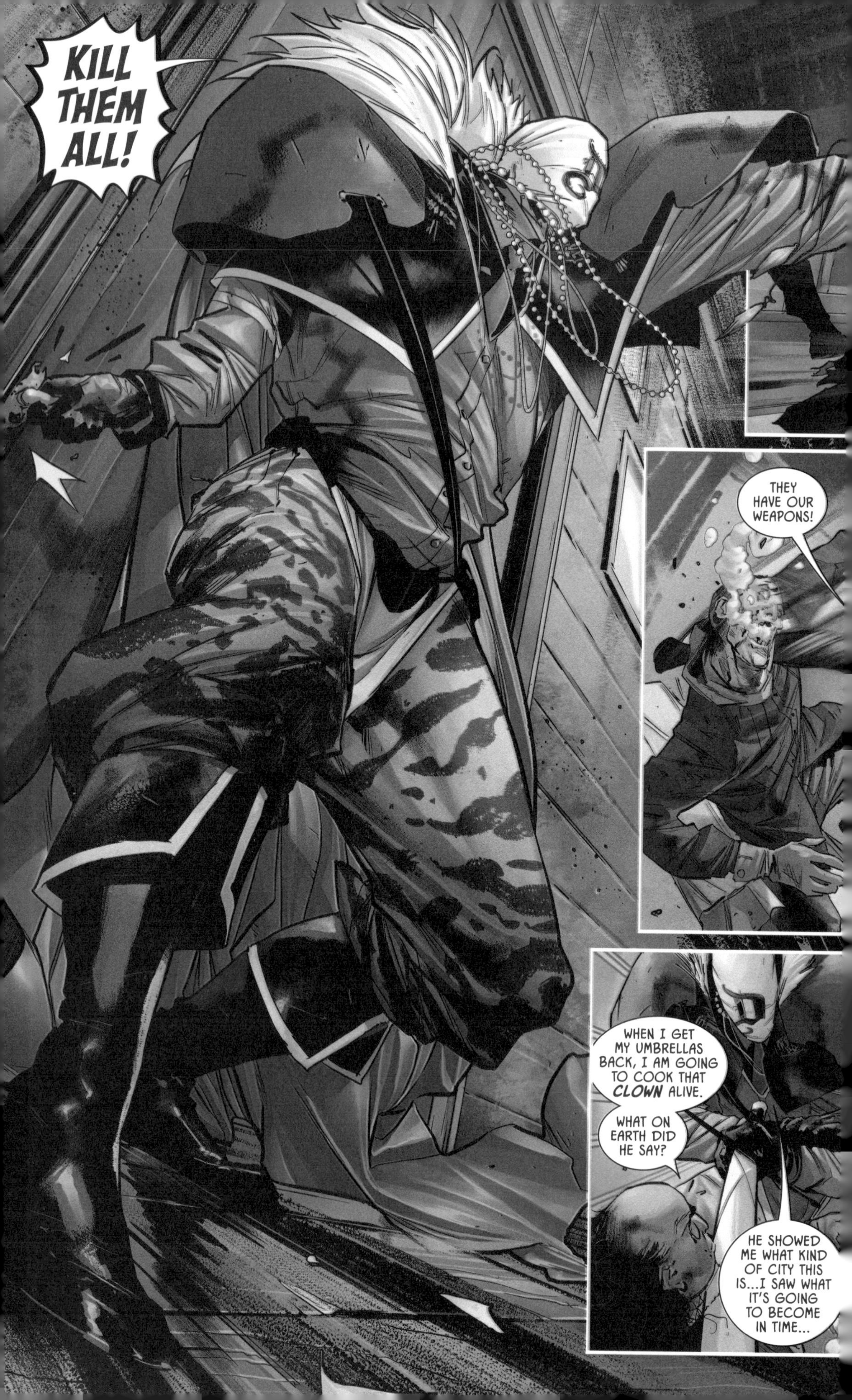
KILL THEM ALL!
THEY HAVE OUR WEAPONS!
WHEN I GET MY UMBRELLAS BACK, I AM GOING TO COOK THAT **CLOWN** ALIVE.
WHAT ON EARTH DID HE SAY?
HE SHOWED ME WHAT KIND OF CITY THIS IS...I SAW WHAT IT'S GOING TO BECOME IN TIME...

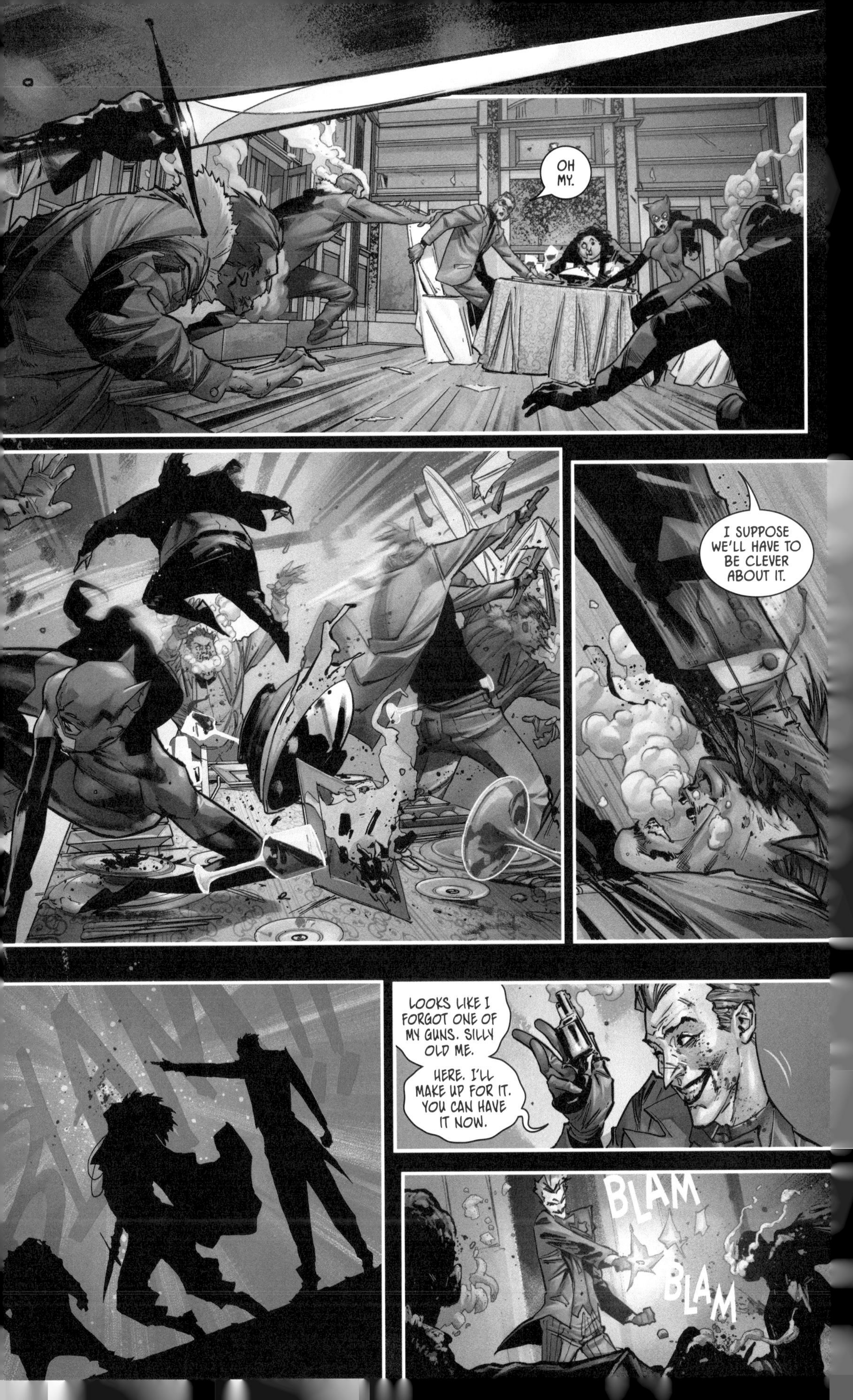
OH MY.
I SUPPOSE WE'LL HAVE TO BE CLEVER ABOUT IT.
LOOKS LIKE I FORGOT ONE OF MY GUNS. SILLY OLD ME.
HERE. I'LL MAKE UP FOR IT. YOU CAN HAVE IT NOW.
BLAM
BLAM

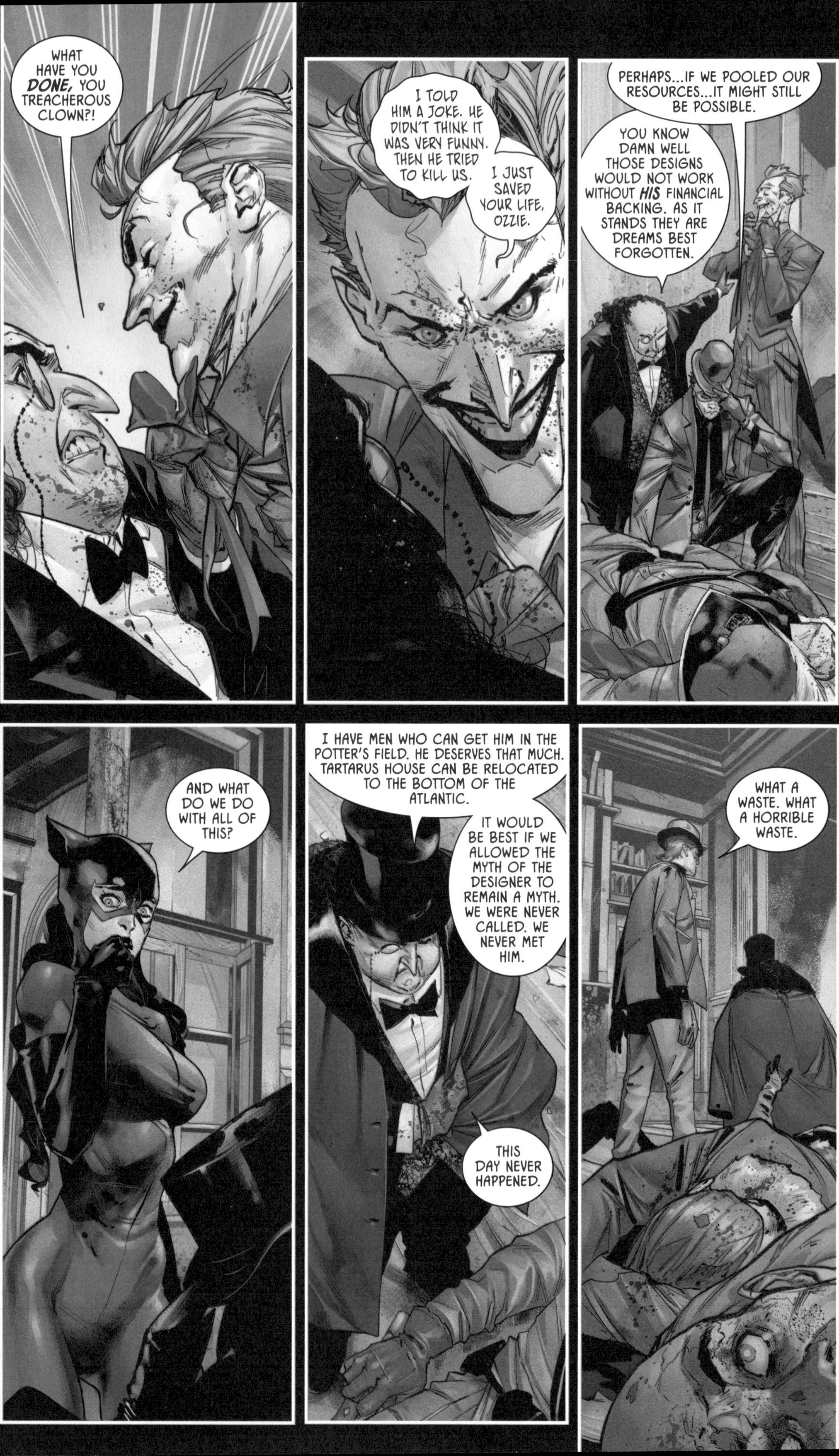
WHAT HAVE YOU *DONE,* YOU TREACHEROUS CLOWN?!
I TOLD HIM A JOKE. HE DIDN'T THINK IT WAS VERY FUNNY. THEN HE TRIED TO KILL US.
I JUST SAVED YOUR LIFE, OZZIE.
PERHAPS...IF WE POOLED OUR RESOURCES...IT MIGHT STILL BE POSSIBLE.
YOU KNOW DAMN WELL THOSE DESIGNS WOULD NOT WORK WITHOUT *HIS* FINANCIAL BACKING. AS IT STANDS THEY ARE DREAMS BEST FORGOTTEN.
AND WHAT DO WE DO WITH ALL OF THIS?
I HAVE MEN WHO CAN GET HIM IN THE POTTER'S FIELD. HE DESERVES THAT MUCH. TARTARUS HOUSE CAN BE RELOCATED TO THE BOTTOM OF THE ATLANTIC.
IT WOULD BE BEST IF WE ALLOWED THE MYTH OF THE DESIGNER TO REMAIN A MYTH. WE WERE NEVER CALLED. WE NEVER MET HIM.
THIS DAY NEVER HAPPENED.
WHAT A WASTE. WHAT A HORRIBLE WASTE.

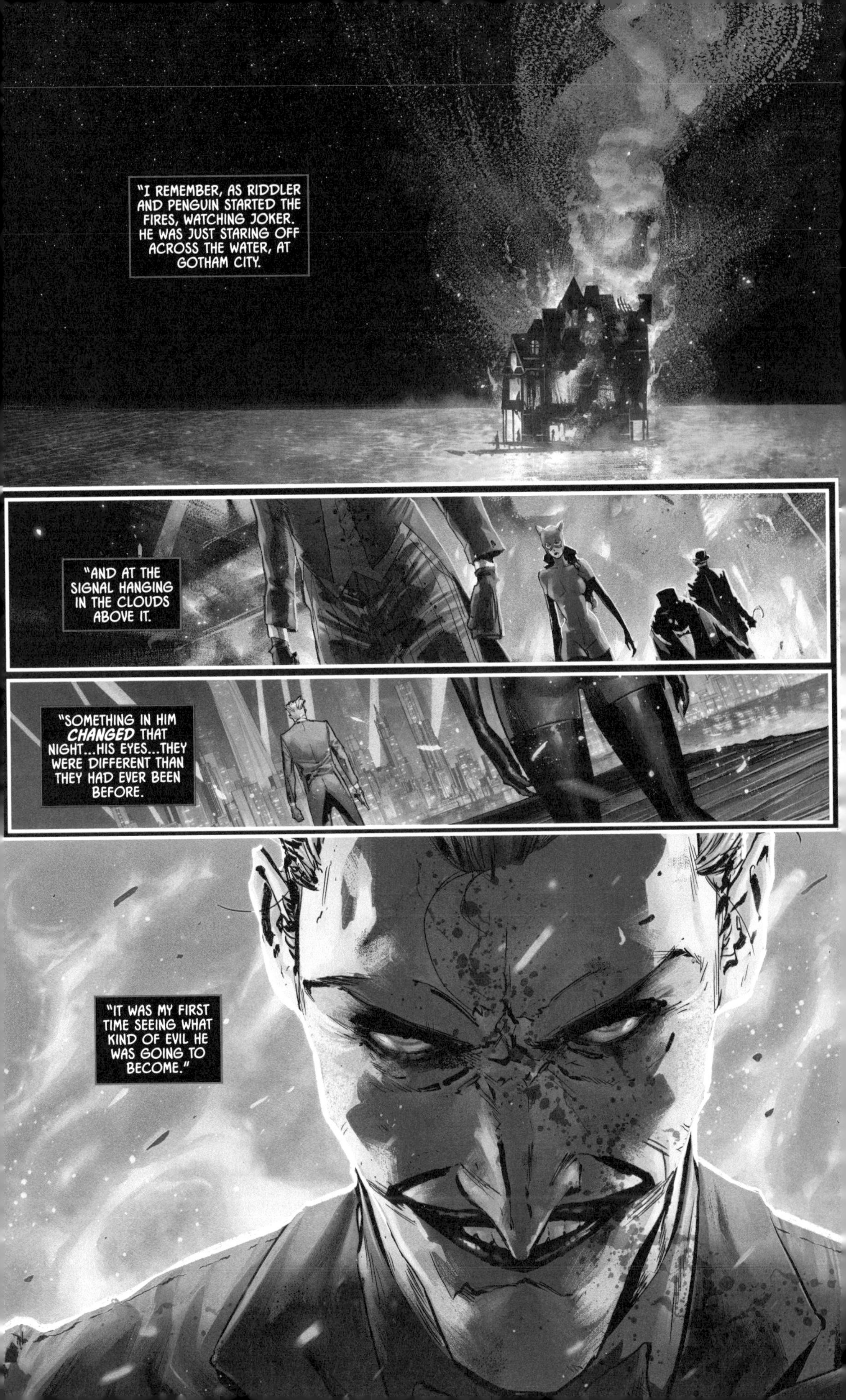
"I REMEMBER, AS RIDDLER AND PENGUIN STARTED THE FIRES, WATCHING JOKER. HE WAS JUST STARING OFF ACROSS THE WATER, AT GOTHAM CITY.
"AND AT THE SIGNAL HANGING IN THE CLOUDS ABOVE IT.
"SOMETHING IN HIM *CHANGED* THAT NIGHT...HIS EYES...THEY WERE DIFFERENT THAN THEY HAD EVER BEEN BEFORE.
"IT WAS MY FIRST TIME SEEING WHAT KIND OF EVIL HE WAS GOING TO BECOME."

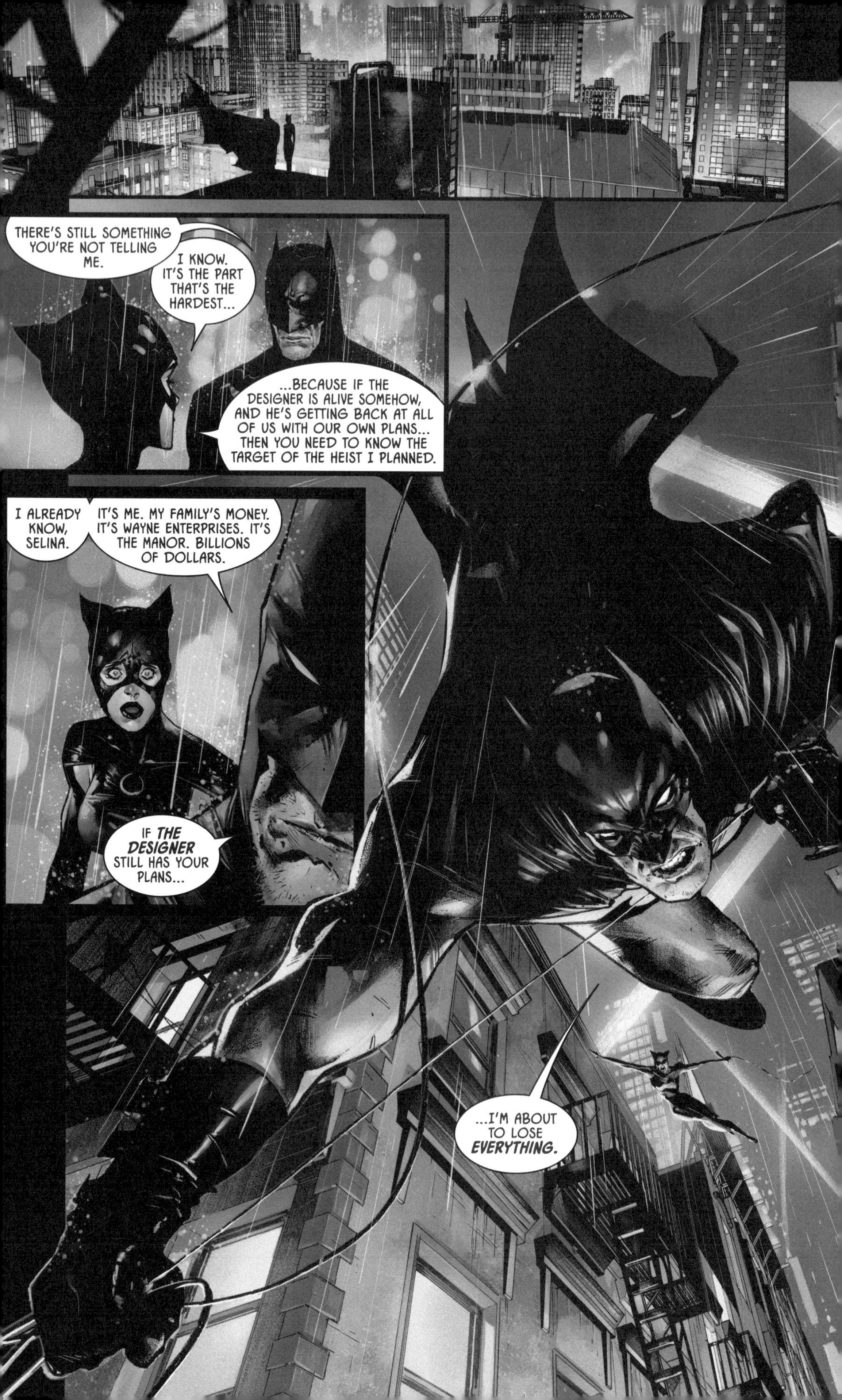
THERE'S STILL SOMETHING YOU'RE NOT TELLING ME.
I KNOW. IT'S THE PART THAT'S THE HARDEST...
...BECAUSE IF THE DESIGNER IS ALIVE SOMEHOW, AND HE'S GETTING BACK AT ALL OF US WITH OUR OWN PLANS... THEN YOU NEED TO KNOW THE TARGET OF THE HEIST I PLANNED.
I ALREADY KNOW, SELINA.
IT'S ME. MY FAMILY'S MONEY. IT'S WAYNE ENTERPRISES. IT'S THE MANOR. BILLIONS OF DOLLARS.
IF *THE DESIGNER* STILL HAS YOUR PLANS...
...I'M ABOUT TO LOSE *EVERYTHING.*

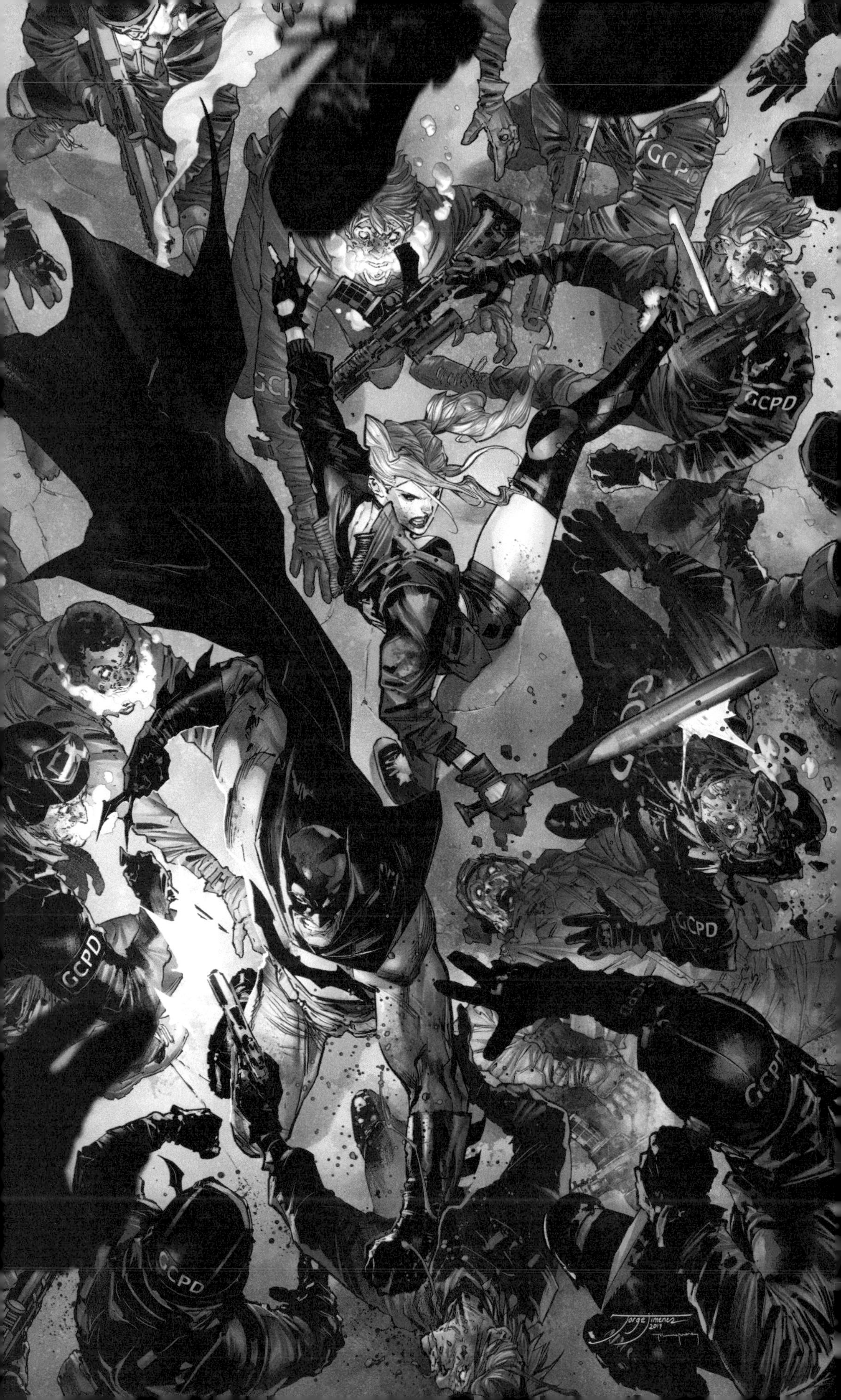
GCPD
GCPD
GCPD
GCPD
GCPD
Jorge Jimenez 2019

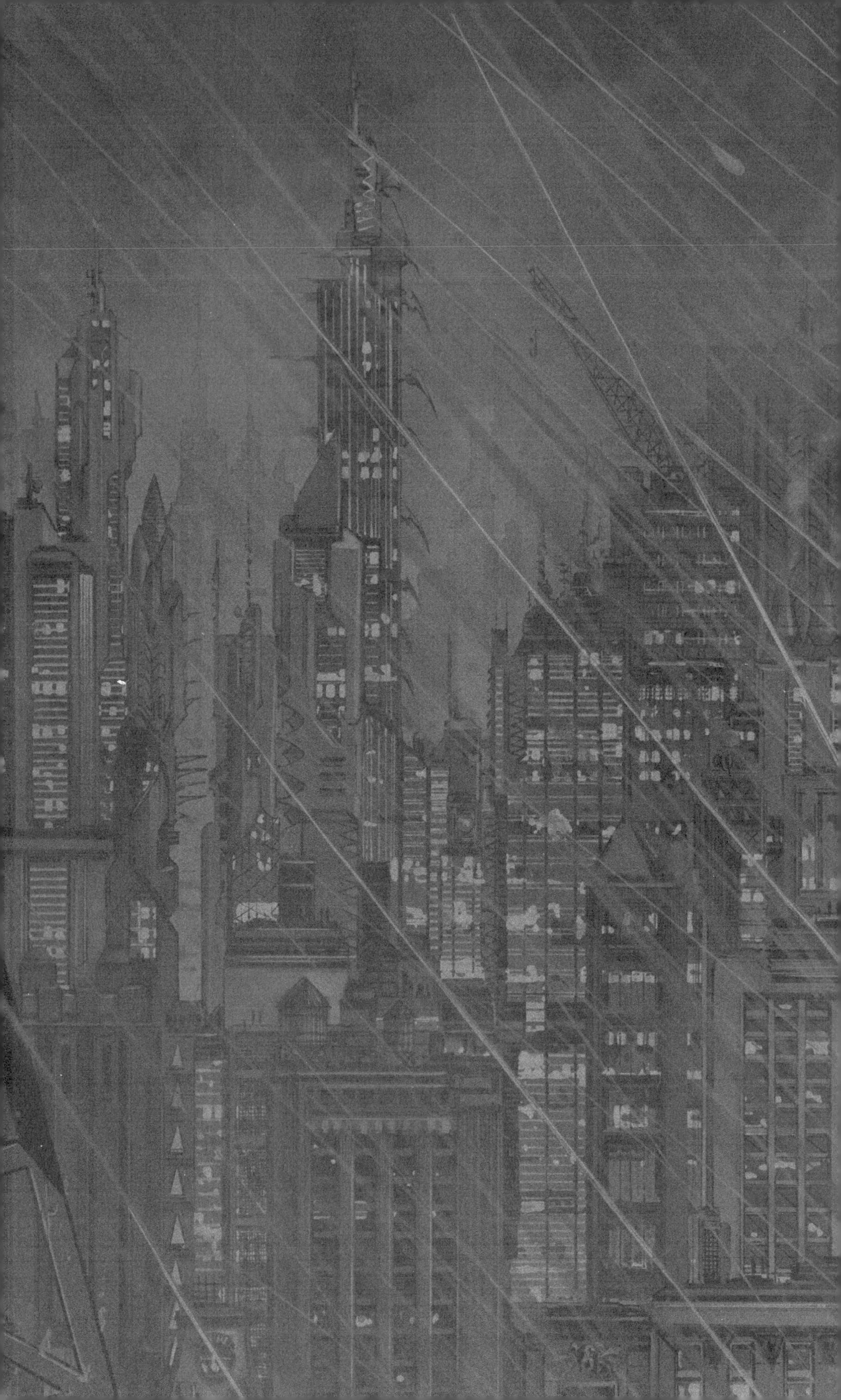

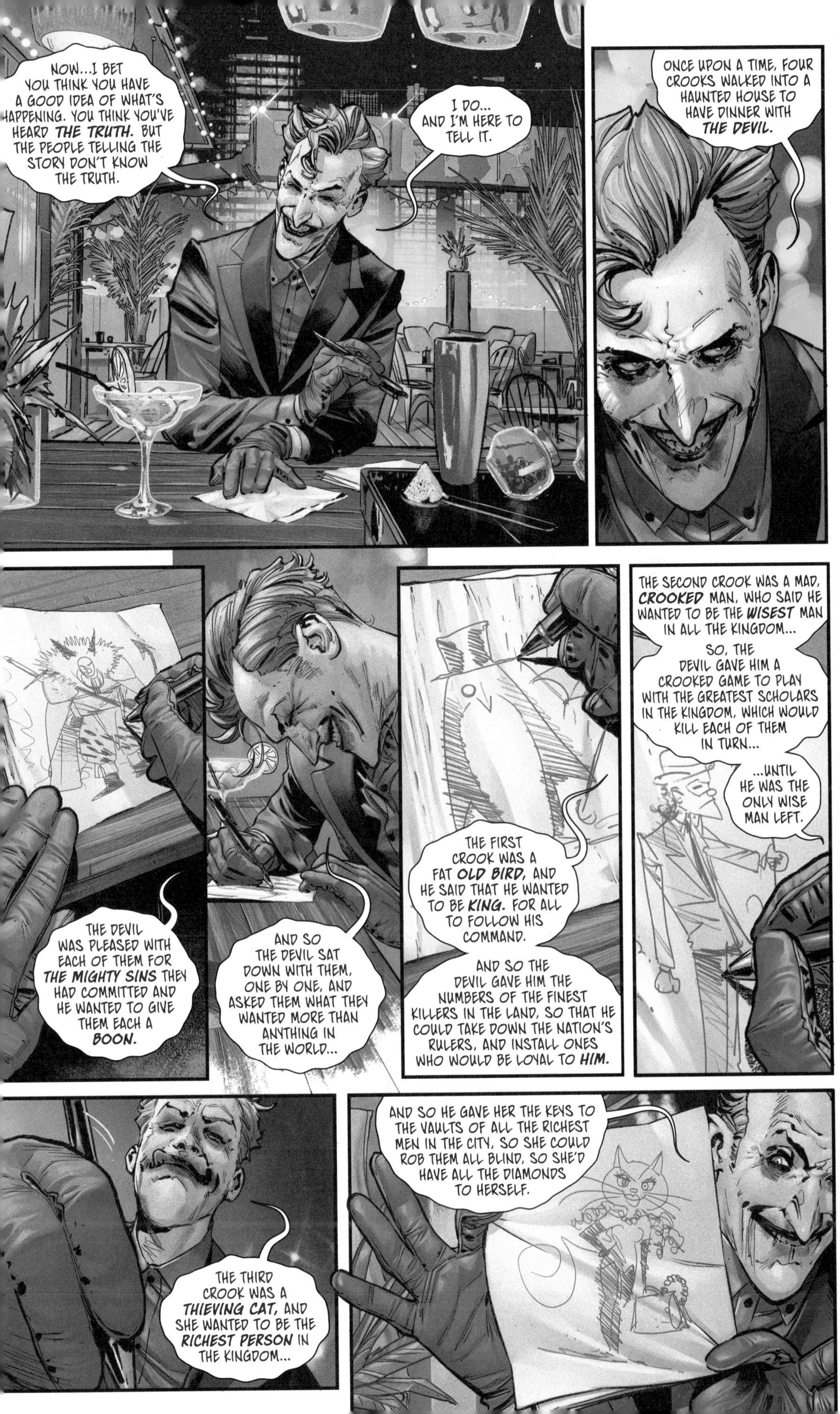
NOW...I BET YOU THINK YOU HAVE A GOOD IDEA OF WHAT'S HAPPENING. YOU THINK YOU'VE HEARD THE TRUTH. BUT THE PEOPLE TELLING THE STORY DON'T KNOW THE TRUTH.
I DO... AND I'M HERE TO TELL IT.
ONCE UPON A TIME, FOUR CROOKS WALKED INTO A HAUNTED HOUSE TO HAVE DINNER WITH THE DEVIL.
THE DEVIL WAS PLEASED WITH EACH OF THEM FOR THE MIGHTY SINS THEY HAD COMMITTED AND HE WANTED TO GIVE THEM EACH A BOON.
AND SO THE DEVIL SAT DOWN WITH THEM, ONE BY ONE, AND ASKED THEM WHAT THEY WANTED MORE THAN ANYTHING IN THE WORLD...
THE FIRST CROOK WAS A FAT OLD BIRD, AND HE SAID THAT HE WANTED TO BE KING. FOR ALL TO FOLLOW HIS COMMAND.
AND SO THE DEVIL GAVE HIM THE NUMBERS OF THE FINEST KILLERS IN THE LAND, SO THAT HE COULD TAKE DOWN THE NATION'S RULERS, AND INSTALL ONES WHO WOULD BE LOYAL TO HIM.
THE SECOND CROOK WAS A MAD, CROOKED MAN, WHO SAID HE WANTED TO BE THE WISEST MAN IN ALL THE KINGDOM...
SO, THE DEVIL GAVE HIM A CROOKED GAME TO PLAY WITH THE GREATEST SCHOLARS IN THE KINGDOM, WHICH WOULD KILL EACH OF THEM IN TURN...
...UNTIL HE WAS THE ONLY WISE MAN LEFT.
THE THIRD CROOK WAS A THIEVING CAT, AND SHE WANTED TO BE THE RICHEST PERSON IN THE KINGDOM...
AND SO HE GAVE HER THE KEYS TO THE VAULTS OF ALL THE RICHEST MEN IN THE CITY, SO SHE COULD ROB THEM ALL BLIND, SO SHE'D HAVE ALL THE DIAMONDS TO HERSELF.

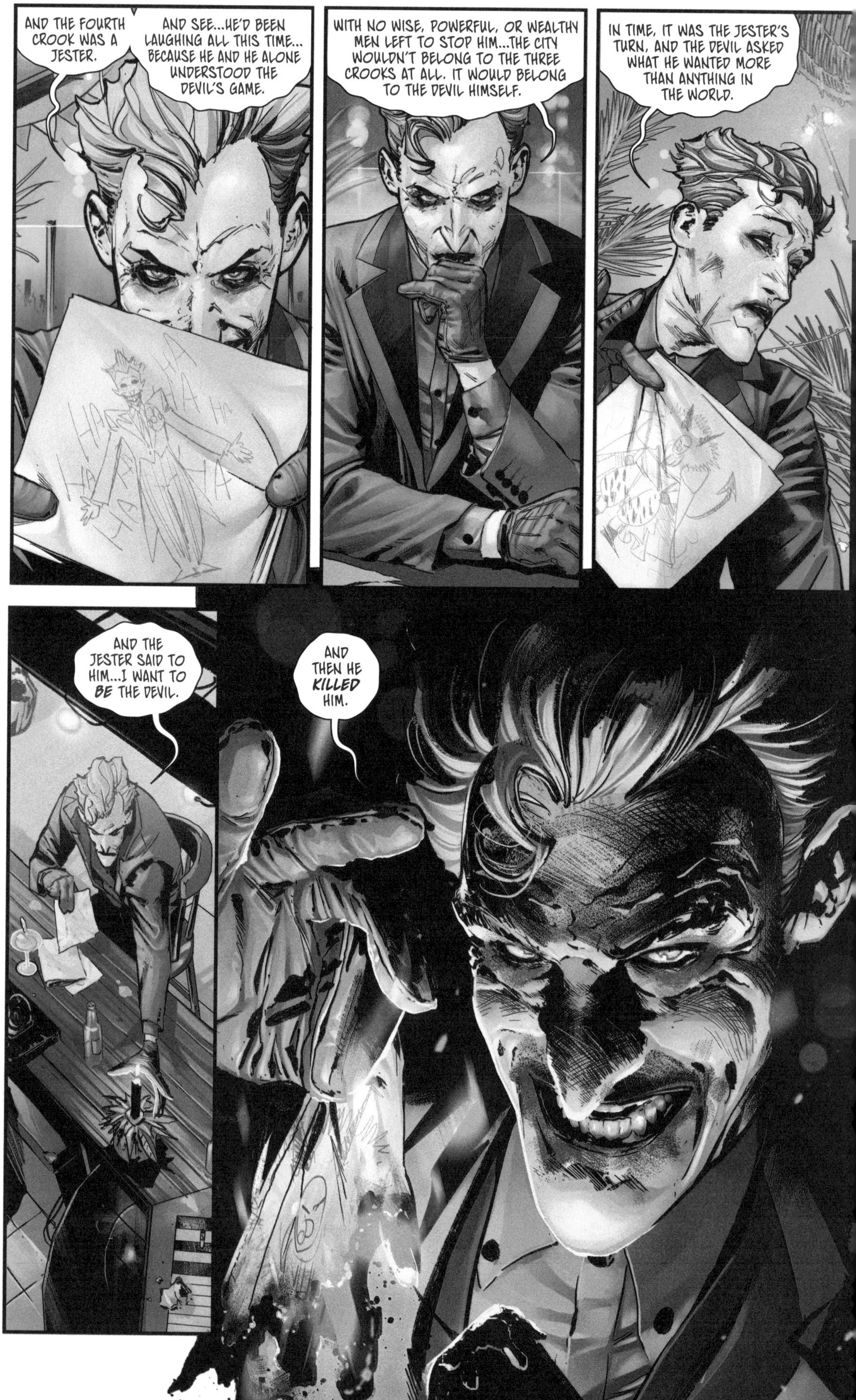
AND THE FOURTH CROOK WAS A JESTER.
AND SEE...HE'D BEEN LAUGHING ALL THIS TIME... BECAUSE HE AND HE ALONE UNDERSTOOD THE DEVIL'S GAME.
WITH NO WISE, POWERFUL, OR WEALTHY MEN LEFT TO STOP HIM...THE CITY WOULDN'T BELONG TO THE THREE CROOKS AT ALL. IT WOULD BELONG TO THE DEVIL HIMSELF.
IN TIME, IT WAS THE JESTER'S TURN, AND THE DEVIL ASKED WHAT HE WANTED MORE THAN ANYTHING IN THE WORLD.
AND THE JESTER SAID TO HIM...I WANT TO *BE* THE DEVIL.
AND THEN HE *KILLED* HIM.

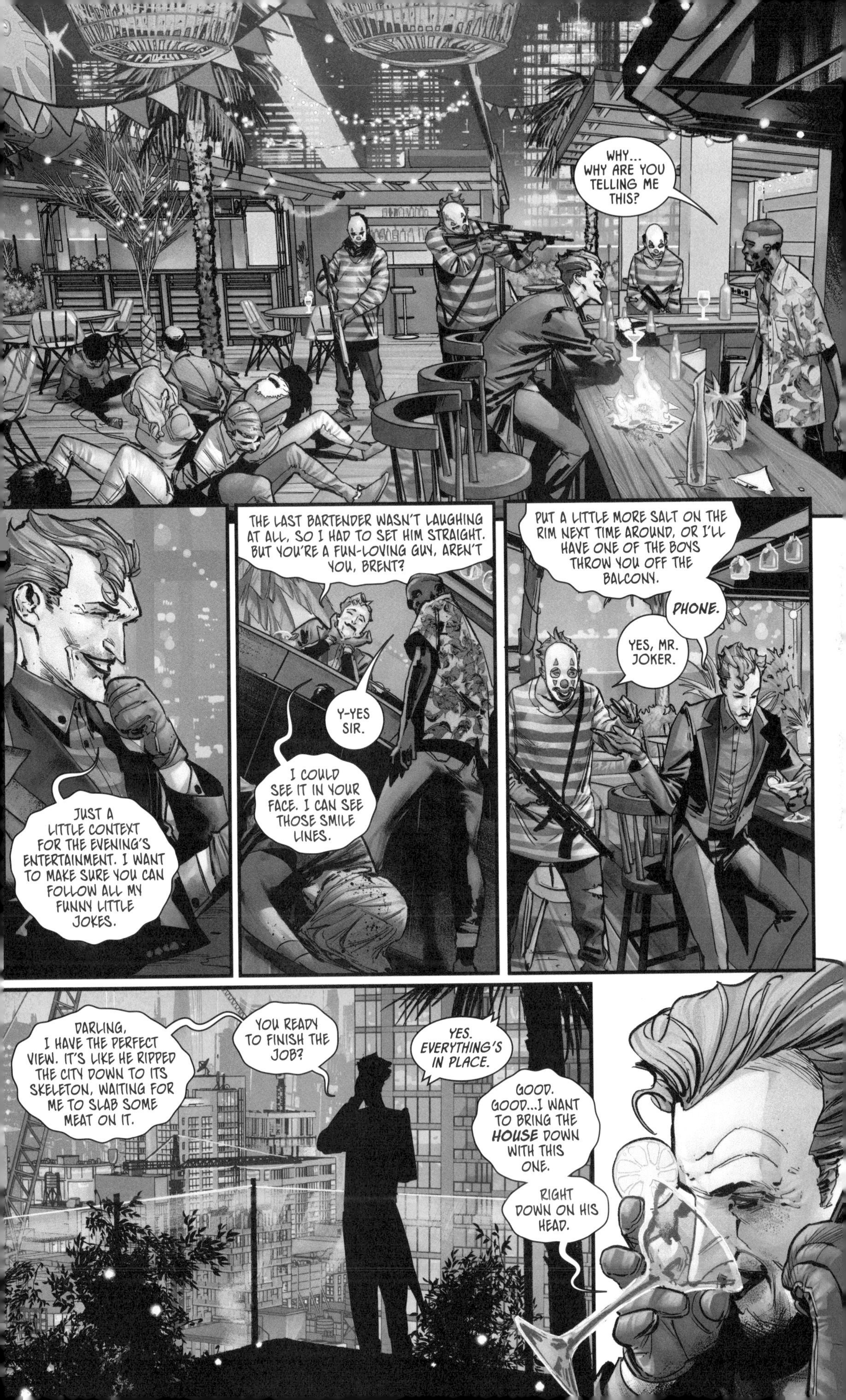

WHY... WHY ARE YOU TELLING ME THIS?
JUST A LITTLE CONTEXT FOR THE EVENING'S ENTERTAINMENT. I WANT TO MAKE SURE YOU CAN FOLLOW ALL MY FUNNY LITTLE JOKES.
THE LAST BARTENDER WASN'T LAUGHING AT ALL, SO I HAD TO SET HIM STRAIGHT. BUT YOU'RE A FUN-LOVING GUY, AREN'T YOU, BRENT?
Y-YES SIR.
I COULD SEE IT IN YOUR FACE. I CAN SEE THOSE SMILE LINES.
PUT A LITTLE MORE SALT ON THE RIM NEXT TIME AROUND, OR I'LL HAVE ONE OF THE BOYS THROW YOU OFF THE BALCONY.
PHONE.
YES, MR. JOKER.
DARLING, I HAVE THE PERFECT VIEW. IT'S LIKE HE RIPPED THE CITY DOWN TO ITS SKELETON, WAITING FOR ME TO SLAB SOME MEAT ON IT.
YOU READY TO FINISH THE JOB?
YES. EVERYTHING'S IN PLACE.
GOOD. GOOD...I WANT TO BRING THE HOUSE DOWN WITH THIS ONE.
RIGHT DOWN ON HIS HEAD.

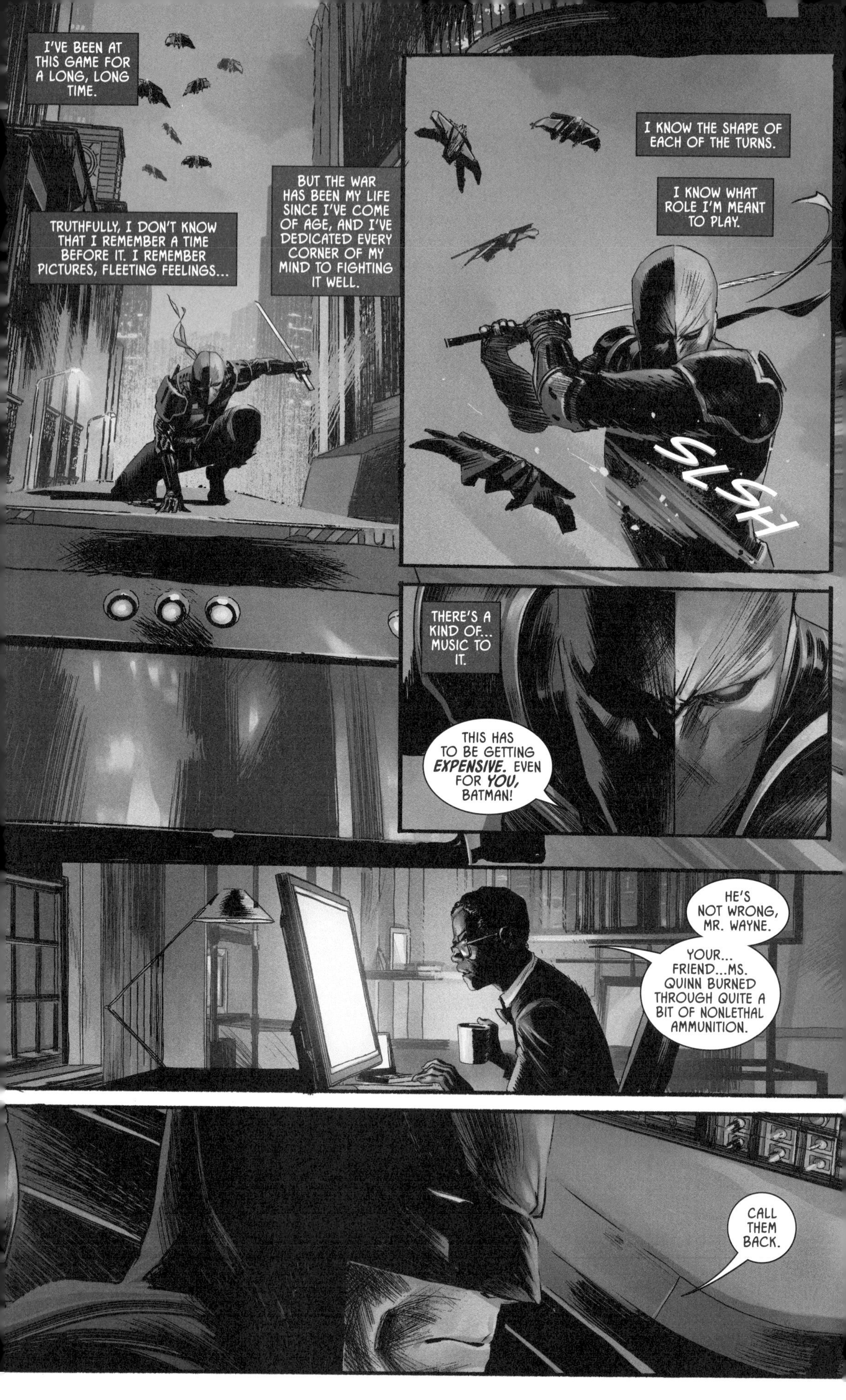
I'VE BEEN AT THIS GAME FOR A LONG, LONG TIME.
TRUTHFULLY, I DON'T KNOW THAT I REMEMBER A TIME BEFORE IT. I REMEMBER PICTURES, FLEETING FEELINGS...
BUT THE WAR HAS BEEN MY LIFE SINCE I'VE COME OF AGE, AND I'VE DEDICATED EVERY CORNER OF MY MIND TO FIGHTING IT WELL.
I KNOW THE SHAPE OF EACH OF THE TURNS.
I KNOW WHAT ROLE I'M MEANT TO PLAY.
SLSH
THERE'S A KIND OF... MUSIC TO IT.
THIS HAS TO BE GETTING EXPENSIVE. EVEN FOR YOU, BATMAN!
HE'S NOT WRONG, MR. WAYNE.
YOUR... FRIEND...MS. QUINN BURNED THROUGH QUITE A BIT OF NONLETHAL AMMUNITION.
CALL THEM BACK.

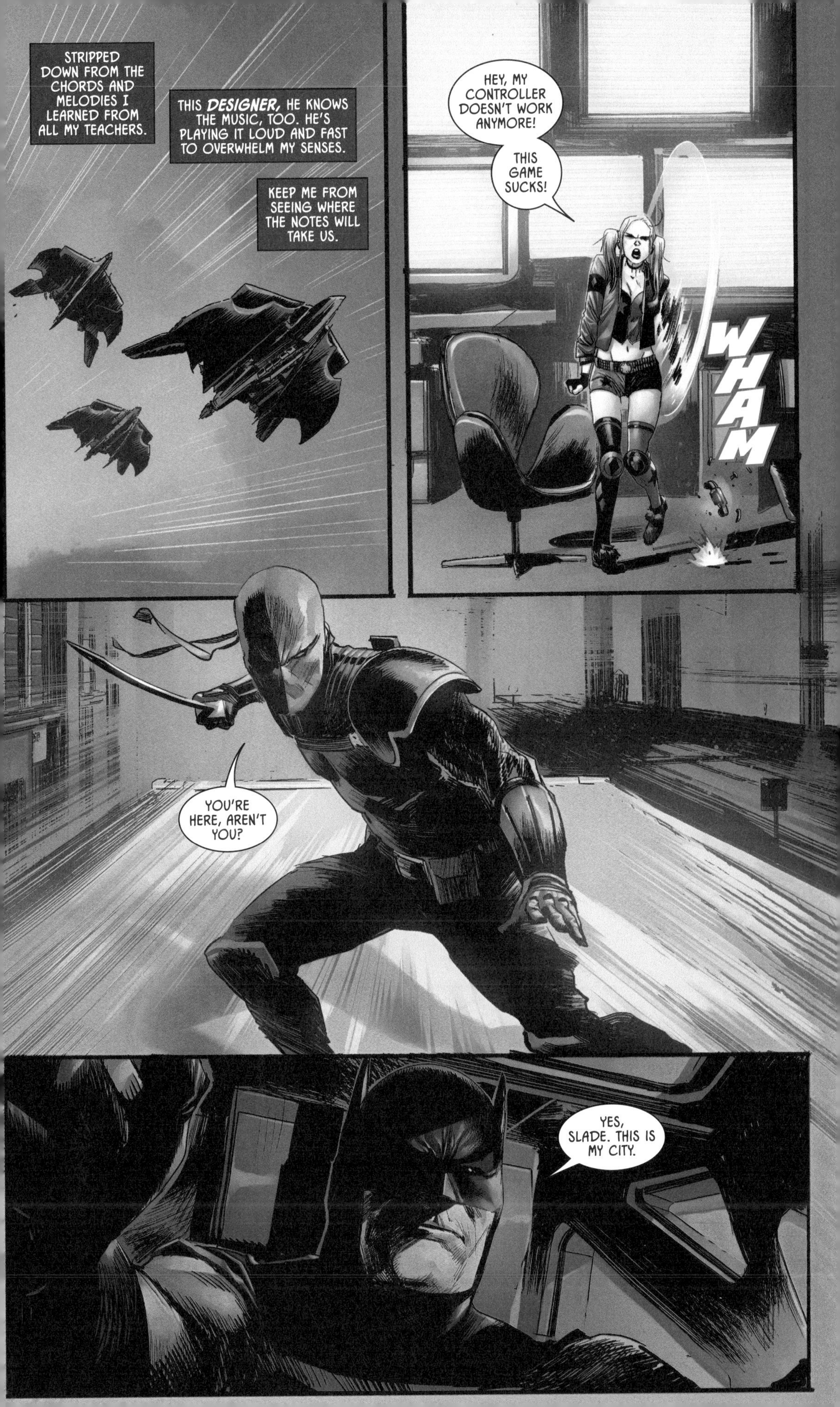
STRIPPED DOWN FROM THE CHORDS AND MELODIES I LEARNED FROM ALL MY TEACHERS.
THIS DESIGNER, HE KNOWS THE MUSIC, TOO. HE'S PLAYING IT LOUD AND FAST TO OVERWHELM MY SENSES.
KEEP ME FROM SEEING WHERE THE NOTES WILL TAKE US.
HEY, MY CONTROLLER DOESN'T WORK ANYMORE!
THIS GAME SUCKS!
WHAM
YOU'RE HERE, AREN'T YOU?
YES, SLADE. THIS IS MY CITY.

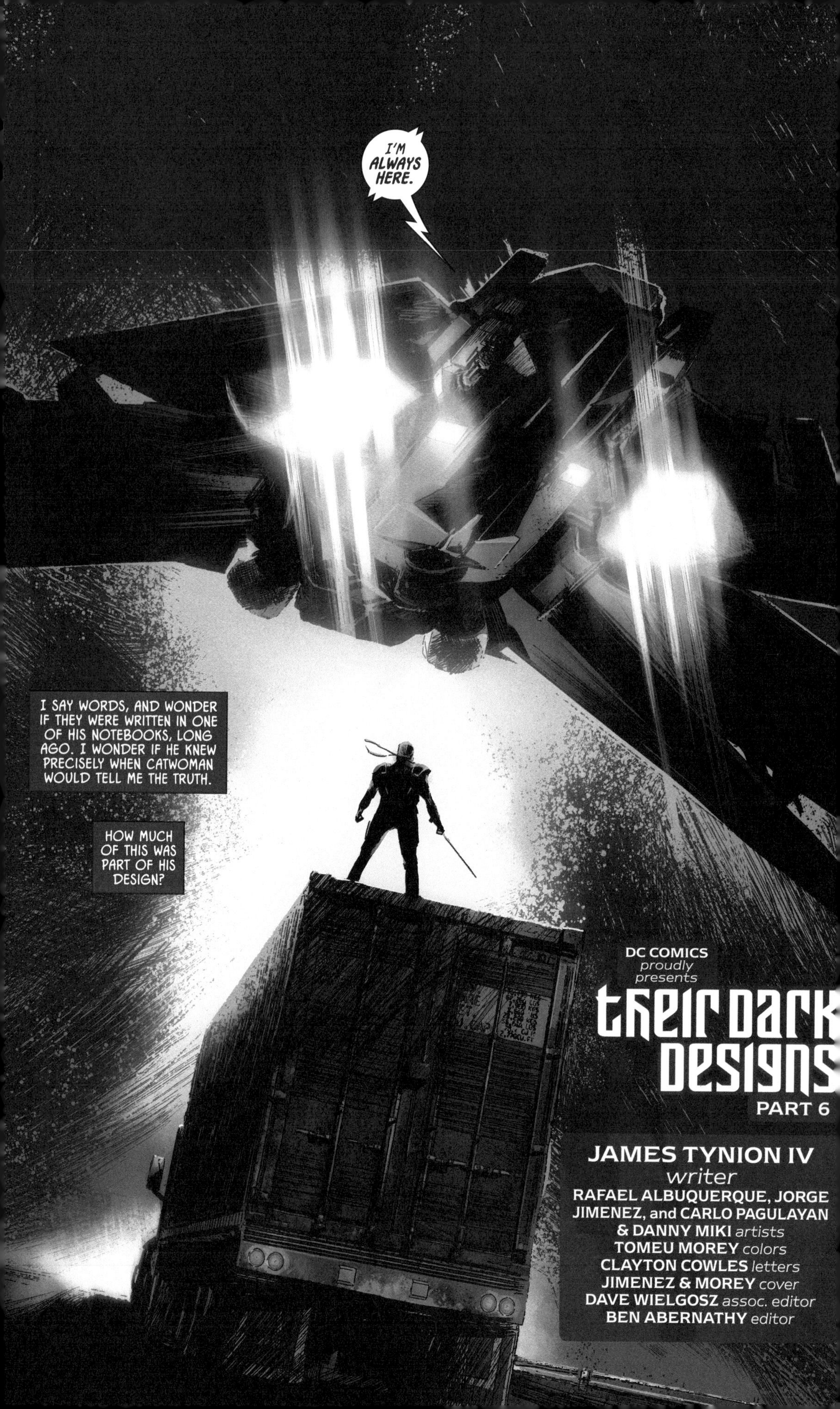

I'M ALWAYS HERE.
I SAY WORDS, AND WONDER IF THEY WERE WRITTEN IN ONE OF HIS NOTEBOOKS, LONG AGO. I WONDER IF HE KNEW PRECISELY WHEN CATWOMAN WOULD TELL ME THE TRUTH.
HOW MUCH OF THIS WAS PART OF HIS DESIGN?
DC COMICS proudly presents
THEIR DARK DESIGNS
PART 6
JAMES TYNION IV writer
RAFAEL ALBUQUERQUE, JORGE JIMENEZ, and CARLO PAGULAYAN & DANNY MIKI artists
TOMEU MOREY colors
CLAYTON COWLES letters
JIMENEZ & MOREY cover
DAVE WIELGOSZ assoc. editor
BEN ABERNATHY editor

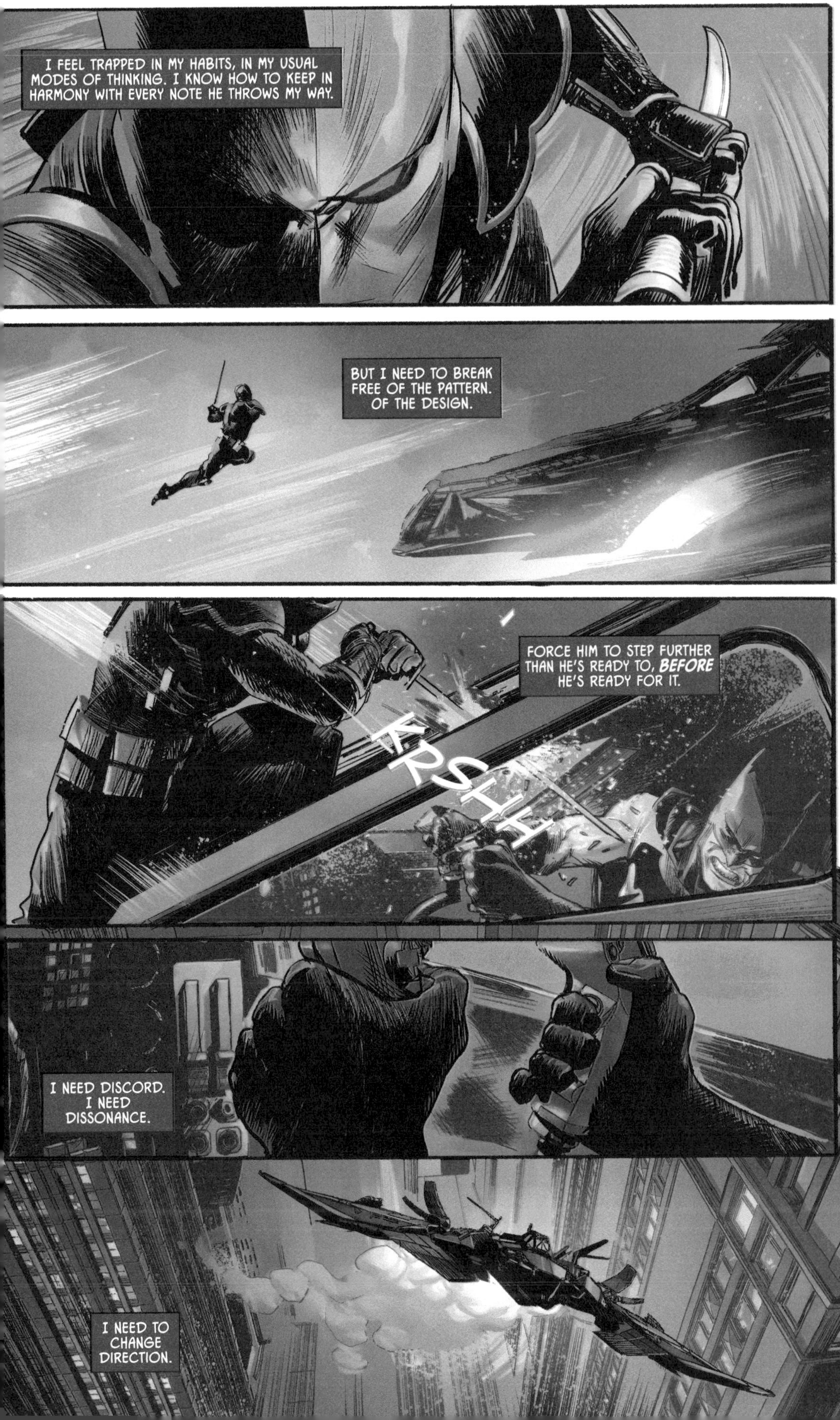
I FEEL TRAPPED IN MY HABITS, IN MY USUAL MODES OF THINKING. I KNOW HOW TO KEEP IN HARMONY WITH EVERY NOTE HE THROWS MY WAY.
BUT I NEED TO BREAK FREE OF THE PATTERN. OF THE DESIGN.
FORCE HIM TO STEP FURTHER THAN HE'S READY TO, *BEFORE* HE'S READY FOR IT.
KRSHH
I NEED DISCORD. I NEED DISSONANCE.
I NEED TO CHANGE DIRECTION.

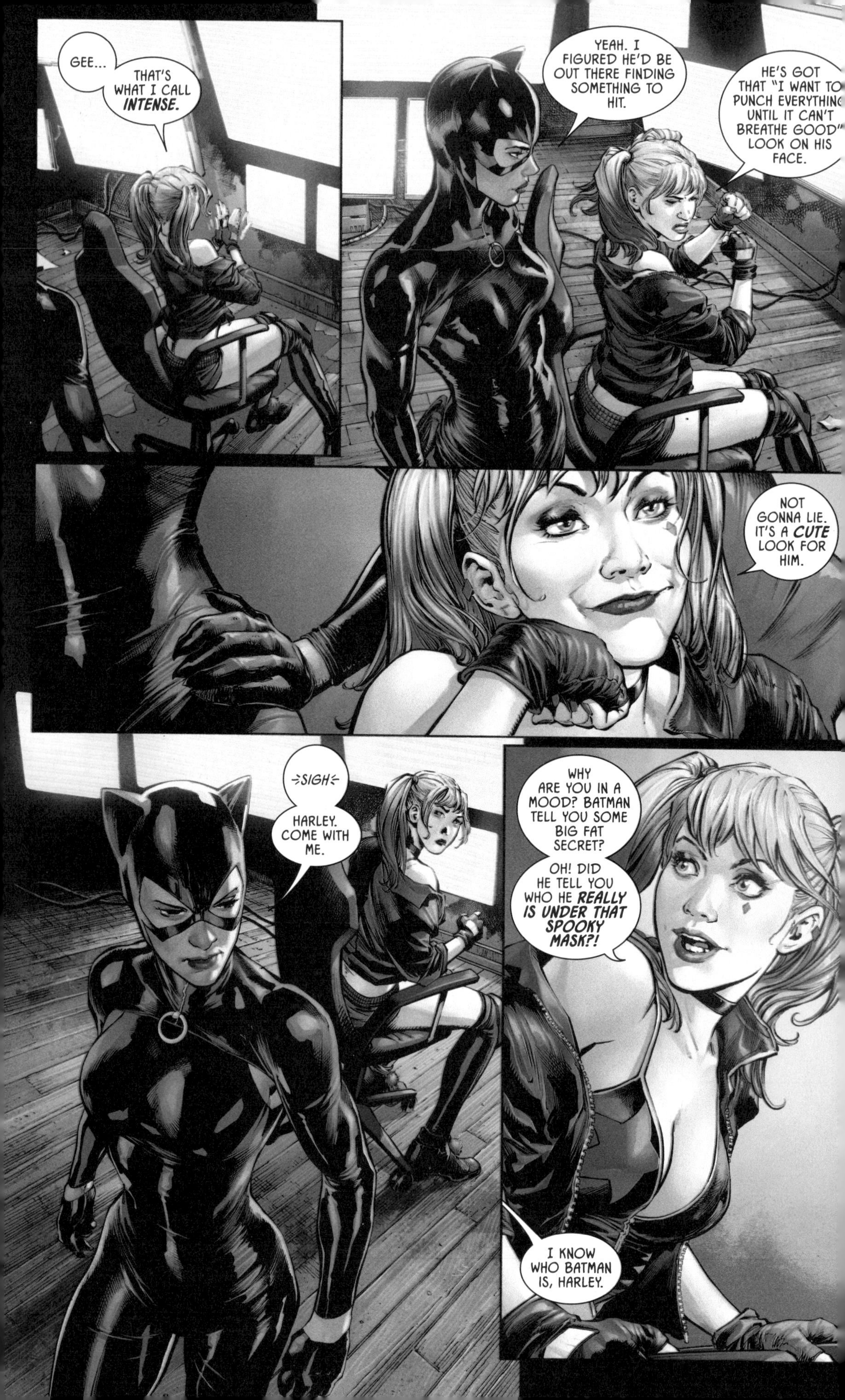
GEE...
THAT'S WHAT I CALL INTENSE.
YEAH. I FIGURED HE'D BE OUT THERE FINDING SOMETHING TO HIT.
HE'S GOT THAT "I WANT TO PUNCH EVERYTHING UNTIL IT CAN'T BREATHE GOOD" LOOK ON HIS FACE.
NOT GONNA LIE. IT'S A CUTE LOOK FOR HIM.
SIGH
HARLEY. COME WITH ME.
WHY ARE YOU IN A MOOD? BATMAN TELL YOU SOME BIG FAT SECRET?
OH! DID HE TELL YOU WHO HE REALLY IS UNDER THAT SPOOKY MASK?!
I KNOW WHO BATMAN IS, HARLEY.

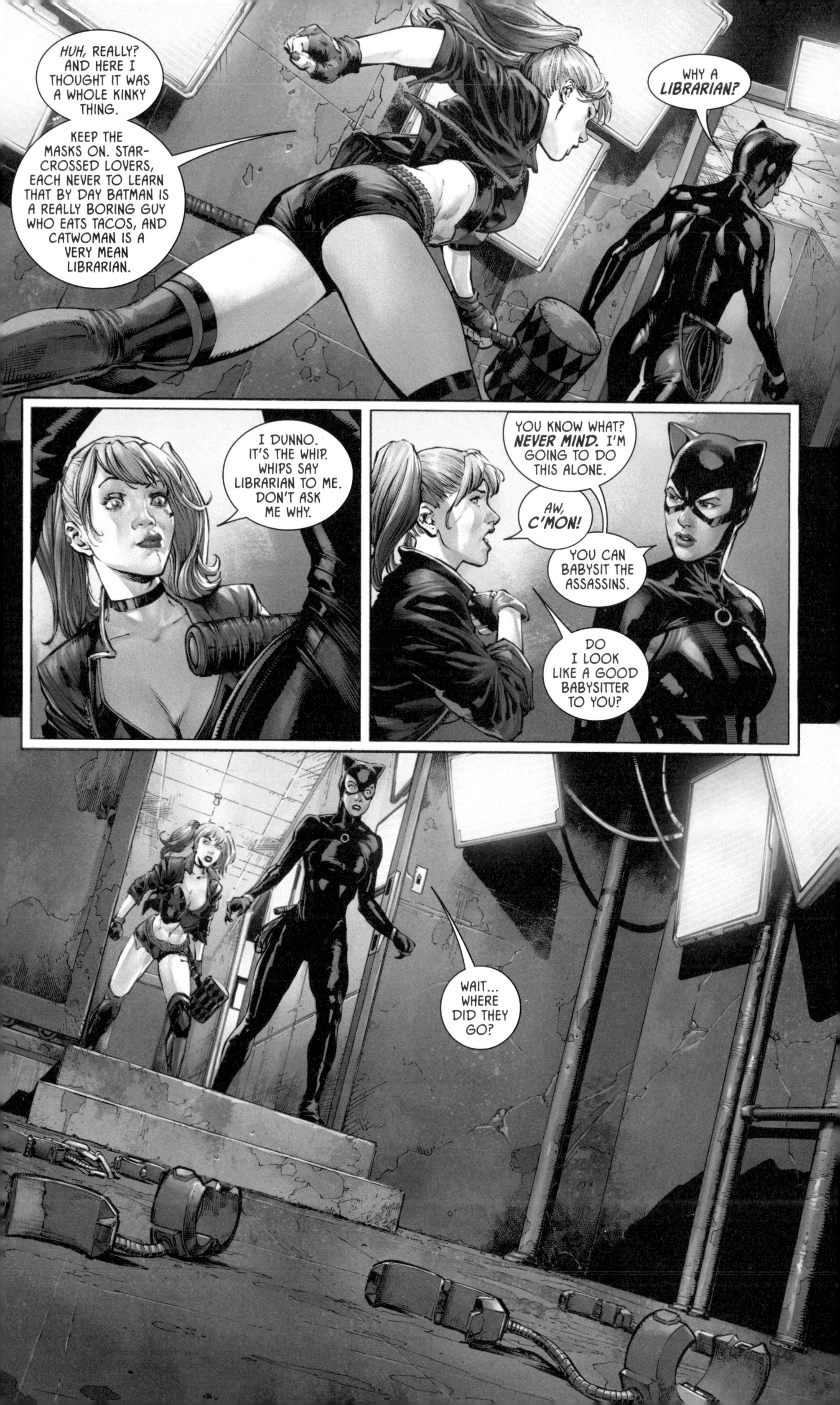

HUH, REALLY? AND HERE I THOUGHT IT WAS A WHOLE KINKY THING.
KEEP THE MASKS ON. STAR-CROSSED LOVERS, EACH NEVER TO LEARN THAT BY DAY BATMAN IS A REALLY BORING GUY WHO EATS TACOS, AND CATWOMAN IS A VERY MEAN LIBRARIAN.
WHY A LIBRARIAN?
I DUNNO. IT'S THE WHIP. WHIPS SAY LIBRARIAN TO ME. DON'T ASK ME WHY.
YOU KNOW WHAT? NEVER MIND. I'M GOING TO DO THIS ALONE.
AW, C'MON!
YOU CAN BABYSIT THE ASSASSINS.
DO I LOOK LIKE A GOOD BABYSITTER TO YOU?
WAIT... WHERE DID THEY GO?

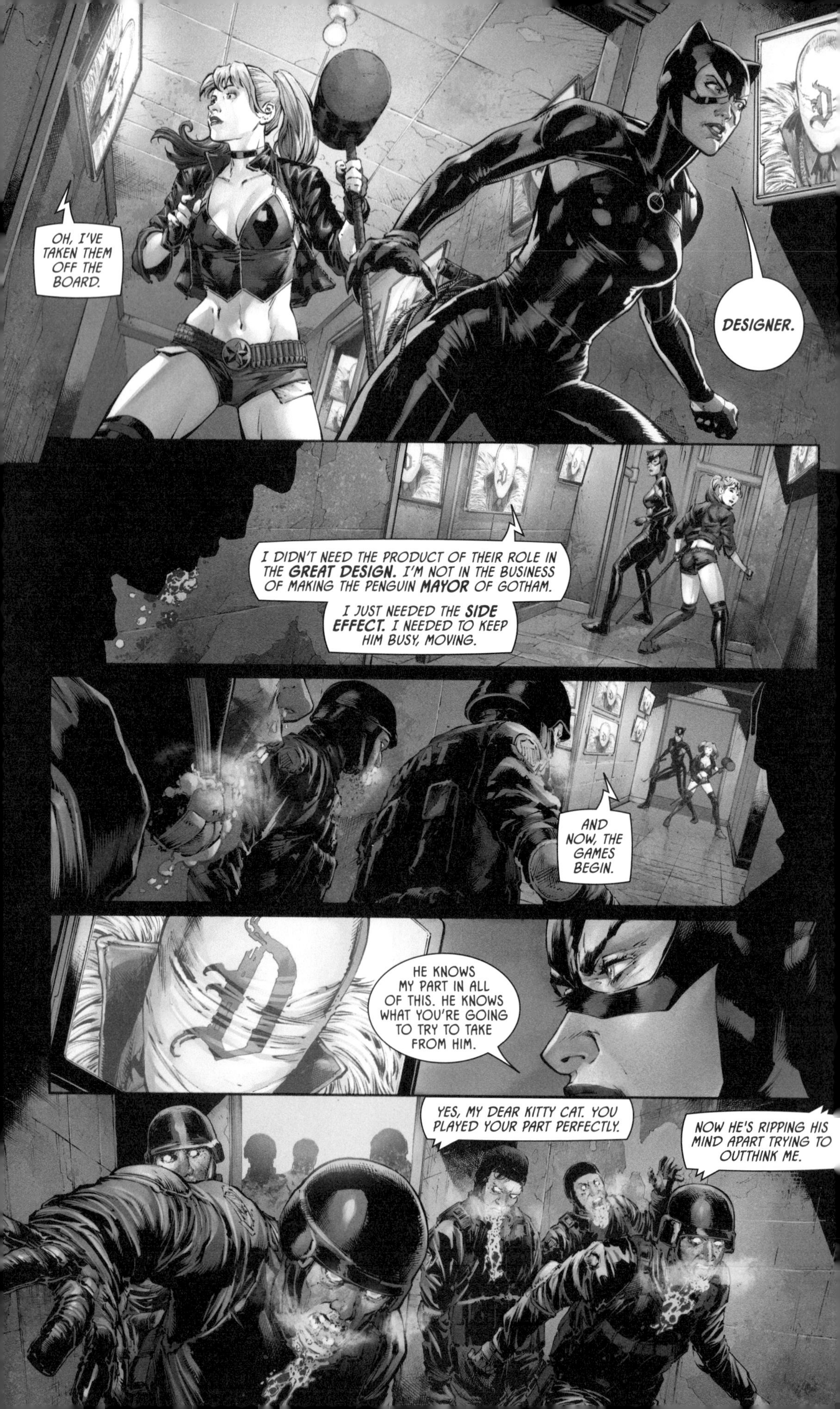

OH, I'VE TAKEN THEM OFF THE BOARD.
DESIGNER.
I DIDN'T NEED THE PRODUCT OF THEIR ROLE IN THE GREAT DESIGN. I'M NOT IN THE BUSINESS OF MAKING THE PENGUIN MAYOR OF GOTHAM.
I JUST NEEDED THE SIDE EFFECT. I NEEDED TO KEEP HIM BUSY, MOVING.
AND NOW, THE GAMES BEGIN.
HE KNOWS MY PART IN ALL OF THIS. HE KNOWS WHAT YOU'RE GOING TO TRY TO TAKE FROM HIM.
YES, MY DEAR KITTY CAT. YOU PLAYED YOUR PART PERFECTLY.
NOW HE'S RIPPING HIS MIND APART TRYING TO OUTTHINK ME.

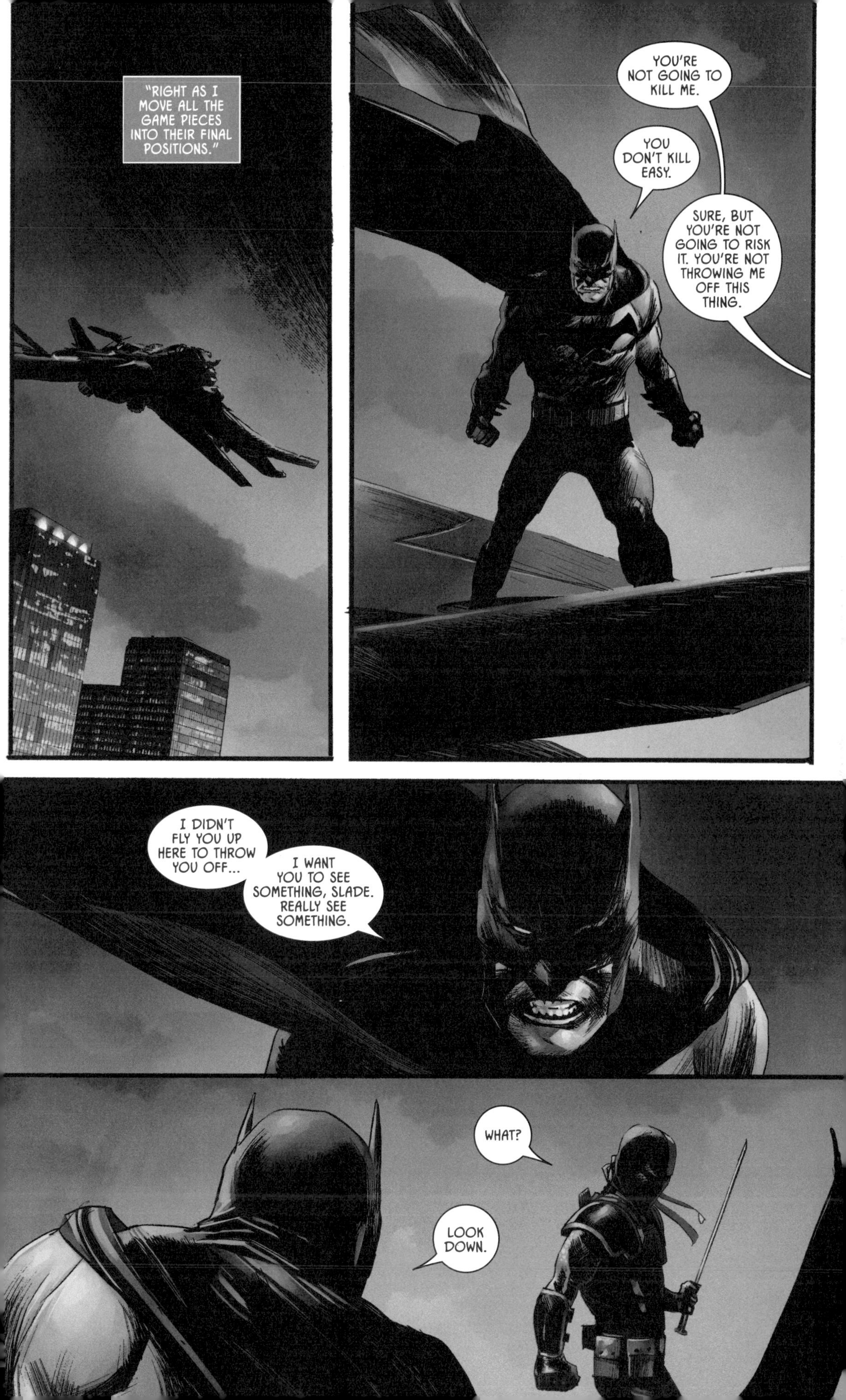
"RIGHT AS I MOVE ALL THE GAME PIECES INTO THEIR FINAL POSITIONS."
YOU'RE NOT GOING TO KILL ME.
YOU DON'T KILL EASY.
SURE, BUT YOU'RE NOT GOING TO RISK IT. YOU'RE NOT THROWING ME OFF THIS THING.
I DIDN'T FLY YOU UP HERE TO THROW YOU OFF...
I WANT YOU TO SEE SOMETHING, SLADE. REALLY SEE SOMETHING.
WHAT?
LOOK DOWN.

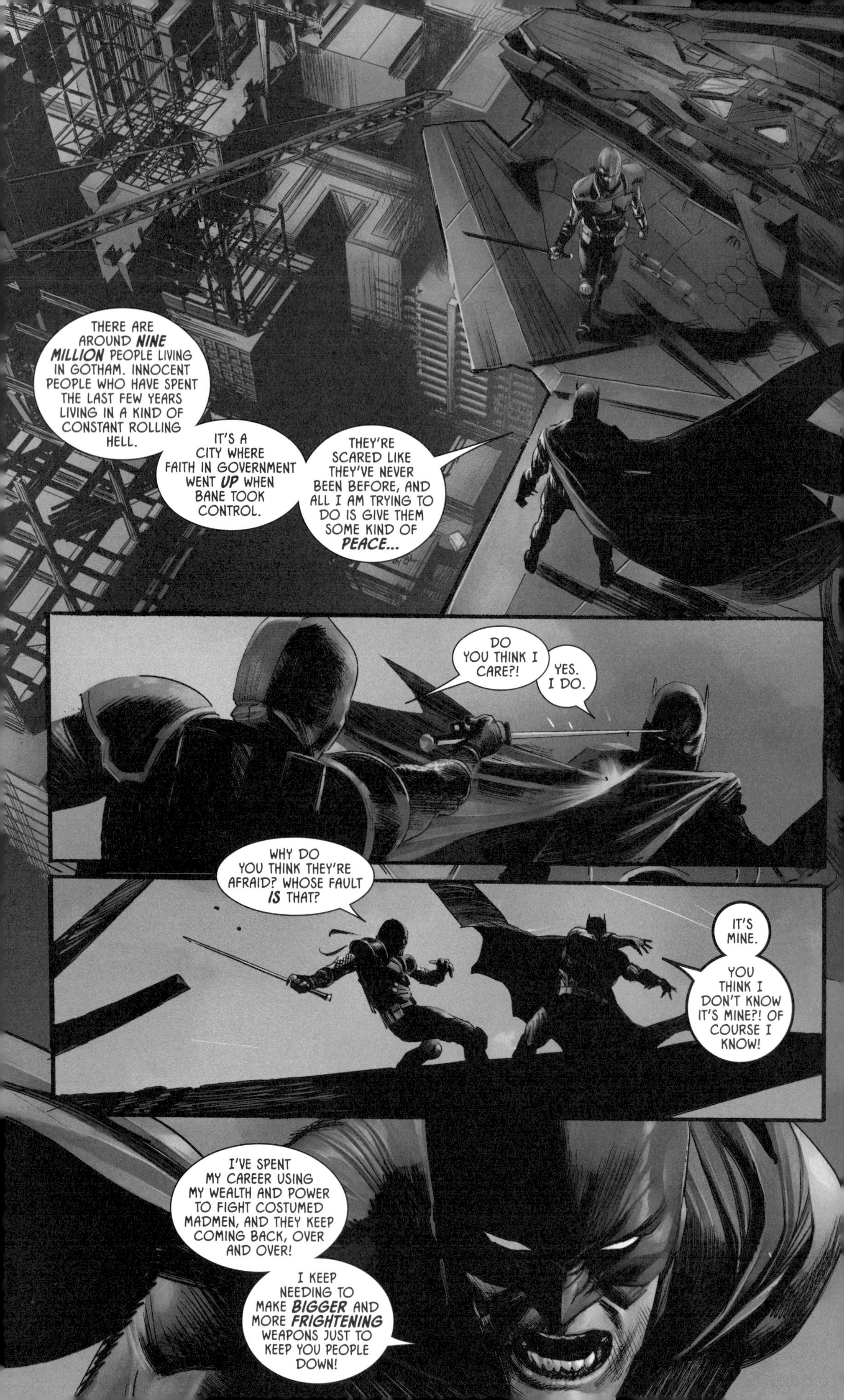
THERE ARE AROUND NINE MILLION PEOPLE LIVING IN GOTHAM. INNOCENT PEOPLE WHO HAVE SPENT THE LAST FEW YEARS LIVING IN A KIND OF CONSTANT ROLLING HELL.
IT'S A CITY WHERE FAITH IN GOVERNMENT WENT UP WHEN BANE TOOK CONTROL.
THEY'RE SCARED LIKE THEY'VE NEVER BEEN BEFORE, AND ALL I AM TRYING TO DO IS GIVE THEM SOME KIND OF PEACE...
DO YOU THINK I CARE?!
YES. I DO.
WHY DO YOU THINK THEY'RE AFRAID? WHOSE FAULT IS THAT?
IT'S MINE.
YOU THINK I DON'T KNOW IT'S MINE?! OF COURSE I KNOW!
I'VE SPENT MY CAREER USING MY WEALTH AND POWER TO FIGHT COSTUMED MADMEN, AND THEY KEEP COMING BACK, OVER AND OVER!
I KEEP NEEDING TO MAKE BIGGER AND MORE FRIGHTENING WEAPONS JUST TO KEEP YOU PEOPLE DOWN!

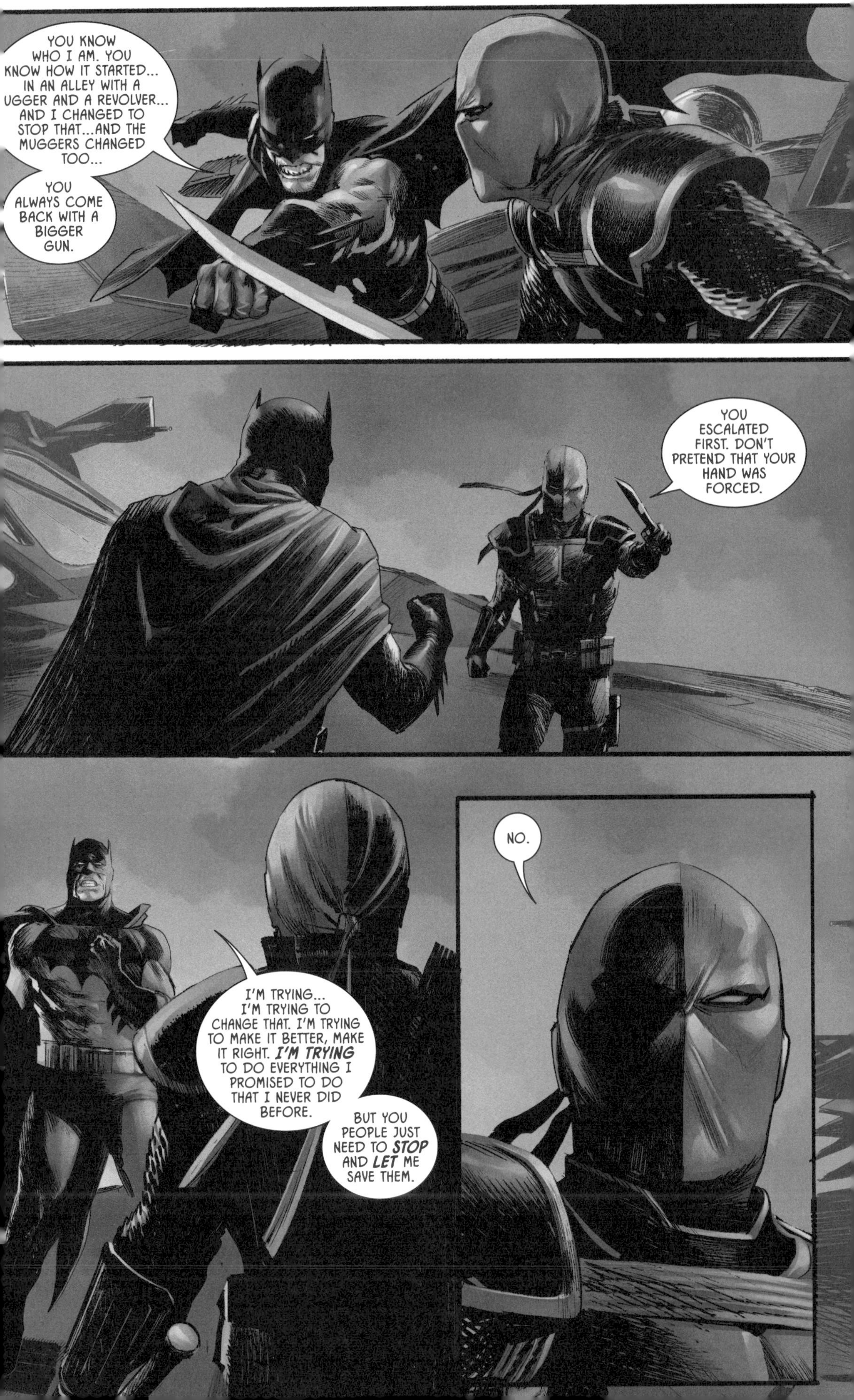

YOU KNOW WHO I AM. YOU KNOW HOW IT STARTED... IN AN ALLEY WITH A UGGER AND A REVOLVER... AND I CHANGED TO STOP THAT...AND THE MUGGERS CHANGED TOO...
YOU ALWAYS COME BACK WITH A BIGGER GUN.
YOU ESCALATED FIRST. DON'T PRETEND THAT YOUR HAND WAS FORCED.
I'M TRYING... I'M TRYING TO CHANGE THAT. I'M TRYING TO MAKE IT BETTER, MAKE IT RIGHT. ***I'M TRYING*** TO DO EVERYTHING I PROMISED TO DO THAT I NEVER DID BEFORE.
BUT YOU PEOPLE JUST NEED TO ***STOP*** AND ***LET*** ME SAVE THEM.
NO.

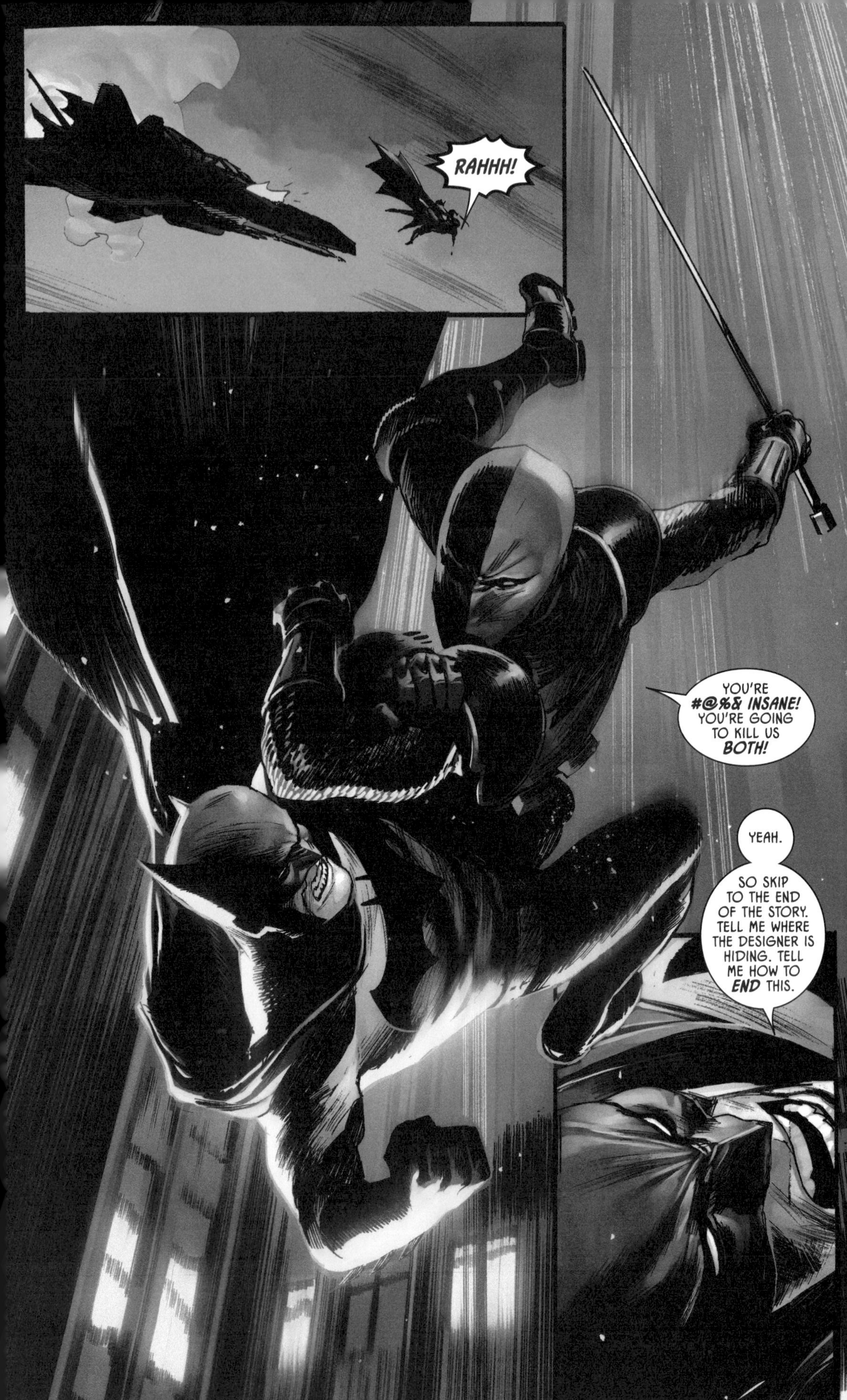
RAHHH!
YOU'RE #@%& INSANE! YOU'RE GOING TO KILL US BOTH!
YEAH.
SO SKIP TO THE END OF THE STORY. TELL ME WHERE THE DESIGNER IS HIDING. TELL ME HOW TO END THIS.

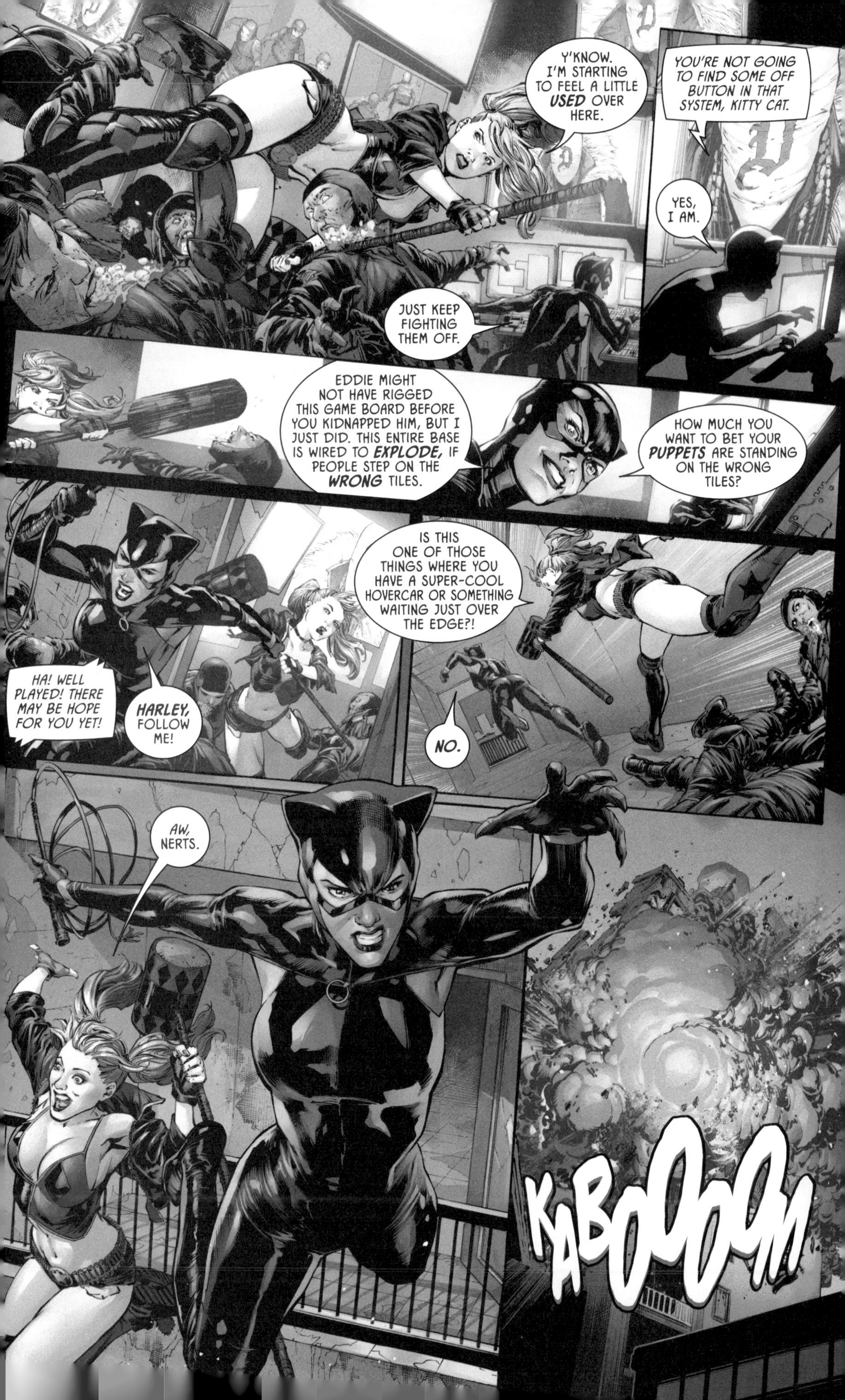
Y'KNOW. I'M STARTING TO FEEL A LITTLE USED OVER HERE.
JUST KEEP FIGHTING THEM OFF.
YOU'RE NOT GOING TO FIND SOME OFF BUTTON IN THAT SYSTEM, KITTY CAT.
YES, I AM.
EDDIE MIGHT NOT HAVE RIGGED THIS GAME BOARD BEFORE YOU KIDNAPPED HIM, BUT I JUST DID. THIS ENTIRE BASE IS WIRED TO EXPLODE, IF PEOPLE STEP ON THE WRONG TILES.
HOW MUCH YOU WANT TO BET YOUR PUPPETS ARE STANDING ON THE WRONG TILES?
HA! WELL PLAYED! THERE MAY BE HOPE FOR YOU YET!
HARLEY, FOLLOW ME!
IS THIS ONE OF THOSE THINGS WHERE YOU HAVE A SUPER-COOL HOVERCAR OR SOMETHING WAITING JUST OVER THE EDGE?!
NO.
AW, NERTS.
KABOOOOM

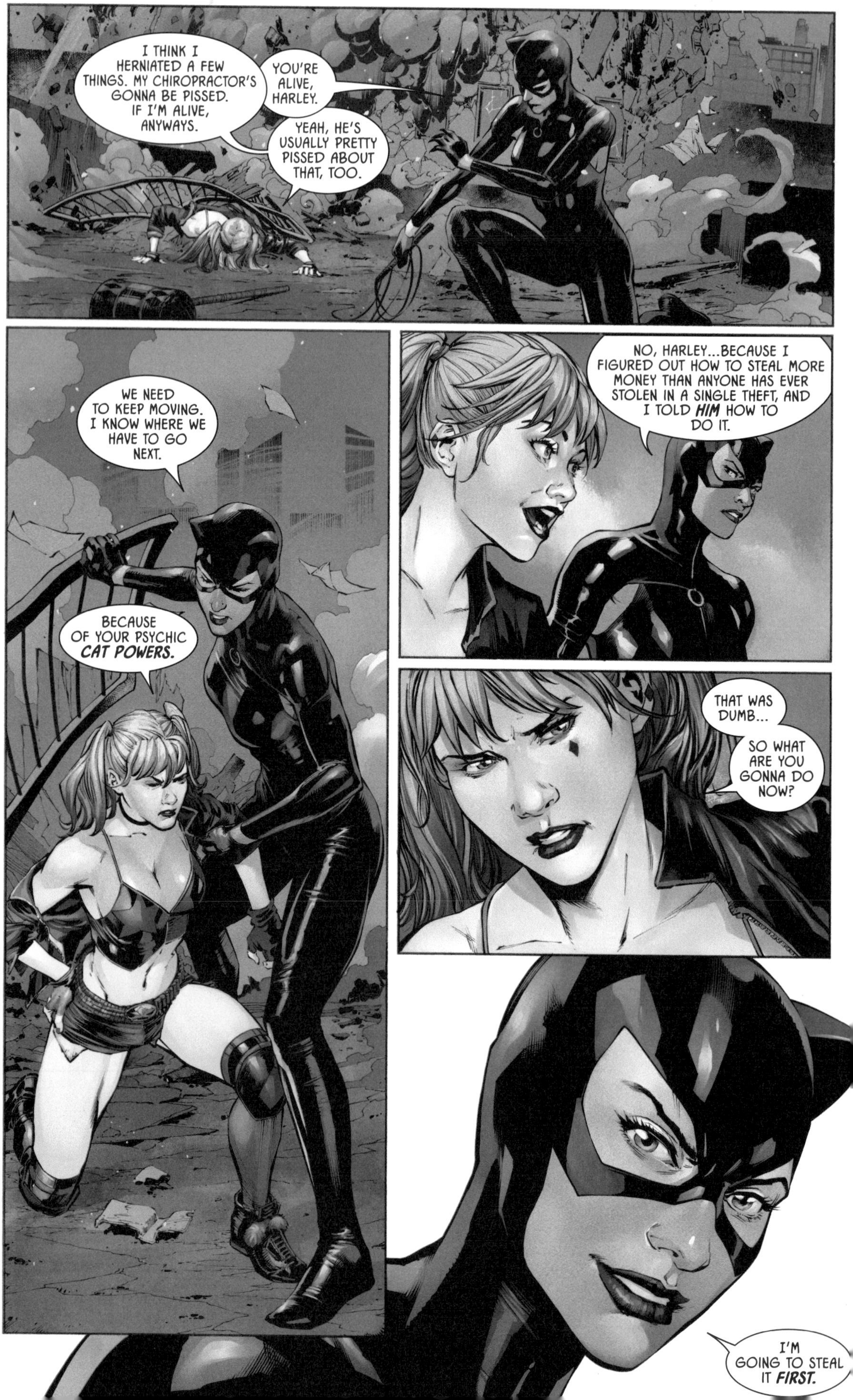

I THINK I HERNIATED A FEW THINGS. MY CHIROPRACTOR'S GONNA BE PISSED. IF I'M ALIVE, ANYWAYS.
YOU'RE ALIVE, HARLEY.
YEAH, HE'S USUALLY PRETTY PISSED ABOUT THAT, TOO.
WE NEED TO KEEP MOVING. I KNOW WHERE WE HAVE TO GO NEXT.
BECAUSE OF YOUR PSYCHIC *CAT POWERS.*
NO, HARLEY...BECAUSE I FIGURED OUT HOW TO STEAL MORE MONEY THAN ANYONE HAS EVER STOLEN IN A SINGLE THEFT, AND I TOLD *HIM* HOW TO DO IT.
THAT WAS DUMB...
SO WHAT ARE YOU GONNA DO NOW?
I'M GOING TO STEAL IT *FIRST.*

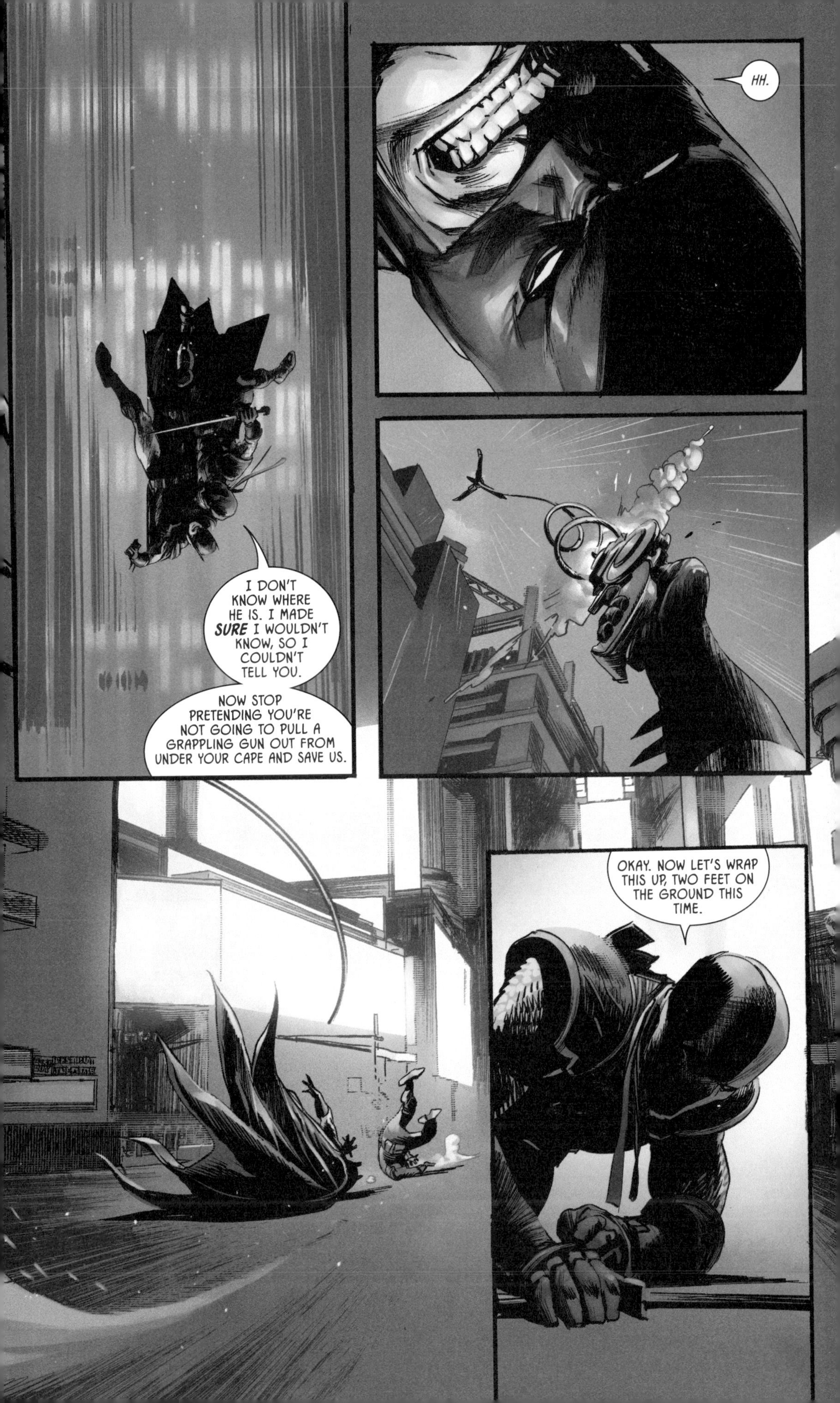
HH.
I DON'T KNOW WHERE HE IS. I MADE **SURE** I WOULDN'T KNOW, SO I COULDN'T TELL YOU.
NOW STOP PRETENDING YOU'RE NOT GOING TO PULL A GRAPPLING GUN OUT FROM UNDER YOUR CAPE AND SAVE US.
OKAY. NOW LET'S WRAP THIS UP, TWO FEET ON THE GROUND THIS TIME.

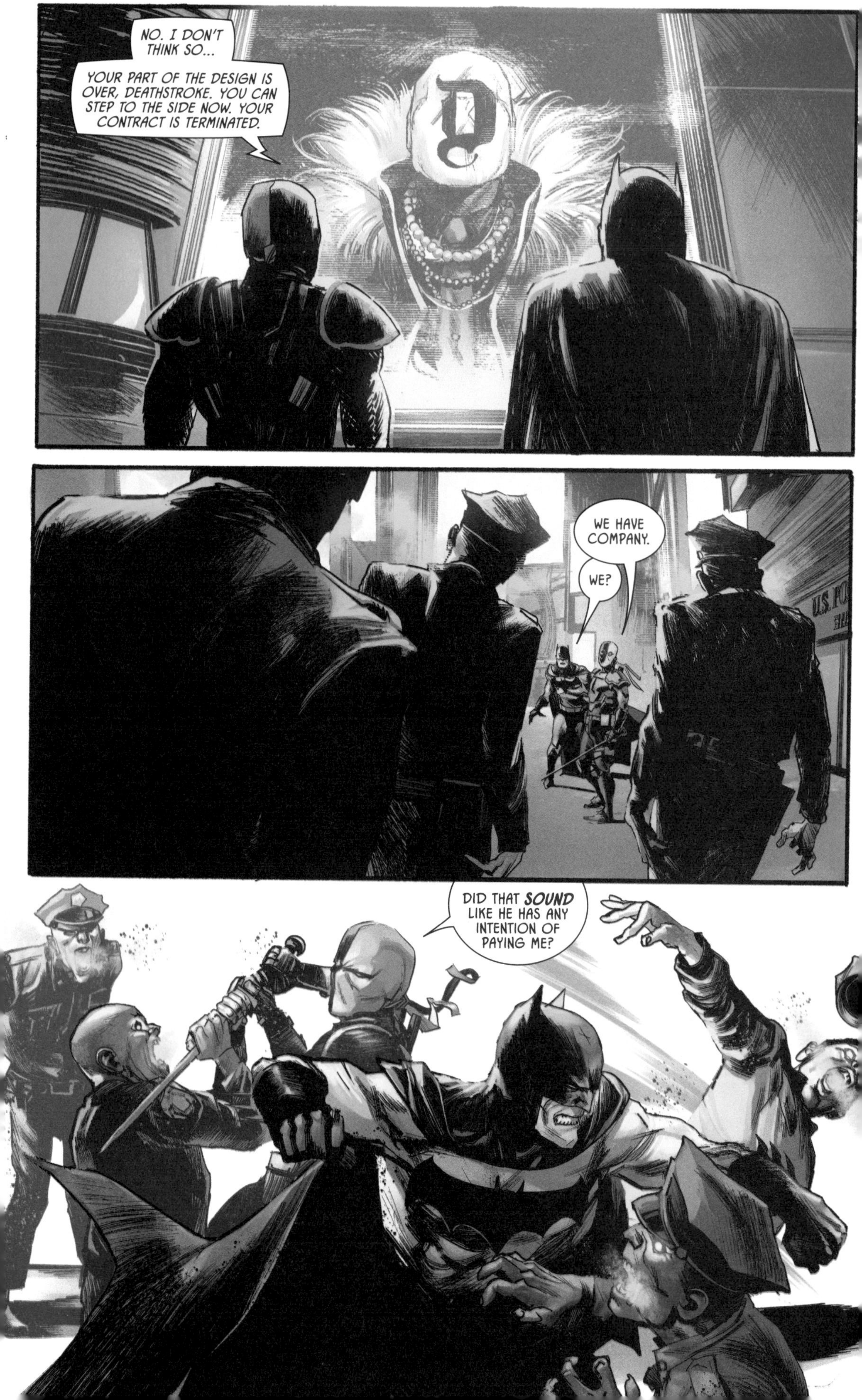
NO. I DON'T THINK SO...
YOUR PART OF THE DESIGN IS OVER, DEATHSTROKE. YOU CAN STEP TO THE SIDE NOW. YOUR CONTRACT IS TERMINATED.
WE HAVE COMPANY.
WE?
DID THAT SOUND LIKE HE HAS ANY INTENTION OF PAYING ME?

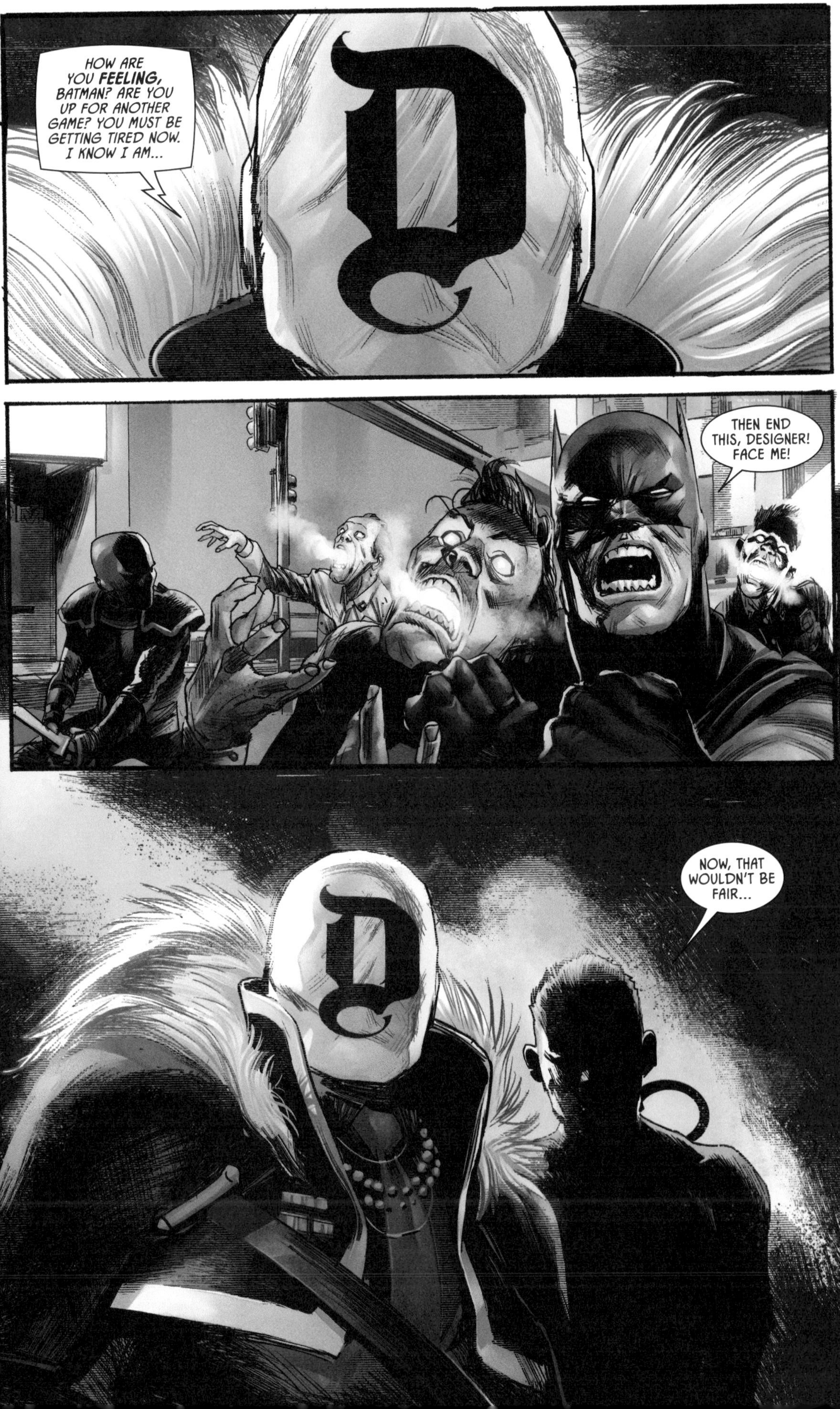
HOW ARE YOU **FEELING,** BATMAN? ARE YOU UP FOR ANOTHER GAME? YOU MUST BE GETTING TIRED NOW. I KNOW I AM...
THEN END THIS, DESIGNER! FACE ME!
NOW, THAT WOULDN'T BE FAIR...

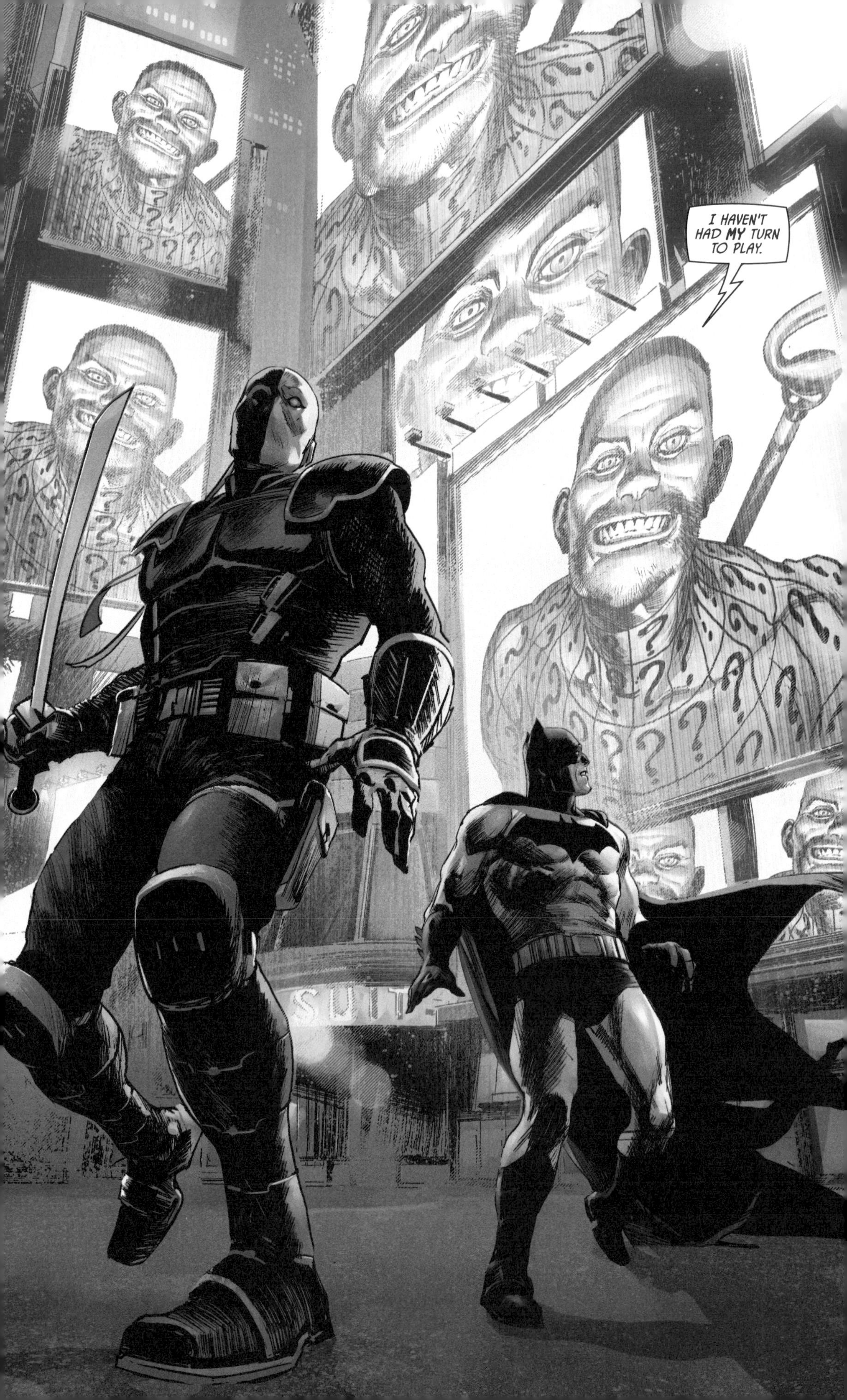
I HAVEN'T HAD MY TURN TO PLAY.
SUIT

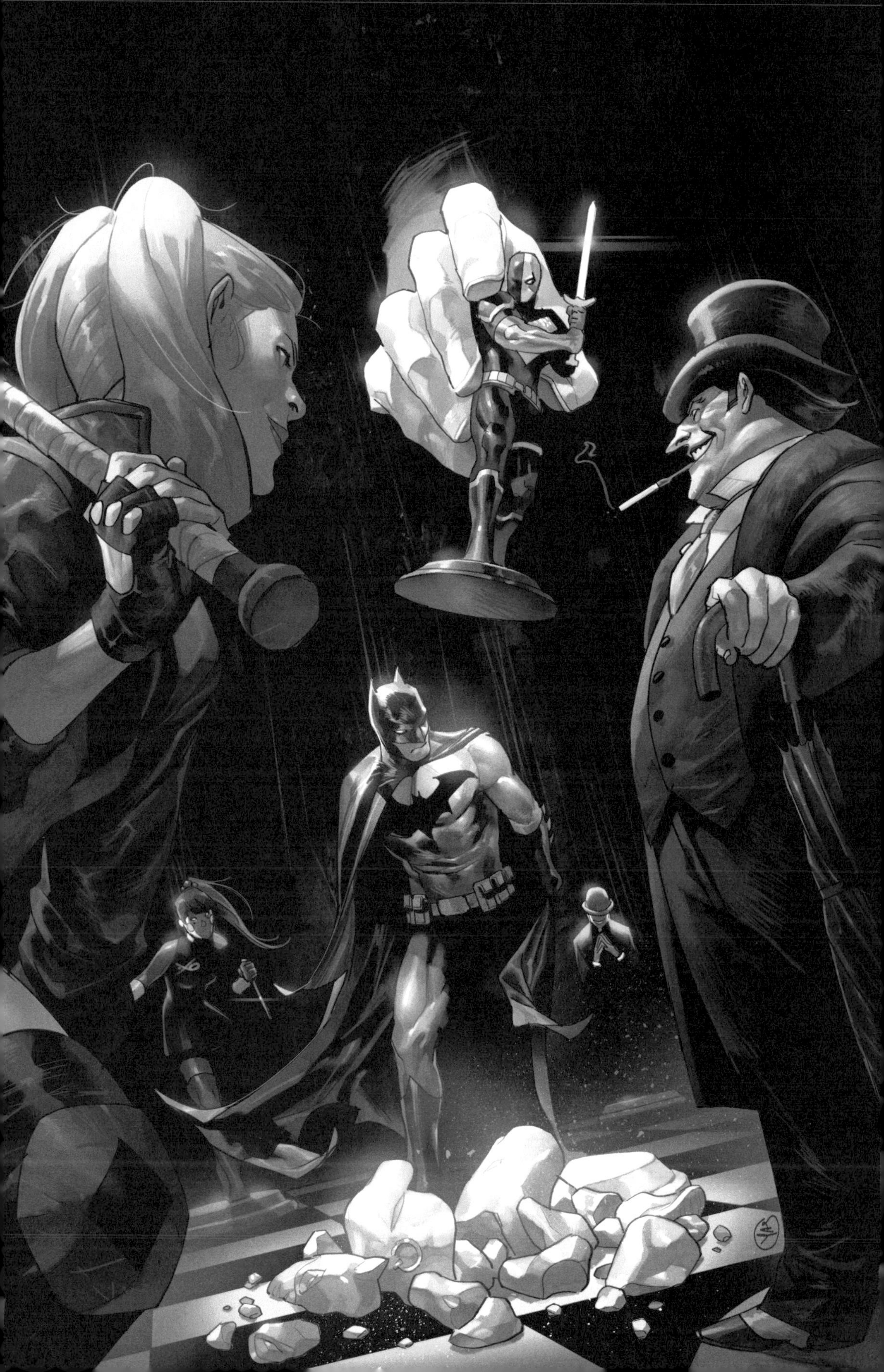

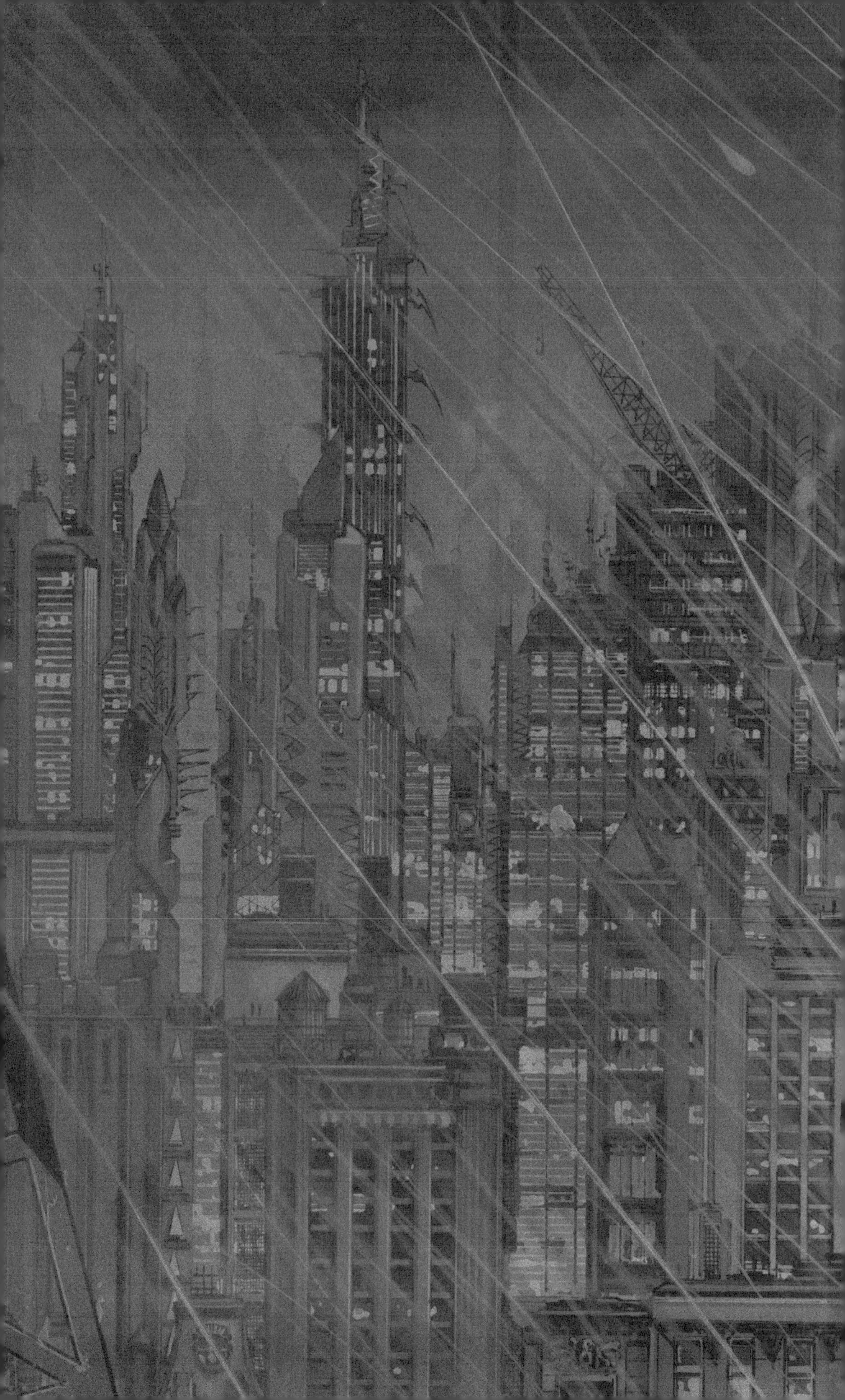

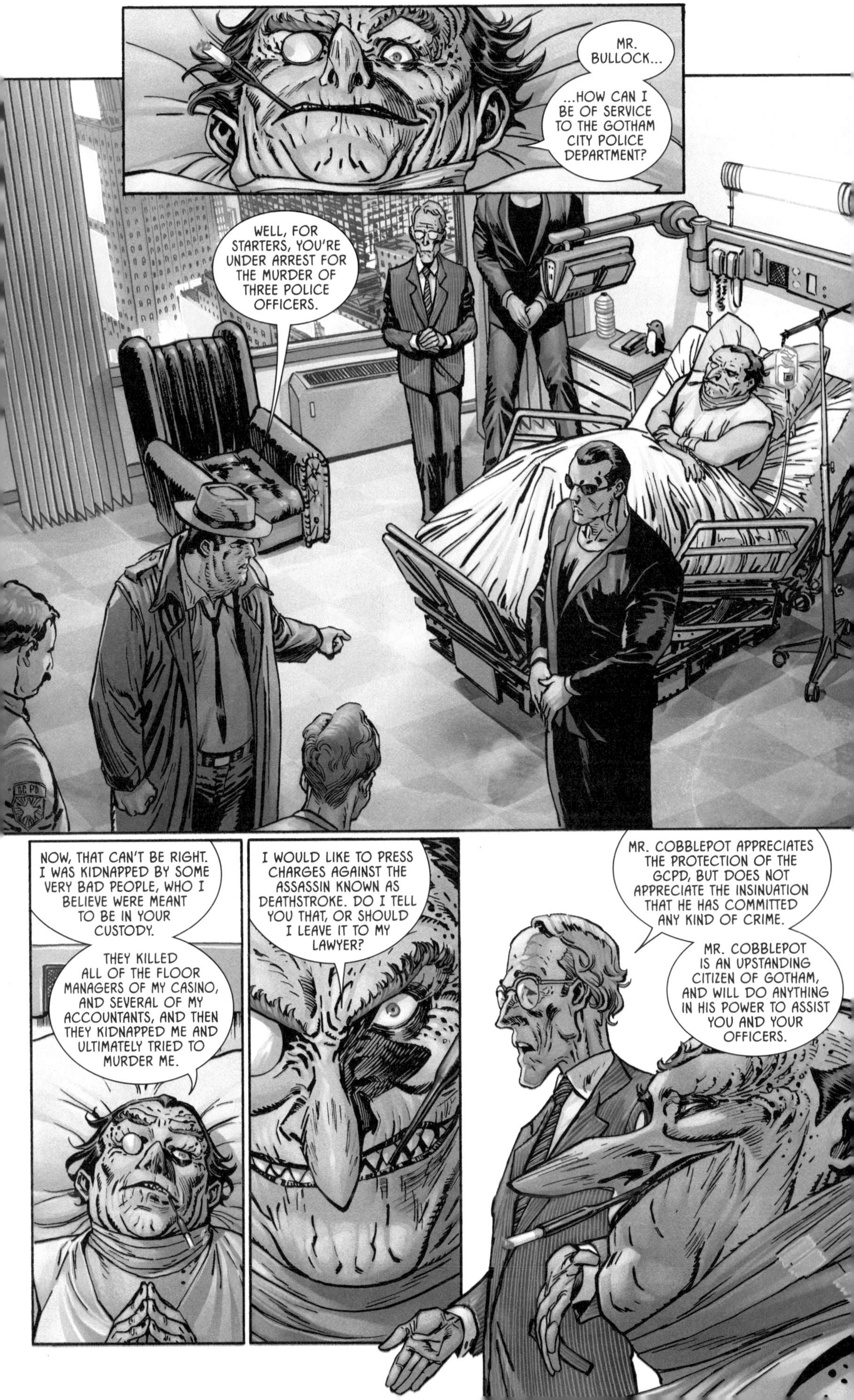
MR. BULLOCK...
...HOW CAN I BE OF SERVICE TO THE GOTHAM CITY POLICE DEPARTMENT?
WELL, FOR STARTERS, YOU'RE UNDER ARREST FOR THE MURDER OF THREE POLICE OFFICERS.
GC PD
NOW, THAT CAN'T BE RIGHT. I WAS KIDNAPPED BY SOME VERY BAD PEOPLE, WHO I BELIEVE WERE MEANT TO BE IN YOUR CUSTODY.
THEY KILLED ALL OF THE FLOOR MANAGERS OF MY CASINO, AND SEVERAL OF MY ACCOUNTANTS, AND THEN THEY KIDNAPPED ME AND ULTIMATELY TRIED TO MURDER ME.
I WOULD LIKE TO PRESS CHARGES AGAINST THE ASSASSIN KNOWN AS DEATHSTROKE. DO I TELL YOU THAT, OR SHOULD I LEAVE IT TO MY LAWYER?
MR. COBBLEPOT APPRECIATES THE PROTECTION OF THE GCPD, BUT DOES NOT APPRECIATE THE INSINUATION THAT HE HAS COMMITTED ANY KIND OF CRIME.
MR. COBBLEPOT IS AN UPSTANDING CITIZEN OF GOTHAM, AND WILL DO ANYTHING IN HIS POWER TO ASSIST YOU AND YOUR OFFICERS.

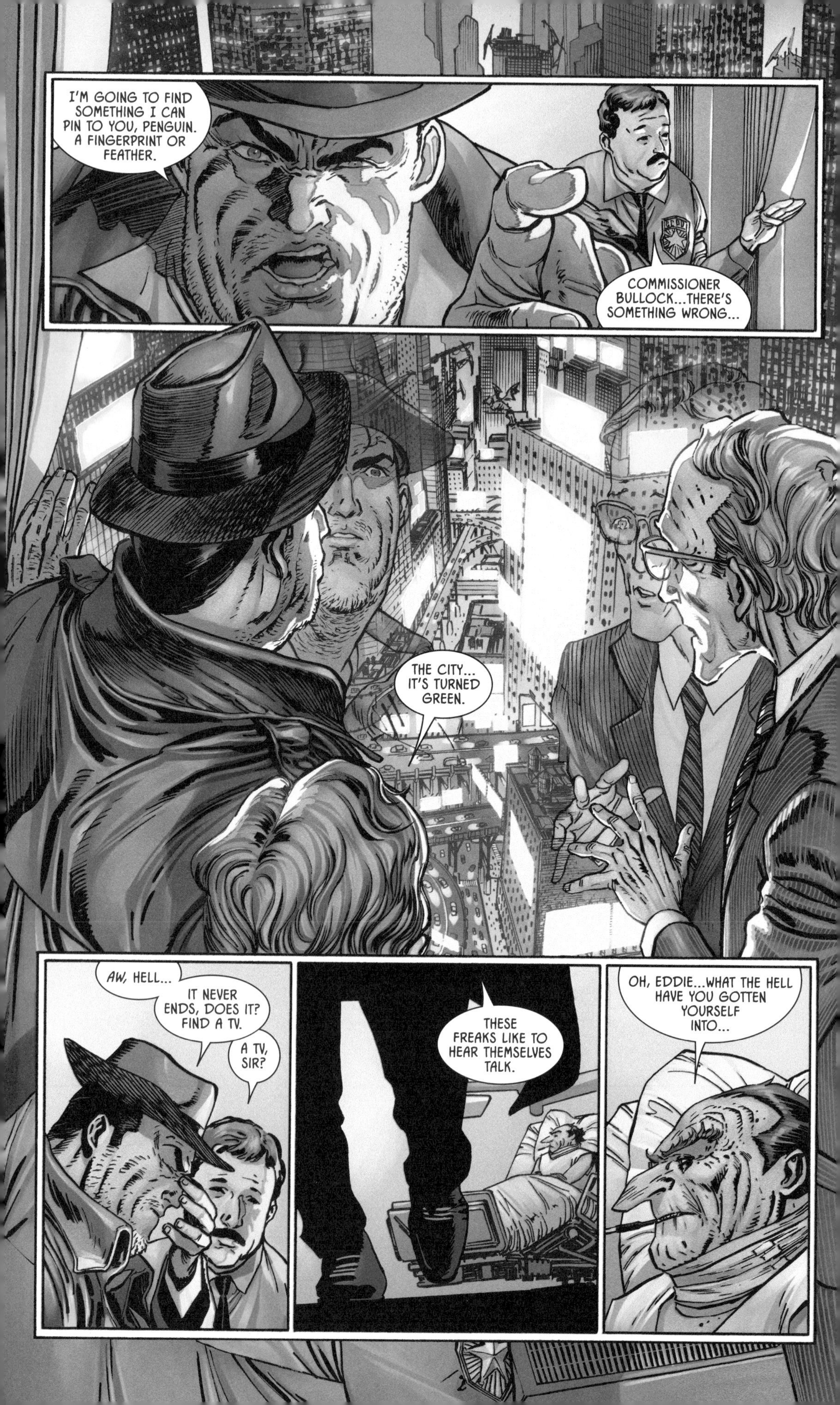
I'M GOING TO FIND SOMETHING I CAN PIN TO YOU, PENGUIN. A FINGERPRINT OR FEATHER.
COMMISSIONER BULLOCK...THERE'S SOMETHING WRONG...
THE CITY... IT'S TURNED GREEN.
AW, HELL...
IT NEVER ENDS, DOES IT? FIND A TV.
A TV, SIR?
THESE FREAKS LIKE TO HEAR THEMSELVES TALK.
OH, EDDIE...WHAT THE HELL HAVE YOU GOTTEN YOURSELF INTO...

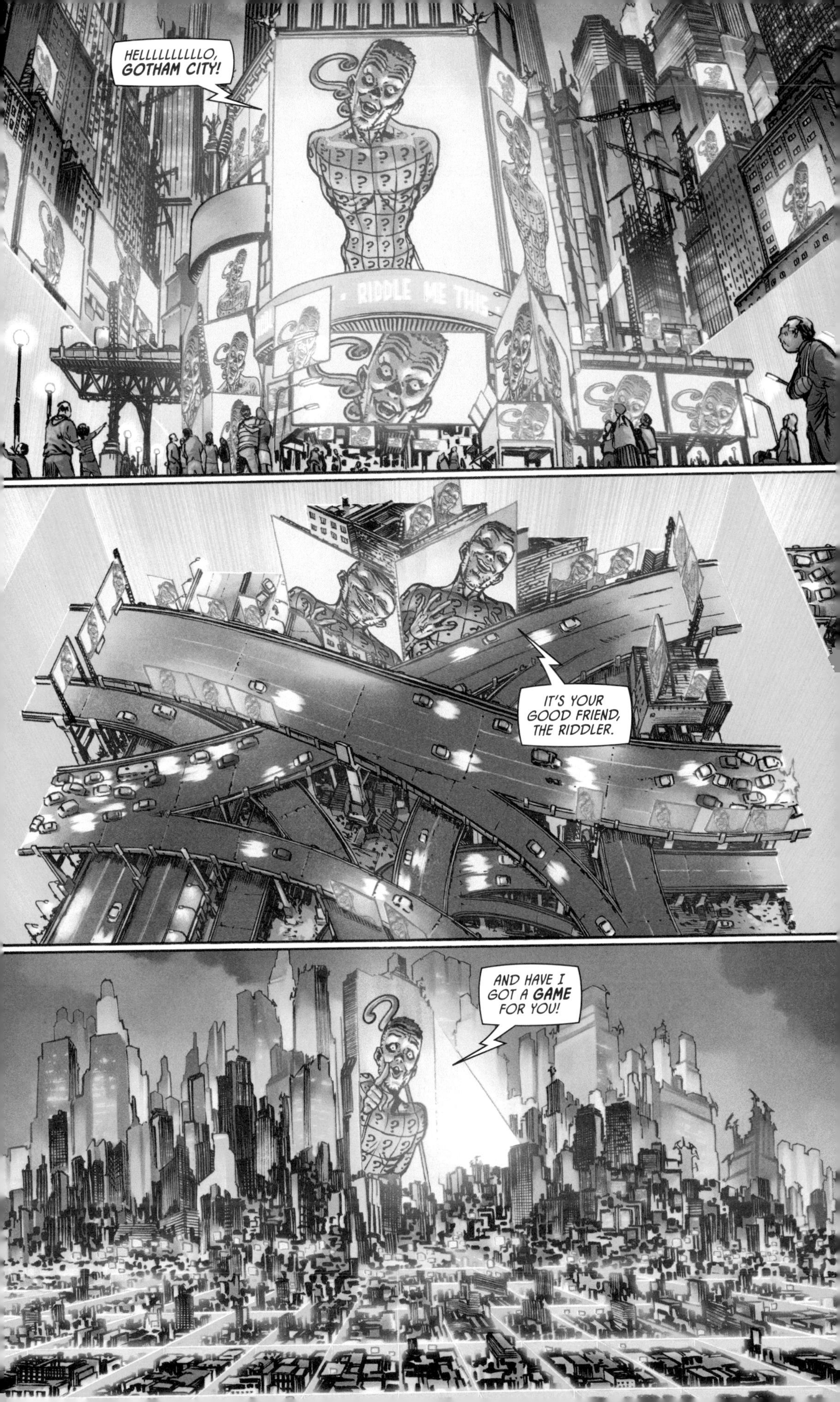
HELLLLLLLLLLLO, **GOTHAM CITY!**
RIDDLE ME THIS
IT'S YOUR GOOD FRIEND, THE RIDDLER.
AND HAVE I GOT A **GAME** FOR YOU!

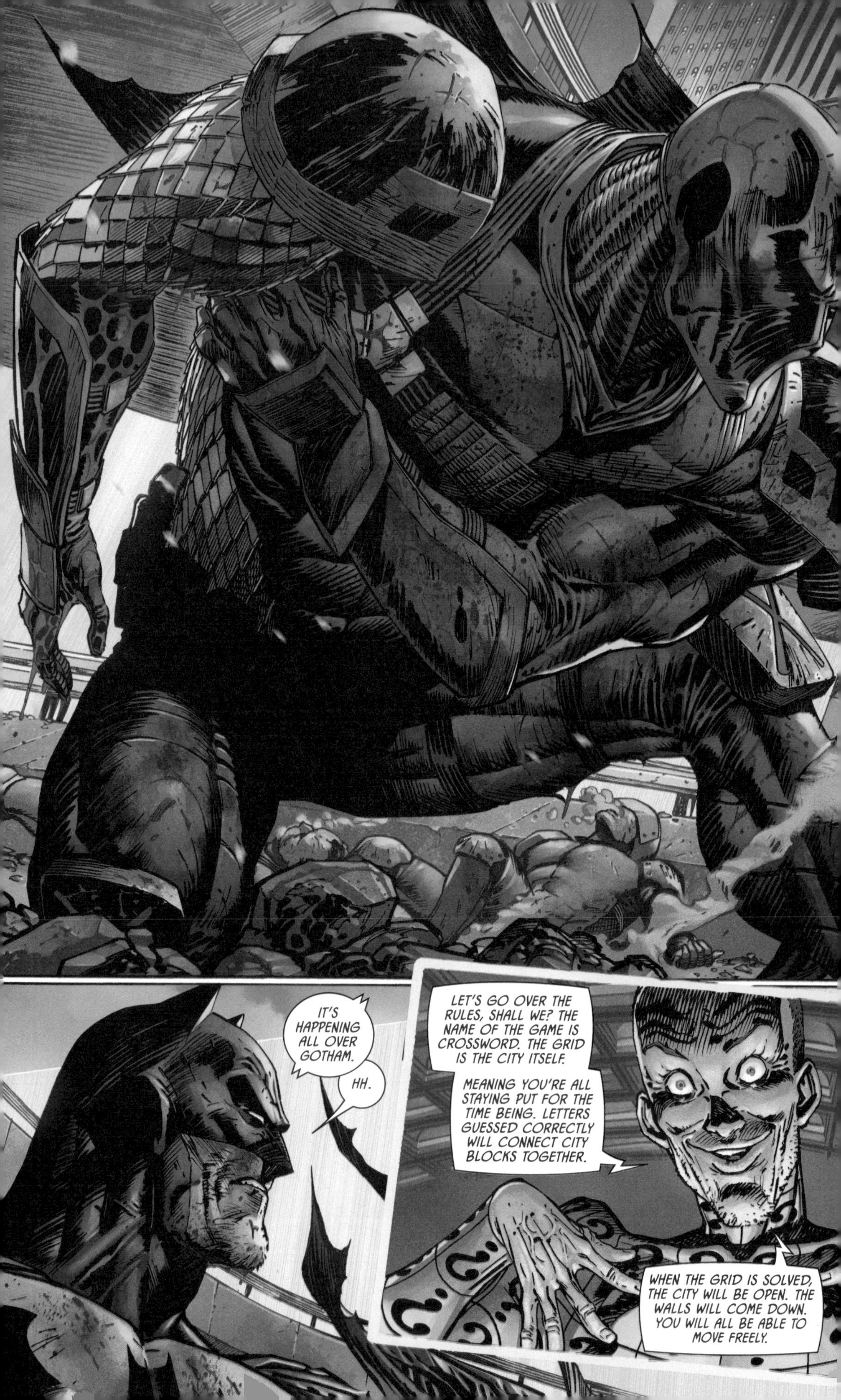
IT'S HAPPENING ALL OVER GOTHAM.
HH.
LET'S GO OVER THE RULES, SHALL WE? THE NAME OF THE GAME IS CROSSWORD. THE GRID IS THE CITY ITSELF.
MEANING YOU'RE ALL STAYING PUT FOR THE TIME BEING. LETTERS GUESSED CORRECTLY WILL CONNECT CITY BLOCKS TOGETHER.
WHEN THE GRID IS SOLVED, THE CITY WILL BE OPEN. THE WALLS WILL COME DOWN. YOU WILL ALL BE ABLE TO MOVE FREELY.

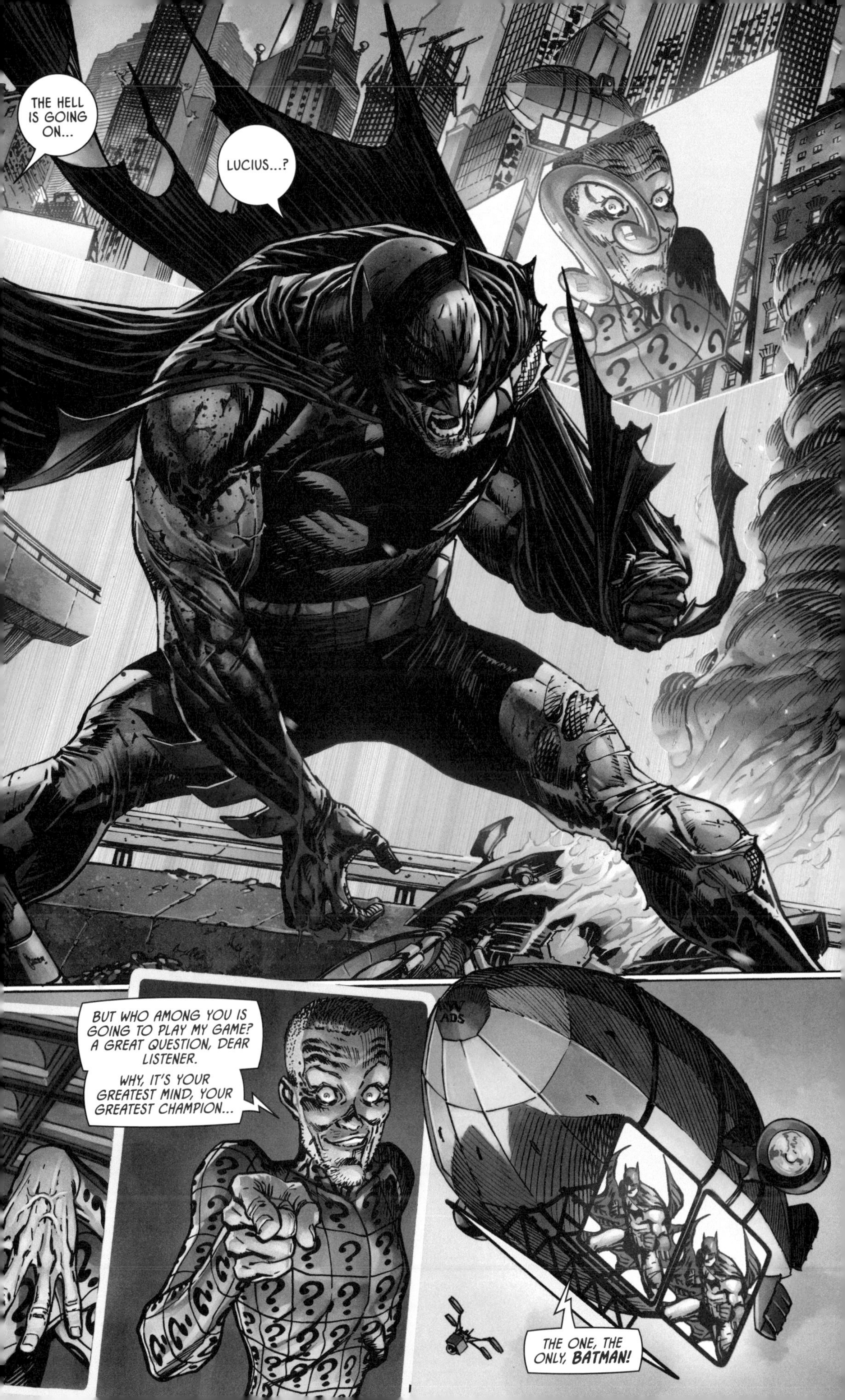
THE HELL IS GOING ON...
LUCIUS...?
BUT WHO AMONG YOU IS GOING TO PLAY MY GAME? A GREAT QUESTION, DEAR LISTENER.
WHY, IT'S YOUR GREATEST MIND, YOUR GREATEST CHAMPION...
THE ONE, THE ONLY, BATMAN!

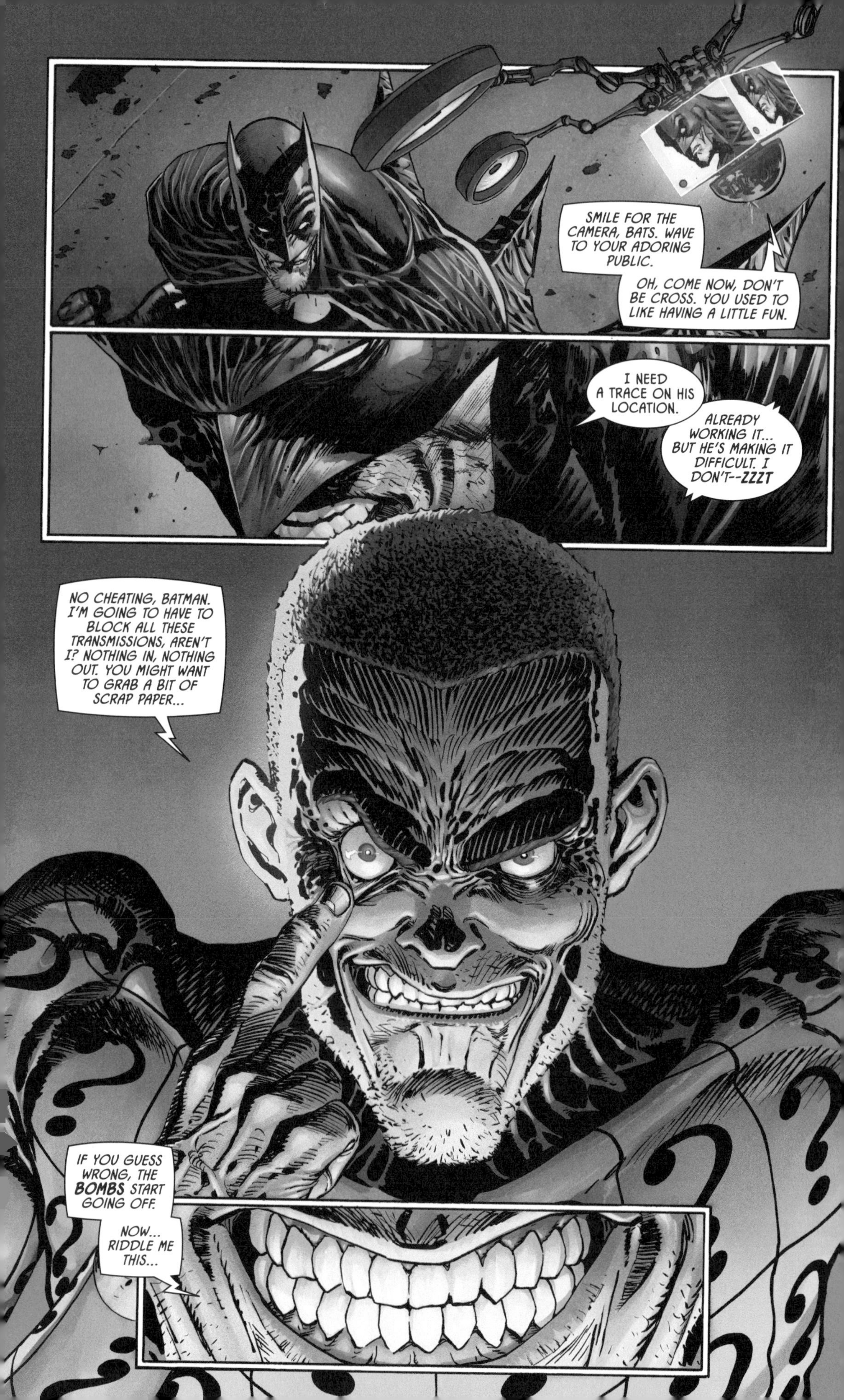
SMILE FOR THE CAMERA, BATS. WAVE TO YOUR ADORING PUBLIC.
OH, COME NOW, DON'T BE CROSS. YOU USED TO LIKE HAVING A LITTLE FUN.
I NEED A TRACE ON HIS LOCATION.
ALREADY WORKING IT... BUT HE'S MAKING IT DIFFICULT. I DON'T--ZZZT
NO CHEATING, BATMAN. I'M GOING TO HAVE TO BLOCK ALL THESE TRANSMISSIONS, AREN'T I? NOTHING IN, NOTHING OUT. YOU MIGHT WANT TO GRAB A BIT OF SCRAP PAPER...
IF YOU GUESS WRONG, THE BOMBS START GOING OFF.
NOW... RIDDLE ME THIS...

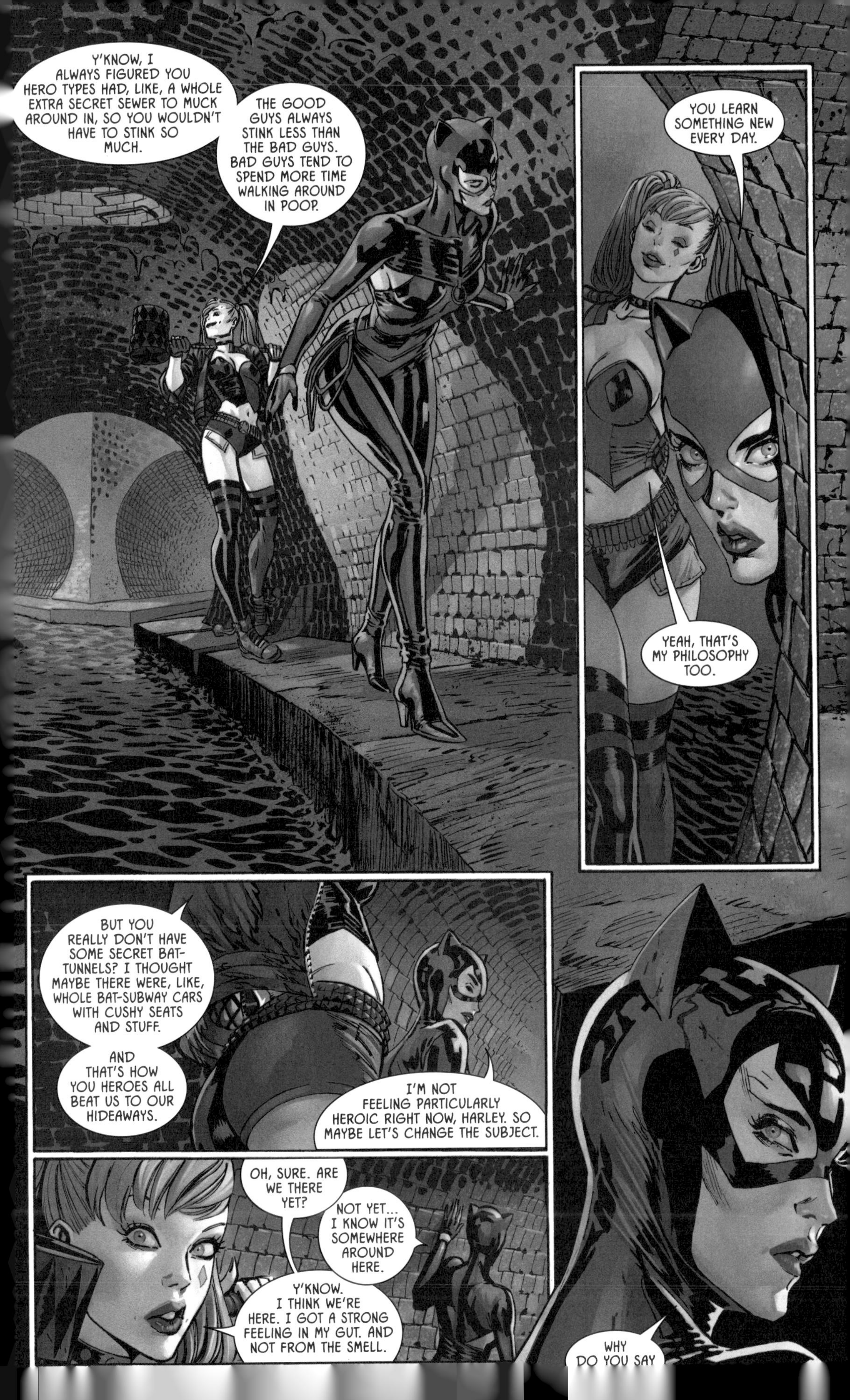
Y'KNOW, I ALWAYS FIGURED YOU HERO TYPES HAD, LIKE, A WHOLE EXTRA SECRET SEWER TO MUCK AROUND IN, SO YOU WOULDN'T HAVE TO STINK SO MUCH.
THE GOOD GUYS ALWAYS STINK LESS THAN THE BAD GUYS. BAD GUYS TEND TO SPEND MORE TIME WALKING AROUND IN POOP.
YOU LEARN SOMETHING NEW EVERY DAY.
YEAH, THAT'S MY PHILOSOPHY TOO.
BUT YOU REALLY DON'T HAVE SOME SECRET BAT-TUNNELS? I THOUGHT MAYBE THERE WERE, LIKE, WHOLE BAT-SUBWAY CARS WITH CUSHY SEATS AND STUFF.
AND THAT'S HOW YOU HEROES ALL BEAT US TO OUR HIDEAWAYS.
I'M NOT FEELING PARTICULARLY HEROIC RIGHT NOW, HARLEY. SO MAYBE LET'S CHANGE THE SUBJECT.
OH, SURE. ARE WE THERE YET?
NOT YET... I KNOW IT'S SOMEWHERE AROUND HERE.
Y'KNOW. I THINK WE'RE HERE. I GOT A STRONG FEELING IN MY GUT. AND NOT FROM THE SMELL.
WHY DO YOU SAY

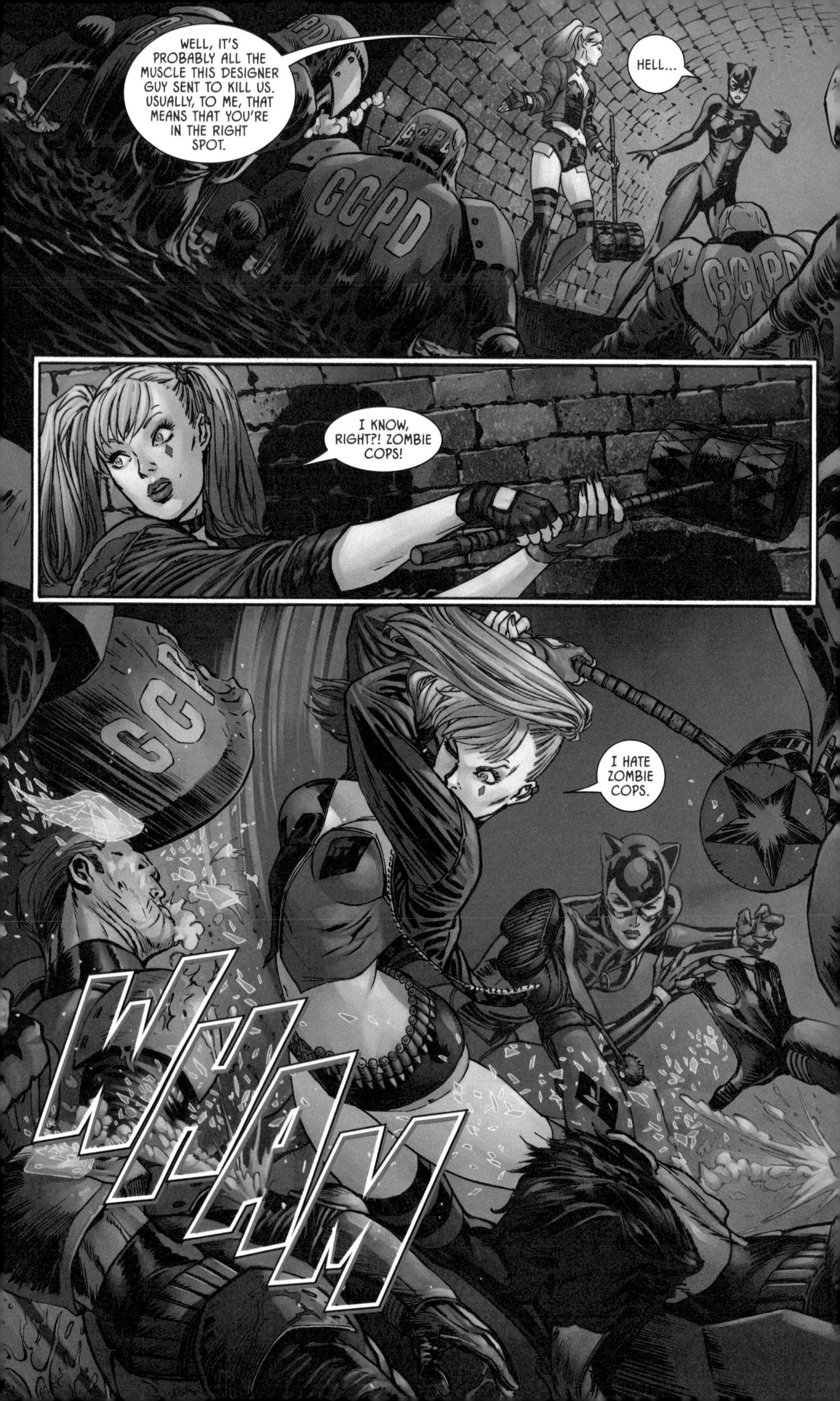
WELL, IT'S PROBABLY ALL THE MUSCLE THIS DESIGNER GUY SENT TO KILL US. USUALLY, TO ME, THAT MEANS THAT YOU'RE IN THE RIGHT SPOT.
HELL...
GCPD
GCPD
I KNOW, RIGHT?! ZOMBIE COPS!
I HATE ZOMBIE COPS.
WHAM

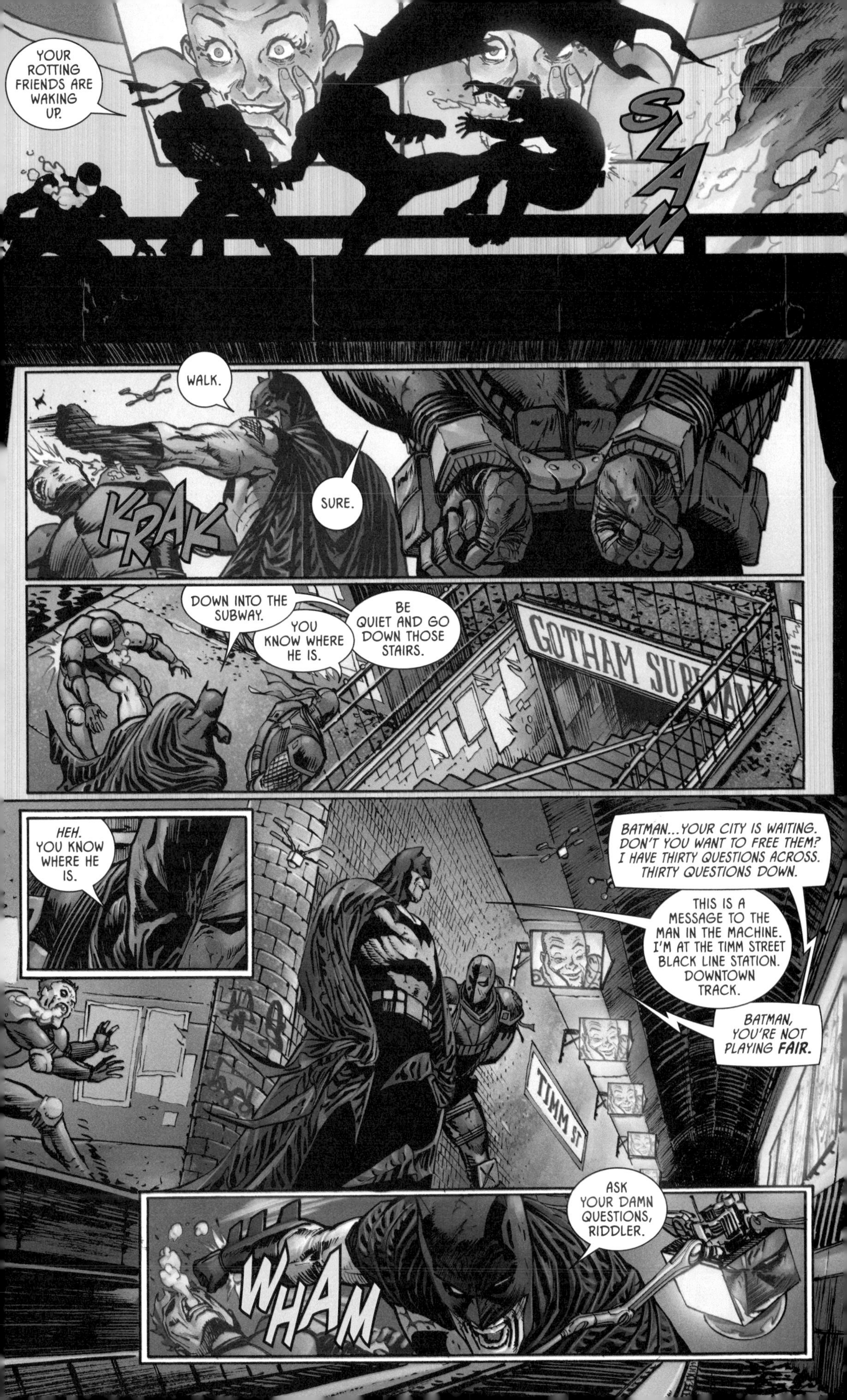

YOUR ROTTING FRIENDS ARE WAKING UP.
SLAM
WALK.
KRAK
SURE.
DOWN INTO THE SUBWAY.
YOU KNOW WHERE HE IS.
BE QUIET AND GO DOWN THOSE STAIRS.
GOTHAM SUBWAY
HEH. YOU KNOW WHERE HE IS.
BATMAN...YOUR CITY IS WAITING. DON'T YOU WANT TO FREE THEM? I HAVE THIRTY QUESTIONS ACROSS. THIRTY QUESTIONS DOWN.
THIS IS A MESSAGE TO THE MAN IN THE MACHINE. I'M AT THE TIMM STREET BLACK LINE STATION. DOWNTOWN TRACK.
BATMAN, YOU'RE NOT PLAYING FAIR.
TIMM ST
ASK YOUR DAMN QUESTIONS, RIDDLER.
WHAM

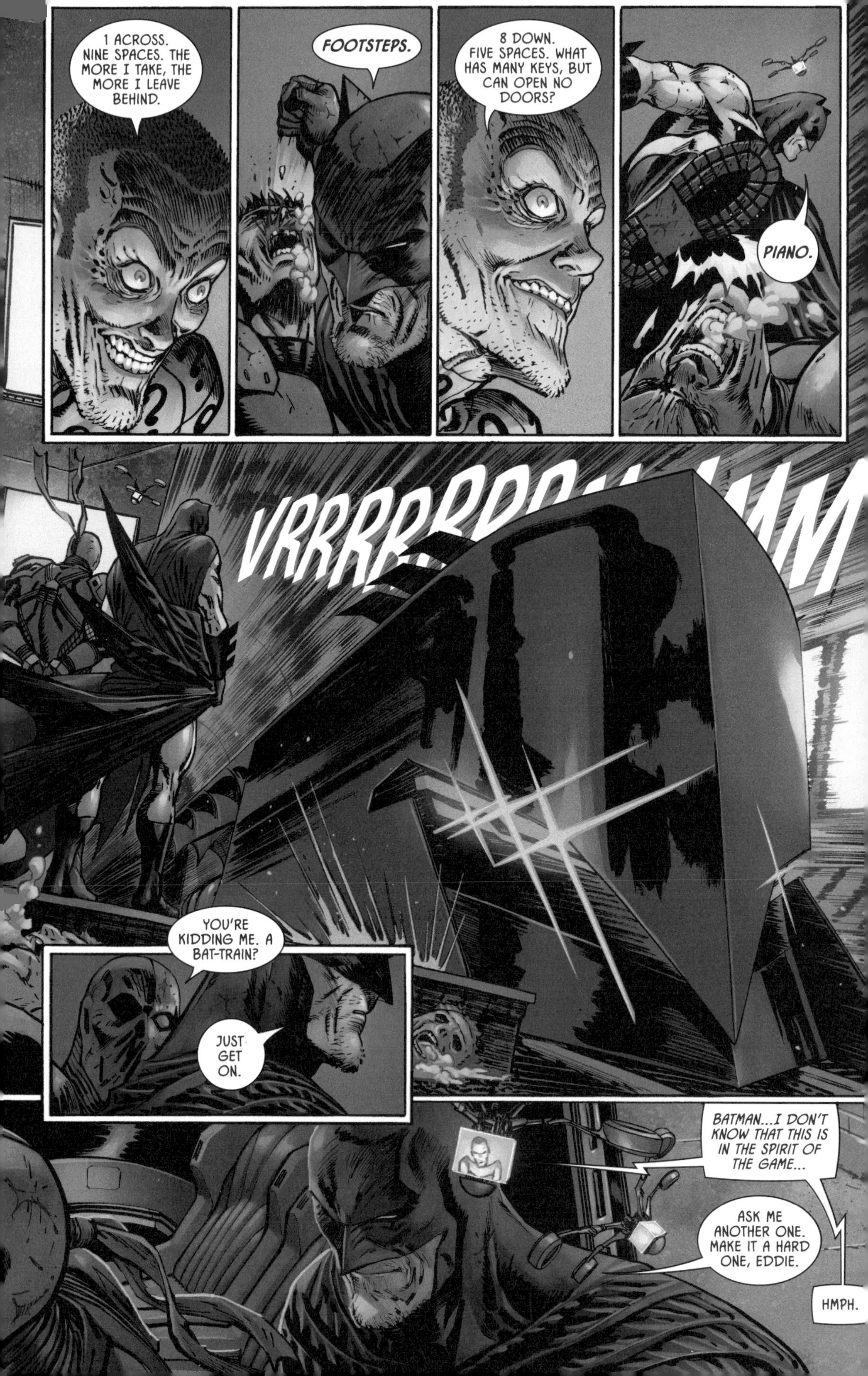
1 ACROSS. NINE SPACES. THE MORE I TAKE, THE MORE I LEAVE BEHIND.
FOOTSTEPS.
8 DOWN. FIVE SPACES. WHAT HAS MANY KEYS, BUT CAN OPEN NO DOORS?
PIANO.
VRRRRRRRMMM
YOU'RE KIDDING ME. A BAT-TRAIN?
JUST GET ON.
BATMAN...I DON'T KNOW THAT THIS IS IN THE SPIRIT OF THE GAME...
ASK ME ANOTHER ONE. MAKE IT A HARD ONE, EDDIE.
HMPH.

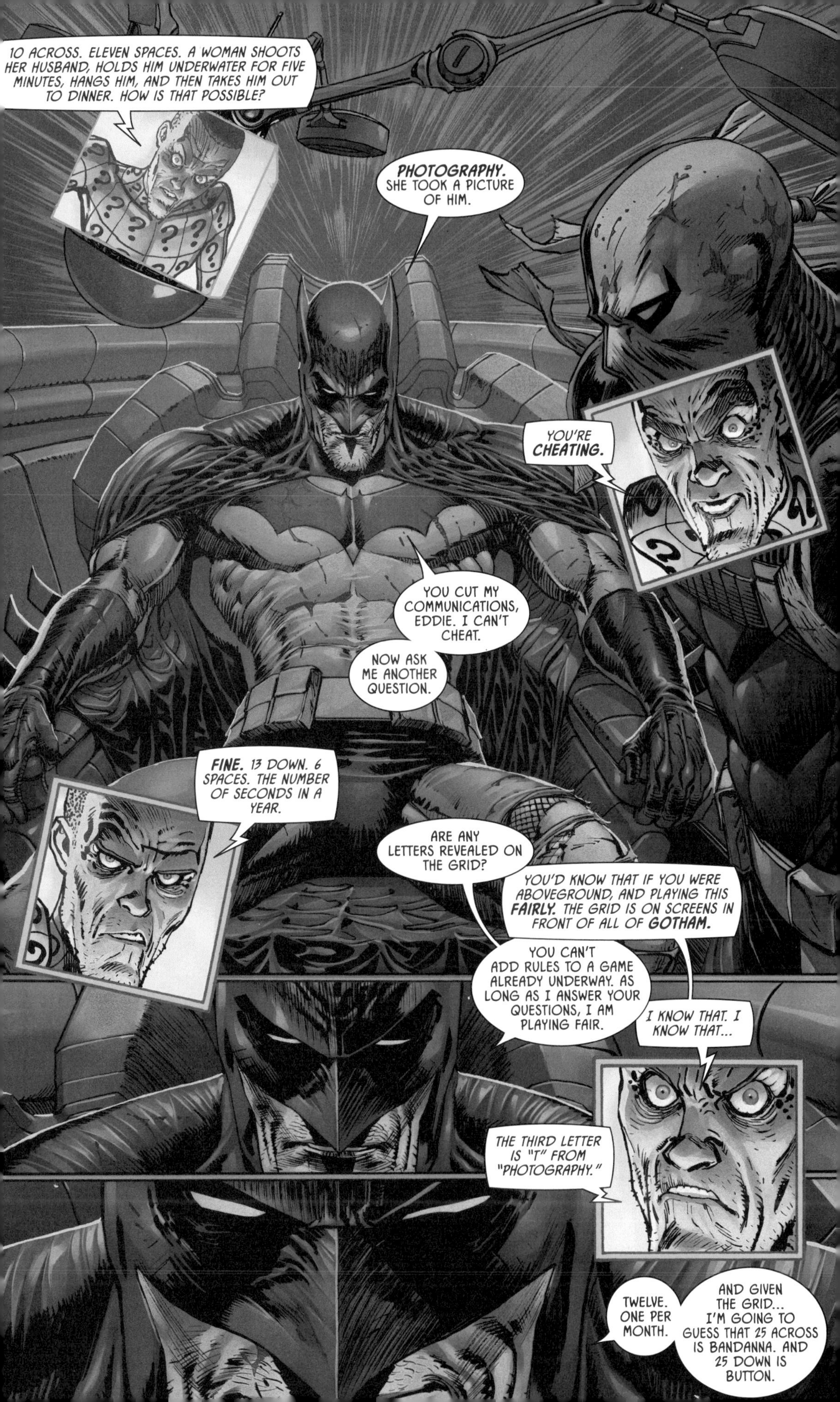
10 ACROSS. ELEVEN SPACES. A WOMAN SHOOTS HER HUSBAND, HOLDS HIM UNDERWATER FOR FIVE MINUTES, HANGS HIM, AND THEN TAKES HIM OUT TO DINNER. HOW IS THAT POSSIBLE?
PHOTOGRAPHY. SHE TOOK A PICTURE OF HIM.
YOU'RE CHEATING.
YOU CUT MY COMMUNICATIONS, EDDIE. I CAN'T CHEAT.
NOW ASK ME ANOTHER QUESTION.
FINE. 13 DOWN. 6 SPACES. THE NUMBER OF SECONDS IN A YEAR.
ARE ANY LETTERS REVEALED ON THE GRID?
YOU'D KNOW THAT IF YOU WERE ABOVEGROUND, AND PLAYING THIS FAIRLY. THE GRID IS ON SCREENS IN FRONT OF ALL OF GOTHAM.
YOU CAN'T ADD RULES TO A GAME ALREADY UNDERWAY. AS LONG AS I ANSWER YOUR QUESTIONS, I AM PLAYING FAIR.
I KNOW THAT. I KNOW THAT...
THE THIRD LETTER IS "T" FROM "PHOTOGRAPHY."
TWELVE. ONE PER MONTH.
AND GIVEN THE GRID... I'M GOING TO GUESS THAT 25 ACROSS IS BANDANNA. AND 25 DOWN IS BUTTON.

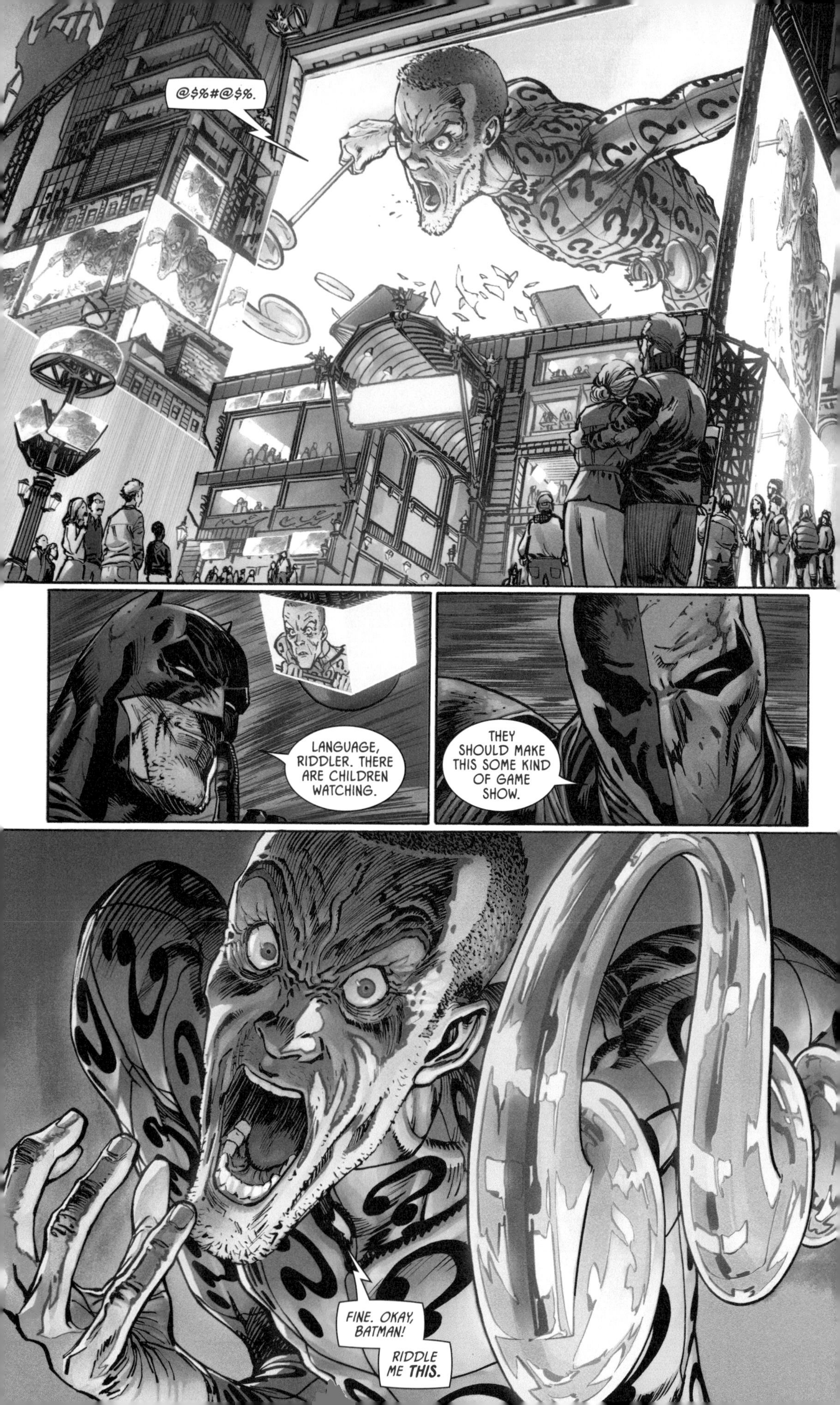
@$%#@$%.
LANGUAGE, RIDDLER. THERE ARE CHILDREN WATCHING.
THEY SHOULD MAKE THIS SOME KIND OF GAME SHOW.
FINE. OKAY, BATMAN!
RIDDLE ME THIS.

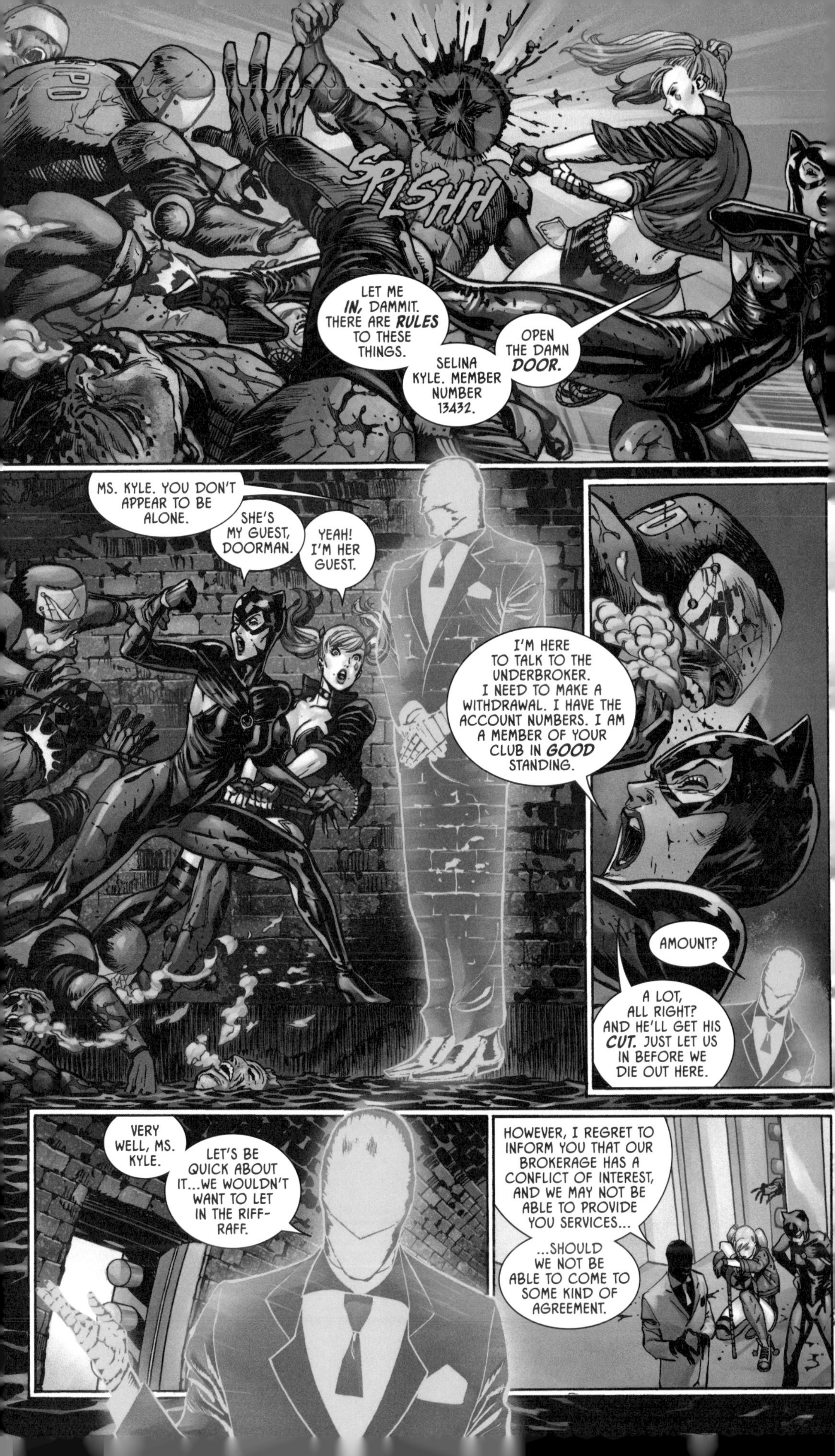
SPLSHH
LET ME IN, DAMMIT. THERE ARE RULES TO THESE THINGS.
SELINA KYLE. MEMBER NUMBER 13432.
OPEN THE DAMN DOOR.
MS. KYLE. YOU DON'T APPEAR TO BE ALONE.
SHE'S MY GUEST, DOORMAN.
YEAH! I'M HER GUEST.
I'M HERE TO TALK TO THE UNDERBROKER. I NEED TO MAKE A WITHDRAWAL. I HAVE THE ACCOUNT NUMBERS. I AM A MEMBER OF YOUR CLUB IN GOOD STANDING.
AMOUNT?
A LOT, ALL RIGHT? AND HE'LL GET HIS CUT. JUST LET US IN BEFORE WE DIE OUT HERE.
VERY WELL, MS. KYLE.
LET'S BE QUICK ABOUT IT...WE WOULDN'T WANT TO LET IN THE RIFF-RAFF.
HOWEVER, I REGRET TO INFORM YOU THAT OUR BROKERAGE HAS A CONFLICT OF INTEREST, AND WE MAY NOT BE ABLE TO PROVIDE YOU SERVICES...
...SHOULD WE NOT BE ABLE TO COME TO SOME KIND OF AGREEMENT.

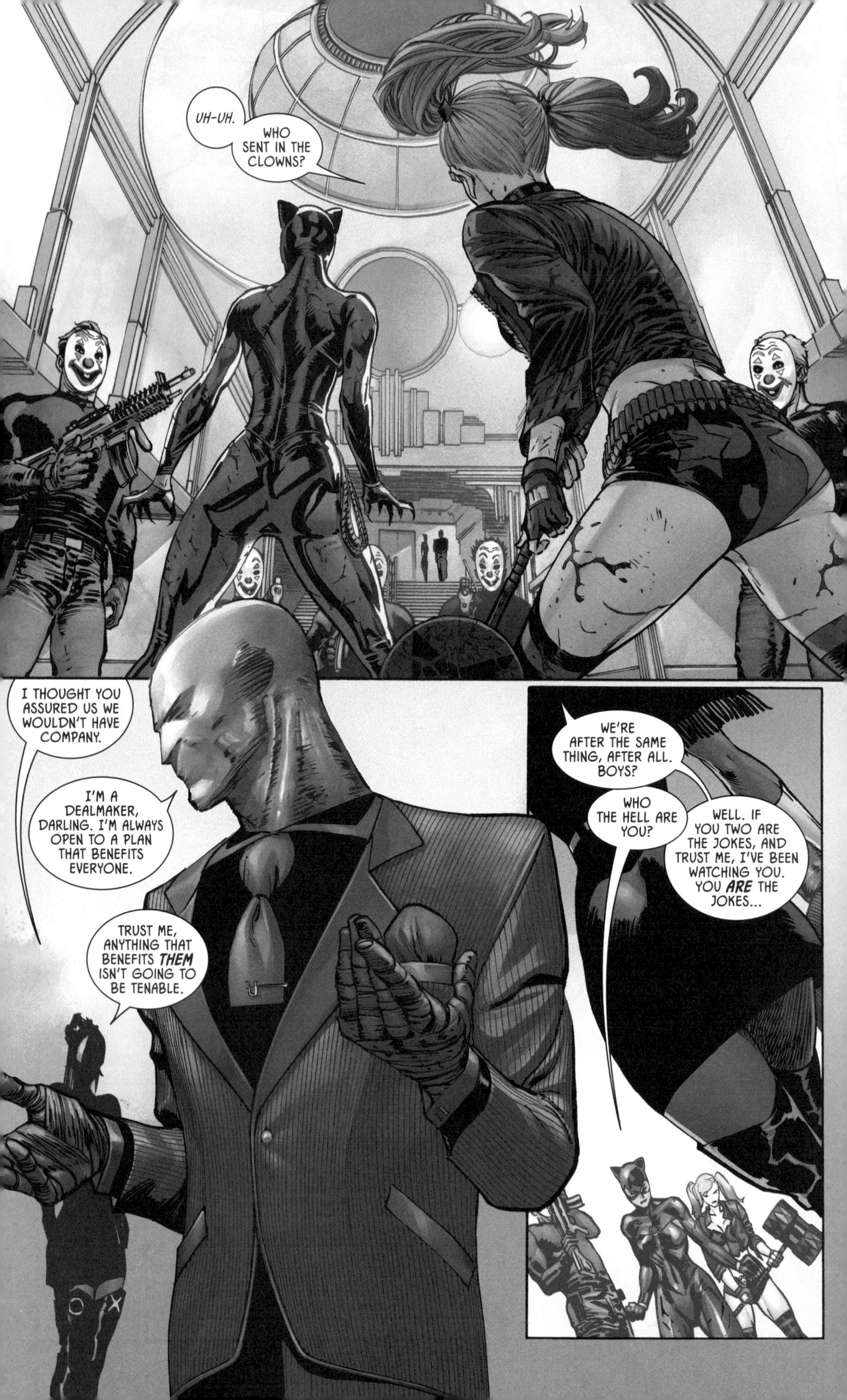
UH-UH.
WHO SENT IN THE CLOWNS?
I THOUGHT YOU ASSURED US WE WOULDN'T HAVE COMPANY.
I'M A DEALMAKER, DARLING. I'M ALWAYS OPEN TO A PLAN THAT BENEFITS EVERYONE.
TRUST ME, ANYTHING THAT BENEFITS *THEM* ISN'T GOING TO BE TENABLE.
WE'RE AFTER THE SAME THING, AFTER ALL. BOYS?
WHO THE HELL ARE YOU?
WELL. IF YOU TWO ARE THE JOKES, AND TRUST ME, I'VE BEEN WATCHING YOU. YOU *ARE* THE JOKES...

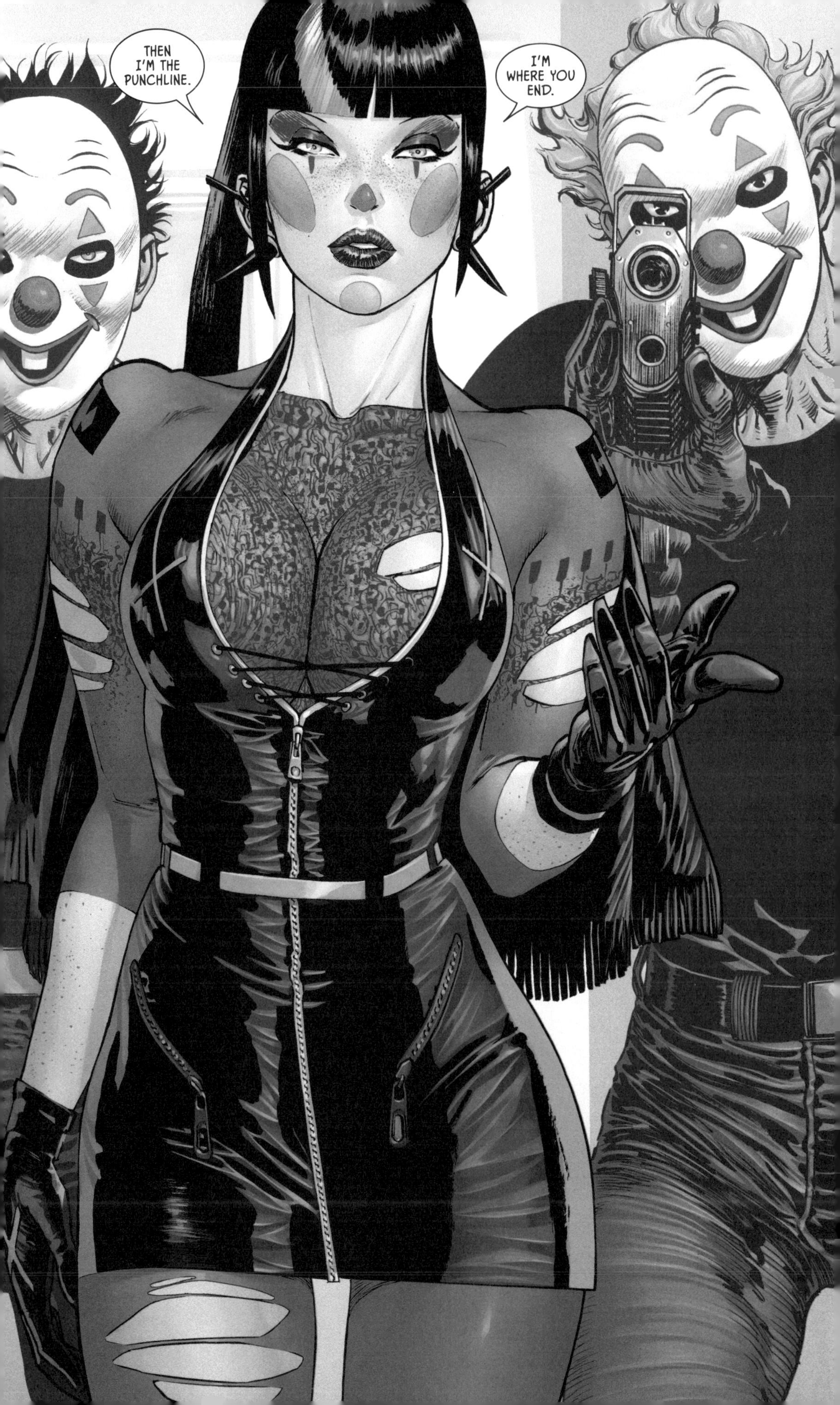
THEN I'M THE PUNCHLINE.
I'M WHERE YOU END.

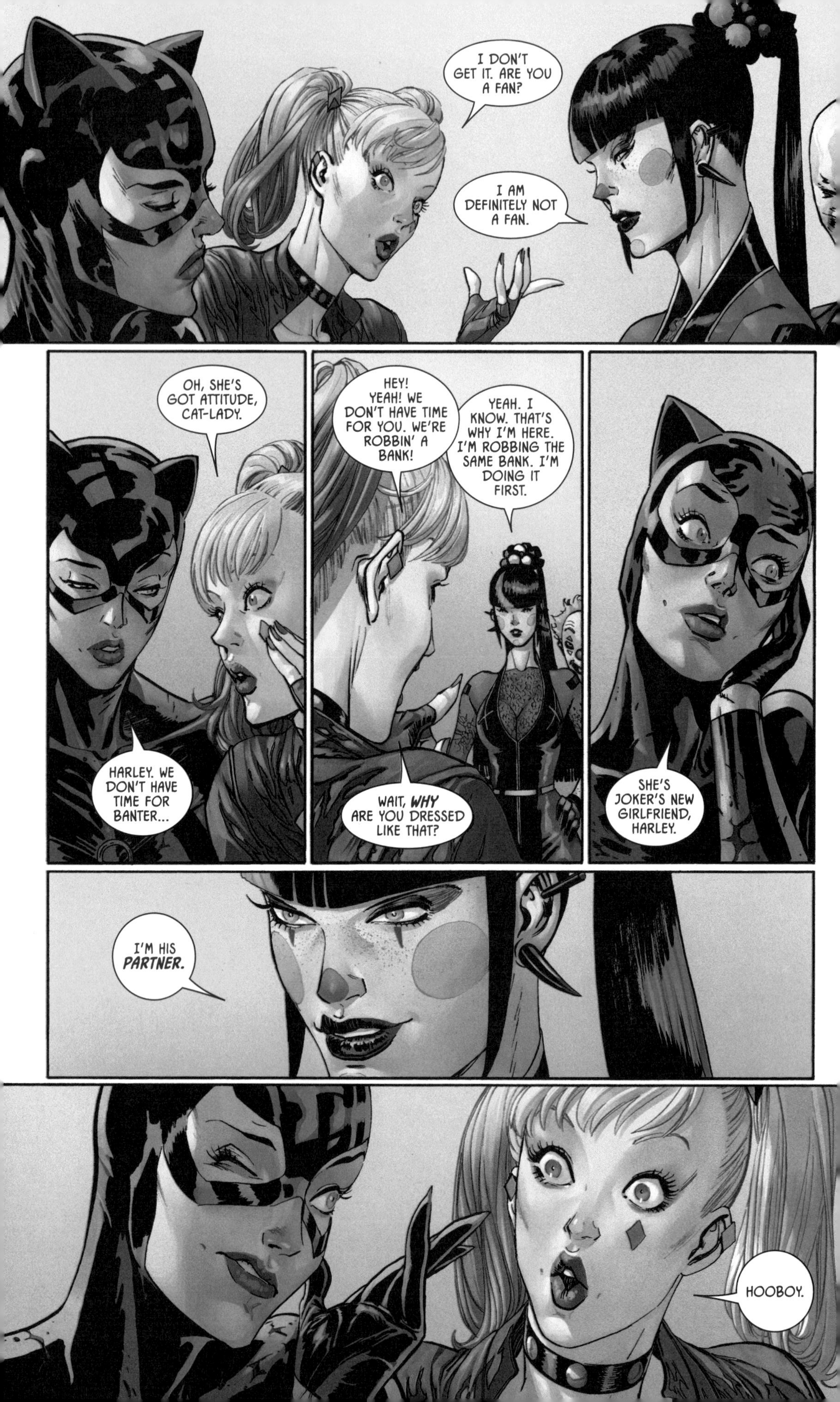
I DON'T GET IT. ARE YOU A FAN?
I AM DEFINITELY NOT A FAN.
OH, SHE'S GOT ATTITUDE, CAT-LADY.
HARLEY. WE DON'T HAVE TIME FOR BANTER...
HEY! YEAH! WE DON'T HAVE TIME FOR YOU. WE'RE ROBBIN' A BANK!
YEAH. I KNOW. THAT'S WHY I'M HERE. I'M ROBBING THE SAME BANK. I'M DOING IT FIRST.
WAIT, *WHY* ARE YOU DRESSED LIKE THAT?
SHE'S JOKER'S NEW GIRLFRIEND, HARLEY.
I'M HIS ***PARTNER.***
HOOBOY.

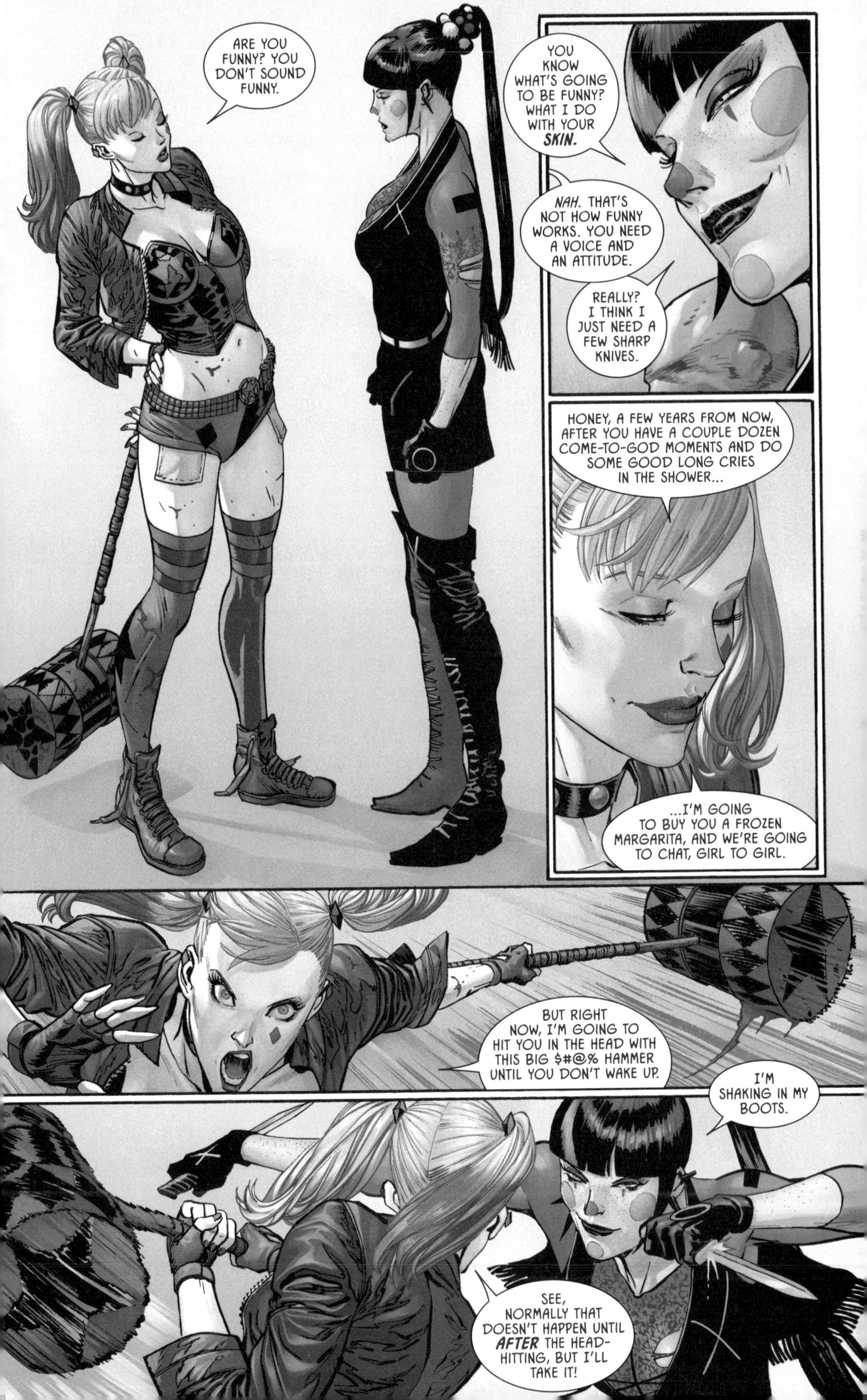
ARE YOU FUNNY? YOU DON'T SOUND FUNNY.
YOU KNOW WHAT'S GOING TO BE FUNNY? WHAT I DO WITH YOUR *SKIN.*
NAH. THAT'S NOT HOW FUNNY WORKS. YOU NEED A VOICE AND AN ATTITUDE.
REALLY? I THINK I JUST NEED A FEW SHARP KNIVES.
HONEY, A FEW YEARS FROM NOW, AFTER YOU HAVE A COUPLE DOZEN COME-TO-GOD MOMENTS AND DO SOME GOOD LONG CRIES IN THE SHOWER...
...I'M GOING TO BUY YOU A FROZEN MARGARITA, AND WE'RE GOING TO CHAT, GIRL TO GIRL.
BUT RIGHT NOW, I'M GOING TO HIT YOU IN THE HEAD WITH THIS BIG $#@% HAMMER UNTIL YOU DON'T WAKE UP.
I'M SHAKING IN MY BOOTS.
SEE, NORMALLY THAT DOESN'T HAPPEN UNTIL ***AFTER*** THE HEAD-HITTING, BUT I'LL TAKE IT!

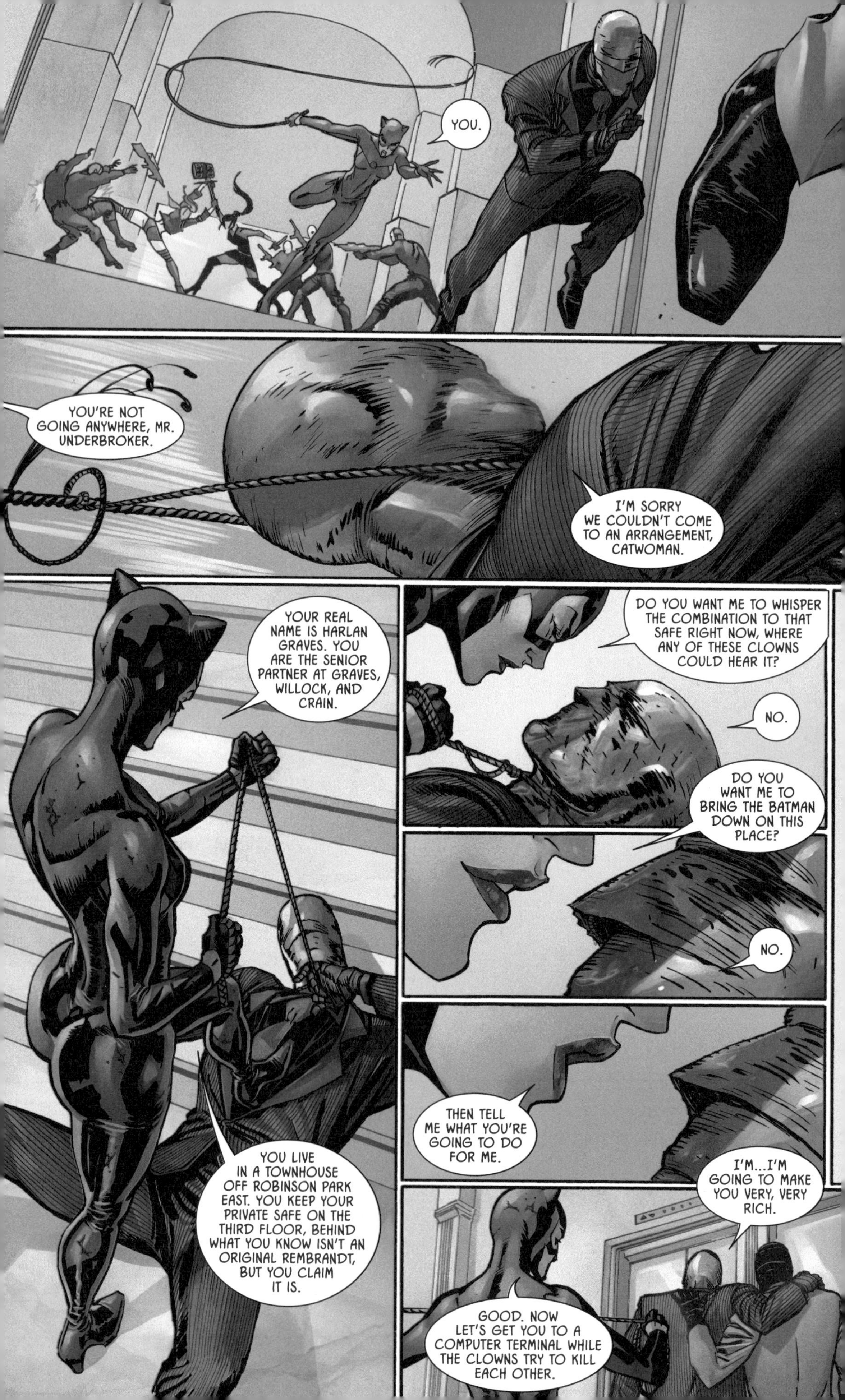
YOU.
YOU'RE NOT GOING ANYWHERE, MR. UNDERBROKER.
I'M SORRY WE COULDN'T COME TO AN ARRANGEMENT, CATWOMAN.
YOUR REAL NAME IS HARLAN GRAVES. YOU ARE THE SENIOR PARTNER AT GRAVES, WILLOCK, AND CRAIN.
YOU LIVE IN A TOWNHOUSE OFF ROBINSON PARK EAST. YOU KEEP YOUR PRIVATE SAFE ON THE THIRD FLOOR, BEHIND WHAT YOU KNOW ISN'T AN ORIGINAL REMBRANDT, BUT YOU CLAIM IT IS.
DO YOU WANT ME TO WHISPER THE COMBINATION TO THAT SAFE RIGHT NOW, WHERE ANY OF THESE CLOWNS COULD HEAR IT?
NO.
DO YOU WANT ME TO BRING THE BATMAN DOWN ON THIS PLACE?
NO.
THEN TELL ME WHAT YOU'RE GOING TO DO FOR ME.
I'M...I'M GOING TO MAKE YOU VERY, VERY RICH.
GOOD. NOW LET'S GET YOU TO A COMPUTER TERMINAL WHILE THE CLOWNS TRY TO KILL EACH OTHER.

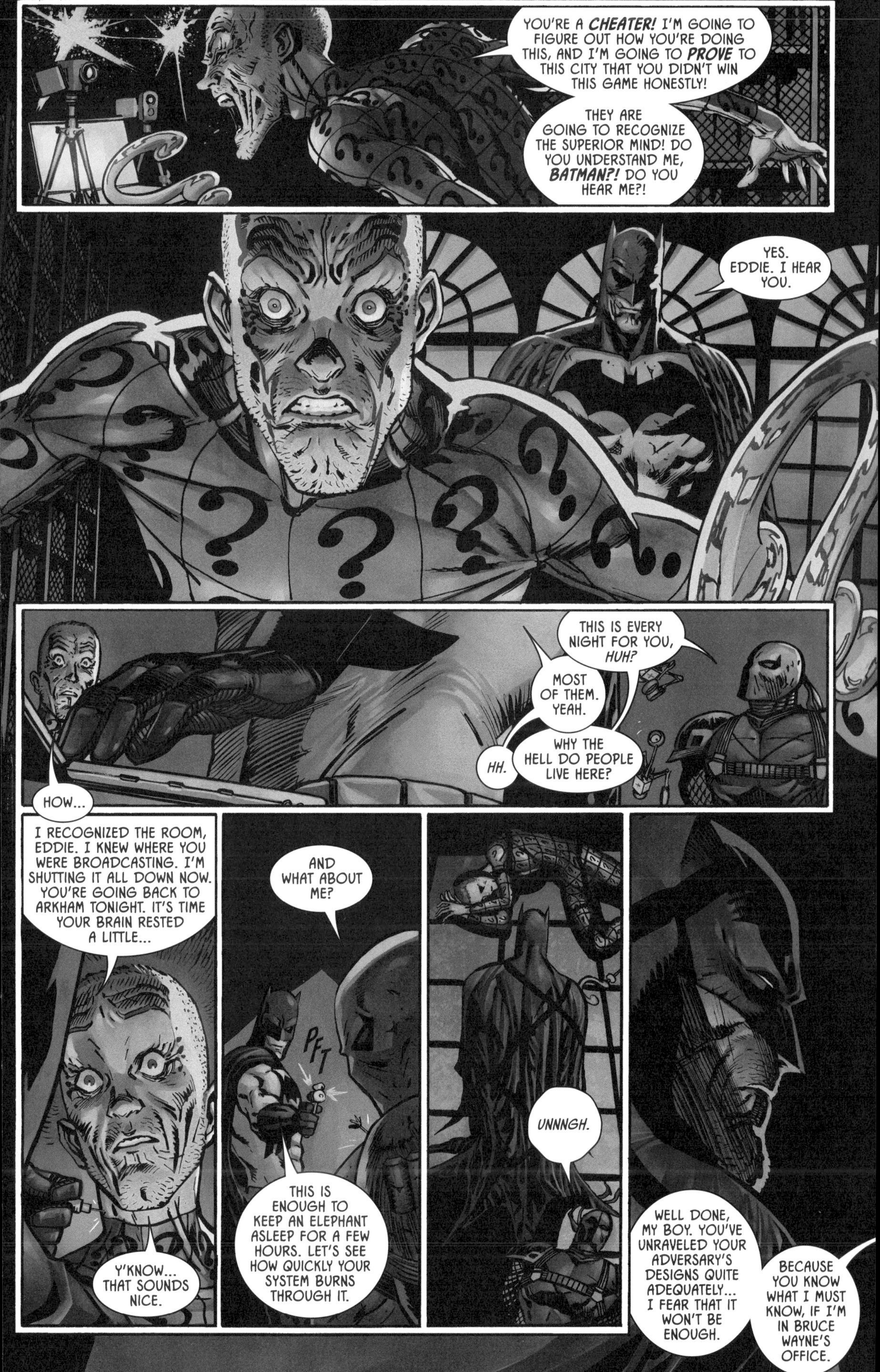
YOU'RE A CHEATER! I'M GOING TO FIGURE OUT HOW YOU'RE DOING THIS, AND I'M GOING TO PROVE TO THIS CITY THAT YOU DIDN'T WIN THIS GAME HONESTLY!
THEY ARE GOING TO RECOGNIZE THE SUPERIOR MIND! DO YOU UNDERSTAND ME, BATMAN?! DO YOU HEAR ME?!
YES. EDDIE. I HEAR YOU.
HOW...
THIS IS EVERY NIGHT FOR YOU, HUH?
MOST OF THEM. YEAH.
HH.
WHY THE HELL DO PEOPLE LIVE HERE?
I RECOGNIZED THE ROOM, EDDIE. I KNEW WHERE YOU WERE BROADCASTING. I'M SHUTTING IT ALL DOWN NOW. YOU'RE GOING BACK TO ARKHAM TONIGHT. IT'S TIME YOUR BRAIN RESTED A LITTLE...
Y'KNOW... THAT SOUNDS NICE.
AND WHAT ABOUT ME?
PFFT
THIS IS ENOUGH TO KEEP AN ELEPHANT ASLEEP FOR A FEW HOURS. LET'S SEE HOW QUICKLY YOUR SYSTEM BURNS THROUGH IT.
UNNNGH.
WELL DONE, MY BOY. YOU'VE UNRAVELED YOUR ADVERSARY'S DESIGNS QUITE ADEQUATELY... I FEAR THAT IT WON'T BE ENOUGH.
BECAUSE YOU KNOW WHAT I MUST KNOW, IF I'M IN BRUCE WAYNE'S OFFICE.

HELLO, BRUCE.
PLEASE COME IN. WE SHOULD TALK A LITTLE BEFORE I KILL YOU.
DC COMICS proudly presents
THEIR DARK DESIGNS
PART 7
JAMES TYNION IV writer GUILLEM MARCH artist
TOMEU MOREY colors CLAYTON COWLES letters
YASMINE PUTRI w/ TONY DANIEL cover
DAVE WIELGOSZ assoc. editor BEN ABERNATHY editor

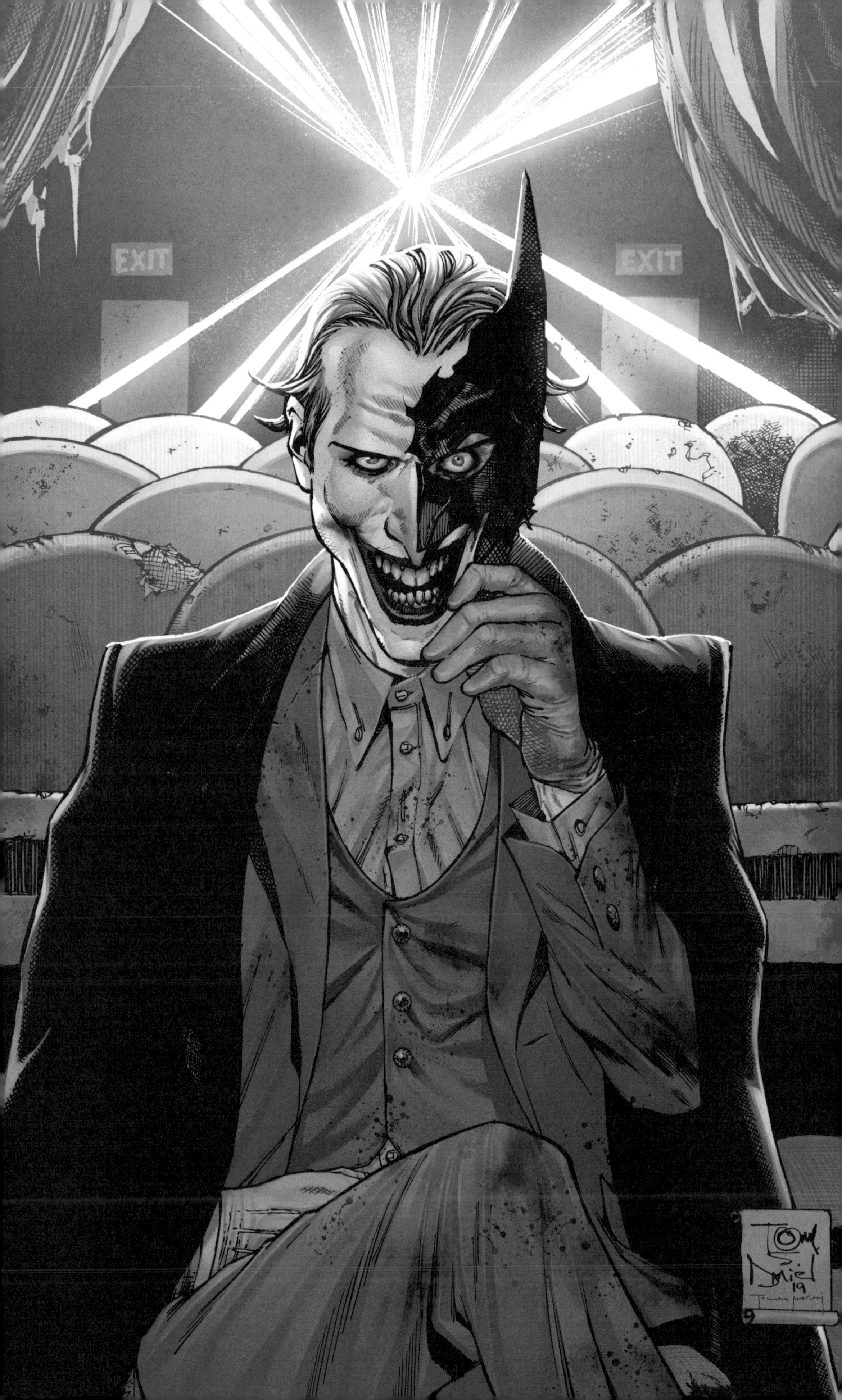
EXIT
EXIT

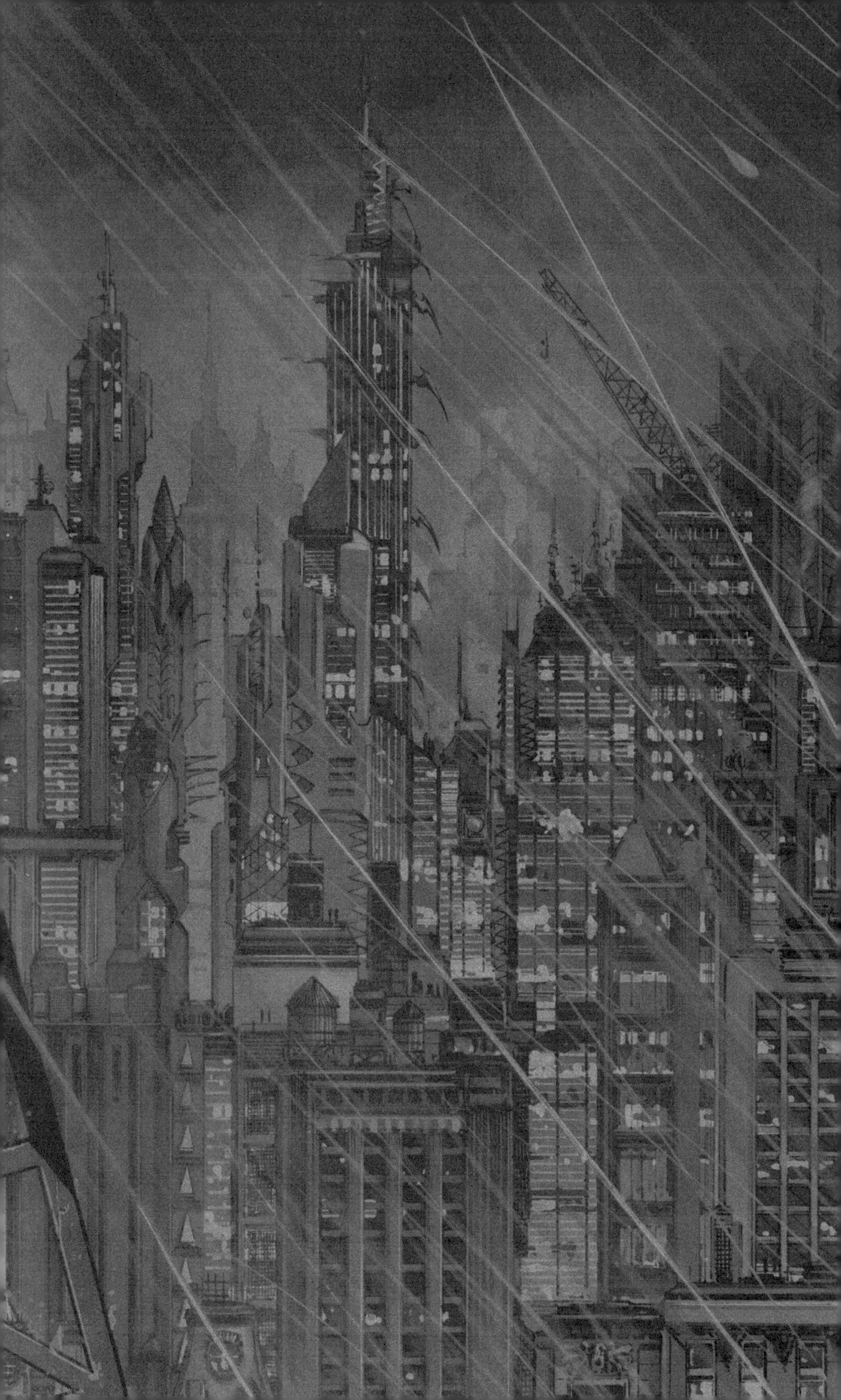

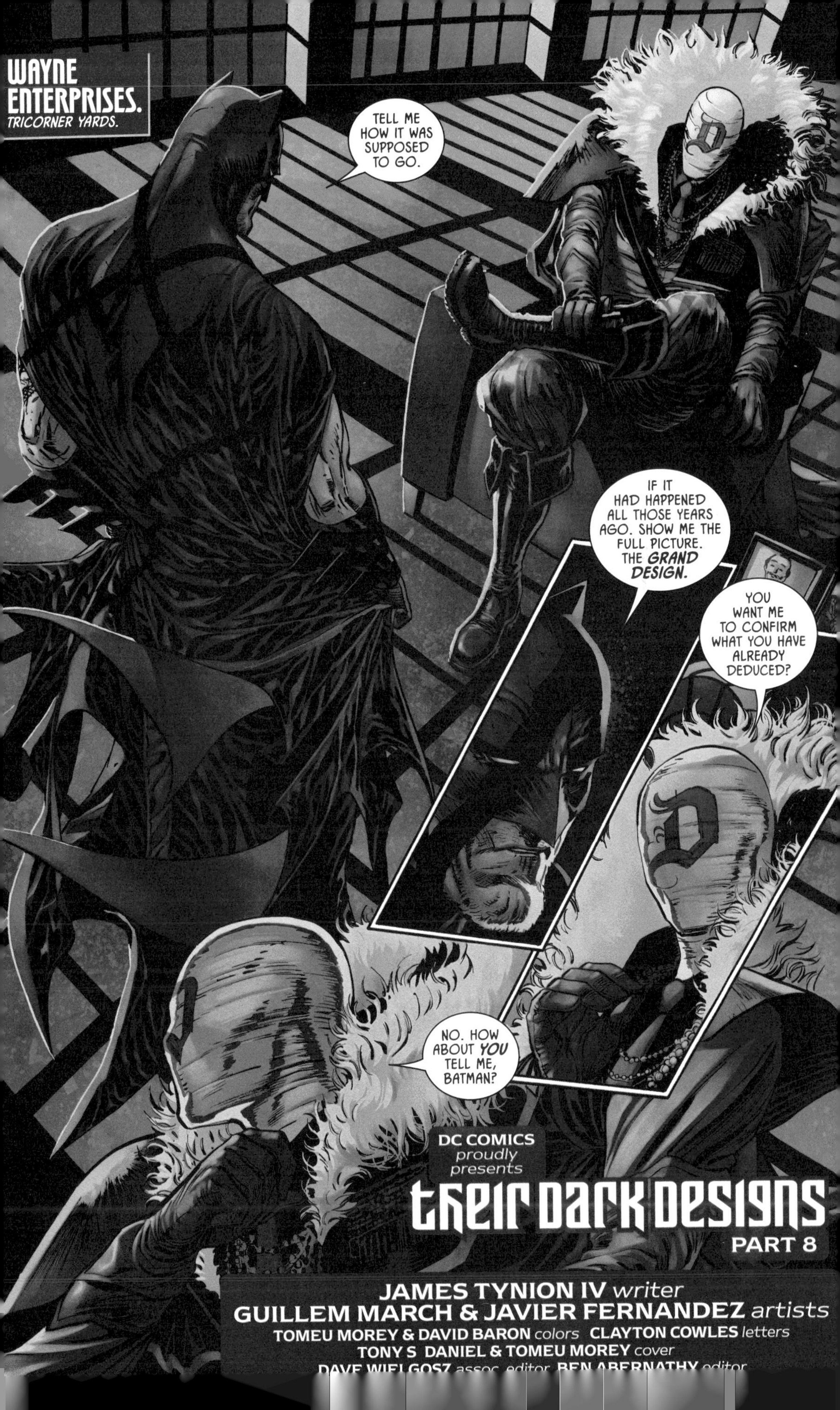

WAYNE ENTERPRISES.
TRICORNER YARDS.
TELL ME HOW IT WAS SUPPOSED TO GO.
IF IT HAD HAPPENED ALL THOSE YEARS AGO. SHOW ME THE FULL PICTURE. THE GRAND DESIGN.
YOU WANT ME TO CONFIRM WHAT YOU HAVE ALREADY DEDUCED?
NO. HOW ABOUT YOU TELL ME, BATMAN?
DC COMICS proudly presents
THEIR DARK DESIGNS
PART 8
JAMES TYNION IV writer
GUILLEM MARCH & JAVIER FERNANDEZ artists
TOMEU MOREY & DAVID BARON colors CLAYTON COWLES letters
TONY S DANIEL & TOMEU MOREY cover

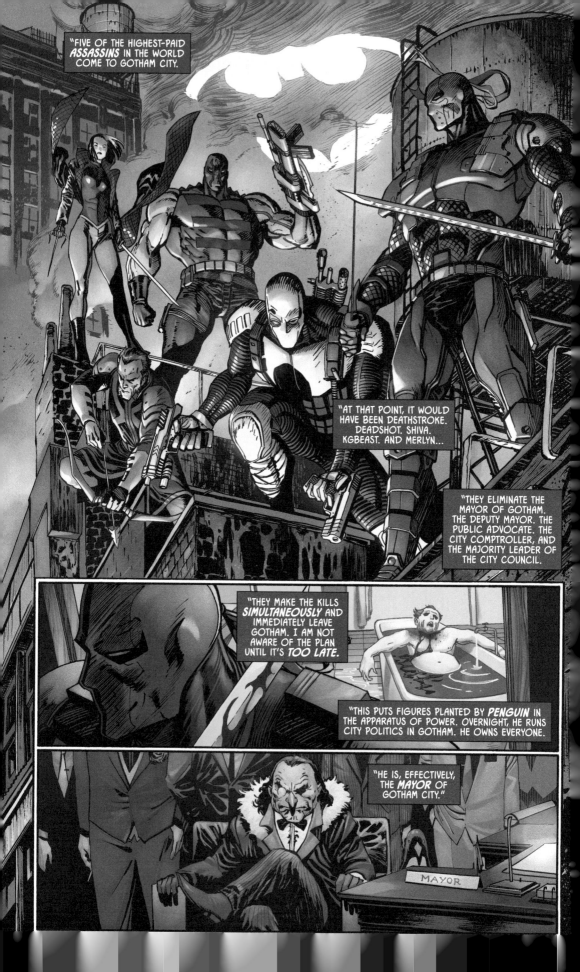

"FIVE OF THE HIGHEST-PAID *ASSASSINS* IN THE WORLD COME TO GOTHAM CITY.

"AT THAT POINT, IT WOULD HAVE BEEN DEATHSTROKE. DEADSHOT. SHIVA. KGBEAST. AND MERLYN...

"THEY ELIMINATE THE MAYOR OF GOTHAM. THE DEPUTY MAYOR. THE PUBLIC ADVOCATE. THE CITY COMPTROLLER, AND THE MAJORITY LEADER OF THE CITY COUNCIL.

"THEY MAKE THE KILLS *SIMULTANEOUSLY* AND IMMEDIATELY LEAVE GOTHAM. I AM NOT AWARE OF THE PLAN UNTIL IT'S *TOO LATE.*

"THIS PUTS FIGURES PLANTED BY *PENGUIN* IN THE APPARATUS OF POWER. OVERNIGHT, HE RUNS CITY POLITICS IN GOTHAM. HE OWNS EVERYONE.

"HE IS, EFFECTIVELY, THE *MAYOR* OF GOTHAM CITY."

MAYOR

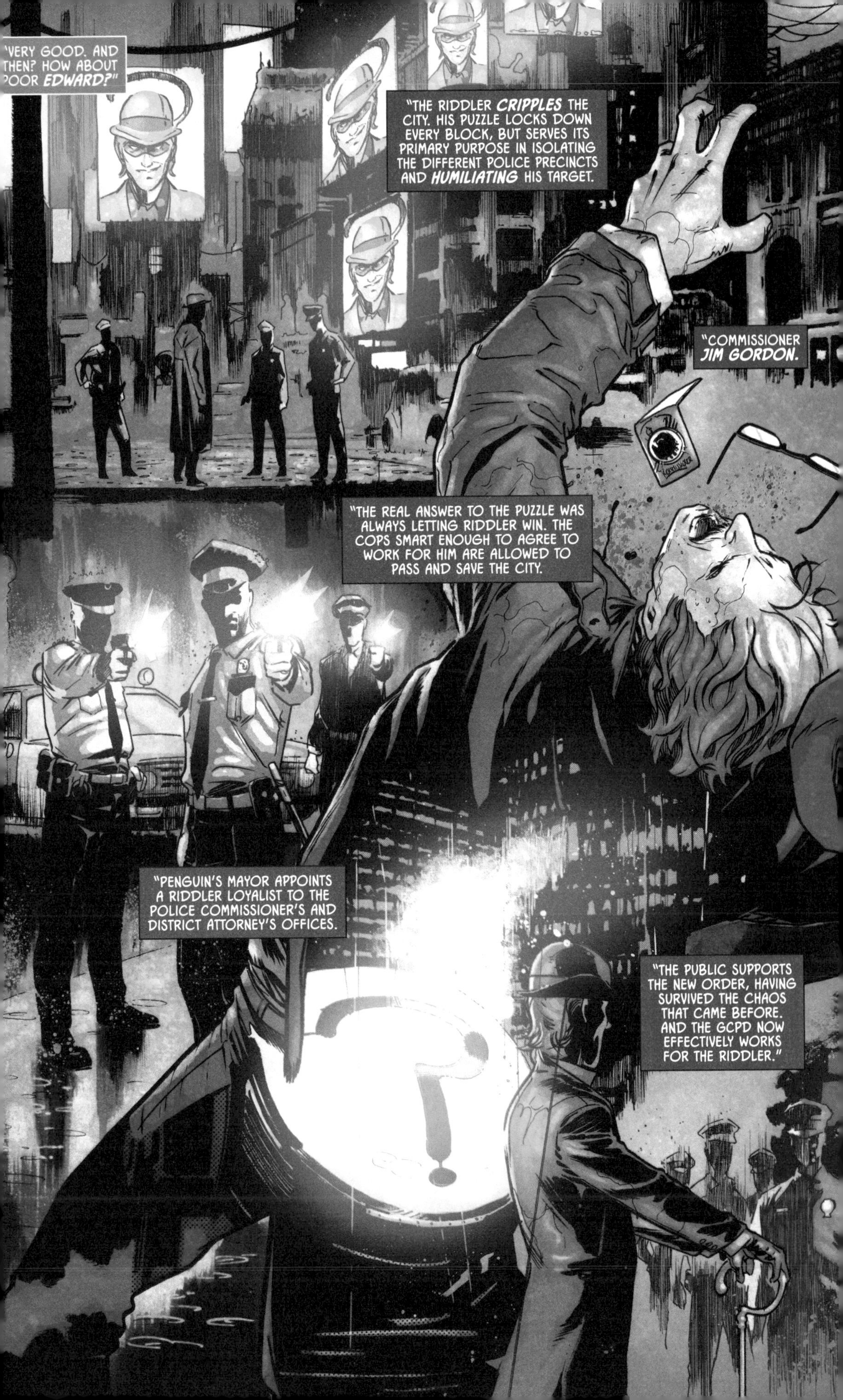
"VERY GOOD. AND THEN? HOW ABOUT POOR EDWARD?"
"THE RIDDLER CRIPPLES THE CITY. HIS PUZZLE LOCKS DOWN EVERY BLOCK, BUT SERVES ITS PRIMARY PURPOSE IN ISOLATING THE DIFFERENT POLICE PRECINCTS AND HUMILIATING HIS TARGET.
"COMMISSIONER JIM GORDON.
"THE REAL ANSWER TO THE PUZZLE WAS ALWAYS LETTING RIDDLER WIN. THE COPS SMART ENOUGH TO AGREE TO WORK FOR HIM ARE ALLOWED TO PASS AND SAVE THE CITY.
"PENGUIN'S MAYOR APPOINTS A RIDDLER LOYALIST TO THE POLICE COMMISSIONER'S AND DISTRICT ATTORNEY'S OFFICES.
"THE PUBLIC SUPPORTS THE NEW ORDER, HAVING SURVIVED THE CHAOS THAT CAME BEFORE. AND THE GCPD NOW EFFECTIVELY WORKS FOR THE RIDDLER."

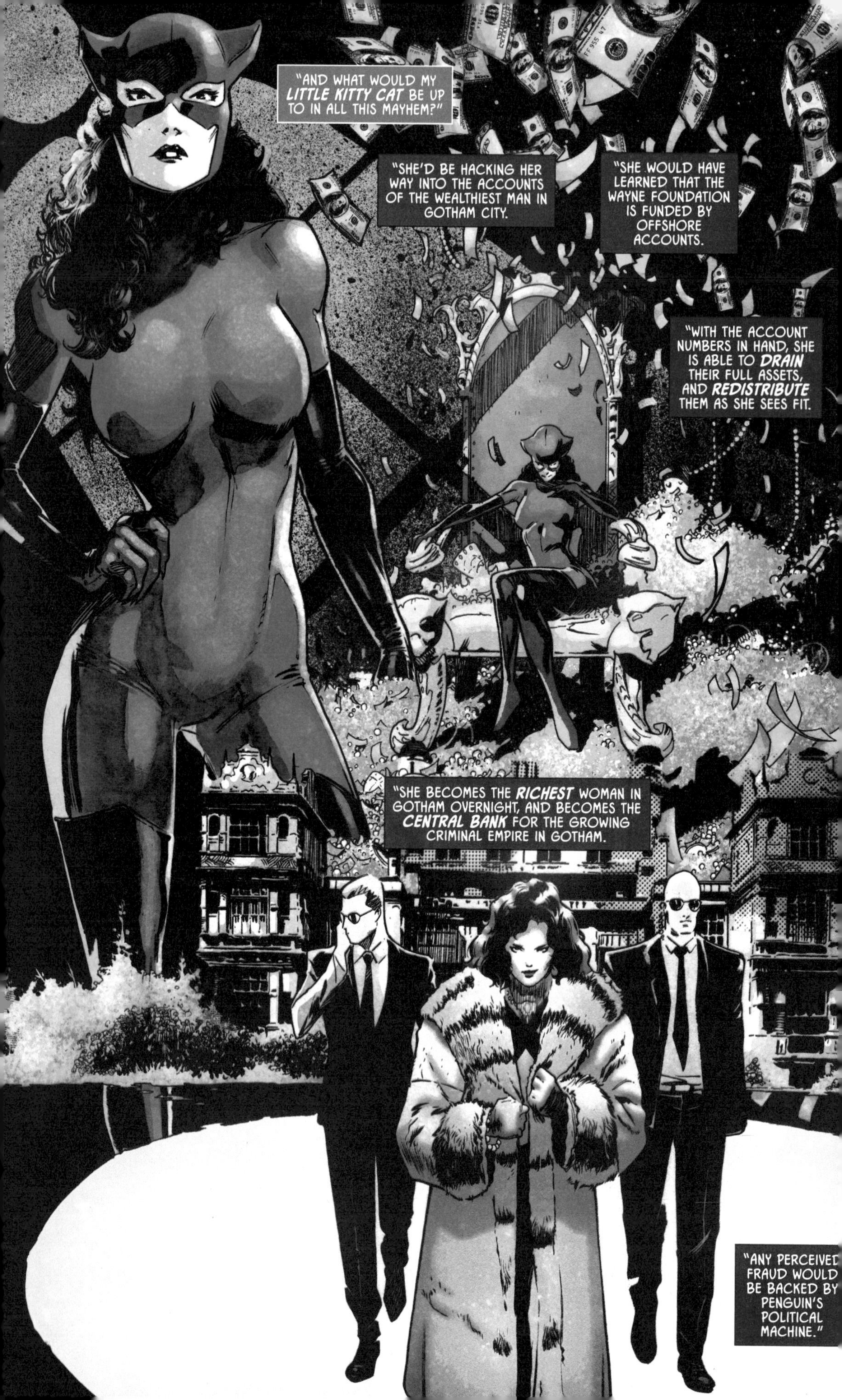
"AND WHAT WOULD MY *LITTLE KITTY CAT* BE UP TO IN ALL THIS MAYHEM?"
"SHE'D BE HACKING HER WAY INTO THE ACCOUNTS OF THE WEALTHIEST MAN IN GOTHAM CITY.
"SHE WOULD HAVE LEARNED THAT THE WAYNE FOUNDATION IS FUNDED BY OFFSHORE ACCOUNTS.
"WITH THE ACCOUNT NUMBERS IN HAND, SHE IS ABLE TO *DRAIN* THEIR FULL ASSETS, AND *REDISTRIBUTE* THEM AS SHE SEES FIT.
"SHE BECOMES THE *RICHEST* WOMAN IN GOTHAM OVERNIGHT, AND BECOMES THE *CENTRAL BANK* FOR THE GROWING CRIMINAL EMPIRE IN GOTHAM.
"ANY PERCEIVED FRAUD WOULD BE BACKED BY PENGUIN'S POLITICAL MACHINE."

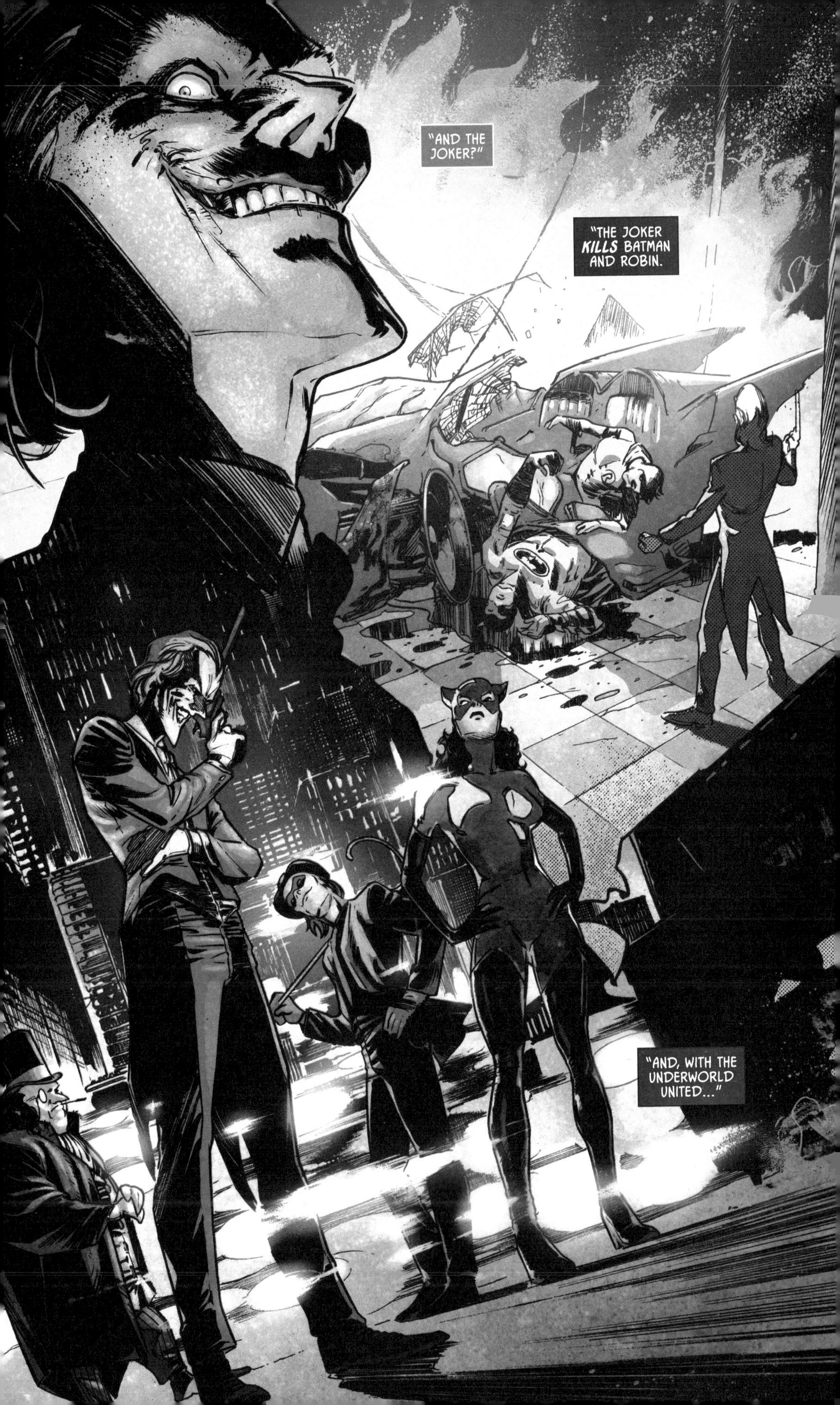
"AND THE JOKER?"
"THE JOKER KILLS BATMAN AND ROBIN.
"AND, WITH THE UNDERWORLD UNITED..."

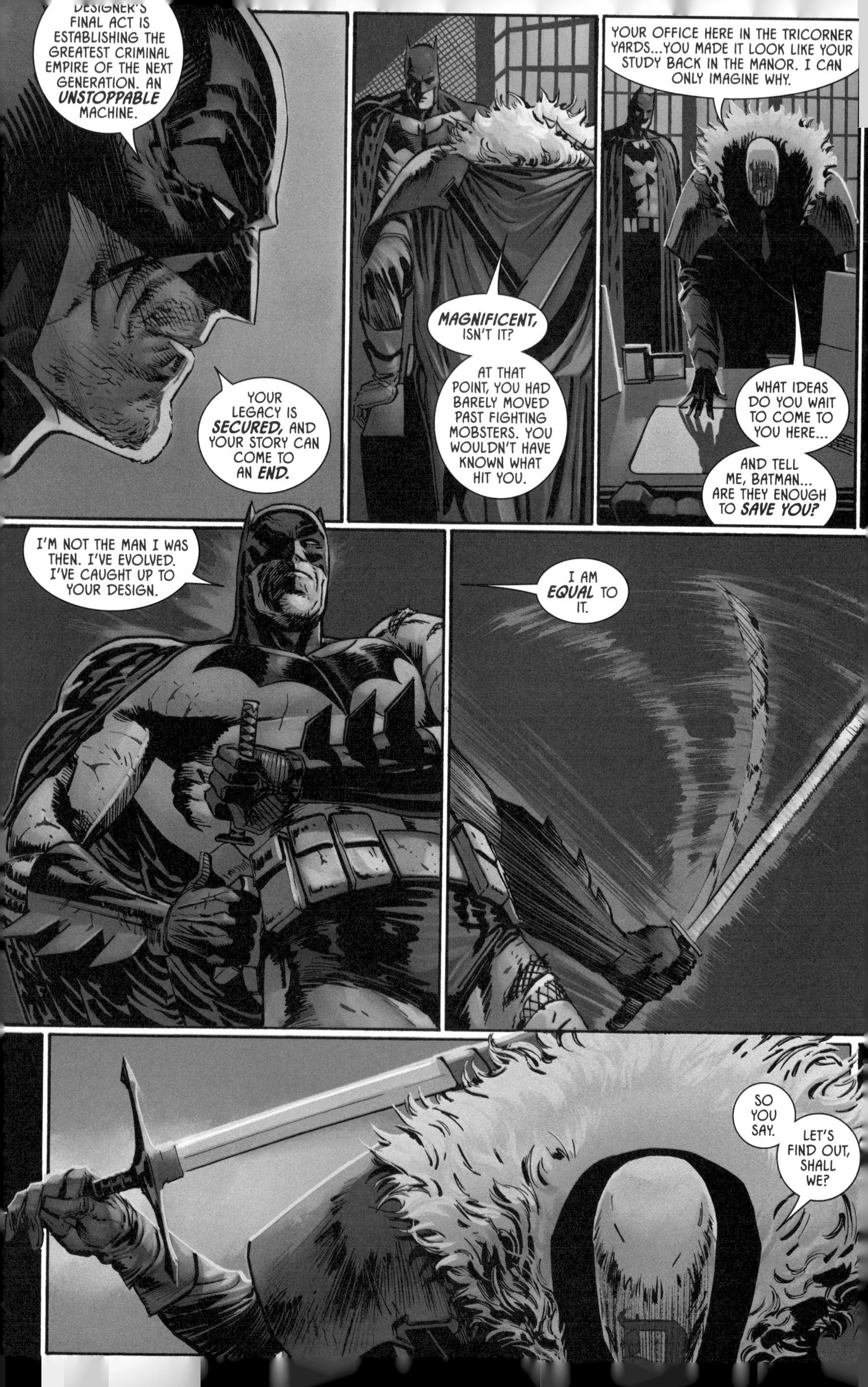
DESIGNER'S FINAL ACT IS ESTABLISHING THE GREATEST CRIMINAL EMPIRE OF THE NEXT GENERATION. AN UNSTOPPABLE MACHINE.
YOUR LEGACY IS SECURED, AND YOUR STORY CAN COME TO AN END.
MAGNIFICENT, ISN'T IT?
AT THAT POINT, YOU HAD BARELY MOVED PAST FIGHTING MOBSTERS. YOU WOULDN'T HAVE KNOWN WHAT HIT YOU.
YOUR OFFICE HERE IN THE TRICORNER YARDS...YOU MADE IT LOOK LIKE YOUR STUDY BACK IN THE MANOR. I CAN ONLY IMAGINE WHY.
WHAT IDEAS DO YOU WAIT TO COME TO YOU HERE...
AND TELL ME, BATMAN... ARE THEY ENOUGH TO SAVE YOU?
I'M NOT THE MAN I WAS THEN. I'VE EVOLVED. I'VE CAUGHT UP TO YOUR DESIGN.
I AM EQUAL TO IT.
SO YOU SAY.
LET'S FIND OUT, SHALL WE?

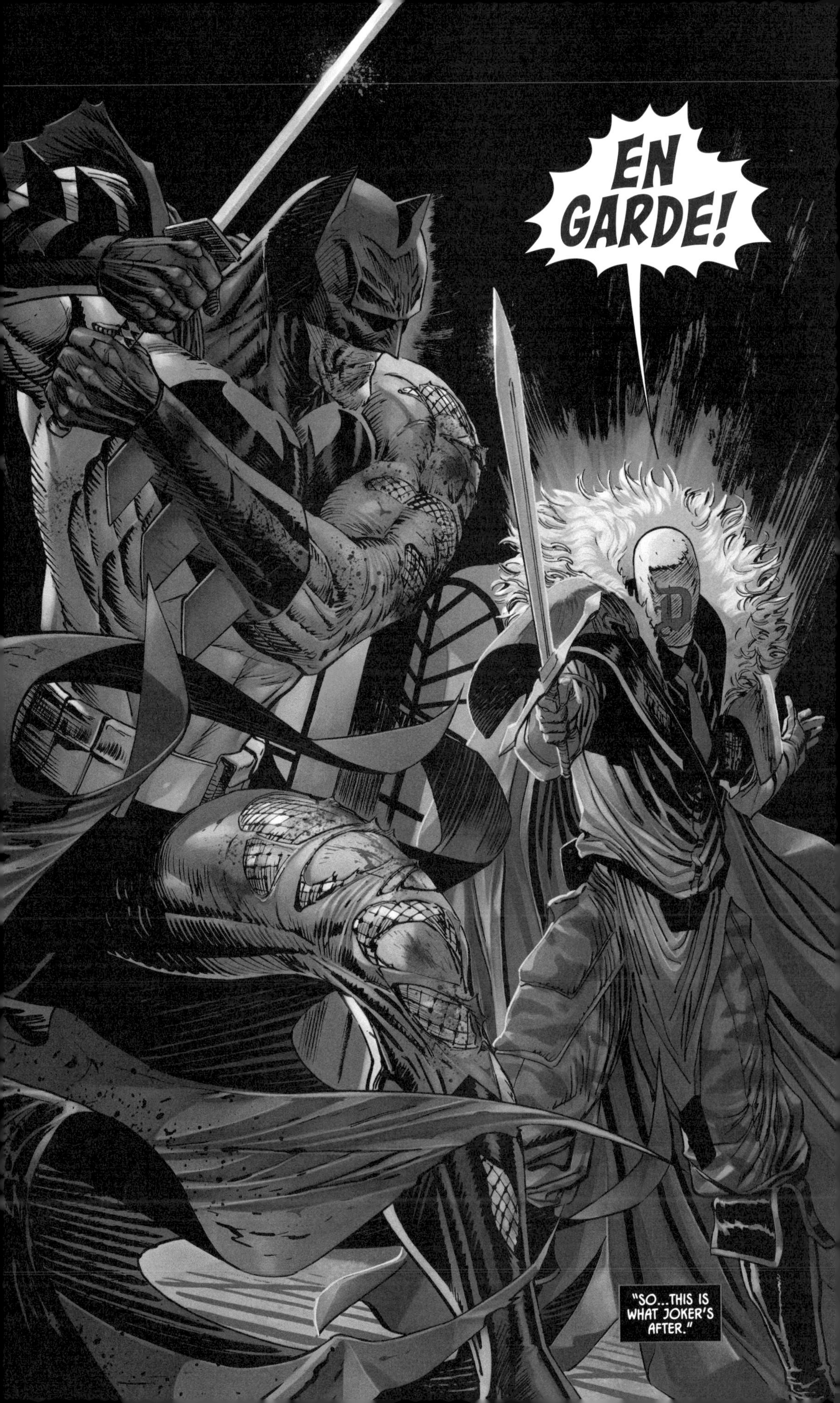
EN GARDE!
"SO...THIS IS WHAT JOKER'S AFTER."

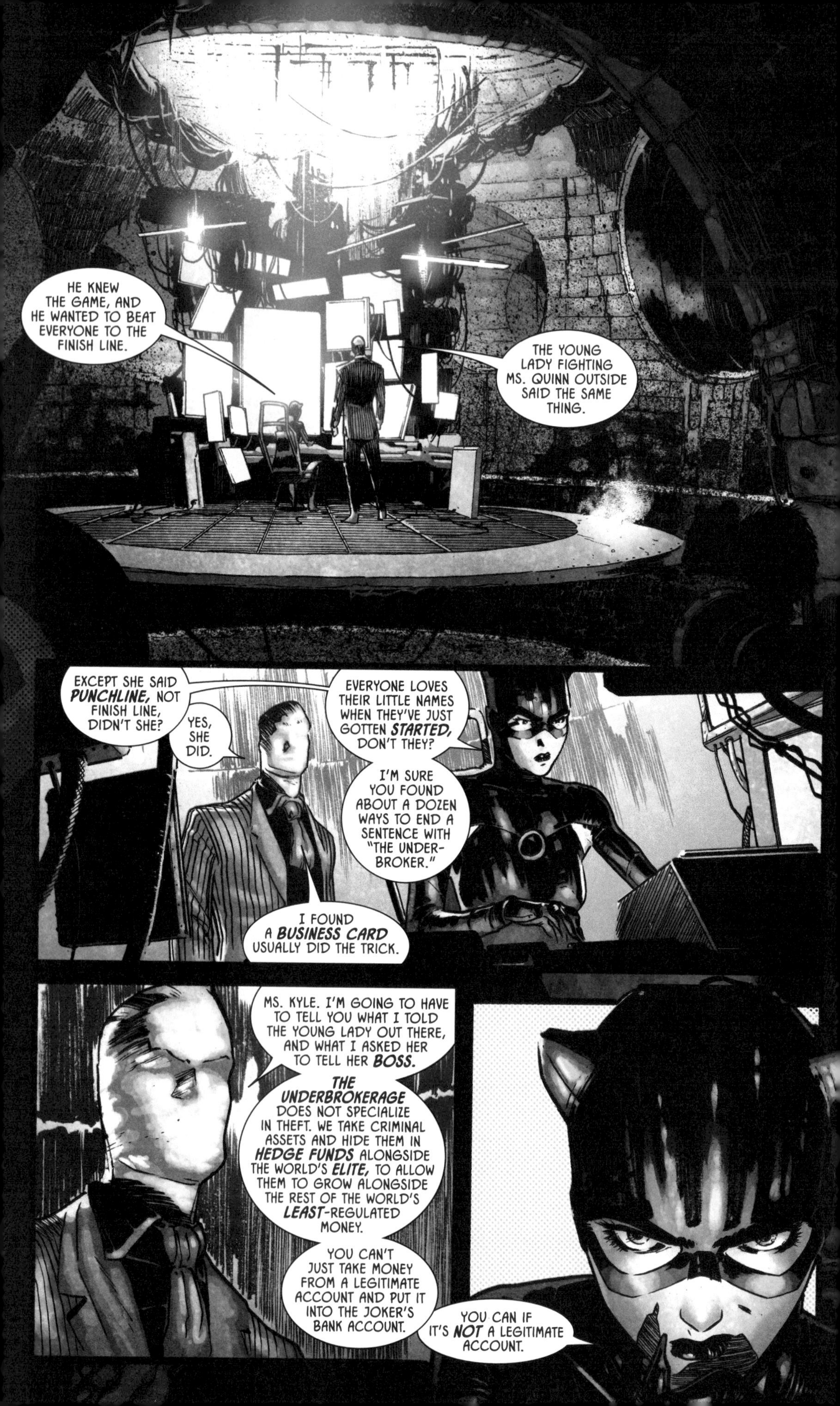
HE KNEW THE GAME, AND HE WANTED TO BEAT EVERYONE TO THE FINISH LINE.
THE YOUNG LADY FIGHTING MS. QUINN OUTSIDE SAID THE SAME THING.
EXCEPT SHE SAID PUNCHLINE, NOT FINISH LINE, DIDN'T SHE?
YES, SHE DID.
EVERYONE LOVES THEIR LITTLE NAMES WHEN THEY'VE JUST GOTTEN STARTED, DON'T THEY?
I'M SURE YOU FOUND ABOUT A DOZEN WAYS TO END A SENTENCE WITH "THE UNDER-BROKER."
I FOUND A BUSINESS CARD USUALLY DID THE TRICK.
MS. KYLE. I'M GOING TO HAVE TO TELL YOU WHAT I TOLD THE YOUNG LADY OUT THERE, AND WHAT I ASKED HER TO TELL HER BOSS.
THE UNDERBROKERAGE DOES NOT SPECIALIZE IN THEFT. WE TAKE CRIMINAL ASSETS AND HIDE THEM IN HEDGE FUNDS ALONGSIDE THE WORLD'S ELITE, TO ALLOW THEM TO GROW ALONGSIDE THE REST OF THE WORLD'S LEAST-REGULATED MONEY.
YOU CAN'T JUST TAKE MONEY FROM A LEGITIMATE ACCOUNT AND PUT IT INTO THE JOKER'S BANK ACCOUNT.
YOU CAN IF IT'S NOT A LEGITIMATE ACCOUNT.

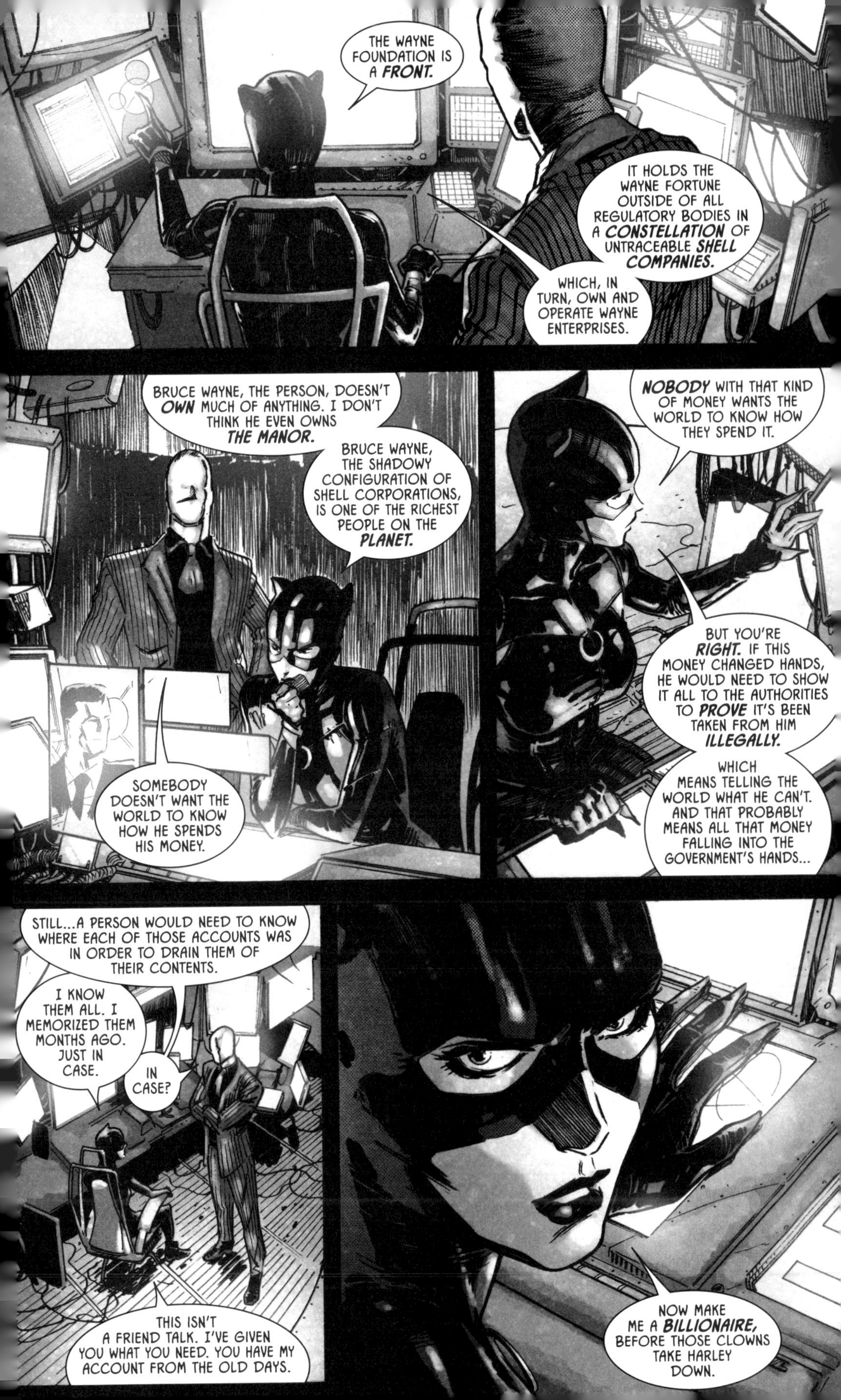
THE WAYNE FOUNDATION IS A FRONT.
IT HOLDS THE WAYNE FORTUNE OUTSIDE OF ALL REGULATORY BODIES IN A CONSTELLATION OF UNTRACEABLE SHELL COMPANIES.
WHICH, IN TURN, OWN AND OPERATE WAYNE ENTERPRISES.
BRUCE WAYNE, THE PERSON, DOESN'T OWN MUCH OF ANYTHING. I DON'T THINK HE EVEN OWNS THE MANOR.
BRUCE WAYNE, THE SHADOWY CONFIGURATION OF SHELL CORPORATIONS, IS ONE OF THE RICHEST PEOPLE ON THE PLANET.
SOMEBODY DOESN'T WANT THE WORLD TO KNOW HOW HE SPENDS HIS MONEY.
NOBODY WITH THAT KIND OF MONEY WANTS THE WORLD TO KNOW HOW THEY SPEND IT.
BUT YOU'RE RIGHT. IF THIS MONEY CHANGED HANDS, HE WOULD NEED TO SHOW IT ALL TO THE AUTHORITIES TO PROVE IT'S BEEN TAKEN FROM HIM ILLEGALLY.
WHICH MEANS TELLING THE WORLD WHAT HE CAN'T. AND THAT PROBABLY MEANS ALL THAT MONEY FALLING INTO THE GOVERNMENT'S HANDS...
STILL...A PERSON WOULD NEED TO KNOW WHERE EACH OF THOSE ACCOUNTS WAS IN ORDER TO DRAIN THEM OF THEIR CONTENTS.
I KNOW THEM ALL. I MEMORIZED THEM MONTHS AGO. JUST IN CASE.
IN CASE?
THIS ISN'T A FRIEND TALK. I'VE GIVEN YOU WHAT YOU NEED. YOU HAVE MY ACCOUNT FROM THE OLD DAYS.
NOW MAKE ME A BILLIONAIRE, BEFORE THOSE CLOWNS TAKE HARLEY DOWN.

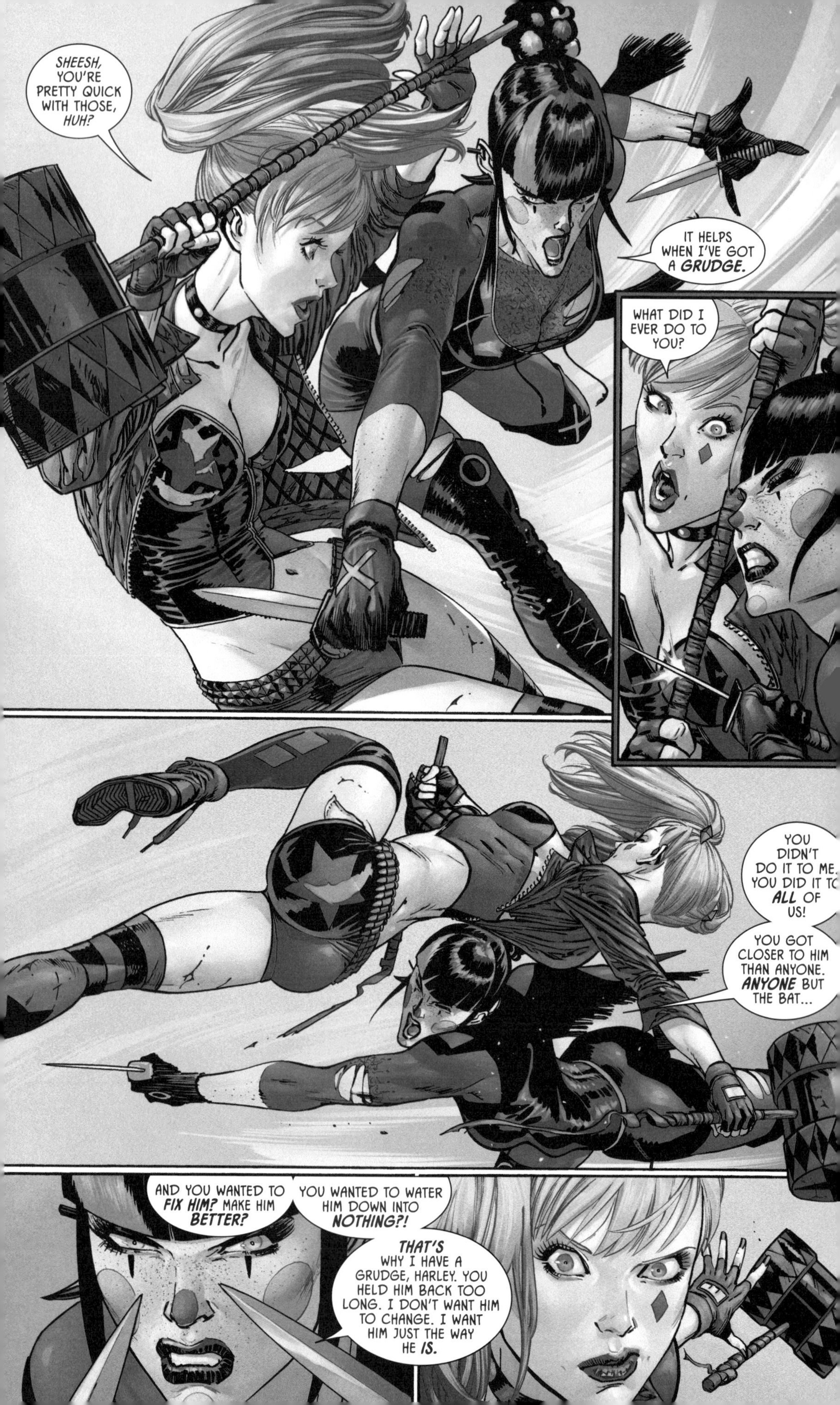

SHEESH, YOU'RE PRETTY QUICK WITH THOSE, HUH?
IT HELPS WHEN I'VE GOT A GRUDGE.
WHAT DID I EVER DO TO YOU?
YOU DIDN'T DO IT TO ME. YOU DID IT TO ALL OF US!
YOU GOT CLOSER TO HIM THAN ANYONE. ANYONE BUT THE BAT...
AND YOU WANTED TO FIX HIM? MAKE HIM BETTER?
YOU WANTED TO WATER HIM DOWN INTO NOTHING?!
THAT'S WHY I HAVE A GRUDGE, HARLEY. YOU HELD HIM BACK TOO LONG. I DON'T WANT HIM TO CHANGE. I WANT HIM JUST THE WAY HE IS.

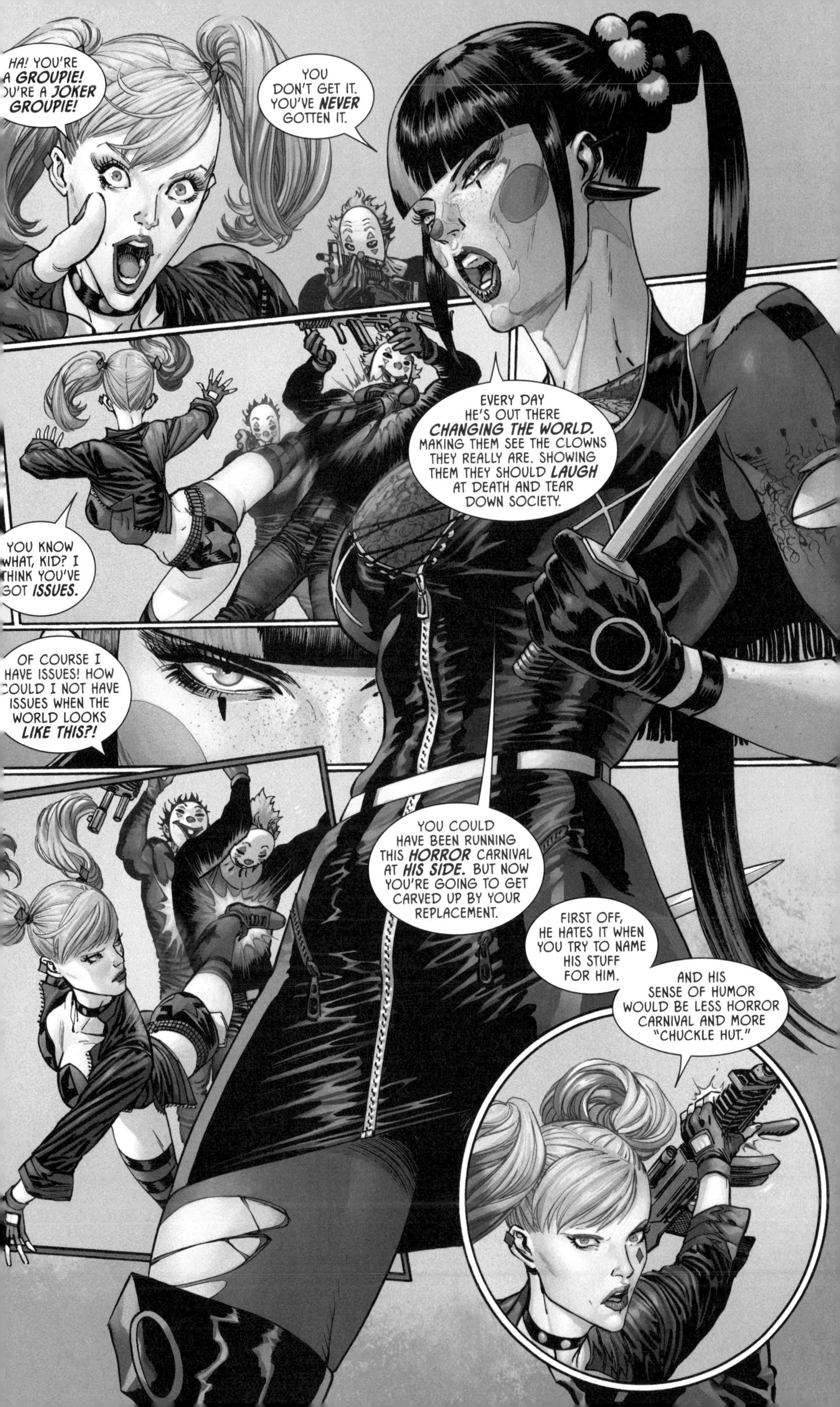

HA! YOU'RE A GROUPIE! YOU'RE A JOKER GROUPIE!
YOU DON'T GET IT. YOU'VE NEVER GOTTEN IT.
EVERY DAY HE'S OUT THERE CHANGING THE WORLD. MAKING THEM SEE THE CLOWNS THEY REALLY ARE. SHOWING THEM THEY SHOULD LAUGH AT DEATH AND TEAR DOWN SOCIETY.
YOU KNOW WHAT, KID? I THINK YOU'VE GOT ISSUES.
OF COURSE I HAVE ISSUES! HOW COULD I NOT HAVE ISSUES WHEN THE WORLD LOOKS LIKE THIS?!
YOU COULD HAVE BEEN RUNNING THIS HORROR CARNIVAL AT HIS SIDE. BUT NOW YOU'RE GOING TO GET CARVED UP BY YOUR REPLACEMENT.
FIRST OFF, HE HATES IT WHEN YOU TRY TO NAME HIS STUFF FOR HIM.
AND HIS SENSE OF HUMOR WOULD BE LESS HORROR CARNIVAL AND MORE "CHUCKLE HUT."

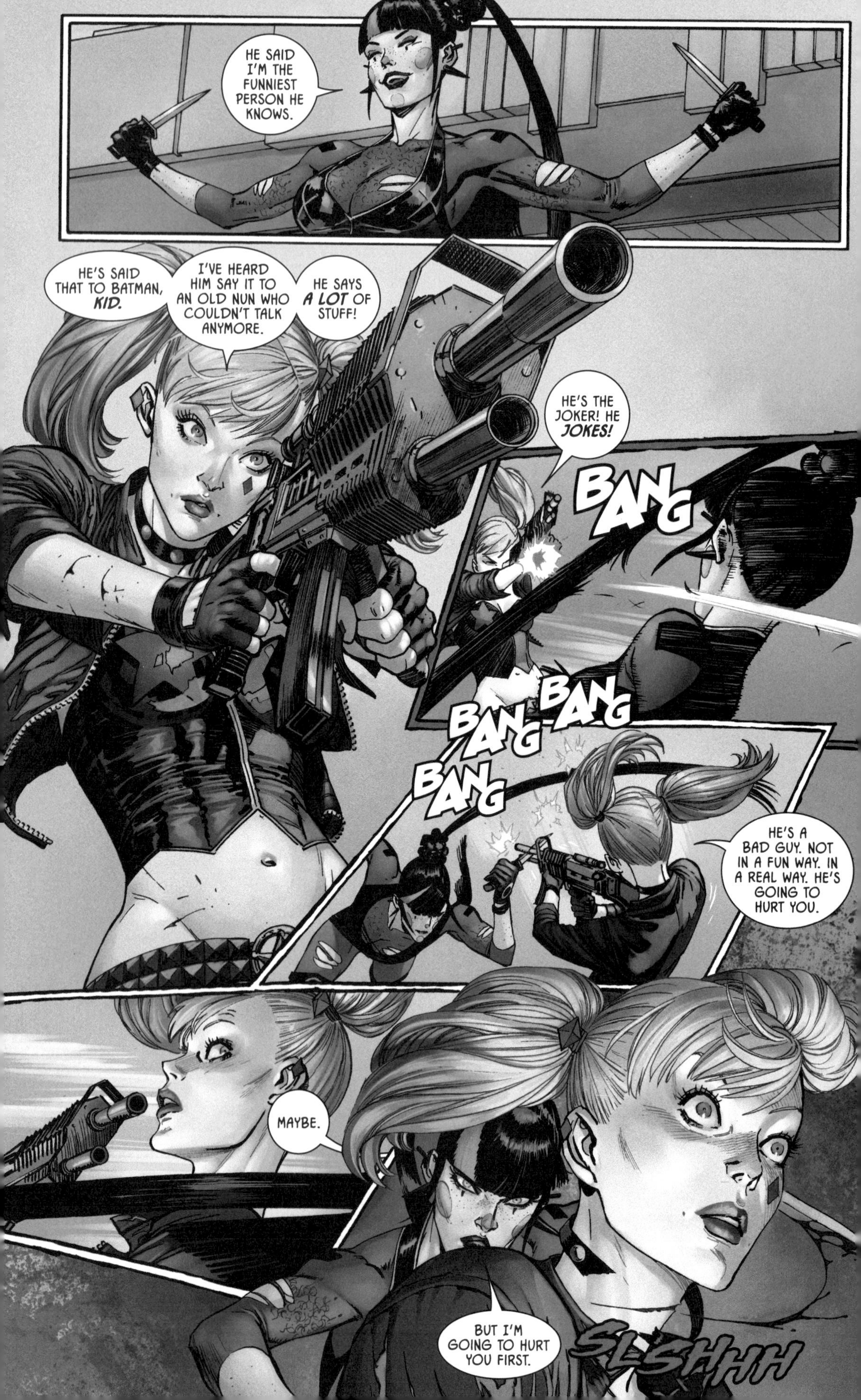

HE SAID I'M THE FUNNIEST PERSON HE KNOWS.
HE'S SAID THAT TO BATMAN, KID.
I'VE HEARD HIM SAY IT TO AN OLD NUN WHO COULDN'T TALK ANYMORE.
HE SAYS A LOT OF STUFF!
HE'S THE JOKER! HE JOKES!
BANG
BANG
BANG
BANG
HE'S A BAD GUY. NOT IN A FUN WAY. IN A REAL WAY. HE'S GOING TO HURT YOU.
MAYBE.
BUT I'M GOING TO HURT YOU FIRST.
SLSHHH

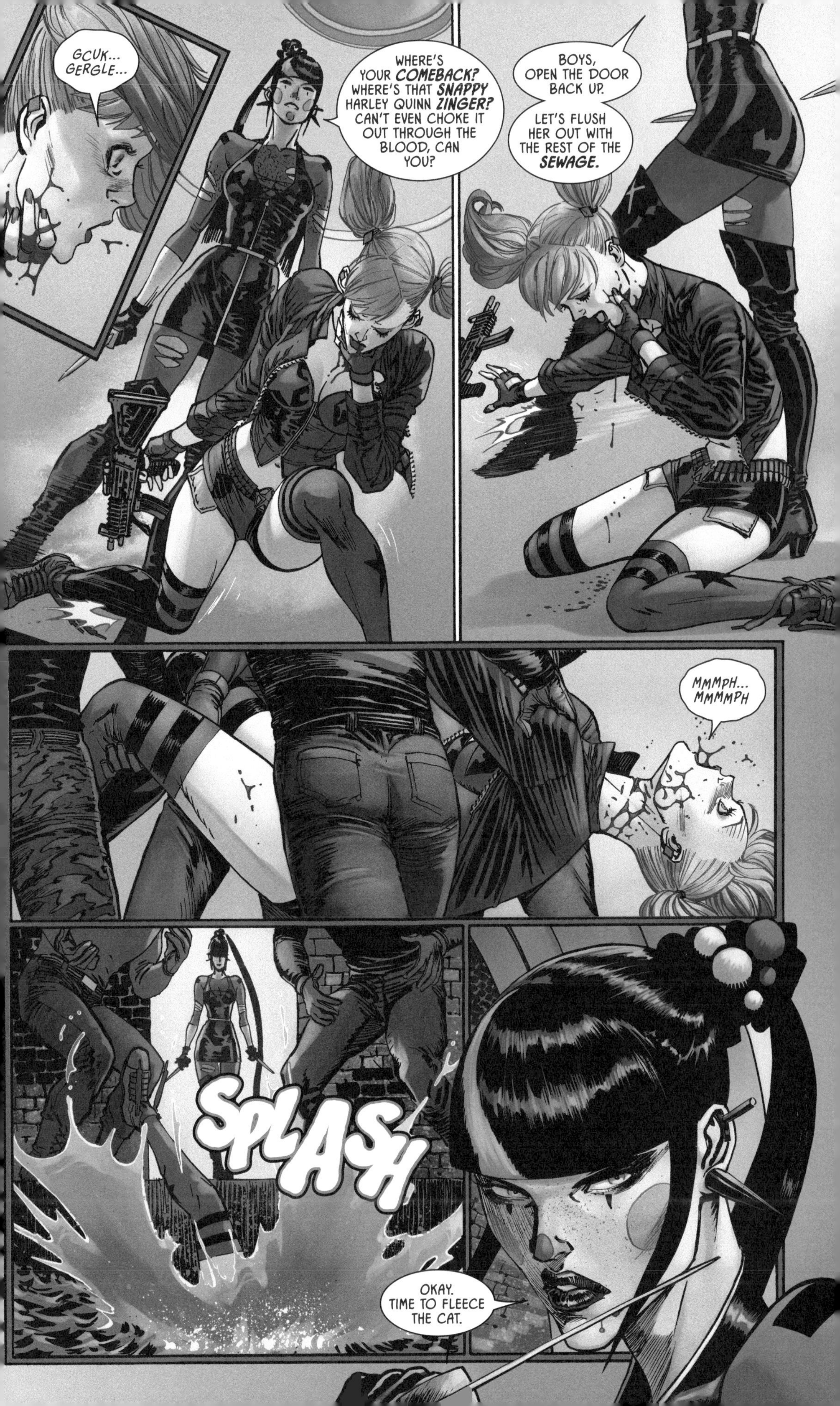
GCUK...
GERGLE...
WHERE'S YOUR COMEBACK? WHERE'S THAT SNAPPY HARLEY QUINN ZINGER? CAN'T EVEN CHOKE IT OUT THROUGH THE BLOOD, CAN YOU?
BOYS, OPEN THE DOOR BACK UP.
LET'S FLUSH HER OUT WITH THE REST OF THE SEWAGE.
MMMPH... MMMMPH
SPLASH
OKAY. TIME TO FLEECE THE CAT.

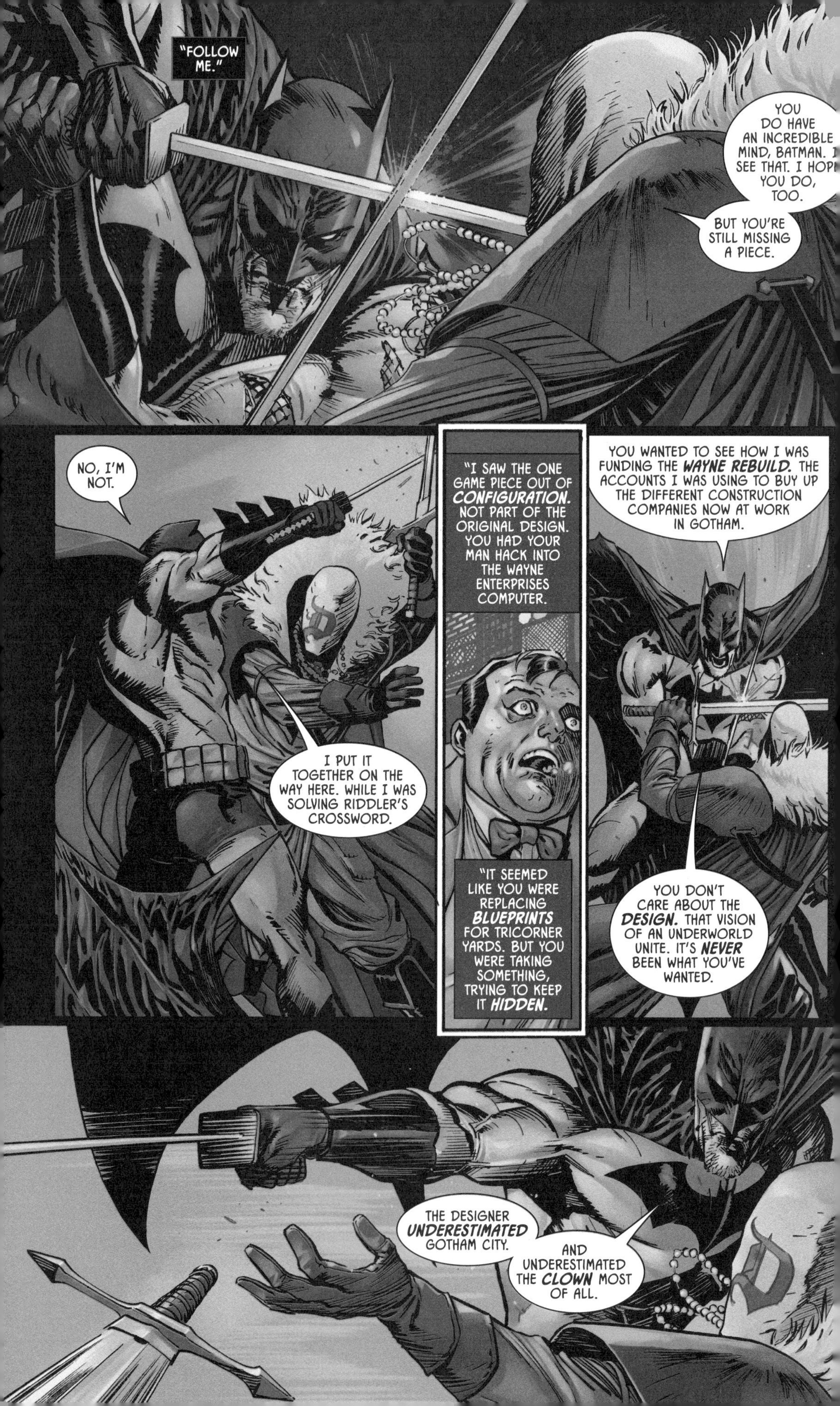
"FOLLOW ME."
YOU DO HAVE AN INCREDIBLE MIND, BATMAN. I SEE THAT. I HOPE YOU DO, TOO.
BUT YOU'RE STILL MISSING A PIECE.
NO, I'M NOT.
I PUT IT TOGETHER ON THE WAY HERE. WHILE I WAS SOLVING RIDDLER'S CROSSWORD.
"I SAW THE ONE GAME PIECE OUT OF CONFIGURATION. NOT PART OF THE ORIGINAL DESIGN. YOU HAD YOUR MAN HACK INTO THE WAYNE ENTERPRISES COMPUTER.
"IT SEEMED LIKE YOU WERE REPLACING BLUEPRINTS FOR TRICORNER YARDS. BUT YOU WERE TAKING SOMETHING, TRYING TO KEEP IT HIDDEN.
YOU WANTED TO SEE HOW I WAS FUNDING THE WAYNE REBUILD. THE ACCOUNTS I WAS USING TO BUY UP THE DIFFERENT CONSTRUCTION COMPANIES NOW AT WORK IN GOTHAM.
YOU DON'T CARE ABOUT THE DESIGN. THAT VISION OF AN UNDERWORLD UNITE. IT'S NEVER BEEN WHAT YOU'VE WANTED.
THE DESIGNER UNDERESTIMATED GOTHAM CITY.
AND UNDERESTIMATED THE CLOWN MOST OF ALL.

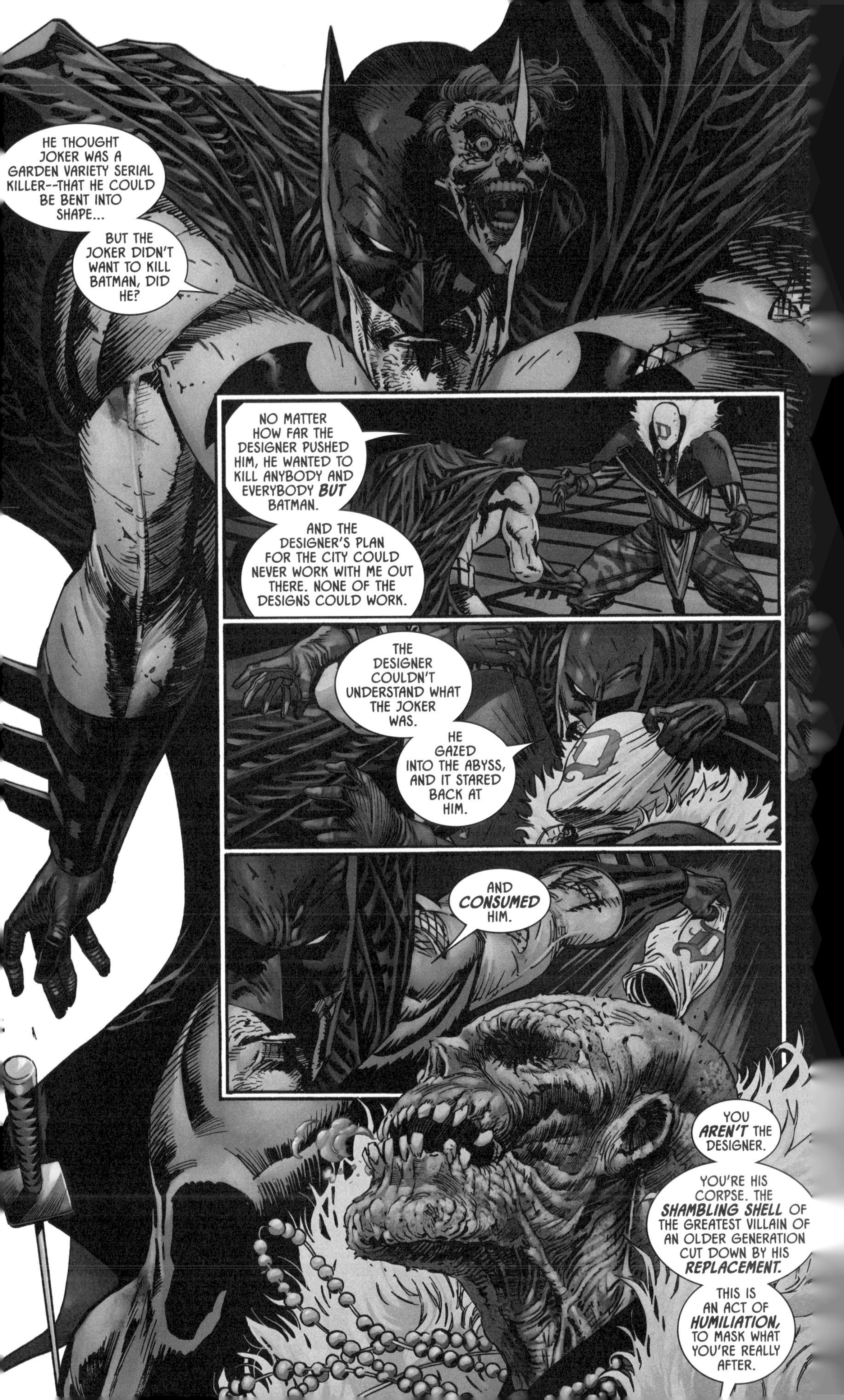
HE THOUGHT JOKER WAS A GARDEN VARIETY SERIAL KILLER--THAT HE COULD BE BENT INTO SHAPE...
BUT THE JOKER DIDN'T WANT TO KILL BATMAN, DID HE?
NO MATTER HOW FAR THE DESIGNER PUSHED HIM, HE WANTED TO KILL ANYBODY AND EVERYBODY ***BUT*** BATMAN.
AND THE DESIGNER'S PLAN FOR THE CITY COULD NEVER WORK WITH ME OUT THERE. NONE OF THE DESIGNS COULD WORK.
THE DESIGNER COULDN'T UNDERSTAND WHAT THE JOKER WAS.
HE GAZED INTO THE ABYSS, AND IT STARED BACK AT HIM.
AND ***CONSUMED*** HIM.
YOU ***AREN'T*** THE DESIGNER.
YOU'RE HIS CORPSE. THE ***SHAMBLING SHELL*** OF THE GREATEST VILLAIN OF AN OLDER GENERATION CUT DOWN BY HIS ***REPLACEMENT.***
THIS IS AN ACT OF ***HUMILIATION,*** TO MASK WHAT YOU'RE REALLY AFTER.

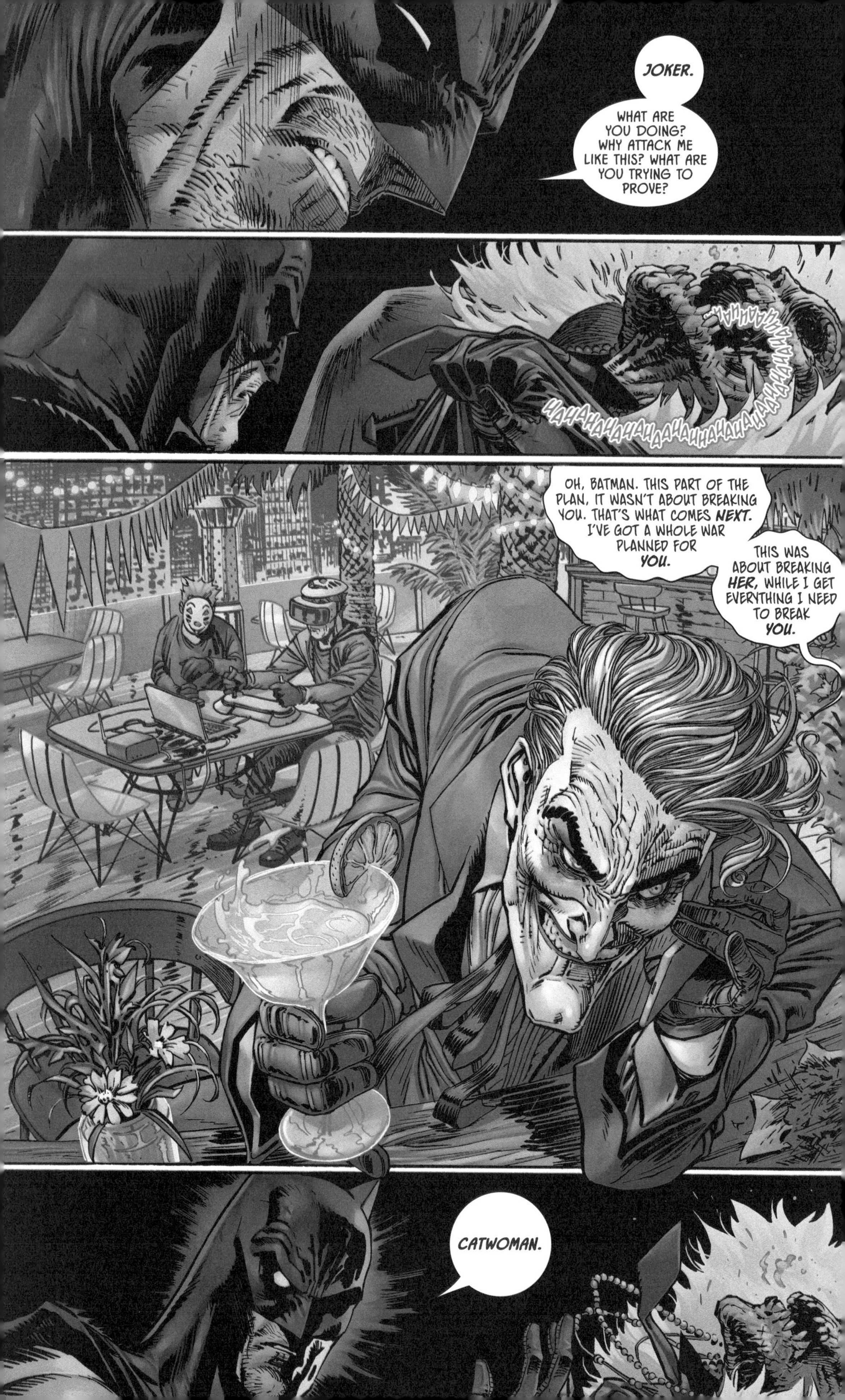

JOKER.
WHAT ARE YOU DOING? WHY ATTACK ME LIKE THIS? WHAT ARE YOU TRYING TO PROVE?
HAHAHAHAHAHAHAAHAHHAHAHAHAHAHAHAHAHAHAHAHAHAHAHAHA
OH, BATMAN. THIS PART OF THE PLAN, IT WASN'T ABOUT BREAKING YOU. THAT'S WHAT COMES NEXT. I'VE GOT A WHOLE WAR PLANNED FOR YOU.
THIS WAS ABOUT BREAKING HER, WHILE I GET EVERYTHING I NEED TO BREAK YOU.
CATWOMAN.

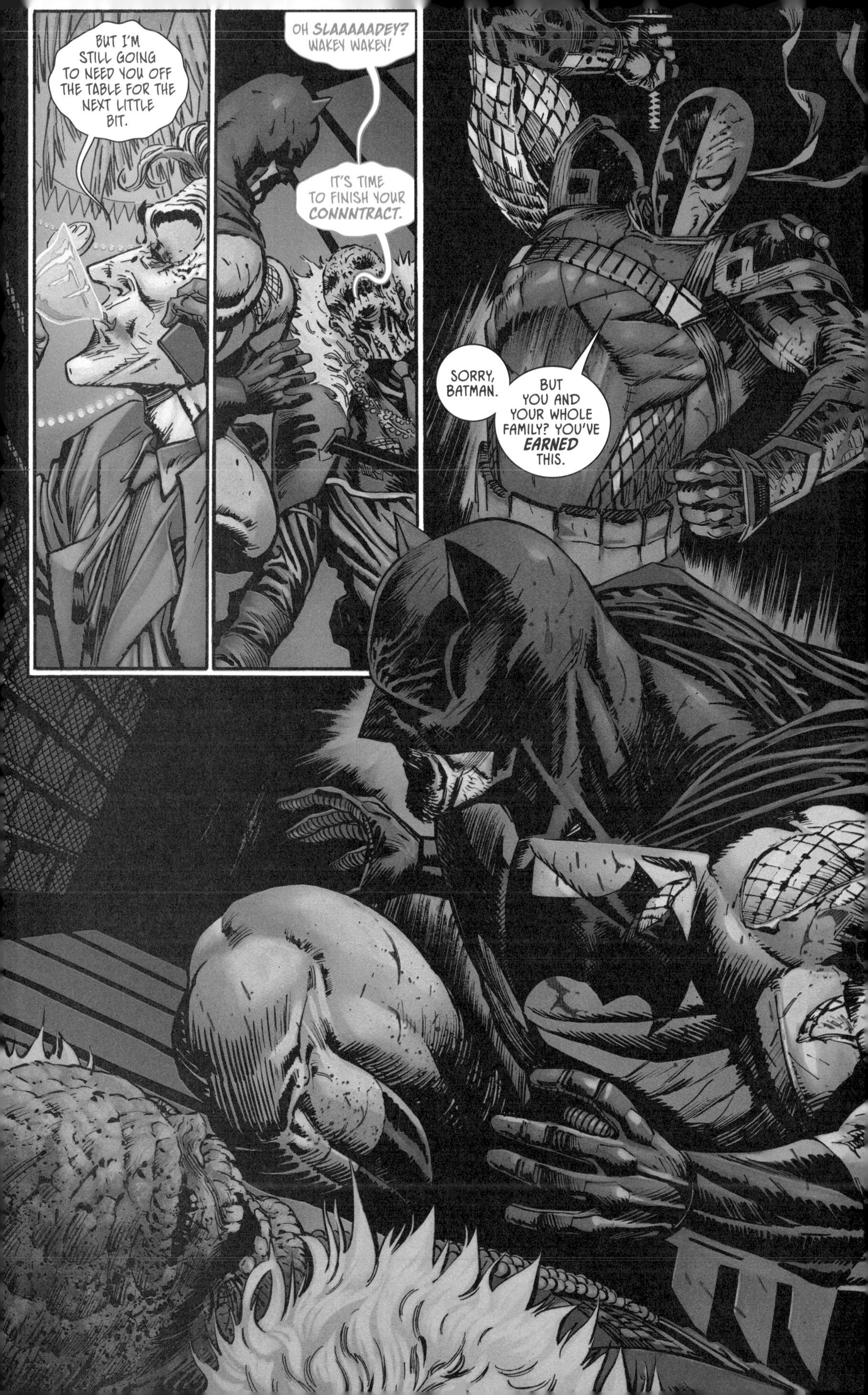
BUT I'M STILL GOING TO NEED YOU OFF THE TABLE FOR THE NEXT LITTLE BIT.
OH SLAAAAADEY? WAKEY WAKEY!
IT'S TIME TO FINISH YOUR CONNNTRACT.
SORRY, BATMAN.
BUT YOU AND YOUR WHOLE FAMILY? YOU'VE EARNED THIS.

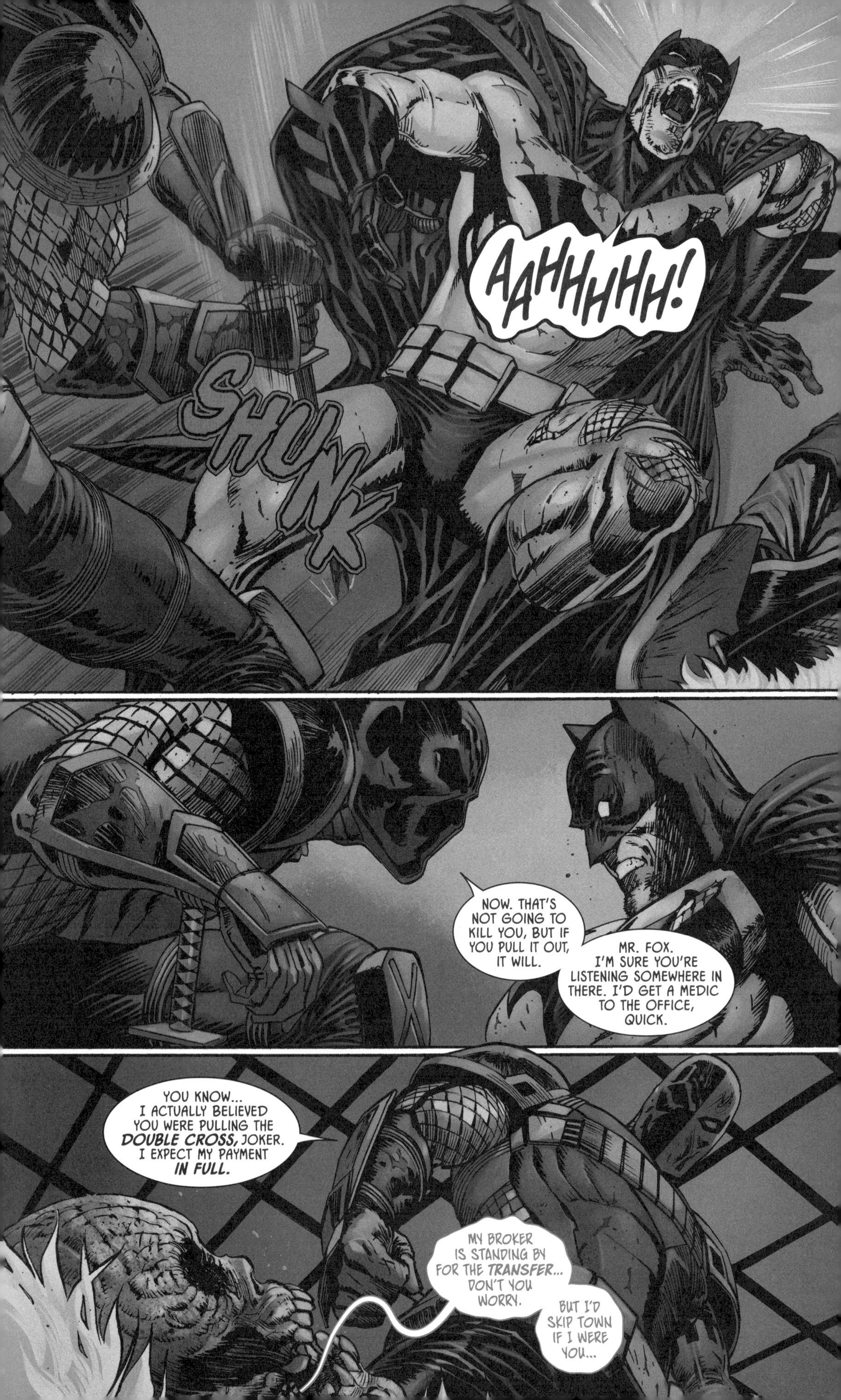
AAHHHHH!
SHUNK
NOW. THAT'S NOT GOING TO KILL YOU, BUT IF YOU PULL IT OUT, IT WILL.
MR. FOX. I'M SURE YOU'RE LISTENING SOMEWHERE IN THERE. I'D GET A MEDIC TO THE OFFICE, QUICK.
YOU KNOW... I ACTUALLY BELIEVED YOU WERE PULLING THE DOUBLE CROSS, JOKER. I EXPECT MY PAYMENT IN FULL.
MY BROKER IS STANDING BY FOR THE TRANSFER... DON'T YOU WORRY.
BUT I'D SKIP TOWN IF I WERE YOU...

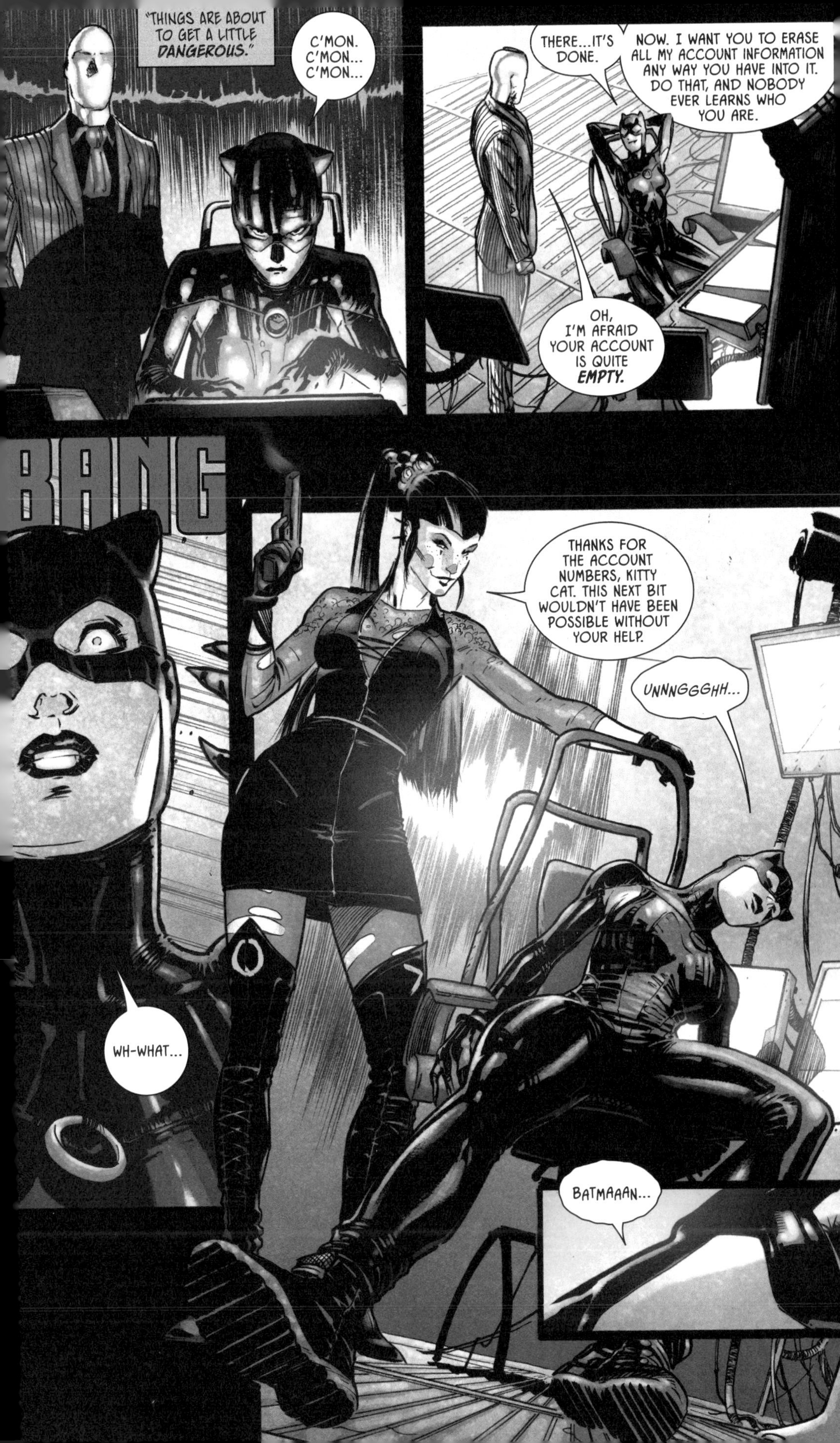
"THINGS ARE ABOUT TO GET A LITTLE DANGEROUS."
C'MON. C'MON... C'MON...
THERE...IT'S DONE.
NOW. I WANT YOU TO ERASE ALL MY ACCOUNT INFORMATION ANY WAY YOU HAVE INTO IT. DO THAT, AND NOBODY EVER LEARNS WHO YOU ARE.
OH, I'M AFRAID YOUR ACCOUNT IS QUITE EMPTY.
BANG
WH-WHAT...
THANKS FOR THE ACCOUNT NUMBERS, KITTY CAT. THIS NEXT BIT WOULDN'T HAVE BEEN POSSIBLE WITHOUT YOUR HELP.
UNNNGGGHH...
BATMAAAN...

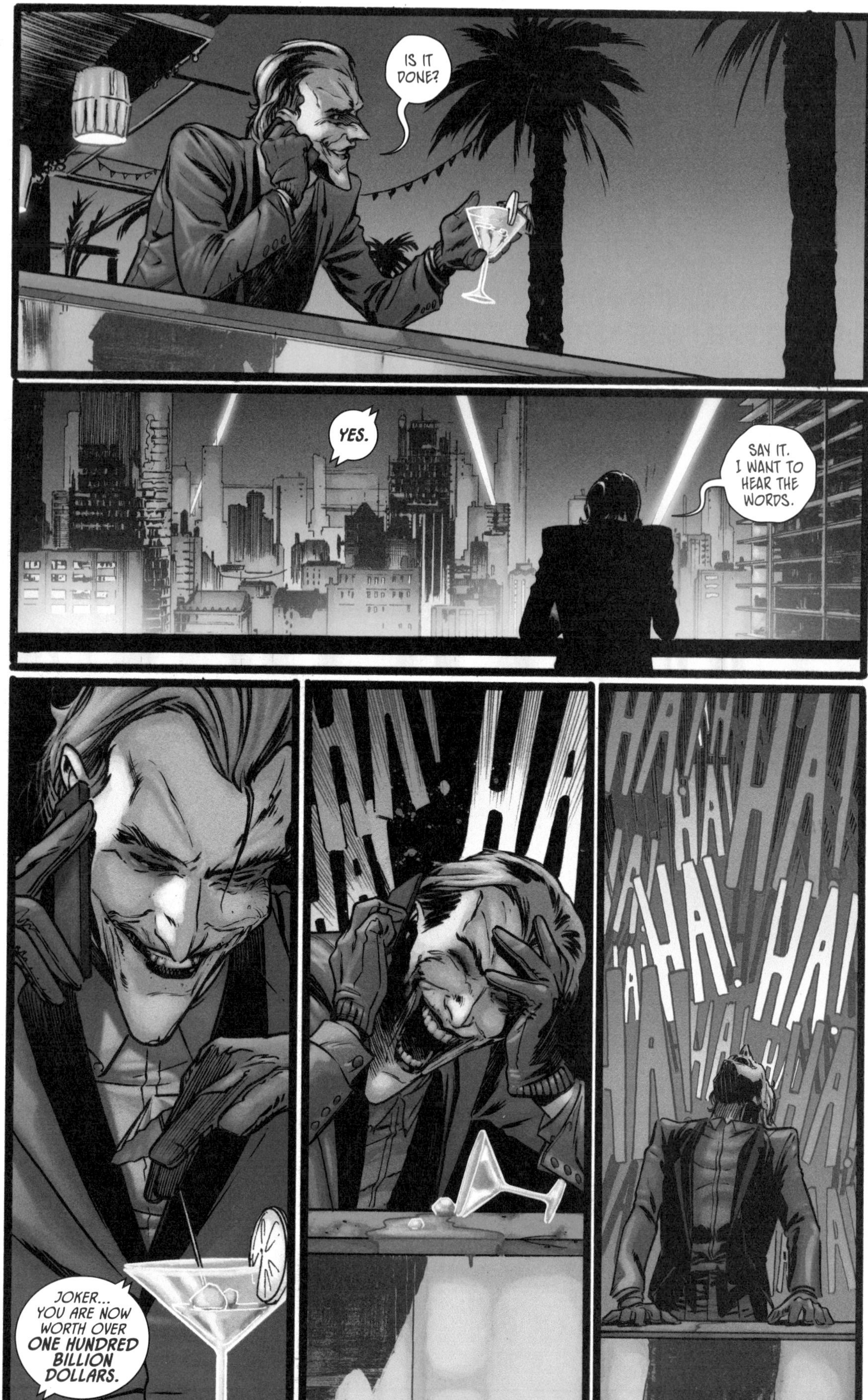
IS IT DONE?
YES.
SAY IT. I WANT TO HEAR THE WORDS.
JOKER... YOU ARE NOW WORTH OVER ONE HUNDRED BILLION DOLLARS.
HA! HA!
HA! HA! HA! HA! HA! HA!

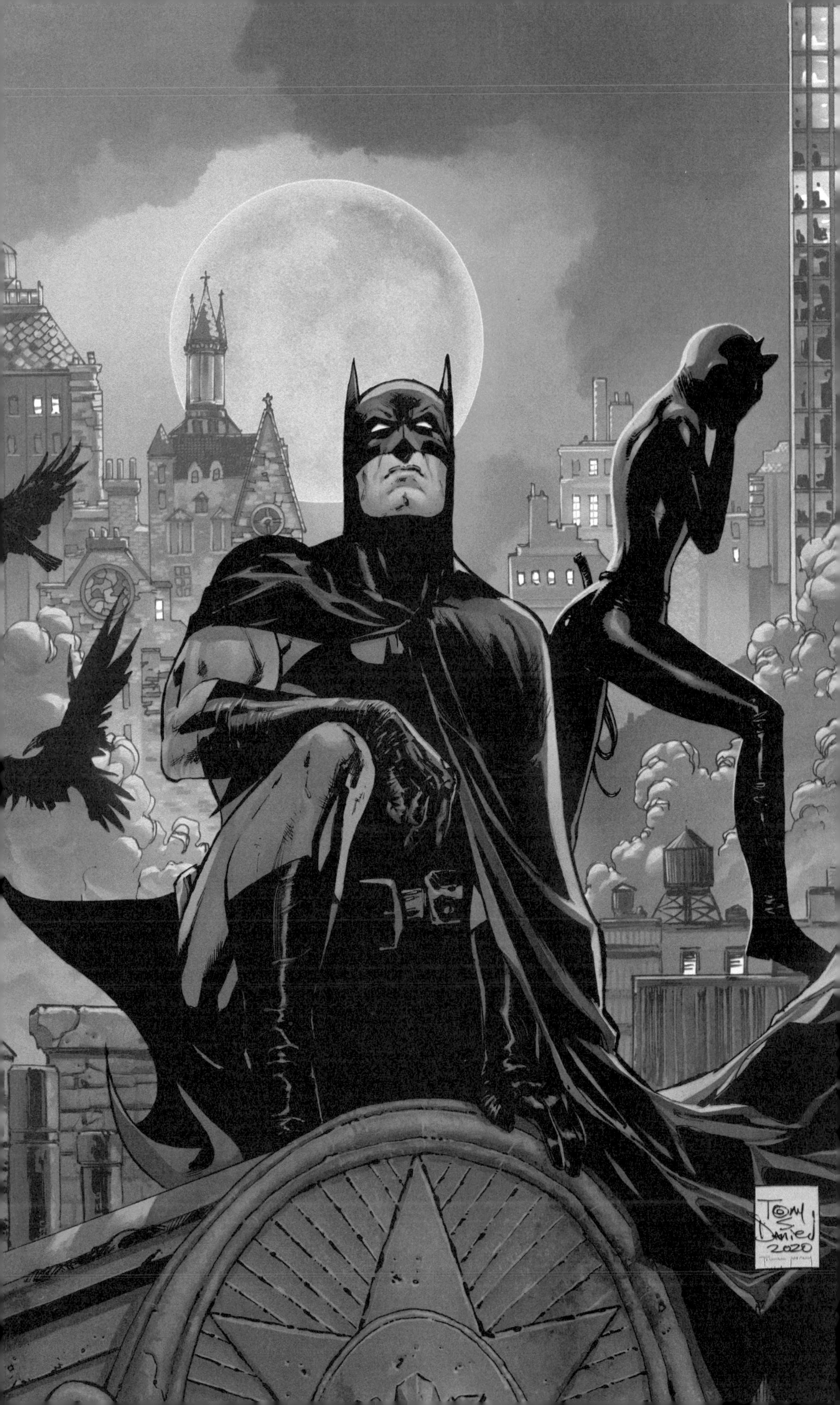

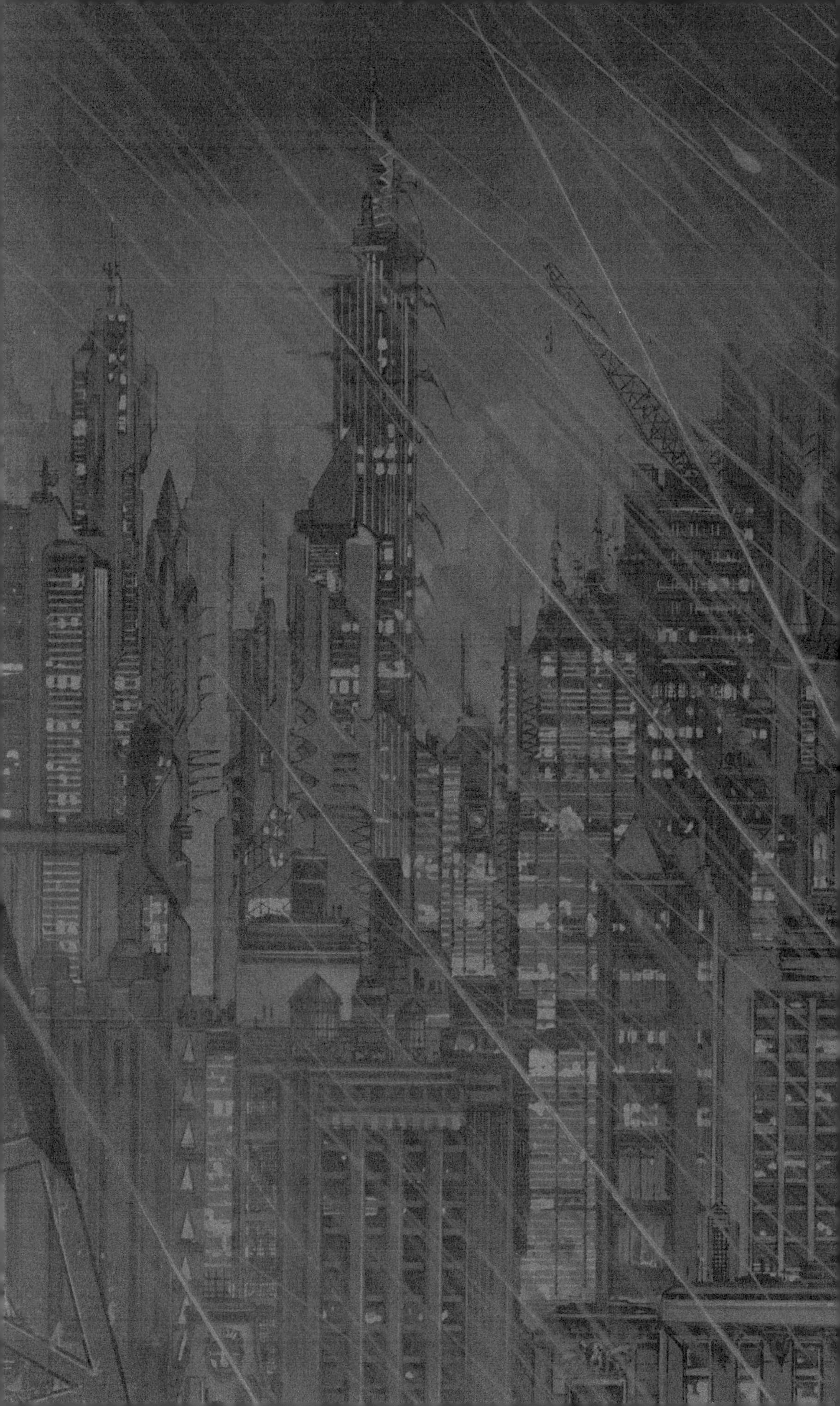

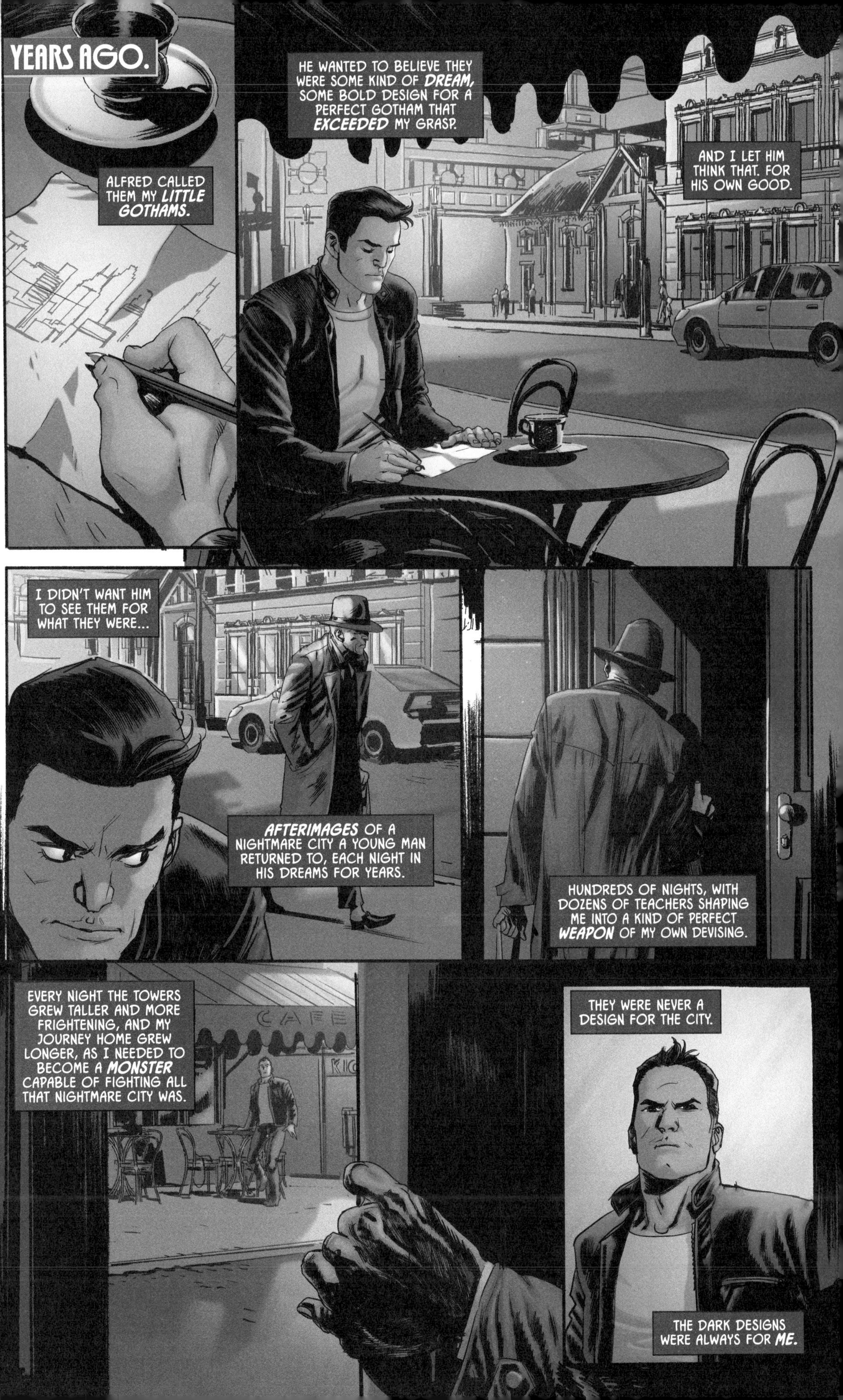
YEARS AGO.
ALFRED CALLED THEM MY *LITTLE GOTHAMS.*
HE WANTED TO BELIEVE THEY WERE SOME KIND OF *DREAM,* SOME BOLD DESIGN FOR A PERFECT GOTHAM THAT *EXCEEDED* MY GRASP.
AND I LET HIM THINK THAT. FOR HIS OWN GOOD.
I DIDN'T WANT HIM TO SEE THEM FOR WHAT THEY WERE...
AFTERIMAGES OF A NIGHTMARE CITY A YOUNG MAN RETURNED TO, EACH NIGHT IN HIS DREAMS FOR YEARS.
HUNDREDS OF NIGHTS, WITH DOZENS OF TEACHERS SHAPING ME INTO A KIND OF PERFECT *WEAPON* OF MY OWN DEVISING.
EVERY NIGHT THE TOWERS GREW TALLER AND MORE FRIGHTENING, AND MY JOURNEY HOME GREW LONGER, AS I NEEDED TO BECOME A *MONSTER* CAPABLE OF FIGHTING ALL THAT NIGHTMARE CITY WAS.
CAFE
THEY WERE NEVER A DESIGN FOR THE CITY.
THE DARK DESIGNS WERE ALWAYS FOR *ME.*

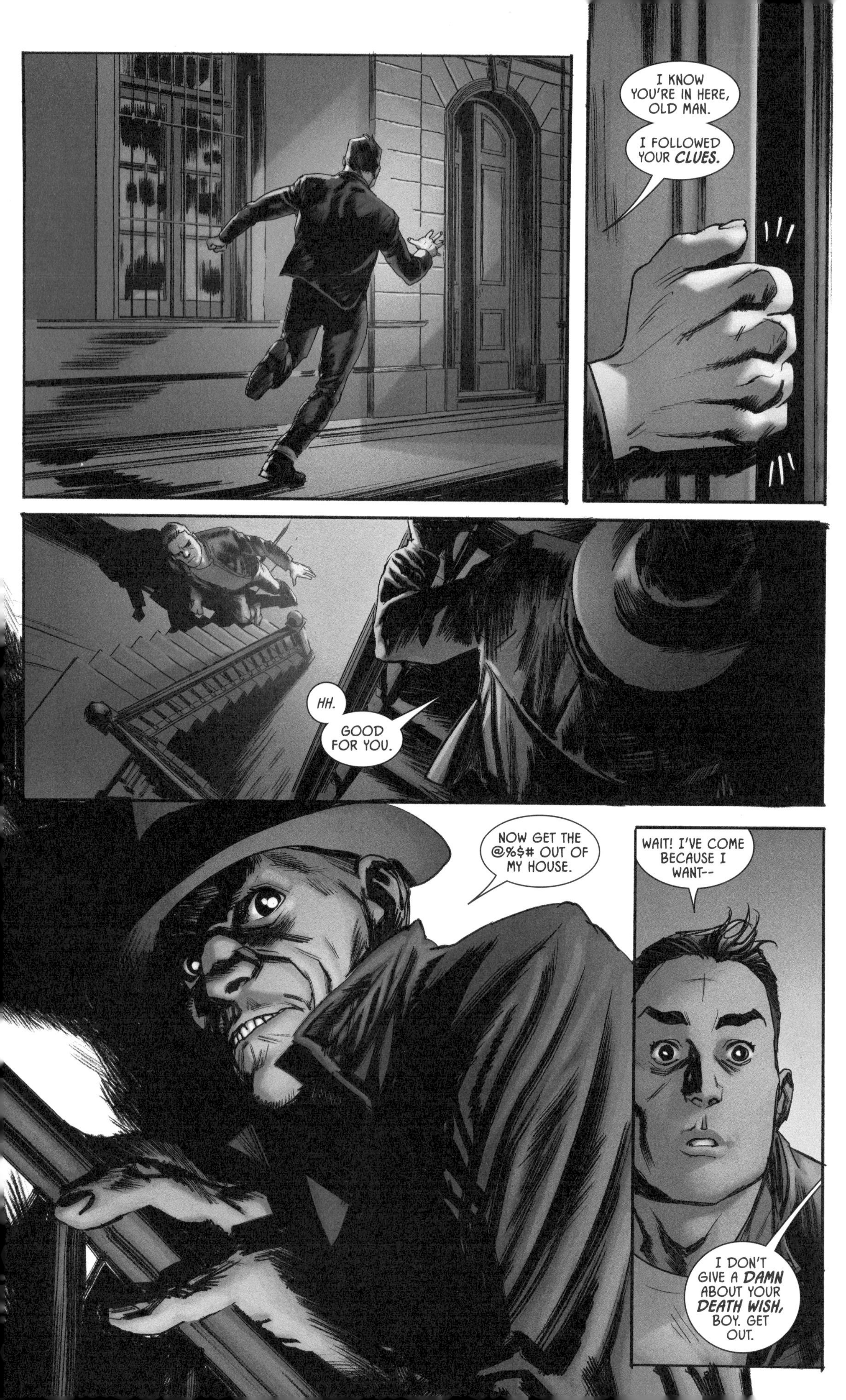
I KNOW YOU'RE IN HERE, OLD MAN.
I FOLLOWED YOUR *CLUES.*
HH.
GOOD FOR YOU.
NOW GET THE @%$# OUT OF MY HOUSE.
WAIT! I'VE COME BECAUSE I WANT--
I DON'T GIVE A *DAMN* ABOUT YOUR *DEATH WISH,* BOY. GET OUT.

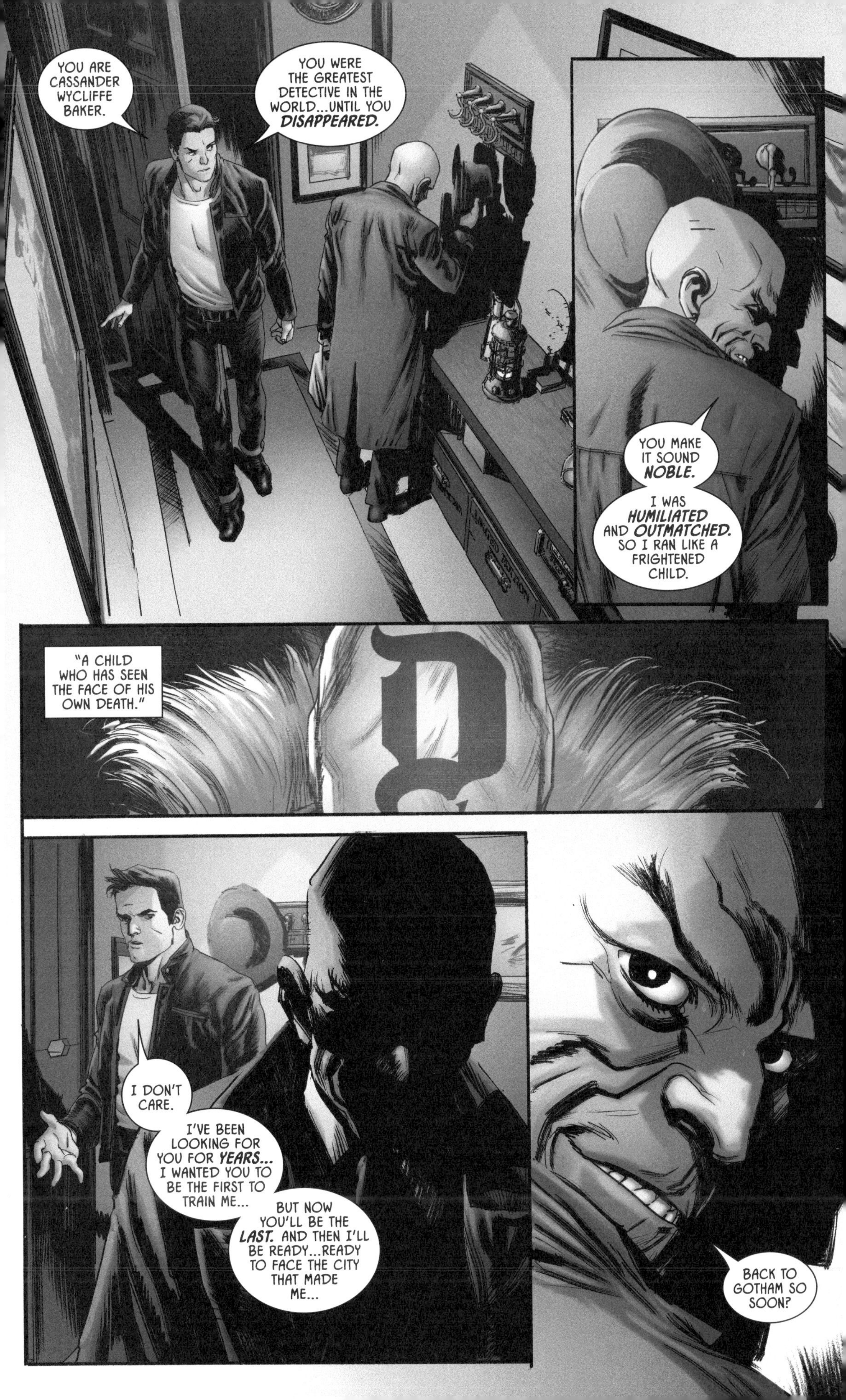
YOU ARE CASSANDER WYCLIFFE BAKER.
YOU WERE THE GREATEST DETECTIVE IN THE WORLD...UNTIL YOU DISAPPEARED.
YOU MAKE IT SOUND NOBLE.
I WAS HUMILIATED AND OUTMATCHED. SO I RAN LIKE A FRIGHTENED CHILD.
"A CHILD WHO HAS SEEN THE FACE OF HIS OWN DEATH."
I DON'T CARE.
I'VE BEEN LOOKING FOR YOU FOR YEARS... I WANTED YOU TO BE THE FIRST TO TRAIN ME...
BUT NOW YOU'LL BE THE LAST. AND THEN I'LL BE READY...READY TO FACE THE CITY THAT MADE ME...
BACK TO GOTHAM SO SOON?

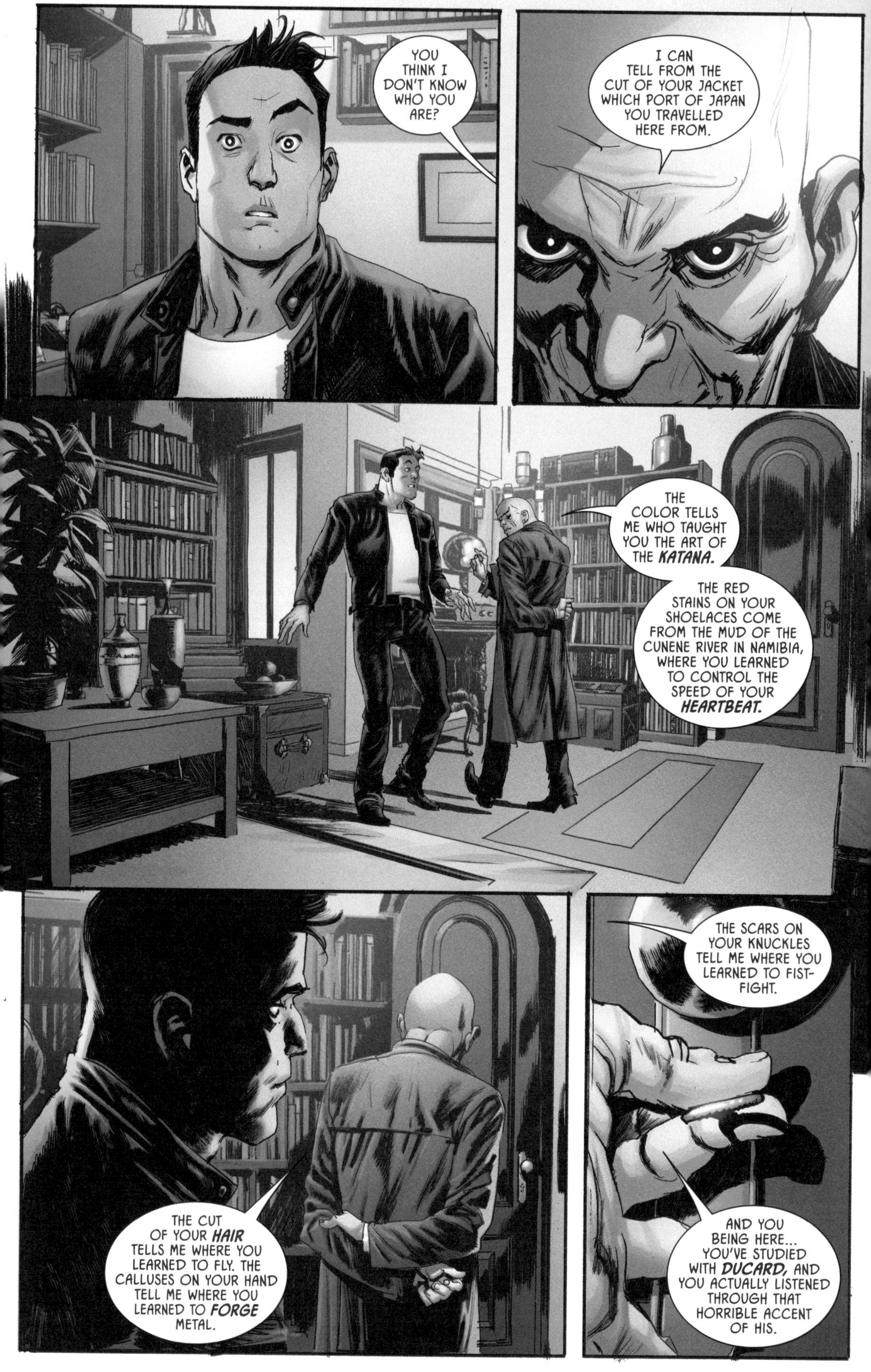
YOU THINK I DON'T KNOW WHO YOU ARE?
I CAN TELL FROM THE CUT OF YOUR JACKET WHICH PORT OF JAPAN YOU TRAVELLED HERE FROM.
THE COLOR TELLS ME WHO TAUGHT YOU THE ART OF THE KATANA.
THE RED STAINS ON YOUR SHOELACES COME FROM THE MUD OF THE CUNENE RIVER IN NAMIBIA, WHERE YOU LEARNED TO CONTROL THE SPEED OF YOUR HEARTBEAT.
THE CUT OF YOUR HAIR TELLS ME WHERE YOU LEARNED TO FLY. THE CALLUSES ON YOUR HAND TELL ME WHERE YOU LEARNED TO FORGE METAL.
THE SCARS ON YOUR KNUCKLES TELL ME WHERE YOU LEARNED TO FIST-FIGHT.
AND YOU BEING HERE... YOU'VE STUDIED WITH DUCARD, AND YOU ACTUALLY LISTENED THROUGH THAT HORRIBLE ACCENT OF HIS.

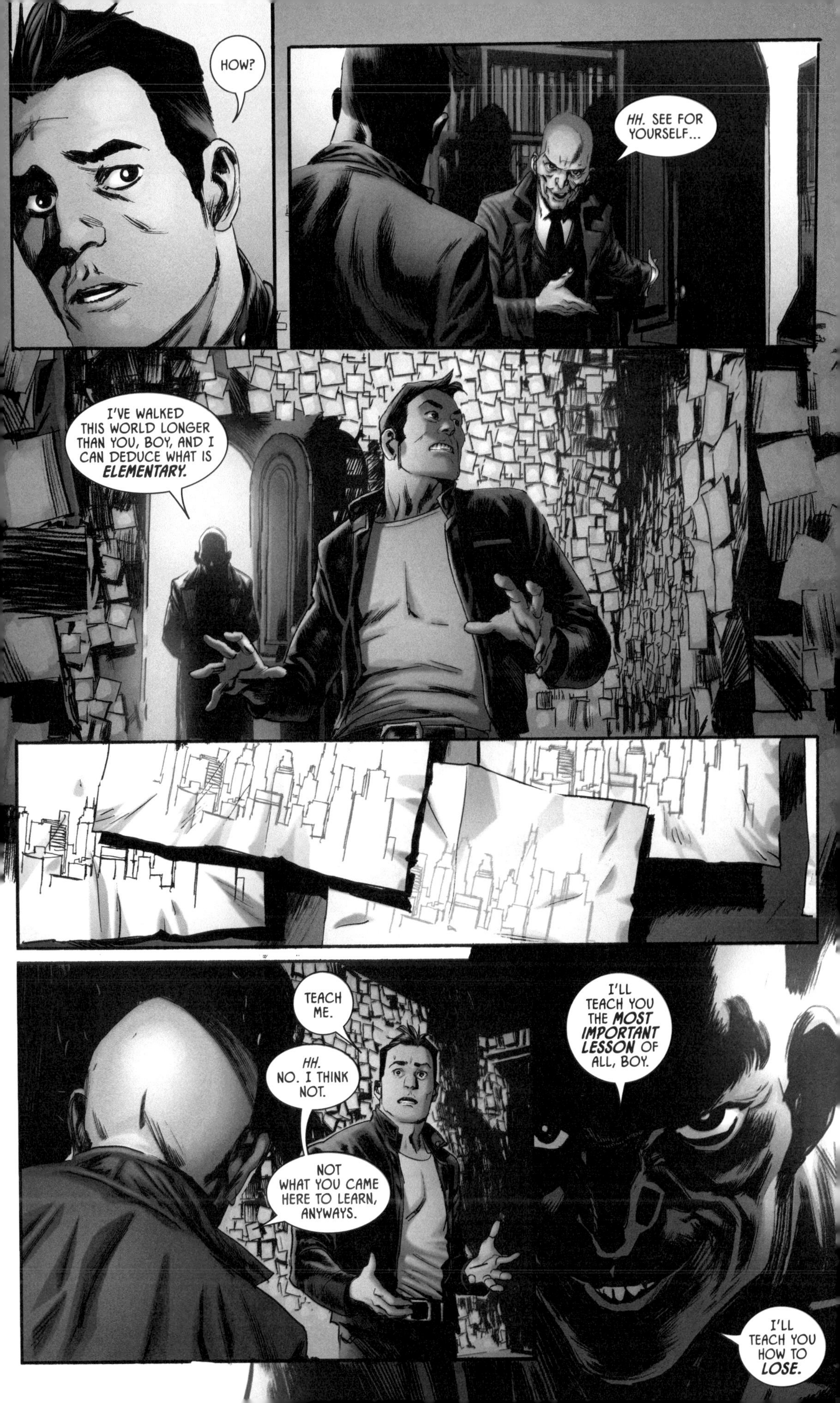
HOW?
HH. SEE FOR YOURSELF...
I'VE WALKED THIS WORLD LONGER THAN YOU, BOY, AND I CAN DEDUCE WHAT IS ***ELEMENTARY.***
TEACH ME.
HH. NO. I THINK NOT.
NOT WHAT YOU CAME HERE TO LEARN, ANYWAYS.
I'LL TEACH YOU THE ***MOST IMPORTANT LESSON*** OF ALL, BOY.
I'LL TEACH YOU HOW TO ***LOSE.***

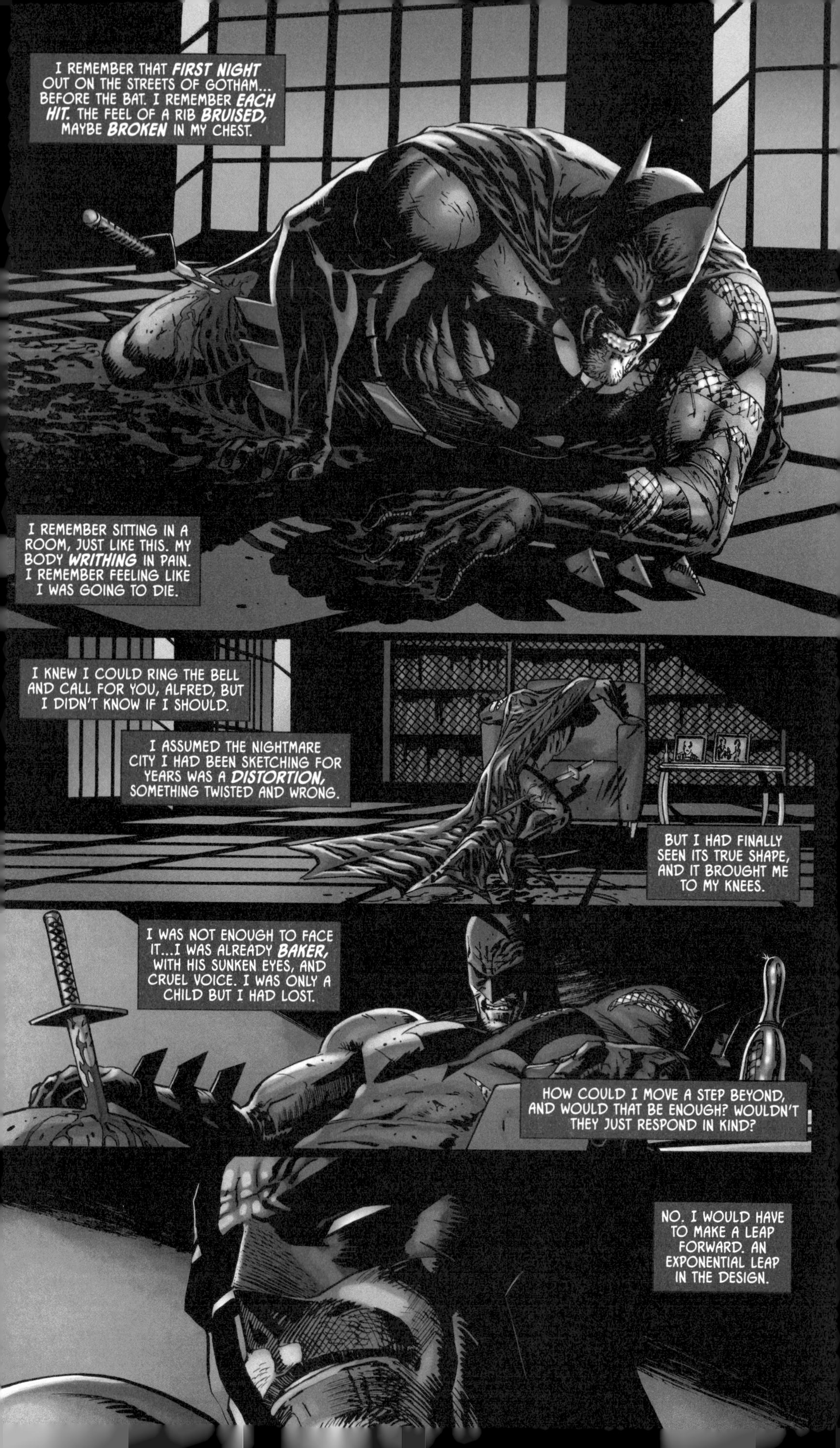
I REMEMBER THAT FIRST NIGHT OUT ON THE STREETS OF GOTHAM... BEFORE THE BAT. I REMEMBER EACH HIT. THE FEEL OF A RIB BRUISED, MAYBE BROKEN IN MY CHEST.
I REMEMBER SITTING IN A ROOM, JUST LIKE THIS. MY BODY WRITHING IN PAIN. I REMEMBER FEELING LIKE I WAS GOING TO DIE.
I KNEW I COULD RING THE BELL AND CALL FOR YOU, ALFRED, BUT I DIDN'T KNOW IF I SHOULD.
I ASSUMED THE NIGHTMARE CITY I HAD BEEN SKETCHING FOR YEARS WAS A DISTORTION, SOMETHING TWISTED AND WRONG.
BUT I HAD FINALLY SEEN ITS TRUE SHAPE, AND IT BROUGHT ME TO MY KNEES.
I WAS NOT ENOUGH TO FACE IT...I WAS ALREADY BAKER, WITH HIS SUNKEN EYES, AND CRUEL VOICE. I WAS ONLY A CHILD BUT I HAD LOST.
HOW COULD I MOVE A STEP BEYOND, AND WOULD THAT BE ENOUGH? WOULDN'T THEY JUST RESPOND IN KIND?
NO. I WOULD HAVE TO MAKE A LEAP FORWARD. AN EXPONENTIAL LEAP IN THE DESIGN.

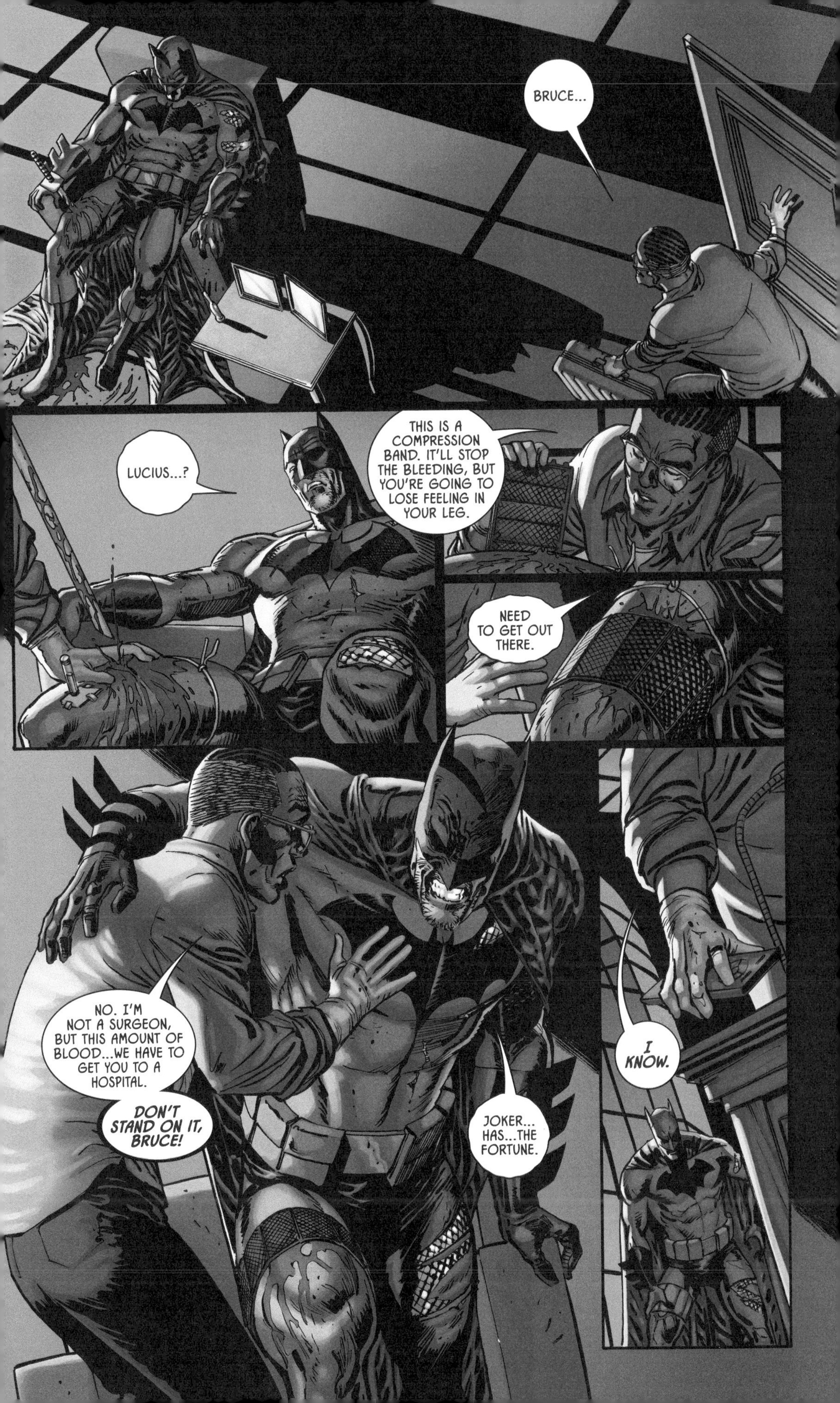
BRUCE...
LUCIUS...?
THIS IS A COMPRESSION BAND. IT'LL STOP THE BLEEDING, BUT YOU'RE GOING TO LOSE FEELING IN YOUR LEG.
NEED TO GET OUT THERE.
NO. I'M NOT A SURGEON, BUT THIS AMOUNT OF BLOOD...WE HAVE TO GET YOU TO A HOSPITAL.
DON'T STAND ON IT, BRUCE!
JOKER... HAS...THE FORTUNE.
I KNOW.

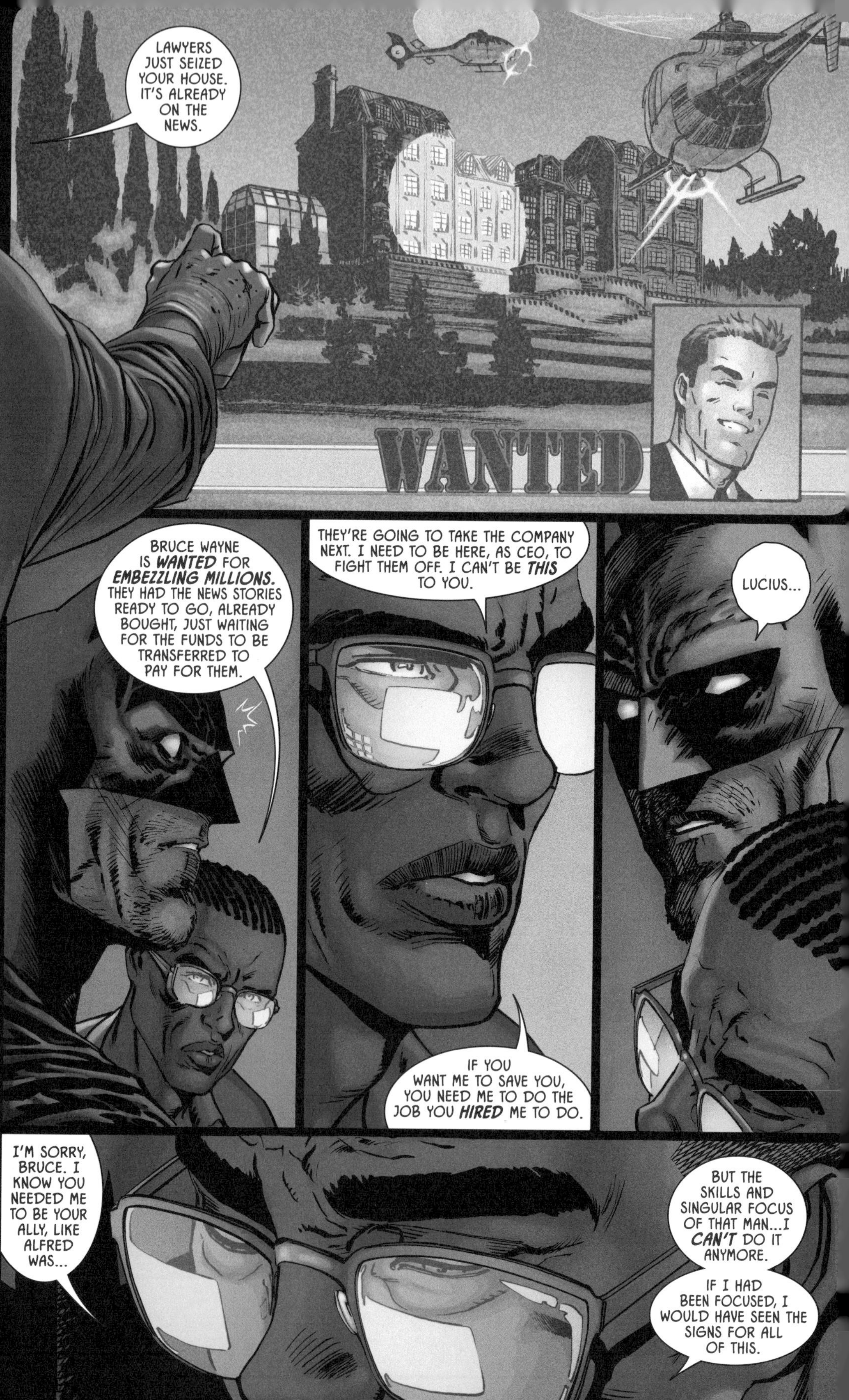
LAWYERS JUST SEIZED YOUR HOUSE. IT'S ALREADY ON THE NEWS.
WANTED
BRUCE WAYNE IS WANTED FOR EMBEZZLING MILLIONS. THEY HAD THE NEWS STORIES READY TO GO, ALREADY BOUGHT, JUST WAITING FOR THE FUNDS TO BE TRANSFERRED TO PAY FOR THEM.
THEY'RE GOING TO TAKE THE COMPANY NEXT. I NEED TO BE HERE, AS CEO, TO FIGHT THEM OFF. I CAN'T BE THIS TO YOU.
IF YOU WANT ME TO SAVE YOU, YOU NEED ME TO DO THE JOB YOU HIRED ME TO DO.
LUCIUS...
I'M SORRY, BRUCE. I KNOW YOU NEEDED ME TO BE YOUR ALLY, LIKE ALFRED WAS...
BUT THE SKILLS AND SINGULAR FOCUS OF THAT MAN...I CAN'T DO IT ANYMORE.
IF I HAD BEEN FOCUSED, I WOULD HAVE SEEN THE SIGNS FOR ALL OF THIS.

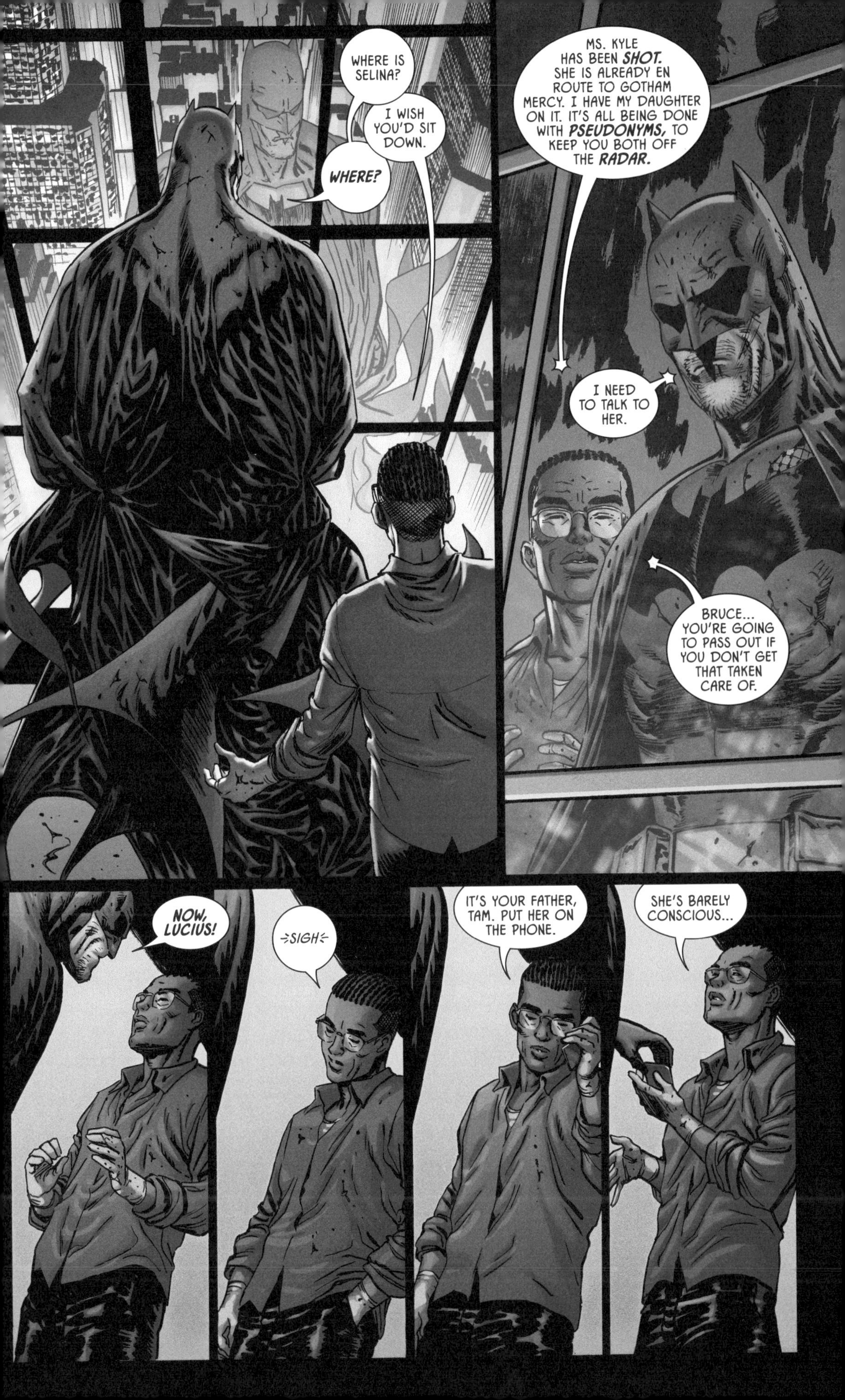
WHERE IS SELINA?
I WISH YOU'D SIT DOWN.
WHERE?
MS. KYLE HAS BEEN SHOT. SHE IS ALREADY EN ROUTE TO GOTHAM MERCY. I HAVE MY DAUGHTER ON IT. IT'S ALL BEING DONE WITH PSEUDONYMS, TO KEEP YOU BOTH OFF THE RADAR.
I NEED TO TALK TO HER.
BRUCE... YOU'RE GOING TO PASS OUT IF YOU DON'T GET THAT TAKEN CARE OF.
NOW, LUCIUS!
SIGH
IT'S YOUR FATHER, TAM. PUT HER ON THE PHONE.
SHE'S BARELY CONSCIOUS...

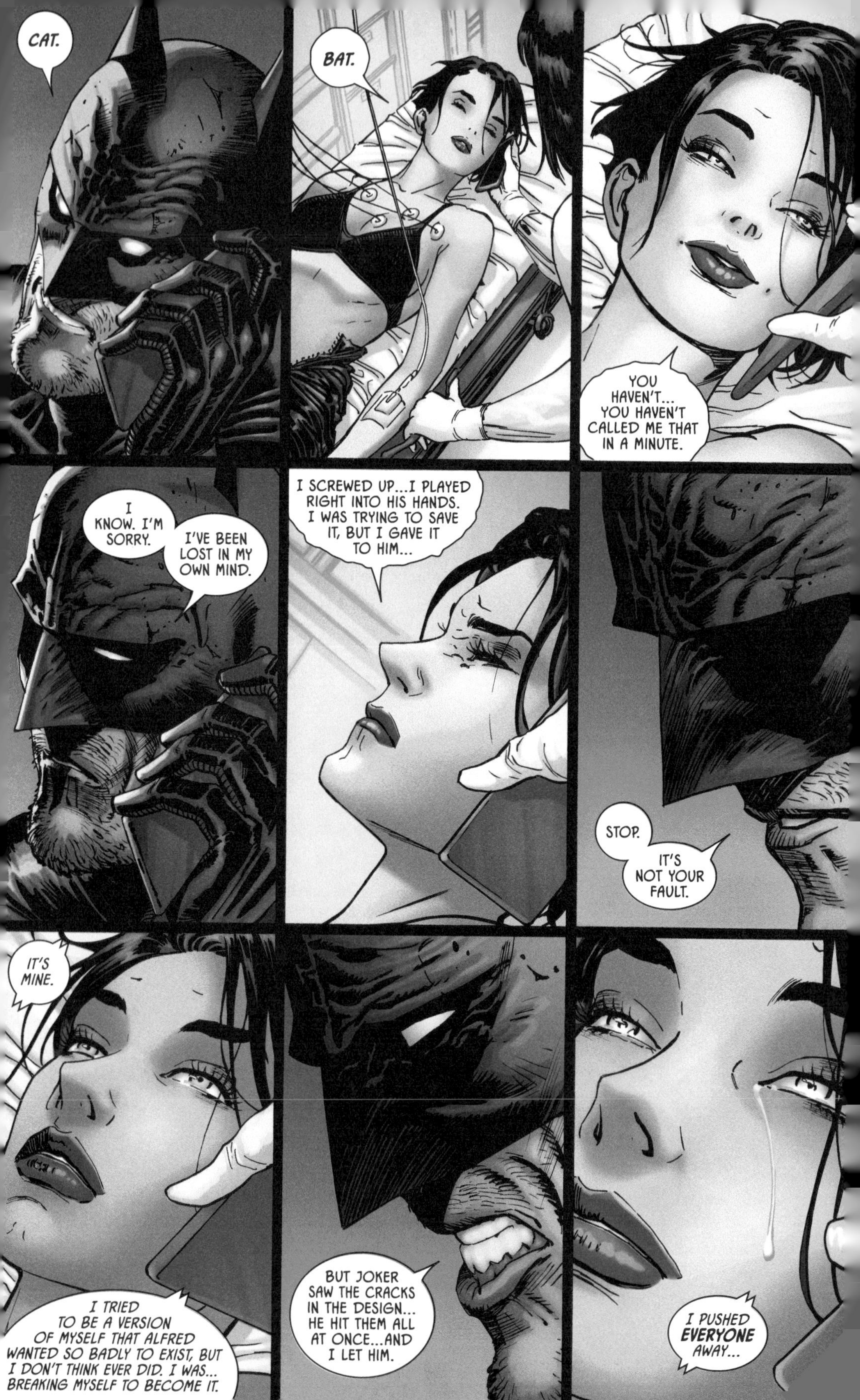
CAT.
BAT.
YOU HAVEN'T... YOU HAVEN'T CALLED ME THAT IN A MINUTE.
I KNOW. I'M SORRY.
I'VE BEEN LOST IN MY OWN MIND.
I SCREWED UP...I PLAYED RIGHT INTO HIS HANDS. I WAS TRYING TO SAVE IT, BUT I GAVE IT TO HIM...
STOP.
IT'S NOT YOUR FAULT.
IT'S MINE.
I TRIED TO BE A VERSION OF MYSELF THAT ALFRED WANTED SO BADLY TO EXIST, BUT I DON'T THINK EVER DID. I WAS... BREAKING MYSELF TO BECOME IT.
BUT JOKER SAW THE CRACKS IN THE DESIGN... HE HIT THEM ALL AT ONCE...AND I LET HIM.
I PUSHED EVERYONE AWAY...

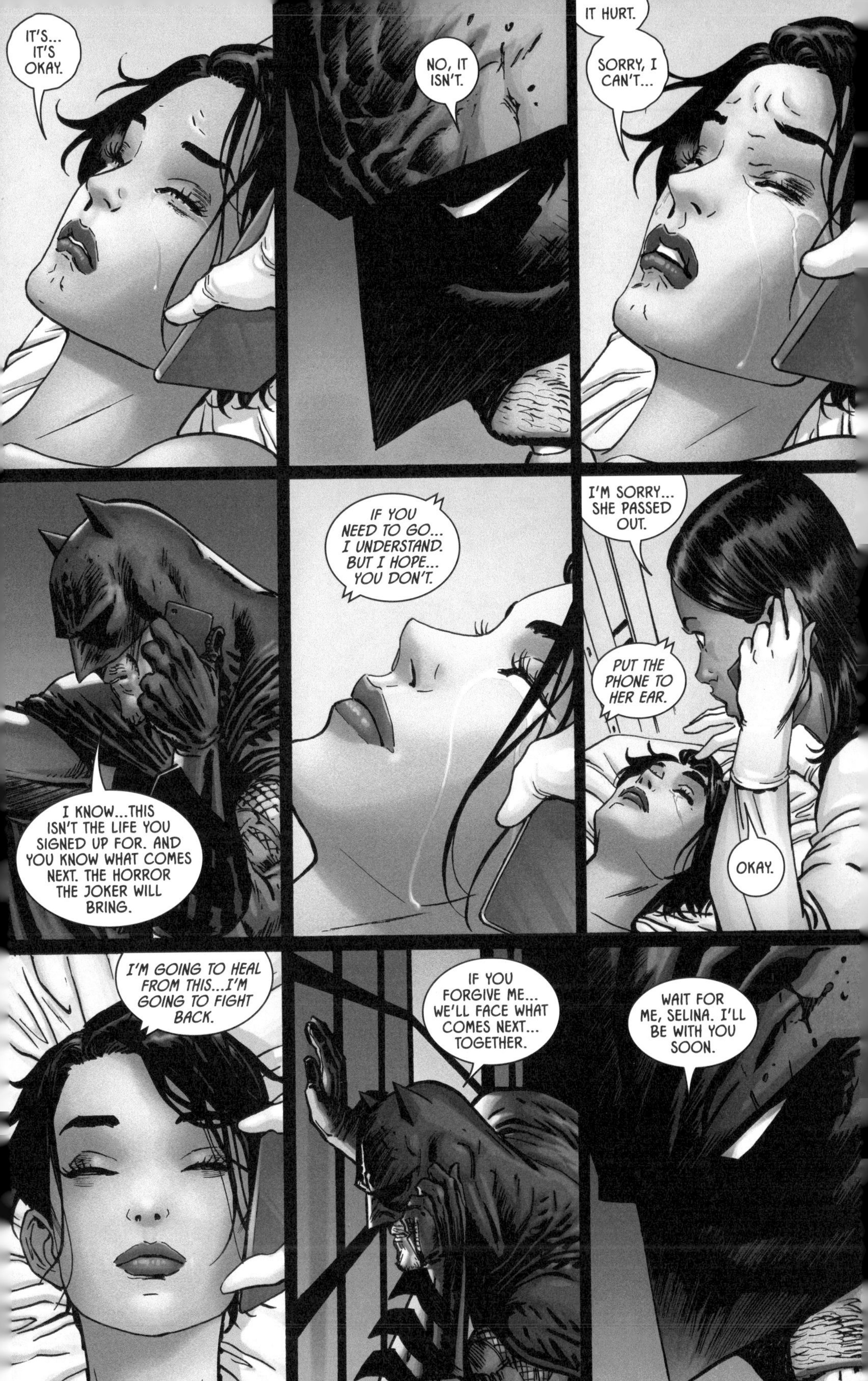
IT'S... IT'S OKAY.
NO, IT ISN'T.
IT HURT.
SORRY, I CAN'T...
IF YOU NEED TO GO... I UNDERSTAND. BUT I HOPE... YOU DON'T.
I KNOW...THIS ISN'T THE LIFE YOU SIGNED UP FOR. AND YOU KNOW WHAT COMES NEXT. THE HORROR THE JOKER WILL BRING.
I'M SORRY... SHE PASSED OUT.
PUT THE PHONE TO HER EAR.
OKAY.
I'M GOING TO HEAL FROM THIS...I'M GOING TO FIGHT BACK.
IF YOU FORGIVE ME... WE'LL FACE WHAT COMES NEXT... TOGETHER.
WAIT FOR ME, SELINA. I'LL BE WITH YOU SOON.

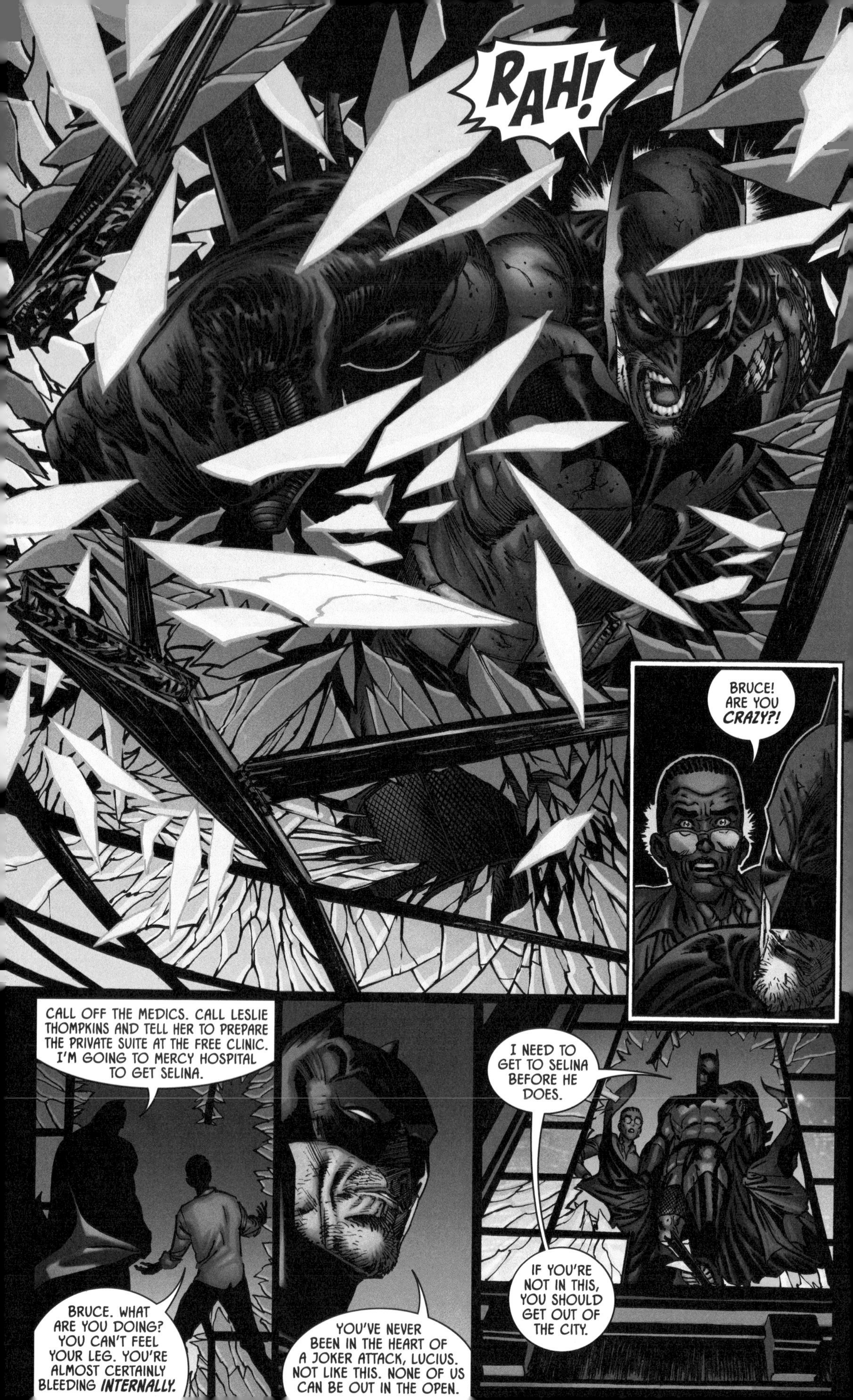
RAH!
BRUCE! ARE YOU CRAZY?!
CALL OFF THE MEDICS. CALL LESLIE THOMPKINS AND TELL HER TO PREPARE THE PRIVATE SUITE AT THE FREE CLINIC. I'M GOING TO MERCY HOSPITAL TO GET SELINA.
BRUCE. WHAT ARE YOU DOING? YOU CAN'T FEEL YOUR LEG. YOU'RE ALMOST CERTAINLY BLEEDING INTERNALLY.
YOU'VE NEVER BEEN IN THE HEART OF A JOKER ATTACK, LUCIUS. NOT LIKE THIS. NONE OF US CAN BE OUT IN THE OPEN.
I NEED TO GET TO SELINA BEFORE HE DOES.
IF YOU'RE NOT IN THIS, YOU SHOULD GET OUT OF THE CITY.

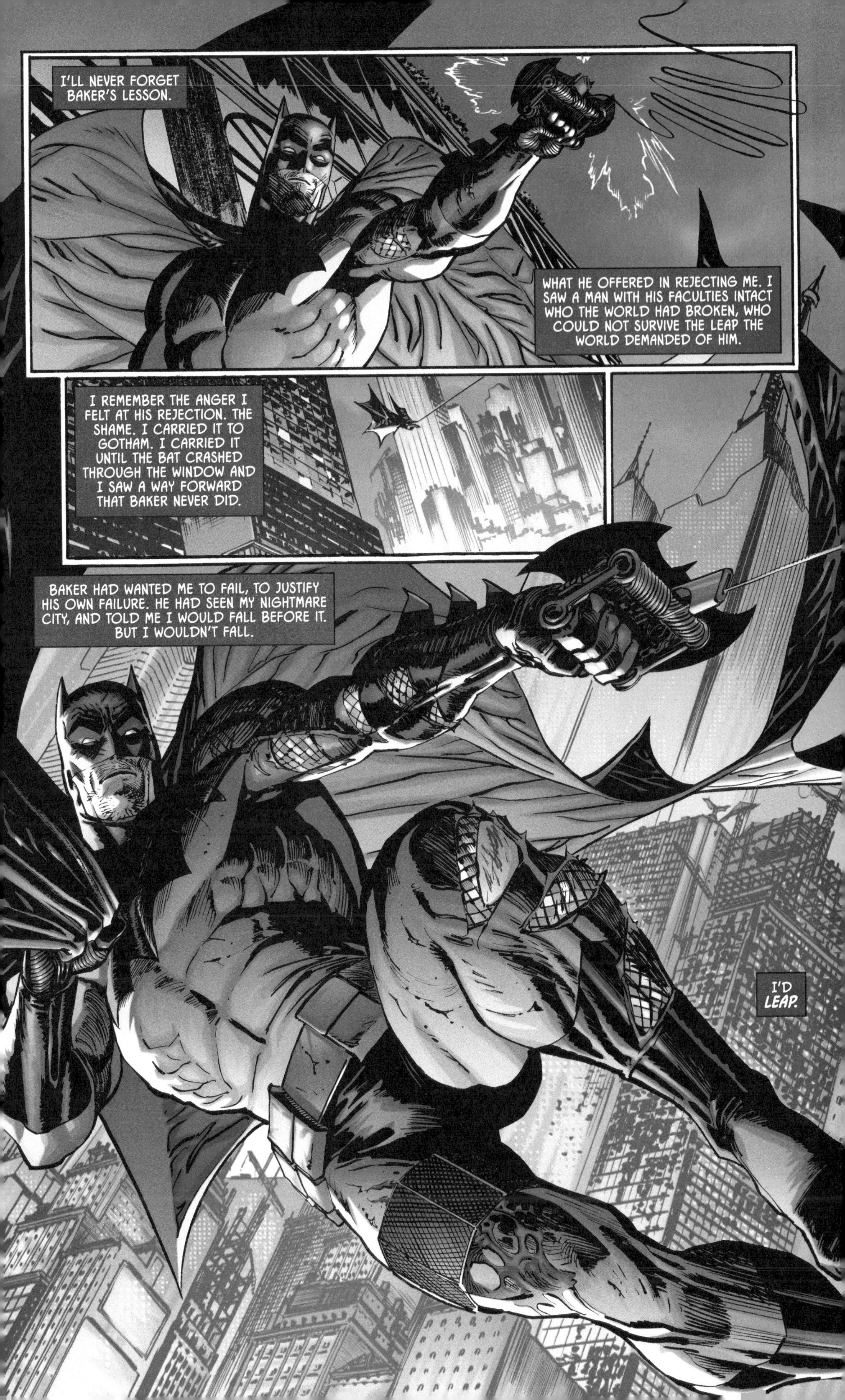
I'LL NEVER FORGET BAKER'S LESSON.
WHAT HE OFFERED IN REJECTING ME. I SAW A MAN WITH HIS FACULTIES INTACT WHO THE WORLD HAD BROKEN, WHO COULD NOT SURVIVE THE LEAP THE WORLD DEMANDED OF HIM.
I REMEMBER THE ANGER I FELT AT HIS REJECTION. THE SHAME. I CARRIED IT TO GOTHAM. I CARRIED IT UNTIL THE BAT CRASHED THROUGH THE WINDOW AND I SAW A WAY FORWARD THAT BAKER NEVER DID.
BAKER HAD WANTED ME TO FAIL, TO JUSTIFY HIS OWN FAILURE. HE HAD SEEN MY NIGHTMARE CITY, AND TOLD ME I WOULD FALL BEFORE IT. BUT I WOULDN'T FALL.
I'D *LEAP.*

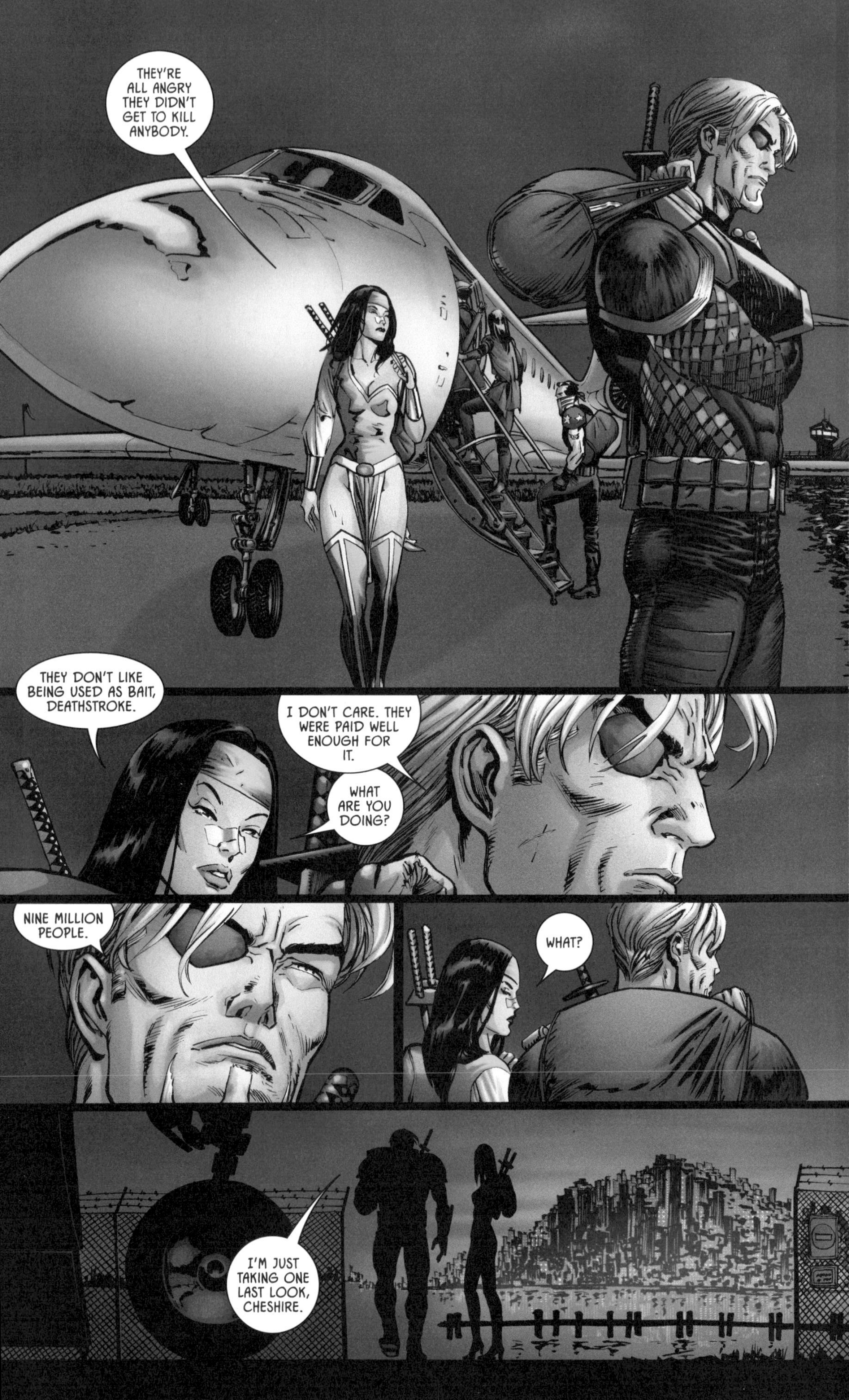

THEY'RE ALL ANGRY THEY DIDN'T GET TO KILL ANYBODY.
THEY DON'T LIKE BEING USED AS BAIT, DEATHSTROKE.
I DON'T CARE. THEY WERE PAID WELL ENOUGH FOR IT.
WHAT ARE YOU DOING?
NINE MILLION PEOPLE.
WHAT?
I'M JUST TAKING ONE LAST LOOK, CHESHIRE.

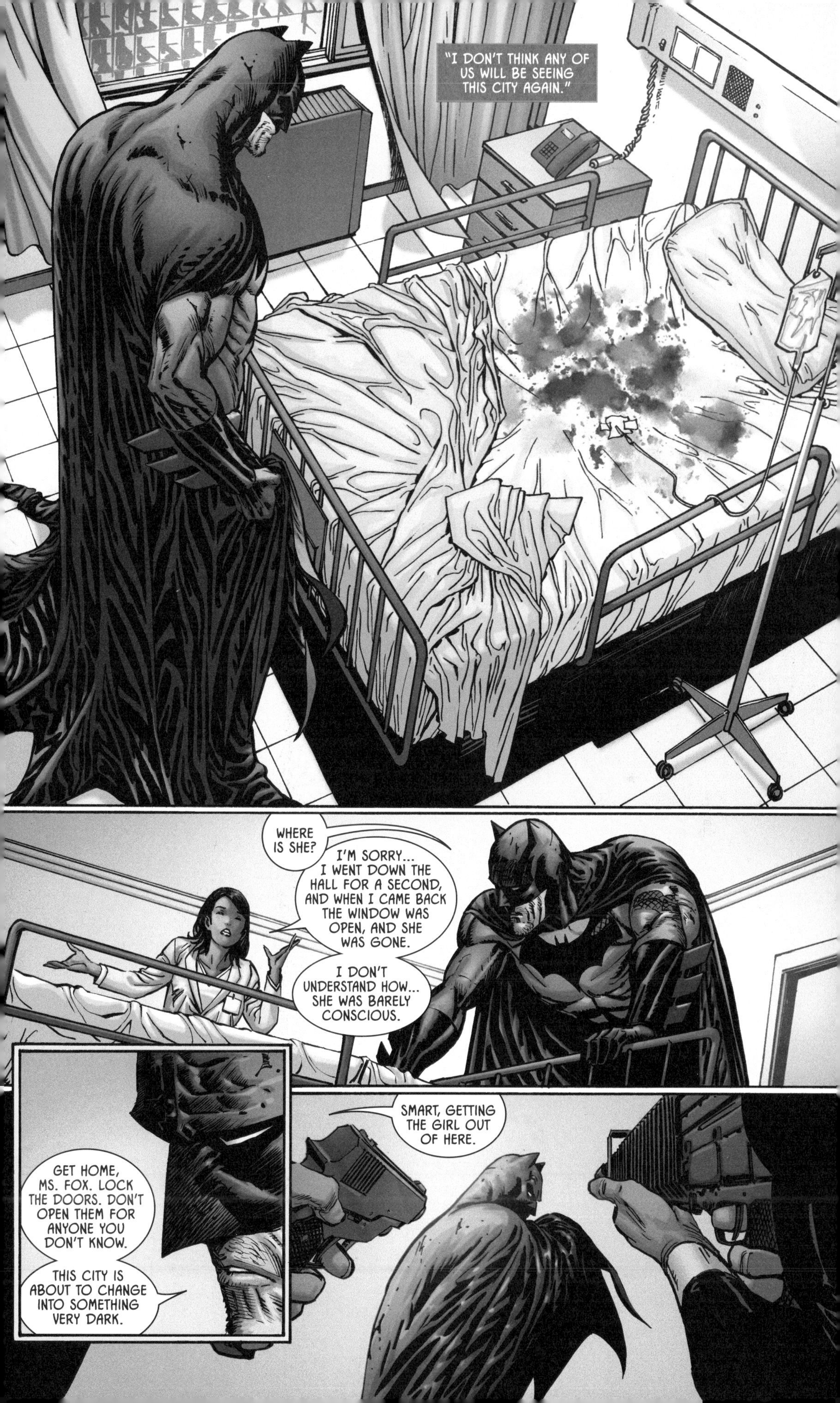
"I DON'T THINK ANY OF US WILL BE SEEING THIS CITY AGAIN."
WHERE IS SHE?
I'M SORRY... I WENT DOWN THE HALL FOR A SECOND, AND WHEN I CAME BACK THE WINDOW WAS OPEN, AND SHE WAS GONE.
I DON'T UNDERSTAND HOW... SHE WAS BARELY CONSCIOUS.
GET HOME, MS. FOX. LOCK THE DOORS. DON'T OPEN THEM FOR ANYONE YOU DON'T KNOW.
THIS CITY IS ABOUT TO CHANGE INTO SOMETHING VERY DARK.
SMART, GETTING THE GIRL OUT OF HERE.

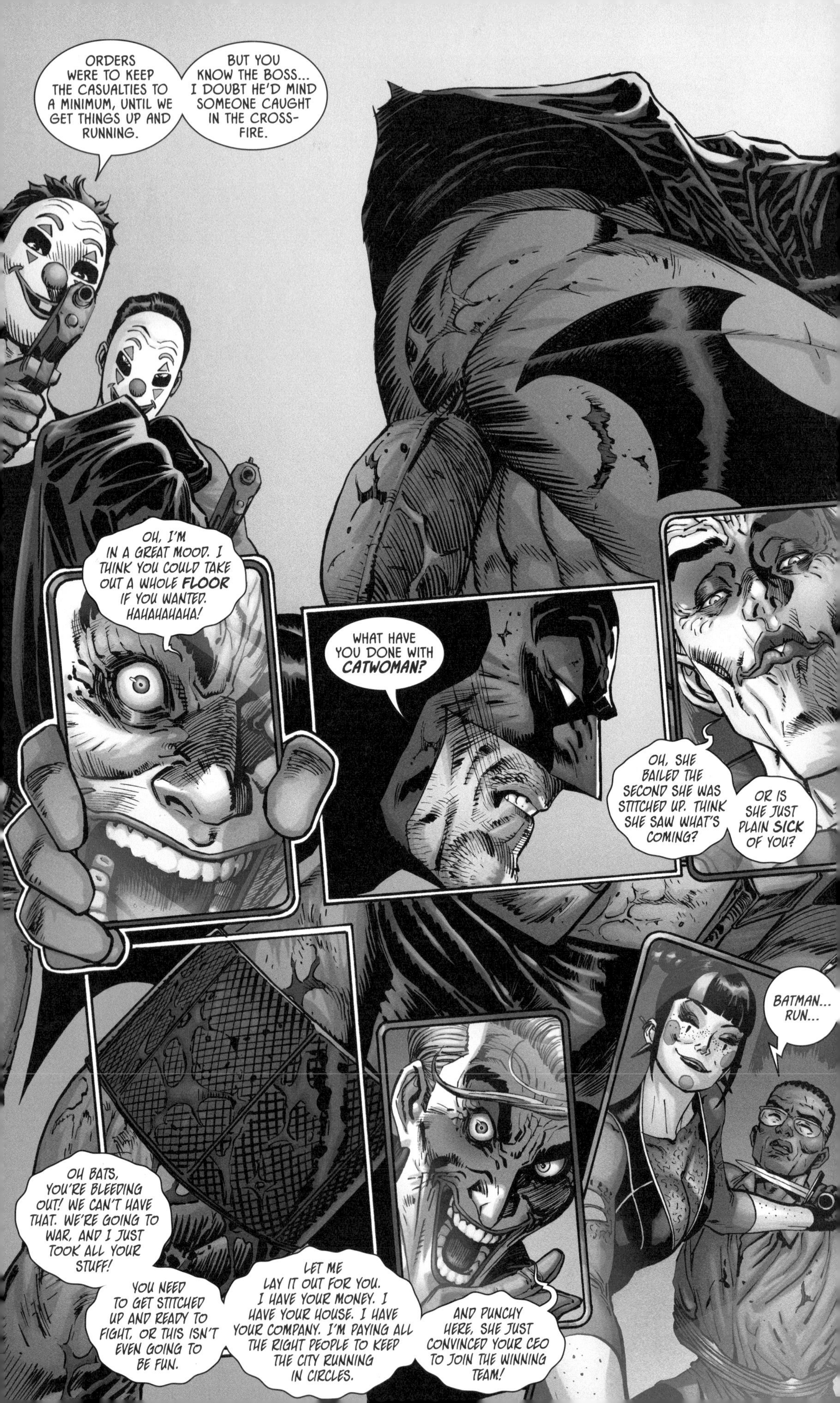
ORDERS WERE TO KEEP THE CASUALTIES TO A MINIMUM, UNTIL WE GET THINGS UP AND RUNNING.
BUT YOU KNOW THE BOSS... I DOUBT HE'D MIND SOMEONE CAUGHT IN THE CROSS-FIRE.
OH, I'M IN A GREAT MOOD. I THINK YOU COULD TAKE OUT A WHOLE FLOOR IF YOU WANTED. HAHAHAHAHA!
WHAT HAVE YOU DONE WITH CATWOMAN?
OH, SHE BAILED THE SECOND SHE WAS STITCHED UP. THINK SHE SAW WHAT'S COMING?
OR IS SHE JUST PLAIN SICK OF YOU?
BATMAN... RUN...
OH BATS, YOU'RE BLEEDING OUT! WE CAN'T HAVE THAT. WE'RE GOING TO WAR, AND I JUST TOOK ALL YOUR STUFF!
YOU NEED TO GET STITCHED UP AND READY TO FIGHT, OR THIS ISN'T EVEN GOING TO BE FUN.
LET ME LAY IT OUT FOR YOU. I HAVE YOUR MONEY. I HAVE YOUR HOUSE. I HAVE YOUR COMPANY. I'M PAYING ALL THE RIGHT PEOPLE TO KEEP THE CITY RUNNING IN CIRCLES.
AND PUNCHY HERE, SHE JUST CONVINCED YOUR CEO TO JOIN THE WINNING TEAM!

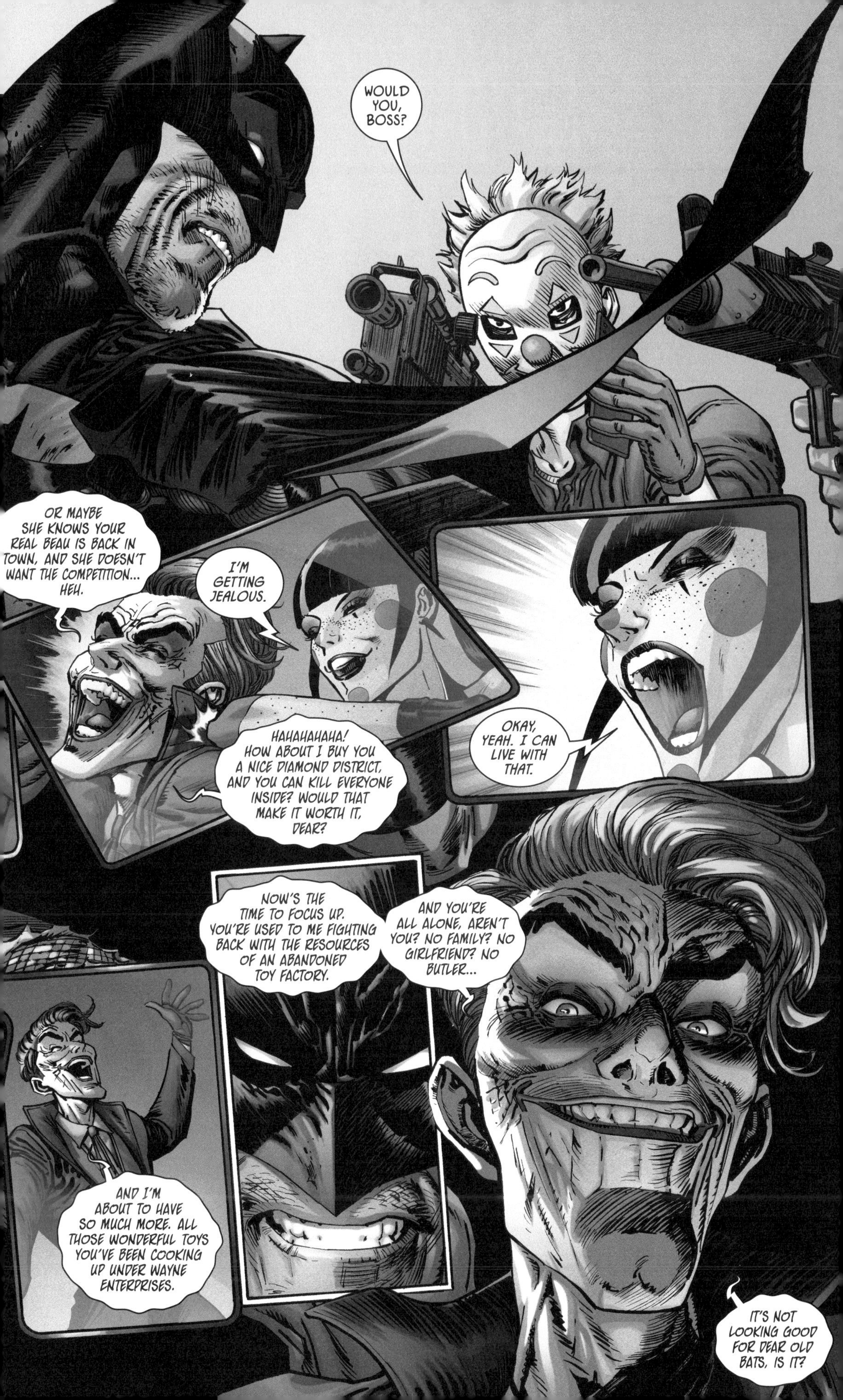
WOULD YOU, BOSS?
OR MAYBE SHE KNOWS YOUR REAL BEAU IS BACK IN TOWN, AND SHE DOESN'T WANT THE COMPETITION... HEH.
I'M GETTING JEALOUS.
HAHAHAHAHA! HOW ABOUT I BUY YOU A NICE DIAMOND DISTRICT, AND YOU CAN KILL EVERYONE INSIDE? WOULD THAT MAKE IT WORTH IT, DEAR?
OKAY, YEAH. I CAN LIVE WITH THAT.
NOW'S THE TIME TO FOCUS UP. YOU'RE USED TO ME FIGHTING BACK WITH THE RESOURCES OF AN ABANDONED TOY FACTORY.
AND YOU'RE ALL ALONE, AREN'T YOU? NO FAMILY? NO GIRLFRIEND? NO BUTLER...
AND I'M ABOUT TO HAVE SO MUCH MORE. ALL THOSE WONDERFUL TOYS YOU'VE BEEN COOKING UP UNDER WAYNE ENTERPRISES.
IT'S NOT LOOKING GOOD FOR DEAR OLD BATS, IS IT?

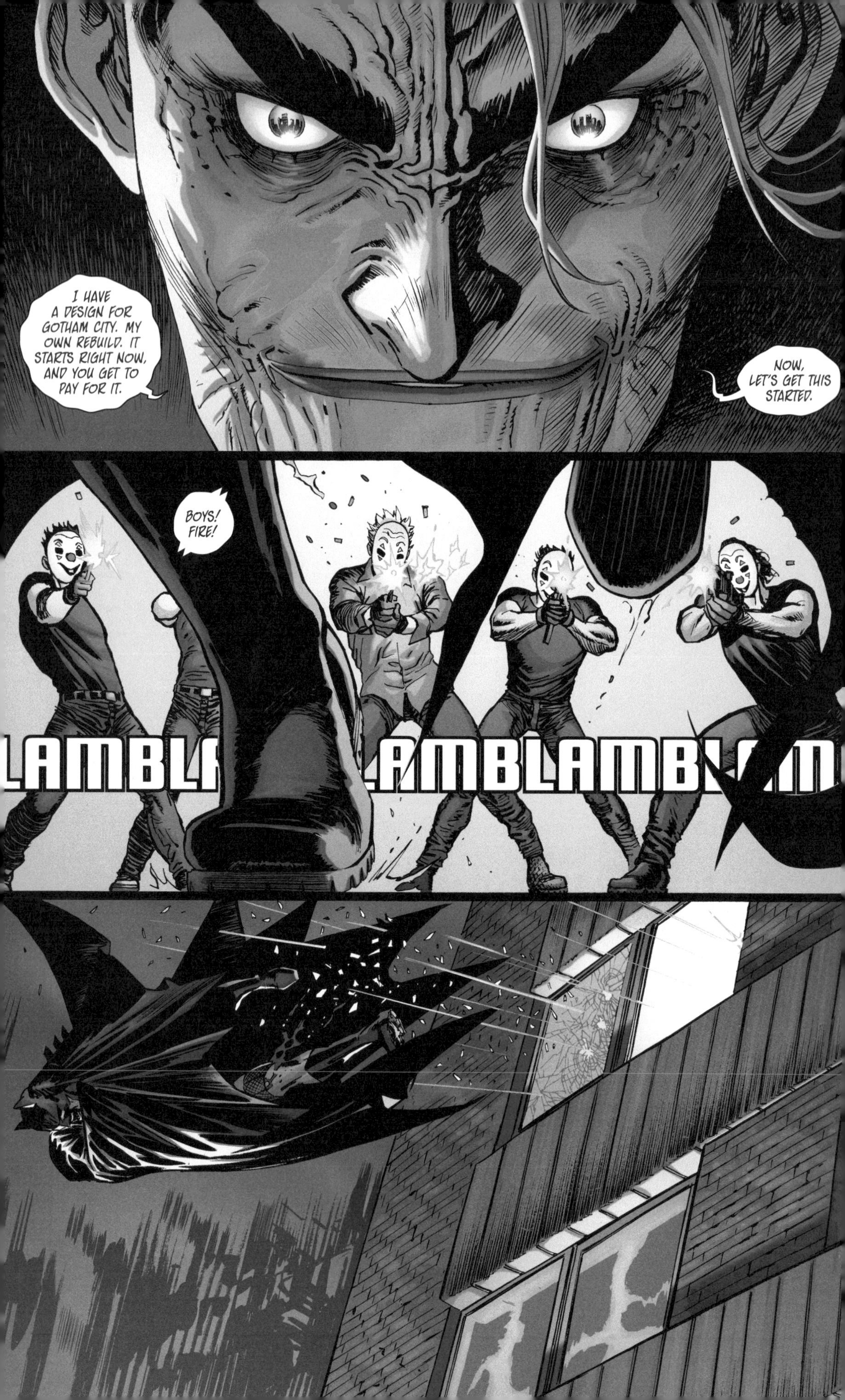
I HAVE A DESIGN FOR GOTHAM CITY. MY OWN REBUILD. IT STARTS RIGHT NOW, AND YOU GET TO PAY FOR IT.
NOW, LET'S GET THIS STARTED.
BOYS! FIRE!
LAMBLAMBLAMBLAMBLAM

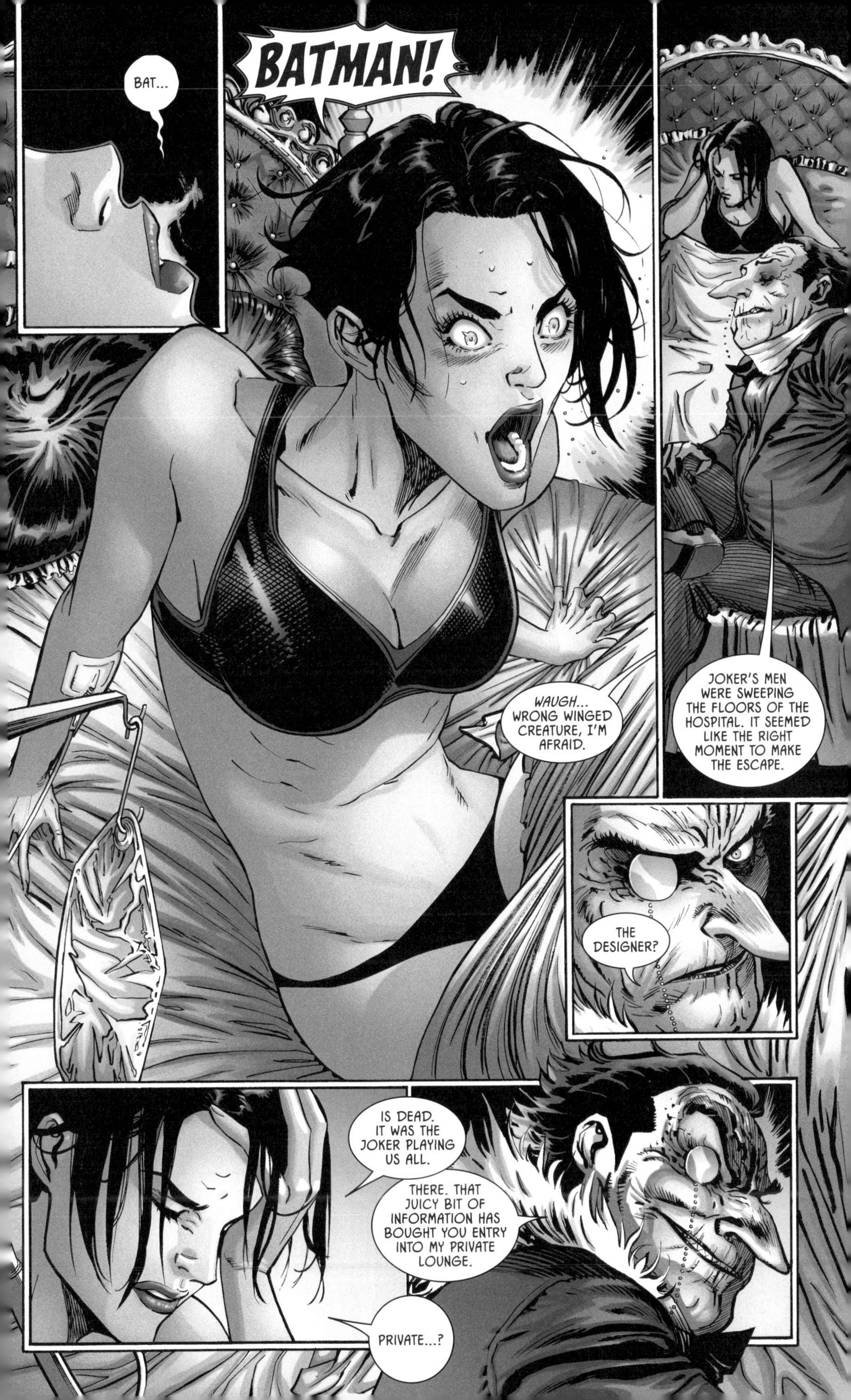
BAT...
BATMAN!
WAUGH... WRONG WINGED CREATURE, I'M AFRAID.
JOKER'S MEN WERE SWEEPING THE FLOORS OF THE HOSPITAL. IT SEEMED LIKE THE RIGHT MOMENT TO MAKE THE ESCAPE.
THE DESIGNER?
IS DEAD. IT WAS THE JOKER PLAYING US ALL.
THERE. THAT JUICY BIT OF INFORMATION HAS BOUGHT YOU ENTRY INTO MY PRIVATE LOUNGE.
PRIVATE...?

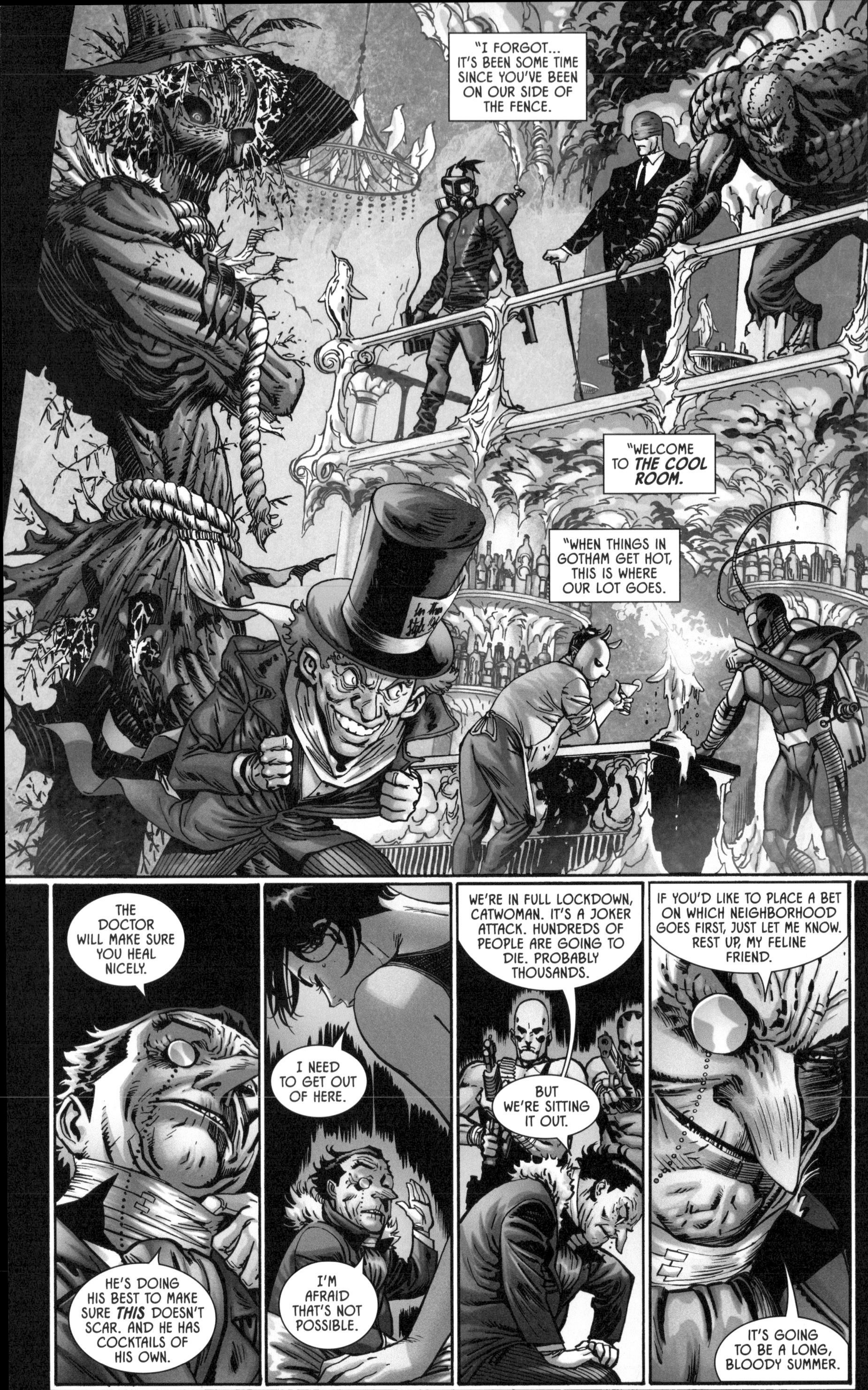
"I FORGOT... IT'S BEEN SOME TIME SINCE YOU'VE BEEN ON OUR SIDE OF THE FENCE.
"WELCOME TO THE COOL ROOM.
"WHEN THINGS IN GOTHAM GET HOT, THIS IS WHERE OUR LOT GOES.
THE DOCTOR WILL MAKE SURE YOU HEAL NICELY.
HE'S DOING HIS BEST TO MAKE SURE THIS DOESN'T SCAR. AND HE HAS COCKTAILS OF HIS OWN.
I NEED TO GET OUT OF HERE.
I'M AFRAID THAT'S NOT POSSIBLE.
WE'RE IN FULL LOCKDOWN, CATWOMAN. IT'S A JOKER ATTACK. HUNDREDS OF PEOPLE ARE GOING TO DIE. PROBABLY THOUSANDS.
BUT WE'RE SITTING IT OUT.
IF YOU'D LIKE TO PLACE A BET ON WHICH NEIGHBORHOOD GOES FIRST, JUST LET ME KNOW. REST UP, MY FELINE FRIEND.
IT'S GOING TO BE A LONG, BLOODY SUMMER.

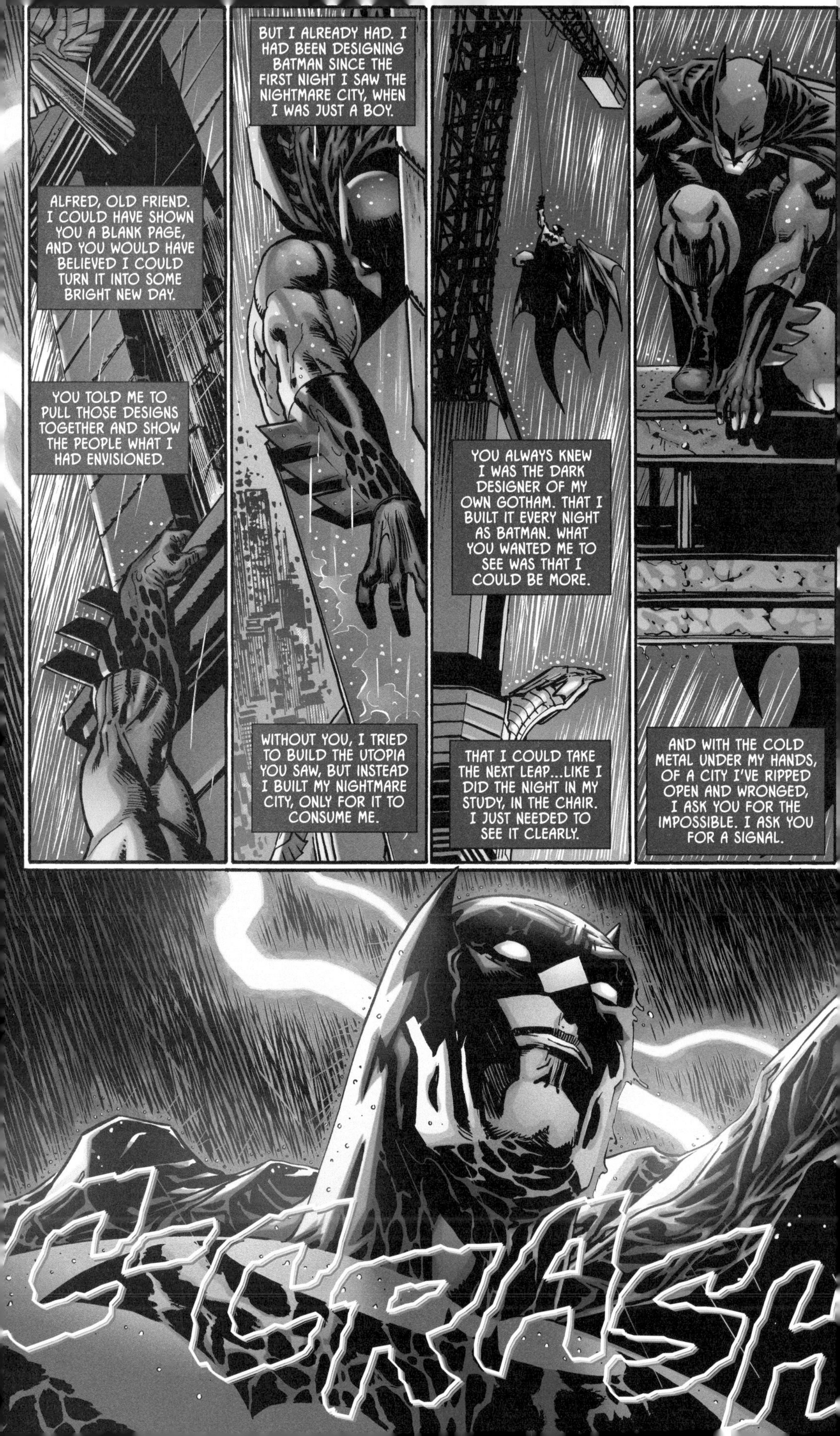
ALFRED, OLD FRIEND. I COULD HAVE SHOWN YOU A BLANK PAGE, AND YOU WOULD HAVE BELIEVED I COULD TURN IT INTO SOME BRIGHT NEW DAY.
YOU TOLD ME TO PULL THOSE DESIGNS TOGETHER AND SHOW THE PEOPLE WHAT I HAD ENVISIONED.
BUT I ALREADY HAD. I HAD BEEN DESIGNING BATMAN SINCE THE FIRST NIGHT I SAW THE NIGHTMARE CITY, WHEN I WAS JUST A BOY.
WITHOUT YOU, I TRIED TO BUILD THE UTOPIA YOU SAW, BUT INSTEAD I BUILT MY NIGHTMARE CITY, ONLY FOR IT TO CONSUME ME.
YOU ALWAYS KNEW I WAS THE DARK DESIGNER OF MY OWN GOTHAM. THAT I BUILT IT EVERY NIGHT AS BATMAN. WHAT YOU WANTED ME TO SEE WAS THAT I COULD BE MORE.
THAT I COULD TAKE THE NEXT LEAP...LIKE I DID THE NIGHT IN MY STUDY, IN THE CHAIR. I JUST NEEDED TO SEE IT CLEARLY.
AND WITH THE COLD METAL UNDER MY HANDS, OF A CITY I'VE RIPPED OPEN AND WRONGED, I ASK YOU FOR THE IMPOSSIBLE. I ASK YOU FOR A SIGNAL.
CCCRASH

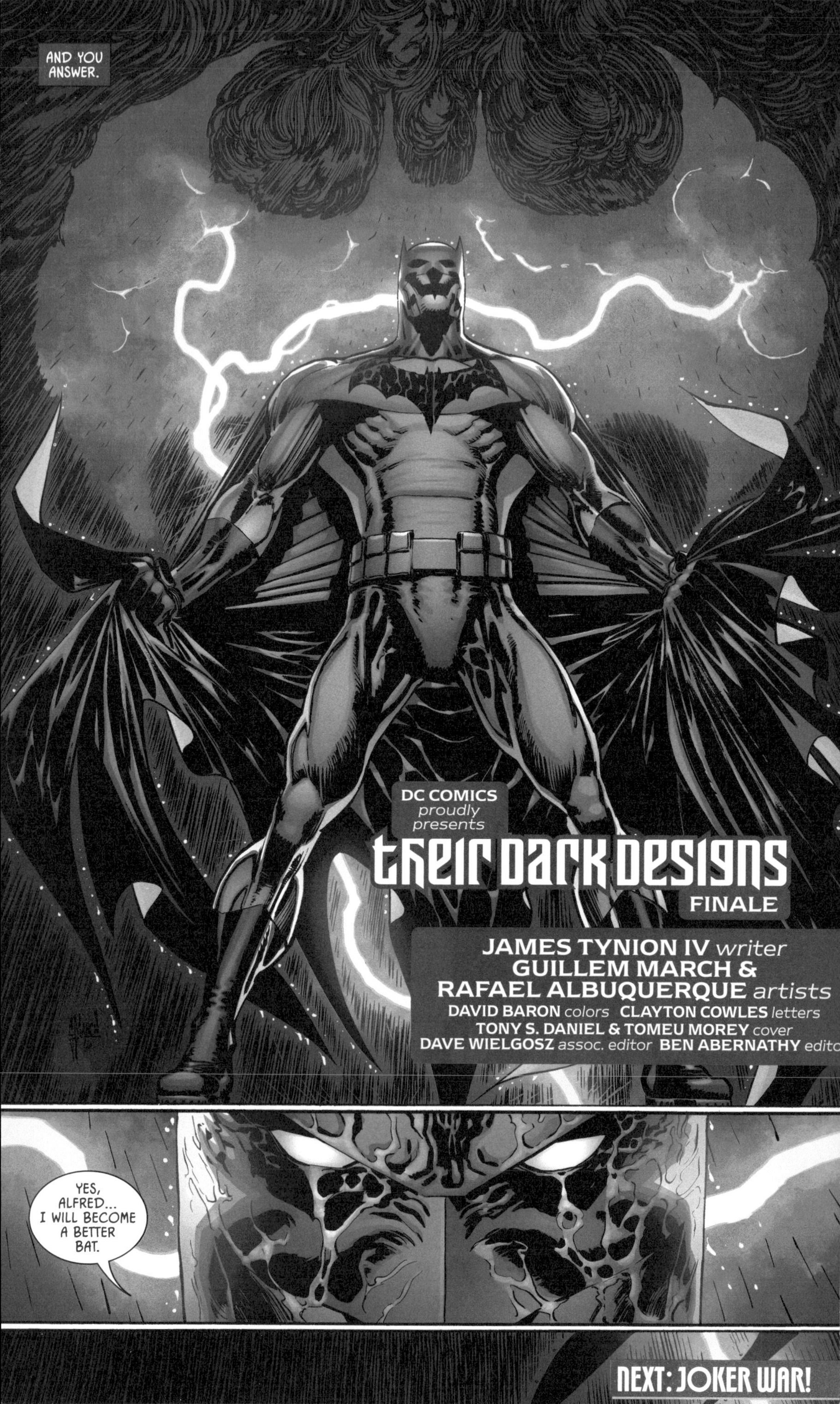
AND YOU ANSWER.
DC COMICS proudly presents
THEIR DARK DESIGNS
FINALE
JAMES TYNION IV writer
GUILLEM MARCH & RAFAEL ALBUQUERQUE artists
DAVID BARON colors CLAYTON COWLES letters
TONY S. DANIEL & TOMEU MOREY cover
DAVE WIELGOSZ assoc. editor BEN ABERNATHY edito
YES, ALFRED... I WILL BECOME A BETTER BAT.
NEXT: JOKER WAR!

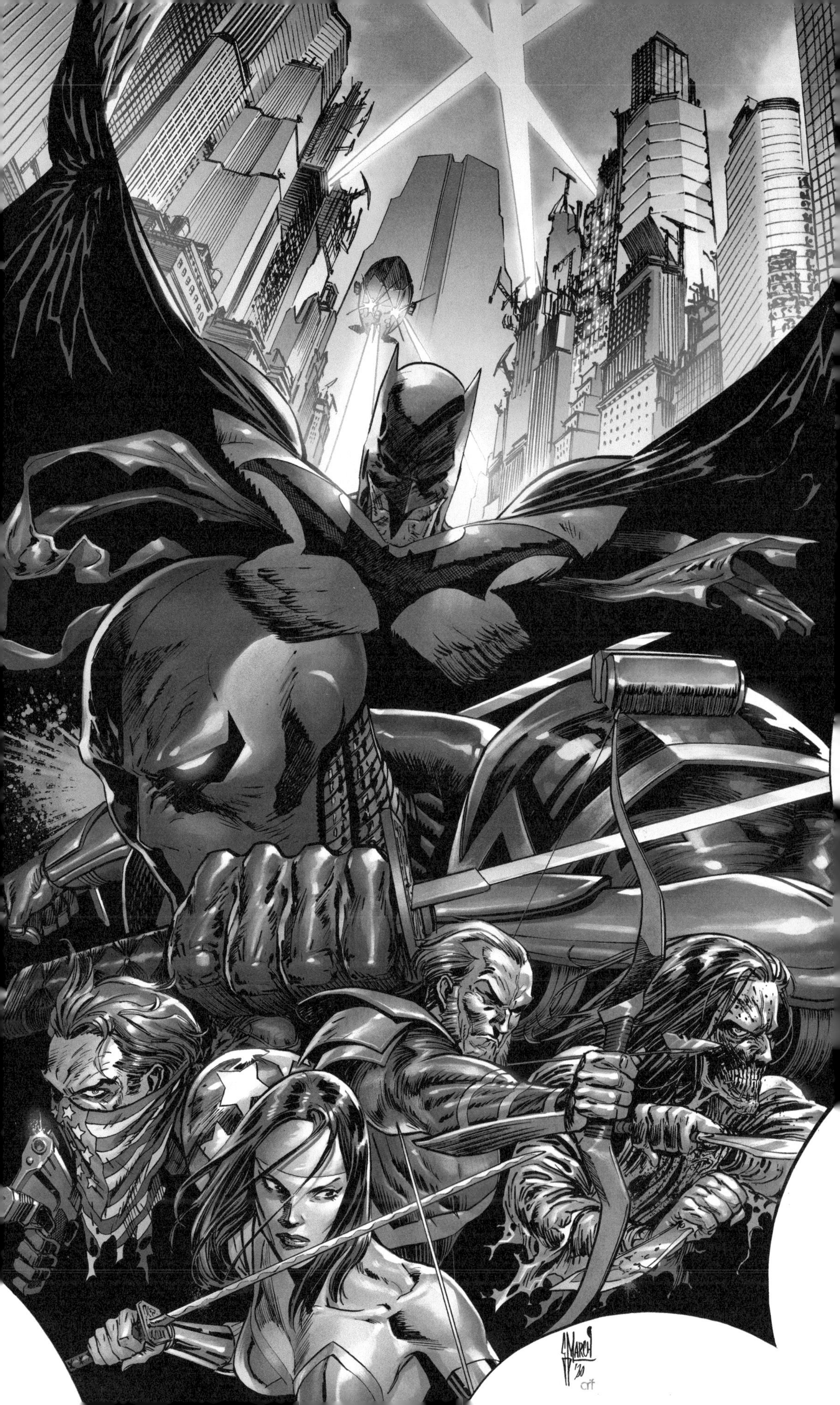

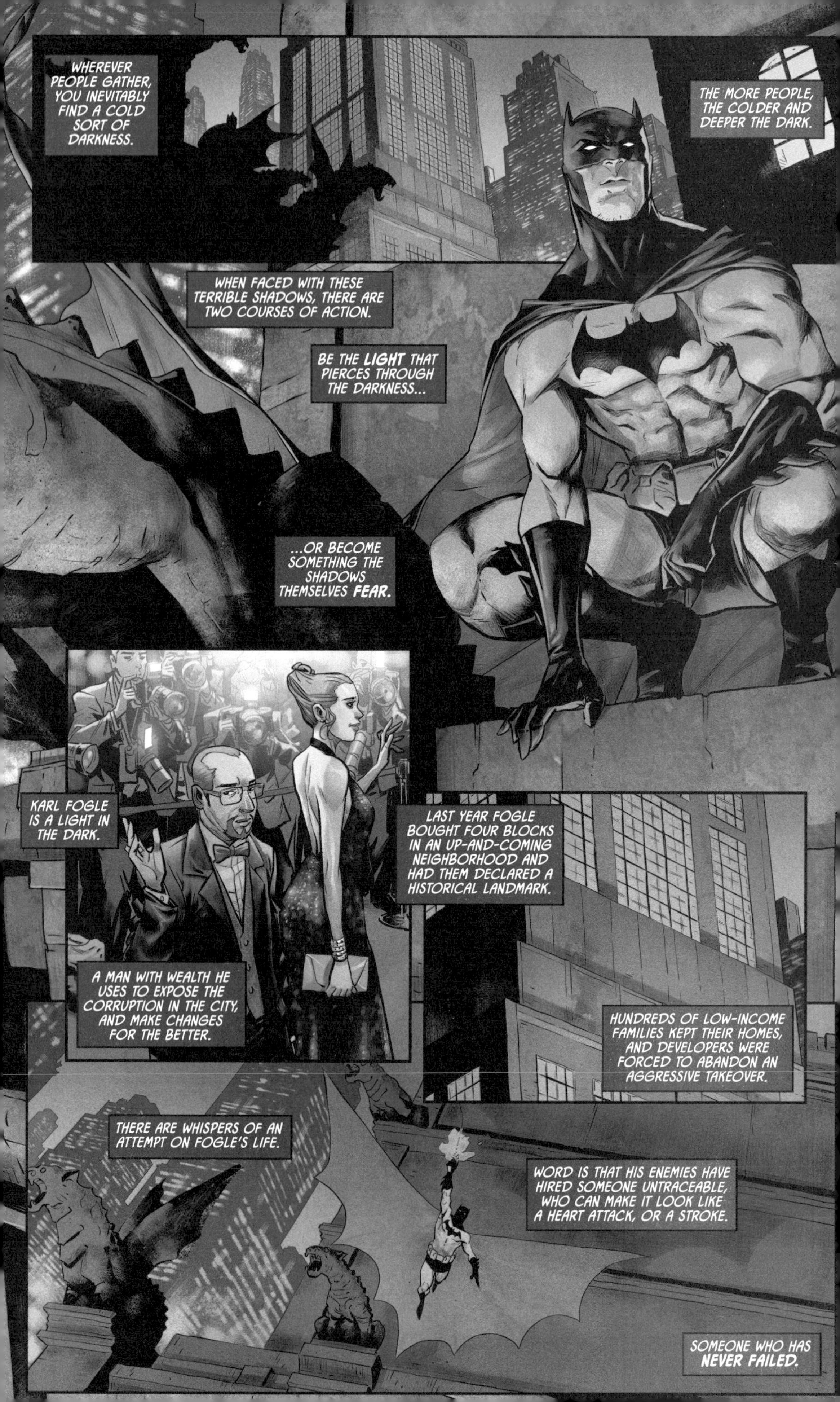
WHEREVER PEOPLE GATHER, YOU INEVITABLY FIND A COLD SORT OF DARKNESS.
THE MORE PEOPLE, THE COLDER AND DEEPER THE DARK.
WHEN FACED WITH THESE TERRIBLE SHADOWS, THERE ARE TWO COURSES OF ACTION.
BE THE **LIGHT** THAT PIERCES THROUGH THE DARKNESS...
...OR BECOME SOMETHING THE SHADOWS THEMSELVES **FEAR.**
KARL FOGLE IS A LIGHT IN THE DARK.
A MAN WITH WEALTH HE USES TO EXPOSE THE CORRUPTION IN THE CITY, AND MAKE CHANGES FOR THE BETTER.
LAST YEAR FOGLE BOUGHT FOUR BLOCKS IN AN UP-AND-COMING NEIGHBORHOOD AND HAD THEM DECLARED A HISTORICAL LANDMARK.
HUNDREDS OF LOW-INCOME FAMILIES KEPT THEIR HOMES, AND DEVELOPERS WERE FORCED TO ABANDON AN AGGRESSIVE TAKEOVER.
THERE ARE WHISPERS OF AN ATTEMPT ON FOGLE'S LIFE.
WORD IS THAT HIS ENEMIES HAVE HIRED SOMEONE UNTRACEABLE, WHO CAN MAKE IT LOOK LIKE A HEART ATTACK, OR A STROKE.
SOMEONE WHO HAS **NEVER FAILED.**

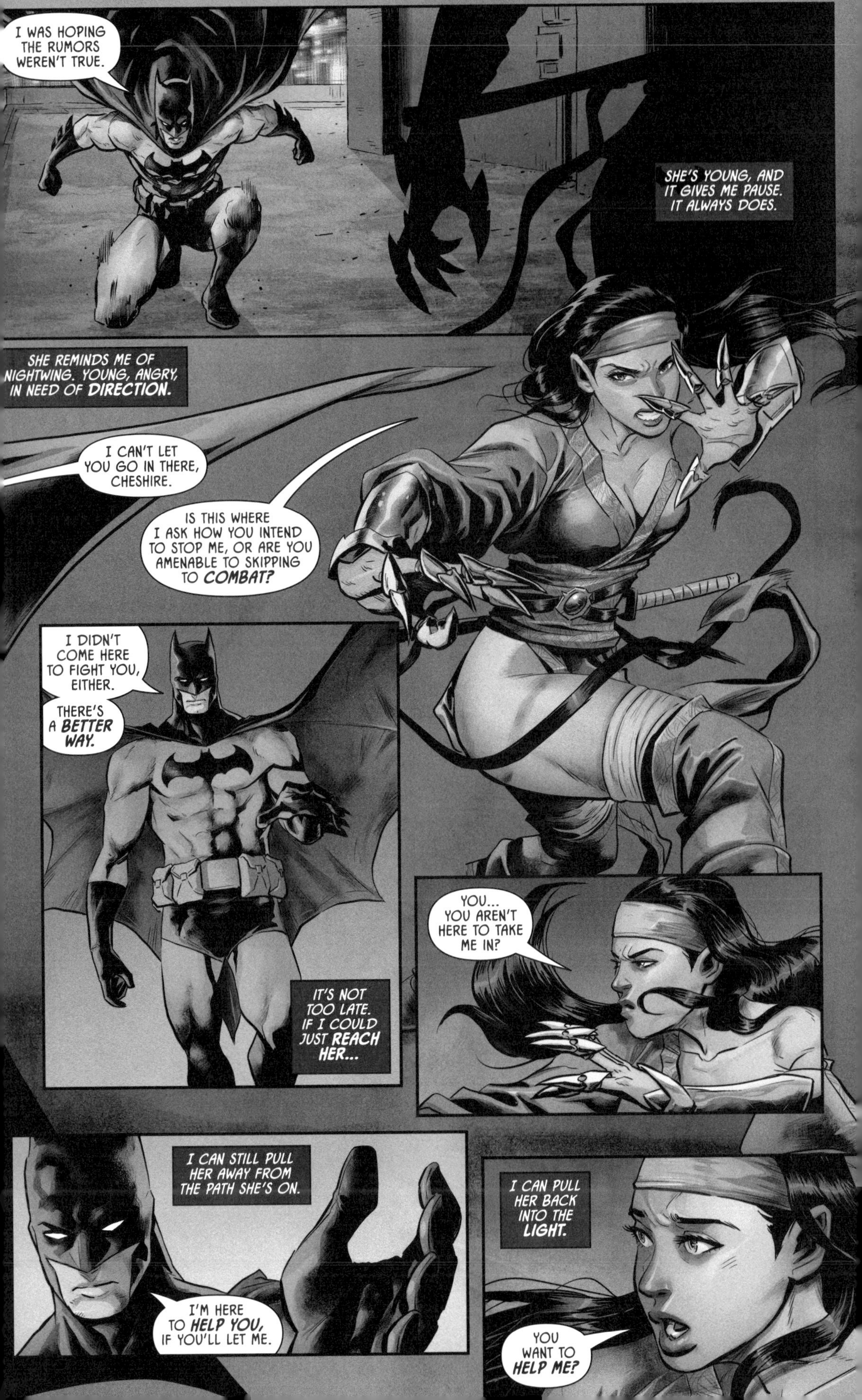

I WAS HOPING THE RUMORS WEREN'T TRUE.
SHE'S YOUNG, AND IT GIVES ME PAUSE. IT ALWAYS DOES.
SHE REMINDS ME OF NIGHTWING. YOUNG, ANGRY, IN NEED OF DIRECTION.
I CAN'T LET YOU GO IN THERE, CHESHIRE.
IS THIS WHERE I ASK HOW YOU INTEND TO STOP ME, OR ARE YOU AMENABLE TO SKIPPING TO COMBAT?
I DIDN'T COME HERE TO FIGHT YOU, EITHER.
THERE'S A BETTER WAY.
IT'S NOT TOO LATE. IF I COULD JUST REACH HER...
YOU... YOU AREN'T HERE TO TAKE ME IN?
I CAN STILL PULL HER AWAY FROM THE PATH SHE'S ON.
I'M HERE TO HELP YOU, IF YOU'LL LET ME.
I CAN PULL HER BACK INTO THE LIGHT.
YOU WANT TO HELP ME?

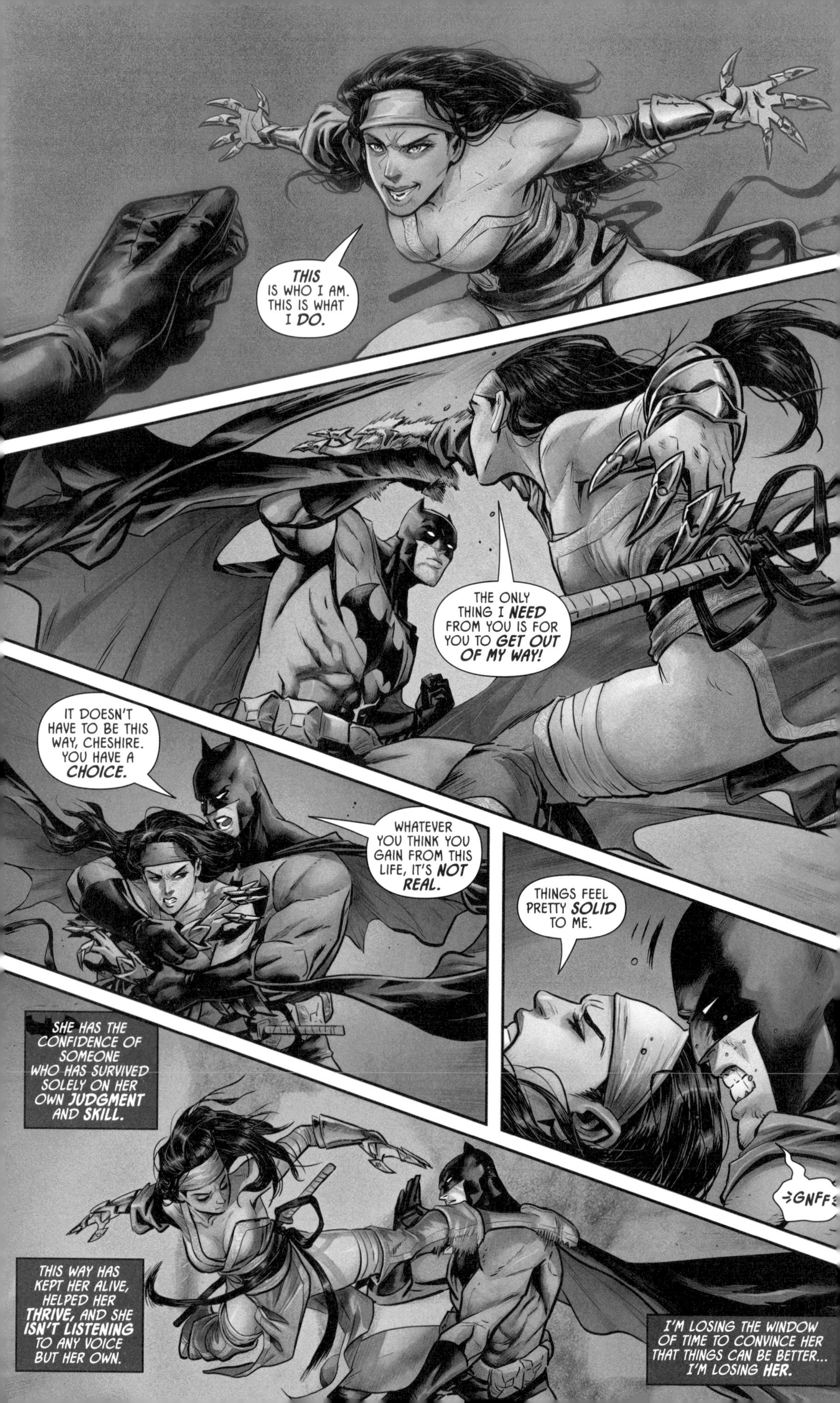
THIS IS WHO I AM. THIS IS WHAT I DO.
THE ONLY THING I NEED FROM YOU IS FOR YOU TO GET OUT OF MY WAY!
IT DOESN'T HAVE TO BE THIS WAY, CHESHIRE. YOU HAVE A CHOICE.
WHATEVER YOU THINK YOU GAIN FROM THIS LIFE, IT'S NOT REAL.
THINGS FEEL PRETTY SOLID TO ME.
SHE HAS THE CONFIDENCE OF SOMEONE WHO HAS SURVIVED SOLELY ON HER OWN JUDGMENT AND SKILL.
GNFF
THIS WAY HAS KEPT HER ALIVE, HELPED HER THRIVE, AND SHE ISN'T LISTENING TO ANY VOICE BUT HER OWN.
I'M LOSING THE WINDOW OF TIME TO CONVINCE HER THAT THINGS CAN BE BETTER... I'M LOSING HER.

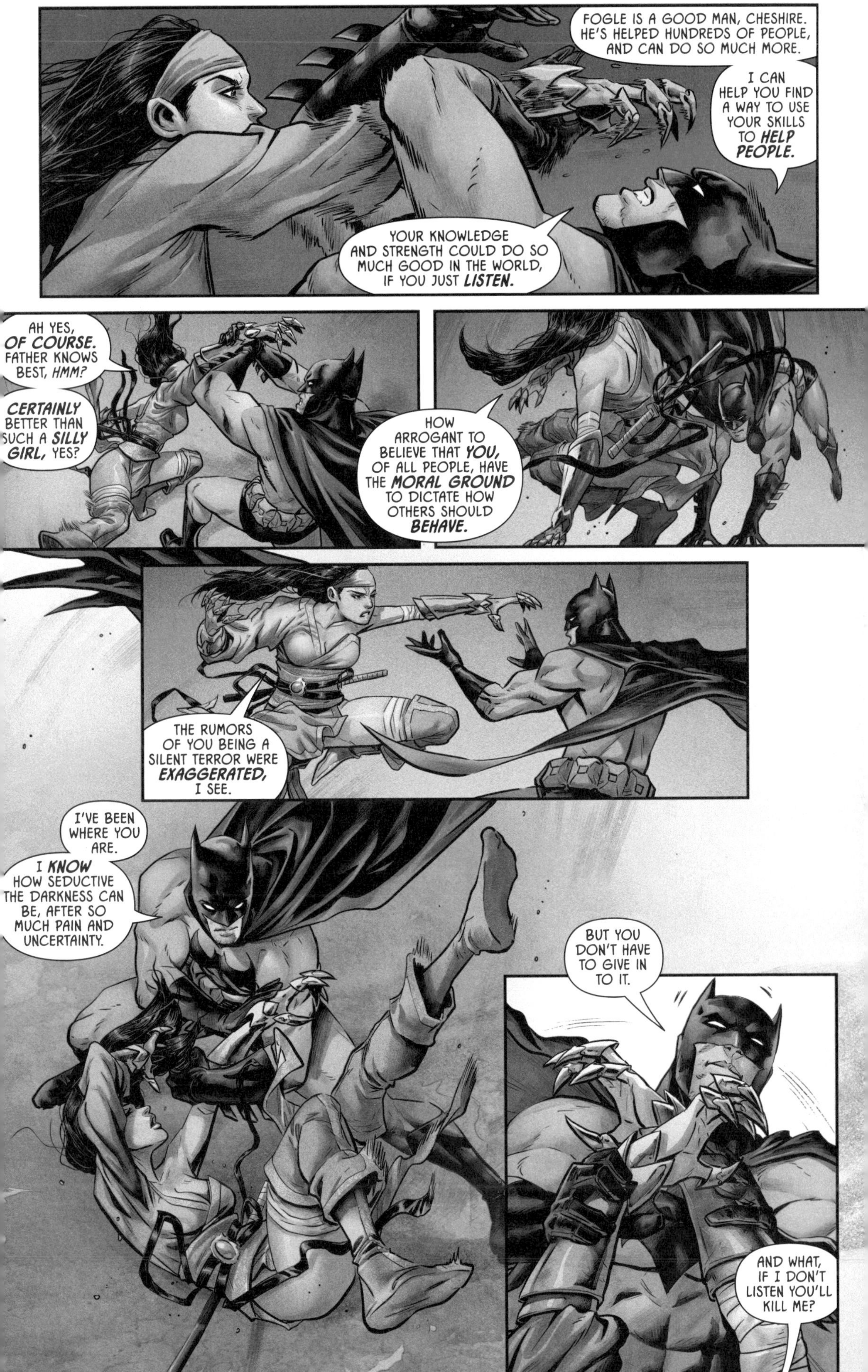

FOGLE IS A GOOD MAN, CHESHIRE. HE'S HELPED HUNDREDS OF PEOPLE, AND CAN DO SO MUCH MORE.
I CAN HELP YOU FIND A WAY TO USE YOUR SKILLS TO HELP PEOPLE.
YOUR KNOWLEDGE AND STRENGTH COULD DO SO MUCH GOOD IN THE WORLD, IF YOU JUST LISTEN.
AH YES, OF COURSE. FATHER KNOWS BEST, HMM?
CERTAINLY BETTER THAN SUCH A SILLY GIRL, YES?
HOW ARROGANT TO BELIEVE THAT YOU, OF ALL PEOPLE, HAVE THE MORAL GROUND TO DICTATE HOW OTHERS SHOULD BEHAVE.
THE RUMORS OF YOU BEING A SILENT TERROR WERE EXAGGERATED, I SEE.
I'VE BEEN WHERE YOU ARE.
I KNOW HOW SEDUCTIVE THE DARKNESS CAN BE, AFTER SO MUCH PAIN AND UNCERTAINTY.
BUT YOU DON'T HAVE TO GIVE IN TO IT.
AND WHAT, IF I DON'T LISTEN YOU'LL KILL ME?

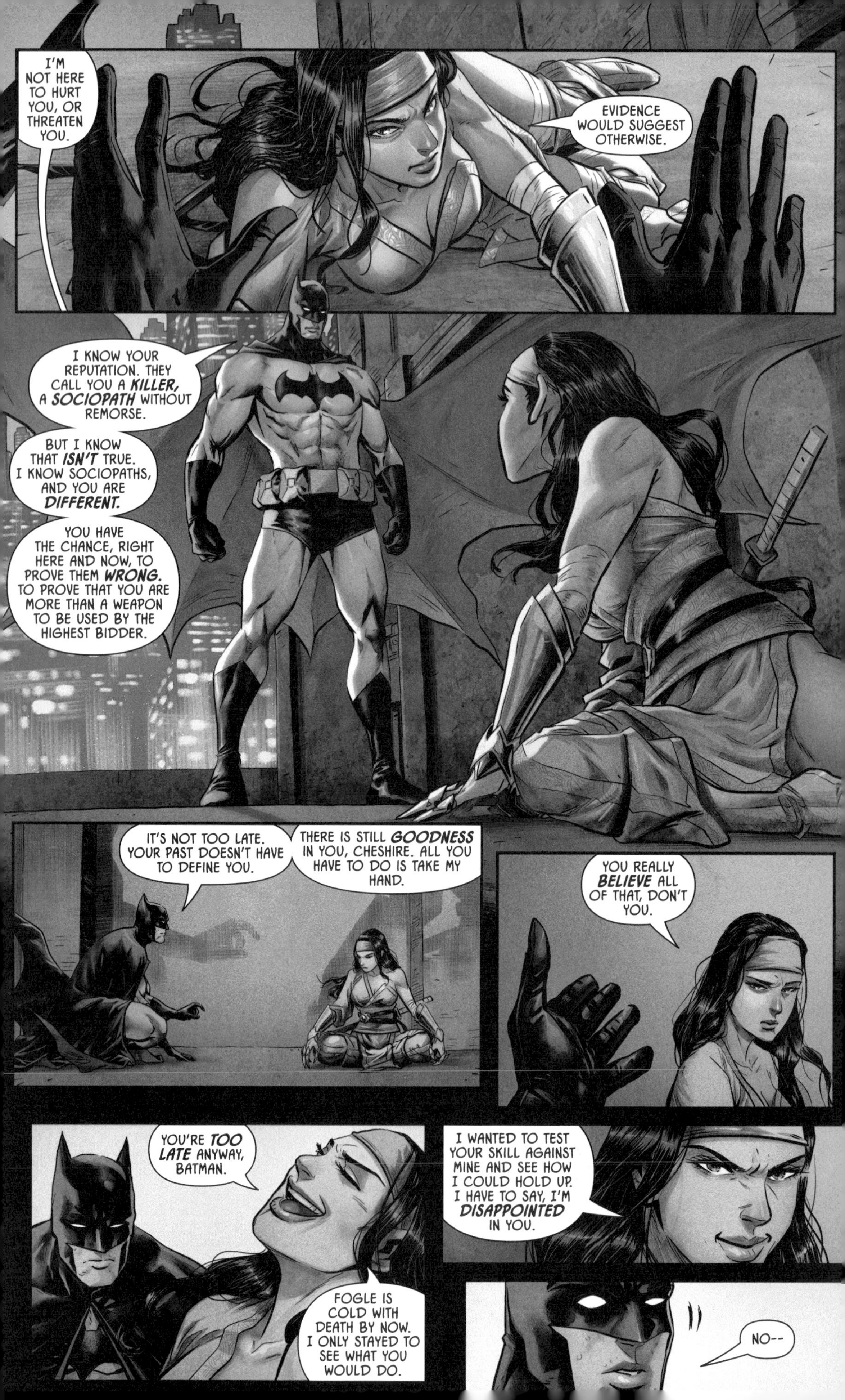
I'M NOT HERE TO HURT YOU, OR THREATEN YOU.
EVIDENCE WOULD SUGGEST OTHERWISE.
I KNOW YOUR REPUTATION. THEY CALL YOU A KILLER, A SOCIOPATH WITHOUT REMORSE.
BUT I KNOW THAT ISN'T TRUE. I KNOW SOCIOPATHS, AND YOU ARE DIFFERENT.
YOU HAVE THE CHANCE, RIGHT HERE AND NOW, TO PROVE THEM WRONG. TO PROVE THAT YOU ARE MORE THAN A WEAPON TO BE USED BY THE HIGHEST BIDDER.
IT'S NOT TOO LATE. YOUR PAST DOESN'T HAVE TO DEFINE YOU.
THERE IS STILL GOODNESS IN YOU, CHESHIRE. ALL YOU HAVE TO DO IS TAKE MY HAND.
YOU REALLY BELIEVE ALL OF THAT, DON'T YOU.
YOU'RE TOO LATE ANYWAY, BATMAN.
FOGLE IS COLD WITH DEATH BY NOW. I ONLY STAYED TO SEE WHAT YOU WOULD DO.
I WANTED TO TEST YOUR SKILL AGAINST MINE AND SEE HOW I COULD HOLD UP. I HAVE TO SAY, I'M DISAPPOINTED IN YOU.
NO--

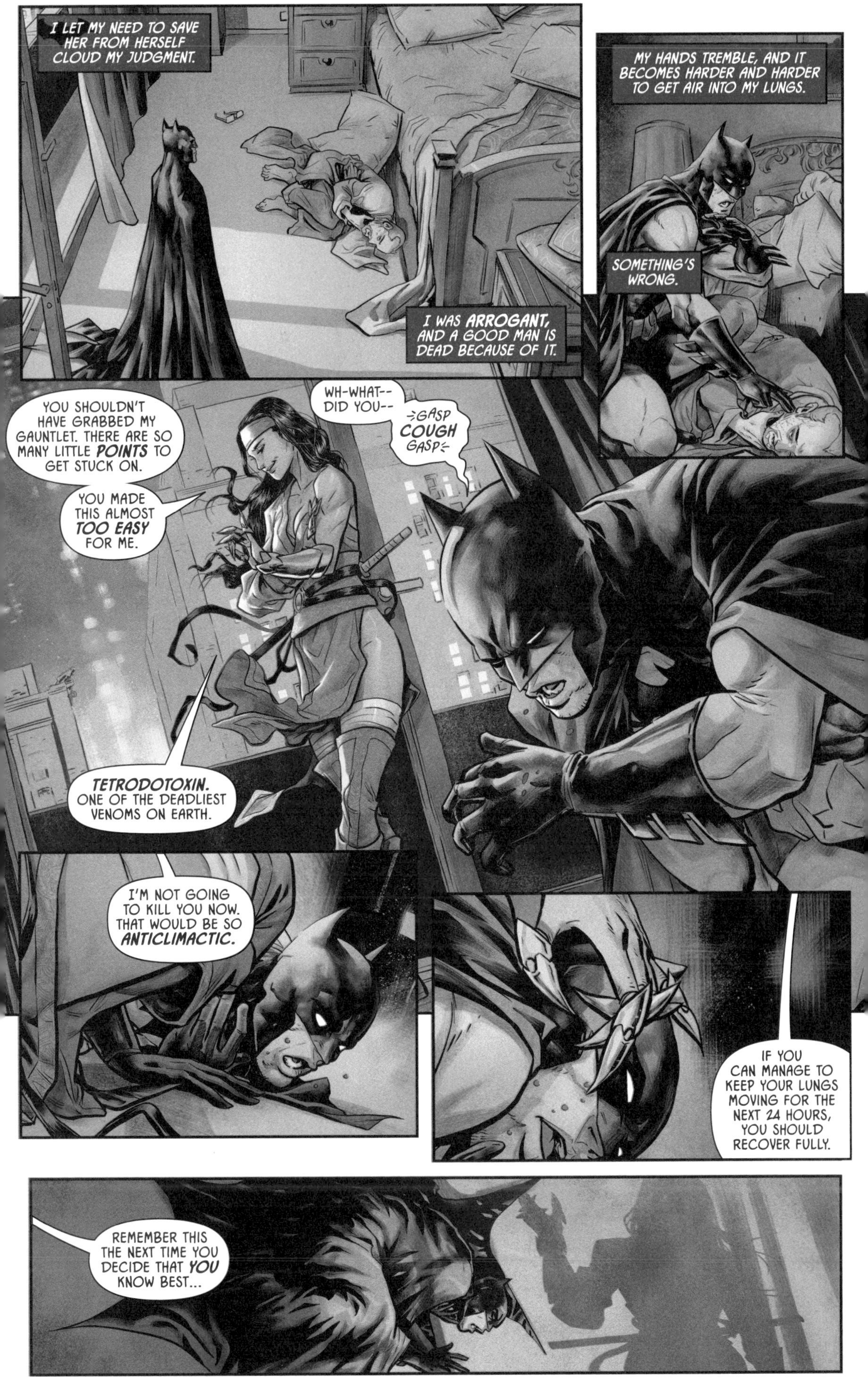
I LET MY NEED TO SAVE HER FROM HERSELF CLOUD MY JUDGMENT.
I WAS ARROGANT, AND A GOOD MAN IS DEAD BECAUSE OF IT.
MY HANDS TREMBLE, AND IT BECOMES HARDER AND HARDER TO GET AIR INTO MY LUNGS.
SOMETHING'S WRONG.
YOU SHOULDN'T HAVE GRABBED MY GAUNTLET. THERE ARE SO MANY LITTLE POINTS TO GET STUCK ON.
YOU MADE THIS ALMOST TOO EASY FOR ME.
WH-WHAT-- DID YOU--
GASP COUGH GASP
TETRODOTOXIN. ONE OF THE DEADLIEST VENOMS ON EARTH.
I'M NOT GOING TO KILL YOU NOW. THAT WOULD BE SO ANTICLIMACTIC.
IF YOU CAN MANAGE TO KEEP YOUR LUNGS MOVING FOR THE NEXT 24 HOURS, YOU SHOULD RECOVER FULLY.
REMEMBER THIS THE NEXT TIME YOU DECIDE THAT YOU KNOW BEST...

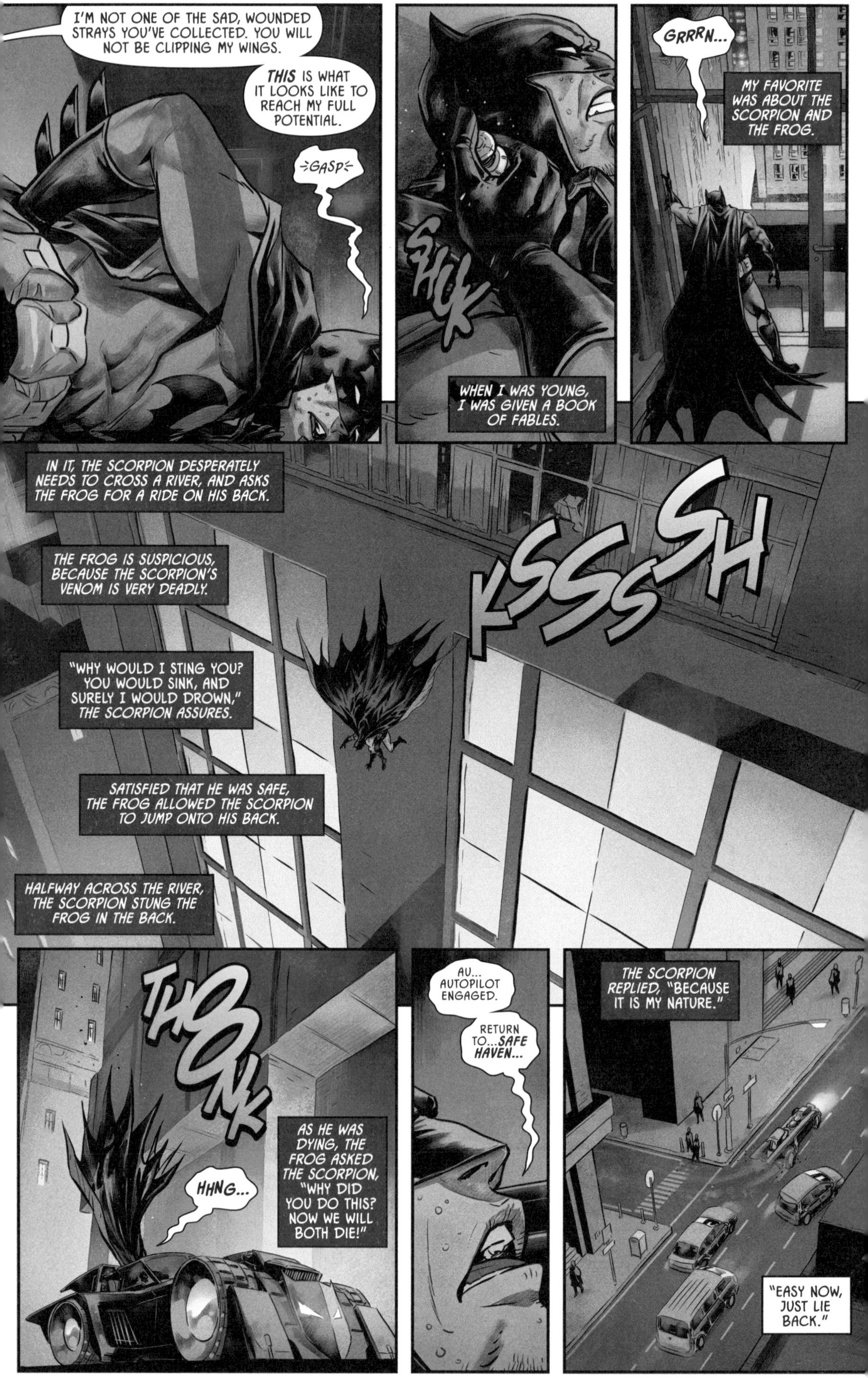
I'M NOT ONE OF THE SAD, WOUNDED STRAYS YOU'VE COLLECTED. YOU WILL NOT BE CLIPPING MY WINGS.
THIS IS WHAT IT LOOKS LIKE TO REACH MY FULL POTENTIAL.
GASP
SHUK
WHEN I WAS YOUNG, I WAS GIVEN A BOOK OF FABLES.
GRRRN...
MY FAVORITE WAS ABOUT THE SCORPION AND THE FROG.
IN IT, THE SCORPION DESPERATELY NEEDS TO CROSS A RIVER, AND ASKS THE FROG FOR A RIDE ON HIS BACK.
THE FROG IS SUSPICIOUS, BECAUSE THE SCORPION'S VENOM IS VERY DEADLY.
KSSSSSH
"WHY WOULD I STING YOU? YOU WOULD SINK, AND SURELY I WOULD DROWN," THE SCORPION ASSURES.
SATISFIED THAT HE WAS SAFE, THE FROG ALLOWED THE SCORPION TO JUMP ONTO HIS BACK.
HALFWAY ACROSS THE RIVER, THE SCORPION STUNG THE FROG IN THE BACK.
THONK
HHNG...
AS HE WAS DYING, THE FROG ASKED THE SCORPION, "WHY DID YOU DO THIS? NOW WE WILL BOTH DIE!"
AU... AUTOPILOT ENGAGED.
RETURN TO...SAFE HAVEN...
THE SCORPION REPLIED, "BECAUSE IT IS MY NATURE."
"EASY NOW, JUST LIE BACK."

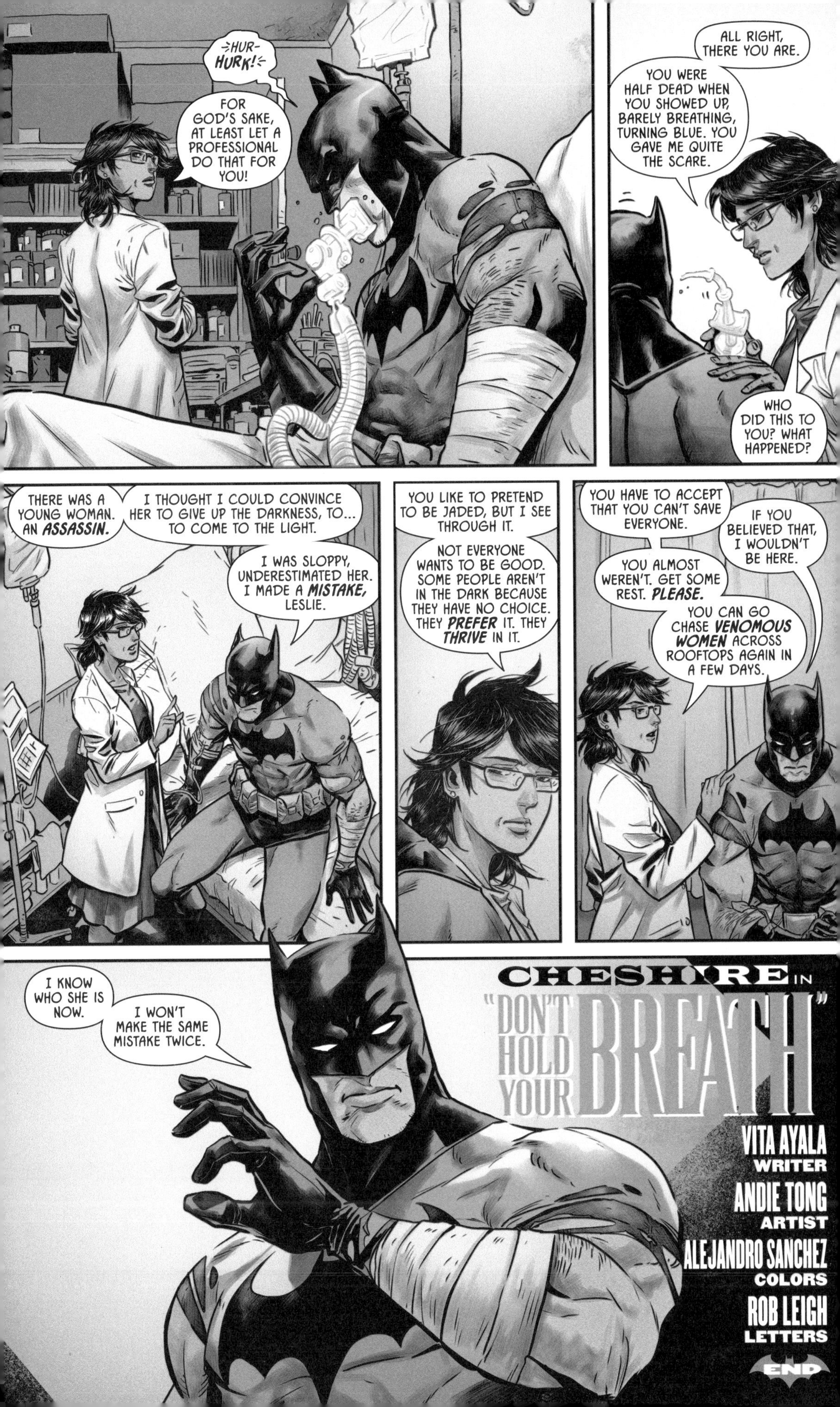

HUR-HURK!
FOR GOD'S SAKE, AT LEAST LET A PROFESSIONAL DO THAT FOR YOU!
ALL RIGHT, THERE YOU ARE.
YOU WERE HALF DEAD WHEN YOU SHOWED UP, BARELY BREATHING, TURNING BLUE. YOU GAVE ME QUITE THE SCARE.
WHO DID THIS TO YOU? WHAT HAPPENED?
THERE WAS A YOUNG WOMAN. AN ASSASSIN.
I THOUGHT I COULD CONVINCE HER TO GIVE UP THE DARKNESS, TO... TO COME TO THE LIGHT.
I WAS SLOPPY, UNDERESTIMATED HER. I MADE A MISTAKE, LESLIE.
YOU LIKE TO PRETEND TO BE JADED, BUT I SEE THROUGH IT.
NOT EVERYONE WANTS TO BE GOOD. SOME PEOPLE AREN'T IN THE DARK BECAUSE THEY HAVE NO CHOICE. THEY PREFER IT. THEY THRIVE IN IT.
YOU HAVE TO ACCEPT THAT YOU CAN'T SAVE EVERYONE.
IF YOU BELIEVED THAT, I WOULDN'T BE HERE.
YOU ALMOST WEREN'T. GET SOME REST. PLEASE.
YOU CAN GO CHASE VENOMOUS WOMEN ACROSS ROOFTOPS AGAIN IN A FEW DAYS.
I KNOW WHO SHE IS NOW.
I WON'T MAKE THE SAME MISTAKE TWICE.
CHESHIRE IN "DON'T HOLD YOUR BREATH"
VITA AYALA WRITER
ANDIE TONG ARTIST
ALEJANDRO SANCHEZ COLORS
ROB LEIGH LETTERS
END

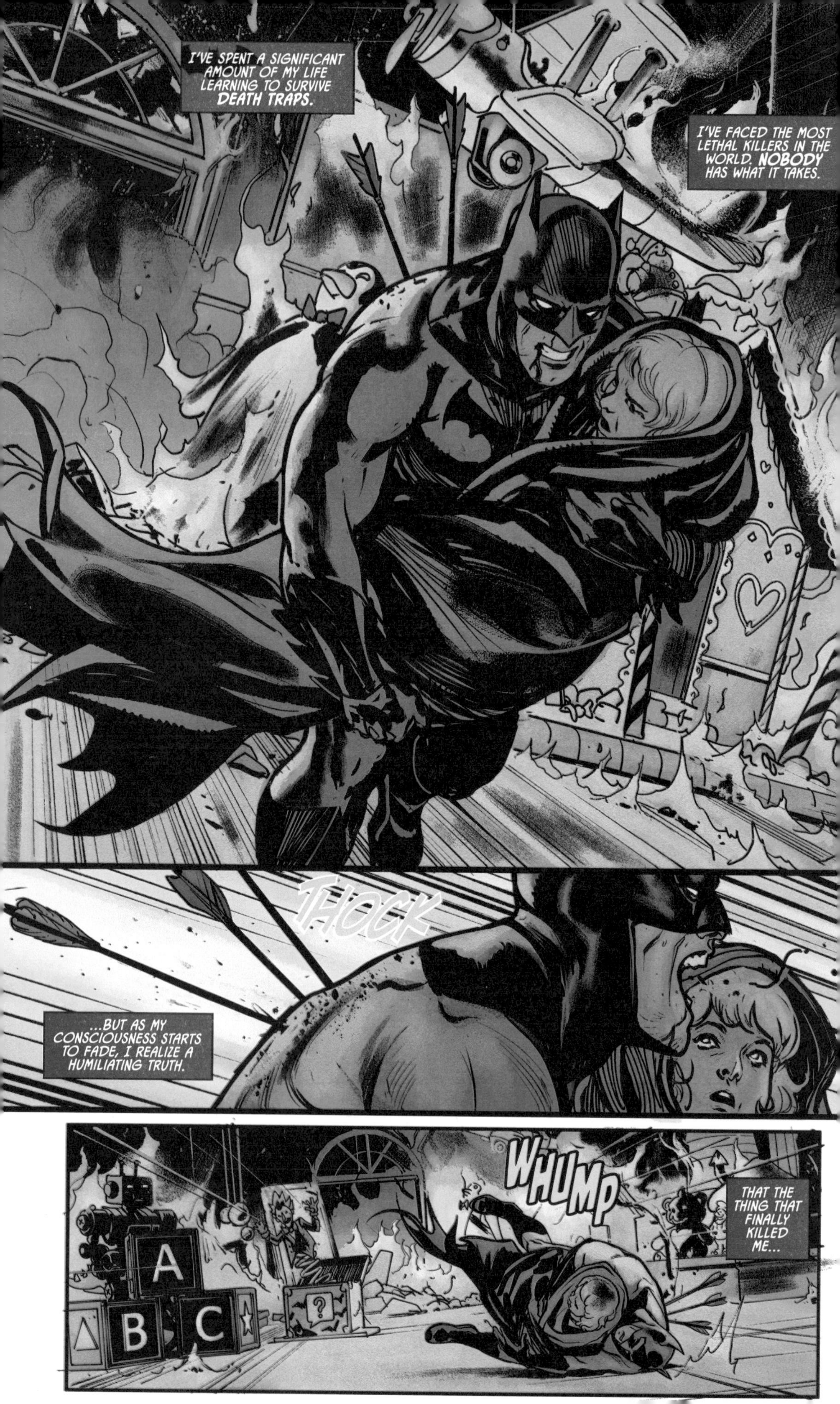
I'VE SPENT A SIGNIFICANT AMOUNT OF MY LIFE LEARNING TO SURVIVE DEATH TRAPS.
I'VE FACED THE MOST LETHAL KILLERS IN THE WORLD. NOBODY HAS WHAT IT TAKES.
THOCK
...BUT AS MY CONSCIOUSNESS STARTS TO FADE, I REALIZE A HUMILIATING TRUTH.
WHUMP
THAT THE THING THAT FINALLY KILLED ME...
A
B
C

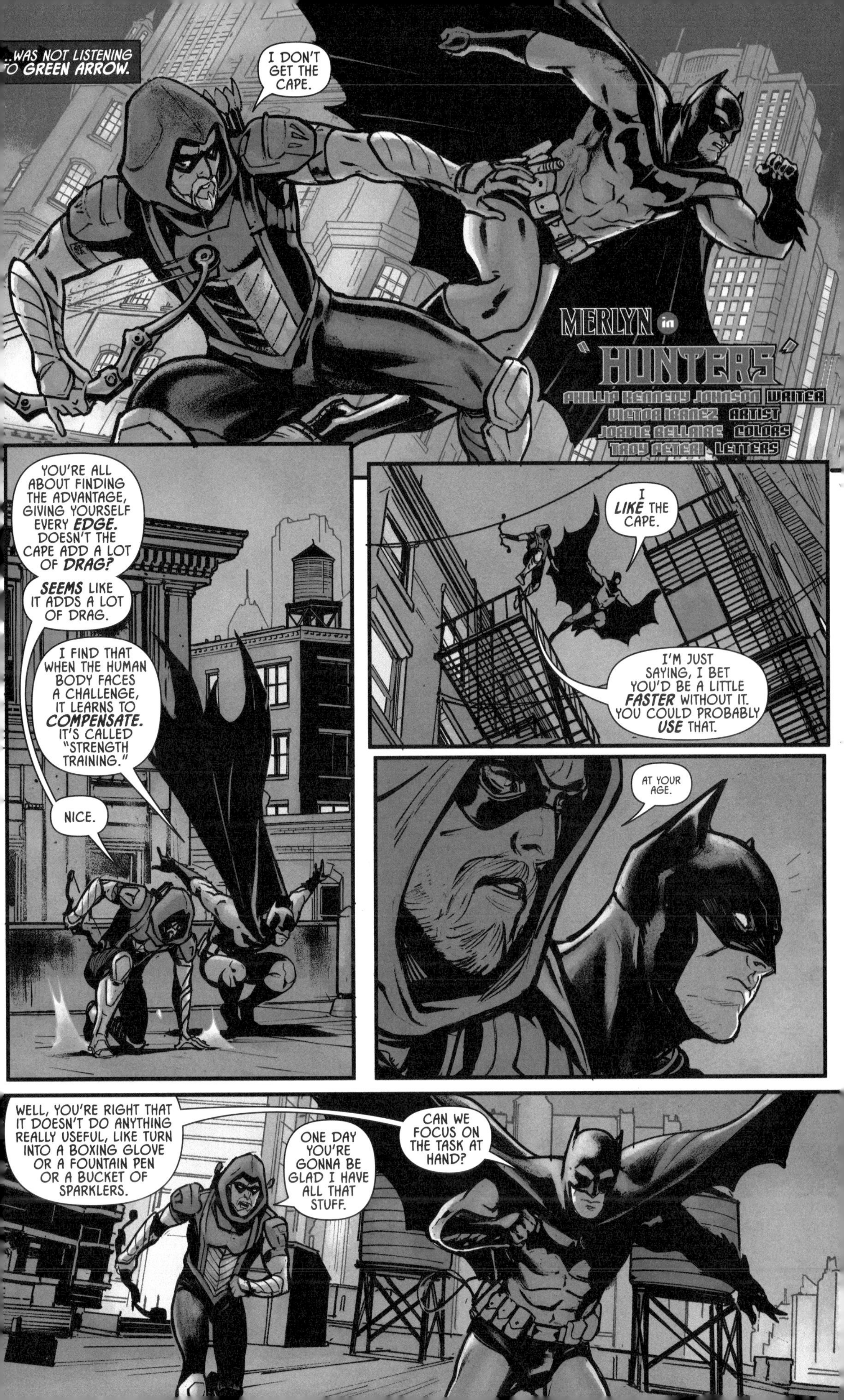
..WAS NOT LISTENING TO GREEN ARROW.
I DON'T GET THE CAPE.
MERLYN in "HUNTERS"
PHILLIP KENNEDY JOHNSON WRITER
VICTOR IBANEZ ARTIST
JORDIE BELLAIRE COLORS
TROY PETERI LETTERS
YOU'RE ALL ABOUT FINDING THE ADVANTAGE, GIVING YOURSELF EVERY EDGE. DOESN'T THE CAPE ADD A LOT OF DRAG?
SEEMS LIKE IT ADDS A LOT OF DRAG.
I FIND THAT WHEN THE HUMAN BODY FACES A CHALLENGE, IT LEARNS TO COMPENSATE. IT'S CALLED "STRENGTH TRAINING."
NICE.
I LIKE THE CAPE.
I'M JUST SAYING, I BET YOU'D BE A LITTLE FASTER WITHOUT IT. YOU COULD PROBABLY USE THAT.
AT YOUR AGE.
WELL, YOU'RE RIGHT THAT IT DOESN'T DO ANYTHING REALLY USEFUL, LIKE TURN INTO A BOXING GLOVE OR A FOUNTAIN PEN OR A BUCKET OF SPARKLERS.
CAN WE FOCUS ON THE TASK AT HAND?
ONE DAY YOU'RE GONNA BE GLAD I HAVE ALL THAT STUFF.

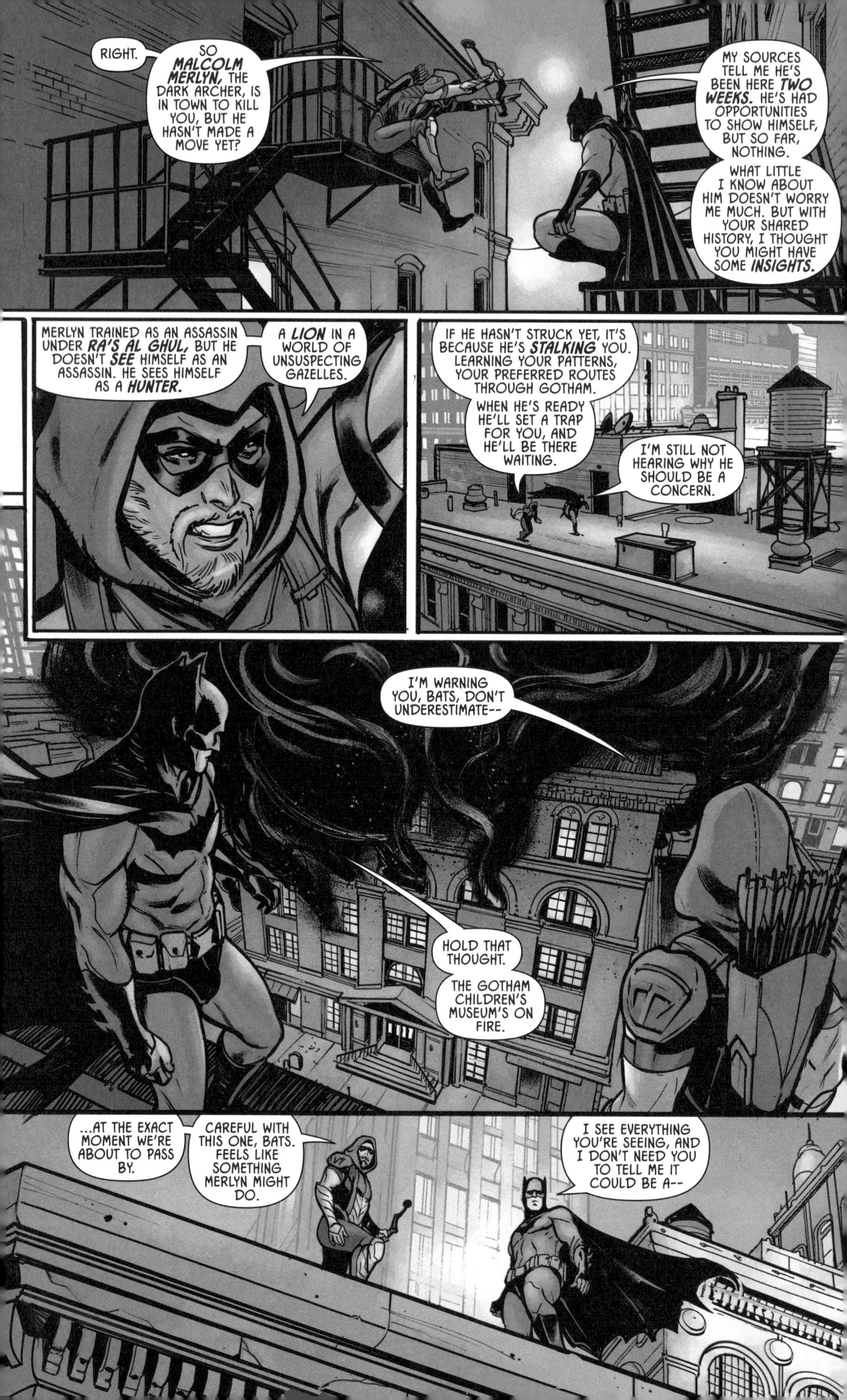

RIGHT.
SO MALCOLM MERLYN, THE DARK ARCHER, IS IN TOWN TO KILL YOU, BUT HE HASN'T MADE A MOVE YET?
MY SOURCES TELL ME HE'S BEEN HERE TWO WEEKS. HE'S HAD OPPORTUNITIES TO SHOW HIMSELF, BUT SO FAR, NOTHING.
WHAT LITTLE I KNOW ABOUT HIM DOESN'T WORRY ME MUCH. BUT WITH YOUR SHARED HISTORY, I THOUGHT YOU MIGHT HAVE SOME INSIGHTS.
MERLYN TRAINED AS AN ASSASSIN UNDER RA'S AL GHUL, BUT HE DOESN'T SEE HIMSELF AS AN ASSASSIN. HE SEES HIMSELF AS A HUNTER.
A LION IN A WORLD OF UNSUSPECTING GAZELLES.
IF HE HASN'T STRUCK YET, IT'S BECAUSE HE'S STALKING YOU. LEARNING YOUR PATTERNS, YOUR PREFERRED ROUTES THROUGH GOTHAM.
WHEN HE'S READY HE'LL SET A TRAP FOR YOU, AND HE'LL BE THERE WAITING.
I'M STILL NOT HEARING WHY HE SHOULD BE A CONCERN.
I'M WARNING YOU, BATS, DON'T UNDERESTIMATE--
HOLD THAT THOUGHT.
THE GOTHAM CHILDREN'S MUSEUM'S ON FIRE.
CAREFUL WITH THIS ONE, BATS. FEELS LIKE SOMETHING MERLYN MIGHT DO.
...AT THE EXACT MOMENT WE'RE ABOUT TO PASS BY.
I SEE EVERYTHING YOU'RE SEEING, AND I DON'T NEED YOU TO TELL ME IT COULD BE A--

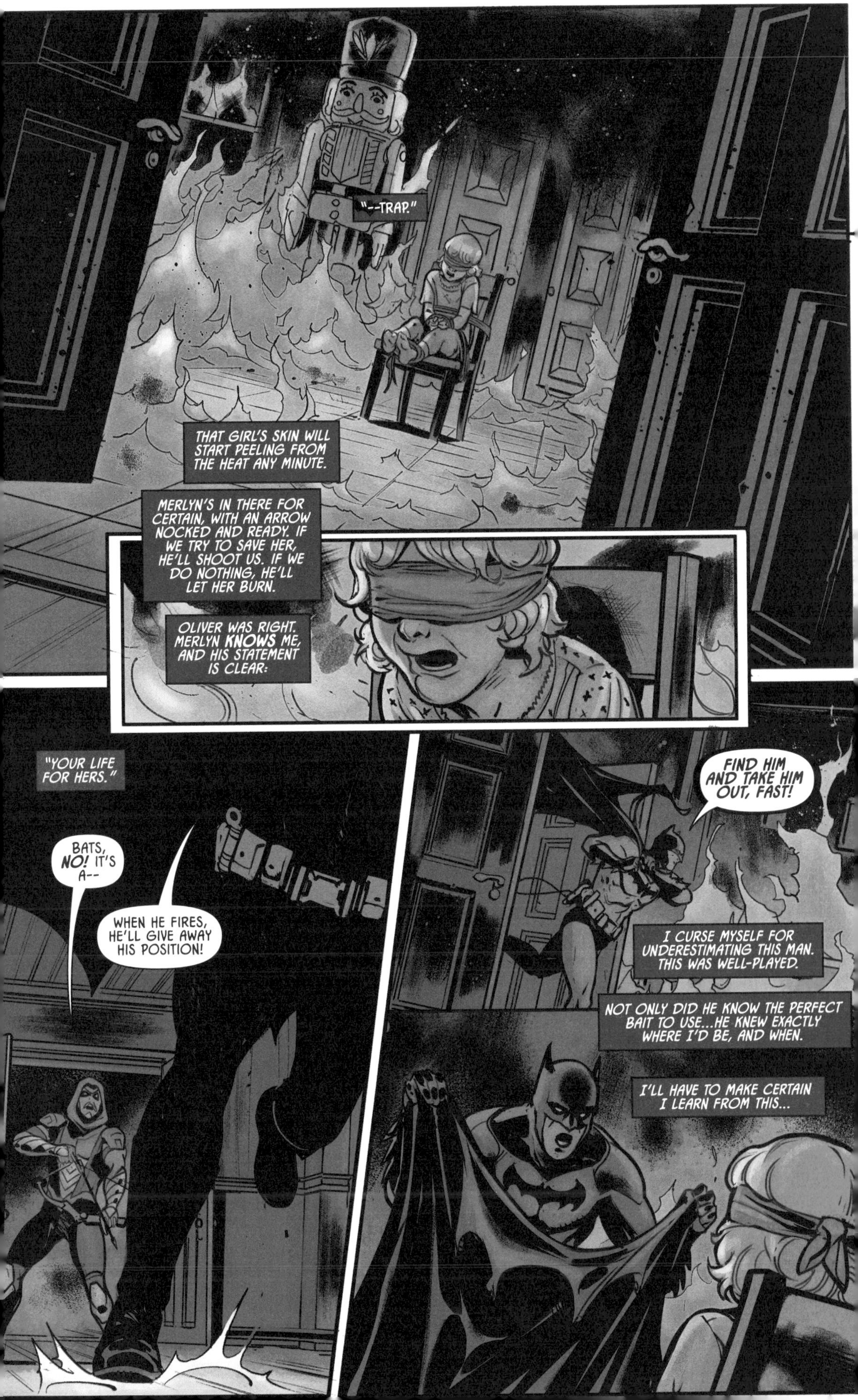

"--TRAP."
THAT GIRL'S SKIN WILL START PEELING FROM THE HEAT ANY MINUTE.
MERLYN'S IN THERE FOR CERTAIN, WITH AN ARROW NOCKED AND READY. IF WE TRY TO SAVE HER, HE'LL SHOOT US. IF WE DO NOTHING, HE'LL LET HER BURN.
OLIVER WAS RIGHT. MERLYN KNOWS ME, AND HIS STATEMENT IS CLEAR:
"YOUR LIFE FOR HERS."
BATS, NO! IT'S A--
WHEN HE FIRES, HE'LL GIVE AWAY HIS POSITION!
FIND HIM AND TAKE HIM OUT, FAST!
I CURSE MYSELF FOR UNDERESTIMATING THIS MAN. THIS WAS WELL-PLAYED.
NOT ONLY DID HE KNOW THE PERFECT BAIT TO USE...HE KNEW EXACTLY WHERE I'D BE, AND WHEN.
I'LL HAVE TO MAKE CERTAIN I LEARN FROM THIS...

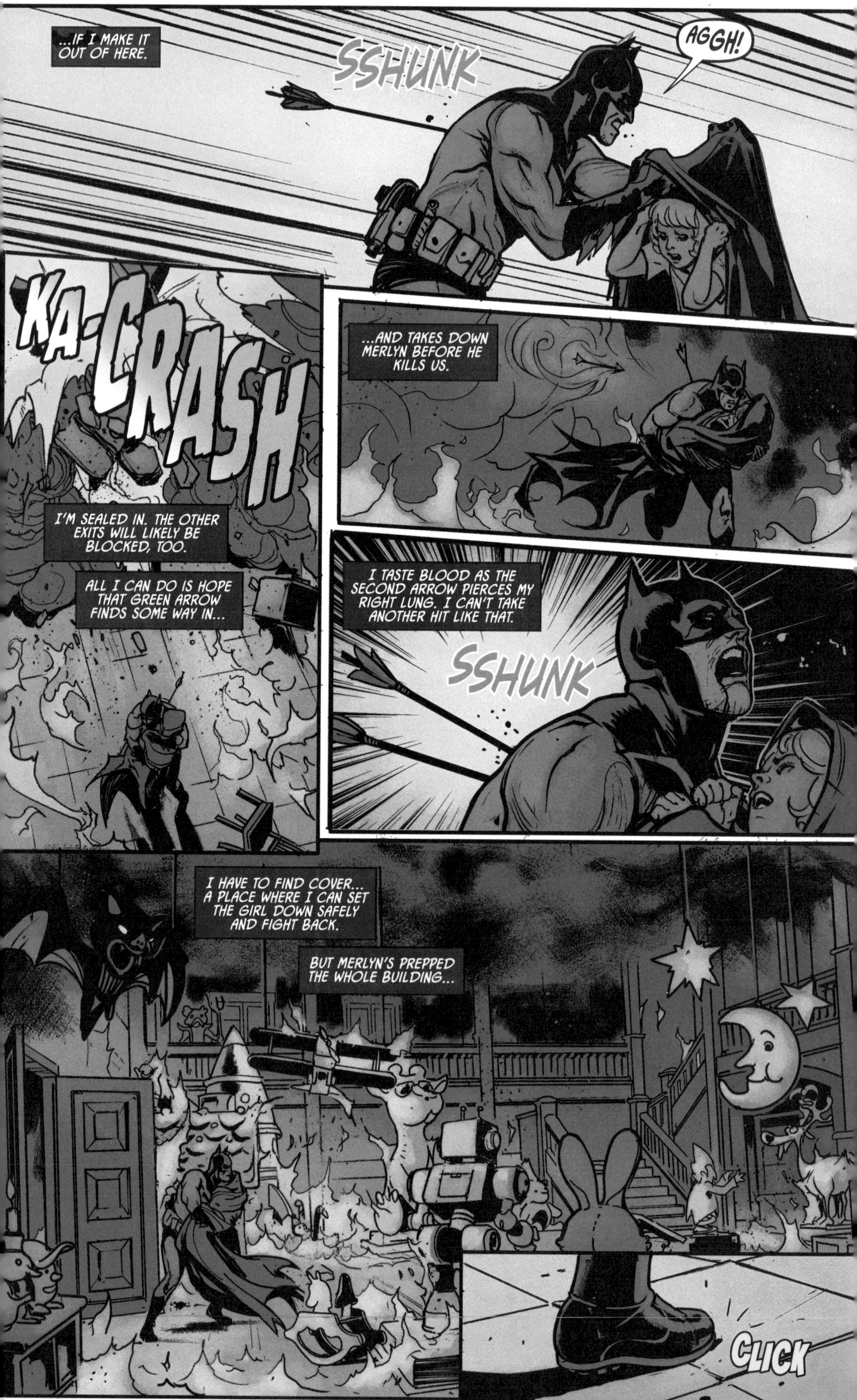
...IF I MAKE IT OUT OF HERE.
SSHUNK
AGGH!
KA-CRASH
I'M SEALED IN. THE OTHER EXITS WILL LIKELY BE BLOCKED, TOO.
ALL I CAN DO IS HOPE THAT GREEN ARROW FINDS SOME WAY IN...
...AND TAKES DOWN MERLYN BEFORE HE KILLS US.
I TASTE BLOOD AS THE SECOND ARROW PIERCES MY RIGHT LUNG. I CAN'T TAKE ANOTHER HIT LIKE THAT.
SSHUNK
I HAVE TO FIND COVER... A PLACE WHERE I CAN SET THE GIRL DOWN SAFELY AND FIGHT BACK.
BUT MERLYN'S PREPPED THE WHOLE BUILDING...
CLICK

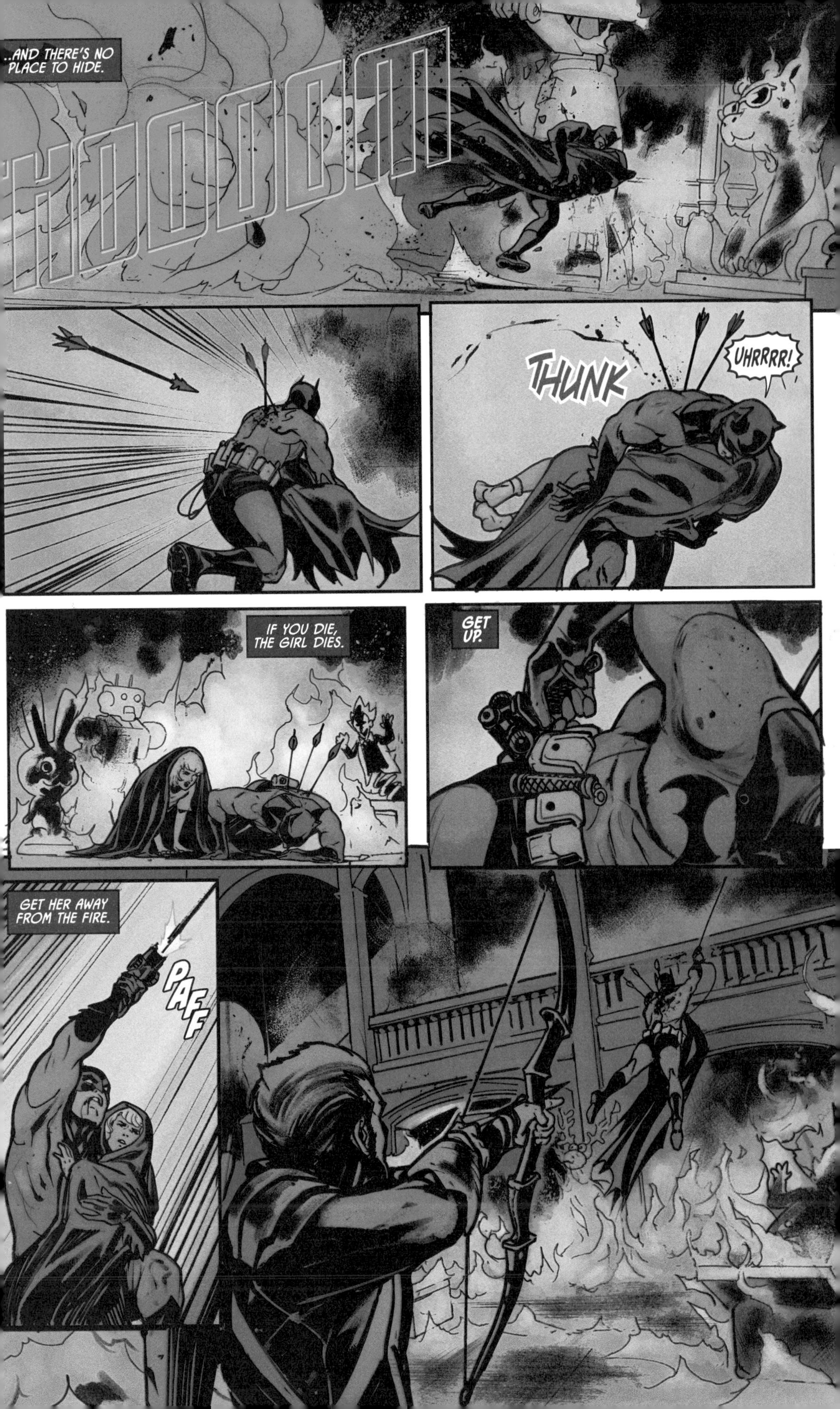

..AND THERE'S NO PLACE TO HIDE.
KHOOOOM
THUNK
UHRRRR!
IF YOU DIE, THE GIRL DIES.
GET UP.
GET HER AWAY FROM THE FIRE.
PAFF

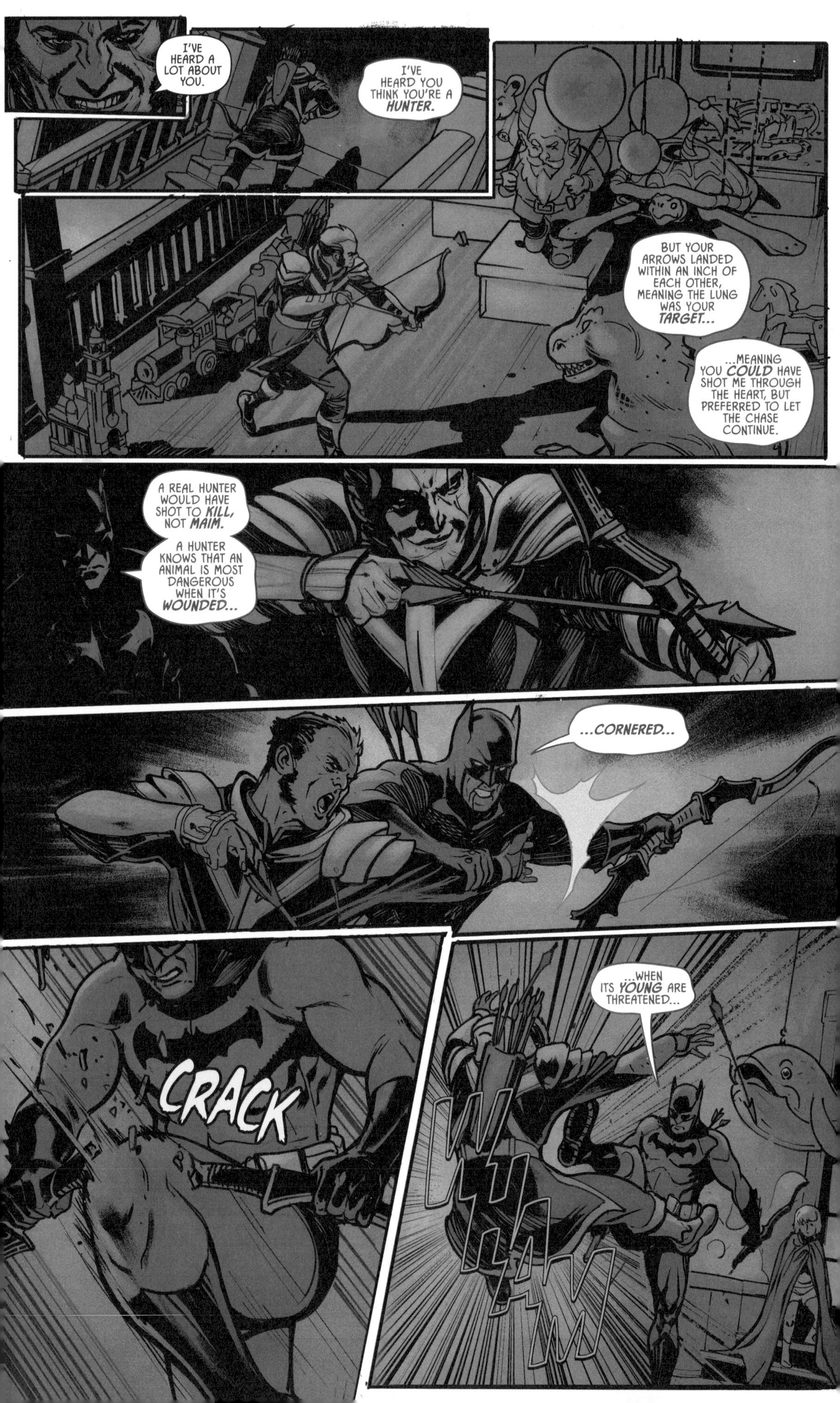
I'VE HEARD A LOT ABOUT YOU.
I'VE HEARD YOU THINK YOU'RE A HUNTER.
BUT YOUR ARROWS LANDED WITHIN AN INCH OF EACH OTHER, MEANING THE LUNG WAS YOUR TARGET...
...MEANING YOU COULD HAVE SHOT ME THROUGH THE HEART, BUT PREFERRED TO LET THE CHASE CONTINUE.
A REAL HUNTER WOULD HAVE SHOT TO KILL, NOT MAIM.
A HUNTER KNOWS THAT AN ANIMAL IS MOST DANGEROUS WHEN IT'S WOUNDED...
...CORNERED...
CRACK
...WHEN ITS YOUNG ARE THREATENED...
WHAM

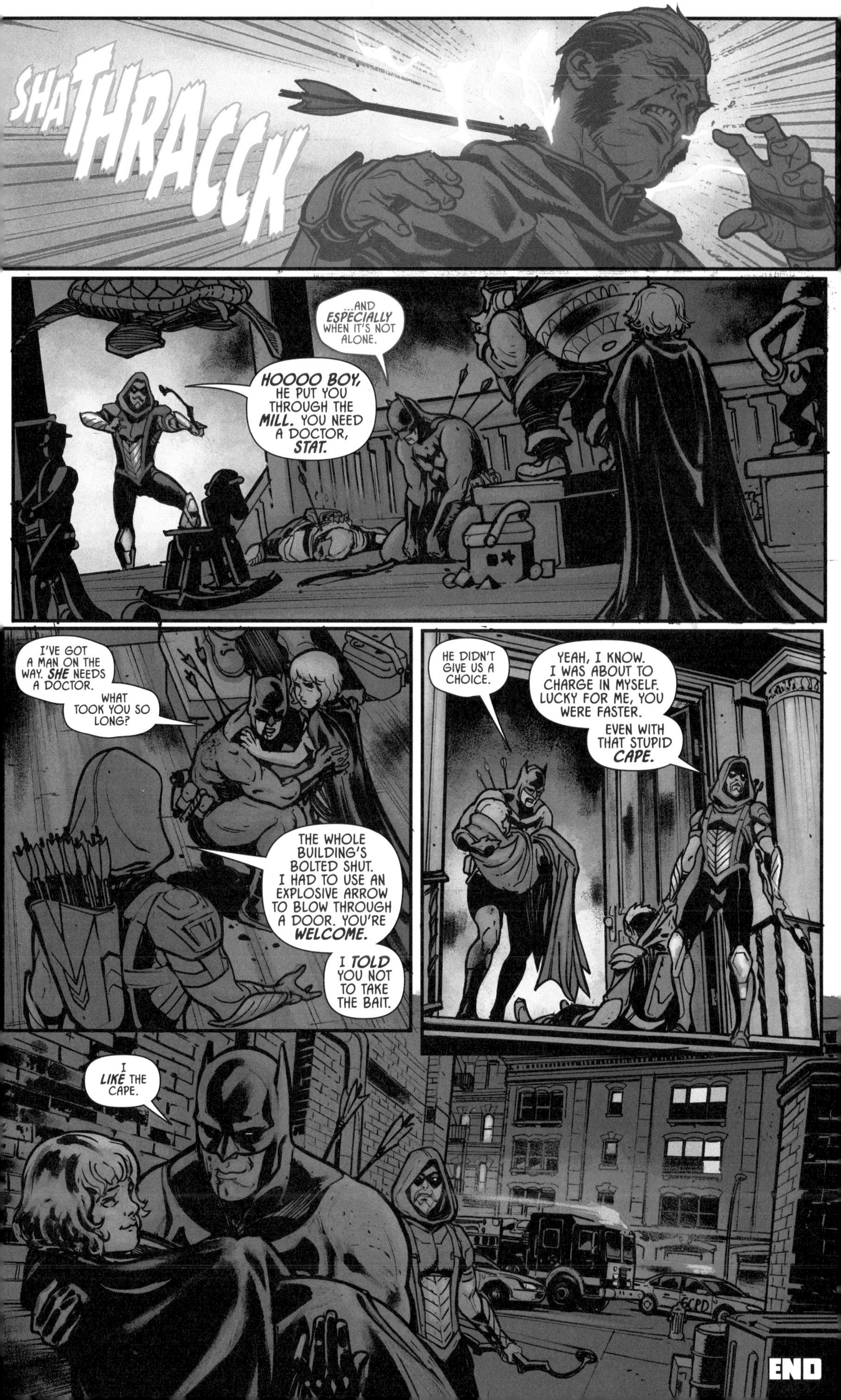

SHATHRACCK
...AND ESPECIALLY WHEN IT'S NOT ALONE.
HOOOO BOY, HE PUT YOU THROUGH THE MILL. YOU NEED A DOCTOR, STAT.
I'VE GOT A MAN ON THE WAY. SHE NEEDS A DOCTOR.
WHAT TOOK YOU SO LONG?
THE WHOLE BUILDING'S BOLTED SHUT. I HAD TO USE AN EXPLOSIVE ARROW TO BLOW THROUGH A DOOR. YOU'RE WELCOME.
I TOLD YOU NOT TO TAKE THE BAIT.
HE DIDN'T GIVE US A CHOICE.
YEAH, I KNOW. I WAS ABOUT TO CHARGE IN MYSELF. LUCKY FOR ME, YOU WERE FASTER.
EVEN WITH THAT STUPID CAPE.
I LIKE THE CAPE.
GCPD
END

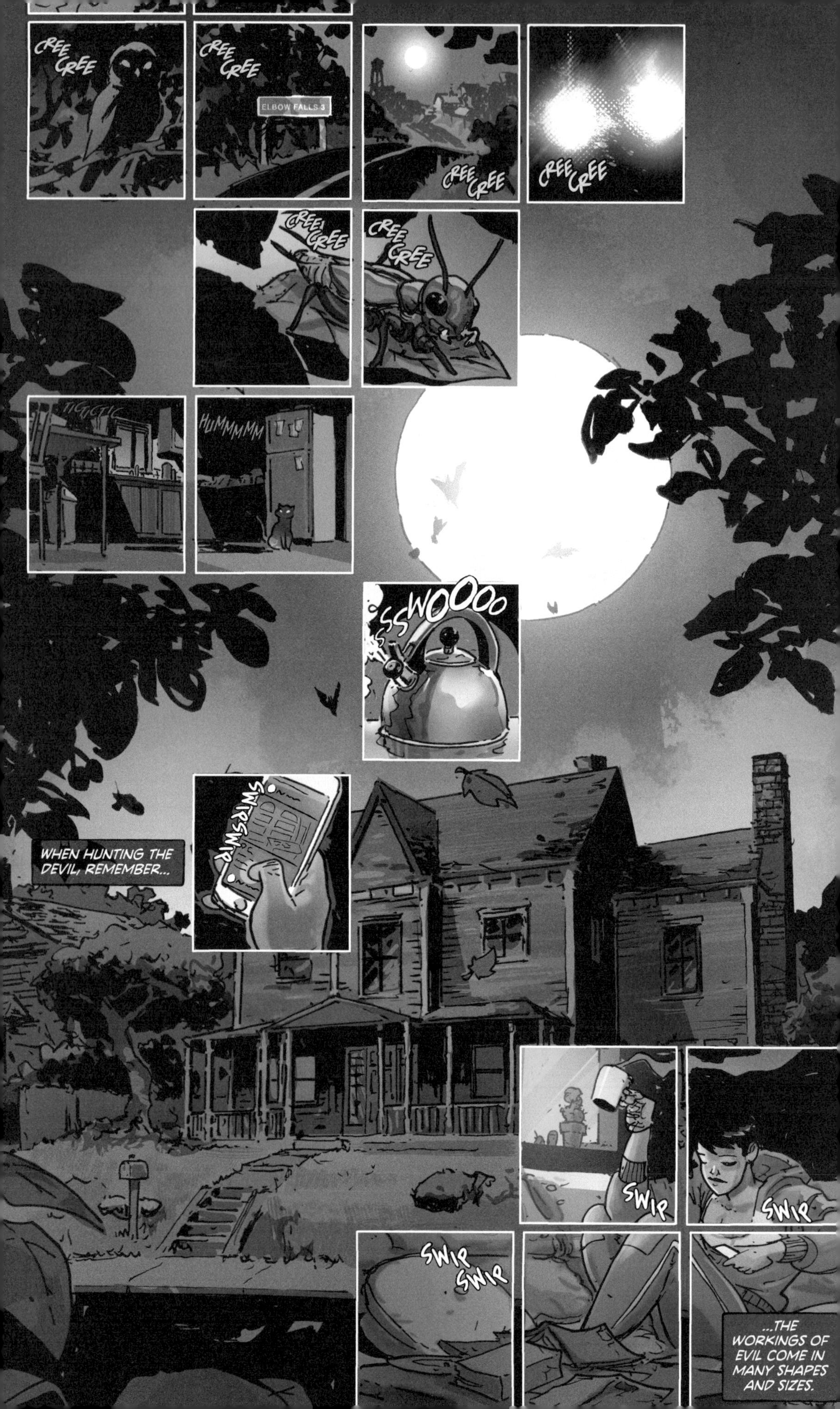

CREE CREE
CREE CREE
ELBOW FALLS 3
CREE CREE
CREE CREE
CREE CREE
CREE CREE
HUMMMMM
SSWOOOO
WHEN HUNTING THE DEVIL, REMEMBER...
SWIPSWIP
SWIP
SWIP
SWIP SWIP
...THE WORKINGS OF EVIL COME IN MANY SHAPES AND SIZES.

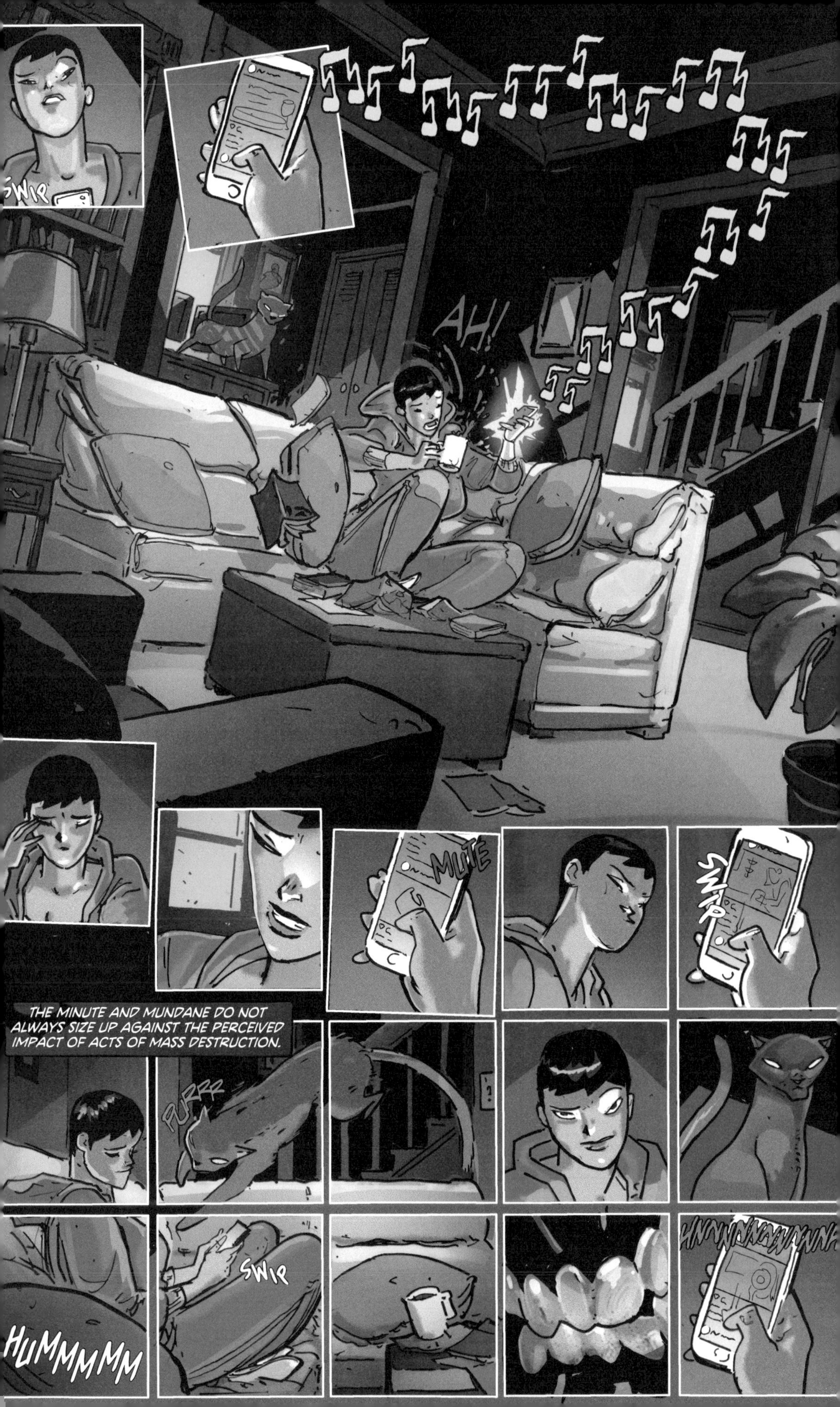
SWIP
AH!
MUTE
SWIP
THE MINUTE AND MUNDANE DO NOT ALWAYS SIZE UP AGAINST THE PERCEIVED IMPACT OF ACTS OF MASS DESTRUCTION.
PURRR
HUMMMMM
SWIP

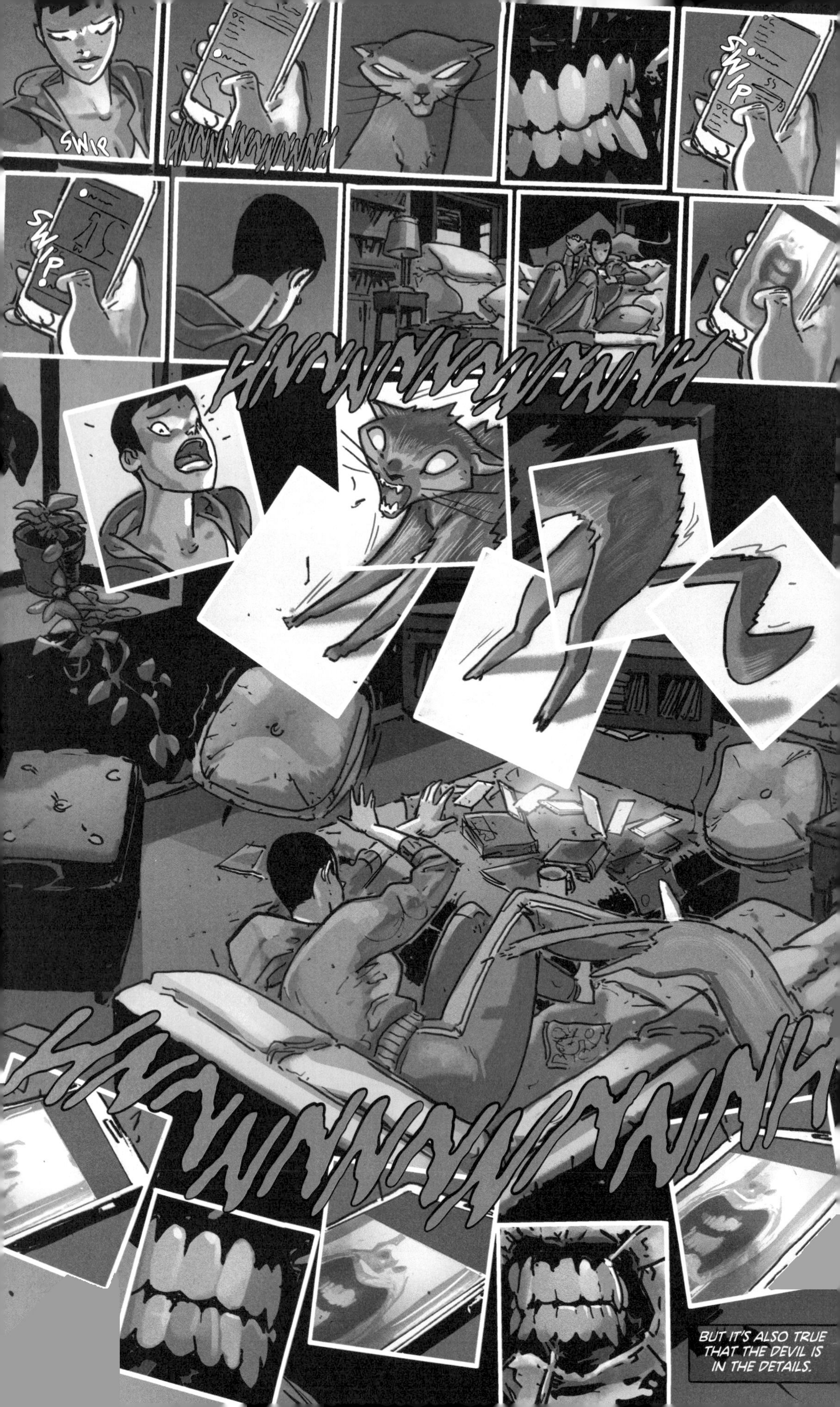
SWIP
HNNNNNNNNNNNNNH
SWIP
SWIP!
HNNNNNNNNNNNNNH
HNNNNNNNNNNNNNNNNNNH
BUT IT'S ALSO TRUE THAT THE DEVIL IS IN THE DETAILS.

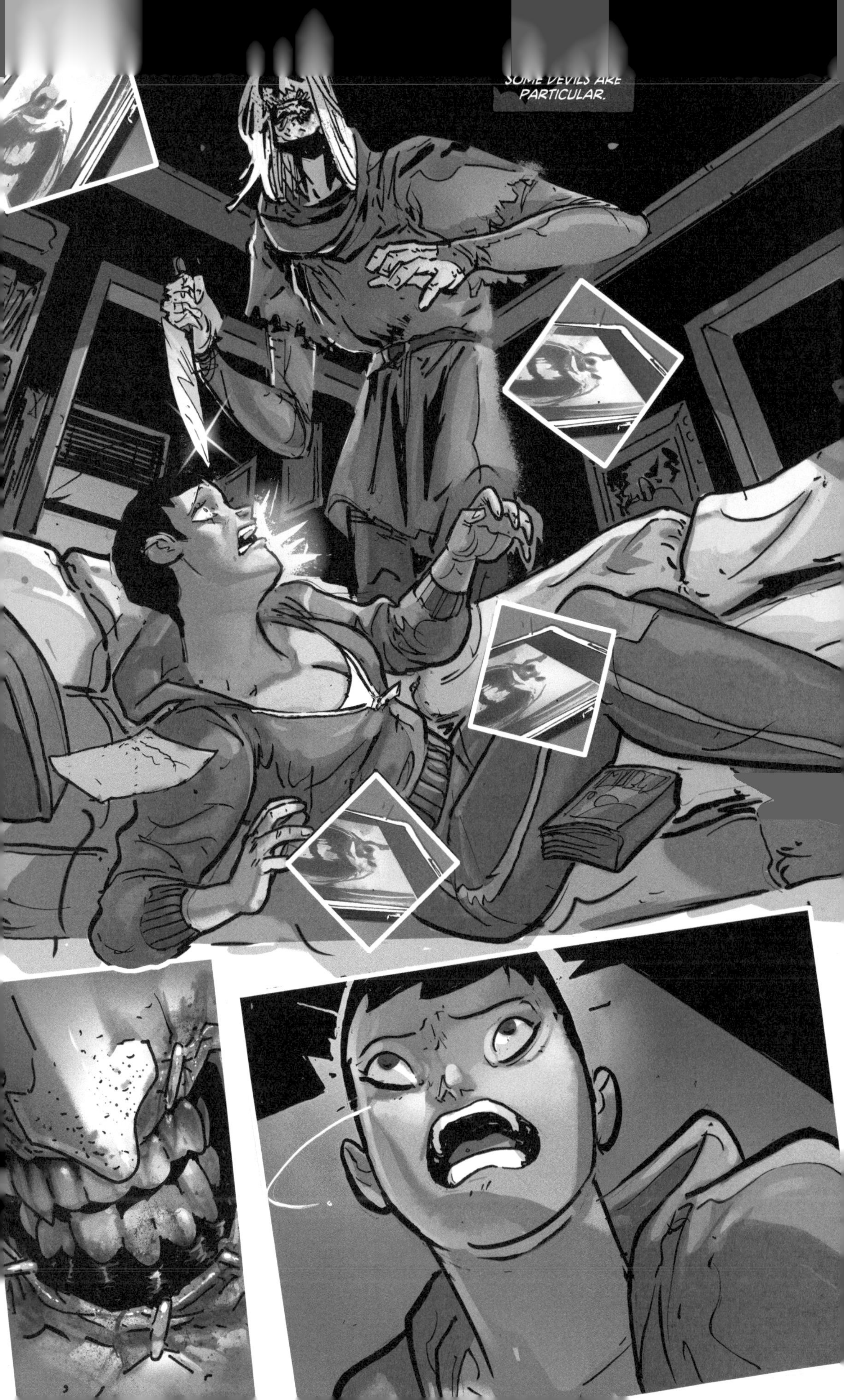
SOME DEVILS ARE PARTICULAR.

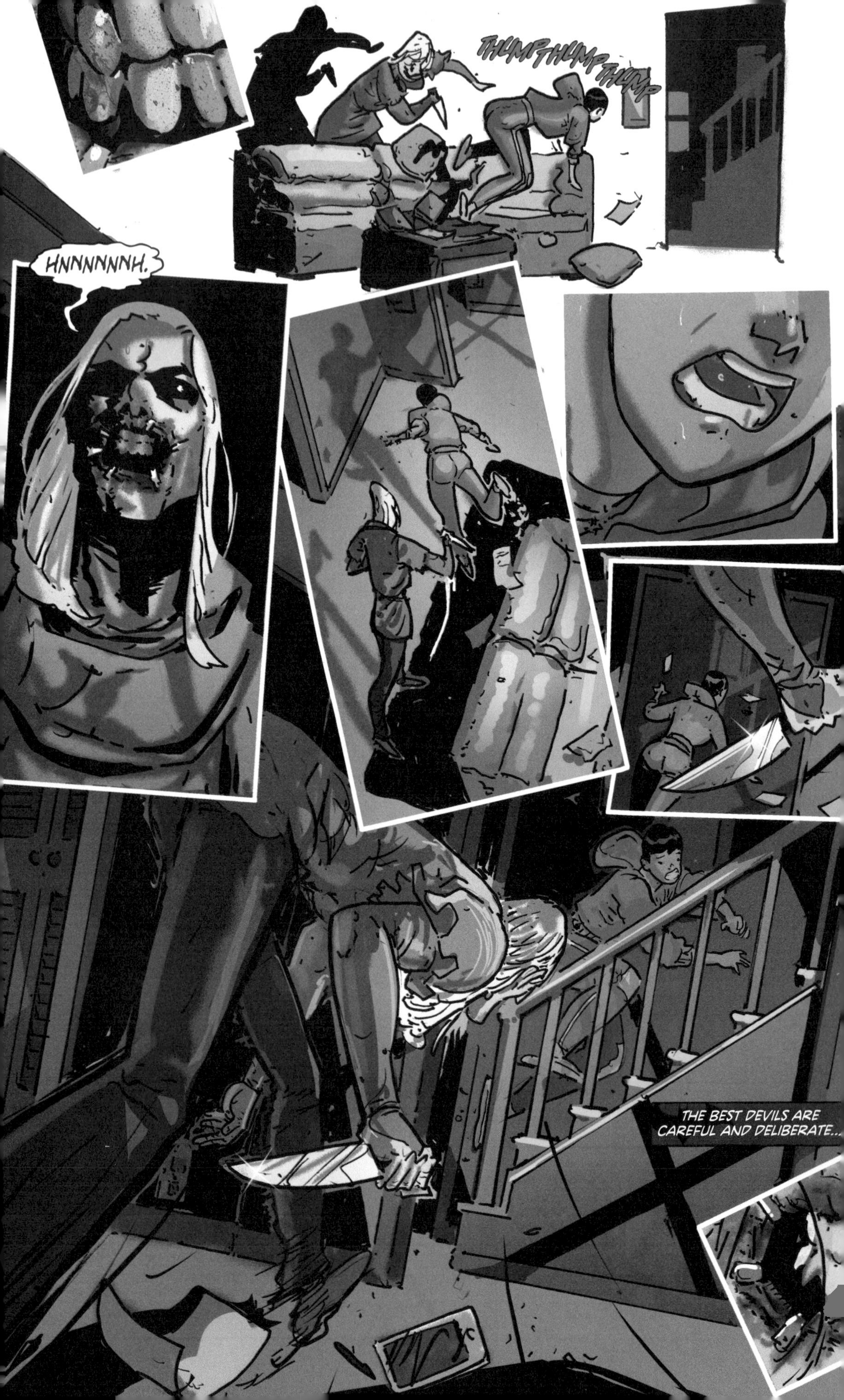
THUMP THUMP THUMP
HNNNNNNH.
THE BEST DEVILS ARE CAREFUL AND DELIBERATE...

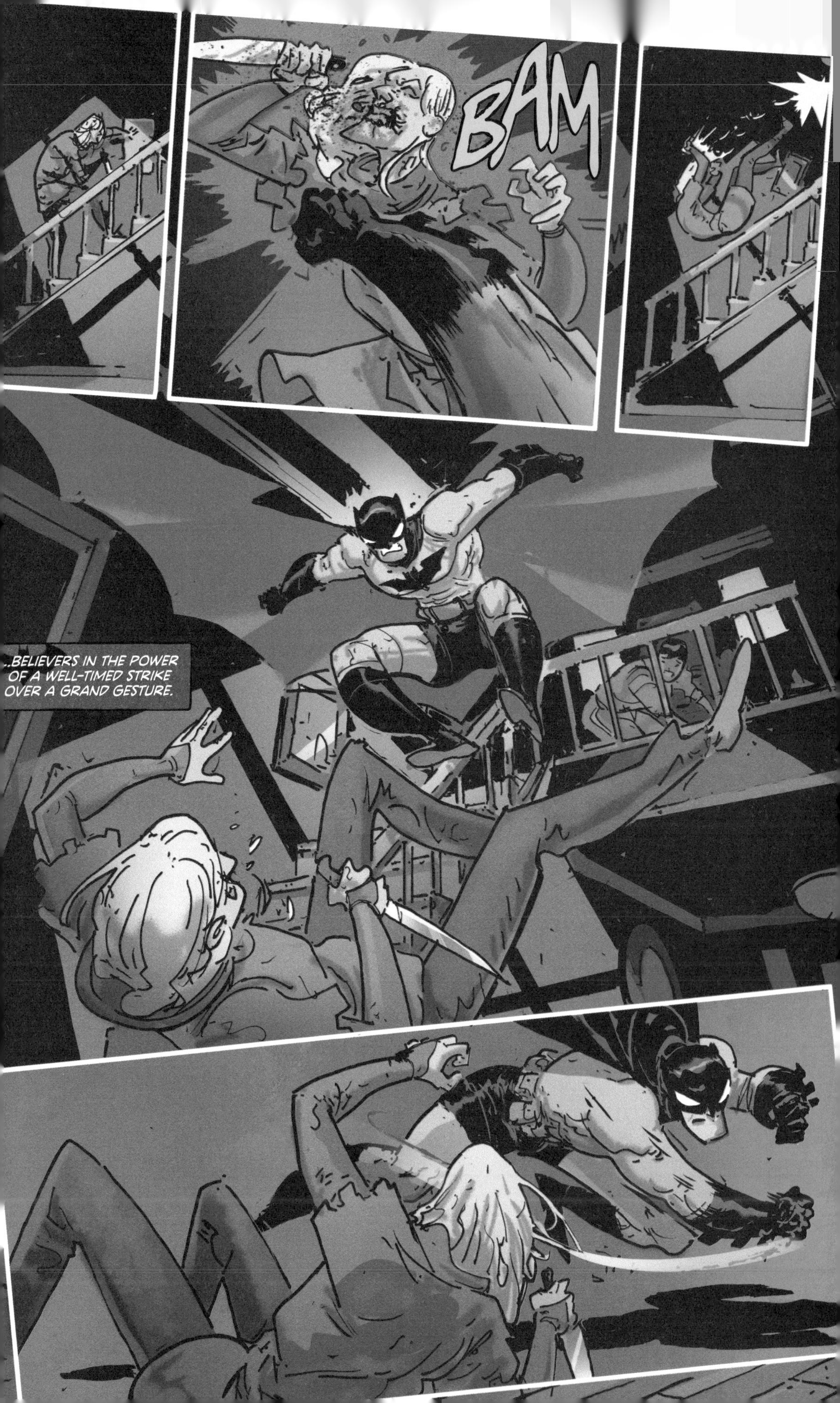
BAM
..BELIEVERS IN THE POWER OF A WELL-TIMED STRIKE OVER A GRAND GESTURE.

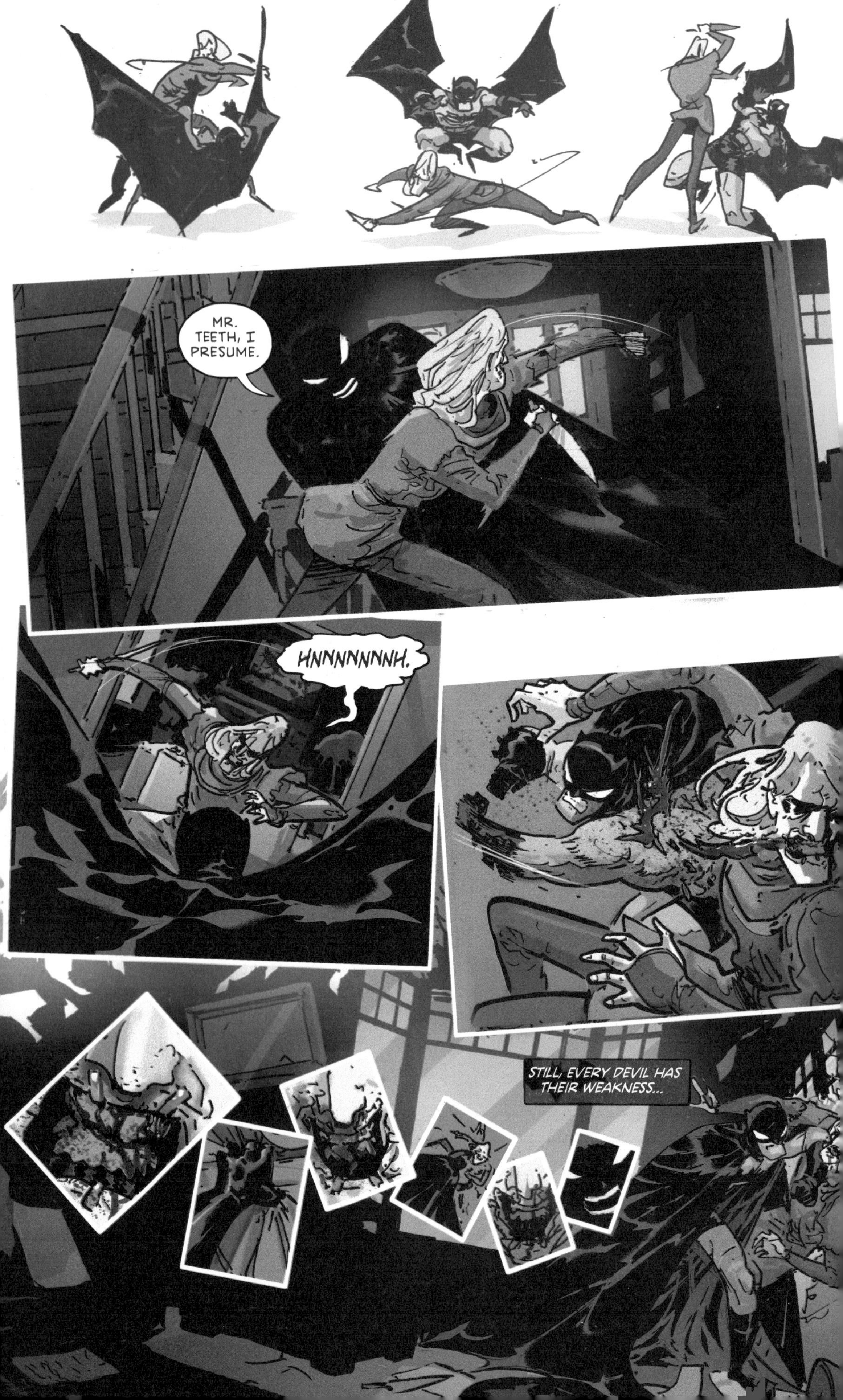
MR. TEETH, I PRESUME.
HNNNNNNNH.
STILL, EVERY DEVIL HAS THEIR WEAKNESS...

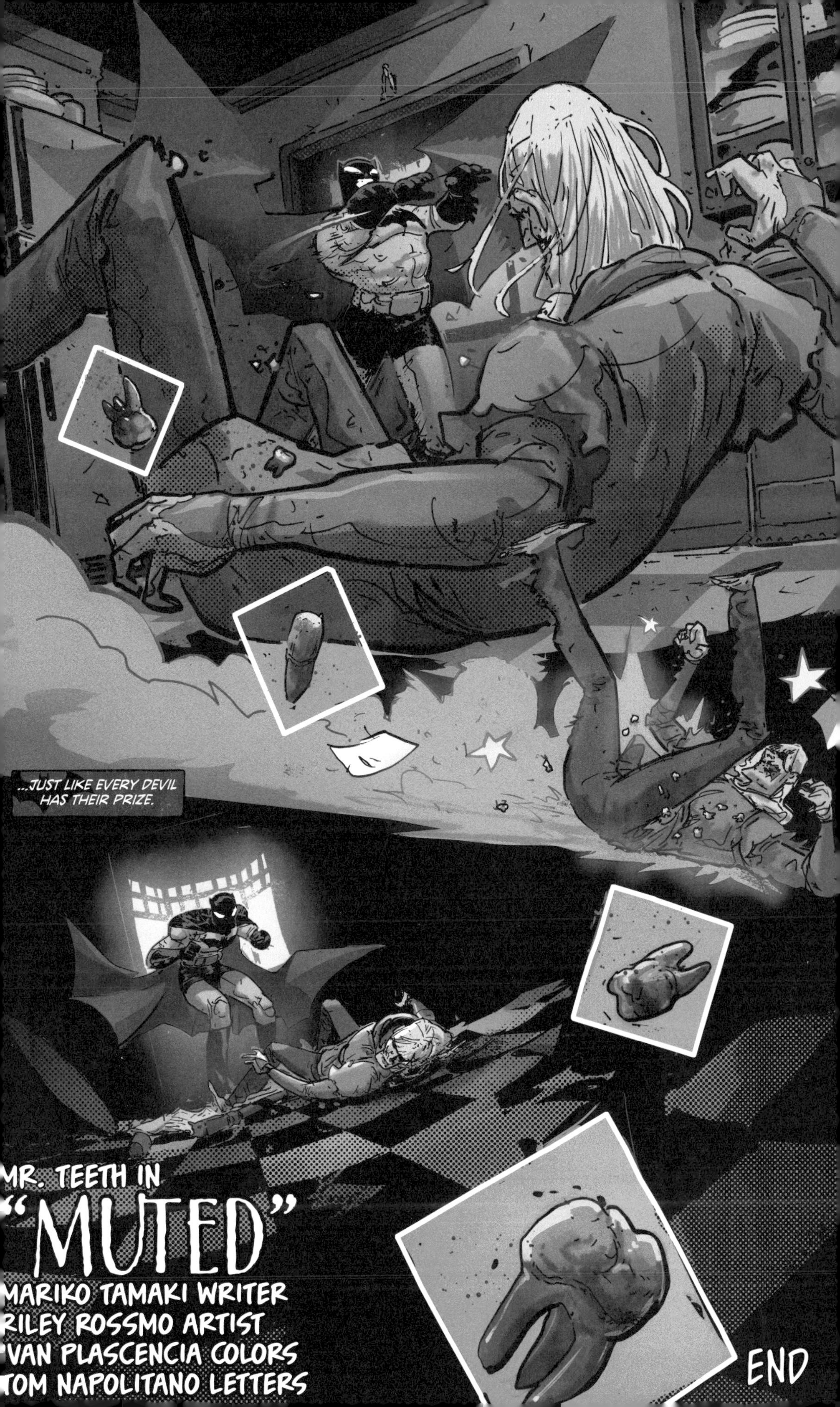
...JUST LIKE EVERY DEVIL HAS THEIR PRIZE.
MR. TEETH IN
"MUTED"
MARIKO TAMAKI WRITER
RILEY ROSSMO ARTIST
IVAN PLASCENCIA COLORS
TOM NAPOLITANO LETTERS
END

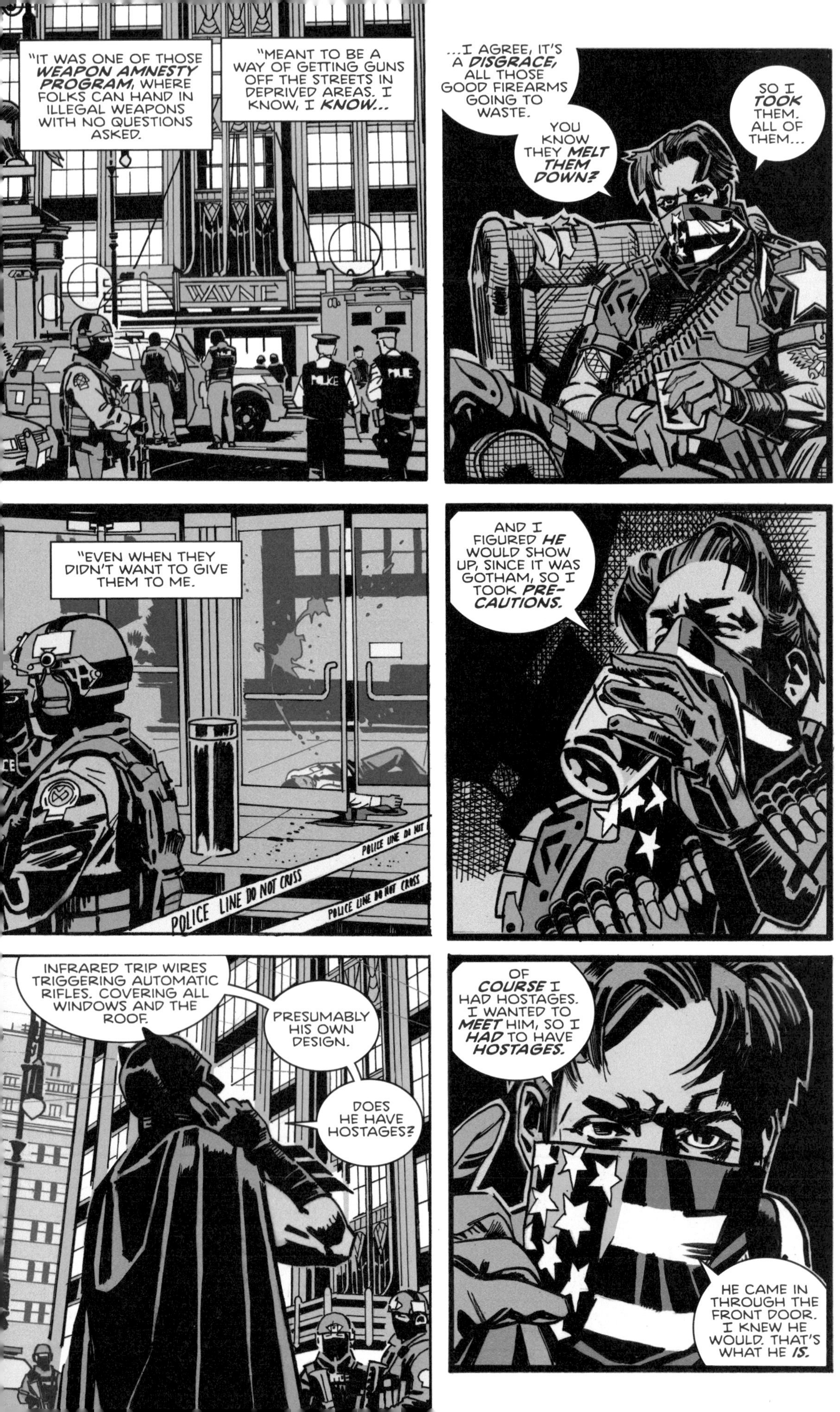
"IT WAS ONE OF THOSE WEAPON AMNESTY PROGRAM, WHERE FOLKS CAN HAND IN ILLEGAL WEAPONS WITH NO QUESTIONS ASKED.
"MEANT TO BE A WAY OF GETTING GUNS OFF THE STREETS IN DEPRIVED AREAS. I KNOW, I KNOW...
WAYNE
...I AGREE, IT'S A DISGRACE, ALL THOSE GOOD FIREARMS GOING TO WASTE.
YOU KNOW THEY MELT THEM DOWN?
SO I TOOK THEM. ALL OF THEM...
"EVEN WHEN THEY DIDN'T WANT TO GIVE THEM TO ME.
POLICE LINE DO NOT CROSS
POLICE LINE DO NOT CROSS
AND I FIGURED HE WOULD SHOW UP, SINCE IT WAS GOTHAM, SO I TOOK PRE-CAUTIONS.
INFRARED TRIP WIRES TRIGGERING AUTOMATIC RIFLES. COVERING ALL WINDOWS AND THE ROOF.
PRESUMABLY HIS OWN DESIGN.
DOES HE HAVE HOSTAGES?
OF COURSE I HAD HOSTAGES. I WANTED TO MEET HIM, SO I HAD TO HAVE HOSTAGES.
HE CAME IN THROUGH THE FRONT DOOR. I KNEW HE WOULD. THAT'S WHAT HE IS.

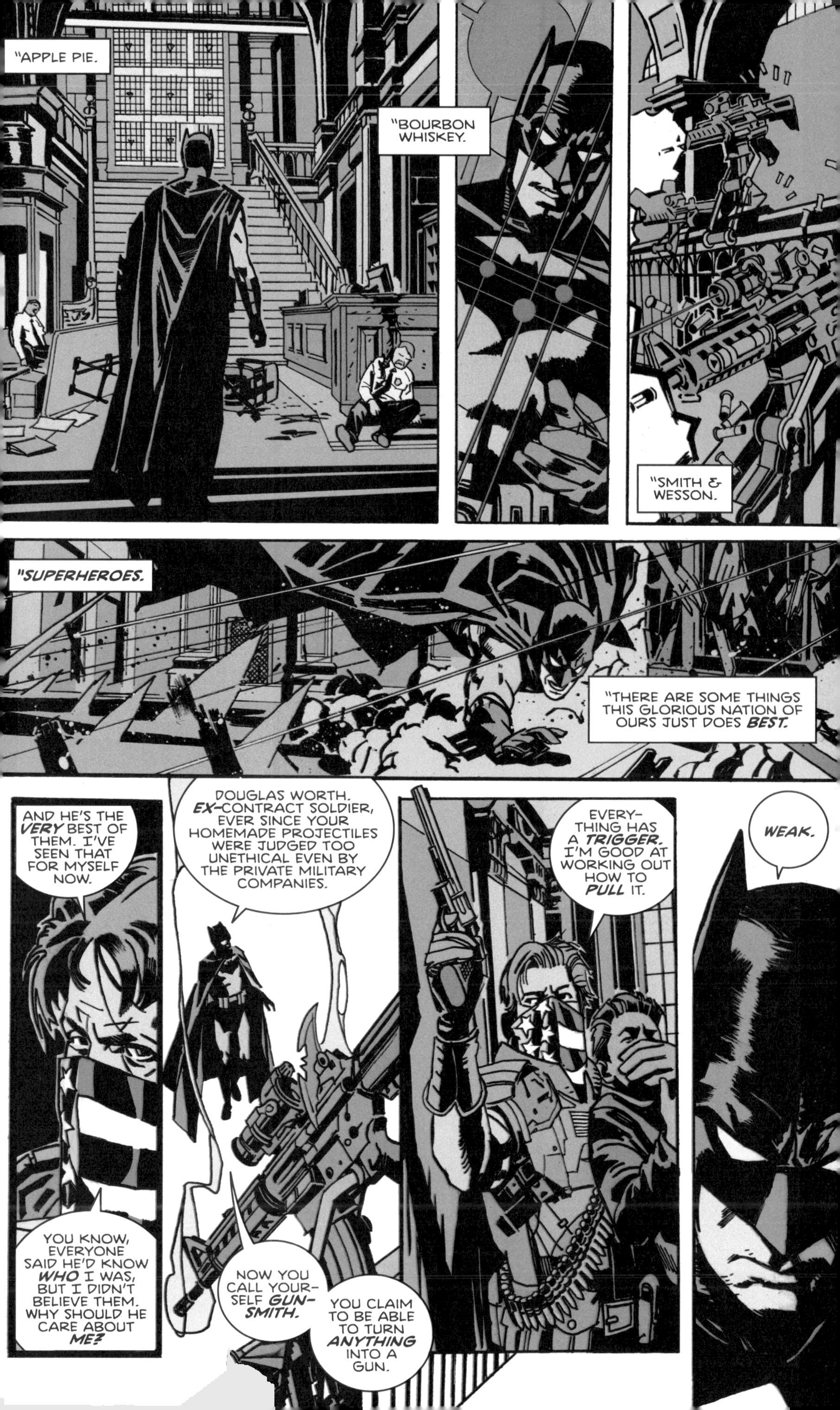

"APPLE PIE.
"BOURBON WHISKEY.
"SMITH & WESSON.
"SUPERHEROES.
"THERE ARE SOME THINGS THIS GLORIOUS NATION OF OURS JUST DOES BEST.
AND HE'S THE VERY BEST OF THEM. I'VE SEEN THAT FOR MYSELF NOW.
YOU KNOW, EVERYONE SAID HE'D KNOW WHO I WAS, BUT I DIDN'T BELIEVE THEM. WHY SHOULD HE CARE ABOUT ME?
DOUGLAS WORTH. EX-CONTRACT SOLDIER, EVER SINCE YOUR HOMEMADE PROJECTILES WERE JUDGED TOO UNETHICAL EVEN BY THE PRIVATE MILITARY COMPANIES.
NOW YOU CALL YOURSELF GUNSMITH.
YOU CLAIM TO BE ABLE TO TURN ANYTHING INTO A GUN.
EVERYTHING HAS A TRIGGER. I'M GOOD AT WORKING OUT HOW TO PULL IT.
WEAK.

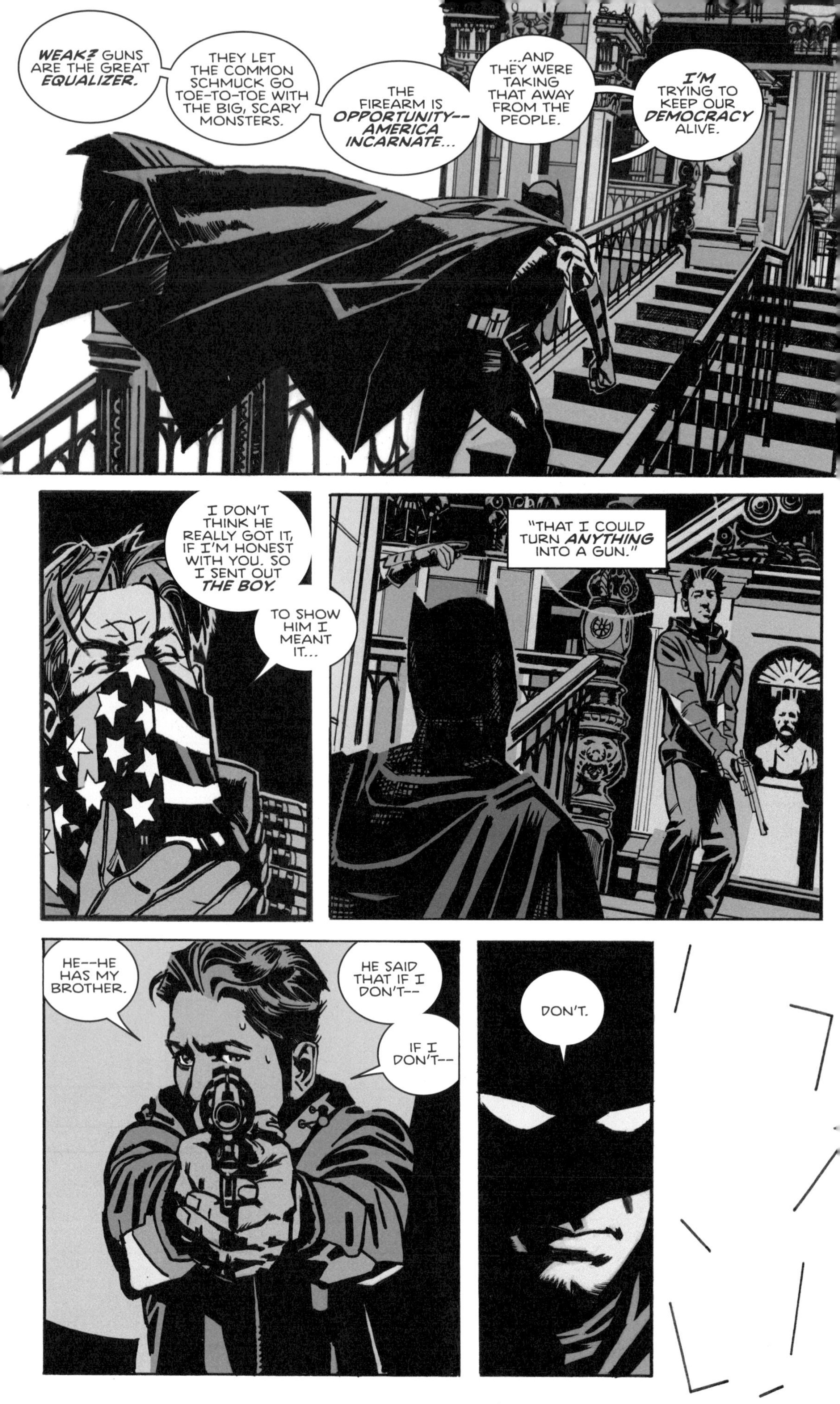
WEAK? GUNS ARE THE GREAT EQUALIZER.
THEY LET THE COMMON SCHMUCK GO TOE-TO-TOE WITH THE BIG, SCARY MONSTERS.
THE FIREARM IS OPPORTUNITY-- AMERICA INCARNATE...
...AND THEY WERE TAKING THAT AWAY FROM THE PEOPLE.
I'M TRYING TO KEEP OUR DEMOCRACY ALIVE.
I DON'T THINK HE REALLY GOT IT, IF I'M HONEST WITH YOU. SO I SENT OUT THE BOY.
TO SHOW HIM I MEANT IT...
"THAT I COULD TURN ANYTHING INTO A GUN."
HE--HE HAS MY BROTHER.
HE SAID THAT IF I DON'T--
IF I DON'T--
DON'T.

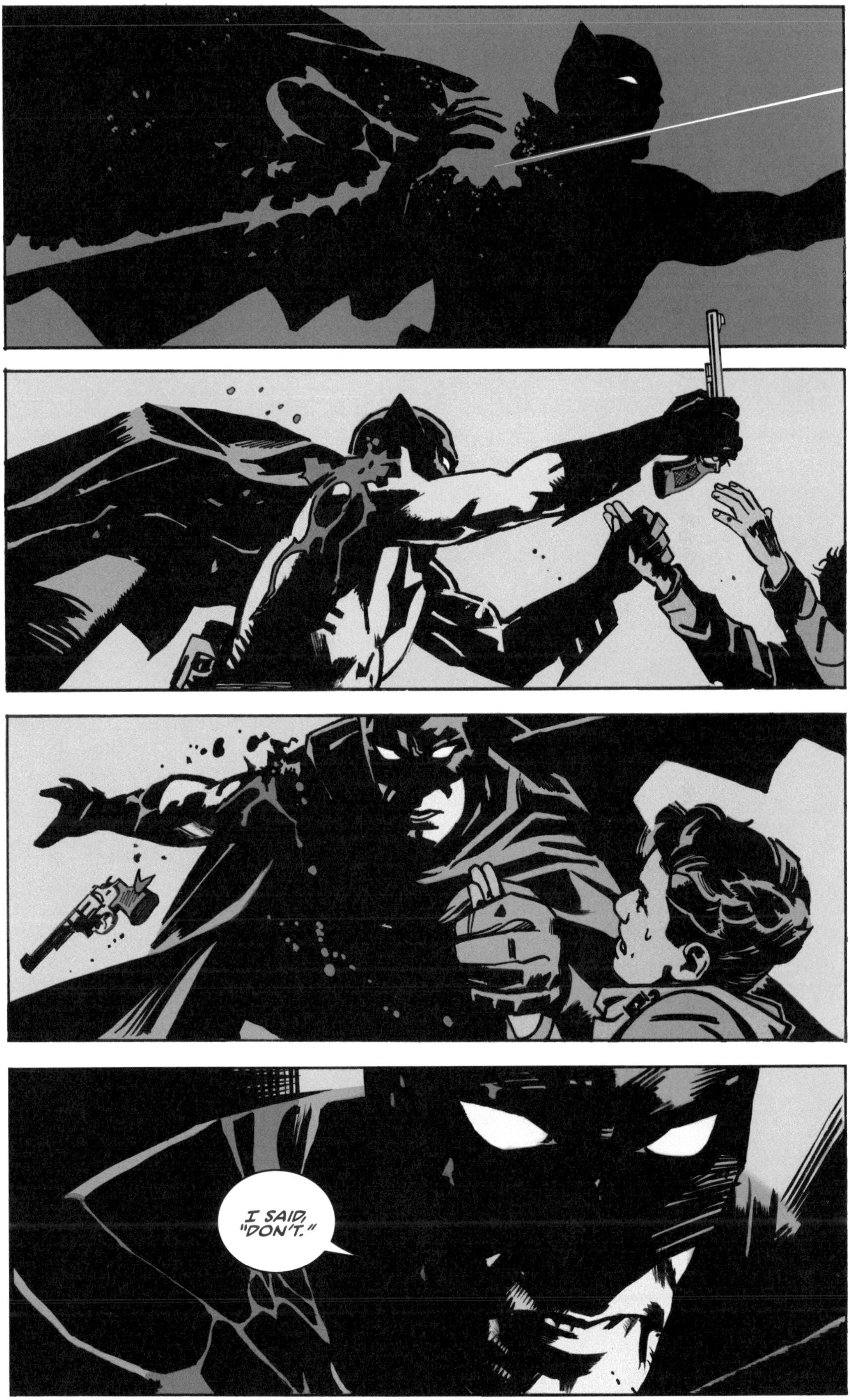
I SAID, "DON'T."

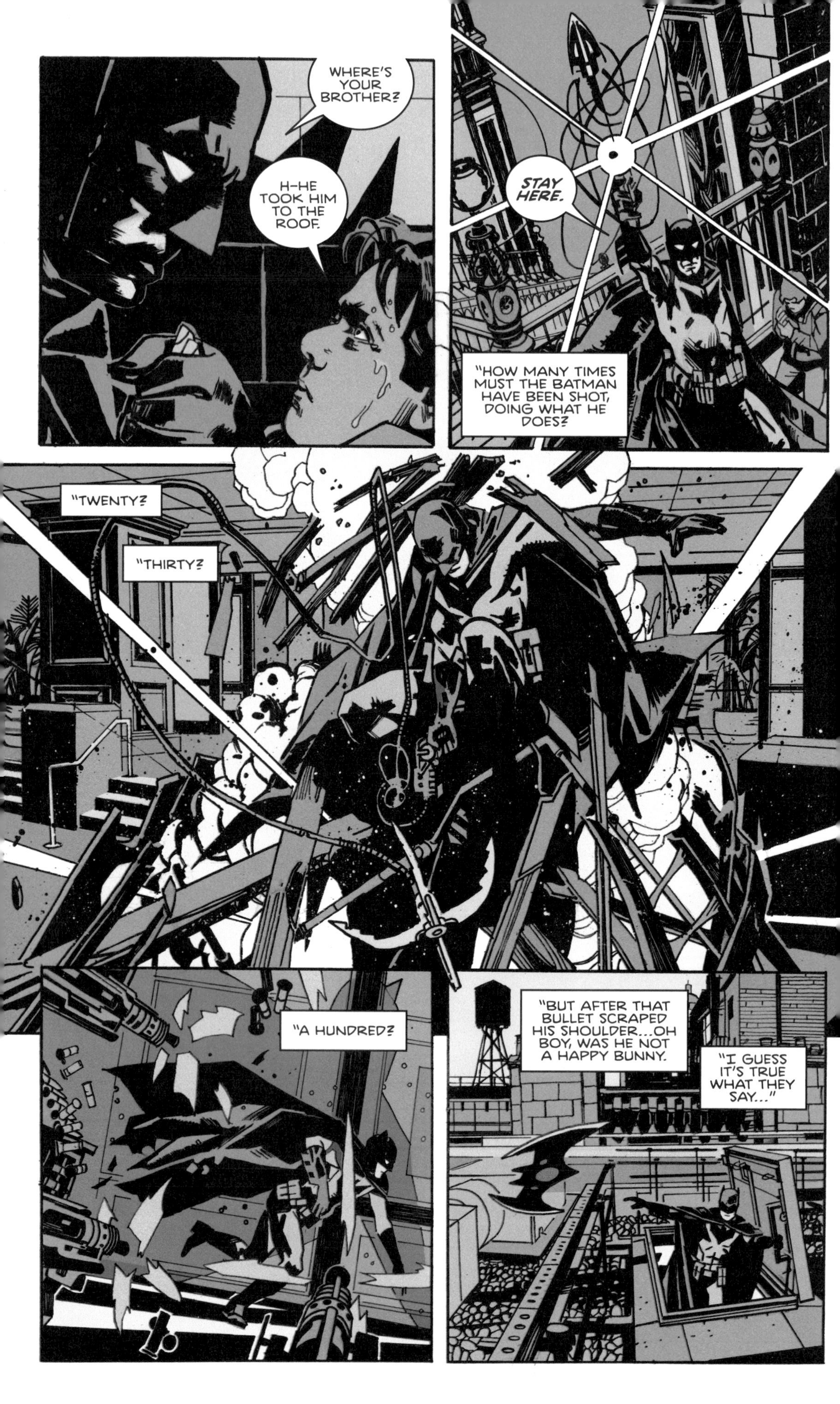
WHERE'S YOUR BROTHER?
H-HE TOOK HIM TO THE ROOF.
STAY HERE.
"HOW MANY TIMES MUST THE BATMAN HAVE BEEN SHOT, DOING WHAT HE DOES?
"TWENTY?
"THIRTY?
"A HUNDRED?
"BUT AFTER THAT BULLET SCRAPED HIS SHOULDER...OH BOY, WAS HE NOT A HAPPY BUNNY.
"I GUESS IT'S TRUE WHAT THEY SAY..."

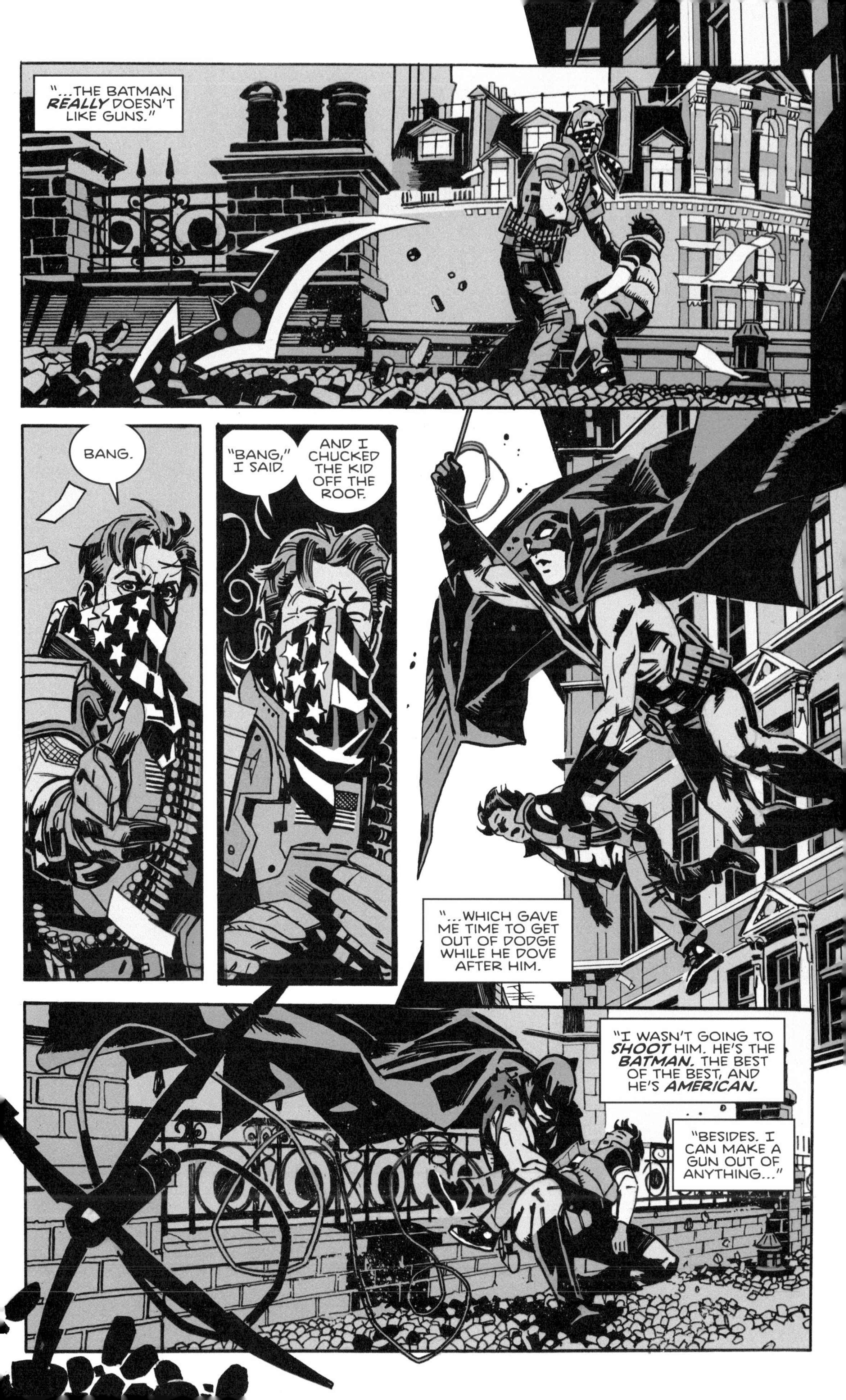
"...THE BATMAN REALLY DOESN'T LIKE GUNS."
BANG.
"BANG," I SAID.
AND I CHUCKED THE KID OFF THE ROOF.
"...WHICH GAVE ME TIME TO GET OUT OF DODGE WHILE HE DOVE AFTER HIM.
"I WASN'T GOING TO SHOOT HIM. HE'S THE BATMAN. THE BEST OF THE BEST, AND HE'S AMERICAN.
"BESIDES. I CAN MAKE A GUN OUT OF ANYTHING..."

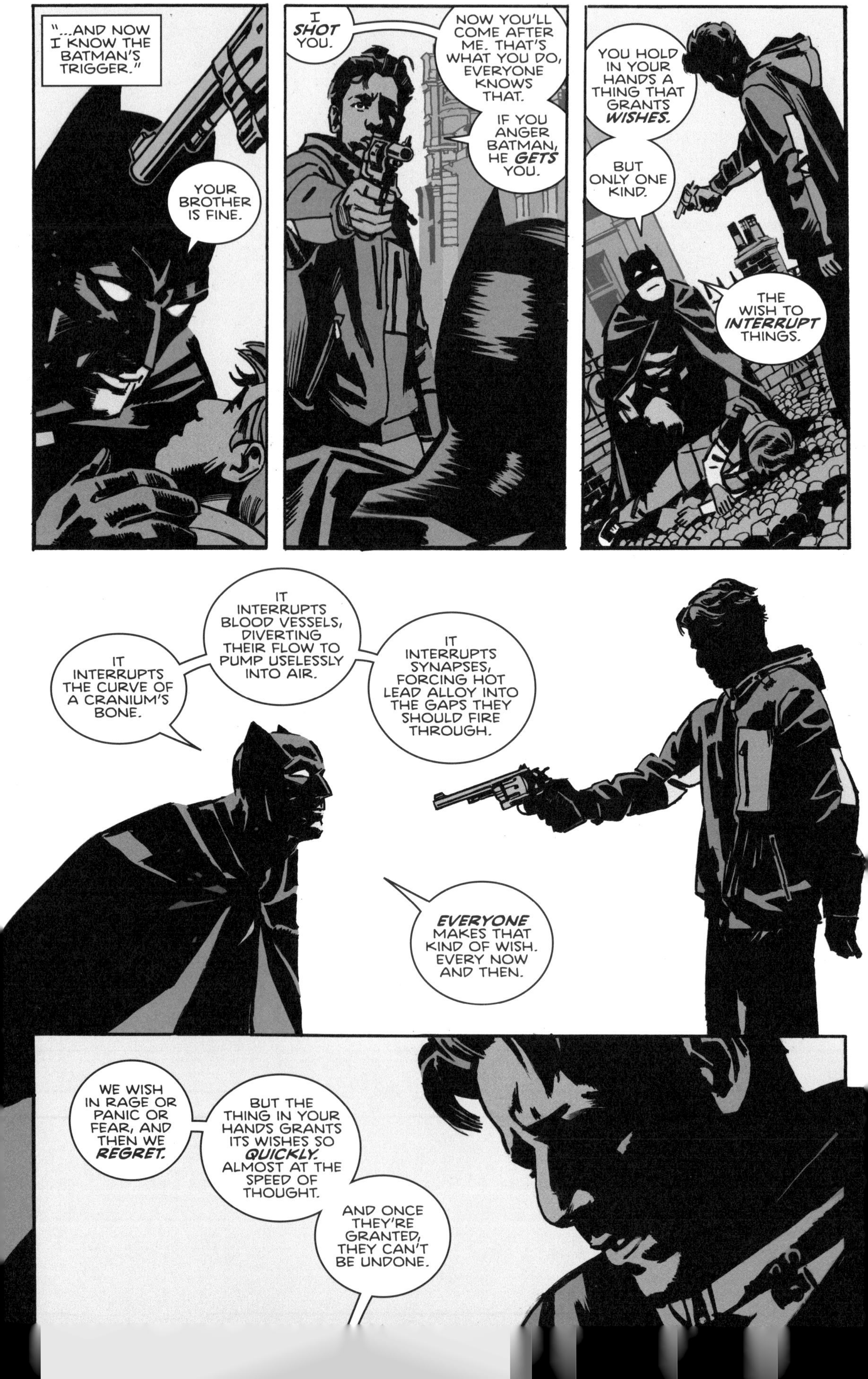
"...AND NOW I KNOW THE BATMAN'S TRIGGER."
YOUR BROTHER IS FINE.
I *SHOT* YOU.
NOW YOU'LL COME AFTER ME. THAT'S WHAT YOU DO, EVERYONE KNOWS THAT.
IF YOU ANGER BATMAN, HE *GETS* YOU.
YOU HOLD IN YOUR HANDS A THING THAT GRANTS *WISHES.*
BUT ONLY ONE KIND.
THE WISH TO *INTERRUPT* THINGS.
IT INTERRUPTS THE CURVE OF A CRANIUM'S BONE.
IT INTERRUPTS BLOOD VESSELS, DIVERTING THEIR FLOW TO PUMP USELESSLY INTO AIR.
IT INTERRUPTS SYNAPSES, FORCING HOT LEAD ALLOY INTO THE GAPS THEY SHOULD FIRE THROUGH.
EVERYONE MAKES THAT KIND OF WISH. EVERY NOW AND THEN.
WE WISH IN RAGE OR PANIC OR FEAR, AND THEN WE *REGRET.*
BUT THE THING IN YOUR HANDS GRANTS ITS WISHES SO *QUICKLY.* ALMOST AT THE SPEED OF THOUGHT.
AND ONCE THEY'RE GRANTED, THEY CAN'T BE UNDONE.

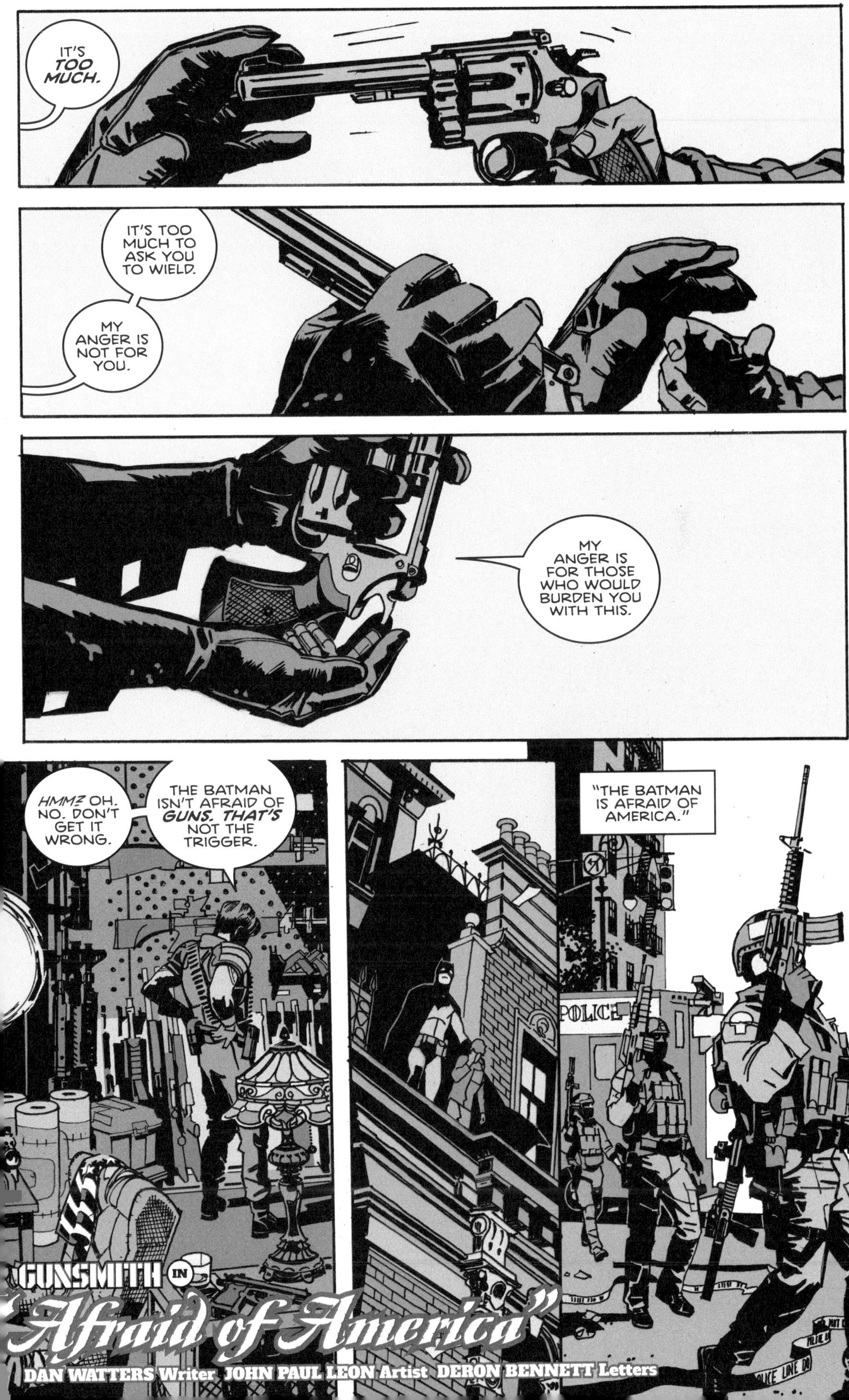
IT'S TOO MUCH.
IT'S TOO MUCH TO ASK YOU TO WIELD.
MY ANGER IS NOT FOR YOU.
MY ANGER IS FOR THOSE WHO WOULD BURDEN YOU WITH THIS.
HMM? OH. NO. DON'T GET IT WRONG.
THE BATMAN ISN'T AFRAID OF GUNS. THAT'S NOT THE TRIGGER.
"THE BATMAN IS AFRAID OF AMERICA."
POLICE
GUNSMITH IN
"Afraid of America"
DAN WATTERS Writer JOHN PAUL LEON Artist DERON BENNETT Letters

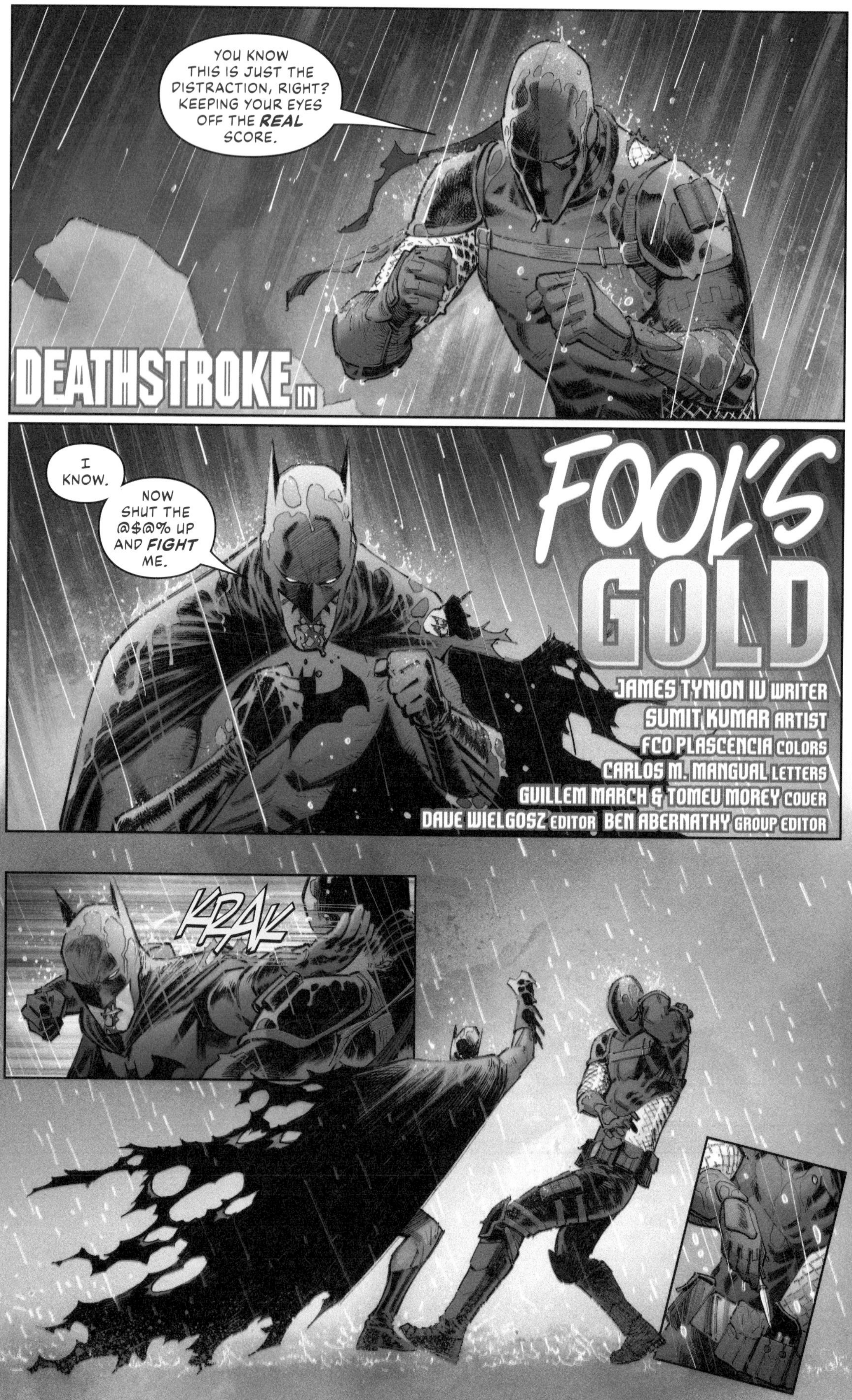
YOU KNOW THIS IS JUST THE DISTRACTION, RIGHT? KEEPING YOUR EYES OFF THE REAL SCORE.
DEATHSTROKE IN
I KNOW.
NOW SHUT THE @$@% UP AND FIGHT ME.
FOOL'S GOLD
JAMES TYNION IV WRITER
SUMIT KUMAR ARTIST
FCO PLASCENCIA COLORS
CARLOS M. MANGUAL LETTERS
GUILLEM MARCH & TOMEU MOREY COVER
DAVE WIELGOSZ EDITOR BEN ABERNATHY GROUP EDITOR
KRAK

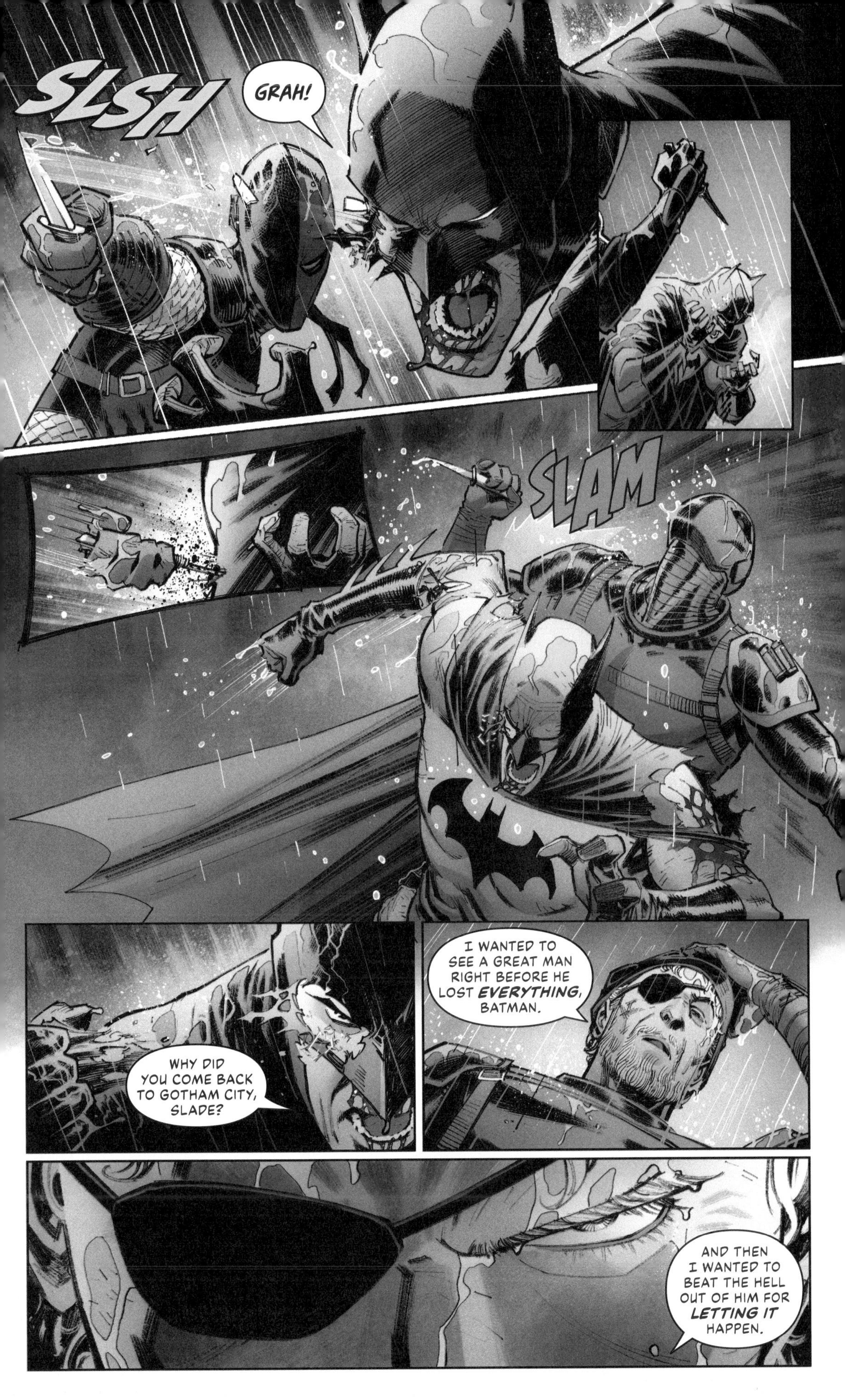
SLSH
GRAH!
SLAM
WHY DID YOU COME BACK TO GOTHAM CITY, SLADE?
I WANTED TO SEE A GREAT MAN RIGHT BEFORE HE LOST EVERYTHING, BATMAN.
AND THEN I WANTED TO BEAT THE HELL OUT OF HIM FOR LETTING IT HAPPEN.

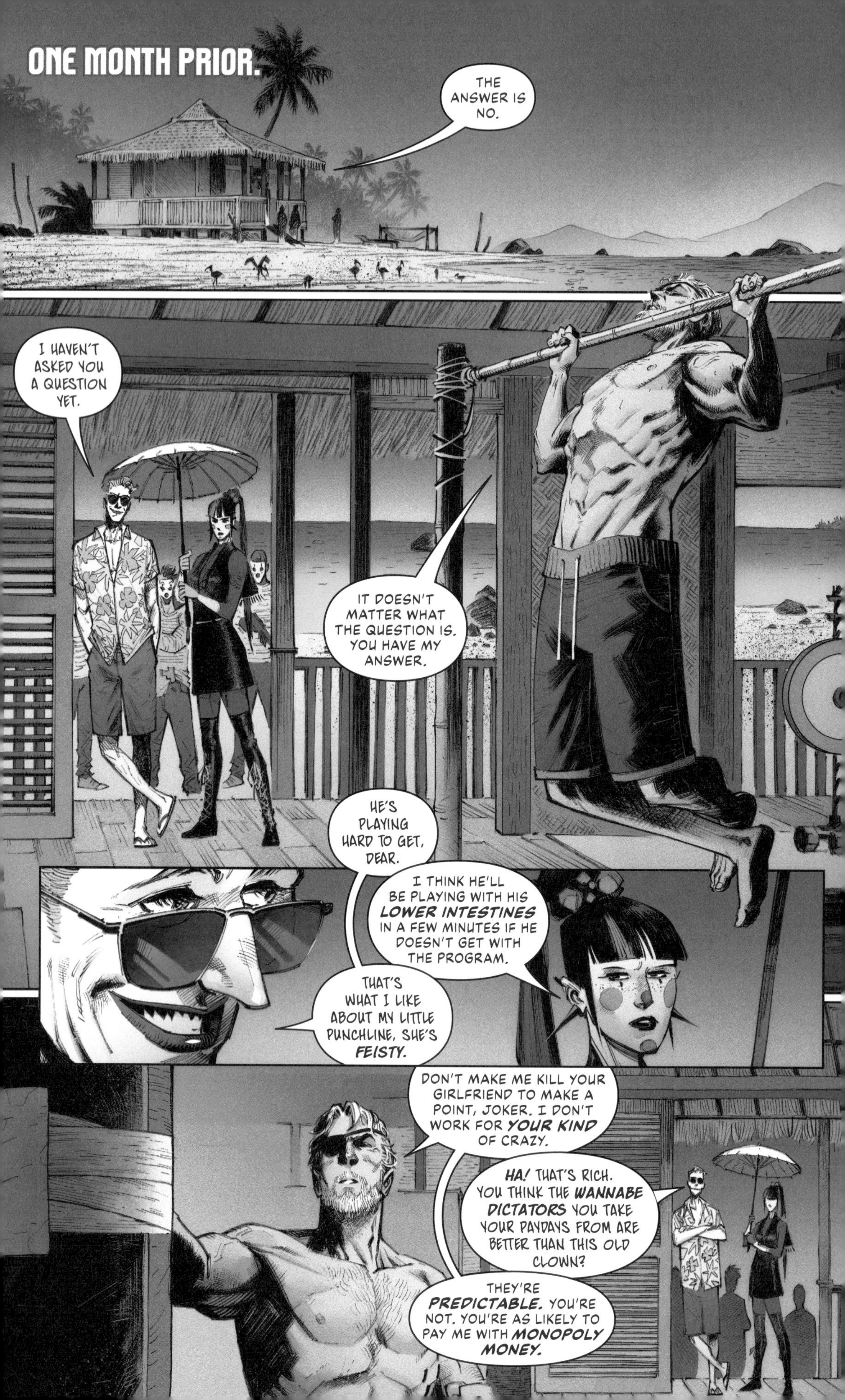
ONE MONTH PRIOR.
THE ANSWER IS NO.
I HAVEN'T ASKED YOU A QUESTION YET.
IT DOESN'T MATTER WHAT THE QUESTION IS. YOU HAVE MY ANSWER.
HE'S PLAYING HARD TO GET, DEAR.
I THINK HE'LL BE PLAYING WITH HIS LOWER INTESTINES IN A FEW MINUTES IF HE DOESN'T GET WITH THE PROGRAM.
THAT'S WHAT I LIKE ABOUT MY LITTLE PUNCHLINE, SHE'S FEISTY.
DON'T MAKE ME KILL YOUR GIRLFRIEND TO MAKE A POINT, JOKER. I DON'T WORK FOR YOUR KIND OF CRAZY.
HA! THAT'S RICH. YOU THINK THE WANNABE DICTATORS YOU TAKE YOUR PAYDAYS FROM ARE BETTER THAN THIS OLD CLOWN?
THEY'RE PREDICTABLE. YOU'RE NOT. YOU'RE AS LIKELY TO PAY ME WITH MONOPOLY MONEY.

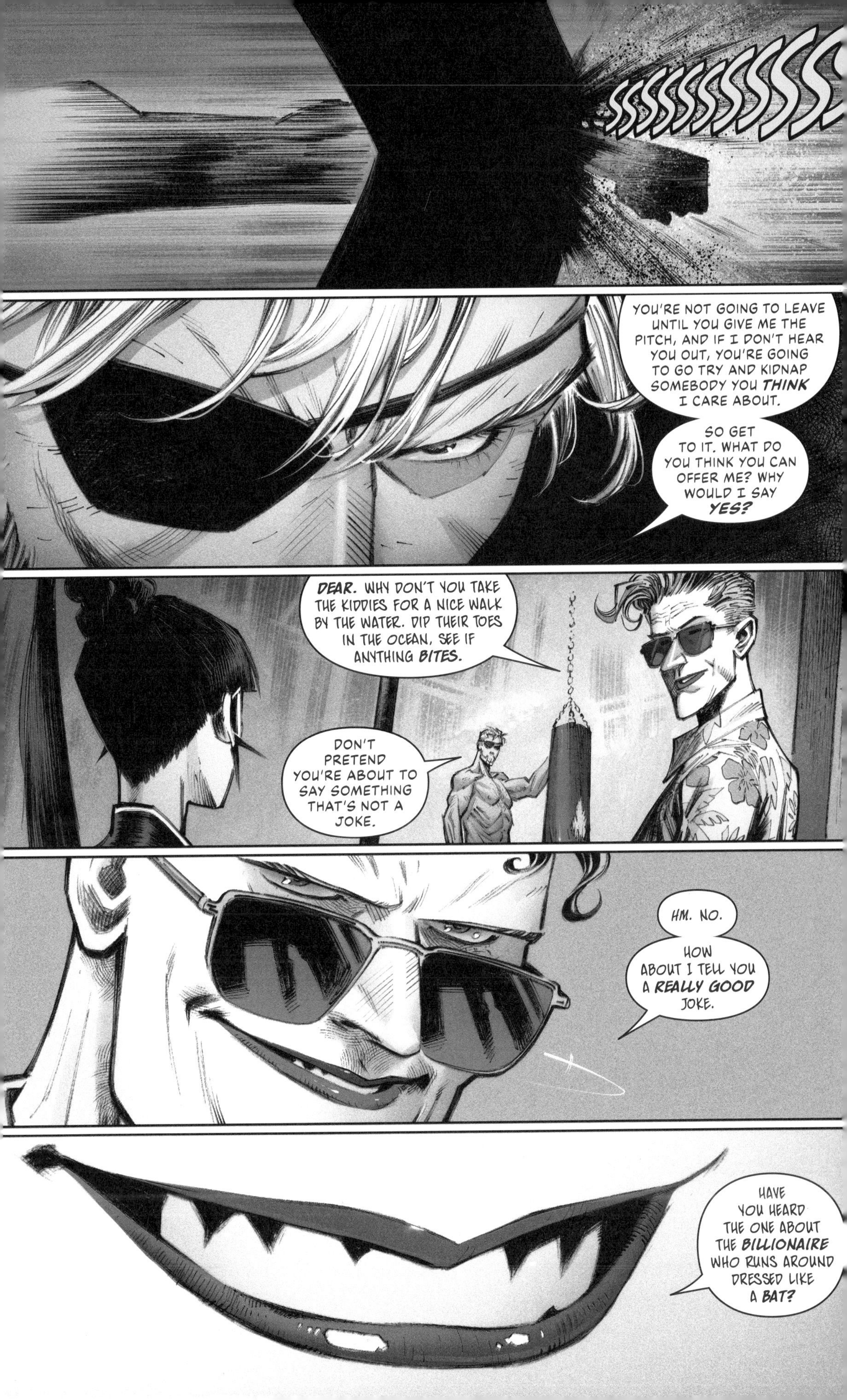
SSSSSSSSS
YOU'RE NOT GOING TO LEAVE UNTIL YOU GIVE ME THE PITCH, AND IF I DON'T HEAR YOU OUT, YOU'RE GOING TO GO TRY AND KIDNAP SOMEBODY YOU THINK I CARE ABOUT.
SO GET TO IT. WHAT DO YOU THINK YOU CAN OFFER ME? WHY WOULD I SAY YES?
DEAR. WHY DON'T YOU TAKE THE KIDDIES FOR A NICE WALK BY THE WATER. DIP THEIR TOES IN THE OCEAN, SEE IF ANYTHING BITES.
DON'T PRETEND YOU'RE ABOUT TO SAY SOMETHING THAT'S NOT A JOKE.
HM. NO.
HOW ABOUT I TELL YOU A REALLY GOOD JOKE.
HAVE YOU HEARD THE ONE ABOUT THE BILLIONAIRE WHO RUNS AROUND DRESSED LIKE A BAT?

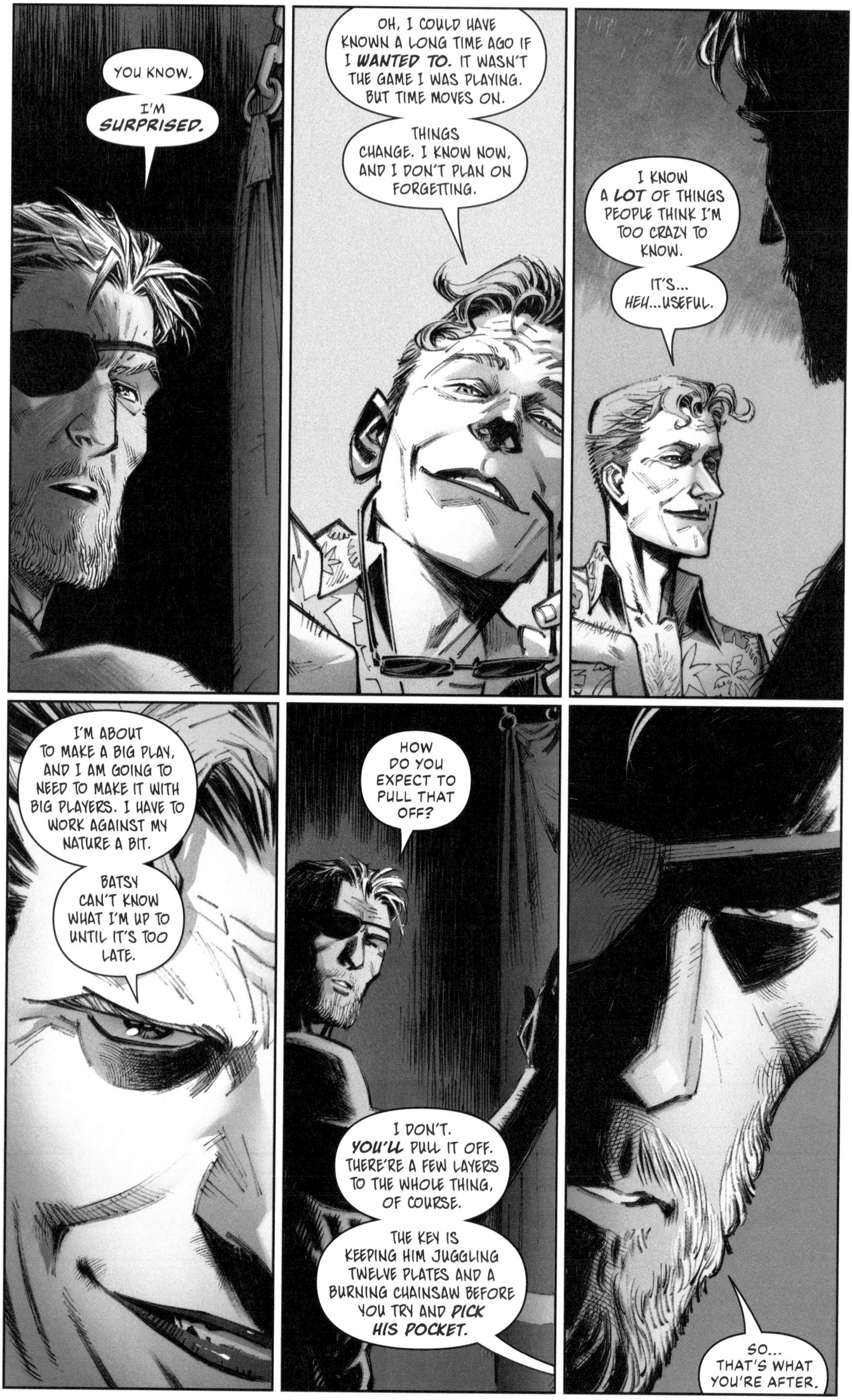
YOU KNOW.
I'M SURPRISED.
OH, I COULD HAVE KNOWN A LONG TIME AGO IF I WANTED TO. IT WASN'T THE GAME I WAS PLAYING. BUT TIME MOVES ON.
THINGS CHANGE. I KNOW NOW, AND I DON'T PLAN ON FORGETTING.
I KNOW A LOT OF THINGS PEOPLE THINK I'M TOO CRAZY TO KNOW.
IT'S... HEH...USEFUL.
I'M ABOUT TO MAKE A BIG PLAY, AND I AM GOING TO NEED TO MAKE IT WITH BIG PLAYERS. I HAVE TO WORK AGAINST MY NATURE A BIT.
BATSY CAN'T KNOW WHAT I'M UP TO UNTIL IT'S TOO LATE.
HOW DO YOU EXPECT TO PULL THAT OFF?
I DON'T. YOU'LL PULL IT OFF. THERE'RE A FEW LAYERS TO THE WHOLE THING, OF COURSE.
THE KEY IS KEEPING HIM JUGGLING TWELVE PLATES AND A BURNING CHAINSAW BEFORE YOU TRY AND PICK HIS POCKET.
SO... THAT'S WHAT YOU'RE AFTER.

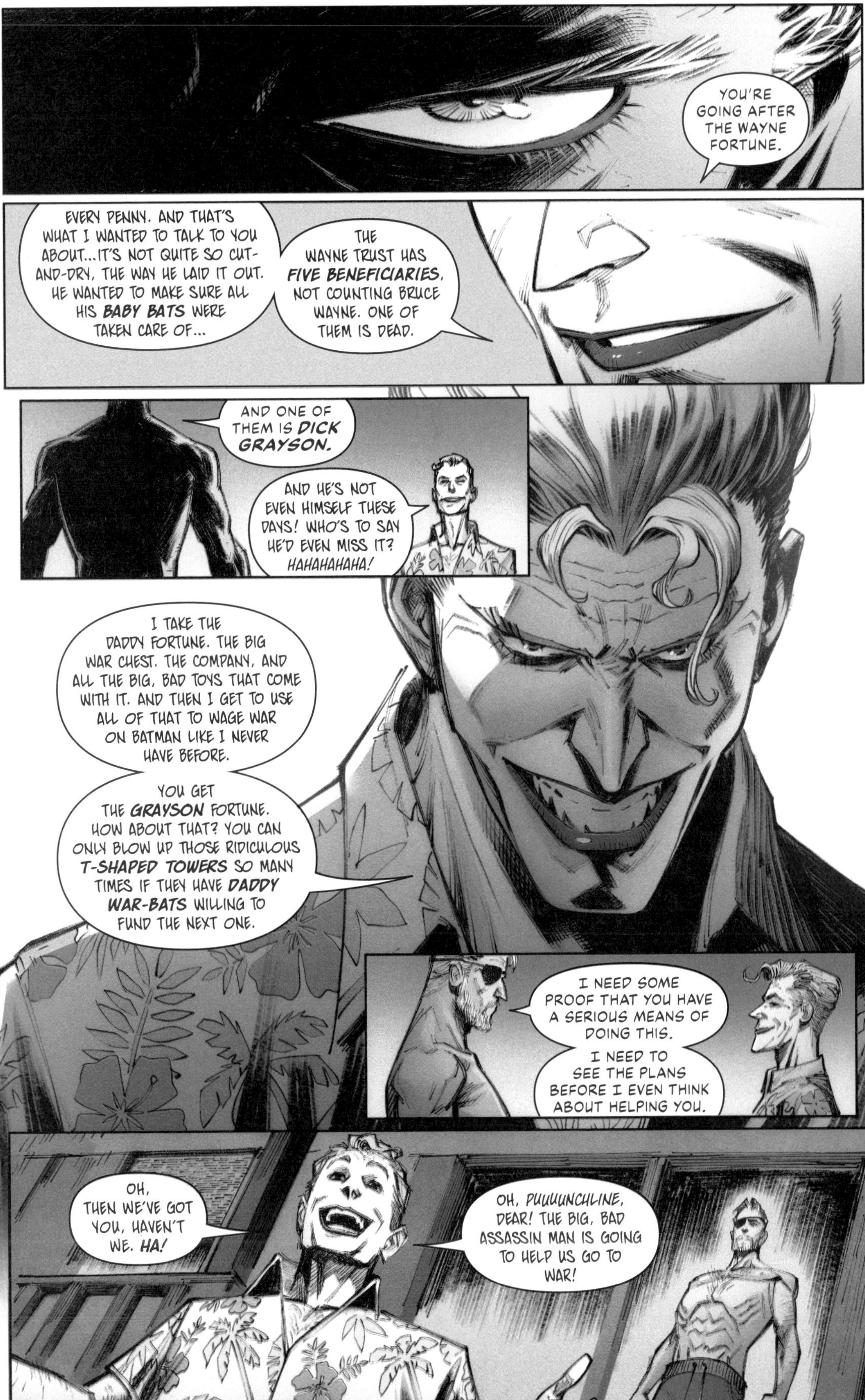
YOU'RE GOING AFTER THE WAYNE FORTUNE.
EVERY PENNY. AND THAT'S WHAT I WANTED TO TALK TO YOU ABOUT...IT'S NOT QUITE SO CUT-AND-DRY, THE WAY HE LAID IT OUT. HE WANTED TO MAKE SURE ALL HIS BABY BATS WERE TAKEN CARE OF...
THE WAYNE TRUST HAS FIVE BENEFICIARIES, NOT COUNTING BRUCE WAYNE. ONE OF THEM IS DEAD.
AND ONE OF THEM IS DICK GRAYSON.
AND HE'S NOT EVEN HIMSELF THESE DAYS! WHO'S TO SAY HE'D EVEN MISS IT? HAHAHAHAHA!
I TAKE THE DADDY FORTUNE. THE BIG WAR CHEST. THE COMPANY, AND ALL THE BIG, BAD TOYS THAT COME WITH IT. AND THEN I GET TO USE ALL OF THAT TO WAGE WAR ON BATMAN LIKE I NEVER HAVE BEFORE.
YOU GET THE GRAYSON FORTUNE. HOW ABOUT THAT? YOU CAN ONLY BLOW UP THOSE RIDICULOUS T-SHAPED TOWERS SO MANY TIMES IF THEY HAVE DADDY WAR-BATS WILLING TO FUND THE NEXT ONE.
I NEED SOME PROOF THAT YOU HAVE A SERIOUS MEANS OF DOING THIS.
I NEED TO SEE THE PLANS BEFORE I EVEN THINK ABOUT HELPING YOU.
OH, THEN WE'VE GOT YOU, HAVEN'T WE. HA!
OH, PUUUUNCHLINE, DEAR! THE BIG, BAD ASSASSIN MAN IS GOING TO HELP US GO TO WAR!

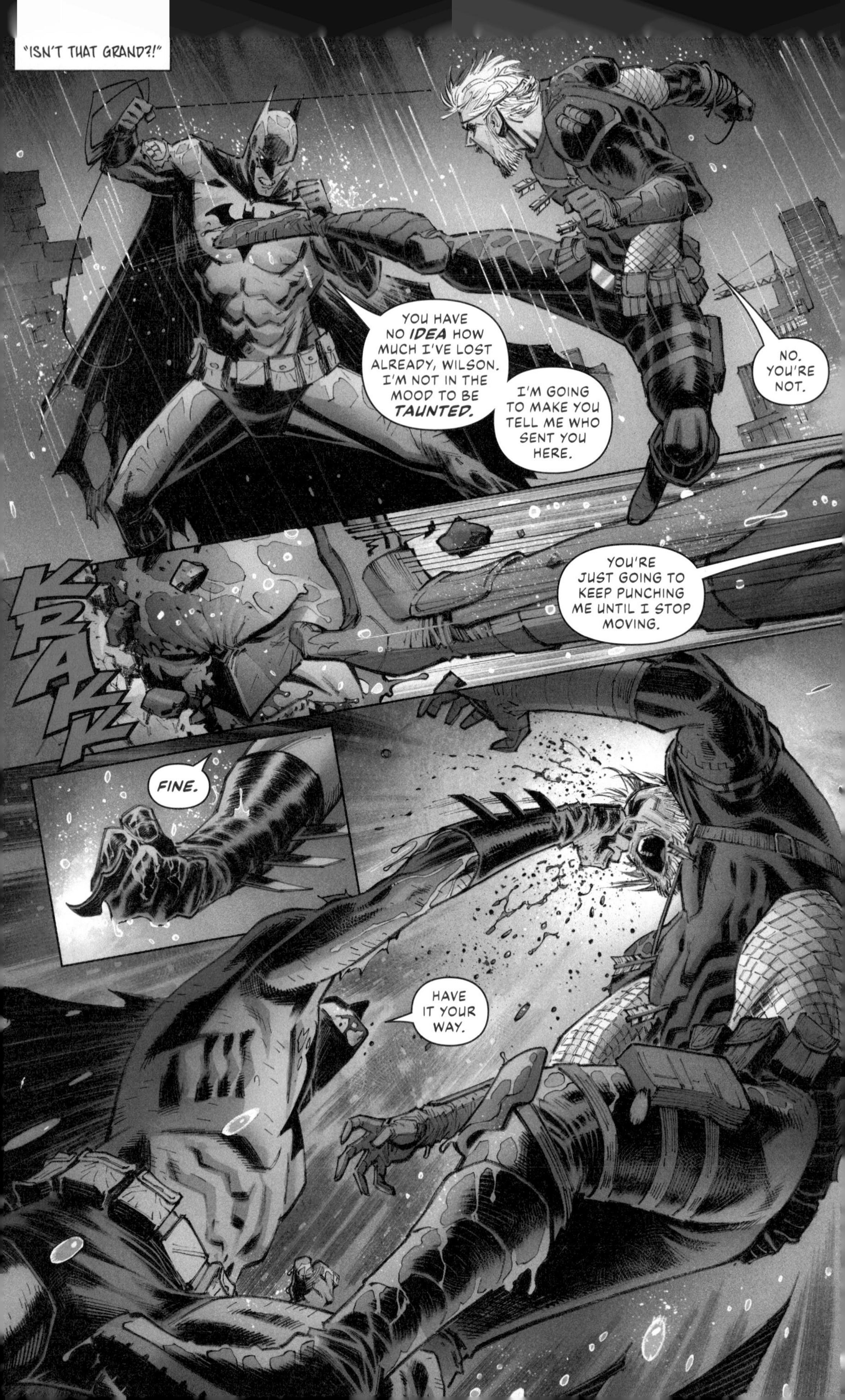
"ISN'T THAT GRAND?!"
YOU HAVE NO IDEA HOW MUCH I'VE LOST ALREADY, WILSON. I'M NOT IN THE MOOD TO BE TAUNTED.
I'M GOING TO MAKE YOU TELL ME WHO SENT YOU HERE.
NO. YOU'RE NOT.
KRAKK
YOU'RE JUST GOING TO KEEP PUNCHING ME UNTIL I STOP MOVING.
FINE.
HAVE IT YOUR WAY.

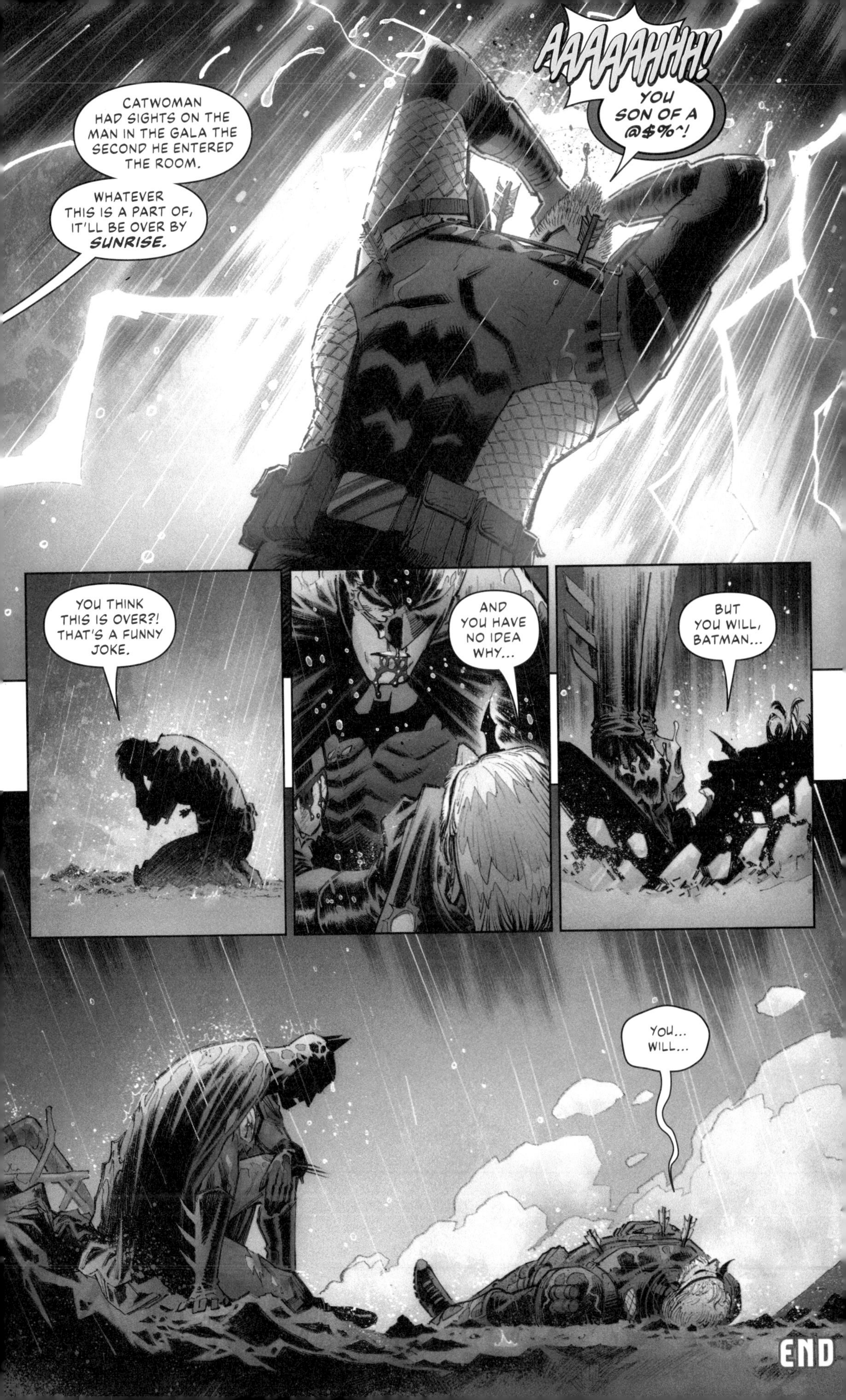
AAAAAHHH!
YOU SON OF A @$%^!
CATWOMAN HAD SIGHTS ON THE MAN IN THE GALA THE SECOND HE ENTERED THE ROOM.
WHATEVER THIS IS A PART OF, IT'LL BE OVER BY SUNRISE.
YOU THINK THIS IS OVER?! THAT'S A FUNNY JOKE.
AND YOU HAVE NO IDEA WHY...
BUT YOU WILL, BATMAN...
YOU... WILL...
END

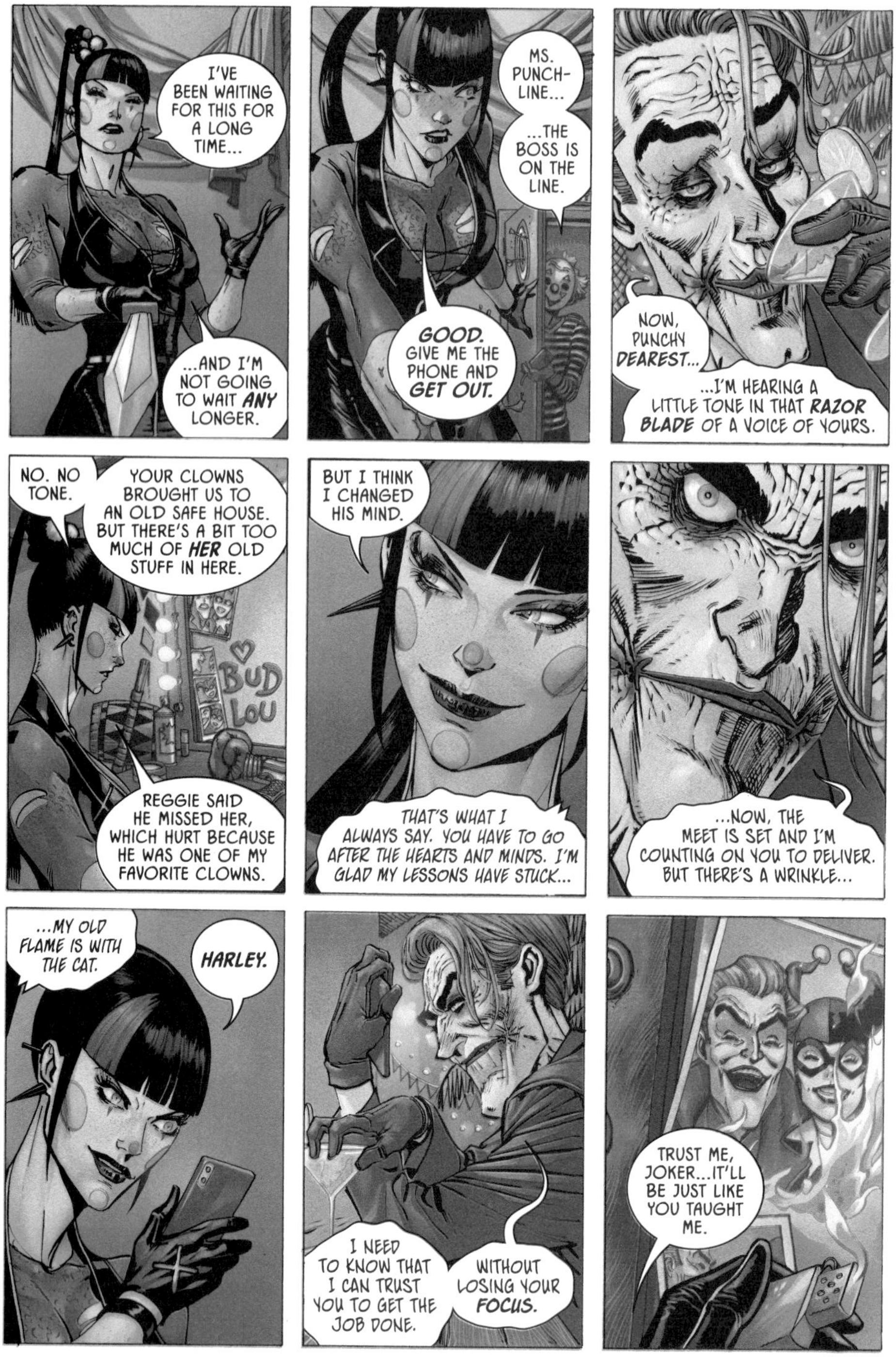
I'VE BEEN WAITING FOR THIS FOR A LONG TIME...
...AND I'M NOT GOING TO WAIT ANY LONGER.
MS. PUNCH-LINE...
...THE BOSS IS ON THE LINE.
GOOD. GIVE ME THE PHONE AND GET OUT.
NOW, PUNCHY DEAREST...
...I'M HEARING A LITTLE TONE IN THAT RAZOR BLADE OF A VOICE OF YOURS.
NO. NO TONE.
YOUR CLOWNS BROUGHT US TO AN OLD SAFE HOUSE. BUT THERE'S A BIT TOO MUCH OF HER OLD STUFF IN HERE.
BUD
LOU
REGGIE SAID HE MISSED HER, WHICH HURT BECAUSE HE WAS ONE OF MY FAVORITE CLOWNS.
BUT I THINK I CHANGED HIS MIND.
THAT'S WHAT I ALWAYS SAY. YOU HAVE TO GO AFTER THE HEARTS AND MINDS. I'M GLAD MY LESSONS HAVE STUCK...
...NOW, THE MEET IS SET AND I'M COUNTING ON YOU TO DELIVER. BUT THERE'S A WRINKLE...
...MY OLD FLAME IS WITH THE CAT.
HARLEY.
I NEED TO KNOW THAT I CAN TRUST YOU TO GET THE JOB DONE.
WITHOUT LOSING YOUR FOCUS.
TRUST ME, JOKER...IT'LL BE JUST LIKE YOU TAUGHT ME.

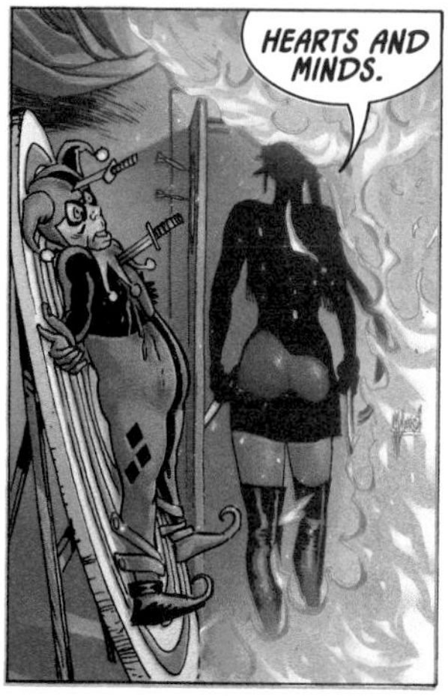
HEARTS AND MINDS.

JAMES TYNION IV *writer*

GUILLEM MARCH *artist*

TOMEU MOREY *colors*

CLAYTON COWLES *letters*

DAVE WIELGOSZ *assoc. editor*

BEN ABERNATHY *editor*

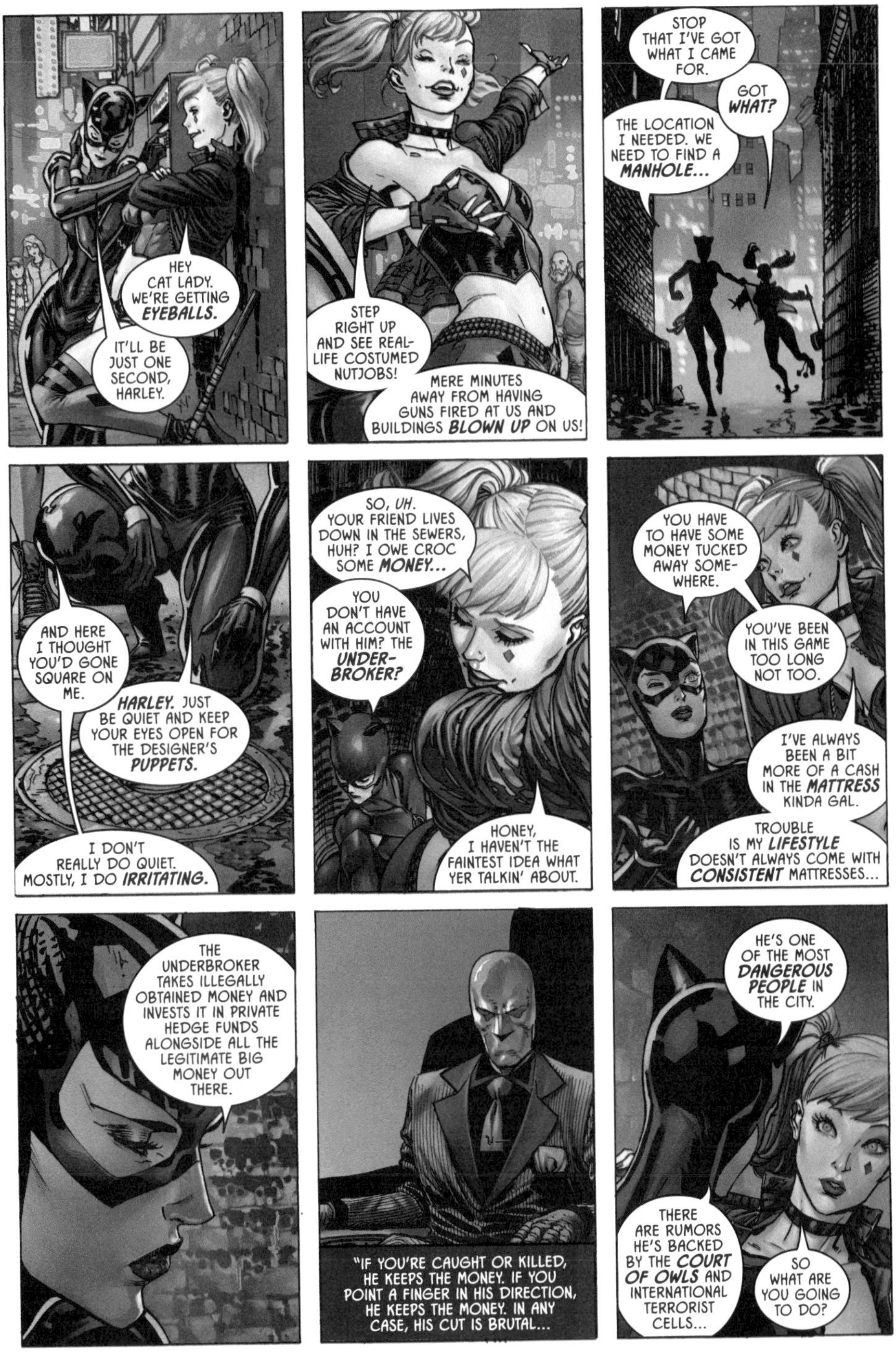
HEY CAT LADY. WE'RE GETTING EYEBALLS.
IT'LL BE JUST ONE SECOND, HARLEY.
STEP RIGHT UP AND SEE REAL-LIFE COSTUMED NUTJOBS!
MERE MINUTES AWAY FROM HAVING GUNS FIRED AT US AND BUILDINGS BLOWN UP ON US!
STOP THAT I'VE GOT WHAT I CAME FOR.
GOT WHAT?
THE LOCATION I NEEDED. WE NEED TO FIND A MANHOLE...
AND HERE I THOUGHT YOU'D GONE SQUARE ON ME.
HARLEY. JUST BE QUIET AND KEEP YOUR EYES OPEN FOR THE DESIGNER'S PUPPETS.
I DON'T REALLY DO QUIET. MOSTLY, I DO IRRITATING.
SO, UH. YOUR FRIEND LIVES DOWN IN THE SEWERS, HUH? I OWE CROC SOME MONEY...
YOU DON'T HAVE AN ACCOUNT WITH HIM? THE UNDER-BROKER?
HONEY, I HAVEN'T THE FAINTEST IDEA WHAT YER TALKIN' ABOUT.
YOU HAVE TO HAVE SOME MONEY TUCKED AWAY SOME-WHERE.
YOU'VE BEEN IN THIS GAME TOO LONG NOT TOO.
I'VE ALWAYS BEEN A BIT MORE OF A CASH IN THE MATTRESS KINDA GAL.
TROUBLE IS MY LIFESTYLE DOESN'T ALWAYS COME WITH CONSISTENT MATTRESSES...
THE UNDERBROKER TAKES ILLEGALLY OBTAINED MONEY AND INVESTS IT IN PRIVATE HEDGE FUNDS ALONGSIDE ALL THE LEGITIMATE BIG MONEY OUT THERE.
"IF YOU'RE CAUGHT OR KILLED, HE KEEPS THE MONEY. IF YOU POINT A FINGER IN HIS DIRECTION, HE KEEPS THE MONEY. IN ANY CASE, HIS CUT IS BRUTAL...
HE'S ONE OF THE MOST DANGEROUS PEOPLE IN THE CITY.
THERE ARE RUMORS HE'S BACKED BY THE COURT OF OWLS AND INTERNATIONAL TERRORIST CELLS...
SO WHAT ARE YOU GOING TO DO?

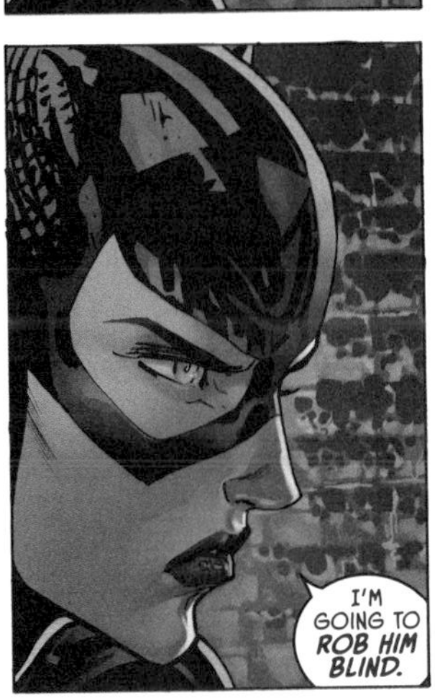
I'M GOING TO ROB HIM BLIND.

JAMES TYNION IV *writer*

GUILLEM MARCH *artist*

TOMEU MOREY *colors*

CLAYTON COWLES *letters*

DAVE WIELGOSZ *assoc. editor*

BEN ABERNATHY *editor*

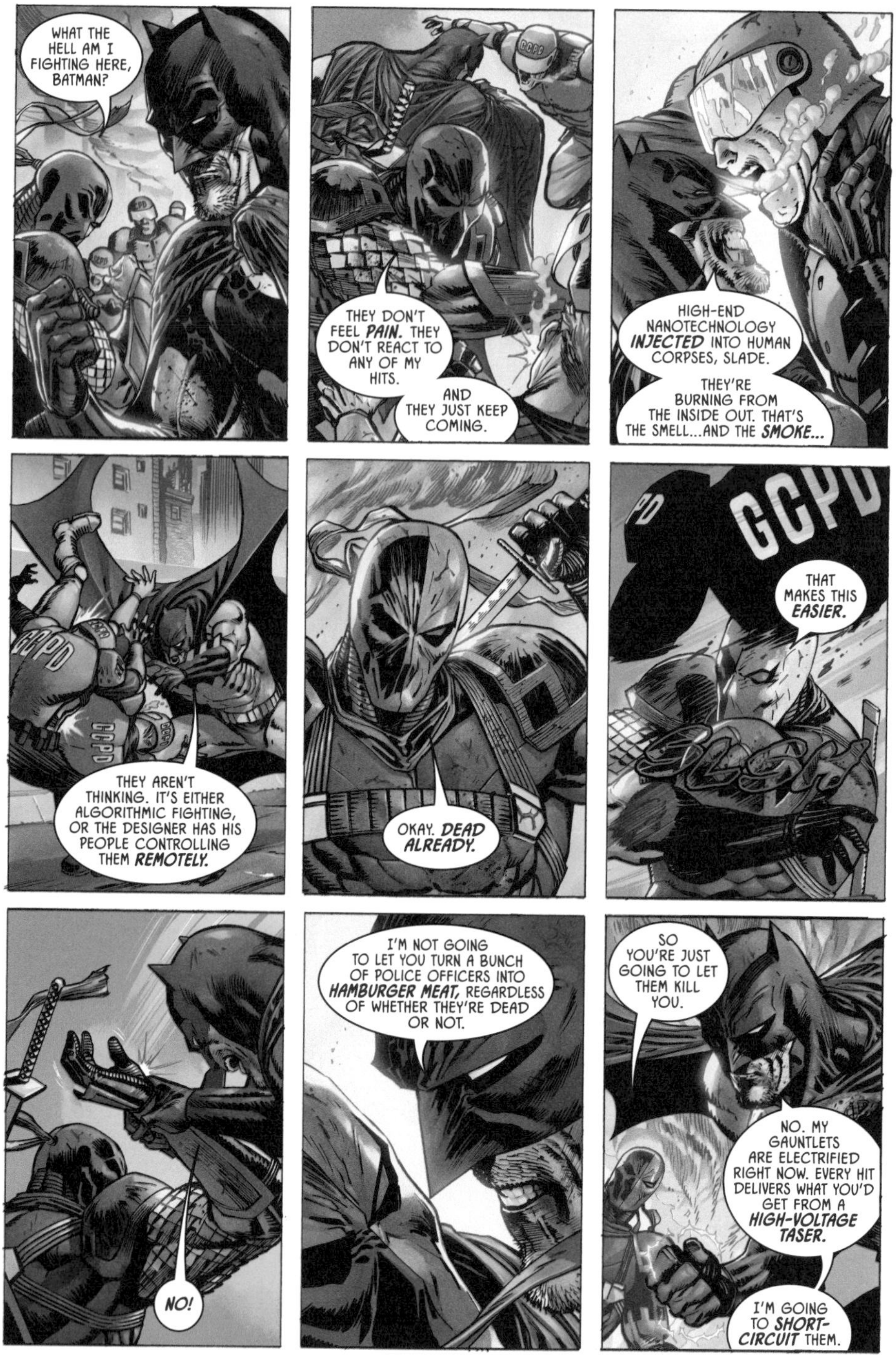

WHAT THE HELL AM I FIGHTING HERE, BATMAN?
THEY DON'T FEEL PAIN. THEY DON'T REACT TO ANY OF MY HITS.
AND THEY JUST KEEP COMING.
HIGH-END NANOTECHNOLOGY INJECTED INTO HUMAN CORPSES, SLADE.
THEY'RE BURNING FROM THE INSIDE OUT. THAT'S THE SMELL...AND THE SMOKE...
THEY AREN'T THINKING. IT'S EITHER ALGORITHMIC FIGHTING, OR THE DESIGNER HAS HIS PEOPLE CONTROLLING THEM REMOTELY.
OKAY. DEAD ALREADY.
THAT MAKES THIS EASIER.
NO!
I'M NOT GOING TO LET YOU TURN A BUNCH OF POLICE OFFICERS INTO HAMBURGER MEAT, REGARDLESS OF WHETHER THEY'RE DEAD OR NOT.
SO YOU'RE JUST GOING TO LET THEM KILL YOU.
NO. MY GAUNTLETS ARE ELECTRIFIED RIGHT NOW. EVERY HIT DELIVERS WHAT YOU'D GET FROM A HIGH-VOLTAGE TASER.
I'M GOING TO SHORT-CIRCUIT THEM.

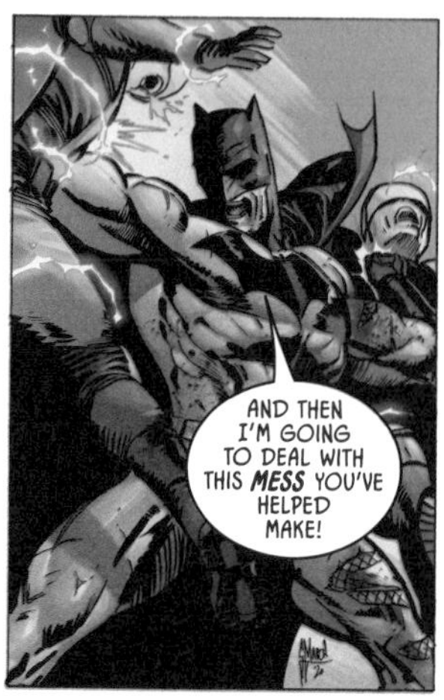

AND THEN I'M GOING TO DEAL WITH THIS MESS YOU'VE HELPED MAKE!

JAMES TYNION IV *writer*

GUILLEM MARCH *artist*

TOMEU MOREY *colors*

CLAYTON COWLES *letters*

DAVE WIELGOSZ *assoc. editor*

BEN ABERNATHY *editor*

Batman #86 variant cover by FRANCESCO MATTINA

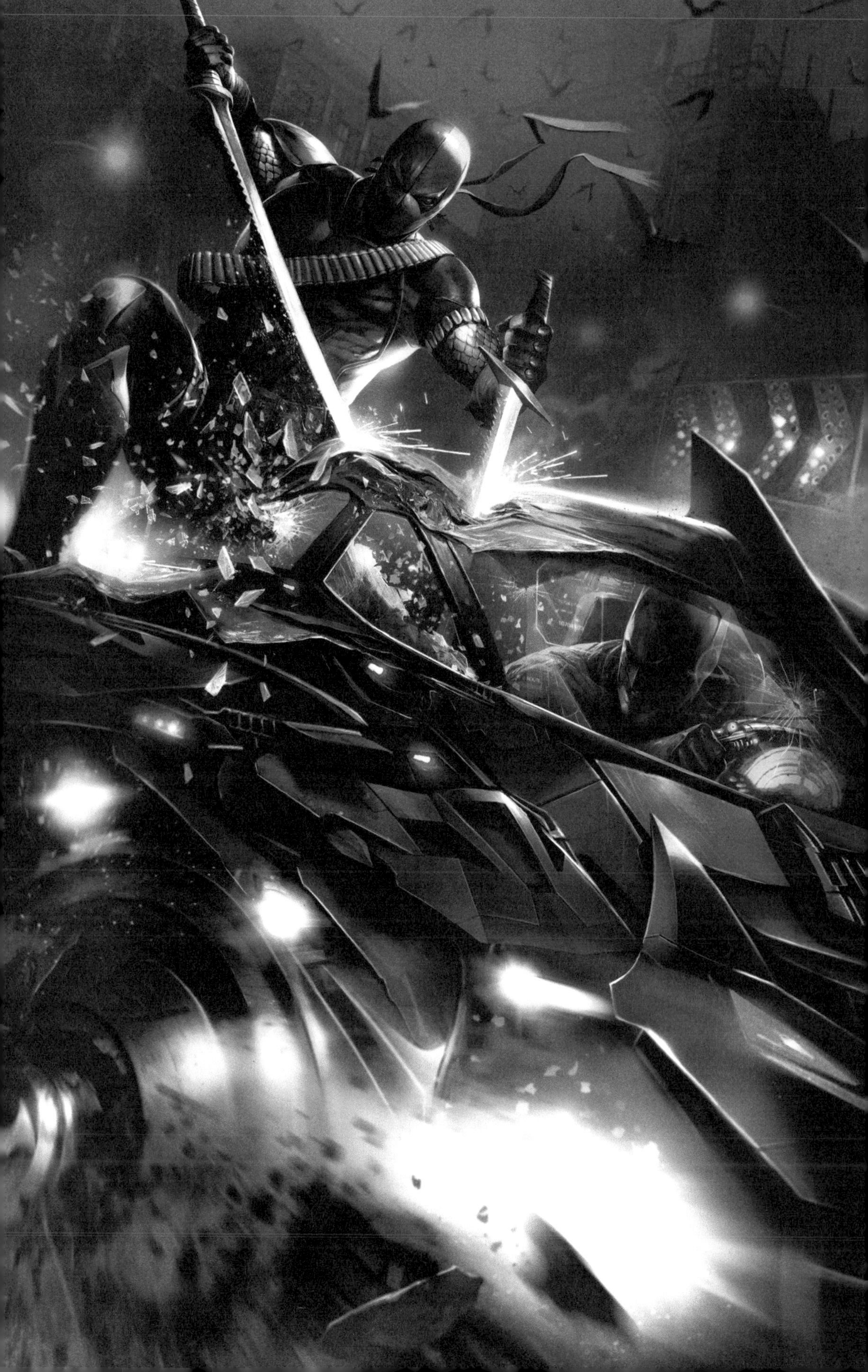

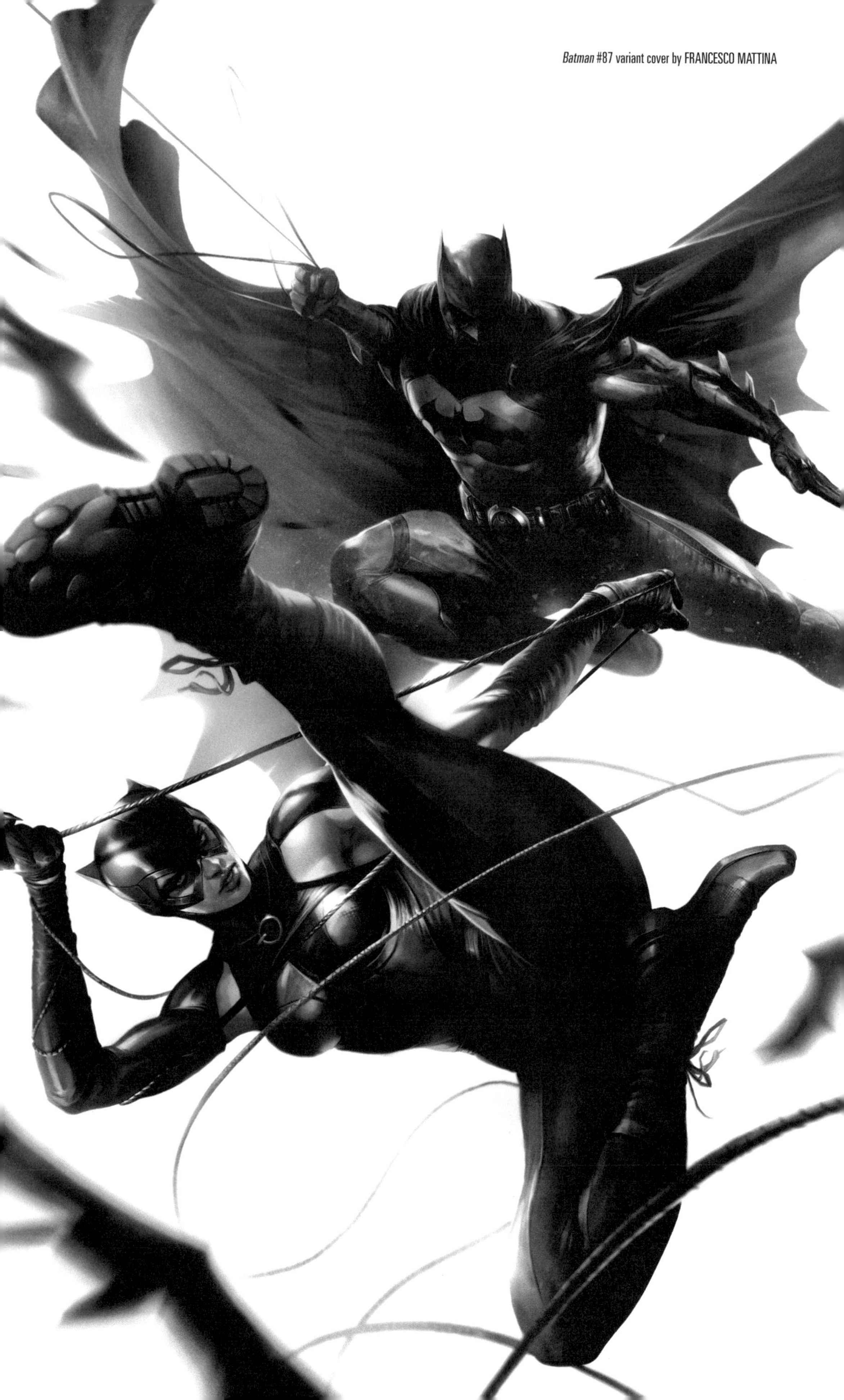

Batman #87 variant cover by FRANCESCO MATTINA

Batman #88 variant cover by FRANCESCO MATTINA

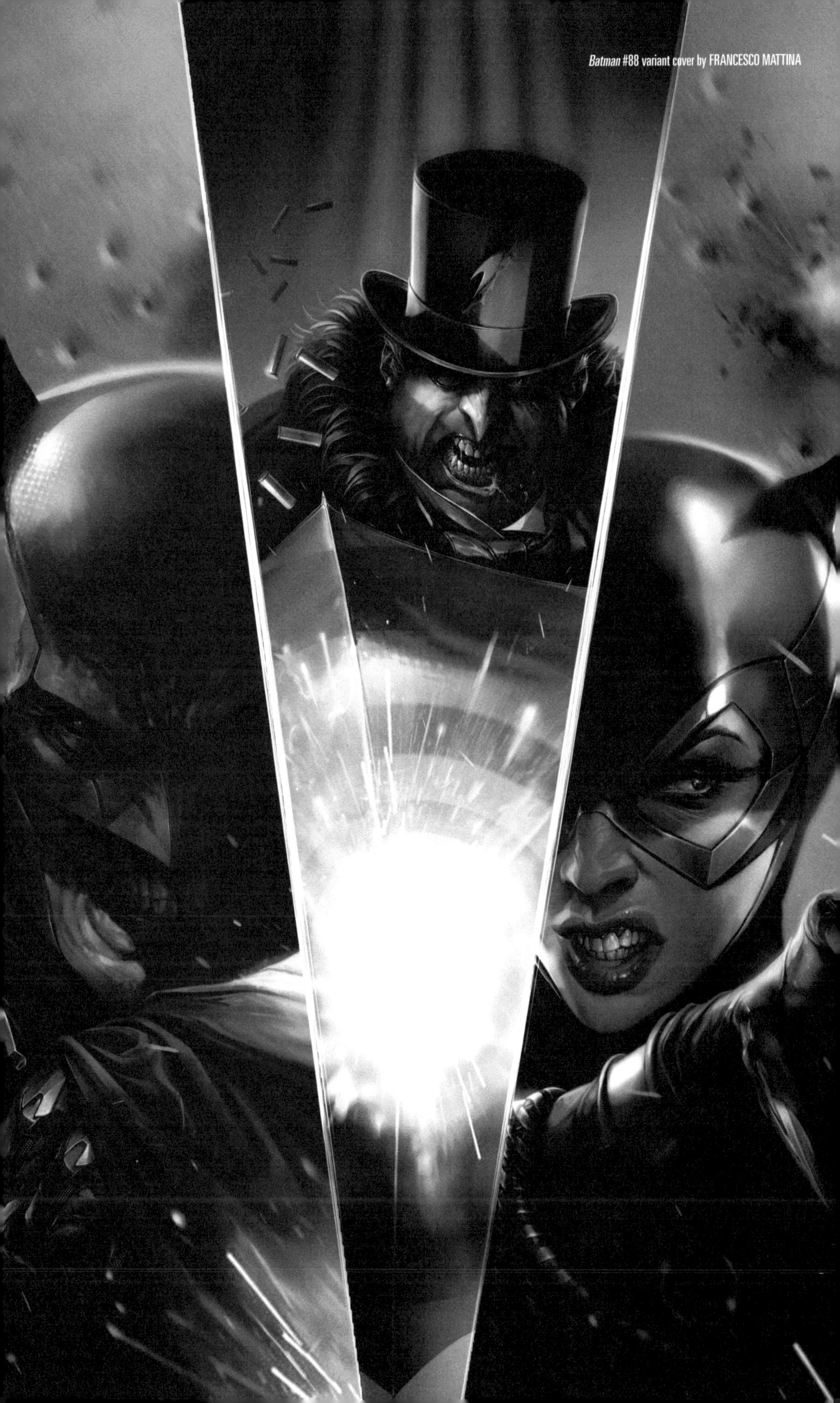

Batman #89 variant cover by FRANCESCO MATTINA

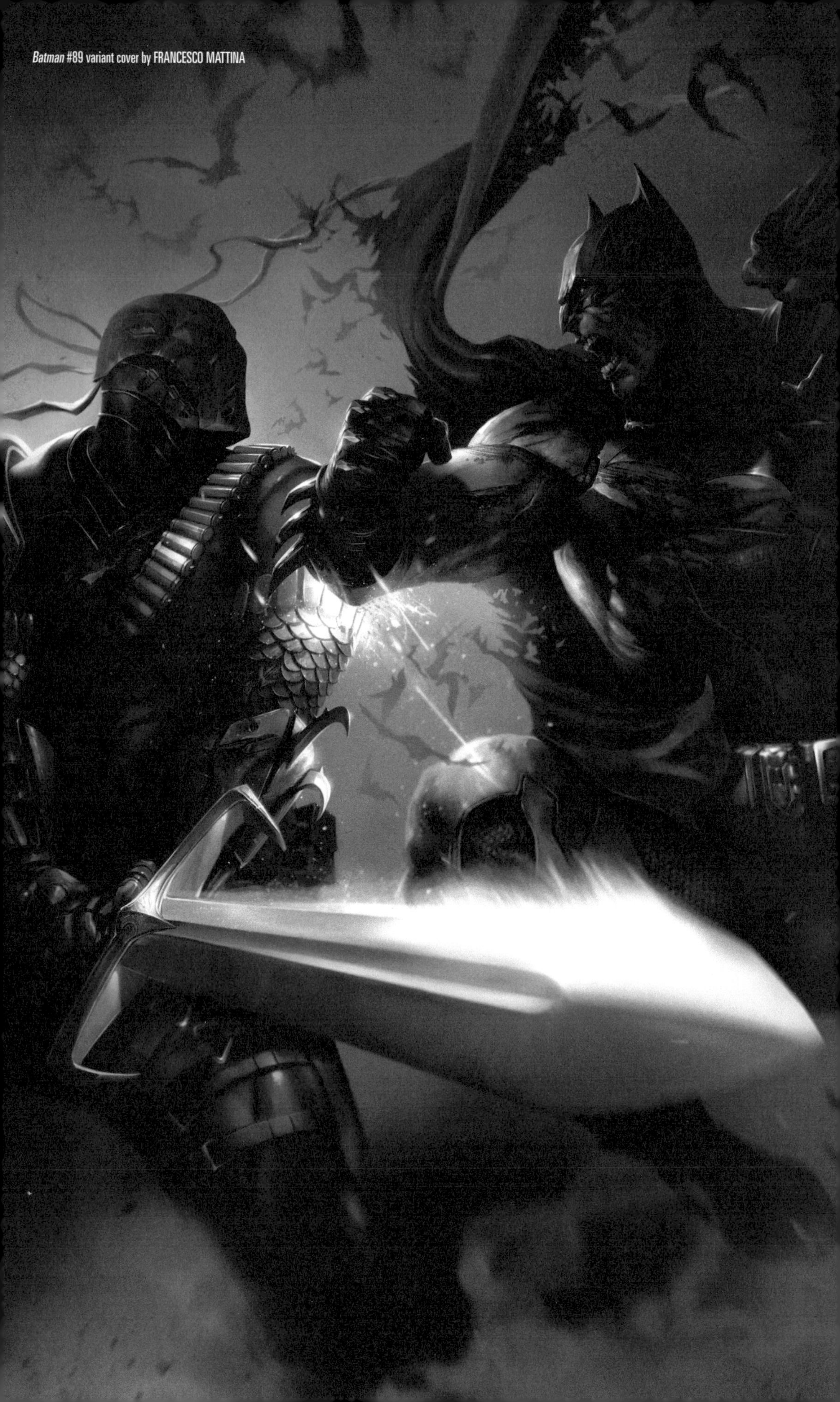

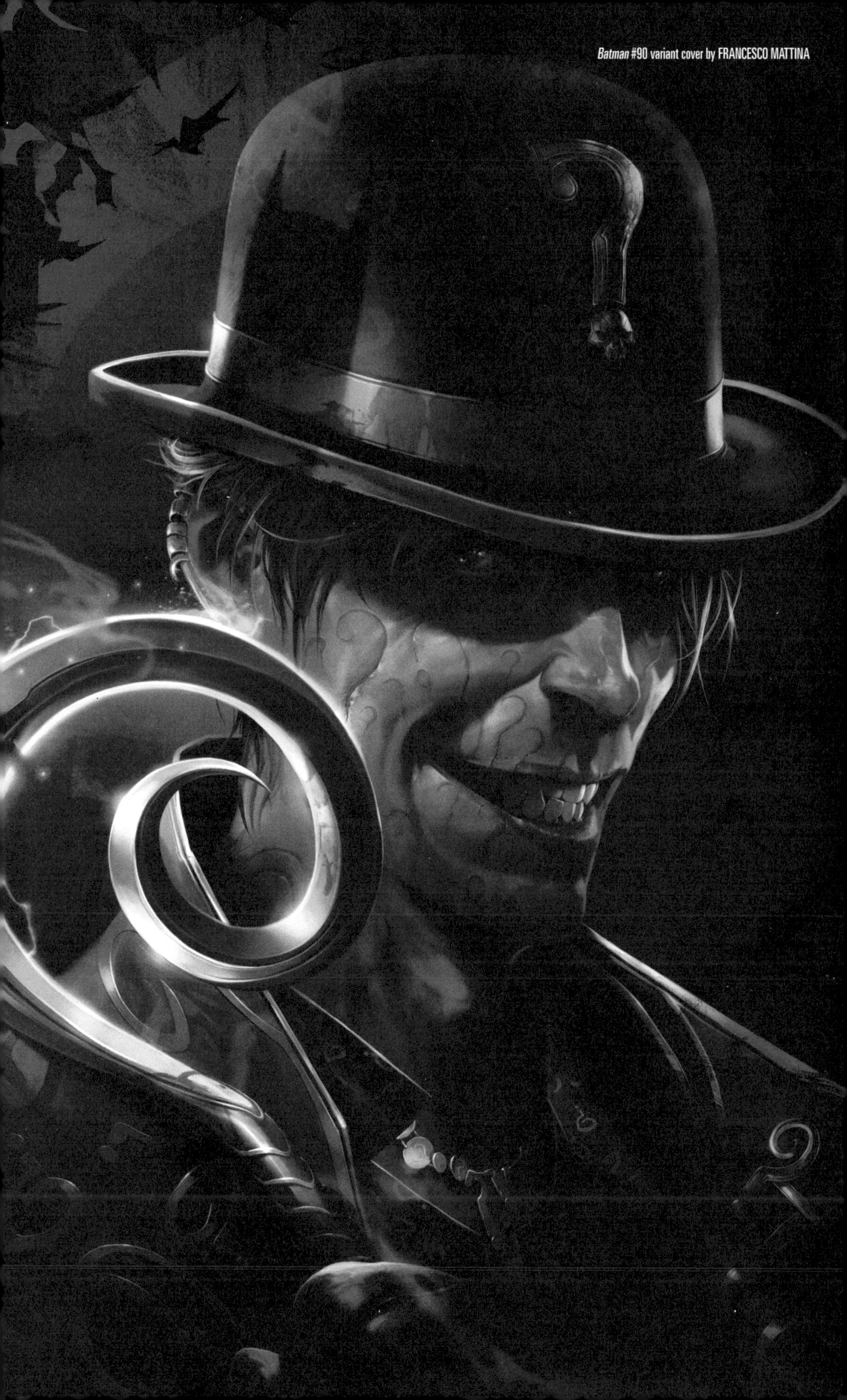

Batman #90 variant cover by FRANCESCO MATTINA

Batman #91 variant cover by FRANCESCO MATTINA

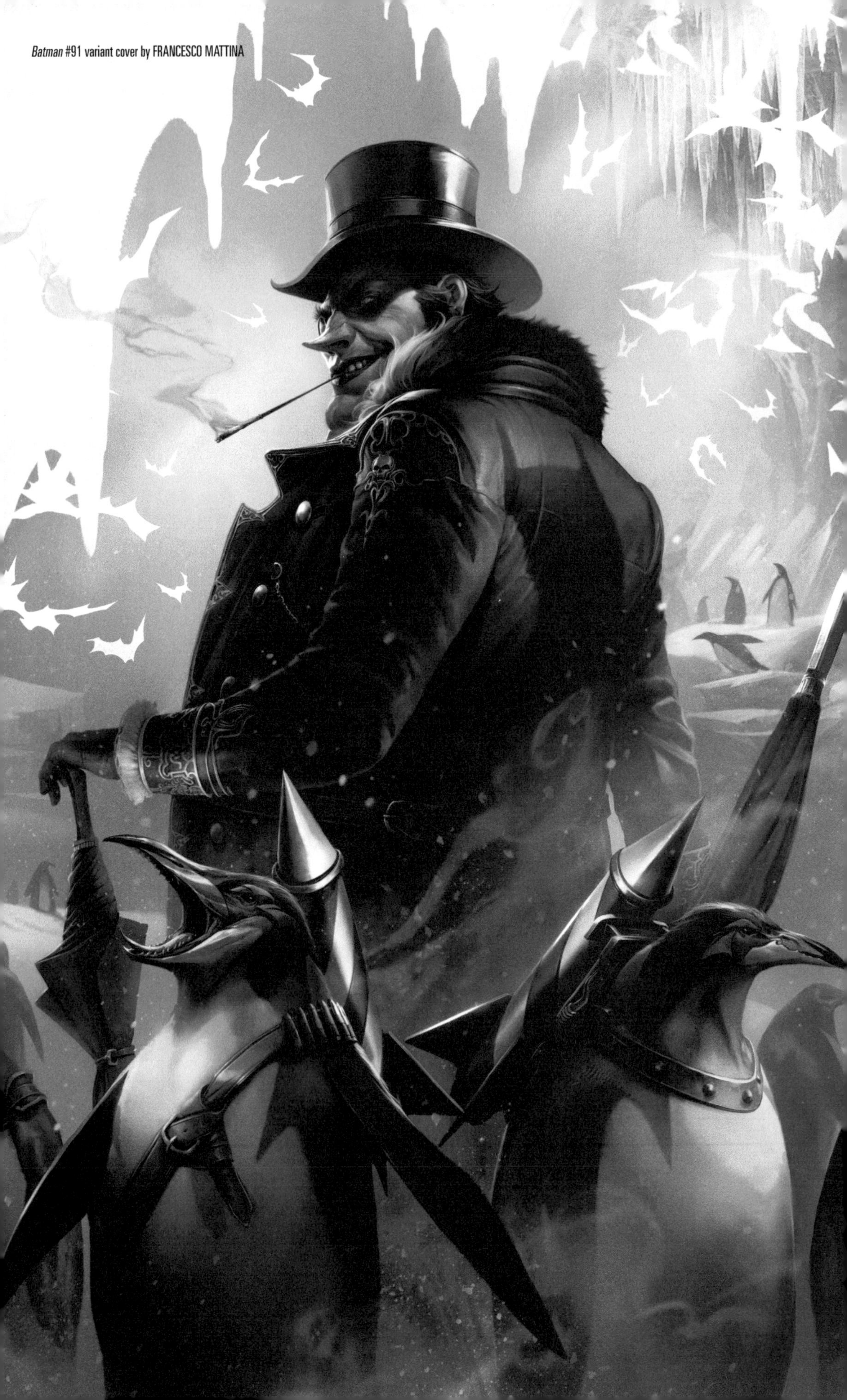

Batman #92 variant cover by STANLEY "ARTGERM" LAU

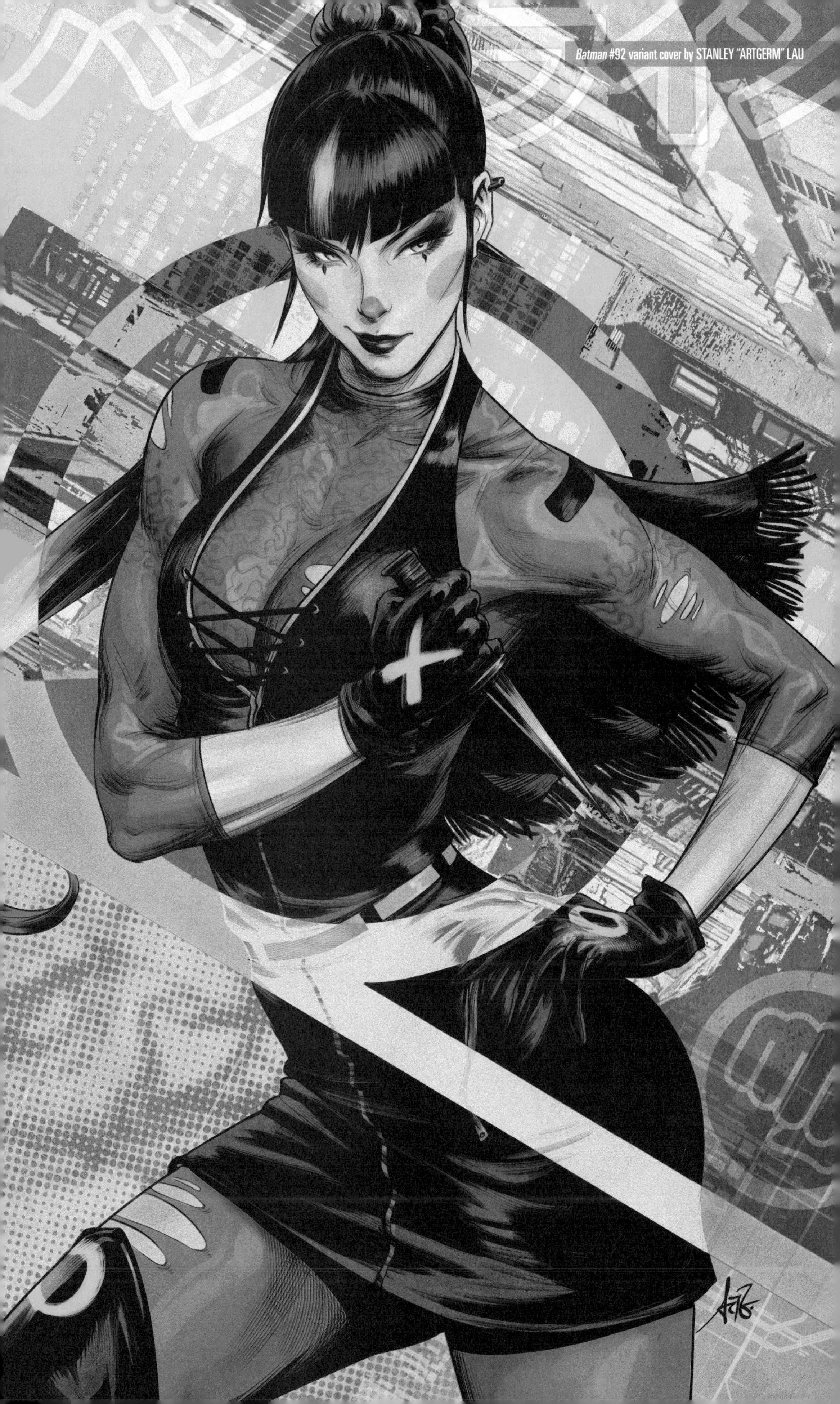

Batman #93 variant cover by FRANCESCO MATTINA

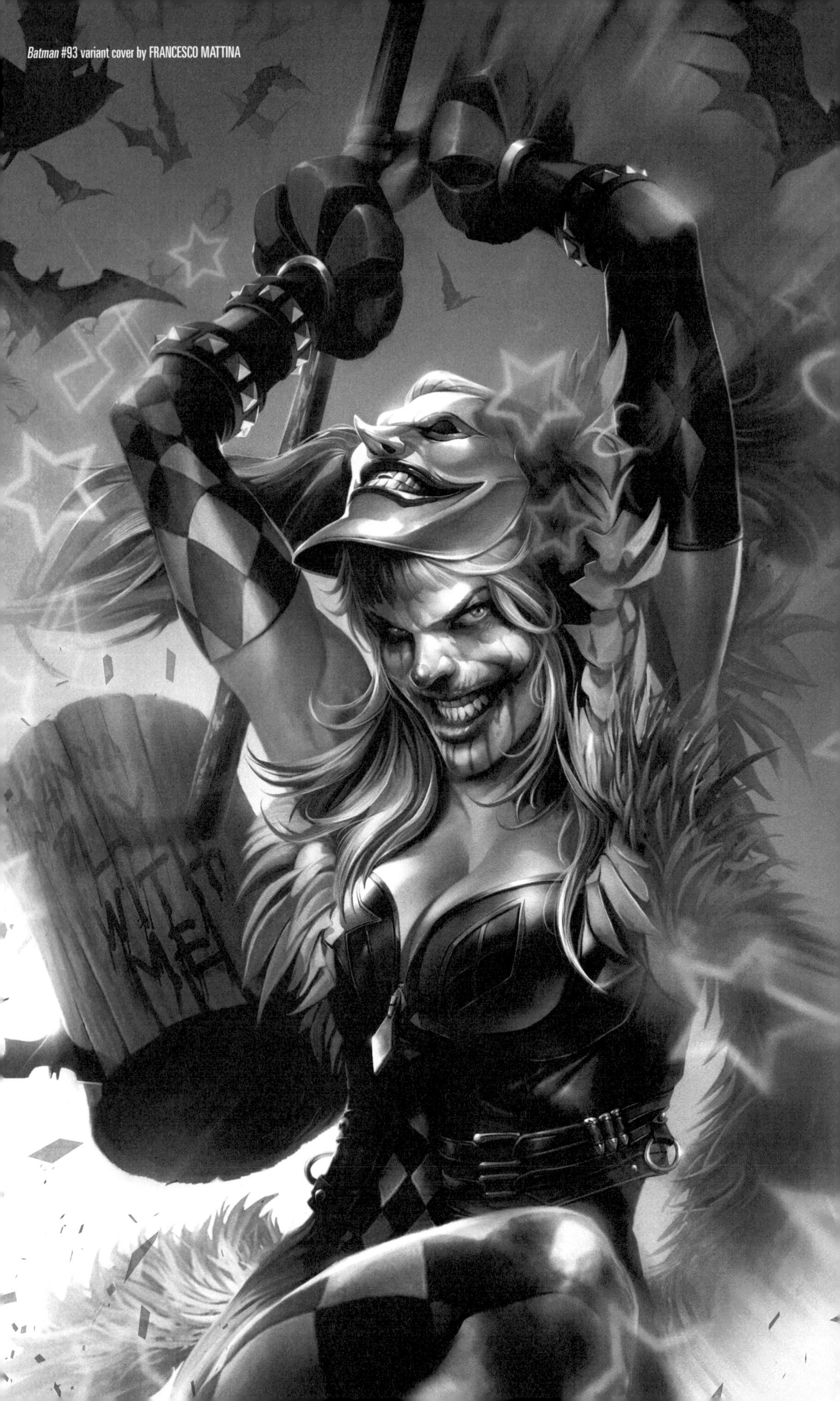

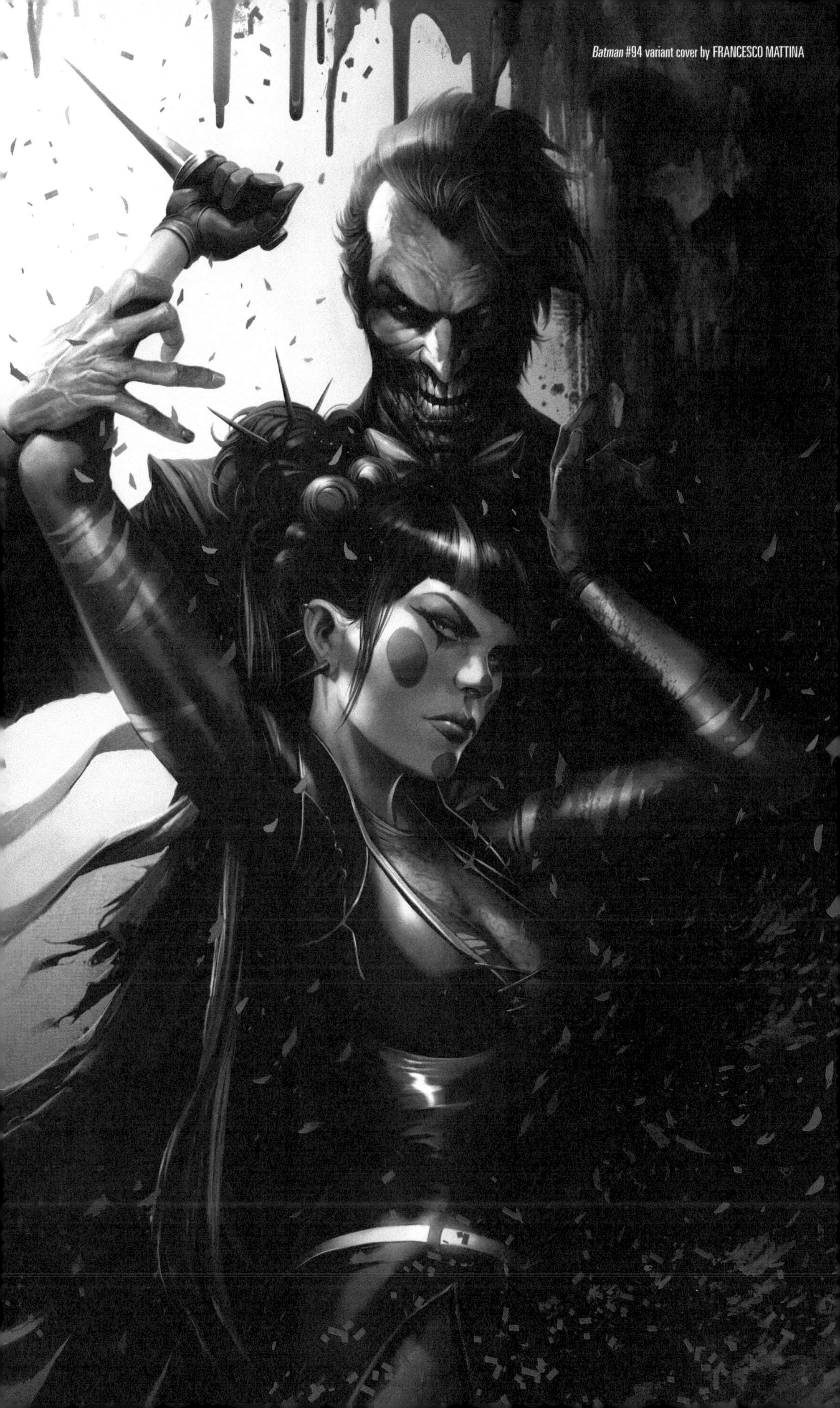

Batman #94 variant cover by FRANCESCO MATTINA

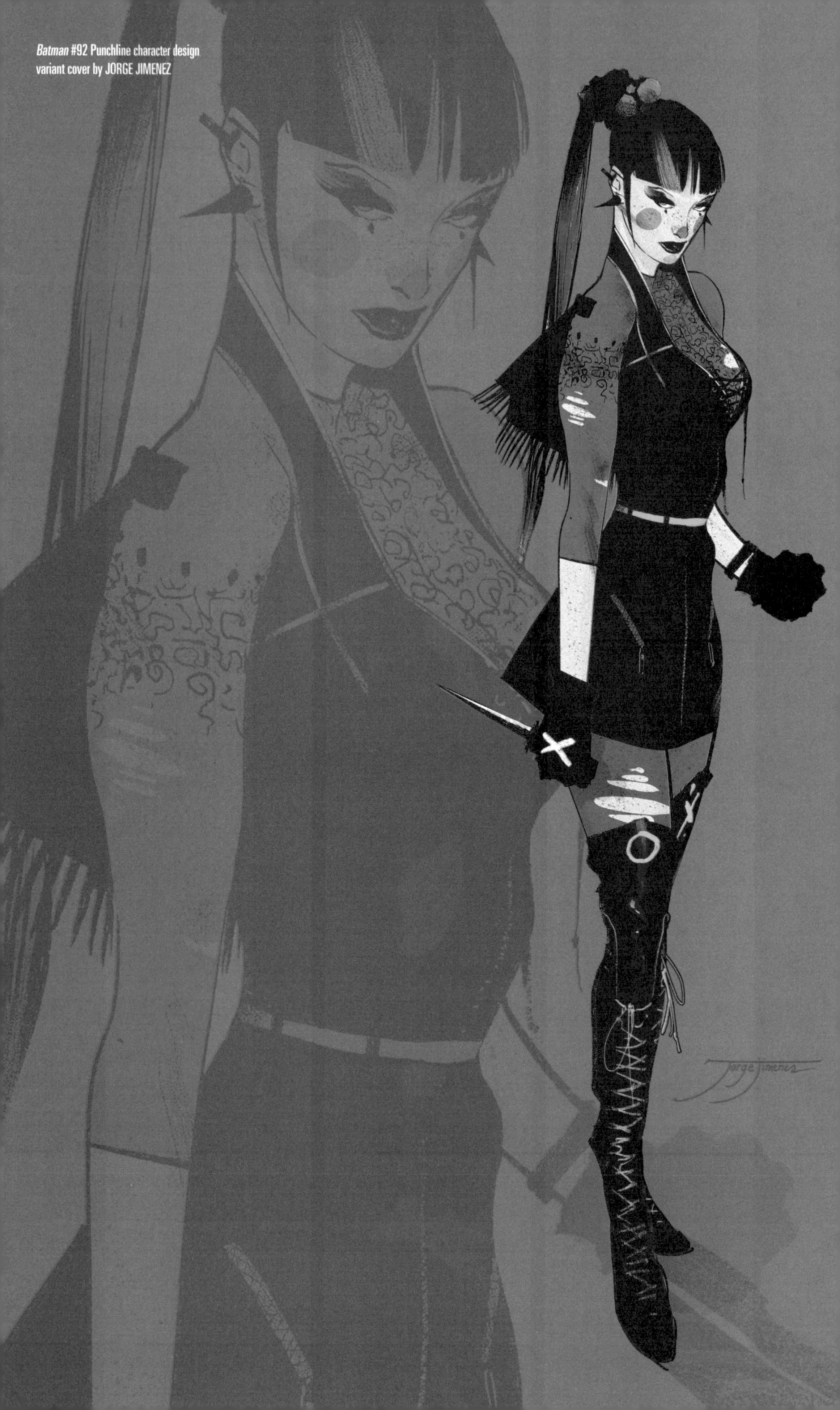
Jorge Jimenez

Batman #92 Punchline character design variant cover by JORGE JIMENEZ

Batman #93 The Designer character design
variant cover by JORGE JIMENEZ

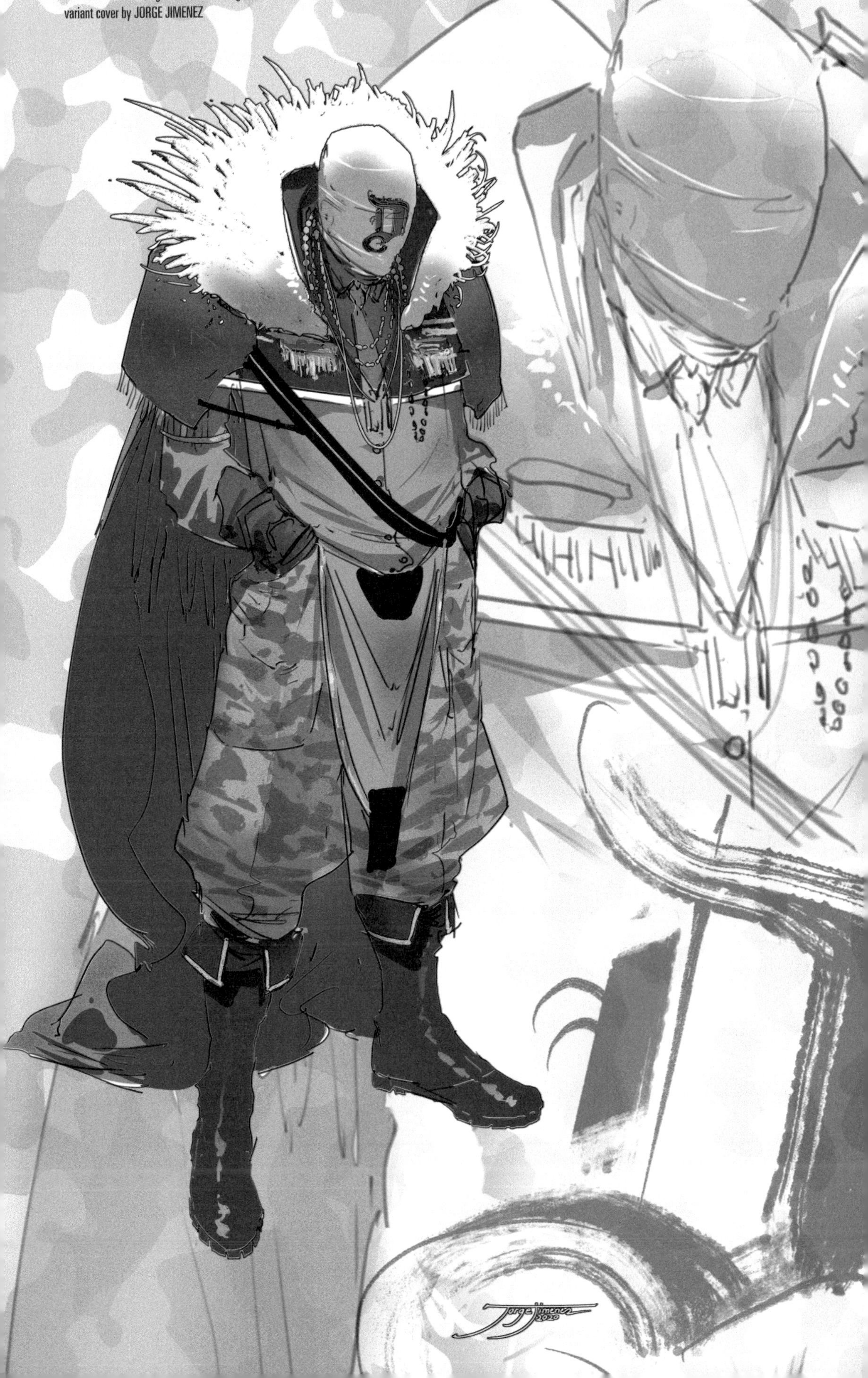
Jorge Jimenez
2020